HOW TO TOEFL® *i*BT
120
LISTENING

넥서스

The Best Solution for TOEFL iBT

HOW TO TOEFL® iBT 120 LISTENING

지은이 허다인
펴낸이 안용백
펴낸곳 (주) 넥서스

초판 1쇄 2007년 7월 5일
초판 4쇄 2008년 12월 25일

2판 1쇄 인쇄 2011년 6월 15일
2판 1쇄 발행 2011년 6월 20일

출판신고 1992년 4월 3일 제311-2002-2호
121-840 서울시 마포구 서교동 394-2
Tel (02)330-5500 Fax (02)330-5555

ISBN 978-89-5797-654-8   18740
       978-89-5797-651-7   (세트)

가격은 뒤표지에 있습니다.
잘못 만들어진 책은 구입처에서 바꾸어 드립니다.
본 책은 〈TOEFL iBT Final 120 listening〉의 개정판입니다.

www.nexusbook.com

The Best Solution for TOEFL iBT

HOW
TO
TOEFL ®

iBT

120
LISTENING

허다인 지음

머리말

　미국 대학이나 대학원으로의 유학을 준비하는 학생들의 미국 대학에서의 학습 능력 정도를 평가하는 것이 원래 목적이었던 TOEFL은 오늘날 미국 외 기타 영어권 국가로의 유학생뿐만 아니라 국내 수험생들의 전반적인 영어 능력을 평가하는 가장 중요하면서도 공신력 있는 영어시험의 하나로 자리잡았다. 기존 TOEFL CBT에서 고득점을 얻고도 막상 원어로 이루어지는 수업을 따라가지 못하거나 토론에 참여하지 못하고 에세이를 쓰는 데 많은 어려움을 겪는 유학생들로 인해 수업 상황에서의 실질적인 영어 실력을 총체적으로, 그리고 최대한 객관적으로 평가할 수 있도록 TOEFL iBT가 도입되었다.

　TOEFL iBT의 가장 큰 특징은 기존 TOEFL에는 없었던 Speaking 섹션이 추가되었다는 것이며, Listening, Reading, Speaking, Writing 네 가지 언어적 능력을 통합적으로 평가하는 Integrated 문제 유형이 도입되었다는 것이다. 또한 CBT 시절 많은 수험자들이 애용하던 일명 '후기'만으로는 고득점이 어려워졌다. 단기간에 집중적으로 기출 문제만을 외워서 고득점을 받는 것을 방지하는 것을 통해 수험자의 실질적 영어 실력을 평가할 수 있게 되었다.

　TOEFL iBT에는 Reading, Listening, Speaking, Writing의 네 섹션이 순서대로 출제된다. 그 중에서도 Listening은 Speaking과 Writing 섹션에도 통합 문제로 포함되어 출제되기 때문에 탄탄한 Listening 실력이 TOEFL iBT에서의 고득점을 좌우하는 열쇠가 되었다. 지문을 대충 듣고 개략적인 내용을 이해하는 것이 아니라 지문의 주제, 화자의 태도나 의도 등 총체적인 것을 이해하고, 정확하고 빠르게 정보를 메모하고 수집된 정보를 바탕으로 문제를 풀어야 고득점에 이를 수 있는 것이다.

　본 실전서는 이러한 TOEFL iBT의 특징과 문제 유형을 면밀히 분석하여 유형별로 챕터를 구성하였으며, 각각의 문제 유형에 완벽히 대비할 수 있는 구체적인 학습 전략을 제시하였다. 새롭게 등장한 문제 유형에 충분히 대비하고 실전 감각을 익힐 수 있도록 각 유형당 풍부한 양의 문제를 수록하였고, 실제 TOEFL iBT 수준을 반영하는 실전 문제를 수록하여 보다 철저하게 실전에 대비할 수 있도록 하였다. 또한 Notetaking 및 Dictation을 연습할 수 있는 부록을 수록하여 보다 효과적인 Listening 대비를 가능하게끔 하였다.

언어는 정복해야 하는 대상이 아니라 평생 배워나가야 하는 것이지만, TOEFL iBT의 경우에는 결코 넘을 수 없는 산은 아니다. 이 책이 여러분이 TOEFL iBT라는 산을 쉽게 정복할 수 있도록 도와주는 가이드가 되었으면 하는 바람이다.

허다인

교재의 구성

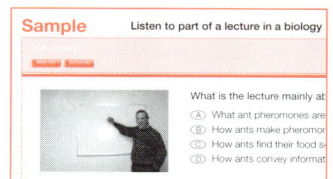

Sample

짧은 지문을 통해 각 문제 유형별로 출제되는 문제를 소개함으로써 문제 유형을 쉽고 빠르게 이해할 수 있도록 했다.

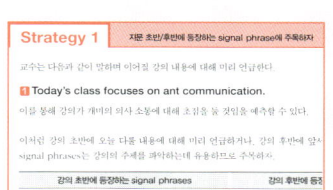

Strategy

특정 문제 유형을 어떻게 이해하고 접근해야 하는지에 대한 구체적인 전략을 설명하였으며, Sample 부분에서 출제된 문제 풀이 방법 또한 설명하여 학습 전략의 적용 방안을 이해할 수 있도록 했다.

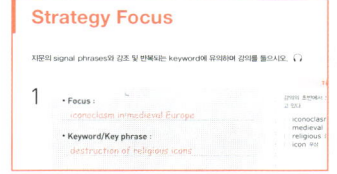

Strategy Focus

짧은 연습 지문을 통해 앞서 설명한 전략을 실전 문제에 활용할 수 있도록 하였으며 문제를 올바르게 풀 수 있는 팁과 중요 단어 및 뜻을 추가했다.

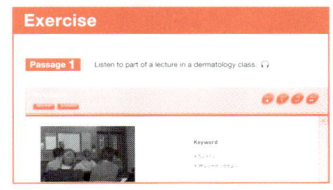

Exercise

iBT TOEFL의 새로운 경향을 반영한 다양한 주제와 길이의 지문을 통해 실전 감각을 익힐 수 있도록 풍부한 분량의 문제를 수록했다.

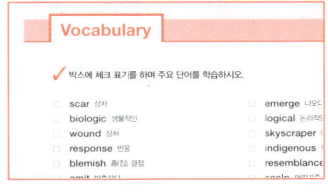

Vocabulary

Exercise의 지문에서 출제된 단어와 뜻을 수록하여 핵심 단어를 익힐 수 있도록 했다.

Vocabulary Test

Vocabulary 섹션에서 출제된 단어들을 반복 학습하고 학습한 어휘를 평가할 수 있도록 어휘 테스트를 수록했다.

교재의 특징

Professionalism

ETS의 문제 유형을 완벽히 파악하여 문제 유형별로 챕터를 구성하였으며, 풍부한 양의 문제를 제공하였다.

Diversity

다양한 분야의 강의 지문을 수록하였으며 여러 가지 학습 환경에서 발생하는 대화 지문을 출제하였다.

Technique

문제 유형별로 주목해야 할 특징들을 제공함으로 실전에 대비할 수 있는 구체적인 기술을 늘릴 수 있도록 하였다.

Readiness

해당 챕터의 문제 유형에 포인트를 주어 쉽고 빠르게 해당 문제 유형에 주목할 수 있도록 했다.

Practicality

미국식 발음 외에 영국식 발음을 녹음 대본에 포함하여 실전에 충분히 대비할 수 있도록 했다.

Efficiency

리스닝 학습의 효율성을 도모하기 위해 Listening Skill Workbook을 별도로 제공하여 노트필기 및 받아쓰기 연습을 충분히 할 수 있도록 했다.

목차

Part 1

Lecture

Chapter 1

Main Idea

1 Main Idea 지문의 전반적인 주제 및 목적 찾기

문제유형

- What is the topic of the lecture(discussion)?
- What is the lecture(discussion) mainly about?
- What aspect of... does the professor mainly discuss?
- What is the main purpose of the lecture(discussion)?
- Why is the professor discussing...?

Sample

Listen to part of a lecture in a biology class. 🎧

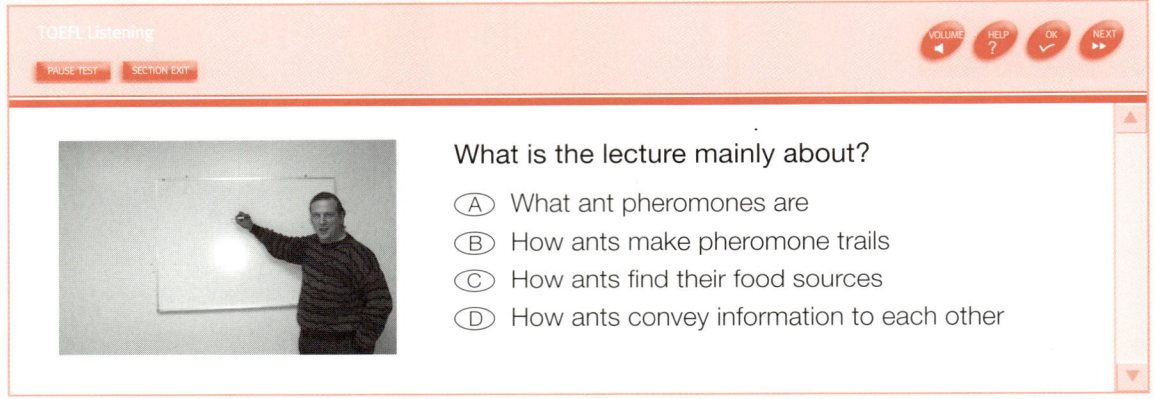

What is the lecture mainly about?

- Ⓐ What ant pheromones are
- Ⓑ How ants make pheromone trails
- Ⓒ How ants find their food sources
- Ⓓ How ants convey information to each other

표기된 signal phrases 및 keyword에 주목하며 강의를 다시 한번 들으시오. 🎧

1 Today's class focuses on **ant communication**. Well, ants, basically, communicate primarily through chemicals called pheromones. You've heard a lot about pheromones, right? Something about animals trying to attract the other sex and things like that. Well, **2** ants use the **pheromone** in order to help the ant and its recruited nest mates find their way back to a food source or prey they plan to kill. For example, let's say this one ant found food. This forager will leave a pheromone trail along the ground on her way home. In a short time, other ants will follow this trail of pheromone. Moving to and fro, they reinforce this same trail which in turn attracts more ants until the food is completely consumed or removed to their nest. When the food is exhausted, the trail is no longer reinforced and slowly dissipates.

지문 초반/후반에 등장하는 signal phrase에 주목하자

교수는 다음과 같이 말하며 이어질 강의 내용에 대해 미리 언급한다.

1 Today's class focuses on ant communication.

이를 통해 강의가 개미의 의사 소통에 대해 초점을 둘 것임을 예측할 수 있다.

이처럼 강의 초반에 오늘 다룰 내용에 대해 미리 언급하거나, 강의 후반에 앞서 설명한 내용에 대해 요약하는 signal phrases는 강의의 주제를 파악하는데 유용하므로 주목하자.

강의 초반에 등장하는 signal phrases	강의 후반에 등장하는 signal phrases
• Today, we're going to talk about~ • Today's class will focus on~ • Let's continue our discussion on~ • Lets turn our attention to~ • Before we go on to the next topic, let's review what we talked about last time~	• To summarize what we've been talking about~ • Today we talked about~ • In short, ~ is~ • Let's go over the main points before we wrap up~ • So the gist of ~ is ~

Strategy 2 주제와 관련되는 단어/구에 주목하여 topic을 유추하자

주제와 관련된 단어를 keyword라고 하며, 구를 key phrase라고 한다. Keyword는 강의에서 자주 언급되거나 강조되는 단어이며 key phrase는 keyword와 밀접하게 관련된 구이다.

위 강의에서는 communicate, pheromone이라는 단어가 자주 등장하므로, 이 둘의 관계에 주목해야 한다. Pheromone이 communication에서 행하는 역할을 설명하고 있는 다음 문장이 바로 key phrase임을 알 수 있다.

2 ants use the pheromone in order to help the ant and its recruited nest mates find their way back to food source or prey...

선택지에서는 main topic이 paraphrase(다른 표현으로 바꿔쓰기)되므로 내용상 main topic을 가장 적절히 반영하고 있는 것을 선택해야 한다. 위의 지문에서는 main topic이 개미의 의사 소통이므로, 이를 적절히 바꾸어 표현한 D가 정답이 된다.

지문에 명확하게 main topic이 제시되지 않은 경우에는, 위와 같이 keyword와 key phrase를 통해 지문의 main topic을 유추하는 것이 효과적이다.

Strategy Focus

지문의 signal phrases와 강조 및 반복되는 keyword에 유의하며 강의를 들으시오. 🎧

1

• **Focus :**

iconoclasm in medieval Europe

• **Keyword/Key phrase :**

destruction of religious icons

.

Tip

강의의 초반에서 오늘의 주제를 소개하고 있다.

☐ iconoclasm 성상파괴
☐ medieval 중세의
☐ religious 종교적인
☐ icon 우상

What is the main topic of the lecture?

Ⓐ The examples of icons
Ⓑ The definition of iconoclasm
Ⓒ The origin of the word iconoclasm
Ⓓ Iconoclasm in Europe in the Middle Ages

2

• **Focus :**

• **Keyword/Key phrase :**

알렉산더 벨의 생애에 대해 설명하며 전화기를 발명하게 된 계기에 대해 언급한다.

☐ invention 발명품
☐ biography 전기
☐ elocution 웅변술
☐ acceptable 받아들일 수 있는

What is the main topic of the lecture?

Ⓐ How Alexander Graham Bell came to invent the telephone
Ⓑ Why Alexander Graham Bell is called "the father of the Deaf"
Ⓒ How Alexander Graham Bell became a student teacher at the age of 16
Ⓓ Why Alexander Graham Bell is the most important inventor in history

3

• Focus :

_____

• Keyword/Key phrase :

_____

_____

Tip

강의 초반에서 교수는 패스트푸드에 대해 언급하고 지문 후반에 패스트푸드의 영향, 특히 트랜스 지방에 의한 위험에 대해 언급하고 있다. 마지막 문장에 강의 주제가 담겨 있다.

☐ crave 열망하다
☐ lack 부족, 결핍
☐ unavoidable 피할 수 없는
☐ addictive 중독성의
☐ potential 잠재적인
☐ consume 소모하다

What is the lecture mainly about?

Ⓐ The negative effect of trans fat on the human body
Ⓑ The destructive nature of trans fat on animals
Ⓒ The worldwide popularity of fast food
Ⓓ The addictive nature of fast food

4

• Focus :

_____

• Keyword/Key phrase :

_____

_____

지문 전반에 걸쳐 교수는 음주운전에 대해 설명하며, 꼭 술을 마시지 않아도 음주운전으로 기소될 수 있음을 설명한다.

☐ charge 고소하다; 죄명, 혐의
☐ DUI 음주운전
☐ offense 위반, 범죄
☐ illegal 불법의

What is the main topic of the lecture?

Ⓐ The definition of DUI
Ⓑ The legal consequences of DUI
Ⓒ The origin of the word DUI
Ⓓ The influence of DUI on people's career

Exercise

Passage 1   Listen to part of a lecture in a dermatology class. 🎧

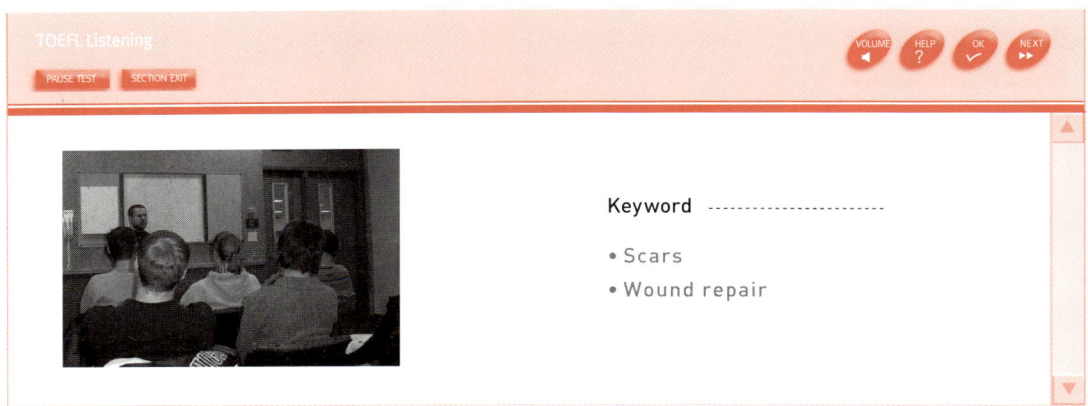

Keyword -----------------------

• Scars
• Wound repair

---

1 What is the topic of the lecture?

Ⓐ How to wrap a bandage on your finger when it is cut

Ⓑ How to remove scars through plastic surgery

Ⓒ What scars are and how they occur

Ⓓ What scar removal treatments involve

2 According to the professor, what is a scar?

Ⓐ Blood oozing out of a cut

Ⓑ Abnormal skin damage by the sun

Ⓒ Uncomfortableness caused by skin trouble

Ⓓ A part of the body's natural response to injury

3 Why does the professor mention his 17-year-old daughter?

Ⓐ To insinuate that he has been married for more than 17 years

Ⓑ To end his explanation about scars and begin the lecture about scar removers

Ⓒ To explain that scars can last for a long time and how some people want to remove them

Ⓓ To demonstrate the fact that scars can be removed only by plastic surgery

Passage 2   Listen to part of a discussion in an engineering class. 🎧

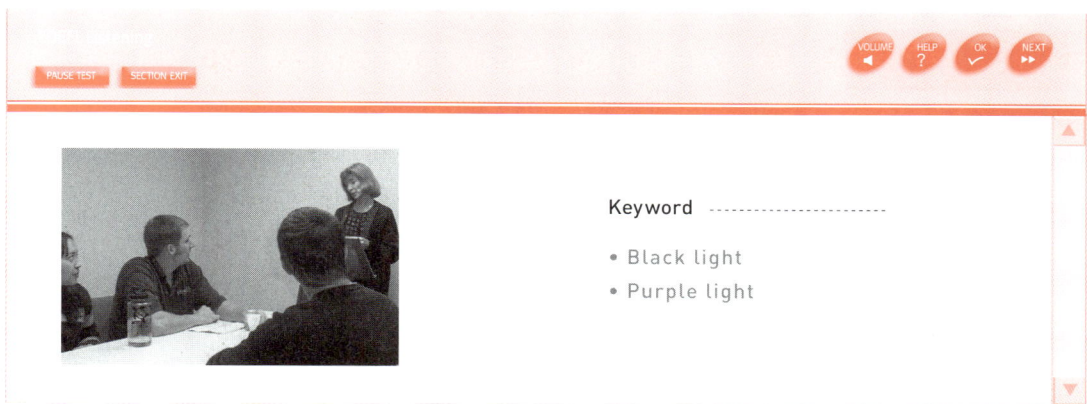

1 What does the professor mainly discuss?
- Ⓐ What black lights are and where they can be found
- Ⓑ What the differences are between black lights and fluorescent lamps
- Ⓒ Why white materials glow in the dark under black lights
- Ⓓ Why black lights are used more often than incandescent light bulbs

2 Listen again to part of the discussion. Then answer the question.
What does the professor mean when she says this: 🎧
- Ⓐ The student will be punished for his ignorance.
- Ⓑ The student has never seen black lights before.
- Ⓒ The student should think beyond its surface meaning.
- Ⓓ The student should always think deeply about the term.

3 What can be said about the professor?
- Ⓐ She is not very interested in today's topic.
- Ⓑ She might probably have black lights in her house.
- Ⓒ She encourages the students to participate in class.
- Ⓓ She does not have sufficient knowledge to teach a college level class.

Passage 3   Listen to part of a discussion in an American literature class. 🎧

1   **What is the main purpose of the discussion?**
   Ⓐ To explain Walt Whitman's life and his poems
   Ⓑ To introduce Walt Whitman's family history
   Ⓒ To exemplify the relationship between Dickinson and Whitman
   Ⓓ To demonstrate how Emily Dickinson affected Walt Whitman's life

2   **What does the professor say about the relationship between Whitman and his family?**
   Ⓐ Whitman despised his family and kept away from them.
   Ⓑ Whitman did not have any type of connection with his family.
   Ⓒ Whitman respected his father and had a close relationship with him.
   Ⓓ Whitman respected his father but relied more on his mother emotionally.

3   **Listen again to part of the discussion. Then answer the question. Why does the professor say this:** 🎧

   Ⓐ To end his suggestion and return to the lecture
   Ⓑ To advise the students to read *Leaves of Grass*
   Ⓒ To comment about the student's procrastination
   Ⓓ To chastise the student for her ignorance on the topic

Passage 4   Listen to part of a lecture in an American history class. 🎧

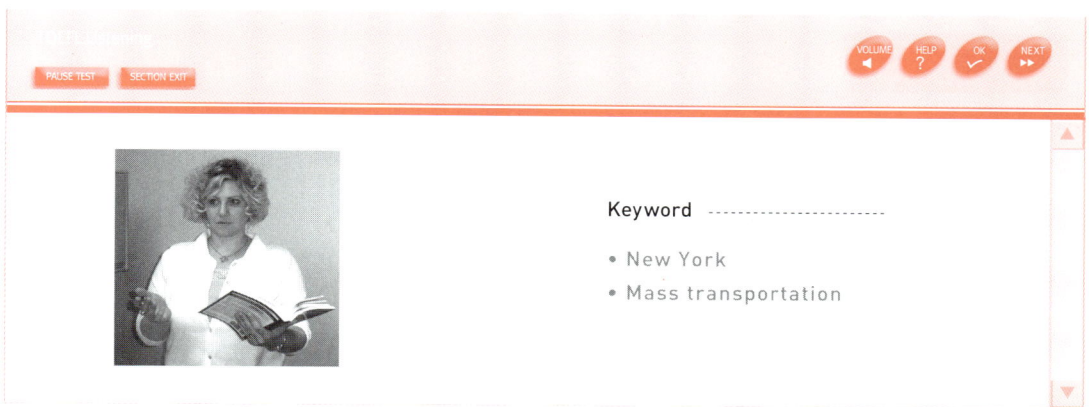

1   **What does the professor mainly discuss?**
  Ⓐ The problems with New York City's mass transportation
  Ⓑ The introduction of New York City's first subway
  Ⓒ The construction of elevated road in New York City
  Ⓓ The underground tunnel for horses in New York City

2   **How does the professor make her point about the transportation situation of New York City in the mid-1800s?**
  Ⓐ By describing transportation problems in the city
  Ⓑ By comparing it with her personal experience
  Ⓒ By explaining the usage of horse drawn carriages
  Ⓓ By contrasting with the transportation situation of other major cities

3   **What did Alfred Beach propose for the transportation problems?**
                                                              Click on 2 answers.

  Ⓐ Expand the roads
  Ⓑ Establish elevated roads
  Ⓒ Build an underground tunnel
  Ⓓ Make detour roads

Passage 5

Listen to part of a lecture in an art history class.

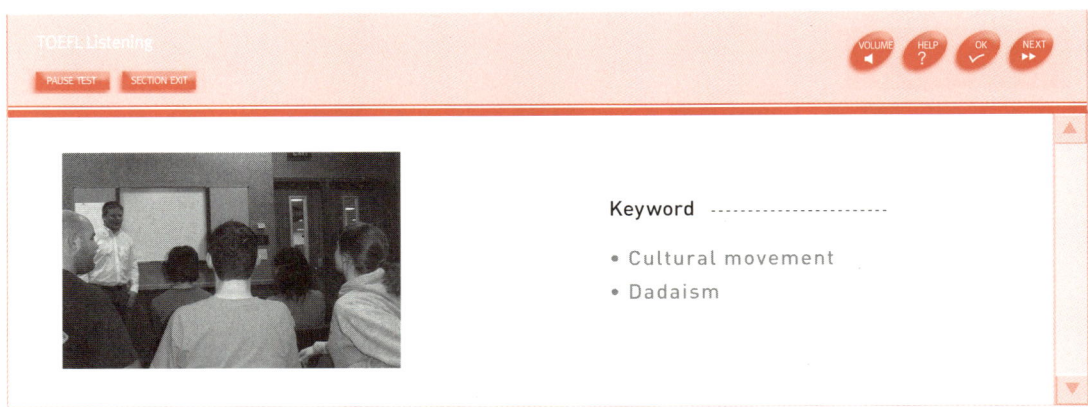

Keyword ------------------

- Cultural movement
- Dadaism

1 **What is the primary purpose of the lecture?**

Ⓐ To facilitate the understanding of Dadaism

Ⓑ To explain how Dadaism had impact on many artists

Ⓒ To demonstrate how surrealism was affected by Dadaism

Ⓓ To explain where the word Dadaism came from

2 **According to the lecture, what can be said about Dadaism?**

Ⓐ Since it began in Switzerland, it did not spread to other countries.

Ⓑ Because it was short-lived, it only flourished among artists and architectures.

Ⓒ Although it lasted for a short period of time, it had a big effect on various fields of art.

Ⓓ Since it began during World War I, it glorified the modern civilization which brought victory to the Western World.

3 **What did many Dadaists grow interested in after Dada faded?**

Ⓐ Romanticism

Ⓑ Modernism

Ⓒ Realism

Ⓓ Surrealism

Passage 6 Listen to part of a discussion in a history class. 🎧

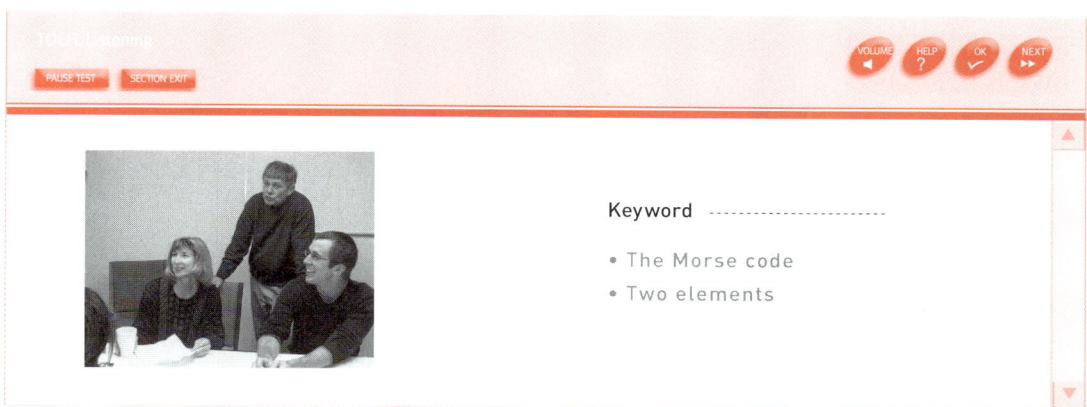

Keyword --------------------------

• The Morse code
• Two elements

1 What is the main topic of the discussion?
- Ⓐ The origin of the word Morse code
- Ⓑ Last week's assignment on the Morse code
- Ⓒ The general operation of the Morse code
- Ⓓ The six elements of the international Morse code

2 Why is the student confused about the Morse code?
- Ⓐ Because this is his first time attending the class
- Ⓑ Because he did not do the assigned reading from last week
- Ⓒ Because he did not know about Morse and Vail's telegraph
- Ⓓ Because he thought that the Morse code was composed of only two elements

3 What will the professor probably discuss next?
- Ⓐ Why the Morse code is composed of six elements
- Ⓑ How Morse and Vail's initial telegraph operated
- Ⓒ Where the Morse code got its name from
- Ⓓ What the Morse code is used for

Passage 7

Listen to part of a discussion in a biology class. 🎧

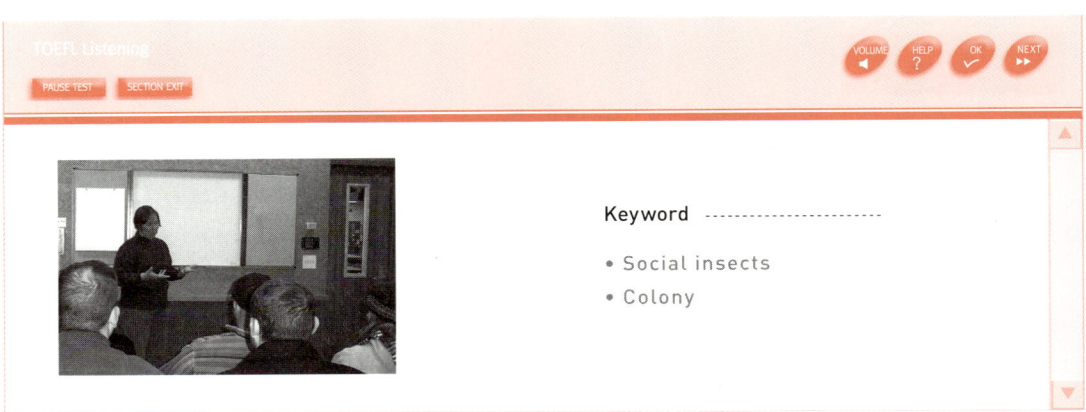

TOEFL Listening

PAUSE TEST   SECTION EXIT

VOLUME   HELP ?   OK ✓   NEXT ▶▶

Keyword -

• Social insects
• Colony

1 **What is the discussion mainly about?**

Ⓐ The definition of a colony
Ⓑ The criteria for bee classification
Ⓒ The construction of a colony
Ⓓ The selection of a queen in a social insects' society

2 **What happens when a new queen emerges in an existing colony?**

Ⓐ She gets killed by the other members of the colony.
Ⓑ She rules the colony together with the other existing queen.
Ⓒ She is forced to leave the colony and start one of her own.
Ⓓ Her reproductive organs are removed by the existing queen.

3 **Which of the following were mentioned as the example of social insects?**

Click on 2 answers.

Ⓐ Termites
Ⓑ Dragonflies
Ⓒ Beetles
Ⓓ Bees

Passage 8   Listen to part of a lecture in an architecture class. 🎧

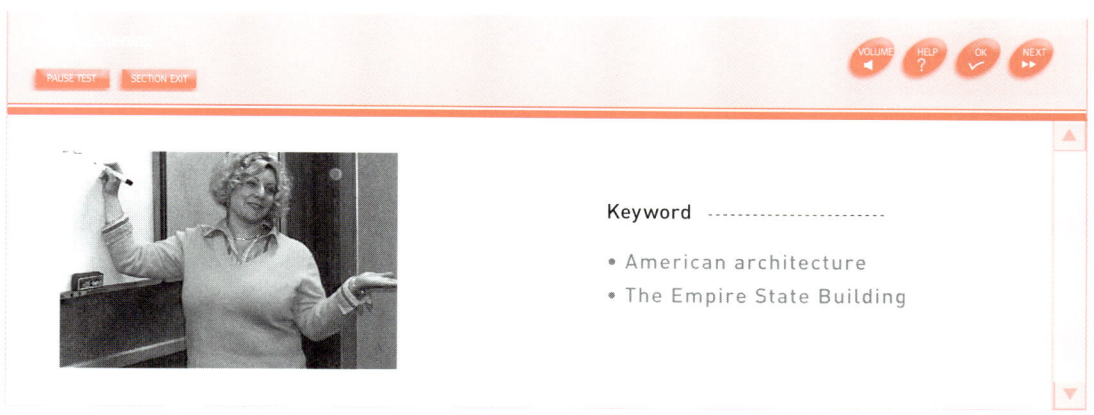

Keyword ----------------------

• American architecture
• The Empire State Building

1 **What is the main topic of the lecture?**
  Ⓐ The construction process of the the Empire State Building
  Ⓑ The status of the Empire State Building in New York City
  Ⓒ The actual height of the Empire State Building
  Ⓓ The collapse the World Trade Center in 2001

2 **According to the professor, what is the current tallest building in the United States?**
  Ⓐ Sears Tower in Chicago
  Ⓑ World Trade Center in New York City
  Ⓒ Empire State Building in New York City
  Ⓓ John Hancock Center in Chicago

3 **Which of the following designers were mentioned in the lecture as the designers of the Empire State Building?**   Click on 2 answers.
  Ⓐ Graham
  Ⓑ Beyer
  Ⓒ Shreve
  Ⓓ Harmon

Passage 9   Listen to part of a lecture in an American history class. 🎧

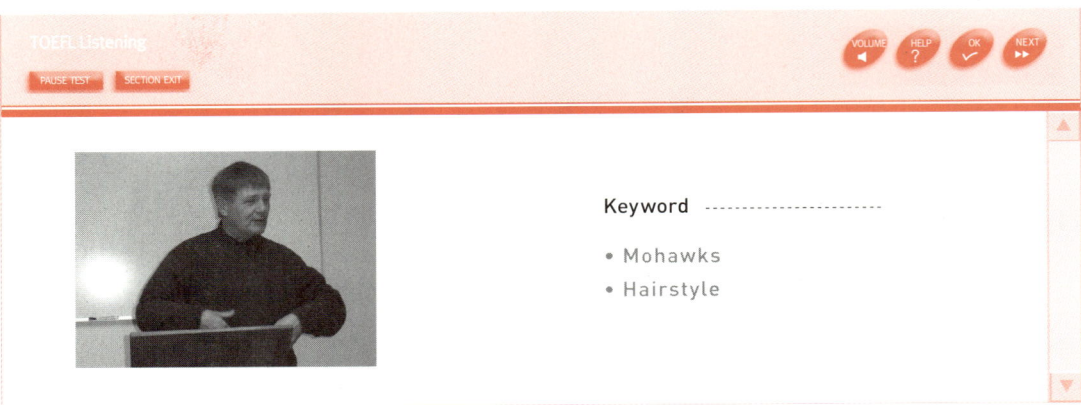

Keyword ----------------------

- Mohawks
- Hairstyle

1 What is the lecture mainly about?
- Ⓐ Mohawks' history and community
- Ⓑ Mohawk warriors and their wars
- Ⓒ Mohawks and their language
- Ⓓ Mohawks' unique clothing style

2 Why does the professor compare the pictures of an American male and a Mohawk warrior?
- Ⓐ To introduce Mohawks' unique culture
- Ⓑ To explain about the Great Lakes region
- Ⓒ To demonstrate the similarity in their hairstyles
- Ⓓ To discuss popular hairstyle among young American male

3 Which member of the Mohawks wore the hairstyle mentioned by the professor?
- Ⓐ Every male in the Mohawk society
- Ⓑ The spiritual leader of a Mohawk tribe
- Ⓒ Male warriors who are about to participate in a war
- Ⓓ Male warriors who gained victory in a previous war

Passage 10

Listen to part of a lecture in a paleontology class. 🎧

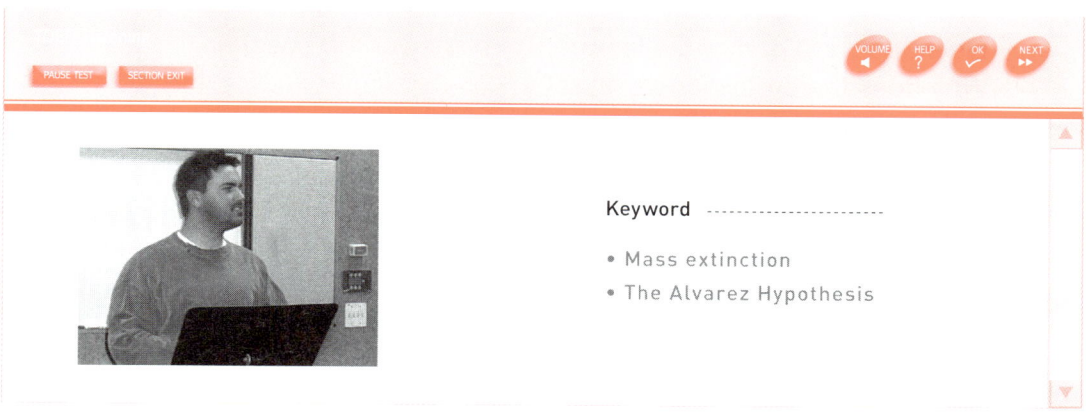

Keyword -----------------------

- Mass extinction
- The Alvarez Hypothesis

1 What is the topic of the lecture?
- Ⓐ Survival of animal species from the massive extinction event
- Ⓑ The life of Luis Alvarez and how he had won the Nobel prize in 1968
- Ⓒ A possible theory on how massive animal species had been wiped out
- Ⓓ The impact of asteroid on animal species of the Earth

2 How does the professor explain the Alvarez Hypothesis?
- Ⓐ By describing a scene from a famous movie
- Ⓑ By providing scientific evidence which supports the theory
- Ⓒ By comparing the theory with another less famous theory
- Ⓓ By giving background information of Luis Alvarez and his research team

3 Why does the professor mention the movie, *Deep Impact*?
- Ⓐ To visualize the massive effect of an asteroid hitting the Earth
- Ⓑ To share his personal experience with the class
- Ⓒ To convince the students to watch the movie
- Ⓓ To enhance students' understanding about Luis Alvarez

4 Listen again to part of the lecture. Then answer the question.
Why does the professor say this: 🎧

   Ⓐ To tell the students that he is a Christian
   Ⓑ To conceal his lack of knowledge on the topic
   Ⓒ To explain the influence on the Earth of the sunlight being blocked
   Ⓓ To indicate that the exact period is unknown

5 According to the lecture, what can be said about the Alvarez Hypothesis?

   Ⓐ It made Luis Alvarez a Nobel Prize laureate.
   Ⓑ It was enthusiastically recognized and approved by all scientists.
   Ⓒ It inspired many famous movies about asteroids hitting the Earth.
   Ⓓ It stems its argument on scientific knowledge and discovery.

6 How does the professor describe the impact of the asteroid collision on Earth 65.5 million years ago?

   Ⓐ He describes it using visual material.
   Ⓑ He compares it with the impact of powerful nuclear weapons.
   Ⓒ He explains the process of the asteroid colliding with the Earth.
   Ⓓ He provides previous examples of an asteroid collision with the Earth.

Vocabulary

✔ 박스에 체크 표기를 하며 주요 단어를 학습하시오.

- ☐ **scar** 상처
- ☐ **biologic** 생물적인
- ☐ **wound** 상처
- ☐ **response** 반응
- ☐ **blemish** 흠(집), 결점
- ☐ **emit** 방출하다
- ☐ **literal** 글자대로의
- ☐ **fluorescent** 형광의
- ☐ **incandescent** 백열의
- ☐ **faint** 희미한, 어렴풋한
- ☐ **influential** 영향력이 있는, 유력한
- ☐ **innovative** 혁신적인
- ☐ **stern** 엄격한, 단호한
- ☐ **affection** 애정
- ☐ **touchstone** 시금석; 표준, 기준
- ☐ **proclaim** 선언하다, 공표하다
- ☐ **transportation** 교통(수단)
- ☐ **expand** 확장하다
- ☐ **practical** 실제의, 실용적인
- ☐ **elevate** 올리다
- ☐ **radical** 급진적인, 혁신적인
- ☐ **initiate** 시작하다
- ☐ **movement** 운동, 동향
- ☐ **involve** 관련시키다
- ☐ **visual** 시각의
- ☐ **deny** 부인하다
- ☐ **disgust** 역겹게 하다
- ☐ **pursue** 추구하다, 쫓다
- ☐ **systematic** 체계적인
- ☐ **surrealism** 초현실주의
- ☐ **renown** 명성
- ☐ **initial** 초기의, 초반의
- ☐ **telegraph** 전보
- ☐ **go into operation** 실행에 들어가다

- ☐ **emerge** 나오다, 나타나다, 드러나다
- ☐ **logical** 논리적인, 이치에 맞는
- ☐ **skyscraper** 마천루, 높은 빌딩
- ☐ **indigenous** 토착의
- ☐ **resemblance** 유사, 닮음
- ☐ **scalp** 머릿가죽, 두피
- ☐ **massive** 거대한, 육중한
- ☐ **extinction** 멸종
- ☐ **perish** 죽다, 소멸하다, 멸망하다
- ☐ **species** (생물) 종
- ☐ **conspicuous** 눈에 잘 띄는
- ☐ **wipe out** 쓸어내다
- ☐ **collide** 충돌하다
- ☐ **fossilize** 화석화되다
- ☐ **sedimentary** 침전물의
- ☐ **concentration** 집결, 집중
- ☐ **dominate** 지배하다
- ☐ **asteroid** 소행성
- ☐ **abundance** 풍부함
- ☐ **extraterrestrial** 지구 밖의, 외계의
- ☐ **comet** 혜성
- ☐ **isotopic** 동위원소의
- ☐ **composition** 구성, 합성
- ☐ **inundate** 범람시키다, 물에 잠기게 하다
- ☐ **detonate** (폭약을) 폭발시키다
- ☐ **vapor** 수증기
- ☐ **intense** 강렬한, 격렬한
- ☐ **combustion** 연소
- ☐ **photosynthesis** 광합성
- ☐ **deplete** 고갈시키다
- ☐ **habitat** 거주지, 서식지
- ☐ **excess** 초과, 여분, 지나침
- ☐ **exterminate** 절멸하다, 몰살하다
- ☐ **controversial** 논란이 되는, 논쟁의 여지가 있는

Vocabulary Test

박스에서 올바른 단어를 골라 빈칸을 채우시오.

indigenous	disgust	conspicuous
influential	extraterrestrial	habitat

1   Considered a military genius with great intellect and a powerful will, Napoleon Bonaparte is considered one of the most _____ leaders of all time.

2   An _____ object which scientists could not figure out where it came from ended up in a small museum somewhere in Nebraska.

3   Ironically, the more George tried to hide his bruises, the more _____ it seemed to his peers.

4   Over the years, five of Chile's original 14 _____ tribes have been lost to the onslaught of colonialism, succumbing to disease, displacement and overuse of their traditional sources of food.

literally	collide	emit
controversial	pursue	resemblance

5   Should euthanasia be legal? Should the death penalty be abolished? These are few of the most _____ topics that still remain to be confirmed.

6   Different atoms _____ and absorb light at precise wavelengths that are unique for each element.

7   During summer time, the populations and the local infrastructure of the beach communities _____ explode.

8   Dr. Houston found a striking _____ between the two species; both animals from the different species had retractable heads and the end of their tails was split into three.

올바른 단어를 골라 문장을 완성하시오.

9 Jason thought there was no point in _____(ing) the rabbit anymore; it had jumped over a hedge and into the woods without leaving any trails.

Ⓐ dominate   Ⓑ deny   Ⓒ pursue   Ⓓ perish

10 If the labor strike at the factory goes on, our stock is expected to be _____ _____(-d/ed).

Ⓐ deplete   Ⓑ radical   Ⓒ excess   Ⓓ collide

11 The natural _____ of many animal and plant species is constantly being destroyed by human activity such as deforestation and so on.

Ⓐ kinship   Ⓑ response   Ⓒ resemblance   Ⓓ habitat

12 Despite the carrot and the stick from the detectives and the attorney, the suspect is still _____(ing) the charge of murdering the little girl.

Ⓐ proclaim   Ⓑ deny   Ⓒ assign   Ⓓ perish

13 Luckily, nobody got seriously injured when the pickup truck _____ _____(-d/ed) into the house.

Ⓐ collide   Ⓑ emit   Ⓒ biologic   Ⓓ disgust

14 Babies, whether they be of human or animals, need constant care and _____ from their parents or care providers.

Ⓐ visual   Ⓑ kinship   Ⓒ response   Ⓓ affection

15 Much to her _____, she discovered a dead body of a possum at the entrance of her driveway.

Ⓐ exterminator   Ⓑ scar   Ⓒ disgust   Ⓓ response

Chapter 2

Supporting Detail

Supporting Detail 지문의 세부적인 정보 찾기

문제유형

- According to the professor(lecture), what is...?
- What does... when...
- What does the professor say about...?
- Where(Why/Who/When/How) did...?
- What is the example of...? Click on 2(3) answers.

Sample

Listen to part of a lecture in a health science class. 🎧

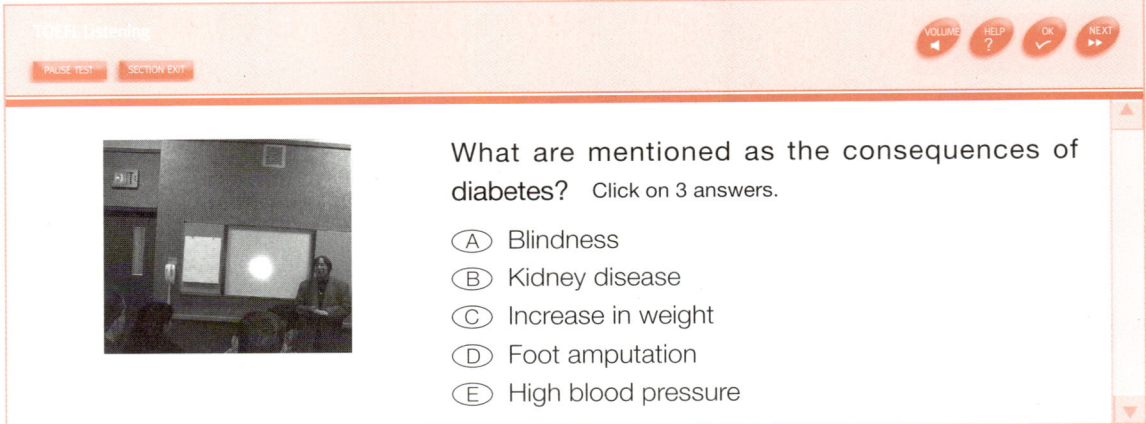

What are mentioned as the consequences of diabetes? Click on 3 answers.

- (A) Blindness
- (B) Kidney disease
- (C) Increase in weight
- (D) Foot amputation
- (E) High blood pressure

주제를 뒷받침하는 세부 사항에 유의하며 강의를 다시 한번 들으시오. 🎧

Although not an infectious disease, **diabetes** seems to be spreading like one. Since 1980, its prevalence in the United States has risen by 47 percent, a trend that's expected to take a space-shuttle trajectory in the next decade. That's because nearly half of Americans, **1** <u>especially men</u>, today either have the condition or are on the verge of developing it. And as you can easily imagine, **2** <u>the **consequences** are considerable</u>. Diabetes is the primary cause of cardiovascular disease, slashing a man's life span by an average of 13 years! Dodge early death and a man could still end up blind, in kidney failure, or, most likely, lose a foot.

Tip 강의나 토론에서 여러 번 언급되거나 열거되는 특징, 내용, 어떠한 현상에 대한 이유 등이 등장하는 경우 답을 2개나 3개 고르는 문제가 출제 될 수 있다.

Strategy

주제를 뒷받침하는 세부 사항들이 제시될 때 등장하는 signal phrase에 주목하자

Keyword와 key phrase를 통해 주제를 파악했다면, 이 주제를 지지하는 세부 정보들에 주목해야 한다. 주제를 뒷받침하는 세부 정보는 다음과 같이 여러 가지 방법으로 지문에 등장한다. 다음을 보면서 주제를 뒷받침하는 세부 정보의 기능과 이를 나타내는 signal phrase를 살펴보자.

정보의 기능	기능에 따라 등장하는 signal phrases
• 이유, 원인	- Because of ~, Due to ~, This is because ~, ~ is the cause of ~
• 설명	- ~ is/are ~, Basically ~, Most importantly ~
• 예시	- For example ~, For instance ~, One example of ~ is ~
• 해결책	- In order to solve this problem, ~ may be proposed
• 결과	- As a result, In consequence, Consequently, Because of ~
• 장점	- One of the strong points of ~ is ~, Some of the merits of ~ are ~
• 단점	- There is a drawback / shortcoming / weak point / defect of ~
• 열거, 반복	- And, Again
• 문제	- The problem of this is ~, There are some problems with ~
• 특징	- The characteristic of ~ is ~, The distinguishing mark of ~ is ~
• 순서	- First, Second, Next, Last, And then, Finally
• 비교	- ~ is similar to ~, ~ is same as ~, ~ and ~ are the same, Likewise
• 대조	- On the other hand, However, In contrast, Unlike

이제 앞서 등장한 지문으로 돌아가자. 강의의 keyword는 diabetes, consequences이며, key phrase 는 **1 especially men**과 **2 the consequences are considerable**이다. 이어 등장하는 문장 (Diabetes is the primary cause of...)을 통해 그 다음에 당뇨병의 합병증이 제시된다는 것을 알 수 있다. 즉, consequences와 primary cause of라는 표현은 결과 제시의 역할을 하고 있다.

강의에서는 당뇨병이 야기하는 여러가지 질병을 열거하고 있다.

> ✔ cardiovascular disease (심장혈관 질환)
> ✔ become blind (시력 상실)
> ✔ a kidney failure (신장 질환)
> ✔ lose a foot (다리 절단)

따라서 답은 A, B, D이다.

강의에는 많은 정보가 다양한 방식으로 제시되므로 이를 가능한 간략하고 한눈에 알아보기 쉽게 필기하는 것이 중요하다. 예를 들어 정보를 열거하거나 강조하는 경우에는 위에서와 같이 체크 표기를 하거나, 비교 및 대조를 하는 경우에는 적절한 화살표를 사용하여 정리해 두는 것이 효과적이다.

Strategy Focus

주제를 뒷받침하는 세부 사항에 유의하며 강의를 들으시오. 🎧

1

- **Focus :**
  paralegals

- **Keyword/Key phrase :**
  let's say, typical tasks include ~

Tip

강의 전반에 걸쳐 변호사 보조원의 업무에 대해 설명하고 있다.

☐ paralegal 변호사 보조원
☐ attorney 변호사
☐ specialty 전문분야
☐ supervision 감독

According to the lecture, which of the following can be performed by a paralegal?

- Ⓐ Give legal advice to clients
- Ⓑ Interview clients for the attorney
- Ⓒ Sign genuine legal documents
- Ⓓ Speak for the client at a court of law

2

- **Focus :**

- **Keyword/Key phrase :**

강의 중간에 등장하는 "This chronic high blood sugar is also known as hyperglycemia"라는 부분에서 답을 추론할 수 있다.

☐ diabetes 당뇨병
☐ bloodstream 혈류
☐ excessive 과도한
☐ resistant 저항하는
☐ chronic 만성의
☐ marker 표적
☐ calamity 큰 불행

According to the lecture, which of the following patients has hyperglycemia?

- Ⓐ A man whose legs are swollen
- Ⓑ A child who is 50 pounds overweight
- Ⓒ A man who has high insulin-resistance
- Ⓓ A woman who has had high blood sugar for a long time

3

• Focus :

....

• Keyword/Key phrase :

....

....

....

Tip

TA는 조직 내에서 움직이는 상품의 속도를 방해하는 병목현상을 제거하는 것이 목적이라는 설명에서 답을 찾을 수 있다.

☐ accounting 회계
☐ approach 접근방법
☐ throughput 작업처리량
☐ alternative 대안(의)
☐ bottleneck 병목현상
☐ profit 이윤
☐ expense 지출, 비용

What does the professor say about Throughput Accounting?

Ⓐ It tries to improve profit performance.

Ⓑ It is another word for Standard Cost Accounting.

Ⓒ It cannot be applied to non-profit organizations.

Ⓓ It hinders the speed of decision making in an organization.

4

• Focus :

....

• Keyword/Key phrase :

....

....

....

강의 초반에서 교수는 광우병에 대해 설명하며 소와 인간에게 미치는 영향에 대해 실례를 들어 설명한다.

☐ progressive 진행하는
☐ degenerative 퇴행성의
☐ fatal 치명적인
☐ nervous 신경의
☐ livestock 가축
☐ infectious 전염성의
☐ contaminated 오염된
☐ variant 변형, 변이체

According to the lecture, what is mentioned about BSE?　Click on 2 answers.

Ⓐ BSE is only detrimental to the cattle, not humans.

Ⓑ Humans become infected with BSE by touching a cow with BSE.

Ⓒ The form of BSE occurring to cattle and humans are different.

Ⓓ Humans might become infected with BSE by eating beef from a cow with BSE.

Exercise

Listen to part of a lecture in an education class. 🎧

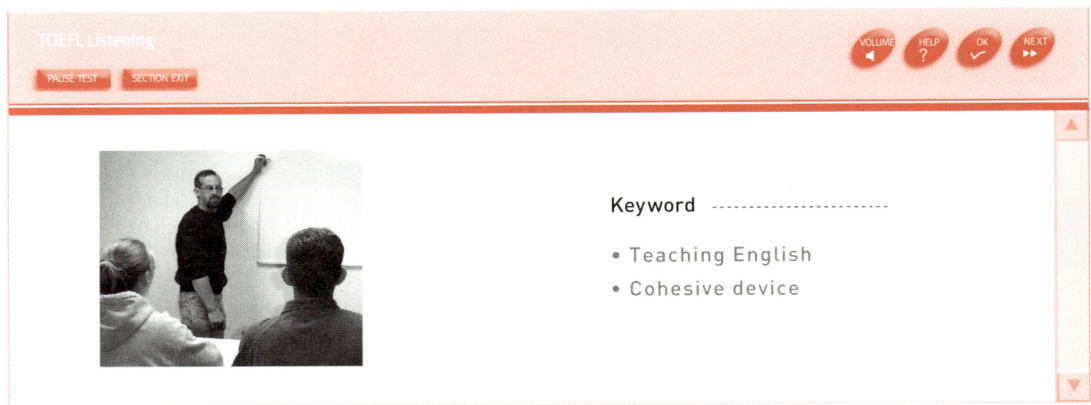

Keyword -

• Teaching English
• Cohesive device

1 What does the professor mainly discuss?

Ⓐ The difficulty of learning cohesive device

Ⓑ ESL students in the United States

Ⓒ Linking devices and their interchangeability

Ⓓ The method to teach cohesive devices to ESL learners

2 According to the professor, what is a cohesive device?

Ⓐ Material device which visualizes one's intention during conversation

Ⓑ Linguistic apparatus which connects separate expressions into related ideas

Ⓒ Mentally produced device which is easy for English language students to learn

Ⓓ Linguistic apparatus which is not helpful in understanding the intent of the writer

3 What can be inferred about the reason why many English learners have problems with learning cohesive devices?

Ⓐ It is difficult to learn a language other than one's own.

Ⓑ Different cohesive devices are used in different settings.

Ⓒ There are not enough writing teachers in schools.

Ⓓ The method of teaching cohesive devices is not fixed according to the age, grade, and proficiency of students.

Passage 2   Listen to part of a lecture in a health science class. 🎧

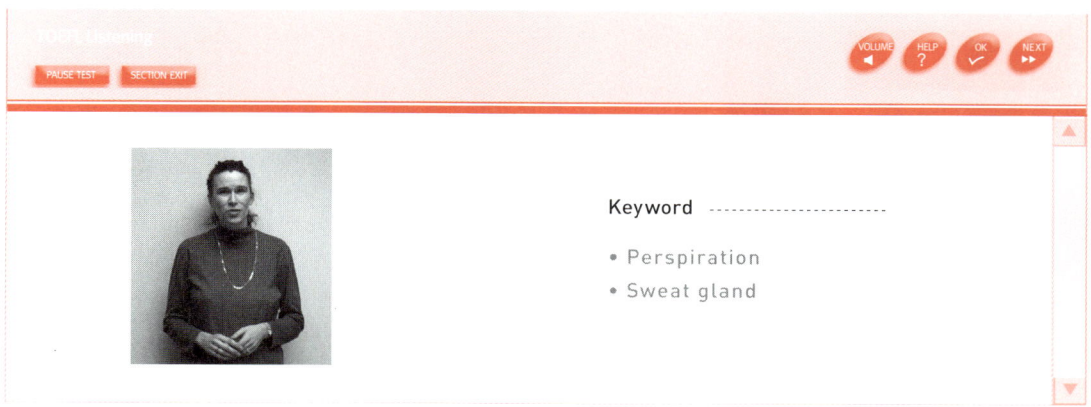

1 What is the main topic of the lecture?
- Ⓐ How to work out at a gym
- Ⓑ What sweat glands look like
- Ⓒ Perspiration and the human body
- Ⓓ The hypothalamus and its functions

2 According to the professor, why do people sweat?
- Ⓐ To enable the brain to function
- Ⓑ To lower the temperature of the body
- Ⓒ To get rid of excessive water in the body
- Ⓓ To eliminate excessive sodium chloride in the body

3 According to the professor, what does human sweat mainly consist of?
- Ⓐ Water and sodium chloride
- Ⓑ Water and table salt
- Ⓒ Sweat gland and water
- Ⓓ Water and hypothalamus

Passage 3

Listen to part of a discussion in a linguistics class.

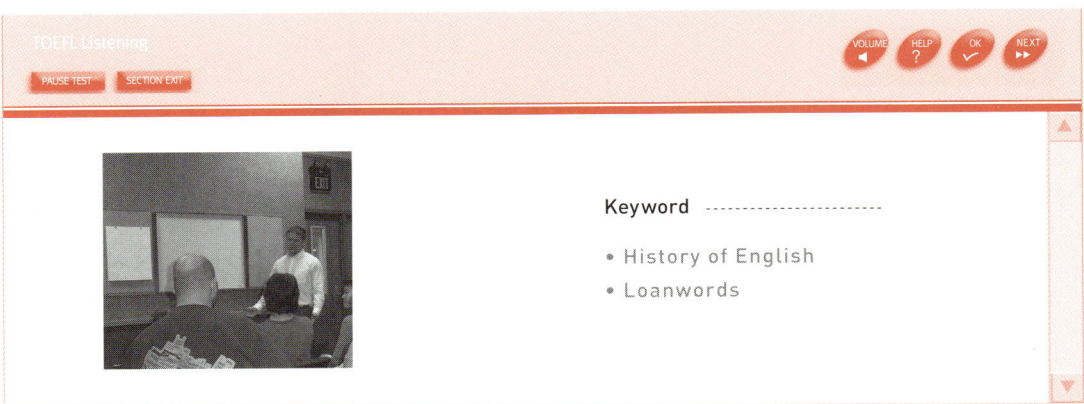

TOEFL Listening

PAUSE TEST   SECTION EXIT

VOLUME   HELP ?   OK   NEXT

Keyword ----------------------

• History of English
• Loanwords

1 What is the main topic of the discussion?

(A) History of England and the language of the English people

(B) Ancestor language of the modern English language

(C) How many words in English were borrowed from the French language

(D) Influence of many foreign languages on the English words

2 According to the discussion, which of the following statements is NOT true?

(A) The loanwords ballet, camouflage and etiquette are from the French language.

(B) The loanwords clock, hamburger and school are from the German language.

(C) The loanwords crayon, mortgage and publicity are from the Spanish language.

(D) The loanwords alcohol, algebra and zero are from the Arabic language.

3 What will the professor probably discuss next?

(A) How Normans were able to conquer the island of Britain

(B) Why English has borrowed so many words from different languages

(C) The similarity between Middle English and Modern English in terms of spelling and grammar

(D) The difference between Old English and Modern English in terms of pronunciation and appearance

Listen to part of a lecture in an art class. 🎧

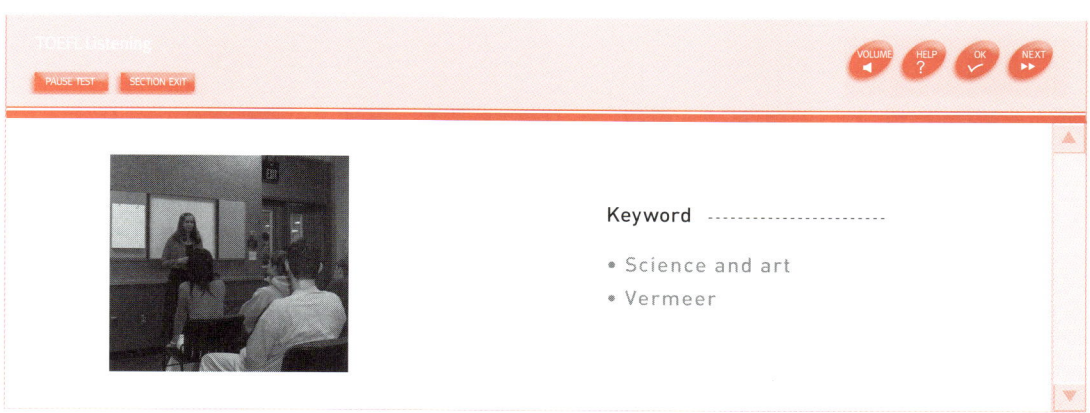

Keyword ----------------------

- Science and art
- Vermeer

1 What does the professor mainly discuss?

Ⓐ The function of X-ray in art field

Ⓑ The scientific analysis of Vermeer's work

Ⓒ Vermeer and his works during his prime time

Ⓓ Technology used in verifying the authenticity of a masterpiece

2 What aspect of a painting do scientists and art historians try to discover in order to verify its authenticity?

Ⓐ The drawing technique

Ⓑ The material that was used for the painting

Ⓒ The time period the painting was created

Ⓓ The place where the painting was created

3 According to the professor, what was mentioned as the method to distinguish the authenticity of *Young Woman Seated at the Virginals*?

Click on 2 answers.

Ⓐ Microscope examination   Ⓑ X-ray examination

Ⓒ Autograph verification   Ⓓ Pigment analysis

Passage 5 Listen to part of a lecture in a botany class. 🎧

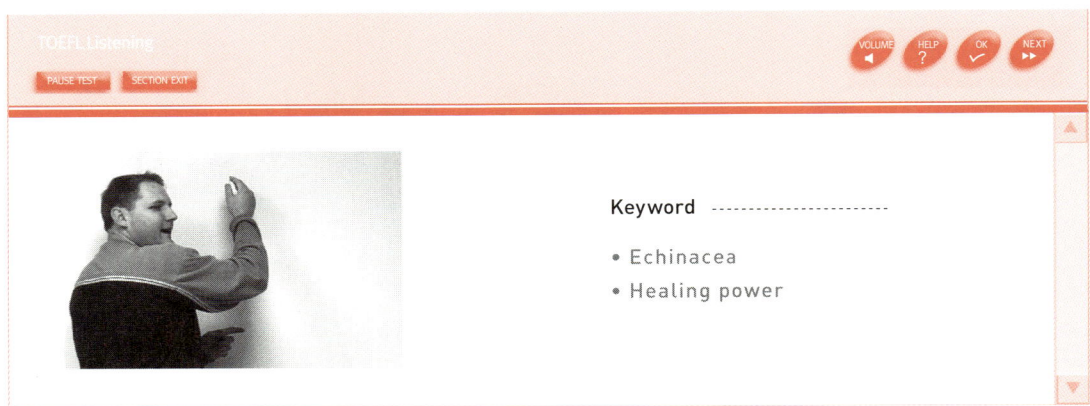

TOEFL Listening
PAUSE TEST   SECTION EXIT
VOLUME HELP ? OK ✓ NEXT ►►

Keyword -

• Echinacea
• Healing power

1 What is the lecture mainly about?
- Ⓐ The habitat of Echinacea
- Ⓑ The current use of Echinacea as medicine
- Ⓒ Similarity between Echinacea and antibiotics
- Ⓓ Use of Echinacea's healing power by the Native Americans

2 What did Native Americans use Echinacea for?
- Ⓐ Medicine
- Ⓑ Food ingredient
- Ⓒ Spice
- Ⓓ Building material

3 According to the lecture, how does Echinacea heal diseases?
- Ⓐ It fiercefully attacks bacteria in the immune cells.
- Ⓑ It needs to be used together with other medical herbs.
- Ⓒ It strengthens the immune cells to fight bacteria more efficiently.
- Ⓓ It has no healing power contrary to common belief.

Passage 6   Listen to part of a lecture in a music history class. 🎧

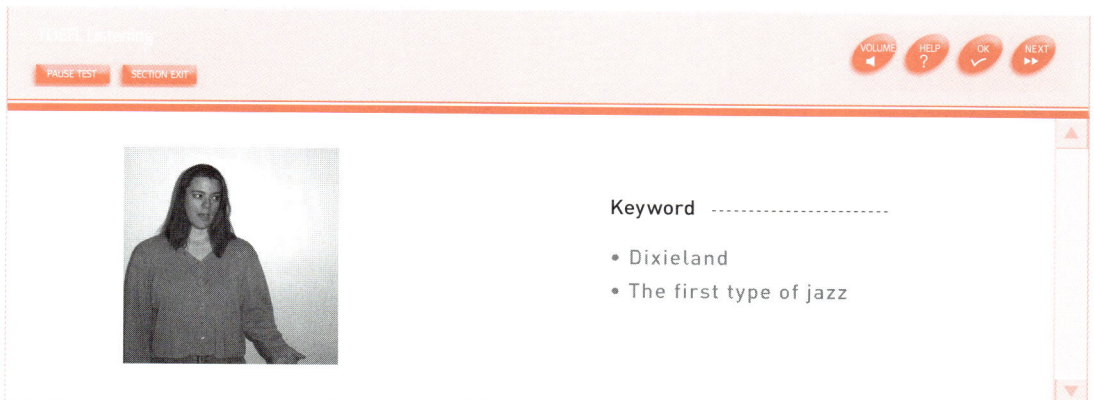

Keyword ----------------------

- Dixieland
- The first type of jazz

1 What is the topic of the lecture?
- Ⓐ Original Dixieland Jazz Band and its members
- Ⓑ Why Dixieland jazz is known as New Orleans jazz
- Ⓒ How Dixieland jazz spread to Chicago
- Ⓓ Dixieland jazz and its origin

2 What is NOT true about Dixieland?
- Ⓐ Its other name is traditional jazz.
- Ⓑ It spread to Chicago, New York, and California.
- Ⓒ It is widely recognized as the first type of jazz.
- Ⓓ It first appeared at the beginning of the 18th century in New Orleans, Louisiana.

3 According to the lecture, where did Dixieland get its name from?
- Ⓐ From the first band that made a jazz recording
- Ⓑ From the city where it first originated from
- Ⓒ From the style of a jazz which it was famous of
- Ⓓ From the name of a recording studio where many jazz musicians recorded

Passage 7 — Listen to part of a lecture in a literature class. 🎧

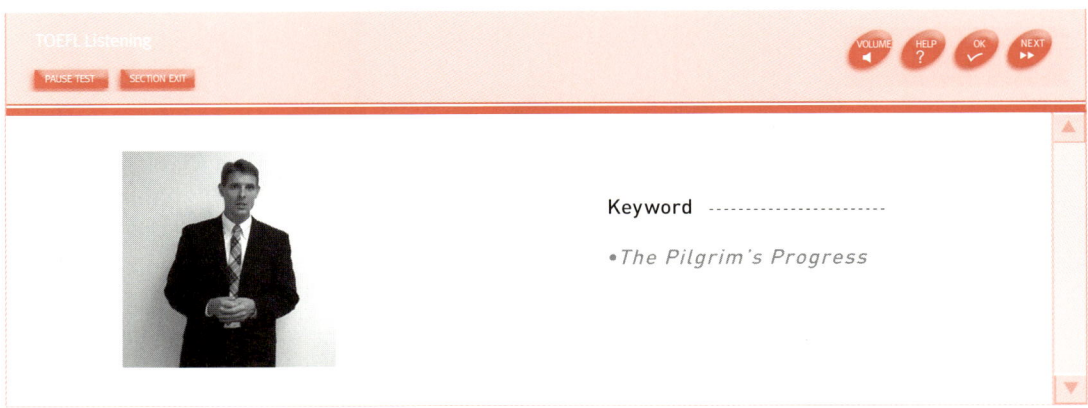

TOEFL Listening

PAUSE TEST   SECTION EXIT

VOLUME   HELP   OK   NEXT

Keyword -------------------------

•*The Pilgrim's Progress*

1 What is the main topic of the lecture?
- Ⓐ John Bunyan and his life as the Puritan writer and preacher
- Ⓑ How John Bunyan became a disestablishmentarian
- Ⓒ John Bunyan's life and his book, *The Pilgrim's Progress*
- Ⓓ Why John Bunyan wrote *The Pilgrim's Progress* in prison

2 Why does the professor mention establishmentarians?
- Ⓐ He was trying to explain why Bunyan opposed to the Anglican Church.
- Ⓑ He wanted to shift the topic from Bunyan to the Anglican Church.
- Ⓒ He wanted to provide the background setting of Bunyan's book.
- Ⓓ He was discussing information not directly related to the main topic.

3 How does the professor feel about *The Pilgrim's Progress*?
- Ⓐ He thinks that it is a timeless Christian classic.
- Ⓑ He feels apathetic that it was written by a Puritan.
- Ⓒ He considers it worthless for the modern world.
- Ⓓ He is enthusiastic because it contains many difficult allegories.

Passage 8   Listen to part of a discussion in a health science class. 🎧

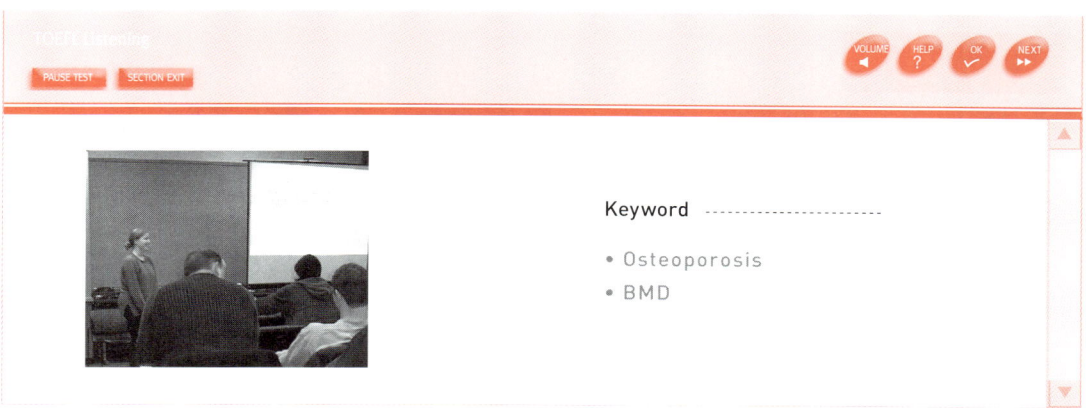

Keyword -----------------

• Osteoporosis
• BMD

1 **What is the discussion mainly about?**
- Ⓐ Relevance of BMD to osteoporosis
- Ⓑ General nature of osteoporosis
- Ⓒ Varying susceptibility to osteoporosis between men and women
- Ⓓ Reasons behind high rates of osteoporosis in pre-menopausal women

2 **Why does the professor mention a sponge during her speech?**
- Ⓐ To contrast the methods of detecting osteoporosis in bone
- Ⓑ To provide a visual image of bone with osteoporosis by comparing it with a sponge
- Ⓒ To explain how osteoporosis progresses in bone by describing how a sponge is created
- Ⓓ To demonstrate how bone with osteoporosis fractures

3 **Why is a woman in her menopause more susceptible to osteoporosis?**
- Ⓐ Because menopausal women usually have a sedentary lifestyle
- Ⓑ Because menopausal women will lose more calcium from her bones than pre-menopausal women
- Ⓒ Because estrogen level will be reduced after menopause
- Ⓓ Because pregnancy and breast-feeding usually alters hormone levels in menopausal women

Exercise

Passage 9   Listen to part of a discussion in a linguistics class. 🎧

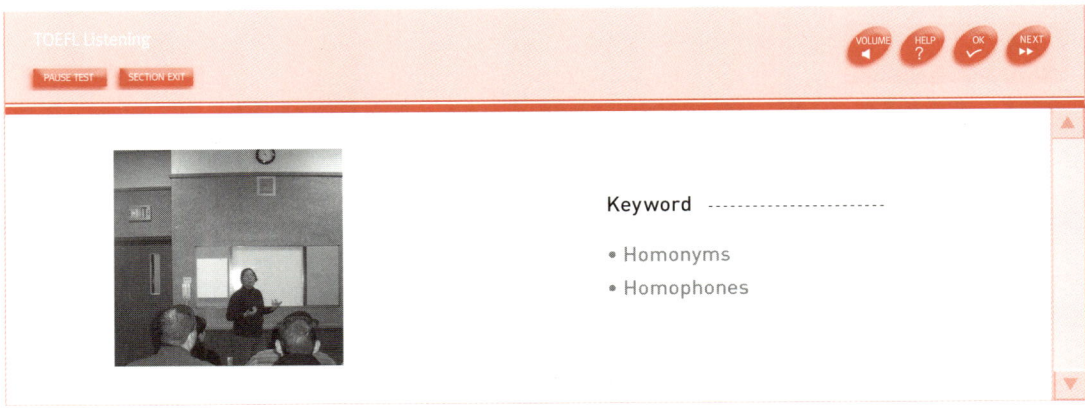

Keyword ----------------------------

• Homonyms
• Homophones

---

1 What is the topic of the discussion?

(A) How homonyms and homophones create complicated structures

(B) The definition of homonyms and homophones

(C) Why buffaloes intimidate other buffaloes

(D) The three definitions of buffalo

2 According to the professor, what is the capitalized Buffalo?

(A) It is a name of an animal.

(B) It is a name of a city in New York.

(C) It is a verb meaning to confuse or to intimidate.

(D) It is a name of a group of bison who dominate other groups of bison.

3 What can be inferred about homonyms and homophones?

(A) They are not complicated at all.

(B) They always clarify the meaning of the sentence.

(C) They are usually used in everyday conversation.

(D) They sometimes create complicated sentence structures.

4   Listen again to part of the discussion. Then answer the question.
    What does the professor want to know when she says this: 🎧
    - (A) Whether the school bell has tolled and the class has ended
    - (B) Whether the students understood the information she just mentioned
    - (C) Whether the information she just mentioned reminded students of anything
    - (D) Whether the students understand that the sentence is grammatically correct

5   Why did the professor mention the sentence, "Don't trouble trouble until
    trouble troubles you"?
    - (A) To provide an advice she has learnt from her past experience
    - (B) To give students a difficult assignment to work on for the week
    - (C) To chastise students who are used to using simple sentence structure
    - (D) To provide an example of how homonyms and homophones generate complexity

Passage10   Listen to part of a lecture in a world history class. 🎧

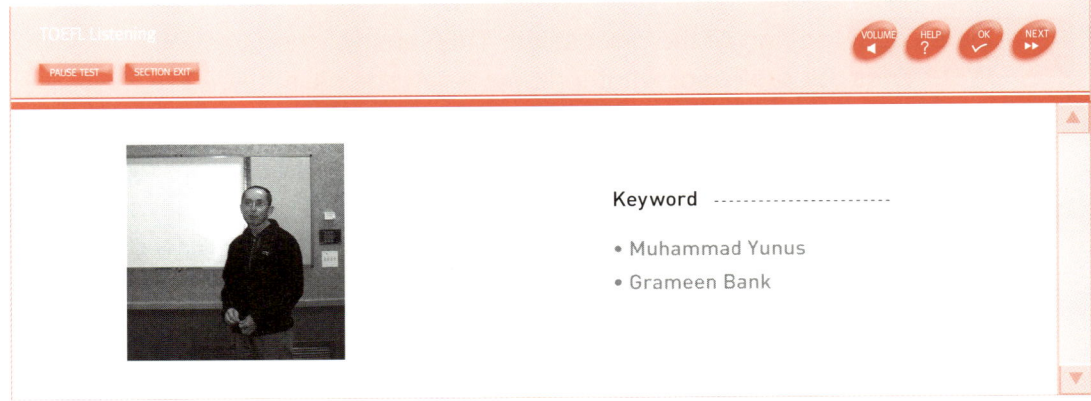

TOEFL Listening

VOLUME   HELP   OK   NEXT

PAUSE TEST   SECTION EXIT

Keyword -----------------------

• Muhammad Yunus
• Grameen Bank

1 What is the professor mainly discussing?

- Ⓐ The personal history of Muhammad Yunus
- Ⓑ The life condition of the poor of Bangladesh
- Ⓒ The foundation of Grameen Bank by Muhammad Yunus
- Ⓓ The creation of the concept of microcredit loan

2 According to the professor, what is the concept of microcredit loan?

- Ⓐ Lending small amount of money with low interest to the poor
- Ⓑ Lending small amount of money with high interest to the poor
- Ⓒ Lending large amount of money with low interest to entrepreneurs
- Ⓓ Lending $30 to everyone who make their living by making bamboo furniture

3 What were mentioned as the reasons for chronic poverty in Bangladesh?

Click on 2 answers.

- Ⓐ The interest rate for the loan was too high.
- Ⓑ The poor could only take a small amount of loan.
- Ⓒ The poor only made very small profit.
- Ⓓ It took the poor too much time to make goods for sale.

Vocabulary

✔ 박스에 체크 표기를 하며 주요 단어를 학습하시오.

- ☐ **cohesive** 결합하는, 응집성의
- ☐ **device** 장치, 기구
- ☐ **crucial** 결정적인, 중대한
- ☐ **problematic** 문제가 있는
- ☐ **misleading** 오해시키는, 혼동케 하는
- ☐ **interchangeable** 호환성이 있는
- ☐ **perspiration** 땀, 발한
- ☐ **gland** 선, 분비기관
- ☐ **period** 시기
- ☐ **original** 원래의
- ☐ **conquest** 정복
- ☐ **appearance** 외관
- ☐ **identical** 동일한
- ☐ **feature** 특징
- ☐ **scam** 사기
- ☐ **quandary** 곤경, 난국
- ☐ **authentic** 진짜의
- ☐ **forge** 위조하다, 날조하다
- ☐ **conventional** 전통적인, 진부한
- ☐ **pin-point** 정확히 짚어내다
- ☐ **distinguish** 구별하다
- ☐ **pigment** 색소
- ☐ **prominent** 저명한
- ☐ **remedy** 치료(요법)
- ☐ **derive** 이끌어내다
- ☐ **stimulate** 자극하다, 격려하다
- ☐ **infection** 감염, 오염
- ☐ **ailment** 병
- ☐ **antibiotic** 항생제
- ☐ **immune** 면역의
- ☐ **abnormal** 비정상의

- ☐ **delve into** ~로 파고들다
- ☐ **puritan** 청교도(의)
- ☐ **preach** 설교하다
- ☐ **imprison** 감옥에 가두다
- ☐ **oppose** 반대하다, 저항하다
- ☐ **allegory** 우화
- ☐ **osteoporosis** 골다공증
- ☐ **disrupt** 분열시키다, 파괴하다
- ☐ **alter** 바꾸다
- ☐ **resorption** (재)흡수
- ☐ **diminish** 줄이다
- ☐ **menopause** 폐경기
- ☐ **fracture** 골절, 좌상
- ☐ **spine** 척추
- ☐ **susceptible** ~하기 쉬운
- ☐ **chock-full of** ~이 많은
- ☐ **deficiency** 결핍, 부족
- ☐ **repetition** 반복
- ☐ **intimidate** 겁주다, 협박하다
- ☐ **prank** 농담, 장난
- ☐ **equivalent** ~과 동등한
- ☐ **deceive** 속이다, 기만하다
- ☐ **bison** 들소
- ☐ **construct** 건설하다, 구성하다
- ☐ **combination** 혼합
- ☐ **drought** 가뭄
- ☐ **socio-political** 사회정치적인
- ☐ **inspire** 영감을 주다
- ☐ **loan** 대출, 차관
- ☐ **generate** 일으키다, 발생시키다
- ☐ **usurious** 고리대금의

Vocabulary Test

박스에서 올바른 단어를 골라 빈칸을 채우시오.

drought	cohesive	repetition
remedy	abnormal	authentic

1. They were trying to find the _____ for insomnia to help people who were being tortured with sleep deprivation.

2. Exposing an advertisement multiple times over a period of time, _____ has been proven to increase recall and comprehension in consumers, particularly if the message is complex.

3. Students who learn English submerged in an English speaking society benefit from many different _____ materials, such as newspapers, magazines, television dramas and so on.

4. The Meteorology Department announced that the _____ that has been going on for more than two months in the region has reached a serious level — more than 45 percent of the region's farmland has dried up.

stimulate	abnormal	prank
immune	imprison	problematic

5. His behavior was _____ today — with disheveled hair, he didn't wear a tie to work, and wore different pairs of socks.

6. When your _____ system does not work properly, your body becomes more vulnerable to attacks from viruses and bacterias.

7. Janet's car got into an accident and had to be sent to the bodyshop; however, the damage turned out to be more _____ than first expected.

8. The police often use force, sometimes overwhelming physical force, to arrest and _____ criminals.

올바른 단어를 골라 문장을 완성하시오.

9 The salesperson said that their DVD player had the lowest price in town, but I found that the other electronics shop had the same model at a cheaper price. I feel like I've been _____(-d/ed).

Ⓐ forge   Ⓑ decevie   Ⓒ distinguish   Ⓓ stimulate

10 Thomas is a very mischievous boy; he likes to play _____(s) on his friends at school.

Ⓐ repetition   Ⓑ prank   Ⓒ fracture   Ⓓ scam

11 Although many citizens _____(-d/ed), the mayor decided to establish a solid gold monument in front of the City Hall, remembering the soldiers who fought in the recent war.

Ⓐ imprison   Ⓑ scam   Ⓒ constuct   Ⓓ oppose

12 In order to kill bacteria and treat infections well, you must follow the doctor's orders and take proper _____ as prescribed by the doctor.

Ⓐ antibiotic   Ⓑ repetition   Ⓒ drought   Ⓓ period

13 It is _____ for business owners and leaders to understand the current market to create profit.

Ⓐ authentic   Ⓑ immune   Ⓒ crucial   Ⓓ abormal

14 The president's remarks about North Korea _____(-d/ed) heated debates among people.

Ⓐ disrupt   Ⓑ stimulate   Ⓒ intake   Ⓓ oppose

15 Mark's cello CD contains not only _____ pieces he wrote but also other pieces of masters such as Beethoven and Bach.

Ⓐ original   Ⓑ allegory   Ⓒ cohesive   Ⓓ repetition

Chapter 3

Organization

3 Organization 지문의 구성과 정보간의 관계 이해하기

문제유형

- How does... emphasize(explain)...?
- How does the professor introduce(organize) his(her) lecture on...?
- In what order does... tell... about...?
- Why does the professor tell the students about...?
- Why does... mention...?

Sample

Listen to a part of a lecture in a health class. 🎧

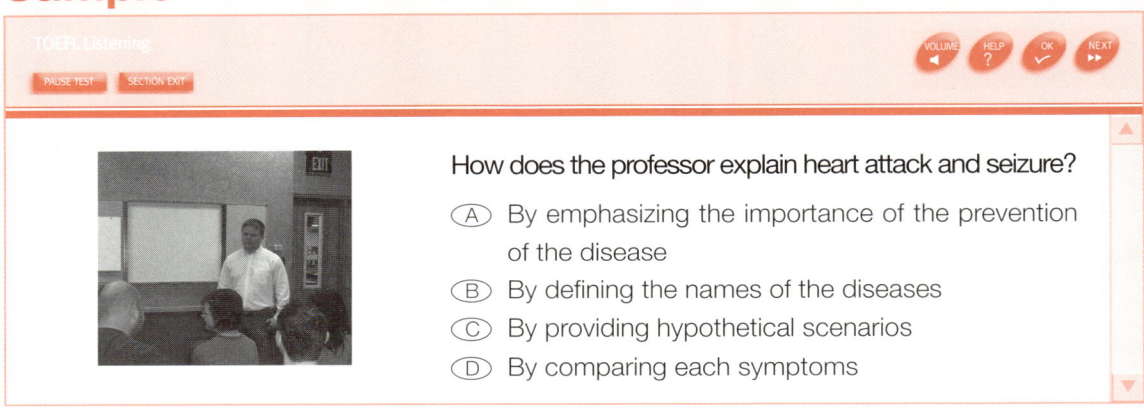

TOEFL Listening

VOLUME ◄ HELP ? OK ✓ NEXT ►►

PAUSE TEST   SECTION EXIT

How does the professor explain heart attack and seizure?

- (A) By emphasizing the importance of the prevention of the disease
- (B) By defining the names of the diseases
- (C) By providing hypothetical scenarios
- (D) By comparing each symptoms

표기된 signal phrases 및 정보간의 관계에 주목하며 다시 한번 들으시오. 🎧

And I saw a lot of people having trouble with understanding these diseases… they confuse heart attacks and seizures, not knowing the symptoms for each and thereby missing the valuable chance to give the right treatment and saving a person's life. **First of all**, heart attack is a disease that occurs when the blood supply to a part of the heart is interrupted, causing heart tissue to die. **1** Symptoms for heart attack, which is the leading cause of death for both men and women all around the globe, are severe chest pain and autonomic phenomena… you know, the patient looking pale, feeling sick, and sweating. **On the other hand**, seizure is a temporary abnormal electrophysiological phenomena of the brain. **2** When a person's muscle suddenly twitches involuntarily or feels numb in some parts of his or her body, you may suspect it's a seizure. When that person shows this symptom, he or she may fall to the ground, lose consciousness, and violently convulse.

Tip Why does ~로 질문이 시작되는 경우에는 선택지가 To emphasize ~, To demonstrate ~, To suggest ~ 등으로 시작된다.

지문 내 정보간의 유기적인 관계를 이해하자

강의에 등장하는 정보들은 다음과 같은 유기적인 관계를 가질 수 있다. 정보간의 관계에 따라 등장할 수 있는 다음과 같은 signal phrase에 주목하자.

정보의 관계	관계에 따라 등장하는 signal phrases
• Definition(Concept) + Explanation(Support)	- For example, For instance, Like, Let me illustrate, In this case, On this occasion, Take the case of
• Compare/Contrast	- On the other hand, Meanwhile, However, Unlike
• Cause and effect	- Because of, Due to, As a result
• Sequence (Process)	- First, Second, Last, Next, Finally
• Addition	- Additionally, Also, Besides, Equally important, Moreover
• Emphasis	- Absolutely, Definitely, Certainly, Extremely, In any case

교수는 심장마비와 발작의 증상을 다음과 같이 비교한다.

1 severe chest pain and autonomic phenomena... the patient looking pale, feeling sick, and sweating

2 person's muscle suddenly twitches involuntarily or feels numb... fall to the ground, lose consciousness, and violently convulse

On the other hand라는 표현으로 보아 Compare/Contrast로 구성되었음을 알 수 있으므로 정답은 D이다.

특정 정보와 전체 강의의 수사학적 관계를 이해하자

전체 강의에서 특정 정보가 구조적인 면에서 어떠한 역할을 하는지 파악하는 것이 중요하다. 각 구조적인 관계에 따라 선택지에 다양한 표현이 사용된다.

구조적 관계	관계에 따라 등장하는 표현
• Topic shift	- To shift/change the topic from A to B
• Relationship between main topic and subtopic	- To explain the relationship between A and B
• Exemplification	- To explain, To demonstrate, To prove, To provide evidence, To give the background of
• Digression	- To digress from the main topic
• Introductory or Concluding remarks	- To introduce/conclude the topic/lecture
• Others	- 기타

Strategy Focus

지문에서 제시된 정보간의 유기적 관계에 유의하며 강의를 들으시오. 🎧

1

• **Focus :**
  Omega-3 fatty acids

• **Role :**
  regulate blood pressure, fight against
  inflammation, immunity, baby's growth

How does the professor explain the food source of the omega-3 fatty acids?

(A) By comparing different food source

(B) By giving examples of the food source

(C) By indicating the importance of consuming the food source

(D) By defining the food group in which the food source is included

Tip

"Present in oily fish like salmon and sardines as well as walnuts, flaxseeds, and dark green vegetables"라는 교수의 말에서 힌트를 찾을 수 있다.

☐ omega-3 fatty acid
   오메가-3 지방산
☐ regulate 조절하다
☐ clot 응고
☐ inflammation 염증
☐ supplement 보충

2

• **Focus :** _____

• **Discovered in :** _____

• **How big :** _____

Why does the professor mention Bode's Law?

(A) To introduce today's topic

(B) To give assignment to the students

(C) To explain about the astronomer, Bode

(D) To conclude the previous lecture and move on

"This is basically what Bode's Law is"에서 지금까지 보데의 법칙에 대해 수업했음을 알 수 있다.

☐ gravitation 중력, 인력
☐ asteroid 소행성
☐ identify 확인하다, 식별하다

3

- Focus : _____

- Harold Foster : _____

- Other adventure comics : _____

Tip

1929년 처음 등장한 타잔을 언급한 후, 그 이후에 등장한 모험 만화의 주인공들을 탄생된 순서대로 소개하고 있다.

☐ adaptation 개조, 각색
☐ legendary 전설의
☐ tycoon (실업계의) 거물

In what order does the professor explain the first adventure comic strips?

(A) From the first appeared to the next
(B) From the most popular to the least
(C) From the most invested to the least
(D) From the least successful to the most

4

- Focus : _____

- Condition : _____

- Used in : _____

"Let's say that"에서 힌트를 찾을 수 있다.

☐ afford ~할 여유가 있다
☐ exchange 교환하다
☐ barter 물물교환
☐ transaction 거래, 매매
☐ monetary 화폐의, 통화의

Why does the professor mention Janet and her CD player?

(A) To introduce a new topic
(B) To scold her for being late to class
(C) To exemplify other monetary systems
(D) To emphasize the importance of new technology

Exercise

Listen to part of a lecture in a world history class. 🎧

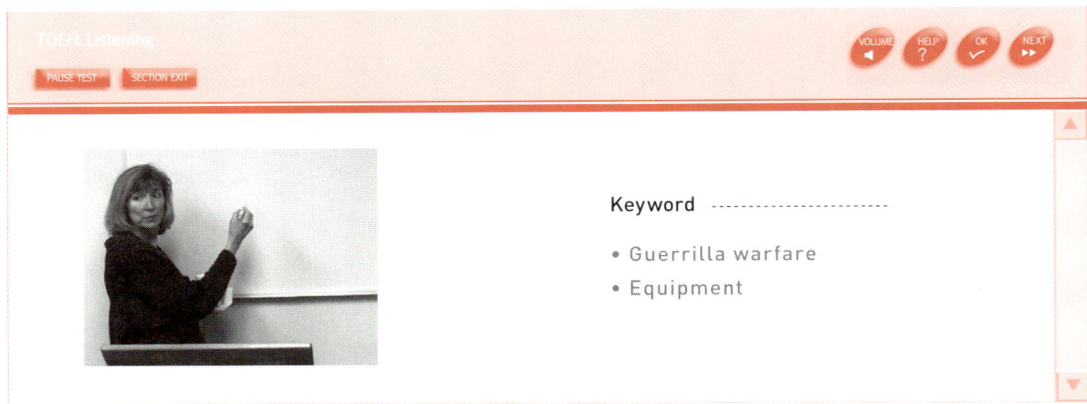

TOEFL Listening

PAUSE TEST   SECTION EXIT

VOLUME   HELP ?   OK ✓   NEXT ▶▶

Keyword ----------------------

• Guerrilla warfare
• Equipment

1 Why does the professor mention the Vietnam War?

Ⓐ To help the students understand guerrilla warfares better

Ⓑ To explain the tactics typically used by guerrillas in a foreign land

Ⓒ To remind the students of an unsuccessful guerrilla warfare

Ⓓ To provide an example of a guerrilla warfare conducted in an unfamiliar landscape

2 What were mentioned in the lecture as the equipment a guerrilla soldier should carry?   Click on 2 answers.

Ⓐ A sleeping bag

Ⓑ A book on tactics

Ⓒ A map

Ⓓ A hammock

3 How does the professor organize the lecture?

Ⓐ She compares one term with another.

Ⓑ She explains a term by explaining its most important supplies.

Ⓒ She defines a term and exemplifies its tactics and necessary supplies.

Ⓓ She defines a term and demonstrates one of its most famous examples.

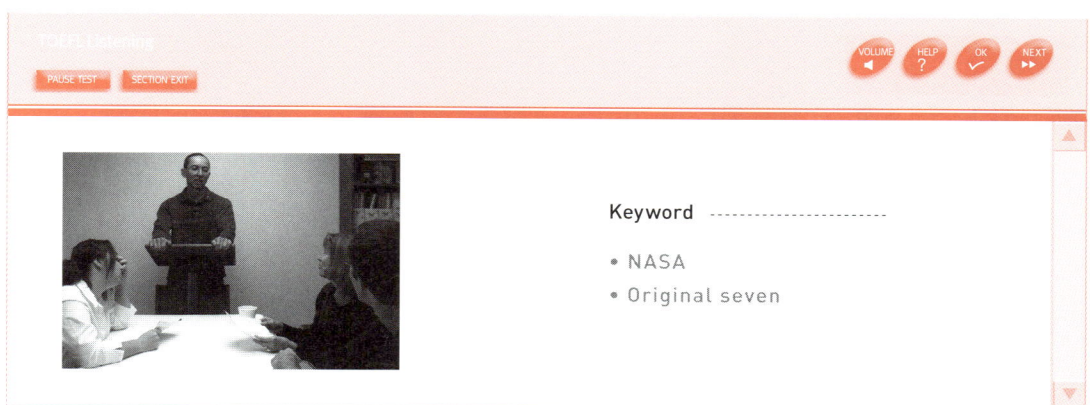

Passage 2   Listen to part of a lecture in an aerospace technology class. 🎧

Keyword ----------------------
• NASA
• Original seven

1 Listen again to part of the lecture. Then answer the question.
What does the professor imply when he says this: 🎧

(A) By coincidence, all seven astronauts' former occupation was a pilot.

(B) NASA intentionally did not recruit pilots as the first astronauts.

(C) NASA thought that military pilots would not be suitable for becoming astronauts.

(D) The occupations of the first astronauts are not known to the general public.

2 What were mentioned in the lecture as the former occupation of astronauts recruited by NASA?   Click on 2 answers.

(A) School teacher

(B) Manager

(C) Doctor

(D) Lawyer

3 In what order does the professor explain the recruit of astronauts by NASA?

(A) From the least recent to the most recent event

(B) From the most famous to the least well-known event

(C) From the most precise to the least precise example

(D) From the least important to the most important event

Passage 3   Listen to part of a discussion in a computer engineering class. 🎧

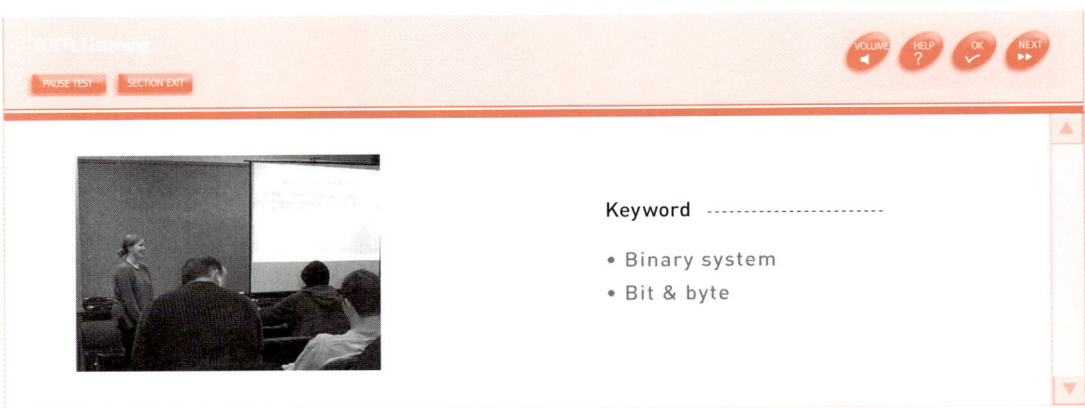

Keyword ------------------------

• Binary system
• Bit & byte

1   According to the professor, why is binary system used for computer systems?
Ⓐ Modern computer systems can only recognize the numbers 1 and 0.
Ⓑ Using binary system takes up less memory of the computer system.
Ⓒ Binary system was applied to the first computer system.
Ⓓ Binary system is easier to apply to computer system.

2   Which of the following are true about bit and byte?   Click on 2 answers.
Ⓐ Bit is the smallest unit of information in a digital world.
Ⓑ One byte equals eight bits.
Ⓒ The term bit is an abbreviation of the term decimal digit.
Ⓓ The term bit was used by many scientists before John Tukey used it in a published paper.

3   Why does the professor mention 11, 101, and 1001?
Ⓐ To show how certain words are indicated in binary logic
Ⓑ To exemplify how certain binary numbers are indicated in decimal logic
Ⓒ To demonstrate the difficulty of indicating decimal numbers in binary logic
Ⓓ To explain how certain decimal numbers are indicated in binary logic

Passage 4   Listen to part of a discussion in a health and food engineering class. 🎧

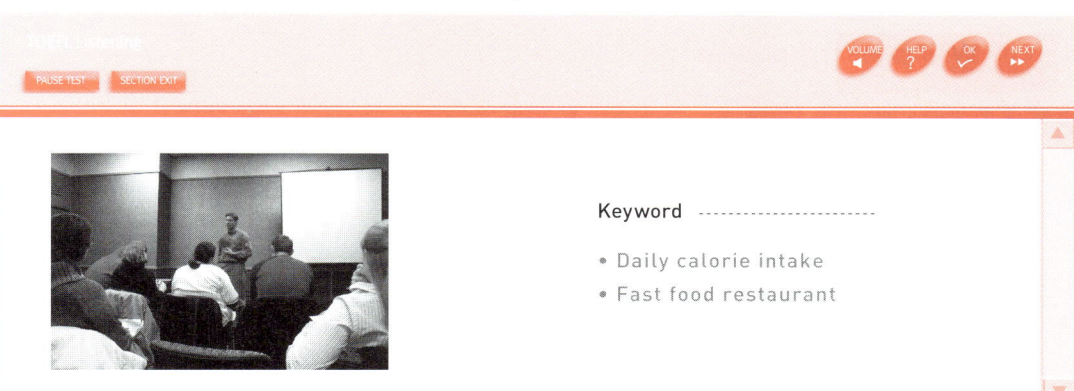

Keyword -

• Daily calorie intake
• Fast food restaurant

1 **What is the main topic of the discussion?**

Ⓐ How to cut down calories when there is less choice given
Ⓑ How much calories a person should consume per day
Ⓒ How to order food at a fast food restaurant
Ⓓ How eating pizza damages your health and growth

2 **What does the professor say about ordering food at a fast food restaurant?**

Ⓐ Order fried fish sandwich instead of grilled beef burger.
Ⓑ Order vegetable pizza instead of meat and cheese pizza.
Ⓒ Order garden green salad and fruit but never order pizza.
Ⓓ Order a large batch of fries and burger with double beef patty.

3 **Why does the professor mention the UK Department of Health and the recommended daily calorie intake?**

Ⓐ To deviate from the main topic
Ⓑ To provide an authority to the topic being discussed
Ⓒ To provide an example of how the calories are calculated
Ⓓ To explain why women should take less calories than men

4 Why does the professor say this:

Ⓐ He remembers visiting a fast food restaurant last week, but does not remember the exact name of the restaurant.

Ⓑ He used to work for the UK Department of Health, but does not remember its location.

Ⓒ He wants to return to the main topic of today's lecture, but does not remember what he was talking about earlier.

Ⓓ He remembers a student asking him a question, but does not remember what the question was about.

5 What were mentioned in the discussion as the factor that affects the personal daily calorie intake?   Click on 3 answers.

Ⓐ Health condition

Ⓑ Age

Ⓒ Intelligence level

Ⓓ Weight

Ⓔ Basic level of daily activity

Passage 5   Listen to part of a lecture in a medical science class. 🎧

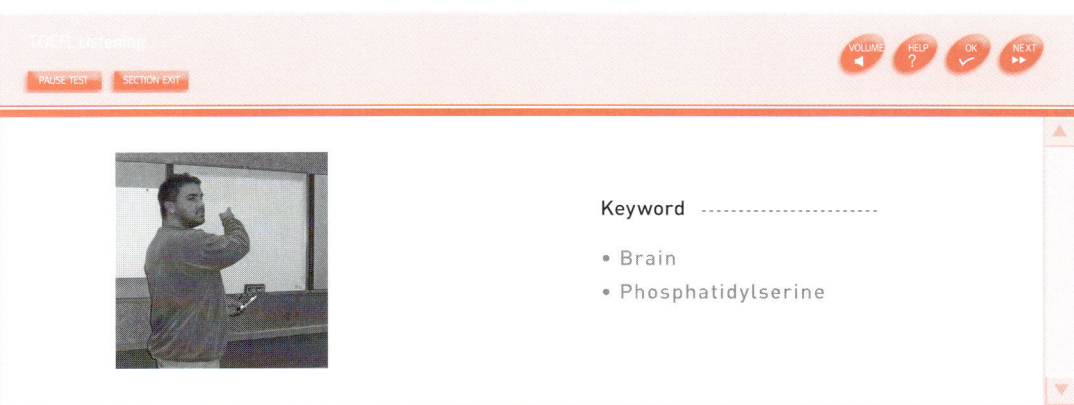

Keyword -----------------------

- Brain
- Phosphatidylserine

1 Listen again to part of the lecture. Then answer the question.
What does the professor mean when he says this: 🎧

Ⓐ He wants the students to write down the spelling of the term now.

Ⓑ He wants the students to memorize the spelling of the term before the lecture starts.

Ⓒ He wants the students to write down the spelling of the term later and focus on the lecture first.

Ⓓ He wants the students to figure out how to spell the term on their own.

2 Why does the professor mention phosphatidylserine?

Ⓐ To ask the students to research more on the substance

Ⓑ To shift the topic from brain health to heart health

Ⓒ To give example of a substance that was discovered to benefit brain health

Ⓓ To conclude the lecture on brain health and move onto another topic

3 According to the lecture, how does the brain maintain optimal health?

Click on 2 answers.

Ⓐ Regular diet   Ⓑ Exercise of the brain

Ⓒ Intake of proper nourishment   Ⓓ Sufficient amount of rest

Exercise

Passage 6   Listen to part of a discussion in a zoology class. 🎧

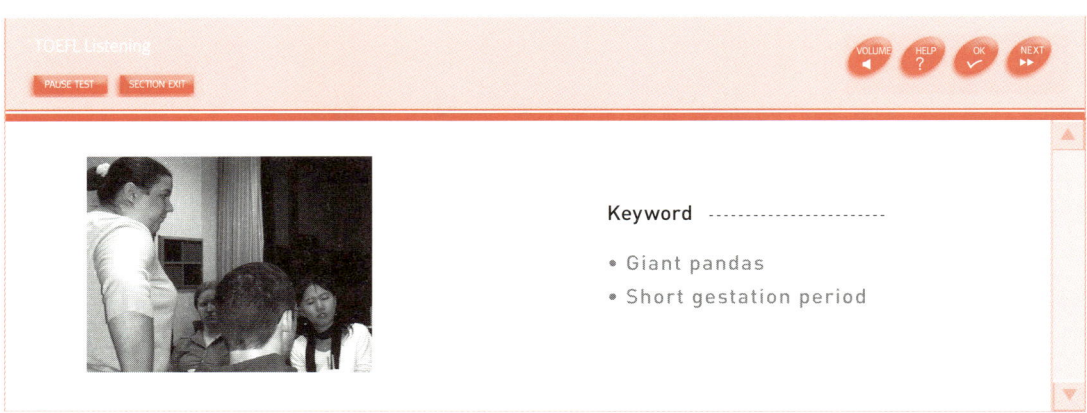

Keyword -----------------------

• Giant pandas
• Short gestation period

1   What is the discussion mainly about?

(A) Giant pandas and the mating procedure

(B) Methods to increase giant pandas' reproduction rate

(C) Low reproduction rate of Giant pandas in captivity

(D) Ling-Ling and Hsing-Hsing, the first pair of pandas in the United States

2   Why does the professor mention the cub of a 9-year-old giant panda that was born on September 6, 2006?

(A) To impress the class with his knowledge on giant pandas

(B) To criticize the ineffective breeding programs of giant pandas in the United States

(C) To demonstrate the low birthrate of giant pandas, especially in captivity

(D) To remind the fact that there are four zoos in the United States that host breeding pairs of giant pandas

3 According to the professor, why is the reproduction rate of giant pandas in zoos so low?

    Ⓐ Because male and female pandas in zoos are kept separate until both are fertile

    Ⓑ Because male pandas in captivity have no source from which to learn how to mate

    Ⓒ Because male pandas in zoos have no other male to compete with

    Ⓓ Because zookeepers do not apply appropriate method to measure the female pandas' gestation period

4 Listen again to part of the discussion. Then answer the question.
Why does the student say this: 🎧

    Ⓐ He is trying to stand out in front of the other students.

    Ⓑ He is confirming that he has understood the professor's remark.

    Ⓒ He is disagreeing with the professor's remark.

    Ⓓ He is adding new information to the professor's explanation.

5 The professor discusses giant pandas and their reproduction rate in nature and in captivity. Based on the information in the discussion, indicate whether each sentence below describes giant pandas in the wild or in captivity.

Click in the correct box.

	In wilderness	In captivity
Male pandas cannot learn how to mate from other pandas' behaviors.		
Male pandas compete for a female during mating season.		
Female pandas give birth every two years for about 15 years.		
The mother panda and the cub are separated six months after birth.		
Male pandas and female pandas live in different domains until the female is fertile.		

Passage 7   Listen to part of a discussion in a health science class. 🎧

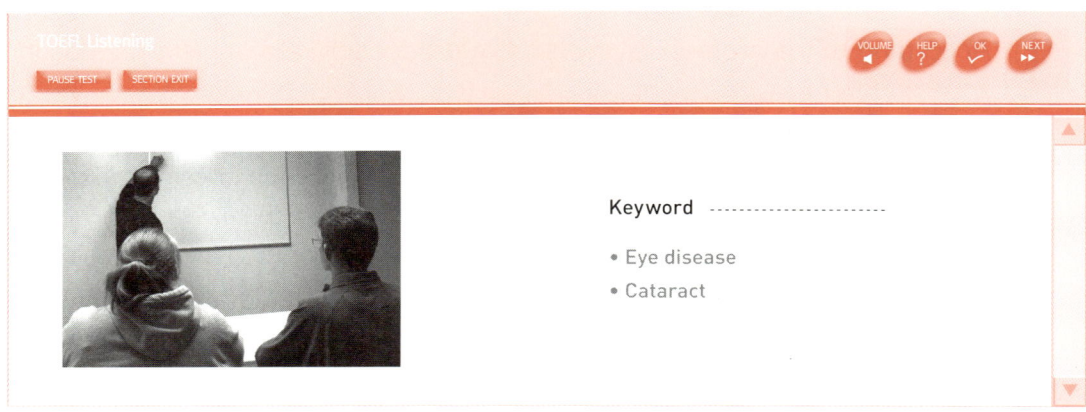

Keyword --------------------------

• Eye disease
• Cataract

---

1   What is the possible subject of the discussion?

Ⓐ Cataract: Definition and symptoms
Ⓑ Cataract: Ways to avoid abusing your eyes
Ⓒ Cataract: Its cause, symptoms and prevention
Ⓓ Cataract: The dreaded disease for the old

2   What were mentioned as the common misconceptions about cataract?

Click on 2 answers.

Ⓐ Cataract is a film over the eye.
Ⓑ Cataract spreads from one eye to the other.
Ⓒ Cataract is caused by overexposure to the sunlight.
Ⓓ Cataract, if mistreated, causes permanent vision loss.

3   Why does the professor mention a frosted window?

Ⓐ To provide an example of having diabetes
Ⓑ To highlight the main cause of cataract
Ⓒ To explain how it feels like to have cataract
Ⓓ To emphasize the importance of keeping your windows clean

4 According to the professor, who is most likely to develop cataract?

- (A) A 20-year-old woman who lost her eye to an accident
- (B) A 75-year-old man who had eye surgery before
- (C) A 15-year-old teenager with diabetes
- (D) A 35-year-old man with leprosy

5 What were mentioned as the common symptoms of cataract?   Click on 3 answers.

- (A) Yellowing of colors
- (B) Poor night vision
- (C) Pain in the eye
- (D) Light insensitivity
- (E) Double vision in one eye

6 According to the professor, how long does it take to develop cataract?

- (A) It usually takes about six months to develop fully.
- (B) It is most likely to develop rapidly within a short period of time.
- (C) It develops over a long period of time, usually from one eye to the other.
- (D) It cannot be predicted since it depends on various conditions.

Passage 8   Listen to part of a lecture in a space science class. 🎧

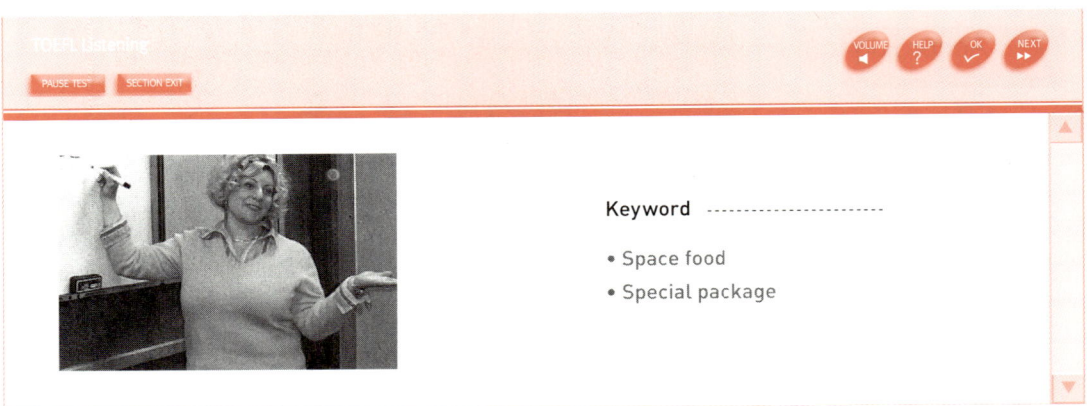

1   What is the lecture mainly about?
- (A) Why astronauts eat particular types of food in space
- (B) What you need to prepare in order to go camping for a month
- (C) Why the United States and Russia are competing over distribution of space food
- (D) What kind of food astronauts eat in space and what is important when preparing space food

2   What are mentioned in the lecture as the necessity for a long-term camping trip?

Click on 3 answers.

- (A) Aluminum foil
- (B) Saran wrap
- (C) Frying pan
- (D) Paper plates
- (E) Garbage bag

3 Why does the professor mention canned food or dried food that is nonperishable when going camping?

- Ⓐ To explain what kind of food is needed in space
- Ⓑ To explain how difficult it is to become an astronaut
- Ⓒ To explain the manufacturers of canned or dried food consumed in space
- Ⓓ To make sure the students are prepared when living in space for a long time

4 How does the professor organize the lecture?

- Ⓐ She puts the ideas in chronological order.
- Ⓑ She provides several examples of space food.
- Ⓒ She compares the space food made by the U.S. and by Russia.
- Ⓓ She gives example of camping and explains important matters of space food.

5 What are mentioned in the lecture about space food?   Click on 2 answers.

- Ⓐ Fruits are prohibited in a space shuttle.
- Ⓑ All space food is stored in a retort bag.
- Ⓒ Space food is provided by both Russia and the U.S.
- Ⓓ Some types of food may be consumed in their natural form.

Passage 9   Listen to part of a lecture in an environmental studies class. 🎧

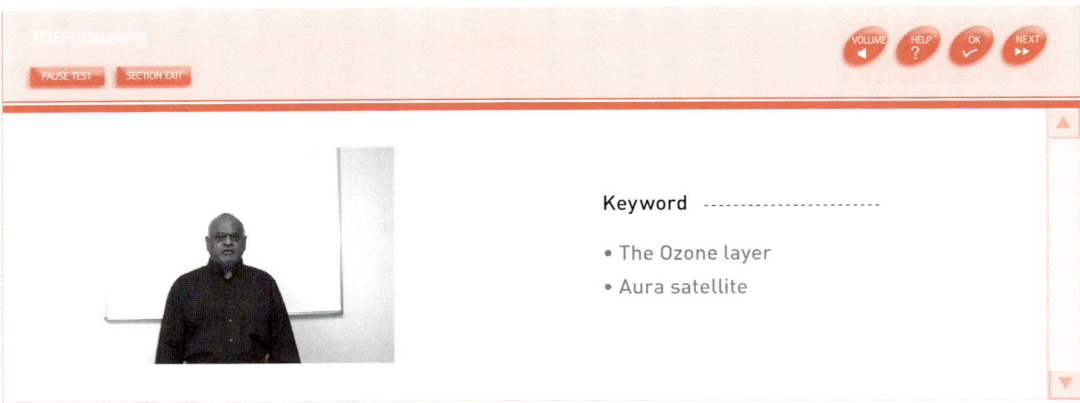

Keyword ------------------------

• The Ozone layer
• Aura satellite

1 What is the lecture mainly about?

Ⓐ Description of the Ozone layer's composition
Ⓑ Explanation of the Ozone layer's functions
Ⓒ Comment of NASA's satellites and recent technology
Ⓓ Illustration on the external form of the Ozone layer

2 Why does the professor mention the meeting with his accountant?

Ⓐ To explain the change in class schedule
Ⓑ To show his deep interest in accounting
Ⓒ To provide a reason for being late to class today
Ⓓ To warn the students about next week's pop quizzes

3 Listen again to part of the lecture. Then answer the question.
Why does the professor say this: 🎧

Ⓐ To explain why he has to miss next Monday's class
Ⓑ To criticize the student for their inattentiveness
Ⓒ To end the announcement and start the lecture
Ⓓ To apologize to the students about the inconvenience caused

4   What are mentioned in the lecture about the Ozone Layer?   Click on 2 answers.

    Ⓐ The sunlight has nothing to do with the creation of ozone.

    Ⓑ 90 percent of the Earth's ozone exists in the stratosphere.

    Ⓒ The Ozone Layer reduces 90 percent of the sun's harmful rays.

    Ⓓ The Ozone Layer is thinning every year due to environmental pollution.

5   According to the lecture, what will probably happen if a living creature is exposed directly to the shorter wavelengths of ultraviolet light from the sun?

    Ⓐ It will probably suffer from serious eye damage only.

    Ⓑ It will not be harmed as long as the creature is a land animal.

    Ⓒ It will probably suffer from genetic damage or physical injury.

    Ⓓ It will probably produce more offspring but eventually die of cancer.

Passage10 Listen to part of a lecture in an entomology class.

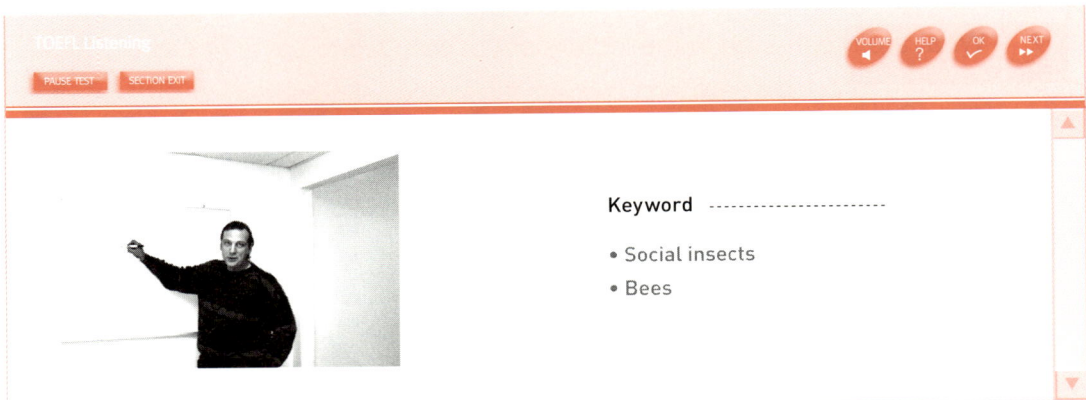

Keyword -

• Social insects
• Bees

1 What does the professor say about the queen bee?

  Ⓐ She is impregnated by several worker bees.

  Ⓑ She makes honey, lays eggs, and protects the hive.

  Ⓒ She cannot produce eggs since she is infertile.

  Ⓓ She usually uses her sting to repel a rival queen.

2 Which of the following are the jobs of the worker bees? Click on 3 answers.

  Ⓐ Laying eggs

  Ⓑ Gathering honey

  Ⓒ Constructing the nest

  Ⓓ Taking care of the queen bee

  Ⓔ Impregnating the queen bee

3 How does the professor organize the lecture on the caste of a typical bee colony?

  Ⓐ He presents information from the most to least important.

  Ⓑ He explains the jobs of each caste of a bee colony.

  Ⓒ He refers to foreign researches on the caste of a bee colony.

  Ⓓ He compares social bees with non-social bees.

Vocabulary

✔ 박스에 체크 표기를 하며 주요 단어를 학습하시오.

☐	**operation** 군사행동, 작전; 운전, 작동	☐	**reluctance** 마지못해함, 꺼림
☐	**territorial** 영토의; 지방의	☐	**incorporate** 구체화하다
☐	**penetrate** 꿰뚫다, 관통하다; 스며들다	☐	**ovulate** 배란하다
☐	**entity** 존재, 실재, 본체	☐	**insemination** 수정
☐	**defensive** 방어적인, 수비의	☐	**cataract** 백내장
☐	**maneuver** 작전, 책략, 술책	☐	**overuse** 과도하게 사용하다
☐	**resistance** 저항(세력)	☐	**misconception** 오해
☐	**tactics** 전술	☐	**blur** 흐리게 하다
☐	**ambush** 매복	☐	**sensitivity** 민감성
☐	**sabotage** 파괴(행위)	☐	**medication** 약제, 약물
☐	**espionage** 스파이 활동, 정탐	☐	**nonperishable** 잘 상하지 않는
☐	**ammo(= ammunition)** 탄약, 무기	☐	**shuttle** 셔틀, 우주왕복선
☐	**rigid** 엄격한; 정확한	☐	**thermostabilize** 열안정화시키다
☐	**screening** 심사, 선발; 집단 검진	☐	**entrée** (주요) 요리
☐	**notation** 표시법, 기수법	☐	**retort** 식품(통조림)의 멸균장치
☐	**decimal** 십진법의	☐	**contamination** 오염
☐	**binary** 이진법의; 둘의	☐	**accountant** 회계사
☐	**intake** 흡입; 섭취량	☐	**absorb** 흡수하다
☐	**alternative** 양자택일	☐	**potentially** 잠재적으로
☐	**fiber** 섬유(질)	☐	**filter** 여과하다
☐	**notion** 관념, 개념	☐	**wavelength** 파장
☐	**batter** 반죽으로 옷을 입히다	☐	**genetic** 유전(상)의
☐	**cutting-edge** 최첨단	☐	**countless** 수없는
☐	**nutrition** 영양(물)	☐	**state-of-the-art** 최첨단의
☐	**youthful** 젊은	☐	**comb** 벌집
☐	**significant** 중요한; 상당한	☐	**secrete** 분비하다
☐	**myriad** 무수한, 막대한	☐	**gland** (분비)샘
☐	**optimal** 최적의	☐	**abdomen** 배, 복부
☐	**breed** (새끼를) 낳다, 사육하다	☐	**colony** 식민지; 군체
☐	**captivity** 포로, 감금, 속박	☐	**caste** 계급; 사회적 지위
☐	**dominant** 유력한, 지배적인	☐	**drone** 수벌
☐	**compelling** 설득력 있는	☐	**ventilate** 환기시키다
☐	**fertile** 번식능력이 있는; 기름진	☐	**impregnate** 임신시키다, 수정시키다
☐	**gestation** 회태, 잉태(기간)	☐	**withdraw** 철회하다, 빼다
☐	**conceive** 수태하다, 새끼를 배다	☐	**barbed** 가시가 있는

Vocabulary Test

🖊 박스에서 올바른 단어를 골라 빈칸을 채우시오.

optimal	overuse	medication
myriad	absorb	contamination

1 The sponge _____(s) water very well — you can get rid of spilt water in just a few seconds with it.

2 Unlike what people generally believe, a proper amount of vitamin C should be taken each day — _____ of vitamin C might result in diarrhea, nausea, burning with urination, skin sensitivities and so on.

3 Many senior citizens are open to adverse drug reactions and misuse of _____.

4 Nutritionists and health experts claim that drinking plenty of water is very important in maintaining _____ physical health.

terrain	countless	abbreviation
dominant	withdraw	drone

5 Years have passed since the U.S. started to send its soldiers to Iraq. Recently, more and more people are raising their voices to _____ the U.S. troops from the region.

6 Although abductions by strangers are quite rare, _____ children are found missing every year, whether temporarily lost in crowded amusement parks or shopping malls or or actually kidnapped by a stranger.

7 While some people raised suspicions that the woman might have been murdered, the _____ view is that she has killed herself.

8 The queen bee, fertilized by the _____ which will soon die after the mating, will start her own colony, laying up to 2,000 eggs per day.

올바른 단어를 골라 문장을 완성하시오.

9   It's extremely hot in here; I think I should _____ the building.

     Ⓐ ventilate   Ⓑ incorporate   Ⓒ overuse   Ⓓ secrete

10   This restaurant has one of the best dishes in town — I'd recommend that you take fillet mignon for _____ and chocolate marquise for dessert.

     Ⓐ drone   Ⓑ diabetes   Ⓒ entrée   Ⓓ sensitivity

11   The Colosseum, originally known as the Flavian Amphitheatre, is constructed with _____ amount of stone and steel.

     Ⓐ dominant   Ⓑ athleric   Ⓒ compelling   Ⓓ significant

12   Some microorganisms associated with degenerative diseases or cancer _____ growth hormones and toxic substances that disrupt normal cellular metabolism and damage the immune system.

     Ⓐ withdraw   Ⓑ secrete   Ⓒ overuse   Ⓓ subsequent

13   Radioactive _____ is typically a result of miscontrol of radioactive materials during the production or use of radioisotopes.

     Ⓐ territorial   Ⓑ resistance   Ⓒ myriad   Ⓓ contamination

14   Friction and gravity are two common types of _____ force.

     Ⓐ resistance   Ⓑ optimal   Ⓒ rigid   Ⓓ medication

15   As the tax season approaches, it is highly difficult to find a good _____ who could help us with a huge tax refund.

     Ⓐ incorproate   Ⓑ accountant   Ⓒ ventilate   Ⓓ reluctance

Chapter 4

Content

Content 지문의 정보를 토대로 추론하고 예측하기

문제유형

- What will the... probably be about?
- What will the professor probably discuss next?
- Indicate whether the following statements each describes... or...
- Based on the information in the lecture, indicate whether the following statements about... are true or false(are characteristics of)...

Sample

Listen to part of a lecture in an economics class. 🎧

TOEFL Listening

PAUSE TEST   SECTION EXIT

VOLUME ◀   HELP ?   OK ✓   NEXT ▶▶

What will the professor probably discuss next?

Ⓐ What credit score is
Ⓑ Who can receive the credit score
Ⓒ How the credit score range was set
Ⓓ Who made the concept of credit score

강의의 전체적인 흐름에 주목하며 강의를 다시 한번 들으시오. 🎧

P: Um, let's, um, let's start. Uh… tonight, we're going to talk about the concept of credit score and how a person's credit score is calculated. First of all, what is a **credit score**? Who can tell me what a credit score is? Yes, Tom?

M: Well, I think it's a number that indicates the measure of a consumer's credit risk at a particular point of time.

P: That's right. Everyone has a credit score — at least if they have a credit history in the United States. Well, uh, the **typical range** for credit scores. It's um, theoretically between 375 and 900, 375 meaning that the person with that score has poor credit, but, um, usually the average credit score in the US is around 680.

W: Um, **1** <u>why is the credit score range between 375 and 900?</u> I mean, it can start from zero or one, or end at 100 or something.

Tip Why does ~, What is the reason for ~ 등으로 문제가 시작되고, 강의에 그 이유가 명백히 드러나 있지 않은 경우, 그 이유를 문맥상 유추하여 답한다.

Strategy 1 강의의 내용 중 세부 정보의 관계를 이해하자

강의에서 제시된 정보들간의 관계를 이해하는 것이 중요하다.

정보의 관계	제시되는 문제의 예
• Cause and Effect	- What is the result of~? Why does~?
• Compare and Contrast	- What can be compared with~? What does A and B have in common~?
• Problem and Solution	- What can be the possible solution of~?
• Process or Procedure	- What is the next possible step of~?

위 강의에서 여학생은 다음과 같이 질문을 한다.

1 why is the credit score range between 375 and 900?

따라서 교수는 원인을 묻는 학생의 질문에 대해 답을 할 것임을 알 수 있다. 신용 점수가 왜 0점과 100점이 아닌, 375점과 900점 사이로 정해지게 되었는지를 설명할 것이므로 정답은 C이다.

Strategy 2 특정 정보를 통해 정보를 유추, 일반화하는 연습을 하자

Supporting Detail 문제와 달리 Content 문제에서는 정보를 연결지어 생각하고 지문에 직접적으로 제시되지 않은 답을 유추해내는 것이 요구된다. 이때 지문 내에서 유추의 근거를 찾아야 한다는 것을 기억하자.

기능	제시되는 문제의 예
• 유추하기	- What can be inferred from ~? What does the professor think about ~?

• 결과/원인/결론 예측하기	- What is the possible result of ~?
	  Why does the professor ~?
	  According to the lecture, why ~?
	  According to the professor, what does ~ demonstrate?
	  What can be concluded from the lecture?

• 일반화하기	- According to the lecture, which of the following is true?
• 다음 단계 예측하기	- What will the professor probably discuss next?

Strategy Focus

강의의 전체적인 흐름에 유의하며 들으시오. 🎧

1

> • **Focus :**
>   hurricanes
>
> • **Keyword/Key phrase :**
>   typhoons or cyclones from in tropical regions

Tip

열대 폭풍의 풍속이 초속 33 마일이 넘으면 허리케인이라고 불리게 된다는 교수의 말에서 힌트를 찾을 수 있다.

- [ ] devastate 황폐화시키다
- [ ] typhoon 태풍
- [ ] cyclone 사이클론
- [ ] tropical 열대의

What can be inferred about hurricanes?

Ⓐ They are concentrated during the summer time, usually in August.

Ⓑ They usually occur in Mexico and Central America and seldom occur in the Caribbean.

Ⓒ The wind velocity of the Hurricane Katrina was at least 33 meters per second.

Ⓓ The disaster caused by the Hurricane Katrina was a man-made disaster.

2

> • **Focus :**
>
> • **Keyword/Key phrase :**

아메리칸 인디언 부족인 나바호족의 언어가 쉽게 해독되지 않는 암호로 사용되었다는 내용에서 힌트를 찾을 수 있다.

- [ ] tragic 비극적인
- [ ] settler 식민자, 이주자
- [ ] slaughter 학살하다
- [ ] misunderstanding 오해
- [ ] retreat 후퇴하다
- [ ] reservation 보호구역

According to the professor, what can be said about the Navajo language?

Ⓐ It was developed by Philip Johnston.

Ⓑ It was comprised of only a few hundred words.

Ⓒ It was easy to be translated into English.

Ⓓ It was unknown to the people outside the tribe.

3

• Focus :

• Keyword/Key phrase :

Tip

지난주에 나눠준 성체 성사에 관한 프린트물을 보자는 교수의 말에서 힌트를 얻을 수 있다.

☐ sacrament 성례전
☐ baptism 세례, 침례
☐ unction 기름부음; 종부성사
☐ communion 성찬식
☐ immersion 담금
☐ recreation 개조, 재현

What will the professor probably discuss next?

Ⓐ The Lord's Supper of the Protestant church
Ⓑ Difference between confirmation and extreme unction
Ⓒ Different forms of baptism of the Protestant church
Ⓓ The Eucharist of the Roman Catholic and Greek Orthodox churches

4

• Focus :

• Keyword/Key phrase :

상품의 외적 가치와 내적 가치의 차이점을 기억하도록 하자.

☐ ethical 윤리적
☐ technical 기술적인, 전문적인
☐ extrinsic 외적의
☐ intrinsic 내적의

What can be said about extrinsic value of a product?

Ⓐ It is usually defined by the monetary value of the product.
Ⓑ It has to do with the owner's relationship with the product.
Ⓒ It stems from the internal beauty and quality of the product.
Ⓓ It cannot be measured by objective means of judgment.

Exercise

Passage 1 Listen to part of a discussion in a psychology class. 🎧

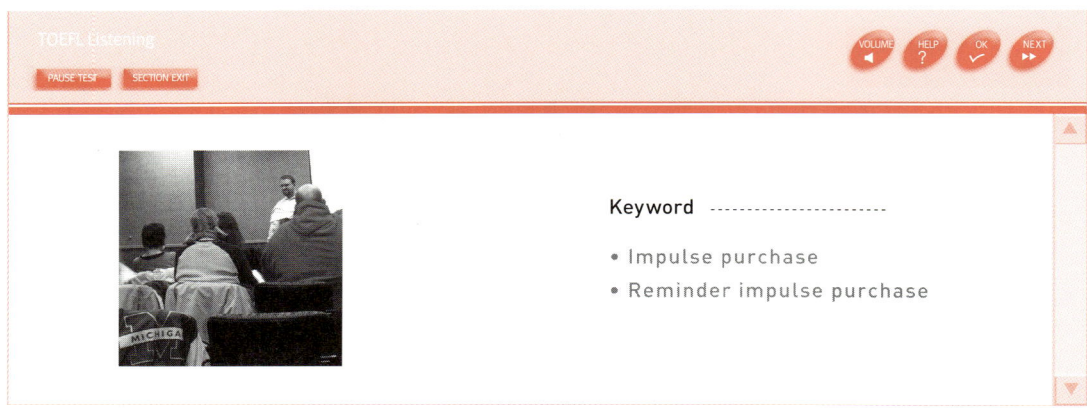

Keyword ----------------------

• Impulse purchase
• Reminder impulse purchase

1 What is the topic of the discussion?

Ⓐ Definition of impulse buying

Ⓑ Several models of impulse buying

Ⓒ General purchasing theory

Ⓓ Examples of reminder impulse purchase

2 Why does the professor mention your mother's birthday?

Ⓐ To shift the topic of the discussion

Ⓑ To digress from today's topic

Ⓒ To introduce the topic of the discussion

Ⓓ To conclude today's discussion

3 According to the discussion, which of the following statements is NOT true about impulse purchase?

Ⓐ It has four different types of sub-models.

Ⓑ It usually occurs spontaneously without a previous purchase plan.

Ⓒ It only occurs when a person is trying to buy a product on-line.

Ⓓ It can also happen when a shopper has suddenly remembered a need to buy a product.

4 What does the professor say about impulse purchase on e-commerce sites?

    Ⓐ It takes up nearly half of all purchases made on-line.

    Ⓑ It is the most important type of purchase made on-line.

    Ⓒ It recently has drawn significant interest of psychologists.

    Ⓓ It particularly represents on-line reminder impulse purchasers.

5 What will the professor discuss during the next class?

    Ⓐ Typical results of impulse purchase

    Ⓑ Examples of pure impulse purchase

    Ⓒ Several models of planned purchase

    Ⓓ The other two models of impulse purchase

Passage 2   Listen to part of a lecture in an ecology class. 🎧

TOEFL Listening

PAUSE TEST   SECTION EXIT

VOLUME   HELP ?   OK ✓   NEXT ▶▶

Keyword ----------------------

• Yellowstone National Park
• Controlled fire

1 Listen again to part of the lecture. Then answer the question.
Why does the professor say this: 🎧

Ⓐ He is trying to introduce the topic of today's lecture.

Ⓑ He wants to know how many of his students have been to Yellowstone National Park.

Ⓒ He is trying to focus the students' attention on the management of Yellowstone National Park.

Ⓓ He wants to conceal the fact that he has actually never been to Yellowstone National Park.

2 Which of the following was mentioned in the lecture as one of the most famous tour sites within Yellowstone National Park?   Click on 2 answers.

Ⓐ The Old Faithful Geyser

Ⓑ The Redwood National Park

Ⓒ The Grand Canyon of the Yellowstone

Ⓓ The Zion Canyon of the Yellowstone

3 What does the professor think about wildfires in national parks?

- (A) He thinks it is too dangerous and disastrous.
- (B) He thinks national parks should only allow controlled wildfires.
- (C) He thinks it is actually beneficial because it helps the ecosystem to change.
- (D) He thinks that some wildfires might be beneficial to the ecosystem but is against the concept of controlled wildfires.

4 The professor discusses Yellowstone National Park and wildfires. Put the sentences below in the order they occurred.

	Order
Yellowstone and other parks instituted a national fire management plan.	
People thought that the wildfire was a destructive force — one to be mastered.	
There was a series of wildfire across much of the ecosystem.	
Ecologists recognized that fire was a primary agent of change in many ecosystems, including the arid mountainous western United States.	
National parks and forests began to experiment with controlled fires.	

Passage 3   Listen to part of a lecture in a nutritional physiology class. 🎧

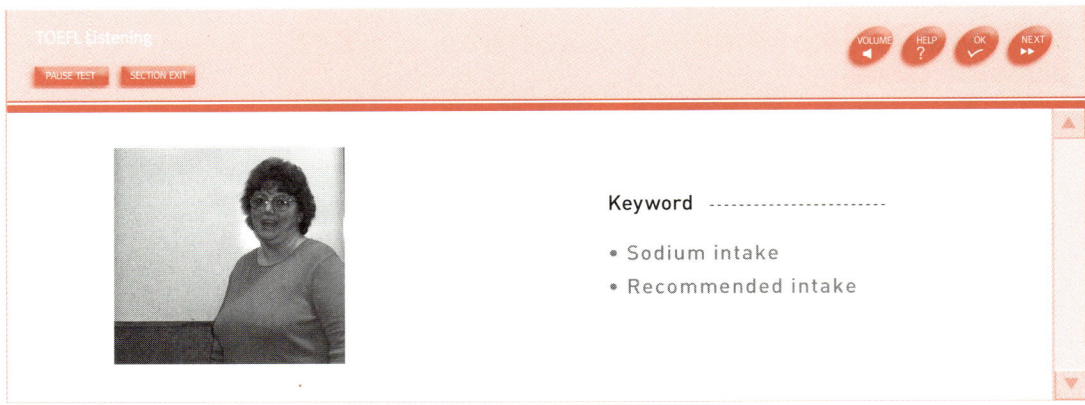

Keyword ---------------------------

• Sodium intake
• Recommended intake

1 What does the professor say about sodium intake?
Ⓐ The majority of Americans consume sodium about 1,500 milligrams a day.
Ⓑ It is recommended that people intake 4,000 milligrams of sodium a day.
Ⓒ Too much intake of sodium may cause a low level of calcium in the bones.
Ⓓ People from underdeveloped countries suffer from a sodium deficiency.

2 What can be inferred about the content of sodium in food?
Ⓐ Food such as cookies and cereal contains the largest amount of sodium.
Ⓑ The average amount of sodium content in each serving is higher than the recommended amount.
Ⓒ Food such as cookies and bread must be avoided to cut down on sodium intake.
Ⓓ Some food that is generally thought to have less sodium may actually contain high quantity of sodium.

3 What will the professor probably discuss next?
Ⓐ Why excessive sodium intake results in heart failure
Ⓑ How much sodium is included in general food
Ⓒ What happened after the FDA was sued
Ⓓ How to avoid eating too much salt

Passage 4   Listen to part of a lecture in a fashion history class. 🎧

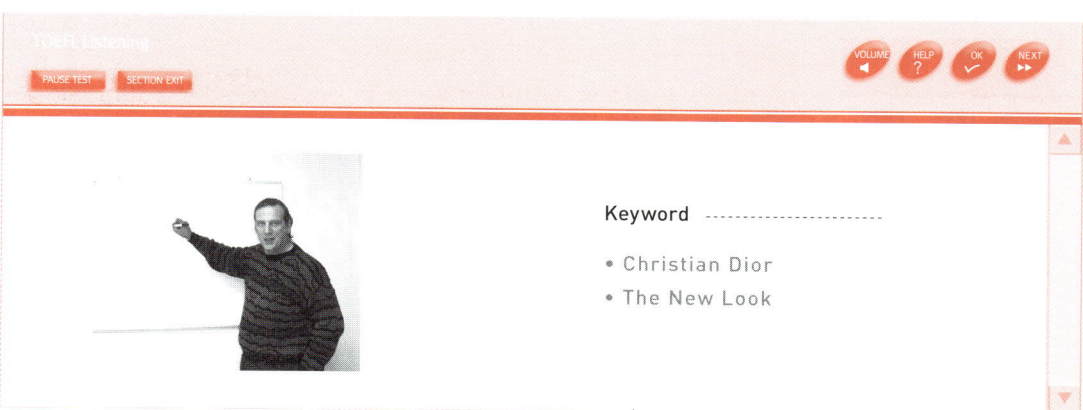

TOEFL Listening

PAUSE TEST   SECTION EXIT

VOLUME ◀ HELP ? OK ✓ NEXT ▶▶

Keyword ----------------------

• Christian Dior
• The New Look

1 **What is the subject of the lecture?**

Ⓐ Christian Dior: The Sketcher who became a Saloon Owner

Ⓑ Christian Dior: The Designer and Soldier

Ⓒ Christian Dior: His Life and Design

Ⓓ Christian Dior: His partnership with Jacques Bonjean

2 **Listen again to part of the lecture. Then answer the question.**
What does the professor mean when he says this: 🎧

Ⓐ Dior was born in a wealthy family.

Ⓑ Dior had physical defects when he was born.

Ⓒ Dior was a needy child when he was young.

Ⓓ Dior was born as a healthy child but became ill later on.

3 **According to the lecture, what can be said about Dior and his New Look?**

Ⓐ His New Look satisfied the women's desire to look more feminine.

Ⓑ He was inspired to create the New Look from the visit to the Soviet Union.

Ⓒ His New Look tried to use as less material as possible.

Ⓓ His New Look was not accepted by the fashion industry because of its sudden
departure from the classic look.

4 The professor talks about the life of the French designer, Christian Dior. Based on the information in the lecture, indicate the order of the following sentences.

	Order
Christian Dior opened an art gallery on rue de la Boetie with his friend, Jacques Bonjean.	
Christian Dior's mother and brother died.	
Christian Dior was born in Grenville, France.	
Christian Dior started working for Robert Piguet at his fashion house as a designer.	
Christian Dior presented his first collection.	

5 What will the professor probably discuss next?

(A) How Dior came up with his revolutionary design

(B) How Dior became a world famous designer

(C) Why Dior's design was called the New Look

(D) How Dior's design changed the fasion industry of Paris

Listen to part of a lecture in an anthropology class. 🎧

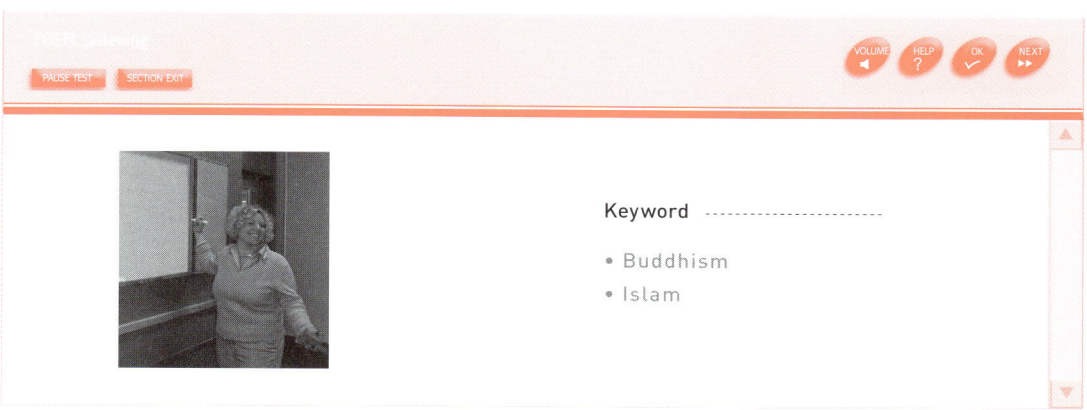

Keyword --------------------

• Buddhism
• Islam

1 What does the professor mainly discuss?

- Ⓐ The origin of Buddhism and Islam
- Ⓑ Sacred places of Muslims
- Ⓒ Holy cities of several religions
- Ⓓ The life of Buddha and Muhammad

2 The professor talks about Buddhism, Islam and the sacred places of both religions. Based on the information in the lecture, indicate whether each statement below is the sacred place of pure Buddhism or of Islam.

Click in the correct box.

	Buddhism	Islam
the Bodhi Tree		
Mecca		
Bodh Gaya		
Kandy		
Medina		

Passage 6

Listen to part of a lecture in an art history class. 🎧

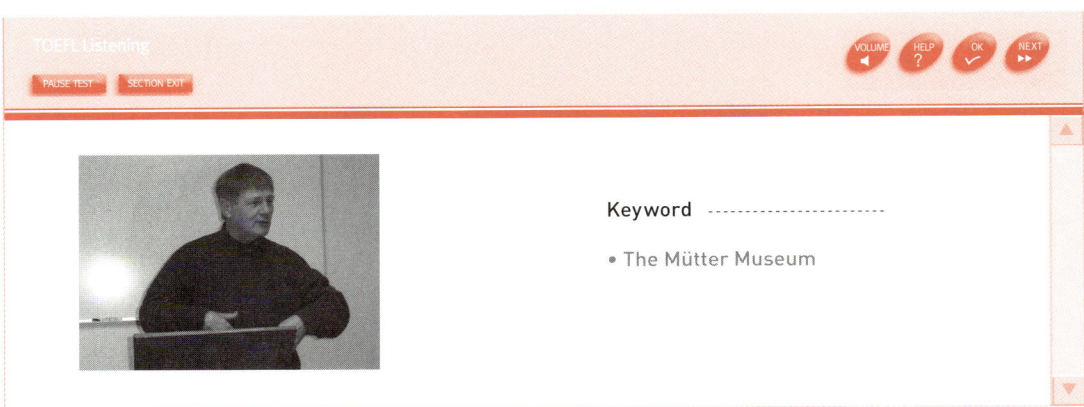

TOEFL Listening

PAUSE TEST   SECTION EXIT

VOLUME   HELP   OK   NEXT

Keyword ----------------------

• The Mütter Museum

1 Why does the professor mention wax and money museums?

Ⓐ To introduce Hollywood Wax Museum

Ⓑ To exemplify different types of museums

Ⓒ To conclude his lecture on the Mütter Museum

Ⓓ To demonstrate his experience on founding a museum

2 The professor talks about the Mütter Museum in Philadelphia. Based on the information in the lecture, indicate whether the following statements are information about the Mütter Museum. Click in the correct box.

	Yes	No
The museum is located in the Jefferson Medical College.		
The museum's collections include preserves of medical oddities, antique medical equipment and biological specimens.		
Only medical doctors are allowed to visit the museum.		
Thomas Dent Mütter played a significant role in establishing the museum in both financial and collectional ways.		
One of the museum's boasted collection items is the mummy of the world-famous Siamese Twins, Chang and Eng Bunker.		

Passage 7   Listen to part of a discussion in a history class. 🎧

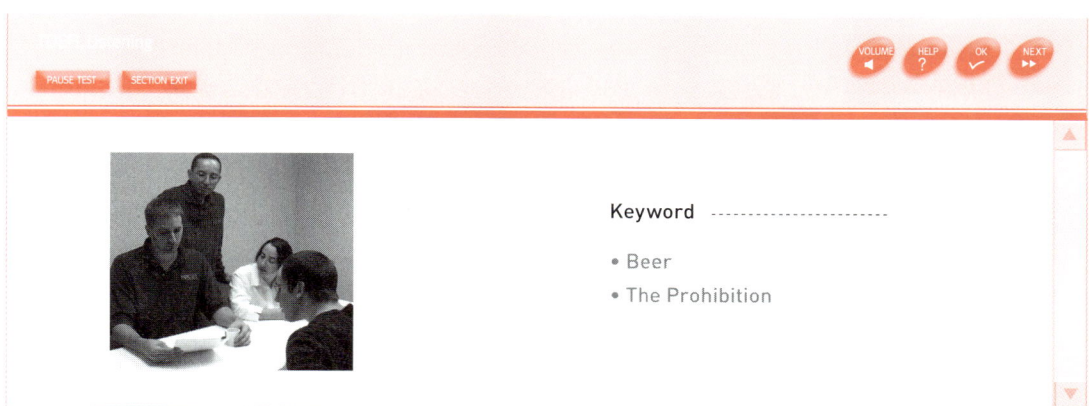

Keyword -

• Beer
• The Prohibition

1 Why does the professor mention watching football on Sunday afternoons?

Ⓐ To digress from the discussion topic
Ⓑ To introduce the topic of today's discussion
Ⓒ To shift the topic from football to beer
Ⓓ To show the relationship between football and beer

2 Listen again to part of the discussion. Then answer the question.
Why does the professor say this: 🎧

Ⓐ Because he thinks that the student is lying
Ⓑ Because the professor himself is fond of drinking beer
Ⓒ Because he knows that many students go out to a movie or a party on Friday nights
Ⓓ Because he thinks that the student's urge to drink beer is not his fault but of the beer company

3 The professor talks about beer brewing and the history of beer in the United States. Based on the information in the discussion, indicate whether the following statements about beer and history about beer are true or false.

Click in the correct box.

	True	False
The basic ingredients for making beer are barley, yeast, sugar, and alcohol.		
In order to make beer, a brewer simply has to mix two of the four basic ingredients.		
In the Middle Ages, it was safer to drink beer than to drink water because of poor sanitation and close quarters.		
Lager was first brewed in Germany in the 1400's.		
The Prohibition on beer lasted from 1920 to 1933 which kicked many small breweries out of business.		

4 What does the professor say about the reason for beer being more important than water in the Middle Ages?

Ⓐ Beer was cheaper than clean water.
Ⓑ Beer was used to convert dirty water into potable water.
Ⓒ People brewed more amount of beer than they produced potable water.
Ⓓ Because beer contained alcohol, it was safer to drink beer than to drink unclean water.

Passage 8

Listen to part of a lecture in a psychology class.

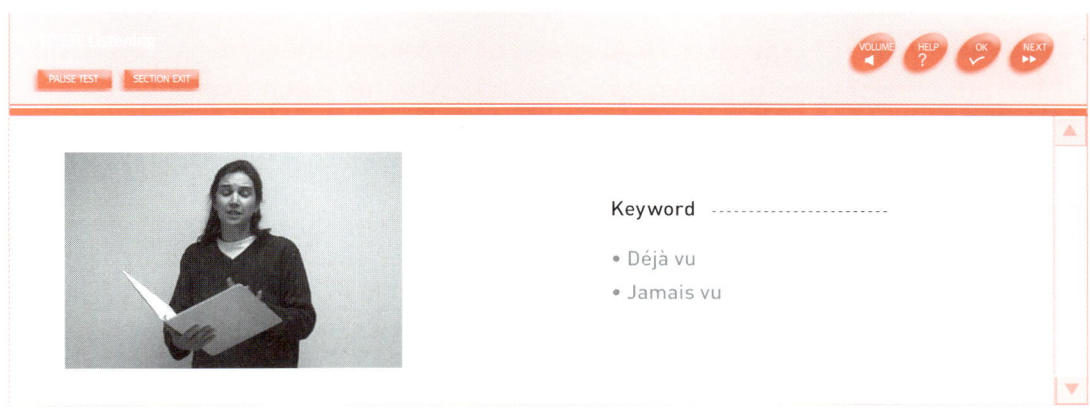

Keyword -

• Déjà vu
• Jamais vu

1 What does the professor mainly discuss?
- (A) General concept of déjà vu
- (B) Specific examples of déjà vu
- (C) Definition of jamais vu
- (D) Origin of the word déjà vu

2 Why does the professor mention visiting your friend's neighborhood?
- (A) To shift the topic
- (B) To digress from the main topic
- (C) To elaborate the feeling of déjà vu
- (D) To show the relationship between déjà vu and jamais vu

3 What can be inferred about déjà vu?
- (A) Only lab researchers can detect déjà vu.
- (B) Déjà vu can only be experienced in science labs.
- (C) It is difficult to have déjà vu voluntarily.
- (D) Only women can experience déjà vu.

4 The professor discusses déjà vu and other related phenomena. Based on the information in the lecture, indicate whether each sentence below describes déjà vu or jamais vu.

Click in the correct box.

	déjà vu	jamais vu
It means "already seen" in French language.		
It means "never seen" in French language.		
According to some researchers, it has three different types.		
This term was first used by Emile Boirac, a French psychic researcher.		
It describes any familiar situation which is not recognized by the observer.		

5 What will the professor probably discuss next?
- Ⓐ Examples of déjà vu
- Ⓑ The three types of déjà vu
- Ⓒ Where the term jamais vu came from .
- Ⓓ Emile Boirac and his book, *The Future of Psychic Sciences*

Passage 9

Listen to part of a lecture in a world history class. 🎧

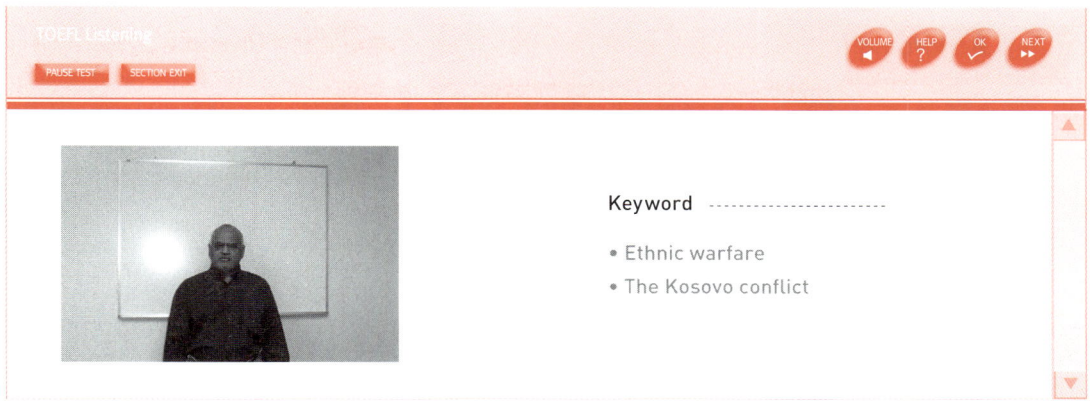

Keyword ------------------------

• Ethnic warfare
• The Kosovo conflict

1 What does the professor mainly discuss?

- (A) Ethnic warfares of the world
- (B) The progress of the Kosovo conflict
- (C) How ethnic cleansing was held across Kosovo
- (D) How Slobodan Milosevic resisted to the NATO force

2 What can be inferred about the definition of ethnic cleansing?

- (A) It means cleaning up houses where Kosovar Albanians used to live in.
- (B) It means dismissal of Kosovar Albanian workers from workplaces.
- (C) It means expulsion of Serbs by Kosovar Albanians.
- (D) It means execution of Kosovar Albanians by Serbs.

3 In what order does the professor explain the warfare?

- (A) From the oldest to the most recent incident
- (B) From the most important to the least important incident
- (C) From the most complete to the least complete incident
- (D) From the most recent to the oldest incident

4 According to the lecture, what can be inferred about the reason for NATO's bombing campaign?

Ⓐ Kosovar Albanian refugees requested NATO for the campaign.

Ⓑ There was no choice but to carry out bombing campaign in the region because of the weather.

Ⓒ Diplomatic efforts to convince Milosevic to permit NATO peacekeeping force to enter Kosovo have failed.

Ⓓ The world expected NATO to commence bombing campaign in the region.

5 The professor talks about the Kosovo Conflict. Based on the information in the lecture, indicate whether the following sentences are true or false.

Click in the correct box.

Sentence	True	False
Rugova was elected as President of Kosovo by the first referendum in June, 1999.		
Slobodan Milosevic, the Serbian leader, eradicated autonomy of Kosovo within the former Yugoslavia and brought it under the direct control of Belgrade.		
The Kosovo Liberation Army (KLA) attacked on Serbian civilians and security personnel simultaneously in several parts of Kosovo.		
A so-called ethnic cleansing campaign was conducted by Kosovar Albanians against Serbs.		
NATO carried on a bombing campaign because a peace agreement could not be reached.		

Passage10   Listen to part of a discussion in a music history class. 🎧

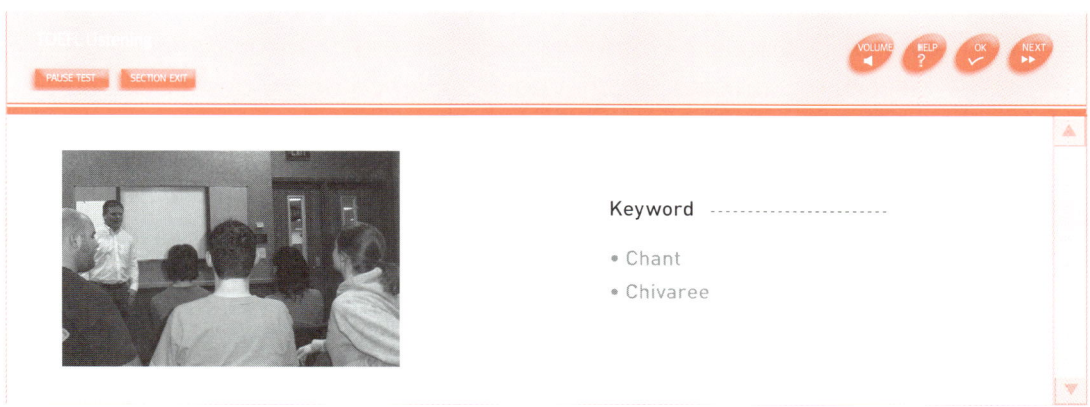

Keyword ----------------

• Chant
• Chivaree

1 According to the professor, why was creating music manuscript difficult during the Middle Ages?

Ⓐ The parchment on which manuscript was written was expensive.
Ⓑ Monophonic songs were impossible to be scribed in manuscript.
Ⓒ Experienced scribes to reproduce the manuscript were hard to find.
Ⓓ Manuscript was created secretly in only churches and monasteries.

2 According to the discussion, when was medieval secular music played the most?

Ⓐ During harvest
Ⓑ During celebrations and festivals
Ⓒ During Mass and prayers
Ⓓ During funerals

3 What can be inferred about medieval people and their secular music?

Ⓐ Music was available to ordinary people only during weddings and festivals.
Ⓑ Ordinary people played and listened to monotonous music called chivaree.
Ⓒ Peasants enjoyed joyful music called chivaree while merchants more enjoyed chants.
Ⓓ Even though ordinary people had less access to standardized music, they enjoyed music of their own.

4 The professor discusses medieval music. Based on the information in the discussion, indicate whether each sentence below describes church music or ordinary people's music.

Click in the correct box.

	Church music	Secular music
Creating manuscript was available which still survives to the current time.		
One type of this is known as Gregorian Chant.		
It was played during times of celebration and festivities.		
It can be represented by the monophonic chant.		
It was called "chivaree."		

5 What will the video strip probably be about?

Ⓐ What kind of instrument was used for chivaree and chant

Ⓑ What kind of dance people enjoyed during festivals and ceremonies

Ⓒ How chivaree was preserved without being recorded on parchment

Ⓓ Why church and monasteries could afford creating music manuscripts

Vocabulary

✓ 박스에 체크 표기를 하며 주요 단어를 학습하시오.

- ☐ **particular** 특별한
- ☐ **impulse** 충동, 변덕
- ☐ **spontaneous** 자발적인, 자연적인
- ☐ **commerce** 상업, 교역
- ☐ **reminder** 상기시키는 것, 신호
- ☐ **geyser** 간헐천
- ☐ **hot spring** 온천
- ☐ **ecosystem** 생태계
- ☐ **mainstream** 주류
- ☐ **destructive** 파괴적인
- ☐ **mountainous** 산이 많은, 산지의
- ☐ **succession** 연속, 계속; 천이
- ☐ **sodium** 나트륨
- ☐ **deficiency** 결핍, 부족
- ☐ **nutrient** 영양분, 영양소
- ☐ **stroke** 발작
- ☐ **hypertension** 고혈압
- ☐ **leach** 걸러지다, 용해하다
- ☐ **intake** 흡입; 섭취량
- ☐ **fertilizer** 비료
- ☐ **compulsory** 강제적인, 의무의
- ☐ **depression** 불경기, 공황
- ☐ **bankruptcy** 파산
- ☐ **tuberculosis** 결핵
- ☐ **milliner** 모자 상인
- ☐ **constricted** 죄어진, 압축된
- ☐ **hemline** 치맛단
- ☐ **severity** 엄숙함
- ☐ **estimate** 추정하다, 평가하다
- ☐ **unsurpassed** 매우 뛰어난, 탁월한
- ☐ **enlightenment** 계발, 개명, 깨달음
- ☐ **sacred** 신성한
- ☐ **destination** 목적지
- ☐ **pilgrimage** 성지 순례

- ☐ **weird** 이상한, 괴상한
- ☐ **oddity** 괴상함, 이상한 물건
- ☐ **specimen** 표본
- ☐ **anatomic** 해부학의
- ☐ **pathological** 병리학의
- ☐ **plaster** 회반죽, 석고
- ☐ **conjoin** 결합하다, 접합하다
- ☐ **preserved** 보존된
- ☐ **brew** (맥주를) 양조하다
- ☐ **ingredient** 성분, 원료, 재료
- ☐ **barley** 보리, 대맥
- ☐ **biochemical** 생화학의
- ☐ **ferment** 발효시키다
- ☐ **staple** 요소, 주요한 테마
- ☐ **quarter** 처소, 숙소
- ☐ **sanitation** 공중 위생
- ☐ **amendment** 개정, 수정
- ☐ **heyday** 전성기, 절정
- ☐ **repeal** 무효로 하다, 폐지하다
- ☐ **distortion** 왜곡
- ☐ **uncanny** 이상한, 섬뜩한
- ☐ **eerie** 기분나쁜, 무시무시한
- ☐ **coin** (신어를) 만들어내다
- ☐ **indicate** 가리키다, 나타내다
- ☐ **ignite** 불붙이다, 생기게하다
- ☐ **empirical** 경험적인
- ☐ **speculative** 이론(추론)적인
- ☐ **psychoanalyst** 정신분석학자
- ☐ **fulfillment** 이행, 완수, 실천
- ☐ **fleeting** 어느덧 지나가는
- ☐ **glimpse** 흘끗 봄
- ☐ **ethnic** (소수)민족의
- ☐ **warfare** 전쟁, 교전
- ☐ **autonomy** 자치(권)

Vocabulary Test

🖋 박스에서 올바른 단어를 골라 빈칸을 채우시오.

distortion	affordable	adverse
amendment	empirical	destructive

1　It was windy and raining. Despite the _____ weather, however, we managed to reach the mountain cabin.

2　One of the highly _____ forces of nature, hurricanes can cause numerous deaths in addition to the millions of dollars of property damage each year due to the intense winds and huge tidal waves.

3　The Honda car is about $20,000. I think it's _____, since we have more than that in our savings account.

4　Science requires that all evidence must be _____, that is, dependent on evidence or consequences that are observable by the senses.

affordable	ingredient	severity
persecution	tension	spontaneous

5　The early Christians in South Korea had to suffer extreme _____; for example, Andrew Kim Taegon, Korea's first Roman Catholic priest, was beheaded at the age of 25.

6　Laura's act last night at the party was pretty natural and _____ — I don't think anybody urged or pushed her to sing and dance in front of the crowd.

7　As the _____ between the two parties prolonged, the two major delegates began to grow weary and tiresome.

8　The _____ and virulence of the poison from the unknown snake caused great concern and interest at the same time in medical circles.

올바른 단어를 골라 문장을 완성하시오.

9 In order to create the most dramatic effect, I'm afraid that we should completely _____ the 10-story building which is located in front of the train station.

    Ⓐ indicate   Ⓑ reproduce   Ⓒ demolish   Ⓓ agitate

10 Reynold's _____ attitude annoyed Anna; not only would he always let Anna make every single decisions on their wedding ceremony but also when and where to have a date.

    Ⓐ passive   Ⓑ constricted   Ⓒ weird   Ⓓ accessible

11 It is illegal to _____, distribute, or sell any photographs taken in this museum without proper written permission.

    Ⓐ staple   Ⓑ reproduce   Ⓒ glimpse   Ⓓ repeal

12 John was acting _____ all day — he was sighing, looking out at the window blankly, picking on his food, and mindlessly staring at the computer monitor without typing or reading anything.

    Ⓐ weird   Ⓑ particular   Ⓒ spontaneous   Ⓓ depression

13 The hotel is readily _____ because it is located right in front of a train station.

    Ⓐ demolish   Ⓑ destructive   Ⓒ affordable   Ⓓ accessible

14 The _____ which started in October, 1929 in most of the world lasted through most of the 1930s and left hundreds of thousands people homeless and unemployed.

    Ⓐ distortion   Ⓑ tension   Ⓒ depression   Ⓓ manuscript

15 Since the clause in the constitution seriously restricts human's rights to express his opinions freely, it needs _____.

    Ⓐ shelter   Ⓑ amendment   Ⓒ persecution   Ⓓ repeal

Chapter 5

Stance

5 Stance 화자의 감정 상태 이해하기

문제유형

- What does(did) the professor(student) feel when he(she) says(said) this?
- What does the professor(student) think about…?
- How does the professor(student) feel about…?
- What is the professor's(student's) attitude towards…?

Sample

Listen to part of a discussion in a history class. 🎧

TOEFL Listening

VOLUME ◀ | HELP ? | OK ✓ | NEXT ▶▶

PAUSE TEST | SECTION EXIT

What does the student think about Cortés?

- Ⓐ She thinks that Cortés legitimately ruled over the Aztecs.
- Ⓑ She thinks that Cortés was the real son of the god Quetzalcoatl.
- Ⓒ She considers Cortés as an intelligent sailor and ruler.
- Ⓓ She thinks that Cortés tricked the Aztecs to have control over them.

억양과 뉘앙스 및 제시되는 지문 내 힌트에 주목하며 강의를 다시 한번 들으시오. 🎧

P: When the Spaniards, under Hernán Cortés, first arrived in 1519, the Aztec civilization was at its peak. Other subject Indian groups were rebellious against Aztec rule, and were highly willing to join the Spanish. The Aztecs believed that the Spaniards were the descendants of the god Quetzalcoatl, the ancient deity and legendary ruler of the Toltec in Mexico who was also believed to be white, bearded and blond, which coincided with… well, how Cortés looked like. So, basically, the last independent Aztec ruler Moctezuma II thought the Spaniard was the incarnation of their god and received him, which **1** Cortés thought was a good opportunity to rule over the Aztecs.

W: **2** I think that was **pretty deceiving**, you know, to **manipulate** the **naïve natives** like that.

Tip 억양과 뉘앙스에는 화자의 태도가 반영되며, 화자가 사용하는 단어의 성질에서도 화자의 태도나 감정 상태를 알 수 있다.

화자의 억양과 뉘앙스에 주목하자

화자의 억양과 뉘앙스를 통해 화자의 태도, 감정 및 확신 정도를 알 수 있다. 같은 표현이라고 해도 상황에 따라 다른 뜻을 가질 수 있다.

상황	사용되는 표현과 예
● 불확실함	- 머뭇거림; 말 끝을 흐림; 말을 더듬기 Um~, I'm not really sure about this but ~, th- that's ~
● 반대	- 톤이 올라감; 강한 부정의 표현을 사용함 Do you really think ~, I don't think ~, I don't agree with ~, Tell me about it ~
● 동의	- 맞장구의 표현을 사용함 Yes, Uh-huh, I think so, too, I agree with ~, Tell me about it ~
● 놀라움	- 끝의 톤이 올라감; 반문과 재확신의 표현을 사용함 Really?, Is that true?, You mean~ is ~?, Are you serious ~?
● 비판/회의	- 비판 혹은 회의의 표현, 부정적 표현을 사용함 I think ~ is pretty bad, ~ was idiotic, ~ shouldn't have ~, I regret ~

Strategy 2 뉘앙스를 뒷받침하는 지문 내 근거에 주목하자

예를 들어 화자의 감정 상태가 '비판적'이라고 판단한 경우, 지문에는 이에 대한 근거가 되는 부분이 담겨 있게 마련이다. 억양 및 뉘앙스에 대한 판단을 할 때 지문에서 이러한 근거를 찾는 것이 중요하다. 이러한 근거는 주로 사용된 단어의 성질이나 표현에서 찾을 수 있다.

위 지문에서, 교수는 에르난 코르테스가 아즈텍 점령에 대해 가진 생각을 다음과 같이 표현하고 있다.

1 Cortés thought was a good opportunity to rule over the Aztecs.

이에 대해 학생은 다음과 같은 단어를 사용하여 주제에 대한 본인의 생각을 드러낸다.

2 I think that was pretty deceiving, you know, to manipulate the naïve natives like that.

학생이 사용하는 deceiving(기만적), manipulate(조종하다), naïve natives(순진한 원주민)이라는 표현을 통해 코르테스에 대한 태도가 상당히 비판적임을 알 수 있다. 따라서 답은 D이다.

Strategy Focus

화자의 억양과 뉘앙스 및 지문 내 힌트에 유의하며 강의를 들으시오. 🎧

1

- **Focus :**
  first American magazines

- **Keyword/Key phrase :**
  1893, the first mass-circulation magazines

Listen again to part of the discussion. Then answer the question.
How does the professor feel when he says this: 🎧

Ⓐ Obligated to tell students current price of magazines
Ⓑ Surprised at the dramatic increase in cost of magazines
Ⓒ Perplexed because he has no knowledge of magazines
Ⓓ Frustrated because magazines today are too expensive

Tip

화자의 말투와 "Wow"라는 감탄사에서 쉽게 답을 알 수 있다.

☐ readership 독자(수, 층)
☐ niche 분야, 영역, 틈새 시장
☐ circulation 유통, 유포

2

- **Focus :**

- **Keyword/Key phrase :**

What is the professor's attitude towards cognitive behavioral therapy(CBT)?

Ⓐ She thinks it is effective and more beneficial than taking medicine constantly.
Ⓑ She thinks taking sedatives is better than taking CBT.
Ⓒ She is skeptical about its effectiveness.
Ⓓ She is surprised to have learned a new fact.

"Luckily"라는 부분에서 힌트를 얻을 수 있다.

☐ elevated 높아진
☐ rupture 파열시키다
☐ clot 응고
☐ insomnia 불면증
☐ sedative 진정제

3

• Focus :

....

....

• Keyword/Key phrase :

....

....

....

Tip

강의의 후반부에서 교수는 뗏집과 뗏집의 생활 조건 등에 대해 비판적으로 이야기하고 있다.

☐ sod 잔디, 떼
☐ frontier 국경지방
☐ prairie 대초원
☐ thatch 이엉
☐ infestation (해충의) 감염

What does the professor think about sod house and its living condition?

Ⓐ People lived in sod houses despite their high prices.

Ⓑ Sod houses were popular because of good sanitation.

Ⓒ It was unhealthy for residents to live in.

Ⓓ It was economical to live in sod houses.

4

• Focus :

....

....

• Keyword/Key phrase :

....

....

....

"Fled for Scotland"라는 부분에서 힌트를 얻을 수 있다.

☐ dispute 논쟁, 분쟁, 쟁의
☐ adversity 어려움, 고난, 역경
☐ amalgamate 통합(합병)하다
☐ union 노동조합, 조합

What is the professor's attitude towards Andrew Carnegie?

Ⓐ Carnegie did not deserve such adversity.

Ⓑ The fact that Carnegie owned a steel company is surprising.

Ⓒ Carnegie was not brave enough to face the workers himself.

Ⓓ The Homestead Strike story is hard to believe.

Exercise

Listen to part of a discussion in an economics class. 🎧

Keyword ---------------------

• Natural commons
• Social commons

1 **What does the professor mainly discuss?**

Ⓐ Methods to manage the commons

Ⓑ The definition of natural commons

Ⓒ Dangers the commons encounter

Ⓓ Several examples of the commons

2 **Listen again to part of the discussion. Then answer the question. How does the student feel when he says this:** 🎧

Ⓐ He is uncertain about his answer.

Ⓑ He is challenging the professor with his answer.

Ⓒ He does not want to be questioned.

Ⓓ He feels extremely confident about his answer.

3 Which of the following are the specific examples of social commons?

Click on 2 answers.

(A) Elephants
(B) English
(C) Wedding
(D) Rain

4 According to the professor, which of the following pose danger on the commons?   Click on 2 answers.

(A) Dismissal from the work force by losing a job
(B) Automobile emissions polluting the air
(C) Exploiting natural resources
(D) Rapid growth in population of an animal's predator

5 What is the professor's attitude towards the commons?

(A) He feels sorry that the commons are provided free.
(B) He thinks that countries should not exploit their social commons.
(C) He thinks that as long as the commons are provided free, people can overuse the commons.
(D) He thinks that people do not take care of the commons well because they do not consider the commons as their own property.

Passage 2 Listen to part of a lecture in a psychology class. 🎧

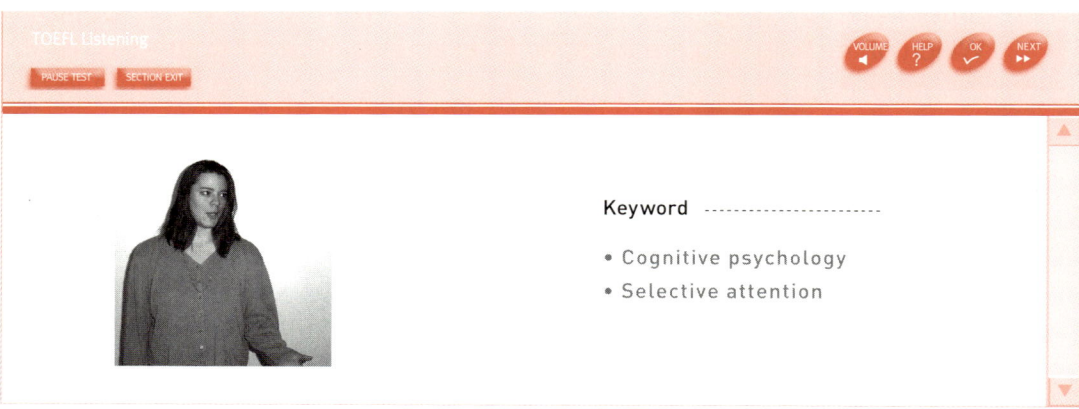

TOEFL Listening

PAUSE TEST   SECTION EXIT

VOLUME   HELP ?   OK ✓   NEXT ▶▶

Keyword -----------------------

• Cognitive psychology
• Selective attention

1 What is the possible subject of the lecture?

Ⓐ Selective attention: What it is and how it happens

Ⓑ Unconscious selective attention: What its results are

Ⓒ Selective attention: Its origins and process

Ⓓ Directions: How to drive a car automatically

2 Which of the following are examples of conscious selective attention?

Click on 2 answers.

Ⓐ A boy sees an orange basketball inside a box filled with white baseballs.

Ⓑ A high school girl who is on a vacation sees a red sports car parked among other silver sports cars.

Ⓒ A little girl who wants to get a Barbie doll for Christmas sees the Barbie doll sitting on a shelf among other dolls in a toy store.

Ⓓ A basketball player at a mall sees a basketball game on a television set in the show window when other sets show other games.

3 Why does the professor mention your friend's television?

   Ⓐ To demonstrate the way of recognizing objects around you

   Ⓑ To provide an example to explain conscious selective attention better

   Ⓒ To explain important features of conscious selective attention

   Ⓓ To provide an example to explain unconscious selective attention better

4 According to the lecture, what is the most possible explanation for simultaneous multi-tasking?

   Ⓐ All of the tasks receive equal amount of awareness and concern.

   Ⓑ Two or three of the multiple tasks receive the most concentration while other tasks are achieved involuntarily.

   Ⓒ One of the multiple tasks receives the most awareness while other tasks are accomplished automatically.

   Ⓓ None of the multiple tasks receives any awareness but all of them are processed mechanically.

5 How does the professor feel when she says this: 🎧

   Ⓐ She does not agree with the opinion that the notion of selective attention stemmed from the question she just mentioned. ·

   Ⓑ She is curious whether human being can attend to more than one thing at a time.

   Ⓒ She feels apologetic because she is not sure where the notion of selective attention stemmed from.

   Ⓓ She feels positive that the notion of selective attention stemmed from the question she just mentioned.

Passage 3   Listen to part of a discussion in a nutrition class.

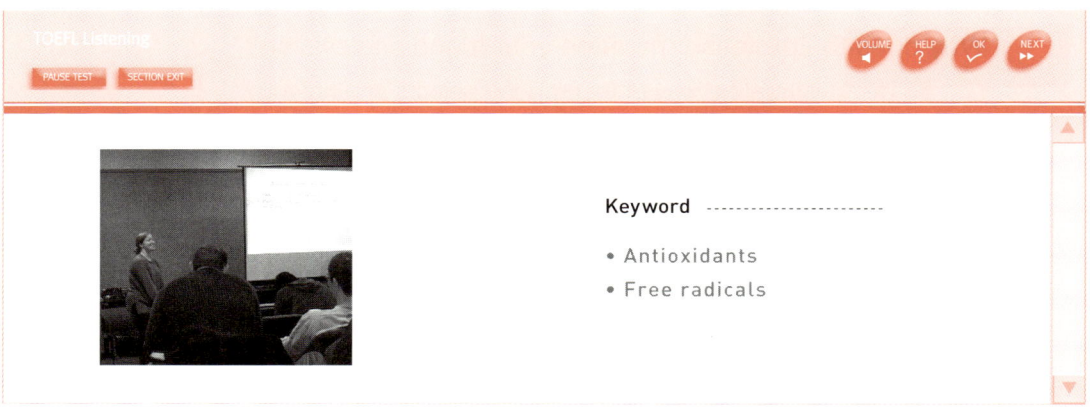

Keyword ------------------------

• Antioxidants
• Free radicals

1   **What is the discussion mainly about?**

(A) Different beneficial components of coffee

(B) Healthy eating habits and exercises

(C) Effect of antioxidant on human body

(D) Ways to maximize the absorption of antioxidants

2   **Why does the professor mention the 11-year study reported in June?**

(A) To shift the topic from caffeinated coffee to decaffeinated coffee

(B) To introduce today's topic by mentioning antioxidant in coffee

(C) To emphasize the benefits of drinking decaffeinated coffee

(D) To draw attention to the effects of coffee on women's diabetes

3   **What does the professor say about antioxidant and free radicals?**

(A) Free radicals can be found mainly in colorful fruits and coffee.

(B) Antioxidant can only be absorbed through eating fruits and vegetables.

(C) When free radicals accumulate in human cell, the human body will grow stronger.

(D) Antioxidant agents can be found in dark green leafy vegetables and fruits with rich colors.

4   Why does the professor say this: 🎧

    Ⓐ To boast about her knowledge on the origin of the word antioxidant

    Ⓑ To provide the origin of a word to promote students' understanding

    Ⓒ To explain the function of antioxidant by providing the origin of the word

    Ⓓ To challenge the students to study more by giving the origin of the word

5   **What is the professor's attitude towards dietary supplement formulas with antioxidants?**

    Ⓐ She agrees that dietary supplement formulas are somewhat helpful for people to stay healthy.

    Ⓑ She believes that people should take dietary supplement formulas three times a day.

    Ⓒ She is skeptical about the efficacy of dietary supplement formulas despite the result of recent researches.

    Ⓓ She feels negative about the effect of dietary supplement formulas.

Exercise

Listen to part of a discussion in a history class. 🎧

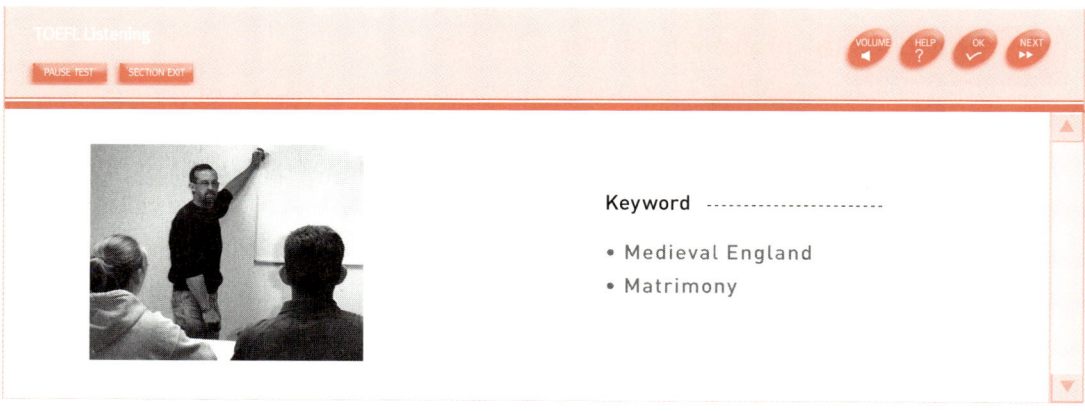

Keyword -

- Medieval England
- Matrimony

1 What is the discussion mainly about?

Ⓐ Feudal society and child raising customs in medieval England

Ⓑ Traditional wedding customs in medieval England

Ⓒ The high death rate of infants in medieval England

Ⓓ Feudal society and matrimony customs in medieval England

2 What can be inferred about the newlyweds in the feudal society?

Ⓐ In England, a man and a woman had to be lucky to get married.

Ⓑ In feudal society, many newborn babies died before they grew up.

Ⓒ In feudal society, a married couple had to have a license to have a baby.

Ⓓ In England, people's average life span was relatively shorter.

3 Listen again to part of the discussion. Then answer the question.
How does the student feel when she says this: 🎧

Ⓐ She does not believe the professor's comment.

Ⓑ She is trying to defy the professor's authority.

Ⓒ She is amazed at the fact that most medieval peasants wedded at such a young age.

Ⓓ She is sorry that she is not married yet even when she is over 19 years old.

4   What does the professor say about the relationship between peasants and a lord of the manor?

   (A) Knights granted the lord of the manor the right to wed peasants.
   (B) Peasants and all of their belongings were owned by the lord of the manor.
   (C) Peasants owned and cultivated the land which was protected by the lord.
   (D) Peasants were owned by the lord only by paper and had more freedom.

5   According to the professor, which of the following is true about medieval weddings?

   (A) Peasants were absolutely not allowed to marry other free people.
   (B) About 3/4 of peasants got married before they reached 24 years old.
   (C) Weddings of peasants as a result of pregnancy were frowned upon.
   (D) Many of the upper class as well as peasants had arranged marriage.

Passage 5

Listen to part of a lecture in a sociolinguistics class. 🎧

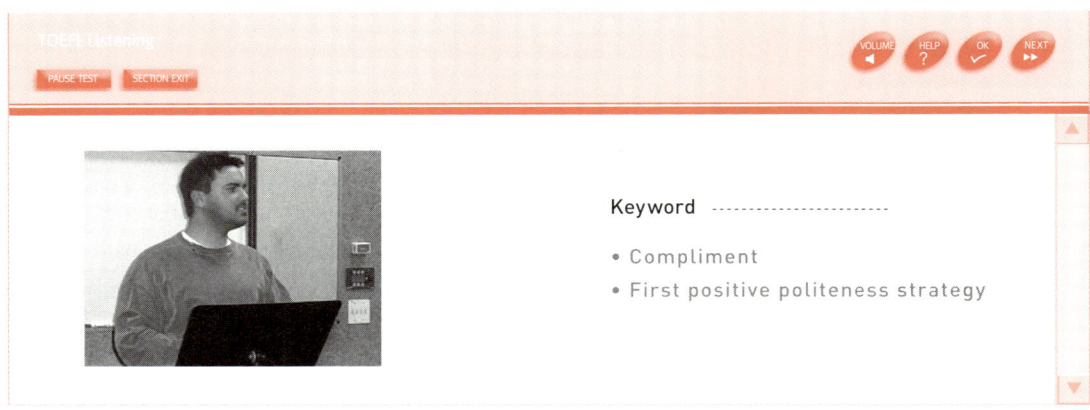

Keyword ------------------

• Compliment
• First positive politeness strategy

1 **What is the lecture mainly about?**

(A) The definition of speech act and its social effect

(B) The reason why people are polite to each other

(C) The relationship between compliment and gender difference

(D) The reason why men and women differ in giving compliments

2 **What is the professor's attitude towards compliment?**

(A) He thinks that men should start complimenting each other more.

(B) He thinks that compliments consolidate relationship between people.

(C) He believes that too much compliment influences relations negatively.

(D) He is uncertain how compliments affect the relationship between people.

3 According to the lecture, which of the following situations is an example of the first positive politeness strategy?

Ⓐ When talking with her friends, Jessica tries to keep her voice down.

Ⓑ In dialogues with other people, Sam tries to listen to them attentively.

Ⓒ When she talks with the elderly, Lily tries to use words in their polite forms.

Ⓓ When he talks to other people, John tries to commend as much as possible.

4 What can be inferred from the result of an experiment in New Zealand?

Ⓐ It is more likely that women in New Zealand compliment each other more than they compliment other men.

Ⓑ It is more likely that men in New Zealand compliment other women more than women in compliment other women.

Ⓒ It can be generalized that men compliment each other more than women compliment each other.

Ⓓ There is no obvious difference in speech act between men and women in New Zealand.

5 Listen again to part of the lecture. Then answer the question.
Why does the professor say this: 🎧

Ⓐ He wants to introduce a subtopic he is about to explain.

Ⓐ He is digressing from the main point of the lecture.

Ⓐ He wants one of the students to answer his question.

Ⓐ He is trying to remember a technical terminology.

Passage 6   Listen to part of a discussion in a history class. 🎧

TOEFL Listening

PAUSE TEST   SECTION EXIT

VOLUME HELP OK NEXT

Keyword ----------------------

• Christopher Columbus
• Discovery of the Americas

1 What is the main idea of the discussion?

ⓐ The results of Christopher Columbus' discovery of the Americas
ⓑ Christopher Columbus and his diary during his four long voyages
ⓒ The process of Christopher Columbus' four voyages and sponsorship
ⓓ The historical significance of Christopher Columbus' voyages to the Americas

2 According to the professor, what can be said about Christopher Columbus?

ⓐ He is the first navigator from a European country to reach the Americas.
ⓑ The name, Christopher Columbus, is not the actual name of the navigator.
ⓒ He landed on the mainlands of the Americas on his first voyage in 1492.
ⓓ His voyages were jointly sponsored by the Vikings and the Catholic Monarchs of Spain.

3 What is the professor's attitude towards Columbus Day?

- (A) She thinks that Columbus Day should be abolished.
- (B) She thinks that Columbus Day should be celebrated worldwide rather than only in some of the American and European countries.
- (C) She thinks that the meaning of Columbus Day should be reconsidered since his arrival at the Americas brought immense tragedy to the original inhabitants.
- (D) She believes that people should pay more attention to Columbus Day.

4 Listen again to part of the discussion. Then answer the question. Why does the professor says this: ∩

- (A) To confirm students' knowledge on the topic
- (B) To divert students' attention from the topic
- (C) To criticize students' ignorance on the topic
- (D) To add information on a student's question

5 According to the professor, what can be inferred about the European conquest?

- (A) It enlightened the primitive world by introducing trade and religion.
- (B) It was extremely difficult for the Europeans to take over the new world.
- (C) It was conducted for academic reasons at first, funded by institutions.
- (D) It introduced unknown diseases into the Americas and the Caribbean region.

Passage 7   Listen to part of a lecture in an ornithology class. 🎧

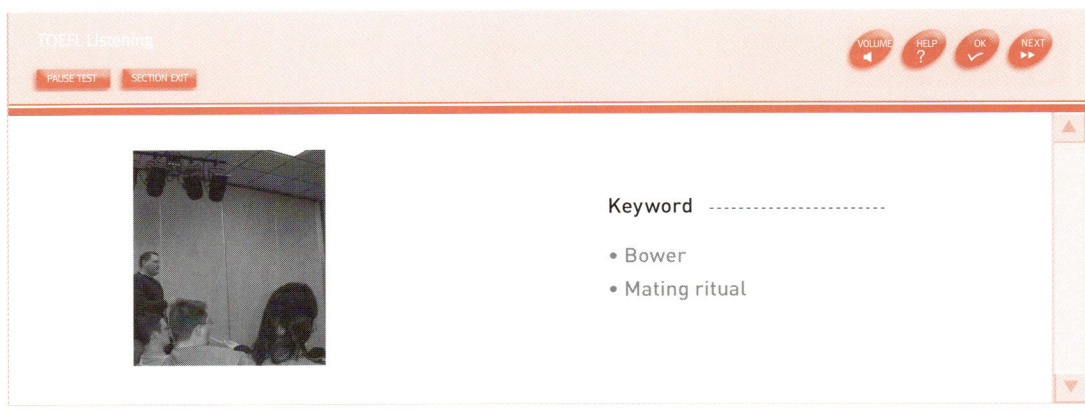

1 According to the lecture, what can be said about bowerbirds?

Ⓐ Female bowerbirds build bowers to attract mates.

Ⓑ Bower builders use various types of materials to make bowers.

Ⓒ Male bowerbirds have the right to choose the mate.

Ⓓ Female bowerbirds perform courtship rituals to attract males.

2 Listen again to part of the lecture. Then answer the question.
What does the professor mean when he says this: 🎧

Ⓐ The male and the female bowerbirds take care of their babies together.

Ⓑ It is extremely difficult for the female bowerbird to mate with a strong male.

Ⓒ The quality of a bower does not reflect the competence of a male bowerbird.

Ⓓ The female bowerbird wants to mate with a strong male for reproduction.

3 What is the professor's attitude towards bowerbirds and their bowers?

Ⓐ He is fascinated by the various materials they use in their bowers.

Ⓑ He feels indifferent since their mating behavior is not particularly interesting.

Ⓒ He is amazed because he expected them to use only artificial objects.

Ⓓ He believes that female bowerbirds should receive more attention than male bowerbirds.

Passage 8   Listen to part of a discussion in a film class. 🎧

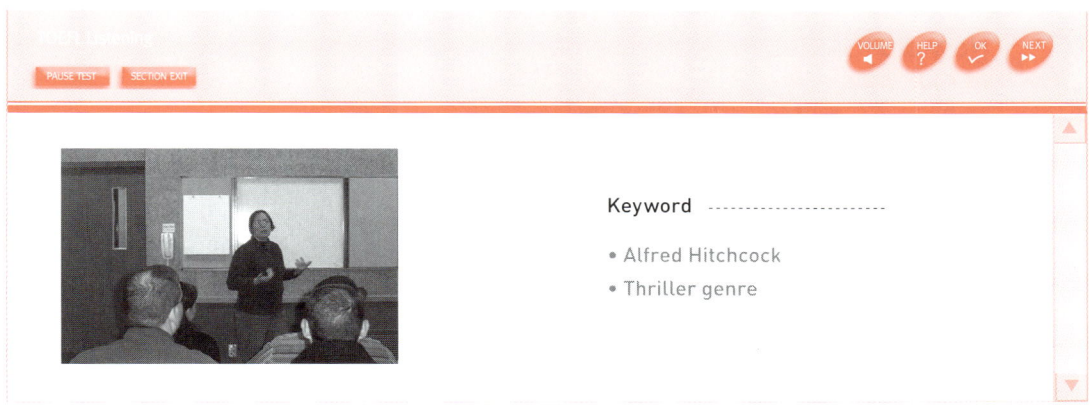

1   What is the discussion mainly about?
- (A) The creation of a new genre by Alfred Hitchcock
- (B) The horror movies created by Alfred Hitchcock
- (C) Commentary on Hitchcock's movies, *Psycho* and *The Birds*
- (D) Famous scenes that create suspense in Alfred Hitchcock's movies

2   What does the professor mention about Hitchcock and his movies?
- (A) Hitchcock is known as the creator of the thriller genre.
- (B) The movie, *The Birds*, was a remake of a movie of the same name.
- (C) Hitchcock created a number of horror films other than *Psycho* and *The Birds*.
- (D) The movie, *The Birds*, is known for one of the scariest scenes in cinema history.

3   Why does the professor mention the list of films directed by Alfred Hitchcock?
- (A) To introduce today's topic on Alfred Hitchcock
- (B) To shift the topic from *The Lodger* to *Rebecca*
- (C) To explain movies she has seen in the past
- (D) To emphasize vast amount of Hitchcock's movies

4 How did the student feel when he first saw the shower scene of the movie, *Psycho*?

   Ⓐ He was disappointed that it was not better than its prequel's similar scene.

   Ⓑ He was amazed by the suspense it created and felt that the scene would never end.

   Ⓒ He felt indifferent by the scene because he already knew what would happen next.

   Ⓓ He felt that it was a mediocre scene that ineffectively showed how Hitchcock had combined close-ups and medium shots.

5 The professor discusses Alfred Hitchcock and his movies. Based on the information in the discussion, indicate whether each sentence below describes the movie *Psycho* or *The Birds*.

Click in the correct box.

	Psycho	*The Birds*
It has no ending card that says, "The End."		
It has the structure which Fellini called a filmic poem.		
It was filmed in 1960.		
The famous scene in this movie is the shower scene, which effectively creates suspense.		
It was based on the novel with the same title by Robert Bloch.		

Passage 9   Listen to part of a lecture in a physics class. 🎧

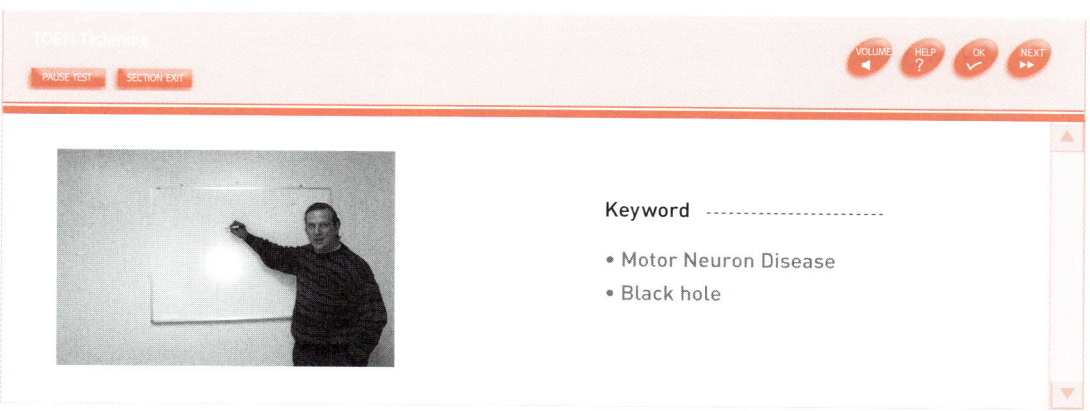

1 What is the lecture mainly about?

Ⓐ Stephen Hawking and his life as a physicist

Ⓑ Stephen Hawking and his books and articles on black holes

Ⓒ Stephen Hawking's life after being struck by Lou Gehrig's Disease

Ⓓ Stephen Hawking's life and his theory about black holes

2 What does the professor say about Lou Gehrig's disease?

Ⓐ It makes the patient unable to see, speak, hear or move.

Ⓑ It paralyzes the mental function but does not affect physical ability.

Ⓒ It degenerates a person's motor skills but does not influence intelligence.

Ⓓ It progressively paralyzes a person's physical and mental function.

3 How does the professor organize the lecture?

Ⓐ He relates Hawking's book to his professional career.

Ⓑ He presents information from least to most recent.

Ⓒ He explains Hawking's life first and then explains his theories.

Ⓓ He compares Hawking's theory on black holes with the theory on massive star collapse.

4 What does the professor mention about black holes?
- Ⓐ Black holes' absorbing power is too great for a light to escape.
- Ⓑ Black holes are clearly visible to bare eyes.
- Ⓒ Black holes are created from a supernova.
- Ⓓ Black holes have low density.

5 What can be inferred about Hawking's book, *A Brief History of Time*?
- Ⓐ It is a fiction which was written by Hawking long time ago.
- Ⓑ It was highly acclaimed in the province of physics.
- Ⓒ It established a new record in the history of time management books.
- Ⓓ It is a book on the history of human being's use of time.

6 Listen again to part of the lecture. Then answer the question.
How does the professor feel when he says this: 🎧
- Ⓐ He feels somewhat disappointed that none of the students has read the well-known book.
- Ⓑ He is excited to have an opportunity to introduce Hawking's bestseller.
- Ⓒ He is angry at the students because they did not finish the assignment.
- Ⓓ He feels sorry for the students who have not heard about the book.

Listen to part of a lecture in a biology class. 🎧

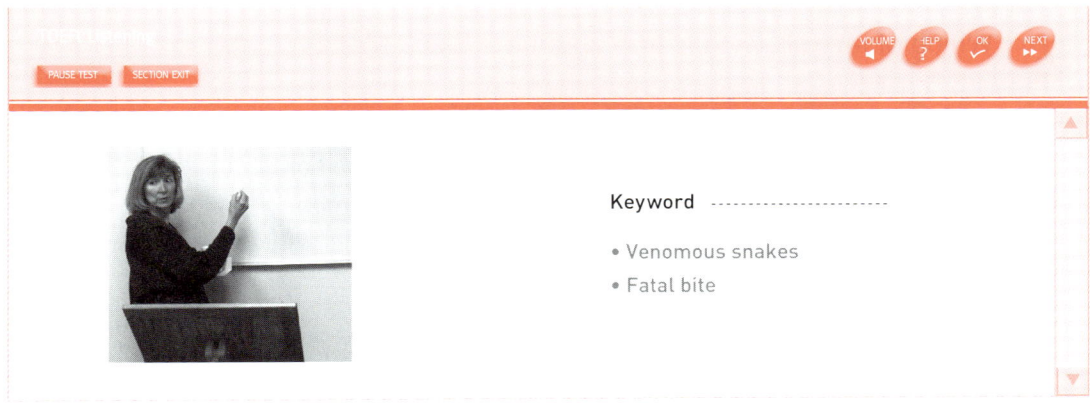

Keyword ------------------------

• Venomous snakes
• Fatal bite

1 How does the professor organize the lecture?

(A) From the least venomous to the most venomous snake

(B) From the most aggressive to the least aggressive snake

(C) From the most venomous to the least venomous snake

(D) From the least popular to the most popular venomous snake

2 What does the professor say about Tiger Snakes?

(A) Tiger Snakes usually live near populated cities in Africa.

(B) Tiger Snakes can be found in forests or grasslands in Australia.

(C) Tiger Snakes are the fastest venomous snakes on earth.

(D) Tiger Snakes are named after the color pattern of their body.

3 According to the professor, why do most venomous snakes attack people?

(A) Because they usually prey on people

(B) Because people threaten or agitate the venomus snakes

(C) Because their habitats are threatened from deforestation

(D) Because people usually poach the youngs of venomous snakes

4   Which of the following is true about the Black Mamba?   Click on 2 answers.

Ⓐ It got its name from the color of its body.
Ⓑ It can travel at the speed of 14 miles per hour on land.
Ⓒ There is no antivenim developed for the Black Mamba bite.
Ⓓ There is no known animal that can kill the Black Mamba.

5   Why does the professor pass the piece of paper to the students at the beginning of the lecture?

Ⓐ To check the attendance of the class
Ⓑ To have the students pick the topic of the next week's presentation
Ⓒ To let the students know which group they are in for the presentation
Ⓓ To inform the students of the presentation guidelines

6   What is the professor's attitude towards Cobra bites on people?

Ⓐ She thinks that although Cobras often do not inject venom, the attacked should be immediately treated medically.
Ⓑ She thinks that only people who were bitten more than 10 times by a Cobra should be sought medical treatment immediately.
Ⓒ She thinks because Cobra bites are not all fatal to people, those who were bitten should rest first before being medically treated.
Ⓓ She thinks that people who were attacked by a Cobra should be tested whether the venom was actually injected or not before being sent to a hospital.

Vocabulary

✔ 박스에 체크 표기를 하며 주요 단어를 학습하시오.

- ☐ **postmodern** 포스트모더니즘의
- ☐ **commons** 공공(재)
- ☐ **deforestation** 산림파괴
- ☐ **degradation** 타락, 퇴보, 퇴화
- ☐ **depletion** 고갈
- ☐ **allocation** 분배
- ☐ **consciousness** 의식, 자각
- ☐ **capacity** 용량
- ☐ **forefront** 맨 앞, 선두
- ☐ **antioxidant** 항산화물질
- ☐ **component** 구성요소, 성분
- ☐ **oxidative** 산화의
- ☐ **reactive** 민감한, 반응이 빠른; 반발의
- ☐ **modify** 변경(수정)하다, 바꾸다
- ☐ **degeneration** 타락, 퇴보, 퇴폐
- ☐ **progression** 진행, 진보, 발달
- ☐ **enzyme** 효소
- ☐ **counteract** 거스르다, 방해하다
- ☐ **absorption** 흡수
- ☐ **supplement** 추가, 보충
- ☐ **legitimate** 합법적인
- ☐ **bestow** 수여하다, 증여하다
- ☐ **liege-lord** 영주
- ☐ **mortality** 사망률
- ☐ **relieving** 걱정이 덜어지는
- ☐ **denote** 표시하다, 나타내다
- ☐ **commendation** 칭찬, 추천
- ☐ **civility** 정중, 공손, 예의바름
- ☐ **affective** 감정적인, 정서적인
- ☐ **informative** 정보를 제공하는
- ☐ **solidarity** 결속, 일치, 단결
- ☐ **addressee** 수취인; 듣는 사람
- ☐ **navigate** 항해하다
- ☐ **imperialism** 제국주의
- ☐ **accomplish** 이루다, 완성하다

- ☐ **perspective** 견해, 관점
- ☐ **devastating** 파괴적인, 압도적인
- ☐ **indigenous** 토착의
- ☐ **eccentric** 이상한, 유별난
- ☐ **courtship** 구애, 구혼
- ☐ **ritual** 의식
- ☐ **titivate** 맵시내다, 몸치장하다, 장식하다
- ☐ **elaborate** 복잡한, 정교한, 공들인
- ☐ **competent** 경쟁력 있는
- ☐ **reproduction** 번식, 생식
- ☐ **acknowledge** 인정하다
- ☐ **tactful** 재치있는, 빈틈없는
- ☐ **suspense** 지속적 긴장감
- ☐ **embezzle** 횡령하다
- ☐ **disturbed** 동요한; 정신(정서) 장애가 있는
- ☐ **deftly** 솜씨 좋게, 교묘히
- ☐ **duration** 지속, 계속, 존속(기간)
- ☐ **sequence** 연속, 연달아 일어남
- ☐ **progressively** 점진적으로
- ☐ **metaphorical** 은유적인
- ☐ **motor** 운동근육(신경)
- ☐ **degenerative** 퇴행성의
- ☐ **disorder** 장애
- ☐ **stabilize** 안정화하다
- ☐ **confined** 한정하다, 제한하다
- ☐ **primordial** 원시의
- ☐ **exhaust** 고갈하다
- ☐ **singularity** 단독
- ☐ **venomous** 독이 있는
- ☐ **aggressive** 공격적인
- ☐ **agitate** 선동하다, 교란하다
- ☐ **invulnerable** 죽지 않는, 이겨낼 수 없는
- ☐ **provoke** 화나게 하다, 자극하다
- ☐ **injection** 주입

Vocabulary Test

📝 박스에서 올바른 단어를 골라 빈칸을 채우시오.

deforestation	modify	rodent
embezzle	scale	stabilize

1 Dolphins' two finlike flippers near the front of the body help _____
  the body in the flowing water and steer the animal as it swims.

2 If a person has the need, opportunity, and rationalization, he or she is apt to
  commit fraud or _____.

3 Despite the fact that many people generally think that fish have the
  _____, many fish, actually, do not have it.

4 Since this contract bears many flaws, you should consider _____
  (ing) it.

confined	deforestation	primordial
invulnerable	disorder	navigate

5 The evolutionist holds the opinion that all creatures share the same genetic
  code, and we have all evolved in the same way from _____ forms
  — perhaps a single form — of life on Earth.

6 The rate of _____ in the Amazon area is so great that many
  scientists worry that it will soon have a serious effect on the world's weather —
  the government as well as the rest of the world should pay much attention on
  this matter if they care about the environment.

7 If a pregnant woman smokes, it is highly possible that her child will be
  born with serious heart disease as well as with other physical and mental
  _____ (s).

8 Jackson was _____ during the debate yesterday — not a single
  participant could defeat his logical retorts.

올바른 단어를 골라 문장을 완성하시오.

9   His life-long goal was to visit at least thirty different countries all over the world; now that he has visited more than forty countries, he considers that he has _____(ed) his goal.

  (A) embezzle   (B) exhaust   (C) modify   (D) accomplish

10 Although some students might think that _____ infestation in college dorms is normal, you must immediately report school officials when you spot mice or rats in your dorm room — it's not normal since it may seriously harm your and your neighbors' health.

  (A) rodent   (B) capacity   (C) implode   (D) render

11 In the 1700's, Lazarro Spallanzani found that bats could fly in total darkness while owls could not; he also found that if the head of a bat was covered, it could not _____ properly.

  (A) inject   (B) elaborate   (C) navigate   (D) accomplish

12 According to this contract, Mr. Simpson is the _____ owner of this property.

  (A) reactive   (B) legitimate   (C) affective   (D) primordial

13 The Kansas crafter's replica of a Native American traditional Dreamcatcher shows off its _____ style with three separate rings embelished delicately with feathers, leather lacing, and beads.

  (A) elaborate   (B) invulnerable   (C) relieving   (D) titivate

14 The dangers of smoking are not _____ to smokers only — their families, friends, whoever near the smoker may be affected by the smoke.

  (A) provoke   (B) confined   (C) embezzle   (D) implode

15 The brain _____ is enormous — they say that we only use three to five percent of our brain.

  (A) civility   (B) referential   (C) scale   (D) capacity

Chapter 6

Function

문제유형

- Why does(did) the professor(student) say this: 🎧
- What does(did) the professor(student) mean when he(she) says this: 🎧
- What does(did) the professor(student) want to know when he(she) says(said) this: 🎧

Sample

Listen to part of a lecture in an entomology class. 🎧

TOEFL Listening

VOLUME ◄ HELP ? OK ✓ NEXT ►►

PAUSE TEST   SECTION EXIT

Why does the professor say this: 🎧

- (A) To check if the students have understood the point of the lesson clearly
- (B) To see if the students brought pictures of ants
- (C) To find out whether the students did the homework
- (D) To make sure the students remember the anatomical parts of the ant body

화자의 의도와 뉘앙스에 유의하며 강의를 다시 한번 들으시오. 🎧

Ant bodies have an **exoskeleton** just like any other insects. Ants have bodies that are externally covered in a protective casing, unlike us humans or other vertebrates that have internal skeletal framework. There are several differences between ants and other small vertebrates, such as marsupials. For one thing, ants don't have lungs. Then how do they breathe? Well, oxygen just passes through tiny pores, the **spiracles**, in their exoskeleton. Carbon dioxide leaves their body through the same hole. Moreover, ants don't have a heart. Ants have **hemolymph**, a colorless blood, running inside their body along a long tube. **1** <u>Everybody got the picture?</u>

Tip 강의나 토론 지문을 들을 때 불평하는 목소리, 강조하는 단어, 머뭇거리거나 자신있어 하는 태도 등에서 문제가 출제될 수 있으므로 주목한다.

Strategy 1   화자의 언급에 담긴 구체적인 의도를 이해하자

교수는 개미의 신체적 구조의 특징으로 exoskeleton(외골격), spiracle(숨구멍), hemolymph(혈액림프)를 언급한 후 다음과 같이 말한다.

1 Everybody got the picture?

Get the picture란 '이해하다'라는 뜻으로 교수는 지금까지의 설명을 학생들이 모두 이해했는지를 확인하고 있다. 따라서 정답은 A이다.

이처럼 강의나 토의에서 화자가 하는 말의 의도를 이해하기 위해서는 지문에서 사용되는 표현과 지문의 전체적인 내용을 이해해야 한다. 아래에서 자주 출제되는 화자의 의도와 그에 대한 예시를 참고하자.

의도	사용되는 표현과 예
• 예시	- Let me give you an example for ~, To demonstrate ~
• 부연 설명	- Further~, What I'm trying to say is~
• 확인하기	- Do you mean~?, Did you say~?, Are you sure~?, ~, right?
• 강조하기	- Absolutely~, Extremely~, Never~, Undeniably ~
• 놀라움 표시	- Really?, Are you serious~?, I didn't know that~, Wow!
• 이해도 질문하기	- Everyone got it?, Got the picture?, Do you follow?, Does everybody understand what I'm trying to say?
• 되돌아가기	- Back to our subject, ~, If we go back to~, Let's go back to~, Anyways, ~

Strategy 2   TPO(Time, Place, Occasion)에 따른 뉘앙스의 차이를 이해하자

같은 단어나 표현이라도 대화나 강의의 상황(context)에 따라 다른 뉘앙스를 갖는다. 다음 예를 살펴보자.

단어/표현	뉘앙스/예
• Ouch	(1) 신체적 아픔을 표현할 때 A: **Ouch**, stop pinching me! That hurts! B: Oh, sorry. (2) 마음의 상처를 입었음을 표현할 때 A: I'm sorry to tell you that Dr. Russell didn't like your paper at all — she said that it was plain and dull. B: **Ouch**.
• Oh, boy	(1) 유쾌함을 표현할 때 A: We'll go to McDonald's for lunch today. B: **Oh, boy!** I love McDonald's! (2) 당황함/안타까움을 표현할 때 A: Mary dropped out of school last week! B: **Oh, boy**, Are you serious?

Strategy Focus

화자의 의도와 뉘앙스에 유의하며 강의를 들으시오. 🎧

1

* Focus :
  baseball and softball

* Keyword/Key phrase :
  judging from the name itself

What does the professor mean when he says this: 🎧

Ⓐ The ball used for softball games is hard.
Ⓑ The ball used for softball games is soft.
Ⓒ Baseball and softball use the same type of ball.
Ⓓ Baseball and softball are the same type of game.

Tip

교수는 softball이라는 이름에서 선수들이 사용하는 공이 어떤 종류인지 알 수 있다고 말한다.

☐ confuse 혼동하다
☐ pitcher 투수

2

* Focus :

* Keyword/Key phrase :

Listen again to part of the discussion. Then answer the question.
What does the professor mean when she says this: 🎧

Ⓐ She wants the student to do his assigned reading.
Ⓑ She is angry because the student does not know the answer.
Ⓒ She will not ask any questions to the student.
Ⓓ She wants the student to make a presentation.

숙제로 내준 책을 읽지 않아 엉뚱한 대답을 한 학생을 간접적으로 꾸짖고 있다.

☐ ape 유인원, 원숭이
☐ assign 할당하다
☐ crucial 매우 중요한

3

- **Focus :**

- **Keyword/Key phrase :**

Tip

"Much controversy"라는 교수의 말에서 힌트를 찾을 수 있다.

- [ ] heritage 유산, 전통
- [ ] controversy 논쟁
- [ ] eradicate 근절하다
- [ ] derogatory 경멸적인

Why does the professor say this: 🎧

- (A) To demonstrate where the term derived from
- (B) To emphasize the importance of American Indians
- (C) To explain that some people do not accept the term
- (D) To elucidate the importance of Christopher Columbus

4

- **Focus :**

- **Keyword/Key phrase :**

기부자의 이름을 딴 대학의 예를 들기 위해 Harvard를 언급하고 있다.

- [ ] adopt 채택하다
- [ ] founder 설립자
- [ ] benefactor 기부자
- [ ] prestigious 훌륭한, 유명한
- [ ] establish 설립하다

Listen again to part of the lecture. Then answer the question.

What does the professor imply when she says this: 🎧

- (A) Harvard University is not very famous.
- (B) Many people wish to attend Harvard University.
- (C) Everyone is familiar with Harvard University.
- (D) Harvard University got its name from one of its benefactors.

Exercise

Listen to part of a lecture in an anthropology class. 🎧

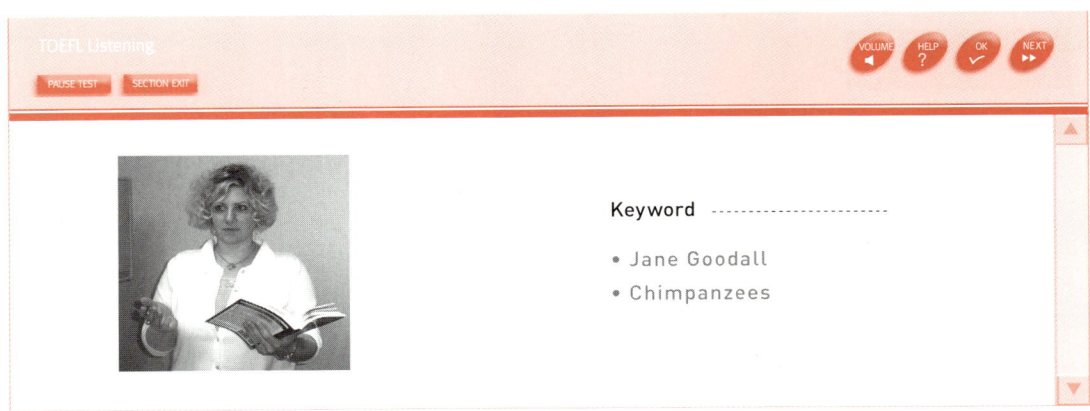

Keyword -

- Jane Goodall
- Chimpanzees

1 What is the main topic of the lecture?
- Ⓐ How Jane Goodall became a primatologist
- Ⓑ The famous long-term chimpanzee study in Tanzania
- Ⓒ The jobs and responsibilities of Jane Goodall Institute
- Ⓓ Jane Goodall's life as the patron of wild chimpanzees

2 What can be inferred about wild chimpanzees before the establishment of the Jane Goodall Institute?
- Ⓐ Chimpanzees enjoyed an extremely safe life.
- Ⓑ The birthrate of chimpanzees was extremely low.
- Ⓒ The study of chimpanzees and their habitat did not exist at all.
- Ⓓ People poached wild chimpanzees and destroyed their habitat.

3 Listen again to part of the lecture. Then answer the question.
What does the professor mean when she says this: 🎧
- Ⓐ Goodall is widely known as the chaperone of chimpanzees.
- Ⓑ Goodall is not very famous among English primatologists.
- Ⓒ Goodall is only known for her scientific achievements.
- Ⓓ Goodall was raised by chimpanzees in the wild.

Passage 2   Listen to part of a lecture in a health science class. 🎧

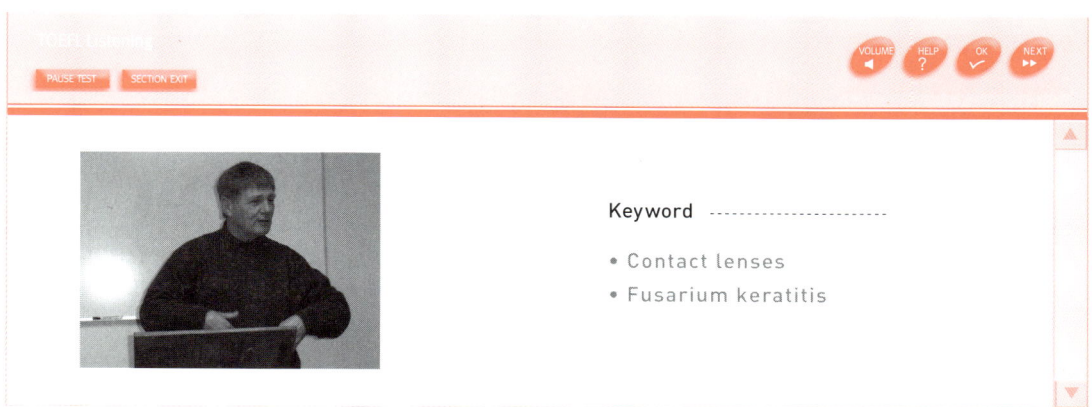

Keyword ------------------------

• Contact lenses
• Fusarium keratitis

1 What is the topic of the lecture?

Ⓐ Why people wear contact lenses

Ⓑ Instructions on how to wear contact lenses

Ⓒ The symptoms of fusarium keratitis and its side effects

Ⓓ Consequences of misusing contact lenses and its prevention

2 According to the lecture, which of the following are the ways to prevent fusarium keratitis?   Click on 2 answers.

Ⓐ Replace lenses before expiration date.

Ⓑ Cleanse your eyes after taking out your lenses.

Ⓒ Take your lenses out before your vision is blurred.

Ⓓ Take your lenses out when your eyes are pink or red.

3 Why does the professor say this: 🎧

Ⓐ To promote the sales of contact lenses

Ⓑ To magnify the benefits of wearing contact lenses

Ⓒ To encourage students to wear contact lenses more often

Ⓓ To explain the reason why people wear contact lenses

Passage 3   Listen to part of a lecture in a history class. 🎧

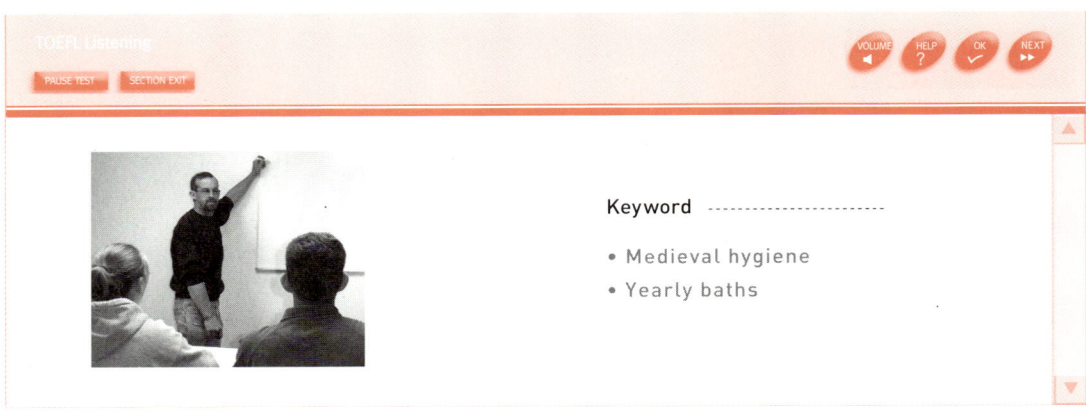

TOEFL Listening

VOLUME ◀   HELP ?   OK ✓   NEXT ▶▶

PAUSE TEST   SECTION EXIT

Keyword -------------------------

- Medieval hygiene
- Yearly baths

---

1   **What is the lecture mainly about?**
- Ⓐ Why medieval people took frequent baths
- Ⓑ Medieval people and festivals
- Ⓒ Hygiene of the medieval people
- Ⓓ The wedding tradition during the Middle Ages

2   **What is the professor about to explain when he says this:** 🎧
- Ⓐ What other methods medieval people used to hide their body odor
- Ⓑ Why medieval people did not cleanse themselves frequently
- Ⓒ How medieval people were ignorant about hygiene
- Ⓓ How medieval people kept themselves clean

3   **Listen again to part of the lecture. Then answer the question.**
Why does the professor say this: 🎧
- Ⓐ To emphasize the importance of public hygiene
- Ⓑ To provide correct information on what many people believe
- Ⓒ To show his anger on people's ignorance on medieval life
- Ⓓ To express his belief that medieval people only had baths once a year

Listen to part of a discussion in an environmental science class. 🎧

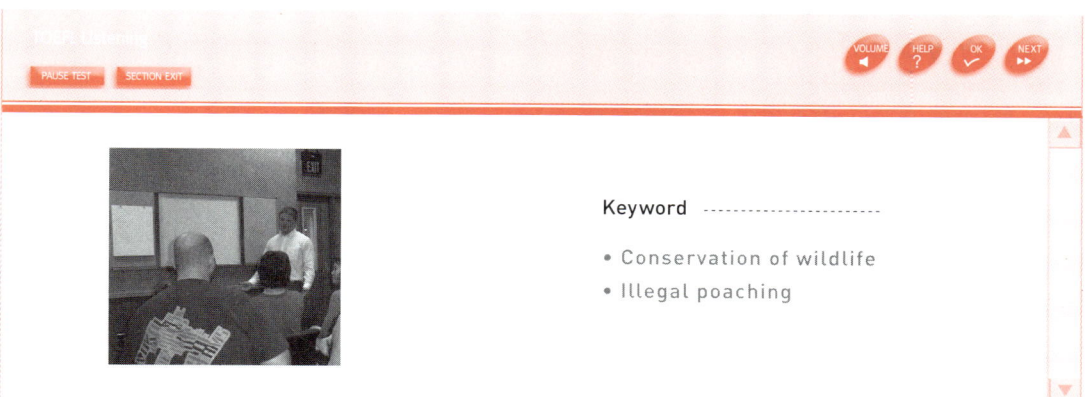

Keyword ------------------------

• Conservation of wildlife
• Illegal poaching

1 What is the discussion mainly about?

  Ⓐ Efforts to preserve wildlife in national parks

  Ⓑ Definition of poaching and illegal trophy trades

  Ⓒ Adverse effect of poaching elephants and white rhinos

  Ⓓ Serengeti National Park's wildlife conservation program

2 According to the discussion, which of the following poses a threat to wildlife within protected areas? Click on 2 answers.

  Ⓐ Poaching

  Ⓑ Enforcement patrols

  Ⓒ Illegal trophy trade

  Ⓓ Destruction of wildlife habitat

3 Why does the professor show pictures of elephant poaching at the beginning of the class?

(A) To explain the violent nature of human beings

(B) To shock the students with extreme pictures of illegal poaching

(C) To keep the promise he made last class that he would show a picture of an illegal poaching

(D) To explain today's topic more effectively by showing the students relevant visual materials

4 Listen again to part of the discussion. Then answer the question.
Why does the professor say this: 🎧

(A) To provide answer to the student's question

(B) To refute the student's theory on poaching

(C) To rebuke the student for his ignorance

(D) To explain an unfamiliar terminology

5 What does the professor say about the conservation program of Serengeti National Park in Tanzania?

(A) It had no effect on poaching and illegal trophy trades in the park.

(B) It contributed to recent increase of wildlife population in the park.

(C) It had harmful influence on the population of elephants and rhinos.

(D) It was a great success because it eradicated poaching in the park.

Passage 5   Listen to part of a lecture in an American history class. 🎧

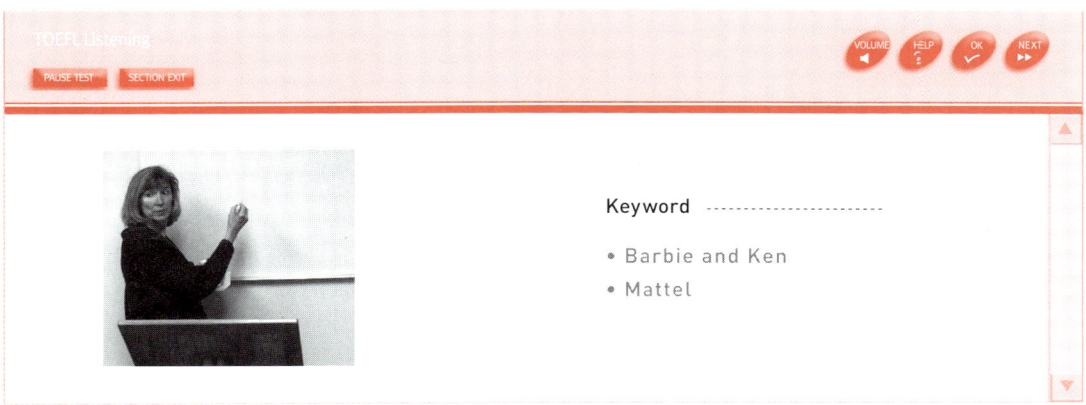

PAUSE TEST   SECTION EXIT   VOLUME   HELP   OK   NEXT

Keyword - - - - - - - - - - - - - - - -

• Barbie and Ken
• Mattel

1 What is the topic of the lecture?

ⓐ The unique design of Ruth Handler

ⓑ The life story of Barbie and Ken

ⓒ The creation of Barbie by Mattel

ⓓ The success story of Ruth and Elliot Handler

2 What is true about the Barbie doll and its creators?

ⓐ Mattel was a family-owned company when it first started.

ⓑ Ruth Handler created the Lilli doll when she lived in Germany.

ⓒ The Handlers and Mattson disagreed in company management.

ⓓ Barbie doll instantly received an avid welcoming from toy buyers.

3 Why does the professor say this: 🎧

ⓐ To explain that Barbie and Ken were actual people who were married

ⓑ To clarify that the dolls got their names from the children of the Handlers

ⓒ To elucidate that Mattel had a difficult time naming its popular dolls

ⓓ To insinuate that she does not know where the dolls got the names from

Passage 6

Listen to part of a lecture in a psychology class.

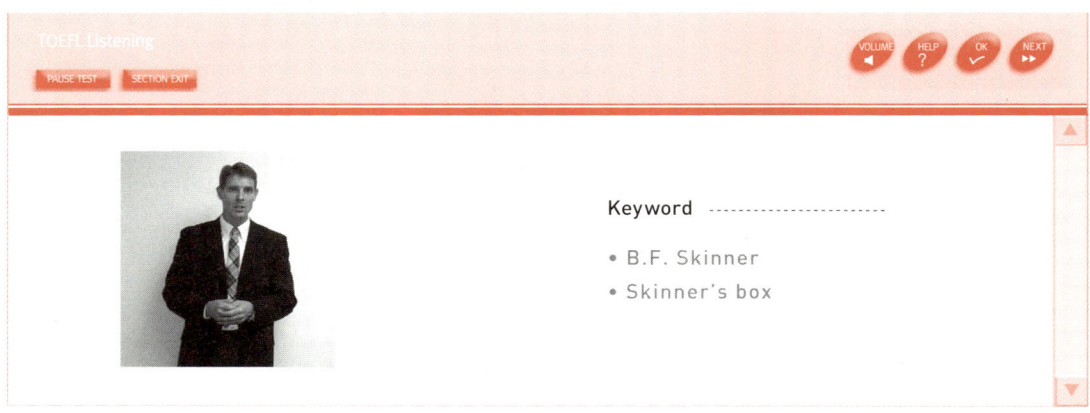

Keyword ---------------------

- B.F. Skinner
- Skinner's box

1 What is the lecture mainly about?

- Ⓐ Skinner and his theory on human learning and behavior
- Ⓑ The mechanism of Skinner's box
- Ⓒ Behaviorism and its famous advocates
- Ⓓ The rat behavior of accumulating food

2 Listen again to part of the lecture. Then answer the question.
Why does the professor say this:

- Ⓐ To describe how children usually obtain goals
- Ⓑ To apologize to the students for being late to class
- Ⓒ To explain the method of teaching language to children
- Ⓓ To provide an example to promote students' understanding

3 What can be inferred about Skinner?

- Ⓐ Pavlov and Skinner were interested in human's respondent behavior.
- Ⓑ Unlike Pavlov, Skinner tried to explain human behavior and learning.
- Ⓒ Pavlov trained his dog to respond using Skinner's reinforcement strategy.
- Ⓓ Skinner was the first psychologist who tried to explain human learning and behavior.

Passage 7   Listen to part of a discussion in an architecture class. 🎧

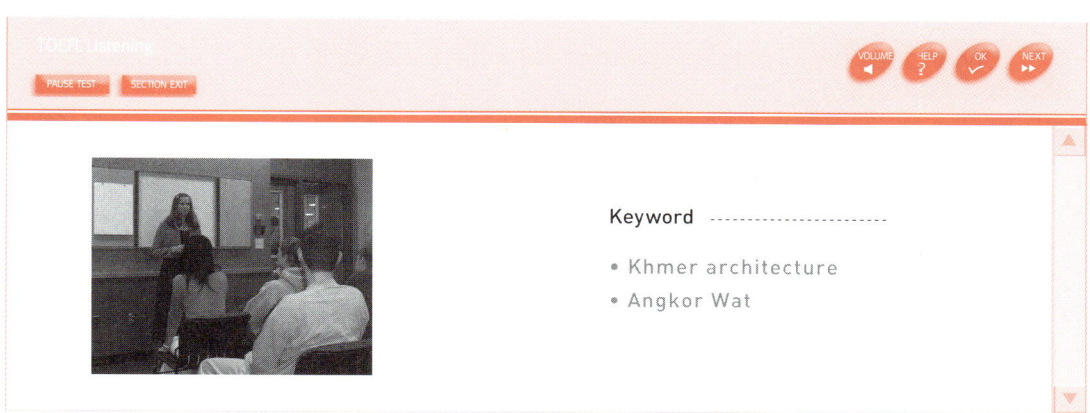

Keyword --------------------------

• Khmer architecture
• Angkor Wat

1 What does the professor mainly discuss?

Ⓐ The geographical location of Angkor Wat

Ⓑ The building materials used in Khmer architecture

Ⓒ The influence of Khmer religion on Indian architecture

Ⓓ The various religions that had impact on Khmer architecture

2 According to the professor, which of the following building materials did Khmer architects mainly use?   Click on 2 answers.

Ⓐ Sandstone

Ⓑ Stone

Ⓒ Laterite

Ⓓ Limestone

3 According to the professor, what is Devaraja?

Ⓐ A type of an architecture which was adopted by the Khmers

Ⓑ A name of a Cambodian empire which lasted from AD 800 to AD 850

Ⓒ A temple which was built for both the king and the Hindu god, Siva

Ⓓ A religion which considers the king as the divine universal ruler

4 Why does the professor mention King Jayavarman II?
- (A) To demonstrate the building process of Angkor Wat
- (B) To clarify the relationship between Cambodians and Indians
- (C) To describe the king's achievements of finishing Angkor Wat
- (D) To explain devaraja and its influence on Khmer architecture

5 Listen again to part of the discussion. Then answer the question. What does the professor imply when she says this: 🎧
- (A) The Cambodians have nothing to do with Khmer architecture.
- (B) The Cambodians were influenced exclusively by Indian culture.
- (C) Other parts of the Cambodian culture were also influenced by Indian culture.
- (D) Angkor Wat was the first temple which was built according to the Indian methods of architecture.

6 Listen again to part of the discussion. Then answer the question. Why does the professor say this: 🎧
- (A) To find out if students have understood her lecture so far
- (B) To prevent any further questions from the students
- (C) To question the students on their knowledge about Khmer architecture
- (D) To see whether she is talking too fast for the students to write down the lecture

Passage 8   Listen to part of a discussion in an astronomy class. 🎧

Keyword ----------------------

• Dark matter
• Gravitational effect

1 What is the main purpose of the discussion?
- Ⓐ To verify the students' understanding on gravity
- Ⓑ To explain what dark matter is and how it is observed
- Ⓒ To require the students to watch *Star Wars* movie
- Ⓓ To give an assignment to the students on dark matter

2 According to the professor, which of the following is true about dark matter?
- Ⓐ It cannot be observed directly.
- Ⓑ It has inspired the *Star Wars* movie.
- Ⓒ It was discovered by mistake.
- Ⓓ It is too bright to be observed.

3 Why does the professor say this: 🎧
- Ⓐ To introduce a new concept in astronmy
- Ⓑ To show off his knowledge on a diffcult subject
- Ⓒ To clarify his previous explanation on a subject
- Ⓓ To divert the students' interest to another subject

4   According to the professor, which of the following explains gravitational lensing?

    Ⓐ The presence of matter which has gravity curves space and light.

    Ⓑ The observed faraway galaxies look fainter than they should be.

    Ⓒ More matter should be observed in the Universe as per scientists' calculations but they are left invisible.

    Ⓓ Images obtained by the distortion field are used to reconstruct the mass distribution of the deflecting intervening matter.

5   Why does the professor mention Darth Vader and Jedi knights from the movie, *Star Wars*?

    Ⓐ To explain the role of Darth Vader in *Star Wars* episodes

    Ⓑ To convince the students to believe that dark matter exists

    Ⓒ To help students understand a difficult scientific concept by making a joke

    Ⓓ To urge the students to take notes on the concept of dark matter

6   Listen again to part of the discussion. Then answer the question. Why does the student say this: 🎧

    Ⓐ To add new information the professor was not aware of

    Ⓑ To make an impression to the professor by showing off

    Ⓒ To disagree with the professor's explanation on dark matter

    Ⓓ To confirm whether he has understood the professor's explanation

Passage 9   Listen to part of a discussion in a zoology class. 🎧

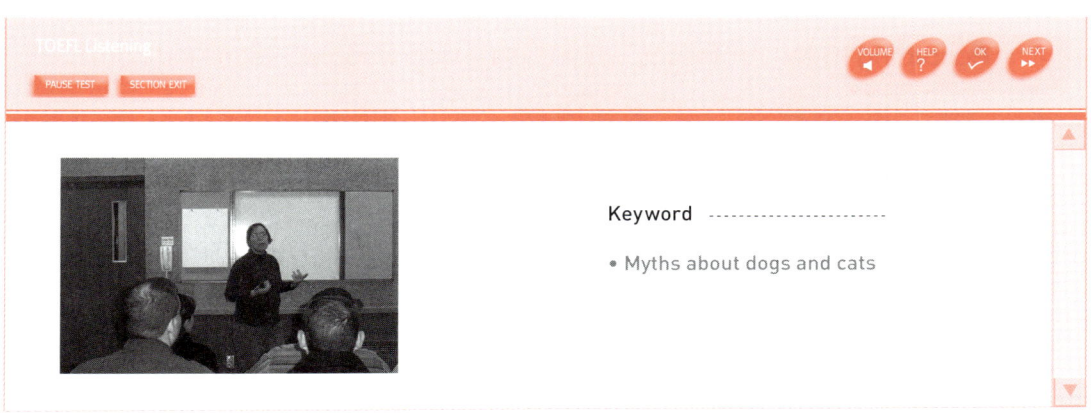

Keyword ------------------------

• Myths about dogs and cats

1 What is the main topic of the discussion?

(A) Why dogs and cats are the most popular pets

(B) Animals that are easy to keep as a pet

(C) What to be aware of in order to keep your pet healthy

(D) False beliefs on dogs and cats commonly held by people

2 Listen again to part of the discussion. Then answer the question.
Why does the professor say this: 🎧

(A) To negate what she has just said

(B) To introduce another erroneous popular information on dogs

(C) To check if the students have finished the assigned reading

(D) To explain that dogs actually cannot see any color at all

3 According to the professor, what kind of color receptors do dogs have?

Click on 2 answers.

(A) Yellow

(B) Blue

(C) Red

(D) Green

4   According to the professor, what does a dog wagging its tail indicate?
    Ⓐ That it is hungry and wants to be fed
    Ⓑ That it is bored and wants to be entertained
    Ⓒ That it is happy, angry, or agitated
    Ⓓ That it has spotted something dead on the ground

5   Why shouldn't cats be allowed to drink too much milk?
    Ⓐ Because too much milk can cause medical problems such as diarrhea
    Ⓑ Because cats can intake sufficient amount of calcium from their daily diet
    Ⓒ Because too much milk can cause cats to suffer from heart attack
    Ⓓ Because cats' cholesterol level may be drastically raised

6   What does the professor say about the source of myths about dogs and cats?
    Ⓐ She does not know where people get myths about dogs and cats from.
    Ⓑ She believes that too many pet owners are overly superstitious.
    Ⓒ She says that pet owners obtain wrongful information from the Internet.
    Ⓓ She thinks that most pet owners do not study enough about their pets.

Passage 10 Listen to part of a discussion in a psychology class.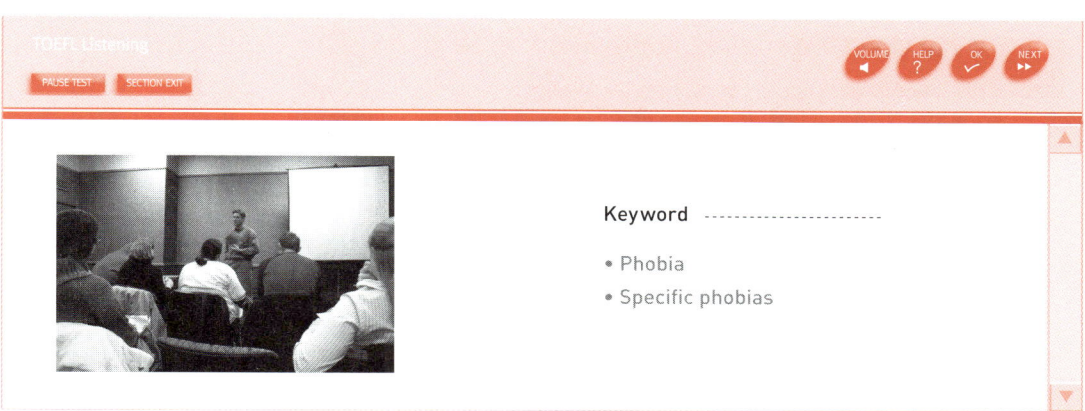

1 **What is the main topic of the discussion?**
- Ⓐ Different types of phobias
- Ⓑ Specific phobias and its possible cures
- Ⓒ Various treatments of phobias
- Ⓓ Dangers of phobia and prevention measures

2 **Listen again to part of the discussion. Then answer the question.**
Why does the student say this:
- Ⓐ She is trying to defy the professor's comment.
- Ⓑ She did not hear what the professor had just said.
- Ⓒ She is trying to show off her knowledge on phobias.
- Ⓓ She wants to make sure whether she has heard the professor's comment correctly.

3 What does the student imply when he says this: 🎧

- Ⓐ He is a flutist in the school orchestra.
- Ⓑ He did not want to join the school orchestra before he played the flute.
- Ⓒ Although he does not have fear of flutes, he fears other musical instruments.
- Ⓓ Because he has a phobia towards the flute, he does not want to play the flute anymore.

4 According to the professor, why do certain people develop specific phobias?

- Ⓐ Because they have inherited those phobias from their parents
- Ⓑ Because they might have experienced something psychologically disturbing in their childhood
- Ⓒ Because they are afraid that the public might criticize their social behavior
- Ⓓ Because they might have experienced something traumatic at an unfamiliar place

5 The professor discusses phobias and three different types of phobia. Based on the information in the discussion, indicate whether each phobia below is an example of social phobias or specific phobias.

Click in the correct box.

	Social phobia	Specific phobia
Obesophobia (fear of gaining weight)		
Arsonphobia (fear of fire)		
Homophobia (fear of blood)		
Psellismophobia (fear of stuttering)		
Muriphobia (fear of mice)		

Vocabulary

✔ 박스에 체크 표기를 하며 주요 단어를 학습하시오.

- ☐ **architecture** 건축(물, 학)
- ☐ **culminate** 최고점에 달하다, 전성의 극에 오르다
- ☐ **cult** 열광적 신흥 종교; 제식, 의식
- ☐ **representative** 대표자, 대리인
- ☐ **indurate** 단단하게 하다, 경화하다
- ☐ **foundation** 기초, 토대
- ☐ **quarry** 채석하다
- ☐ **primatologist** 영장류학자
- ☐ **ethologist** 행동학자
- ☐ **anthropologist** 인류학자
- ☐ **habitat** 서식지, 집
- ☐ **reckless** 무분별한, 무모한
- ☐ **poach** 밀렵하다
- ☐ **harvest** 수확하다, 포획하다
- ☐ **carcass** (짐승의) 시체, 사체
- ☐ **trophy** 전리품, 사냥 기념물
- ☐ **enforcement** 시행, 강제
- ☐ **pristine** 본래의, 원시의, 자연그대로의
- ☐ **preserve** 금렵지구, 보호지역
- ☐ **dire** 무시무시한, 비참한
- ☐ **misuse** 오용하다
- ☐ **blur** 흐리게 하다
- ☐ **inspire** 영감을 주다
- ☐ **surge** 급격히 오르다; 쇄도하다
- ☐ **infinite** 끝없는
- ☐ **ignorant** 무지한, 무식한
- ☐ **medieval** 중세(시대)의
- ☐ **coincide** 동시에 일어나다
- ☐ **ostensible** 표면상의, 허울만의
- ☐ **clandestine** 은밀한, 비밀의
- ☐ **prostitute** 창녀, 매춘부
- ☐ **astronomical** 천문학상의
- ☐ **fundamental** 근본적인, 주요한
- ☐ **discordance** 불일치

- ☐ **conquer** 정복하다, 이기다
- ☐ **detect** 발견하다, 탐지하다
- ☐ **emit** (빛을) 방출하다
- ☐ **infer** 추론하다, 암시하다
- ☐ **stellar** 별의, 항성의
- ☐ **galactic** 은하계의, 성운의
- ☐ **supercluster** 초은하 집단
- ☐ **velocity** 속도
- ☐ **luminous** 빛을 내는, 밝은
- ☐ **distort** 왜곡시키다
- ☐ **behaviorism** 행동주의
- ☐ **rote** 기계적 방법의
- ☐ **repetition** 반복
- ☐ **reinforce** 강화(보강, 증강)하다
- ☐ **devoid of** ~가 없는
- ☐ **apparatus** 기계, 장치
- ☐ **hoard** 저장하다, 축적하다
- ☐ **elicit** 도출하다, 이끌어내다
- ☐ **amphibian** 양서류
- ☐ **reptile** 파충류
- ☐ **specialize** 특수화(전문화)하다
- ☐ **indicate** 가리키다, 나타내다
- ☐ **agitate** 선동하다, 동요시키다
- ☐ **annoy** 화나게 하다
- ☐ **nourish** 기르다, 영양을 주다
- ☐ **qualm** 불안, 염려
- ☐ **phobia** 공포증
- ☐ **persistent** 지속적인, 버티는, 끈덕진
- ☐ **disorder** 무질서; 장애, 병
- ☐ **scrutiny** 정밀한 조사; 뚫어지게 보기; 감시
- ☐ **trigger** 계기, 자극; 방아쇠
- ☐ **traumatic** 잊을수 없을만큼 정신적 충격이 큰
- ☐ **heredity** 유전적 (형질)
- ☐ **genetics** 유전적 특징

Vocabulary Test

박스에서 올바른 단어를 골라 빈칸을 채우시오.

phobia	distort	repetition
nourish	ignorant	inspire

1. The legendary guitarist, singer, and songwriter Jimi Hendrix _____ (ed/-d) a generation of guitarists.

2. In order to _____ your soul, you should read lots of good books.

3. Many tabloids that write about unrealistic things sacrifice and _____ reality to sell news.

4. The city has confronted a disastrous flood last summer; now, the mayor has taken active measures to prevent a _____ of such unfortunate events.

annoy	trigger	repetition
ignorant	infinite	coincide

5. There is an _____ amount of questions in this world that will not be eventually all be answered — knowledge will constantly expand and so will information.

6. The gunman pulled the _____ and shot the buffalo to death.

7. The little boy who seemed _____ at first turned out to be very intelligent and knowledgeable.

8. Since our free time doesn't _____ this week, we should find another time next week.

✎ 올바른 단어를 골라 문장을 완성하시오.

9 A 10-month-old baby swallowed a small coin and was almost _____(ed/-d) — it was really close.

Ⓐ agitate Ⓑ choke Ⓒ coincide Ⓓ inspire

10 A 4-year-old child I was baby-sitting threw a major tantrum last right, crying uncontrollably for hours and hours — it was just impossible to make her hush. She made me really _____(ed/-d).

Ⓐ hoard Ⓑ infer Ⓒ inspire Ⓓ anncy

11 When people find themselves suddenly in danger, sometimes they are overcome with feelings of helplessness, horror, or fear. These events are called _____ experiences, such as being physically attacked, being involved in a serious accident or a combat, or being sexually assaulted.

Ⓐ traumatic Ⓑ ignorant Ⓒ infinite Ⓓ svelte

12 In some parts of the world, poor people illegally _____ animals in order to make more money.

Ⓐ surge Ⓑ agitate Ⓒ poach Ⓓ misuse

13 Dyslexia, a specific difficulty in learning to read, is a brain-based _____ that is likely to have a genetic component.

Ⓐ harvest Ⓑ disorder Ⓒ phobia Ⓓ architecture

14 It became highly difficult for us to find enough referees and umpires to work baseball games due to the recent _____ in the number of Little Baseball Leagues across the United States.

Ⓐ entity Ⓑ repetition Ⓒ trigger Ⓓ surge

15 Jennifer Tomlin usually takes care of construction materials while Ross Crane mainly deals with _____ and design.

Ⓐ architecture Ⓑ habitat Ⓒ splinter Ⓓ dire

Part 2

Conversation

Chapter 1

Main Idea

문제유형

- What is the (main) topic of the conversation?
- What is the conversation mainly about?
- What are the speakers mainly discussing?
- Why has the man(woman/student) come to...?
- Why does the student(professor/man/woman) want to talk with...?

Sample

Listen to part of a conversation between a student and an insurance agent. 🎧

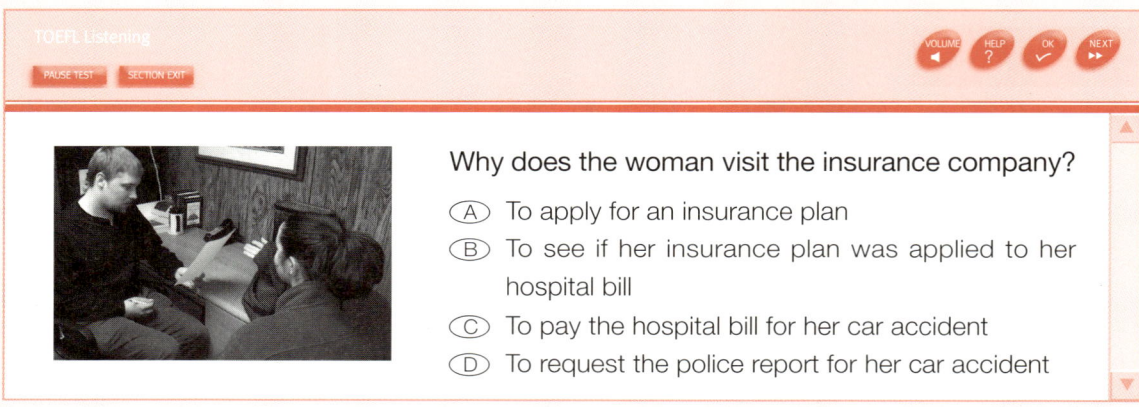

TOEFL Listening

PAUSE TEST   SECTION EXIT

VOLUME   HELP   OK   NEXT

Why does the woman visit the insurance company?

Ⓐ To apply for an insurance plan
Ⓑ To see if her insurance plan was applied to her hospital bill
Ⓒ To pay the hospital bill for her car accident
Ⓓ To request the police report for her car accident

표기된 signal phrases 및 keyword에 주목하며 대화를 다시 한번 들으시오.

W: Hi, **1** I have a question about my **student insurance**.

M: Yes, what can I do for you?

W: Um, I have student insurance with your company, and... um, I was in a car accident two months ago and I had to go to the emergency room. I told the ER that I had insurance with your company but **2** they sent me a huge bill which I don't think the insurance was applied to. So... I was wondering what was going on.

M: Oh, in that case, you have to go to the Customer Service. This is the Policy Service Department.

W: I know, I already visited them, but they sent me over to you.

M: Okay, could you give me your name and your plan number?

W: Sure, it's Sienna Miller, and my plan number is PWL2643475.

Tip 강의나 토론의 주제를 묻는 문제와 달리, 대화의 주제를 묻는 문제는 이 대화가 이루어지는 이유 등의 "목적"을 주로 묻는다.

Strategy 1 — 지문 초반에 등장하는 signal phrase에 주목하자

위의 대화 초반에서 여학생은 다음과 같이 말함으로써 방문한 목적을 제시한다.

1 I have a question about my student insurance.

이어서 학생은 차사고가 났으며 보험이 있음에도 불구하고 병원비가 많이 나왔다는 자신의 상황을 설명하고, 확인하고자 하는 사항을 다음과 같이 제시한다.

2 they sent me a huge bill which I don't think the insurance was applied to. So... I was wondering what's going on.

따라서 학생은 보험이 있음에도 비싼 병원비가 나온 이유에 대한 설명을 듣기 위해 방문했음을 알 수 있으므로, 답은 B이다.

대화의 목적이나 주제는 주로 대화의 초반에 등장하므로 대화 초반부터 주의해서 대화를 듣고, signal phrase에도 주목하도록 하자.

대화에서 등장하는 signal phrases

• I wanted to talk to you about ~	• I heard you wanted to see me ~
• I called you because ~	• Can I talk to you for a minute?
• I was wondering ~	• How's it going with ~?
• I was hoping that I could talk with you about ~	• By the way, have you heard about/did you hear that ~?

Strategy 2 — 주제와 관련되는 단어/구에 주목하여 topic을 유추하자

강의의 경우에서와 마찬가지로, 대화의 초반에서 명확하게 주제나 대화의 목적이 드러나지 않는 경우가 종종 있다. 이럴 때에는 전체적인 대화를 들으면서 가장 빈번하게 등장하는 keyword와 key phrases를 파악하고, 연관된 단어들과 함께 대화의 주제와 목적을 유추해야 한다.

위 대화에서는 student insurance라는 단어가 빈번하게 등장하는데, 이것이 바로 이 다화의 keyword이며, car accident, emergency room(ER)과 huge bill 또한 대화의 목적, 즉 보험 플랜이 있음에도 병원비가 너무 비싸게 나온 이유를 알기 위해 방문했음을 유추할 수 있는 keyword들이다.

Strategy Focus

지문 초반 및 후반의 signal phrases와 강조 및 반복되는 keyword에 유의하며 강의를 들으시오. 🎧

1

• **Focus :**

job fair

• **Keyword/Key phrase :**

job fair, resume, pre-register

Tip

대화 중간중간 주제에서 벗어난 이야기를 하지만, 대화의 주제는 October Job Fair이다.

☐ **job fair** 취업박람회
☐ **resume** 이력서
☐ **rip-off** 사기, 갈취

What are the students mainly talking about?

Ⓐ How to write a good resume

Ⓑ Why the job fair is a rip-off

Ⓒ The job fair which will be held in October

Ⓓ Professor Stevenson and the difficulty of his classes

2

• **Focus :**

• **Keyword/Key phrase :**

대화의 초반부터 남학생은 형법 수업의 어려움을 장황하게 토로하고 결국 여학생이 개인과외를 자청한다.

☐ **GPA** 성적
☐ **tutor** 개인과외하다, 개별지도하다

What is the man's problem?

Ⓐ He is struggling with the Criminal Law class.

Ⓑ He is tired of studying Criminal Law by himself.

Ⓒ He cannot understand Dr. Pico's pronunciation.

Ⓓ He received a low GPA this semester.

3

• Focus :

• Keyword/Key phrase :

Tip

여학생은 룸메이트와 문제가 있음을 이야기한다.

☐ **switch** 바꾸다
☐ **residence** 주거
☐ **irreconcilable** 화해할 수 없는
☐ **accommodate** 숙박시키다, 수용하다

Why does the student go to the residence advisor?

Ⓐ To explain why she is upset about doing the dishes

Ⓑ To explain problems with her dish washer

Ⓒ To explain why she needs to talk with a residence advisor

Ⓓ To find out if it is possible to solve the problem with her roommate

4

• Focus :

• Keyword/Key phrase :

학생의 보고서에 대해 이야기를 나눈 후, 학생을 부른 이유를 언급한다.

☐ **viewpoint** 관점
☐ **eerie** 이상한, 괴상한
☐ **insightful** 통찰력 있는
☐ **genuine** 진짜의, 진품의

Why does the professor want to see the man?

Ⓐ To discuss the use of X-rays to distinguish whether an art work is authentic or not

Ⓑ To ask the man to prepare a presentation

Ⓒ To see how the man got the weird feeling when he was looking at Millet's painting

Ⓓ To praise the man's high-quality paper

Exercise

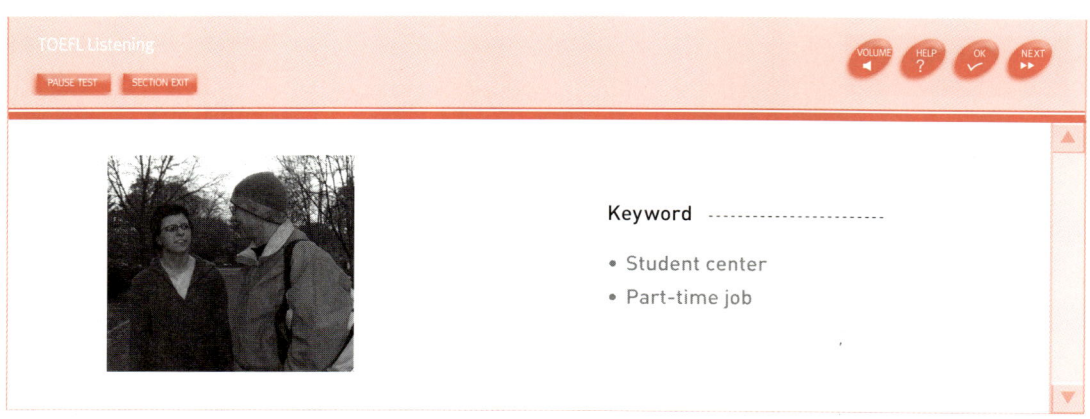

Passage 1   Listen to part of a conversation between two students. 🎧

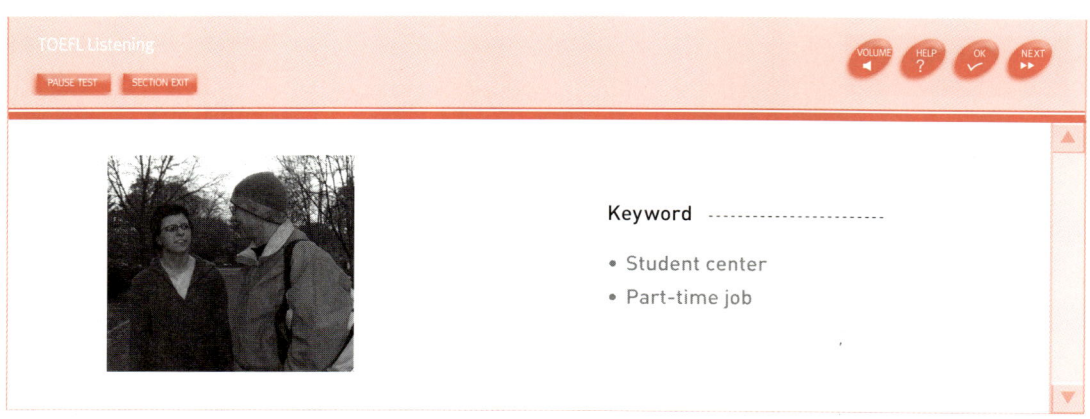

TOEFL Listening

PAUSE TEST   SECTION EXIT

VOLUME   HELP ?   OK ✓   NEXT ▶▶

Keyword -

• Student center
• Part-time job

1 What is the woman's problem?
- Ⓐ The poor grade she received on her term papers
- Ⓑ The promotion problem at her part-time job
- Ⓒ The low payment at the cafeteria as a waitress
- Ⓓ The difficulty she is having with time management

2 Why does the man talk about his ex-roommate?
- Ⓐ To chastise the woman of her idleness
- Ⓑ To introduce the woman a private tutor
- Ⓒ To recommend a way that may help the woman
- Ⓓ To recommend a popular time management method

3 What will the woman probably do next?
- Ⓐ She will buy a jar and try to fill it with rocks, pebbles, and sand.
- Ⓑ She will quit working at the cafeteria and concentrate on her studies.
- Ⓒ She will call Robert and get some help with time management from him.
- Ⓓ She will go to the Student Center and make an appointment with one of the counselors.

Passage 2　Listen to part of a conversation between a student and a student advisor.

Keyword ----------------------

• Graduate school
• Application

1 Why does the student advisor want to see the student?

Ⓐ To inquire the man's intention on applying for scholarship
Ⓑ To recommend a cheap graduate program to the man
Ⓒ To ask the man about the graduate school application status
Ⓓ To ask the how the man is preparing to finance graduate school

2 Listen again to part of the conversation. Then answer the question. What does the student advisor imply when she says this: 🎧

Ⓐ She knows nothing about graduate schools.
Ⓑ She graduated from the school the man wants to apply to.
Ⓒ She does not think that applying to graduate schools is so difficult.
Ⓓ She experienced similar difficulties when she applied to graduate school.

3 Listen again to part of the conversation. Then answer the question. Why does the student say this: 🎧

Ⓐ He is mad because the woman made fun of him.
Ⓑ He is being humble at the woman's compliments.
Ⓒ He is discouraged because of the woman's remarks.
Ⓓ He is frustrated because the woman does not understand his difficulties.

Passage 3   Listen to part of a conversation between two students. 🎧

Keyword ----------------------

• Off-campus housing
• Roommate

1 **What is the woman's problem?**

Ⓐ The problem with exterminators in her dormitory room
Ⓑ The financial problem with moving into an apartment
Ⓒ The cockroach infestation in her dormitory room
Ⓓ The trouble with finding a new roommate

2 **What can be inferred about the man's cousin?**

Ⓐ She teaches students at the business school.
Ⓑ She likes to keep her house very clean.
Ⓒ She used to live with a roommate but lives alone now.
Ⓓ Her off-campus house is right next to the woman's school building.

3 **What will the woman probably do next?**

Ⓐ Go to the Engineering Building to attend a meeting
Ⓑ Go to the school library to drop off some text books
Ⓒ Go to Rowland Hills apartment managing office to sign a contract
Ⓓ Go to the school Book Store with the man to meet the man's cousin sister

Passage 4   Listen to part of a conversation between a student and a librarian.

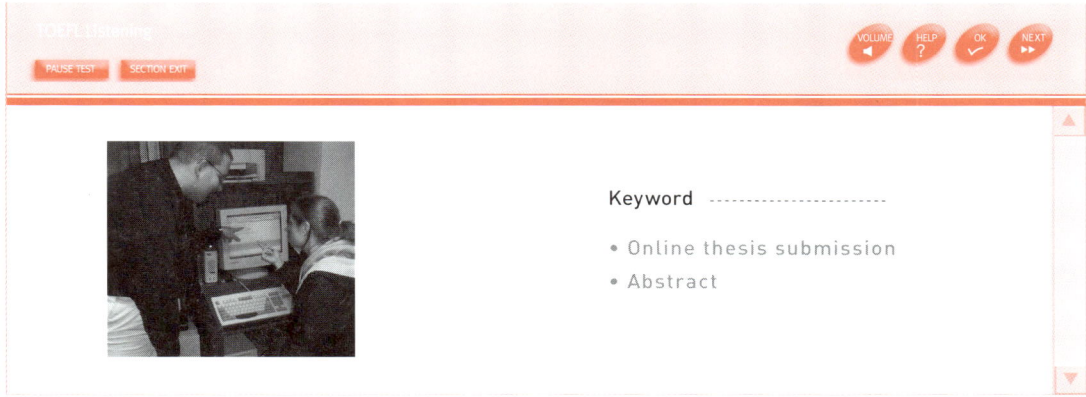

Keyword ------------------------

- Online thesis submission
- Abstract

1 Why does the woman want to talk with the man?
- Ⓐ To borrow a file compressor from the library
- Ⓑ To get a signature from the library for her thesis
- Ⓒ To inquire about uploading thesis file on the online library
- Ⓓ To ask him to upload her thesis file on the online library

2 The librarian explains how to upload the thesis file on the online library. Based on the information in the conversation, indicate whether the following statements are information about uploading the thesis file on the online library.

Click in the correct box.

Statement	Yes	No
Upload the thesis abstract.		
Register at the library information desk.		
Type in thesis title and student information and upload file.		
Log in and click online thesis submission button.		
Print out confirmation form, then click submission complete button.		

Passage 5

Listen to part of a conversation between a student and a professor. 🎧

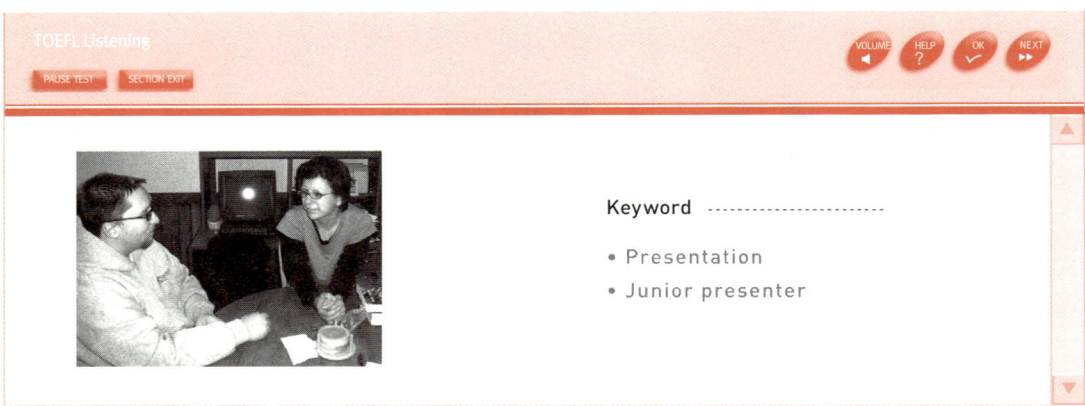

Keyword ---------------------

• Presentation
• Junior presenter

1 Why does the professor want to talk to the student?

Ⓐ To request him to help her research on Actualism

Ⓑ To recommend him to the dean for a school scholarship

Ⓒ To inform him of a recent decision on the Geology Conference

Ⓓ To commend the student's presentation on Actualism at Irvine Hall

2 Listen again to part of the conversation. Then answer the question.
What does the professor mean when she says this: 🎧

Ⓐ The presentation the student made at Irvine Hall cost him a lot of money.

Ⓑ The student made many mistakes while making the presentation at Irvine Hall.

Ⓒ The student got a better opportunity because of the presentation he made at Irvine Hall.

Ⓓ The student will be eligible to receive a scholarship because of the presentation at Irvine Hall.

3 What can be inferred about the student?

Ⓐ He usually takes much time in writing an article.

Ⓑ He feels nervous about making a presentation at Prague.

Ⓒ He has confidence in himself of the presentation at Prague.

Ⓓ He has expected the professor to recommend him as a junior presenter.

4   According to the professor, what will junior presenters do in order to prepare for the conference?

    Ⓐ Plan and manage the order of the presenters
    Ⓑ Write an article and prepare for a presentation
    Ⓒ Assist main presenters to search information
    Ⓓ Create abstract and graphs for main presenters

5   **What will the student most probably do during the summer vacation?**

    Ⓐ Go back home and get a part-time job as a tutor
    Ⓑ Visit Prague and gather information on Actualism
    Ⓒ Gather reference and start writing a draft of his article
    Ⓓ Participate in geology conferences to acquire experience

Vocabulary

✓ 박스에 체크 표기를 하며 주요 단어를 학습하시오.

- ☐ **hectic** 몹시 바쁜
- ☐ **cafeteria** 구내 식당
- ☐ **promotion** 진급
- ☐ **barely** 간신히, 겨우, 가까스로
- ☐ **manage** 간신히 ~하다
- ☐ **management** 관리
- ☐ **workload** 작업량
- ☐ **give a hand** 도와주다
- ☐ **regarding** ~에 관해서
- ☐ **RA (Research Assistant)** 연구 보조원
- ☐ **organization** 기구, 기관
- ☐ **counselor** 상담원
- ☐ **pebble** 조약돌
- ☐ **general** 전반적인
- ☐ **detail** 세부 사항
- ☐ **apply** ~에 지원하다
- ☐ **make up one's mind** 결정하다
- ☐ **graduate school** 대학원
- ☐ **desperate** 절박한, 필사적인
- ☐ **ranking** 순위
- ☐ **faculty** 교수진
- ☐ **extracurricular** 정규 과목 이외의
- ☐ **acceptance** 입학허가
- ☐ **dormitory** 기숙사
- ☐ **insane** 제정신이 아닌
- ☐ **studio** 원룸 아파트
- ☐ **roach (= cockroach)** 바퀴벌레
- ☐ **complain** 불평하다

- ☐ **doctoral** 박사 과정의
- ☐ **candidate** 후보자, 지원자
- ☐ **freak out** 흥분하다, 놀라다
- ☐ **infest** 만연하다, 창궐하다
- ☐ **exterminator** 해충 구제업자
- ☐ **fumigate** 소독하다
- ☐ **upload** 전송하다, 업로드하다
- ☐ **thesis** 논문(주로 대학원 논문. 박사 논문은 dissertation)
- ☐ **register** 등록하다
- ☐ **submission** 제출, 제시
- ☐ **compress** (파일을) 압축하다
- ☐ **abstract** 개요, 발췌, 강령
- ☐ **confirmation** 확인
- ☐ **presentation** 발표
- ☐ **Actualism** 현실설
- ☐ **stammer** 말을 더듬다
- ☐ **conference** 회의, 협의
- ☐ **nervous** 긴장한, 불안한, 겁내는
- ☐ **pay off** ~이 성과를 얻다
- ☐ **dean** 학장
- ☐ **junior** 손아래의, 후배의, 하위의, 하급의
- ☐ **senior** 손위의, 선배의, 선임의, 고참의, 상위의
- ☐ **recommend** 추천하다
- ☐ **reference** 참고 서적
- ☐ **advantageous** 유리한, 이로운
- ☐ **draft** 초고, 초안

Vocabulary Test

✏️ 올바른 단어를 골라 문장을 완성하시오.

1 When I graduate from college, I'd like to work for a law firm as a paralegal or any type of assistant, and after I build up my career for a couple years, I will _____ to law school.

    Ⓐ infest   Ⓑ register   Ⓒ upload   Ⓓ apply

2 My sister is one of the MBA _____(s) who graduate next year.

    Ⓐ candidate   Ⓑ presentation   Ⓒ senior   Ⓓ faculty

3 Mike feels very _____ about the result of last week's exam because he only studied an hour for it.

    Ⓐ insane   Ⓑ hectic   Ⓒ nervous   Ⓓ advantageous

4 Are you planning to go to _____ after you finish college?

    Ⓐ conference   Ⓑ studio   Ⓒ promotion   Ⓓ graduate school

5 I'm having rodent _____ problems in my room; I'd better call the exterminator first thing in the morning.

    Ⓐ infestation   Ⓑ sudmission   Ⓒ conference   Ⓓ presentation

6 Tim wants to go to this university — it's in-state so the tuition is cheap, its campus is beautiful, and it's located near his parents' house so it will be very _____ for him to commute.

    Ⓐ abstract   Ⓑ hectic   Ⓒ convenient   Ⓓ insane

7 There will be a _____ meeting at 5 pm tomorrow; all the professors in the School of Medicine are advised to attend the meeting.

    Ⓐ compress   Ⓑ feculty   Ⓒ pay off   Ⓓ counselor

8 Jessica had to write a 5-page-book report until Monday, but she caught a bad flu on Saturday. She _____ managed to finish the book report, thanks to the help of her best friend.

    Ⓐ desperately   Ⓑ insanely   Ⓒ nervously   Ⓓ barely

Chapter 2

Supporting Detail

문제유형

- Why is(does/has) the man(woman/professor/student)...?
- What does the man(woman) say about...?
- What problem does(did) the man(woman) have?
- What does(did) the man(woman/professor) want the woman(man/student) to do?
- As described by the man(woman/professor), what is...?

Sample   Listen to part of a conversation between two students.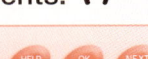

TOEFL Listening

PAUSE TEST   SECTION EXIT

VOLUME ◀   HELP ?   OK ✓   NEXT ▶▶

What does the man say about Dr. Hansen's criticism?

- Ⓐ It is encouraging.
- Ⓑ It will eventually be helpful.
- Ⓒ It is actually unnecessary.
- Ⓓ It is not helpful at all.

표기된 signal phrases 및 keyword에 주목하며 대화를 다시 한번 들으시오.

W: Oh, I'm so nervous about my **presentation** today.

M: That's right, you told me you're supposed to give an oral presentation today at Dr. Hansen's class, right? What's the matter, aren't you ready yet?

W: I am ready, but… you know, **1** Dr. Hansen is known for **criticism** and harsh remarks. I think she's gonna give me a hard time today.

M: Well, she is notorious for her criticism. But as long as you don't freak out and stutter, and have full knowledge on your presentation topic, I'm sure she's gonna give you a good score. Also, if you think about it later, **2** all the harsh feedbacks that she gives you are gonna help you improve your understanding on the topic.

W: Yeah, I guess you're right. But I can't stop being nervous, you know.

Tip 대화 파트에서도 강의 파트와 마찬가지로 지문에서의 중요한 내용이나 특징 등에 대한 질문에 2개나 3개의 답을 고르는 문제가 출제될 수 있다.

여학생은 발표에 대해 긴장하고 있는 이유로 다음과 같이 말한다.

1 Dr. Hansen is known for criticism and harsh remarks.

이에 대해 남학생은 교수의 지적이 다음과 같은 긍정적인 역할을 한다고 말한다.

2 all the harsh feedbacks that she gives you are gonna help you improve your understanding on the topic.

따라서 정답은 B이다.

Keyword와 key phrase를 바탕으로 대화의 주제를 파악했다면, 이와 관련하여 어떠한 세부사항이 언급되는지 주목해야 한다. 대화의 주제에 따라 사용되는 표현들과 signal phrase를 파악하자.

대화의 주제	사용되는 표현과 signal phrases
• 문제가 있을 때	- I'm having a problem/hard time with ~, I don't know how/what ~, ~ is too difficult for me ~, ~ is not going very well ~, There's something wrong with ~
• 수업 과제	- assignment, assigned reading
• 시험 문제	- test, pop quiz, oral exam
• 주거 문제	- apartment, studio, housing manager, move in/out, rent
• 친구(룸메이트) 문제	- I can't stand my roommate anymore because ~, We don't get along ~
• 자동차 관련 문제	- gas tap, brakes, steering wheel, engine oil, leak, body shop
• 프레젠테이션 문제	- presentation in front of the class, questions, feedback
• 아르바이트 문제	- part-time job, too much work
• 기타 비용 문제	- financial problems, student loan, bank, savings account
• 과외(동아리) 활동	- student organization, chairman, volunteer
• 면담/상담할 때	- I have an appointment with ~, I heard that you wanted to see me ~, Could you help me with ~?, I need information on ~, I want to know ~, How ~?
• 교수와의 면담 • 향후 진로 상담	- Research Assistant(RA), Teaching Assistant(TA), dissertation topic, project - graduate from college, graduate school, law school, medical school, dental school, work at a firm, resume, job fair, interview
• 의료기관과의 상담	- appointment, insurance card, fill out forms, prescription
• 도서관에서 책 빌리기	- library, check out/drop off/turn in books, borrow, school ID

대화에서는 주제를 뒷받침하기 위해 다양한 세부 사항들이 등장할 수 있으며, 강의와는 달리 이를 위해 사용되는 signal phrases가 정해져 있지는 않다. 따라서 대화에서 자주 출제되는 주제를 미리 파악해두고 그와 관련된 다양한 표현들과 어휘를 익혀두고, TV나 라디오 등을 통해 일상생활의 대화를 자주 듣는 연습을 하는 것이 효과적이다.

Strategy Focus

주제를 뒷받침하는 세부사항들에 유의하며 강의를 들으시오. 🎧

1

• Focus :

  borrow books

• Keyword/Key phrase :

  library; turn in these books; borrow some

  other books

Tip

남학생의 일을 보는 김에 여학생의 부탁을 들어주게 된다.

☐ turn in 반납하다
☐ check out 대출하다

Why is the man going to the library?

Ⓐ To attend a class at the Beckman Hall
Ⓑ To check out some books for his classes
Ⓒ To return the books that he already finished reading
Ⓓ To see if they have multiple copies of the books that he needs

2

• Focus :

• Keyword/Key phrase :

교수는 이 잡지에 여성과 남성의 성역할에 대한 시각이 잘 나타나 있지 않다는 학생의 의견에 반대한다.

☐ gender 성
☐ subscribe 정기구독하다
☐ dichotomize 이분화하다
☐ buff 강건한, 튼튼한
☐ abs 복부; 복근

What does the professor say about the *Men's Health* magazine?

Ⓐ It argues that men should always drink beer.
Ⓑ It clearly depicts men's and women's gender role.
Ⓒ It insinuates that men should always have well-structured body.
Ⓓ It usually talks about what men should do in order to gain women's interest.

3

• Focus :

• Keyword/Key phrase :

Tip

여자는 교수가 페이퍼의 형식에 매우 엄격하다고 말한다

☐ midterm 중간고사
☐ conference 회의
☐ TA 조교(= teaching assistant)
☐ format 형식

What does the woman say about the midterm paper format?

Ⓐ The format is introduced in the topic list.
Ⓑ The paper should contain 24 lines in one page.
Ⓒ It should be less than ten pages with 12-point word font.
Ⓓ The paper may be graded poorly if it is not written according to the format.

4

• Focus :

• Keyword/Key phrase :

여학생은 도서관에서 학생증과 면허증이 든 지갑을 잃어버렸다.

☐ student ID 학생증
☐ identification 신분증
☐ renewal 갱신

What does the woman say about her driver's license?

Ⓐ She does not have a driver's license.
Ⓑ She lost the license when she lost her student ID.
Ⓒ She accidentally left it at the library bathroom.
Ⓓ She brought the license along with her today.

Exercise

Passage 1 Listen to part of a conversation between a student and a student advisor. 🎧

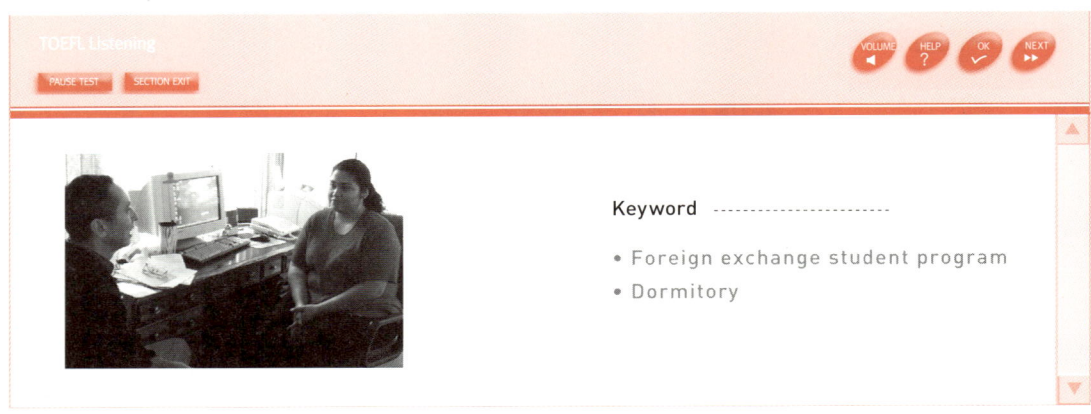

Keyword ----------------------

- Foreign exchange student program
- Dormitory

1 Listen again to part of the conversation. Then answer the question. Why does the man say this: 🎧

(A) He is confused about whether the advisor is joking or not.

(B) He is surprised at the information the advisor just gave.

(C) He is irritated at the advisor's indecisive behavior.

(D) He is frustrated because the advisor is too inconsiderate.

2 Why is the man upset with the foreign exchange student program?

(A) Because the exchange program is too expensive

(B) Because he has to take a year off from his school

(C) Because he cannot go to the school he wanted to attend

(D) Because he cannot go to France because of his bad grades

3 What can be inferred about the man?

(A) He does not want to live anywhere but in an apartment.

(B) He is extremely stingy with tuitions and housing fees.

(C) He has not thought about other exchange programs.

(D) He will probably go to the school next year as an exchange student.

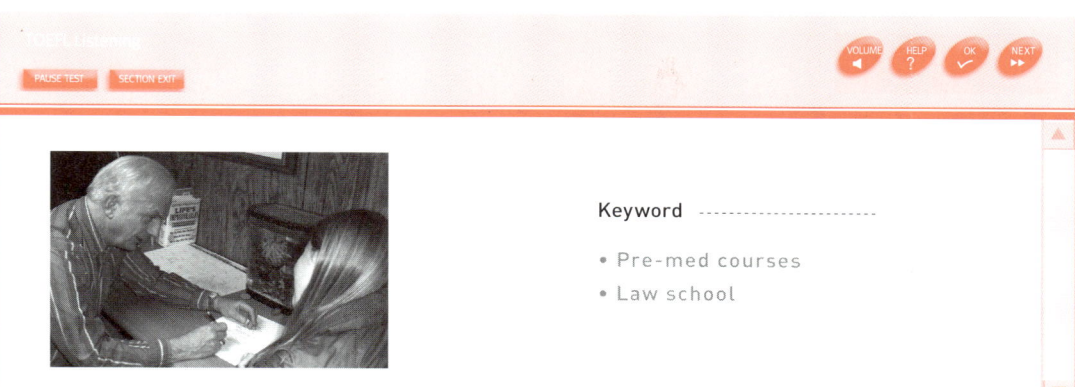

Passage 2   Listen to part of a conversation between a student and a professor.

Keyword -

• Pre-med courses
• Law school

1 Why does the professor want to talk to the woman?
- (A) He wants to encourage the woman by giving proper advice.
- (B) He wants to check if the woman is on track with her academic schedule.
- (C) He wants to persuade the woman to go to law school rather than medical school.
- (D) He wants to know why the woman does not wish to take pre-med courses anymore.

2 What does the student say about becoming a doctor?
- (A) She is not very passionate in becoming a doctor.
- (B) She thinks that doctors do not make enough money.
- (C) She thinks that becoming a doctor is too difficult.
- (D) She says that becoming a doctor will take too much time.

3 According to the professor, what can be said about law schools?
- (A) Law schools usually accept students from abroad.
- (B) Law schools always accept students who studied history.
- (C) Law schools prefer students who studied particular subjects.
- (D) Law schools only accept pre-med courses as prerequisite.

Passage 3   Listen to part of a conversation between a student and a professor. 🎧

TOEFL Listening

PAUSE TEST   SECTION EXIT

VOLUME ◀   HELP ?   OK ✓   NEXT ▶▶

Keyword ------------------------

• APA format
• Plagiarism

1   Why does the professor give a poor grade on the student's paper?
- (A) Because the student cheated on his paper
- (B) Because the student's handwriting is illegible
- (C) Because the student did not conduct a thorough research
- (D) Because the student did not use the standard citation format

2   Listen again to part of the conversation. Then answer the question.
How does the student feel when he says this: 🎧
- (A) He is sorry that he did not know the APA format earlier.
- (B) He feels discouraged because of the professor's criticism on his ignorance.
- (C) He is curious about what the professor might think if he used proper APA format.
- (D) He is worried about getting in trouble for copying other peoples' articles.

3   What kind of penalty does the professor say some students received when they committed plagiarism?
- (A) They had to write more papers.
- (B) They were expelled from the school.
- (C) They were suspended from the school for a year.
- (D) They had to help doctoral students with their dissertations.

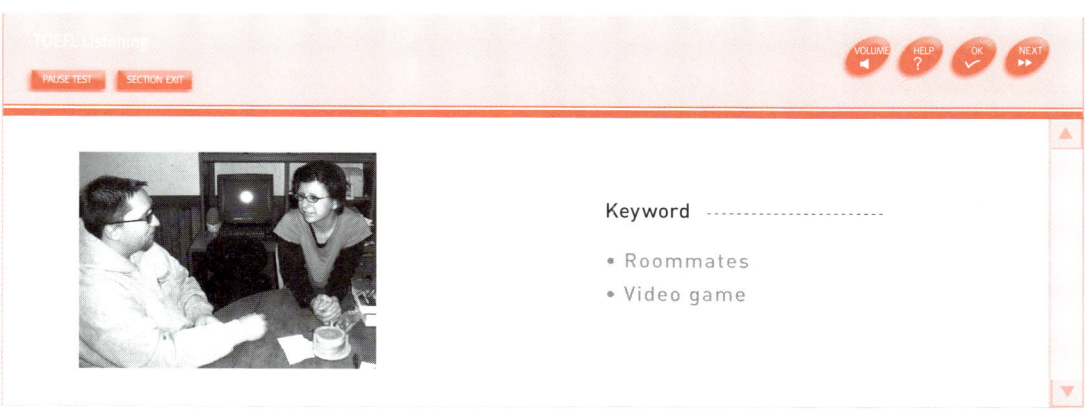

Listen to part of a conversation between a student and a housing manager. 🎧

1 According to the conversation, what is the man's problem?
- Ⓐ Having unclean and lazy roommates
- Ⓑ Having a hard time finding a Calculus tutor
- Ⓒ Having roommates who are addicted to video games
- Ⓓ Having roommates who distract him by playing video games

2 What does the woman say about the man's problem?
- Ⓐ The man should talk to a higher authority.
- Ⓑ She cannot help him because it is not her duty.
- Ⓒ She cannot help him because the man's problem is personal.
- Ⓓ She will try to find a solution when the person in charge returns.

3 Why does the woman mention the Bronz Library?
- Ⓐ To recommend a place where the man can study at night
- Ⓑ To introduce a library that was enlarged to place more books
- Ⓒ To recommend a place where the man can find study partners
- Ⓓ To introduce a place where the man's roommates can play video games

Passage 5

Listen to part of a conversation between a student and a computer assistant. 🎧

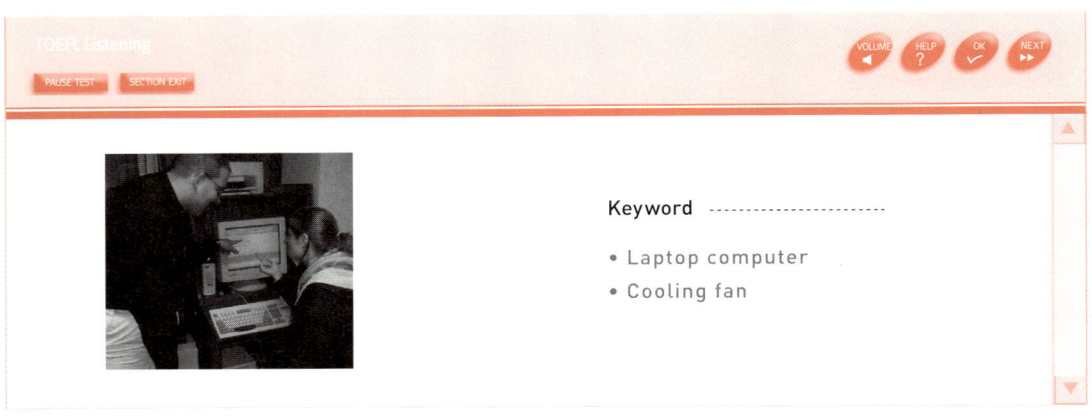

Keyword ----------------------

• Laptop computer
• Cooling fan

1 What is the purpose of the conversation?

Ⓐ The woman is looking for assistance in fixing her laptop computer.

Ⓑ The man is encouraging the woman to learn more about computers.

Ⓒ The man is convincing the woman to send her laptop computer to the manufacturing company.

Ⓓ The woman seeks the man's advice for cooling down the computer's inner temperature.

2 Which of the following were mentioned as alternative recommendations for the woman to use the laptop? Click on 2 answers.

Ⓐ Supply cool air to the hot components directly.

Ⓑ Use a cooling pad while using the laptop.

Ⓒ Use the laptop without the battery.

Ⓓ Put an ice bag on the laptop while using.

3 How does the woman feel about the current situation with her computer?

    Ⓐ She is angry because she does not have enough money to fix it.

    Ⓑ She is annoyed because her computer turns off frequently.

    Ⓒ She is glad because she does not have to write her term paper anymore.

    Ⓓ She thinks that it will be better to get a new computer.

4 According to the conversation, why does it take a long time to fix a laptop computer?

    Ⓐ Because manufacturers do not have enough service centers

    Ⓑ Because it takes more than two weeks to deliver the product

    Ⓒ Because it takes some time for manufacturing companies to fix it

    Ⓓ Because manufacturing companies cannot detect problems in time

5 Listen again to part of the conversation. Then answer the question. Why does the man say this: 🎧

    Ⓐ To advise the woman to always use a cooling pad

    Ⓑ To suggest an alternative method the woman may take

    Ⓒ To rebuke the woman of her ignorance on her computer

    Ⓓ To remind the woman of a means she should have taken

Vocabulary

✔ 박스에 체크 표기를 하며 주요 단어를 학습하시오.

☐ **exchange student** 교환학생
☐ **dormitory** 기숙사
☐ **housing** 주거, 숙소
☐ **tuition** 등록금
☐ **contact** 연락하다
☐ **refund** 환불
☐ **institution** 기관
☐ **linguistics** 언어학
☐ **reconsider** 재고하다, 다시 생각하다
☐ **ridiculous** 터무니 없는
☐ **pre-med** 의학부 예과의
☐ **calling** 천직, 직업; 소명
☐ **constitutional** 헌법의
☐ **accept** 받아들이다
☐ **standard** 기준
☐ **format** 형식
☐ **cite** 인용하다
☐ **source** 출처, 근거
☐ **mention** 언급하다
☐ **plagiarize** 표절하다, 도용하다
☐ **reference** 참조; 참고 문헌

☐ **expel** 추방시키다, 퇴학시키다
☐ **dissertation** (박사) 논문
☐ **article** 기사, 논설; 학술지에 게재된 짧은 논문
☐ **complaint** 불평, 불만
☐ **in charge** 담당하는
☐ **on leave** 휴가 중인
☐ **tutor** 개인 지도하다
☐ **Calculus** 미적분학
☐ **lure** 유혹하다, 꾀어들이다
☐ **freak** 열광자
☐ **distracting** 방해하는, 거슬리는
☐ **personal** 개인적인
☐ **be in one's shoes** ~의 입장에 있다
☐ **activate** 활동화시키다, 작동시키다
☐ **retrieve** 되찾다, 회수하다
☐ **frustrate** 짜증나게 하다
☐ **severely** 극심하게, 심각하게
☐ **overheat** 과열시키다
☐ **detect** 발견하다, 감지하다
☐ **manufacturing** 제조의
☐ **doubt** 미심쩍게 생각하다, 의심하다.

Vocabulary Test

✏️ 올바른 단어를 골라 문장을 완성하시오.

1 Karen used to live in the undergraduate _____ but she moved out to an off-campus apartment.

Ⓐ reference   Ⓑ tuition   Ⓒ dormitory   Ⓓ component

2 Let me _____ what deGaulle had said: A true leader always keeps an element of surprise up his sleeve, which others cannot grasp but which keeps his public excited and breathless.

Ⓐ cite   Ⓑ detect   Ⓒ refuse   Ⓓ expel

3 Talking on the phone while driving seriously _____(-s/es) your attention from the road.

Ⓐ lure   Ⓑ distract   Ⓒ retrieve   Ⓓ activate

4 If you compare this part of the article with Matt's paper, you can clearly see the similarity — he used the same wording from the article. I believe that Matt _____(-d/ed) in his paper.

Ⓐ plagiarize   Ⓑ complaint   Ⓒ distract   Ⓓ require

5 I was extremely _____(-d/ed) by Bobby's behavior at the mall today — he was crying, screaming, lying on the floor and kicking. It was so difficult to calm him down and it was so humiliating.

Ⓐ lure   Ⓑ overheat   Ⓒ ridiculous   Ⓓ frustrate

6 Some of the _____(-s/es) in order to become a cheerleader are: You must be at least 5 feet and 4 inches tall, you should be athletic, and you should expect to spare at least two or three hours a day for practicing.

Ⓐ complaint   Ⓑ requirement   Ⓒ dissertation   Ⓓ reference

7 If we don't behave, we'll be _____(-d/ed) from school.

Ⓐ expel   Ⓑ detect   Ⓒ cite   Ⓓ detour

8 Melissa asked me if I could take her to the school dance next week. I was actually going to ask Stacey, but I couldn't _____ her, so I said yes.

Ⓐ expel   Ⓑ frustrate   Ⓒ source   Ⓓ refuse

Chapter 3

Content

3 Content 대화의 정보를 연결하여 추론하고 결과 예측하기

문제유형

- What will the ... probably be about?
- What will the man(woman/student) probably do next?
- What will the man(woman/student) likely to do next?
- What is the possible reason for...?
- What can be inferred(said) about the man(woman/student/professor)?

Sample

Listen to part of a conversation between a student and a gym personnel. 🎧

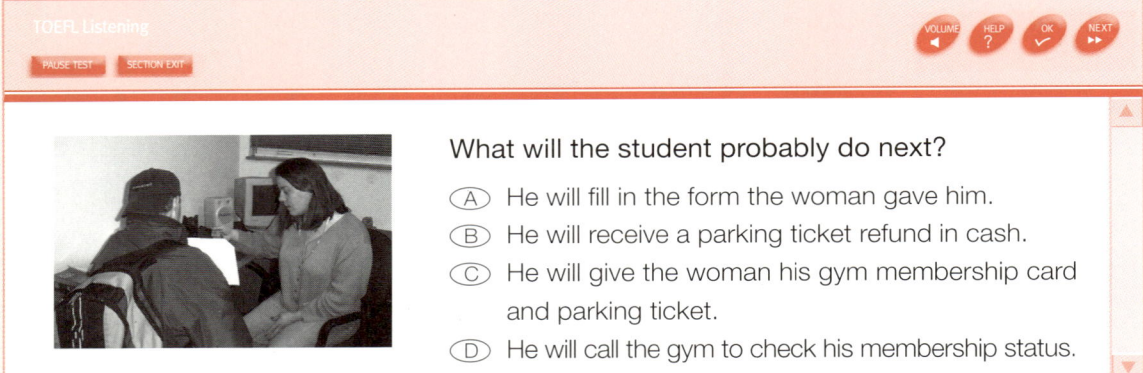

What will the student probably do next?

- Ⓐ He will fill in the form the woman gave him.
- Ⓑ He will receive a parking ticket refund in cash.
- Ⓒ He will give the woman his gym membership card and parking ticket.
- Ⓓ He will call the gym to check his membership status.

전체적인 흐름에 주목하며 대화를 다시 한번 들으시오. 🎧

W: Hello, how can I help you?

M: Hi, um… I used to be a member of this gym, but **my membership's expired**, so I'd like a **refund for my parking ticket**.

W: All right. Do you have your old membership card and your parking ticket?

M: Sure, here you go.

W: Okay. 1 Could you fill out this form for me?

M: Sure, but what is it?

W: It's basically your current home address and your daytime phone number so that we can send your refund in personal check. You can receive it by mail in two or three weeks.

M: Oh, I see. But, uh, I thought I could get the refund by cash right away.

W: Well, the policy changed two months ago. Now, any refund will be done this way.

대화에서 제시되는 정보들의 관계는 강의의 정보간의 관계과 크게 다를 것이 없지만, 이보다 더 간단하다. 대화 중간중간에 제시되는 정보들을 잘 기억하고 그 관계를 유추해야 한다. 유추의 근거는 언제나 지문 내에 명확하게 제공된다는 것을 기억하자.

다음 정보의 관계에 따른 다양한 예시를 살펴보자.

정보의 관계	제시되는 문제 및 표현
• Cause and Effect	- 지문에서 제시된 문제의 원인과 결과 이해하고 예측하기 　Why does the man/woman ~? 　What is the reason for the man's/woman's problem? - 등장하는 표현 　because of ~, due to ~, A is the reason of B
• Problem and Solution	- 제시된 문제와 그 해결책 이해하고 예측하기 　What will the man/woman do to solve the problem? 　What does the man/woman suggest the woman/man do ~? - 등장하는 표현 　I don't know what to do, I have a problem with ~, I'm having problem with ~, A is driving me insane/crazy, What about ~?, Why don't you ~?, How about ~?
• Inference	- 제시된 정보로 원인/세부사항 등을 유추하기 　What can be inferred about the man/woman? 　What does the man/woman think about ~? 　What is true about the man/woman?
• Generalization	- 제시된 정보로 일반화하기 　According to the conversation, which of the following is true?
• Prediction	- 제시된 정보를 통해 다음 행동 예측하기 　What will the man/woman probably do next? 　Where will the man/woman probably go next? *cf)* 유추와 일반화, 예측 문제는 대화의 내용을 연결시켜 접근해야 하므로 따로 사용되는 표현이 없다.

여자가 **1** **Could you fill out this form for me?**라고 요청한 것을 통해 앞으로 이어질 행동은 서류를 작성하는 것임을 알 수 있다. 따라서 정답은 A이다.

Strategy Focus

전체적인 흐름에 유의하며 대화를 들으시오. 🎧

1

- **Focus :**
  assignment

- **Keyword/Key phrase :**
  analyze the style of a house

Tip

대화에서 등장한 building과 style 등의 단어들을 통해 남자와 여자가 수강하는 과목이 무엇인지를 유추할 수 있다.

☐ **observe** 관찰하다
☐ **old-fashioned** 구식의
☐ **represent** 대표하다, 대변하다

What can be inferred about the man?

(A) He will probably team up with the woman.

(B) He has to go on another basketball tour soon.

(C) He does not think he can finish the project until the due date.

(D) He will contact the professor to inquire about finding a team mate.

2

- **Focus :**

- **Keyword/Key phrase :**

여권이 배달되기 전까지의 며칠 동안은 교수의 서명이 들어간 확인서를 가지고 다녀야 한다.

☐ **confirm** 확인하다
☐ **debit card** 데빗 카드(현금 카드)
☐ **photo I.D** 사진이 있는 증명서
☐ **issue** 발급하다

What will the woman probably do in order to attend her classes for the next couple of days?

(A) She will make a photo I.D. from somewhere else.

(B) She will call her parents to send her passport through mail.

(C) She will ask her professors to come to the entrance of the building and prove that she is in their classes.

(D) She will meet her professors and receive notes stating that she is a legitimate student in their classes.

3

• Focus :

_____

• Keyword/Key phrase :

_____

_____

What can be said about the man?

Ⓐ He does not know what Interlibrary Loan is.

Ⓑ He usually does not participate at the class discussion.

Ⓒ He does not actually have an appointment with the professor.

Ⓓ He does not like reading other peoples' books because he likes to read clean books.

4

• Focus :

_____

• Keyword/Key phrase :

_____

_____

What can be inferred about the woman?

Ⓐ She is very forgetful and usually does not remember appointments she made with other friends.

Ⓑ She is a jazz singer and is working on her resume in order to work as a jazz musician.

Ⓒ She has been working on her resume for the last week in order to apply to a job.

Ⓓ She did not go to the student lounge today because she had to buy lunch for another friend.

Tip

대화의 초반에서 남자의 "Is this a bad time?"이라는 말에서 힌트를 얻을 수 있다.

☐ participate 참여하다
☐ copy 사본; 부, 권
☐ photocopy 복사(하다)

그동안 직장을 구하기 위해 이력서를 쓰면서 스트레스를 받았다는 여학생의 말에서 힌트를 얻을 수 있다.

☐ concentrate 집중하다
☐ deprivation 박탈
☐ function 기능하다

Exercise

Listen to part of a conversation between a student and a university housing manager. 🎧

VOLUME ◄ HELP ? OK ✓ NEXT ►►

PAUSE TEST   SECTION EXIT

Keyword --------------------------

• Studio
• Contract

1 The student and the university housing manager discuss signing the contract for an on-campus housing. Indicate whether each phrase below is a step in the process.

Click in the correct box.

	Yes	No
Take a tour around the studios		
Meet the residents		
Meet the housing manager		
Sign the contract		
Pay three months' rent in advance		

2 What will the woman probably do next?

Ⓐ Have a meeting with the housing manager to sign the contract

Ⓑ Leave the manager's office and return later this afternoon to take a tour of the studio rooms

Ⓒ Decide the exact moving in date and inform the housing manager

Ⓓ Read the leasing contract before signing the contract

3   Why does the woman go to see the university housing manager?

    Ⓐ   To arrange a meeting to sign the leasing contract

    Ⓑ   To seek help in searching for an on-campus studio

    Ⓒ   To complain about the high rent of her apartment

    Ⓓ   To seek consultation on applying for a student loan

4   Listen again to part of the conversation. Then answer the question. Why does the woman say this: 🎧

    Ⓐ   To signal that she wants a cheaper on-campus studio

    Ⓑ   To challenge the housing manager of his incompetence

    Ⓒ   To see if there are more studios available in other locations

    Ⓓ   To ask if the housing manager can arrange a larger studio

Passage 2   Listen to part of a conversation between a student and a gym employee. 🎧

Keyword -

• The Spring Marathon
• Gym member

1 Why does the woman want to talk with the man?

(A) To activate her gym membership and issue a membership card
(B) To register for the marathon event at the Stanton River
(C) To ask him about a movie poster she saw on the second floor
(D) To ask him about some more information on the marathon event

2 Why does the woman mention her friend?

(A) To refute what the gym personnel has just said
(B) To inform the gym personnel of her friend's whereabouts
(C) To check the possibility of her friend's participation in the event
(D) To brag about her friend who has won in the last marathon event

3 What can be inferred about the courses at the Spring Marathon?

(A) Everybody has to run 10 miles in order to win the event.
(B) People can run any course according to their running abilities.
(C) Bottled water is only available to the 10-mile-course runners.
(D) The 5-mile-course will be more difficult because the course is steep.

Listen to part of a conversation between a student and a librarian. 🎧

Keyword ----------------------

• Flavell and Miller

1 What does the woman say about the book, *Cognitive Development*?

Ⓐ All seven copies of the book are currently unavailable.

Ⓑ The library does not hold the book but other libraries might have them.

Ⓒ The library used to have the copies, but disposed of them long time ago.

Ⓓ Four copies of the book are available on the fourth floor.

2 According to the woman, which books are currently available at the library?

Click on 2 answers.

Ⓐ *Developmental Psychology*

Ⓑ *Human Development*

Ⓒ *Handbook of Child Psychology*

Ⓓ *Infant Behavior and Development*

3 What will the man probably do next?

Ⓐ He will start working on his book report right away.

Ⓑ He will check the availability of some books on the computer.

Ⓒ He will go to the fourth floor of the library to find some books.

Ⓓ He will send e-mails to those who have checked out the books.

Passage 4

Listen to part of a conversation between a student and a travel agent. 🎧

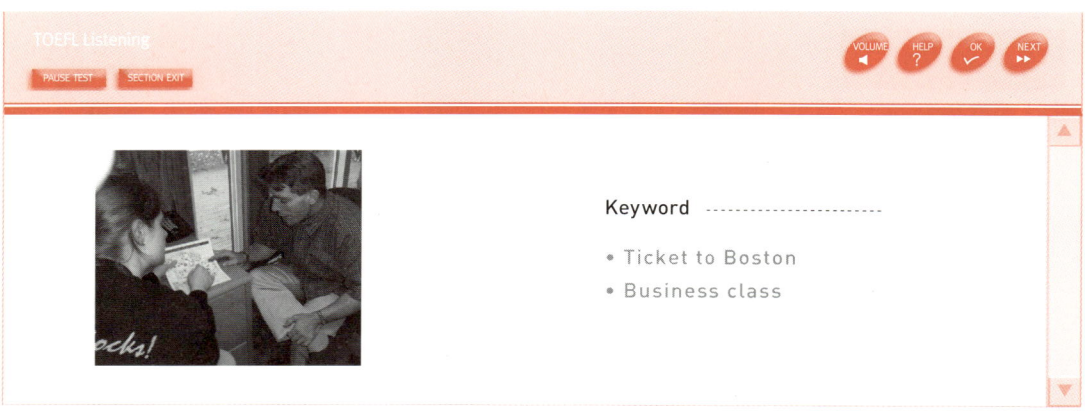

Keyword -

• Ticket to Boston
• Business class

1 According to the conversation, why was the woman late in purchasing her plane ticket?

Ⓐ She already got a plane ticket but had to cancel it.
Ⓑ She did not know her Spring Break schedule.
Ⓒ She has been putting off purchasing a ticket.
Ⓓ She did not know how to book a plane ticket until now.

2 What does the woman say about taking the train to Boston?

Ⓐ It will take too much time to go to Boston.
Ⓑ It is cheap, but the seats are too uncomfortable.
Ⓒ It is more expensive than taking the business class.
Ⓓ It is difficult because she has to transfer multiple times.

3 What will the woman probably do next in order to get to Boston?

Ⓐ She will call a rent-a-car agency to get a car and drive to Boston.
Ⓑ She will call her father to discuss purchasing the business class ticket.
Ⓒ She will change her travel dates in order to take the coach seat.
Ⓓ She will purchase a cheap one way plane ticket to Boston and take the train back.

Passage 5   Listen to part of a conversation between a student and an academic advisor. 🎧

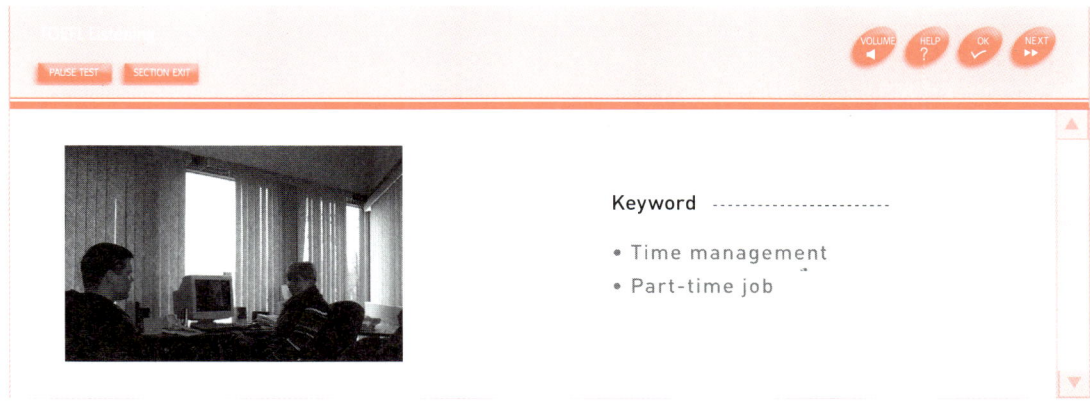

PAUSE TEST   SECTION EXIT

VOLUME   HELP   OK   NEXT

Keyword ------------------------

• Time management
• Part-time job

1   Listen again to part of the conversation. Then answer the question. How does the man feel when he says this: 🎧

Ⓐ He has no idea what the woman is talking about.

Ⓑ He feels frustrated towards the woman's indifference.

Ⓒ He feels lost and discouraged because of his poor time management.

Ⓓ He feels buoyant because the woman is encouraging his endeavors.

2   What can be inferred about the man's current part-time job?

Ⓐ His working hours are pretty flexible.

Ⓑ The pay is higher enough to support his living.

Ⓒ It does not significantly hurt the man's study time.

Ⓓ He receives much tip working as a waiter.

3   Why does the woman mention talking to the dean?

Ⓐ To find a way to support the man's finances

Ⓑ To recommend the man's essay as an award candidate

Ⓒ To punish the man's idleness by sending him to the dean's office

Ⓓ To recommend the man to the dean to work as an assistant

Vocabulary

✔ 박스에 체크 표기를 하며 주요 단어를 학습하시오.

- ☐ **move out** 이사 나가다
- ☐ **on-campus** 캠퍼스 내의(학교에서 운영하는)
- ☐ **studio** 부엌과 침실이 붙어 있는 원룸
- ☐ **available** 이용할 수 있는
- ☐ **prefer** 선호하다
- ☐ **steep** 비싼; 가파른
- ☐ **relatively** 상대적으로
- ☐ **recommend** 추천하다
- ☐ **maintenance** 보수 관리, 정비; 생활비
- ☐ **arrange** 준비하다, 예정을 세우다
- ☐ **leasing** 임대
- ☐ **specific** 상세한, 정확한
- ☐ **inform** 알려주다
- ☐ **in advance** 미리
- ☐ **security money** 보증금
- ☐ **resident** 거주자
- ☐ **check** 수표
- ☐ **work out** 운동하다
- ☐ **gym (= gymnasium)** 체육관, 헬스장
- ☐ **drop by** 들르다
- ☐ **curious** 관심 있는, 호기심 있는
- ☐ **participate** 참가하다, 참여하다
- ☐ **register** 등록하다

- ☐ **beforehand** 먼저, 이전에
- ☐ **relief** 안도, 위안
- ☐ **be aware of** ~을 알다, 유념하다
- ☐ **chilly** (날씨가) 쌀쌀한
- ☐ **alongside** ~을 따라서
- ☐ **on the spot** 현장의, 즉석의
- ☐ **be checked out** 대여중인
- ☐ **company** 동행(자)
- ☐ **round trip** 왕복
- ☐ **book** 예약하다
- ☐ **procrastinate** 늑장부리다, (자꾸) 미루다
- ☐ **coach seat** 일반석
- ☐ **distract** (주의를) 흐트러뜨리다
- ☐ **management** 관리
- ☐ **news stand** 신문 가판대
- ☐ **pay raise** 급여 인상
- ☐ **regret** 후회하다
- ☐ **depend** ~에 의존하다
- ☐ **premise** 전제
- ☐ **devoted** 헌신적인
- ☐ **financial** 재정의
- ☐ **status** 상태
- ☐ **scholarship** 장학금

Vocabulary Test

올바른 단어를 골라 문장을 완성하시오.

1   When I receive my weekly payment, do I get to receive it in cash or by personal
    _____?

    Ⓐ book   Ⓑ scholarship   Ⓒ premise   Ⓓ check

2   My paper is due tomorrow morning at 10 o'clock, but I haven't even started
    writing yet. I know I should have started writing two weeks ago, but I kept
    putting it off... I will never _____ again.

    Ⓐ depend   Ⓑ inform   Ⓒ procrastinate Ⓓ check

3   Melanie was accepted by the graduate school she wanted to go to, but refused
    to go because of financial situations. She _____(s) not going there
    now and wants to get another chance.

    Ⓐ regret   Ⓑ depend   Ⓒ devote   Ⓓ inform

4   I overslept last night, so I missed my flight. When's the next _____
    flight to Washington D.C.?

    Ⓐ arrange   Ⓑ beforehand   Ⓒ available   Ⓓ roundtrip

5   I went to the library yesterday, but two girls who were sitting right across me
    wouldn't stop chatting all day. It was extremely _____(ing).

    Ⓐ distract   Ⓑ inform   Ⓒ lease   Ⓓ participate

6   A: How are you going to pay the tuition next semester?
    B: My parents told me that they'll pay my loan until I graduate.
    A: Man, don't you think you _____ on your parents too much?

    Ⓐ arrange   Ⓑ regret   Ⓒ book   Ⓓ depend

7   I am in charge of _____(ing) meetings in my office.

    Ⓐ submit   Ⓑ arrange   Ⓒ procrastinate Ⓓ distract

8   A: I went to San Francisco last summer and I had a hard time walking around
       on the street because of the hills.
    B: Yeah, the hills of San Francisco are pretty _____.

    Ⓐ chilly   Ⓑ steep   Ⓒ available   Ⓓ devoted

Chapter 4

Stance

4 Stance 화자의 감정 상태 이해하기

문제유형

- How does(did) the man(woman/professor/student) feel when he(she) says this: 🎧
- What does the man(woman/professor/student) think about...?
- How does the man(woman/professor/student) feel about...?
- What is the man's(woman's/professor's/student's) attitude towards...?
- What is the man's(woman's/professor's/student's) opinion of...?

Sample

Listen to part of a conversation between a student and an academic advisor. 🎧

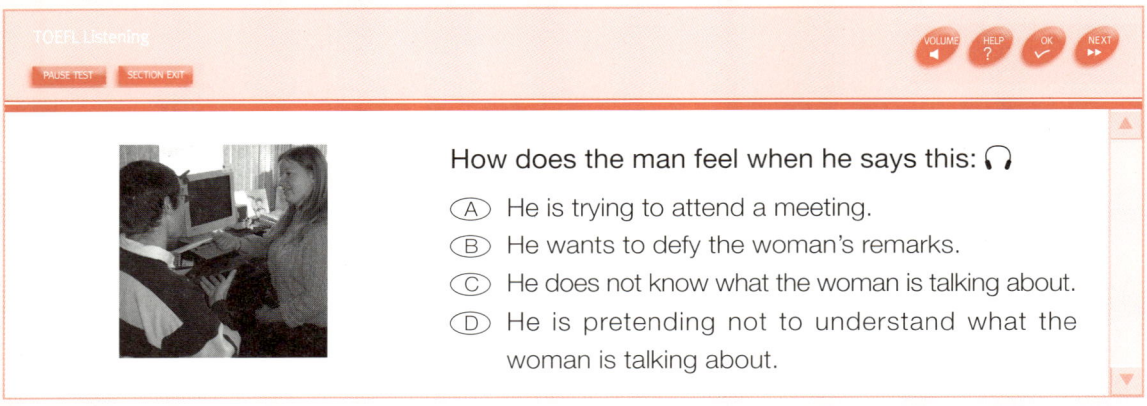

How does the man feel when he says this: 🎧

- Ⓐ He is trying to attend a meeting.
- Ⓑ He wants to defy the woman's remarks.
- Ⓒ He does not know what the woman is talking about.
- Ⓓ He is pretending not to understand what the woman is talking about.

억양과 뉘앙스 및 지문내 힌트에 주목하며 대화를 다시 한번 들으시오. 🎧

W: Jim, how come I didn't see you at the meeting today?

M: Um… I don't understand, Dr. Russell. **1** What… what meeting?

W: Did you forget the **IHT meeting**?

M: The IHT meeting?

W: Jimmy, remember the International House Tutors' meeting? You were supposed to talk about how your class is going on, remember?

M: Oh, gee… Oh, dear, what got into me? I can't believe this!

W: Now you remember? I was worried because you didn't show up.

M: Yeah… oh, I am so sorry, Dr. Russell. This always happens to me when I don't write down my schedule. **2** I'm so forgetful!

> **Tip** 강의에서와 마찬가지로 대화에서 역시 억양과 뉘앙스에 유의해야 한다. 화자의 억양과 뉘앙스 및 화자가 사용하는 단어의 성질에서도 태도나 감정 상태를 추론할 수 있다.

화자의 억양과 뉘앙스에 주목하자

대화 지문에서는 단어의 성질보다는 화자의 억양과 뉘앙스를 통해 화자의 태도와 감정이 더 잘 표출된다. 아래에서 다양한 감정 상태에 따라 사용될 수 있는 표현들을 살펴보자.

상황	사용되는 표현과 예
• 놀라움	- 끝의 톤이 올라가며 반문, 재확신의 표현 사용; 부정의 표현 사용 What?, Are you serious?, No way!, You're kidding me!, No kidding!, You're joking!
• 불확실	- 머뭇거리거나 더듬기 Well, I think, uh… um…, I'm not really sure ~, I guess/think ~
• 재확인	- 잘 듣지 못한 경우 직접 질문하거나 상대방이 했던 얘기를 끝의 톤을 높여 반복함 What did you say?, What's that?, Pardon?, Excuse me?, I'm sorry?, He did what?, Did you say ~?
• 반대	- 강한 부정의 표현을 사용함 I don't think you should ~, I think you shouldn't ~, I don't think so, I can't agree with that
• 동의	- 맞장구의 표현을 사용함 Yeah, I can't agree with you more, I'm with you, You have my support on that ~, I think you're right ~, That is so true
• 부인	- 부인의 표현이나 잘 모르겠다는 표현을 사용함 No, ~ is not ~, I don't know what you're talking about

뉘앙스를 뒷받침하는 지문 내 hint에 주목하자

대화 지문에서는 화자의 억양과 뉘앙스에 주목해야 한다.

지도교수가 미팅에 대해 언급하자 학생은 다음과 같은 반응을 보인다.

1 What… what meeting?

2 I'm so forgetful!

학생은 당황하며 처음에는 전혀 미팅에 대해 기억하지 못하다가, 뒤늦게 깜빡했음을 끼닫고 스스로를 탓한다. 따라서 참석해야 할 미팅을 깜빡하여 불참했음을 알 수 있으므로 정답은 C가 된다. 이처럼 대화 내에서 제공되는 화자의 감정 상태에 대한 근거에 주목해야 한다.

Strategy Focus

화자의 억양과 뉘앙스 및 지문내 힌트에 유의하며 대화를 들으시오. 🎧

1

• **Focus :**

medical school, prerequisite, chemistry, GPA over 3.8

• **Keyword/Key phrase :**

Ugh, still a freshman though!

Listen again to part of the conversation. Then answer the question.
How does the student feel when she says this: 🎧

- Ⓐ Worried because she does not like chemistry
- Ⓑ Perplexed about the professor's advice
- Ⓒ Overwhelmed at the new information
- Ⓓ Angry because the professor does not know her GPA

Tip

학생이 몰랐던 사실을 교수가 가르쳐주고 있다.

☐ medical school 의학대학원
☐ prerequisite 필수(과목)
☐ idle away 게으름을 피우다

2

• **Focus :**

• **Keyword/Key phrase :**

What is the woman's attitude towards the student tutor system?

- Ⓐ She thinks it might help the man's study.
- Ⓑ She thinks it is too expensive for students.
- Ⓒ She thinks it should be taught by professors.
- Ⓓ She thinks graduate students teach better than professors.

여학생은 Student Academic Center의 개인교사 시스템을 활용하라고 조언한다.

☐ biochemistry 생화학
☐ biology 생물학
☐ neurophysiology 신경생리학
☐ tutor 개인교사

3

• Focus :

....

• Keyword/Key phrase :

....

....

Tip

주차관리인은 10가에 있는 길거리 주차장을 추천하지만, 학생은 주민들만을 위한 곳이라며 거절한다.

☐ expire (기한이) 만료되다
☐ residence 주거, 주택
☐ tow 견인하다, 끌다

How does the woman feel about the residence area street parking?

Ⓐ She thinks the 10th street parking area is too dangerous.

Ⓑ She believes the area is unavailable for non-residents.

Ⓒ She thinks it is extremely difficult to find a parking space.

Ⓓ She fears her car might be damaged if she parks there.

4

• Focus :

....

• Keyword/Key phrase :

....

....

학생은 매일 공부하는 건물의 난방이 앞으로 일찍 끊기게 된 것에 대해 불평한다.

☐ proposal 계획(서)
☐ vandalism 기물 파괴 행위

Listen again to part of the conversation. Then answer the question.

How does the man feel when he says this: 🎧

Ⓐ He wants to exaggerate how much he studies.

Ⓑ He feels discouraged with the current weather.

Ⓒ He is discontented with the school's decision.

Ⓓ He is thankful for the woman's advice.

Exercise

Listen to part of a conversation between a student and a car lease agent. 🎧

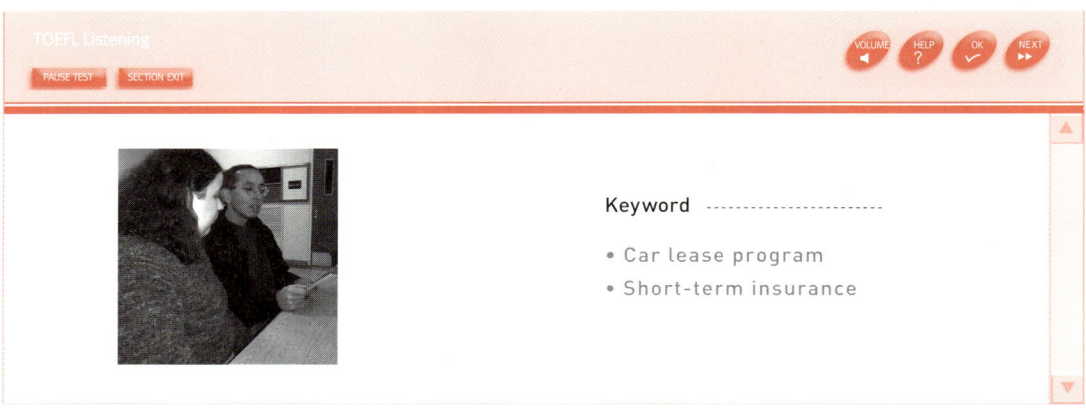

1 Listen again to part of the conversation. Then answer the question. Why does the woman say this: 🎧

Ⓐ To ask the man to repeat what he had just said

Ⓑ To express her frustration towards the man

Ⓒ To confirm her understanding of the man's remark

Ⓓ To ask the man to recommend a suitable program

2 What can be said about the woman?

Ⓐ She is currently working as a student teacher.

Ⓑ She likes to travel on weekends and holidays.

Ⓒ It takes her 30 minutes to go to school if she drives.

Ⓓ She does not have much knowledge about the car leasing program.

3 How does the woman feel about the short-term insurance?

Ⓐ She thinks it is too expensive for her to pay every month.

Ⓑ She thinks it is unfair to be on insurance mandatorily.

Ⓒ She thinks it is unnecessary because she already has an insurance.

Ⓓ She thinks only long-term car leasers should be on insurance.

Passage 2

Listen to part of a conversation between a student and a Student Employment Center employee. 🎧

Keyword ----------------------

- Part-time job
- Housing manager

1 How does the man feel about the job opening at Burger Place?

- Ⓐ He thinks that the wage is not as high as he originally thought.
- Ⓑ He thinks that working as a cashier is too degrading for him.
- Ⓒ He thinks that the working time does not fit his schedule.
- Ⓓ He thinks that he is too inexperienced to get the job.

2 Listen again to part of the conversation. Then answer the question. How does the man feel when he says this: 🎧

- Ⓐ He does not like the job because the pay is too small.
- Ⓑ He is excited to work as a housing manager.
- Ⓒ He feels that he has always been fastidious about his job.
- Ⓓ He is not pleased with the working time but has no other choice.

3 What kind of part-time job will the man probably get?

- Ⓐ A coffee brewer at Coffee House in Levine Hall
- Ⓑ A cashier at Burger Place outside the campus
- Ⓒ A housing manager at the college dormitory
- Ⓓ A construction worker at a campus building

Passage 3   Listen to part of a conversation between a student and a professor. 🎧

TOEFL Listening

PAUSE TEST   SECTION EXIT

VOLUME   HELP   OK   NEXT

Keyword -----------------------

• Thesis proposal
• Financial support

1 What is the purpose of the conversation?

Ⓐ The professor wants to inform the student of the dean's research support.

Ⓑ The student wants to discuss her research subject with the professor.

Ⓒ The professor wants to introduce a research topic to the student.

Ⓓ The student wants the professor to recommend her research to the dean.

2 Listen again to part of the conversation. Then answer the question. Why does the woman say this: 🎧

Ⓐ She is denying what the professor had just said.

Ⓑ She is amazed at what the professor had just told her.

Ⓒ She is asking the professor to repeat what he had just said.

Ⓓ She is trying to conceal the mistakes she made in her proposal.

3 Listen again to part of the conversation. Then answer the question. How does the woman feel when she says this: 🎧

Ⓐ Aggravated at the professor's deceiving manners

Ⓑ Indifferent at the professor's praise for her works

Ⓒ Confused at the professor's previous statement

Ⓓ Frustrated at the professor's unfair treatment

Passage 4   Listen to part of a conversation between a student and a librarian.

Keyword ---------------------

• Return books
• Late fee

1   **Why does the man want to talk with the woman?**

Ⓐ To check the status of the books he needs to borrow

Ⓑ To request a list of books he needs to refer to for his thesis

Ⓒ To get information about the professor at the School of Design

Ⓓ To confirm the content of the e-mail he received from the library

2   **Why does the man need to return the books earlier than the original due date?**

Ⓐ The man did not fill out the proper check-out form.

Ⓑ The books were due three months ago and are late.

Ⓒ A professor needs to refer to the books for his research.

Ⓓ The library wants to replace the books because they are too old.

3   **Listen again to part of the conversation. Then answer the question. How does the man feel when he says this:** 🎧

Ⓐ He feels reluctant towards the woman's suggestion.

Ⓑ He is excited about the fact that he can make a photocopy.

Ⓒ He feels disturbed at the woman's absurd proposal.

Ⓓ He is exhilarated because he got to keep the book.

Passage 5

Listen to part of a conversation between a student and a professor.

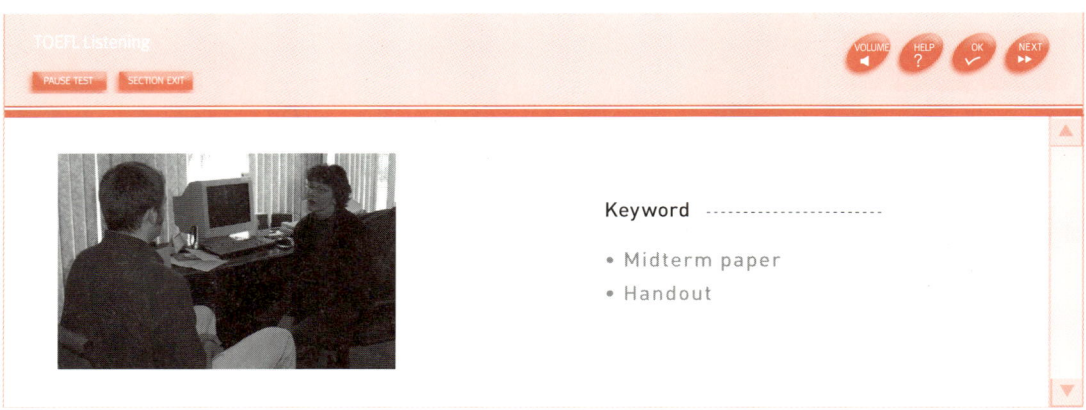

Keyword

• Midterm paper
• Handout

1 Why does the student go to see his professor?

  (A) He was called in to discuss his midterm paper.

  (B) He wanted to ask her about the guidelines for the midterm paper.

  (C) He wanted her to go through his midterm paper before he handed it in.

  (D) He thought he wrongfully received a bad grade for his midterm paper.

2 Listen again to part of the conversation. Then answer the question. How does the student feel when he says this:

  (A) He is angry because the professor is chastising him.

  (B) He feels that the professor is treating him wrongfully for no reason.

  (C) He feels confused because he thought he wrote the paper according to the guideline.

  (D) He does not think that his midterm paper is incomplete.

3 According to the conversation, why did the student miss receiving the model review handout?

    Ⓐ He was absent from the class because he was sick.

    Ⓑ The TA forgot to pass out the model review in class.

    Ⓒ The TA did not give him the model review on purpose.

    Ⓓ He had to miss the class because he worked as an intern at the hospital.

4 According to the professor, why is the student's paper incomplete?

    Ⓐ It is less than three pages long.

    Ⓑ It is not on English teaching methods.

    Ⓒ It does not meet the writing guideline.

    Ⓓ It is not written according to the APA format.

5 Listen again to part of the conversation. Then answer the question. What does the professor mean when she says this: ∩

    Ⓐ Marianne was out of her mind that day.

    Ⓑ Marianne is usually forgetful and clumsy.

    Ⓒ Marianne was acting strangely that day.

    Ⓓ Marianne is good at taking care of handouts.

Vocabulary

✓ 박스에 체크 표기를 하며 주요 단어를 학습하시오.

☐ **lease** 임대하다, 빌리다
☐ **multiple** 복수의, 여러 개의
☐ **short-term** 단기의
☐ **long-term** 장기의
☐ **respectively** 각각, 각자
☐ **commute** 통근하다, 통학하다
☐ **student teacher** 교생, 교육 실습생
☐ **narrow down** (선택의 폭이) 좁혀지다
☐ **compact car** 소형차
☐ **mileage** 주행 거리, 총 마일 수
☐ **contract** 계약서
☐ **desperate** 다급한, 필사적인
☐ **budget** 예산
☐ **cashier** 금전 출납원, 계산원
☐ **brew** (차나 커피를) 끓이다; (맥주를) 양조하다
☐ **shift** 교대 시간
☐ **spare** 예비의, 여분의
☐ **shift** 교대
☐ **tempting** 구미가 당기는, 유혹하는
☐ **picky** 까다로운
☐ **exceptional** 뛰어난, 훌륭한
☐ **dropout** 중퇴자, 탈락자

☐ **analyze** 분석하다
☐ **prevention** 예방, 방지
☐ **district** 지구, 지역, 구역
☐ **apply for** 신청하다
☐ **transcribe** (글씨로) 받아적다, 필기하다, (연설 등을) 문자화하다
☐ **voice-record** 음성 녹음하다
☐ **expense** 비용
☐ **recognize** 인정하다, 알아보다
☐ **calculate** 계산하다
☐ **submit** 제출하다
☐ **urgently** 급히
☐ **refer to~** ~를 참조하다
☐ **unfair** 불공평한
☐ **guideline** 지침, 정책
☐ **incomplete** 불완전한
☐ **review** 평론, 비평, 논평
☐ **handout** 핸드아웃, 수업에서 나눠주는 프린트물
☐ **permission** 허락
☐ **go through~** ~를 살펴보다
☐ **format** 형식
☐ **citation** 인용

Vocabulary Test

올바른 단어를 골라 문장을 완성하시오.

1   In order to be hired as a manager here, _____ skills in sales management and a results-oriented attitude are required.

(A) picky   (B) exceptional   (C) unfair   (D) spare

2   A: There's a mysterious speck on my coffee mug.
    B: It's probably nothing. You're too _____ about everything.

(A) exceptional   (B) incomplete   (C) respective   (D) picky

3   Your research paper is based on _____ information — I advise you to go out there and do some more research.

(A) multiple   (B) unfair   (C) incomplete   (D) compact

4   I share a two-bedroom apartment with my roommate; however, I got the small bedroom while he got the larger one. I think this is _____.

(A) unfair   (B) recognize   (C) shift   (D) picky

5   I'm glad that I finally got a new car. It will drastically cut down my _____ down to about 30 minutes.

(A) shift   (B) lease   (C) commute   (D) prevent

6   At first, he was nothing but a junior high _____ who had no job and lived on the streets. But he decided to go back to school and went to a job training school — now, he works as a medical technician at a local hospital.

(A) arrange   (B) format   (C) cashier   (D) dropout

7   The _____ that Professor Sloan passed out in class yesterday was very helpful for me to understand the difficult economic concepts.

(A) handout   (B) voice-record   (C) format   (D) shift

8   I got a flat tire from traveling to Las Vegas last weekend. I didn't have a _____ tire with me so I had a very hard time coming back home.

(A) exceptional   (B) budget   (C) spare   (D) lease

Chapter 5

Function

문제유형

- Why does(did) the man(woman/professor/student) say this: 🎧
- What does(did) the man(woman/professor/student) mean when he(she) says this: 🎧
- What does(did) the man(woman) want to know when he(she) says(said) this: 🎧

Sample

Listen to part of a conversation between two students. 🎧

TOEFL Listening

VOLUME ◀   HELP ?   OK ✓   NEXT ▶▶

PAUSE TEST   SECTION EXIT

Why does the woman say this: 🎧

- Ⓐ She is trying to encourage the man to do his assignment.
- Ⓑ She wants to correct the man's mistake in the last week's class.
- Ⓑ She is expressing surprise at the man's ignorance.
- Ⓓ She is chastising the man so that he would not leave class early from now on.

강의의 전체적인 흐름에 주목하며 대화를 다시 한번 들으시오. 🎧

W: How's it going with your report for next class?

M: What are you talking about?

W: You know, we're supposed to **submit a 5-page report** on several of the famous sculptures we learned last week, remember?

M: Are you sure? How come I didn't know about this?

W: Didn't you come to class last week?

M: Yeah, I was there, but the professor didn't mention anything about the report when I was there.

W: Well, she told us right before the class ended. I wonder how you missed that if you were in the class that morning.

M: Good gosh. I was late for my part-time job so I had to sneak out five minutes before the class ended. I knew I should've stayed longer!

W: 1 Well, at least you know it now. 2 You still have three days left before turning in the paper.

Tip 대화 지문에서는 여러 상황에 대해 문제가 출제될 수 있으므로 앞뒤 상황과 화자의 뉘앙스 등을 종합적으로 살펴야 한다.

Strategy 1 　화자가 말을 하는 구체적인 의도를 이해하자

대화에서 화자가 하는 말의 의도를 밝힐 때에는 먼저 화자가 사용하는 표현과 앞뒤 상황 등을 이해해야 한다. 다음은 문제에 자주 출제되는 화자의 의도와 그에 대한 예시이다.

의도	예
● 확인하기	- Are you sure that ~?, Is it true that ~?, I heard that ~, So you mean that ~, right?, Am I right?
● 강조하기	- I am absolutely/pretty sure ~, ~ is extremely/never/always ~
● 놀라움 표시	- What?, Say what?, Are you kidding?, Oh, gosh!, I can't believe this!, I can't believe that I ~!, Geez!
● 부탁하기	- Can I ask you a little favor ~?, Could you ~?, May I ~?, I was wondering if I/you could ~,
● 화자의 말을 못 들었을 때	- What's that?, Can you speak a little bit louder/slower please?, I'm sorry?, Excuse me?, Pardon me?, I'm sorry, but, what did you just say?, I didn't hear that

Strategy 2 　표면적 의미를 넘어 화자의 뉘앙스를 이해하자

앞의 대화에서 남학생이 다음 수업에 레포트를 내야 한다는 사실을 뒤늦게 깨닫자 여학생은 **1 Well, at least you know it now**라고 하는데, 이제라도 알았으니 다행이며 걱정하지 말라는 뜻을 담고 있다. 이는 여학생의 다음 대사 **2 You still have three days left before turning in the paper**에서 확인된다. 따라서 정답은 A가 된다.

같은 단어라도 상황에 따라 뉘앙스가 달라진다. 이러한 표현들을 다음의 표에서 살펴보자.

단어 및 표현	뉘앙스 및 예
● Teach a lesson	(1) "손을 봐주다"라는 뜻으로 사용할 때 I'll **teach him a lesson**. (내가 그 사람 손 좀 봐줄게.) (2) "정신을 차리게 하다"라는 뜻으로 사용할 때 That'll **teach him a lesson**. (이제 정신 좀 차리겠지.)
● Attitude	(1) "성격적인 문제"라는 뜻으로 사용할 때 She has an **attitude** problem. (그녀는 성격에 문제가 있어.) (2) "태도"라는 뜻으로 사용할 때 You should have a positive **attitude**. (긍정적인 태도를 가져라.)
● Scene	(1) "소란을 피운다"라는 뜻으로 사용할 때 Stop making a **scene** in public. (사람들 앞에서 추태 부리지 마.) (2) "장면"이라는 뜻으로 사용할 때 This **scene** is my favorite in this movie. (난 이 영화에서 이 장면이 제일 좋아.)
● Guts	(1) "용기"라는 뜻으로 사용할 때 He has no **guts**. (그는 용기가 없어.) (2) "예감"이라는 뜻으로 사용할 때 I have a **gut** feeling that I'll fail the test. (시험에 낙방할 것 같은 예감이 들어.)

Strategy Focus

화자의 의도와 뉘앙스에 유의하며 대화를 들으시오. 🎧

1

• Focus :

Quadrangle Square, moving-in date

• Keyword/Key phrase :

Tip

"Only two days are allowed to move in?"이라는 여학생의 말에서 힌트를 찾을 수 있다.

☐ confusion 혼동
☐ disorder 혼잡
☐ permission 허락

Why does the woman say this: 🎧

Ⓐ Because she is angry at the man's wrong information
Ⓑ Because she is discouraged from missing the orientation
Ⓒ Because she is astonished at the short moving-in days
Ⓓ Because she is frustrated by the man's rude behavior

2

• Focus :

• Keyword/Key phrase :

다음에 이어지는 남자의 말에서 힌트를 얻을 수 있다.

☐ reservation 예약
☐ match 게임. 경기
☐ short notice 급한. 당장에

What does the woman mean when she says this: 🎧

Ⓐ She is trying to gain attention from the man.
Ⓑ She wants the man to confirm her suggestion.
Ⓒ She is trying to confirm the man's hearing ability.
Ⓓ She wants to know whether she is making sense or not.

3

• Focus :

....

• Keyword/Key phrase :

....

....

Tip

"Much controversy"라는 교수의 말에서 힌트를 찾을 수 있다.

☐ in advance 미리, 사전에
☐ move out 이사를 가다

Why does the man say this: 🎧

Ⓐ To convince the woman to take care of his keys for him

Ⓑ To get information on what he should do with his keys

Ⓒ To exchange old keys with new keys for a new room

Ⓓ To deposit his keys in order to borrow a cart

4

• Focus :

....

• Keyword/Key phrase :

....

....

"Follow"는 "따라가다"라는 뜻 외에 "이해하다"라는 뜻을 갖는다.

☐ application 지원
☐ tricky 까다로운, 미묘한
☐ recommendation letter 추천서

Listen again to part of the conversation. Then answer the question.

Why does the woman say this: 🎧

Ⓐ She is trying to change the topic to her internship.

Ⓑ She wants to blame the man for her current situation.

Ⓒ She wants to tell the man to talk more slowly.

Ⓓ She wants the man to elaborate on what he had just said.

Exercise

Listen to part of a conversation between a student and a professor. 🎧

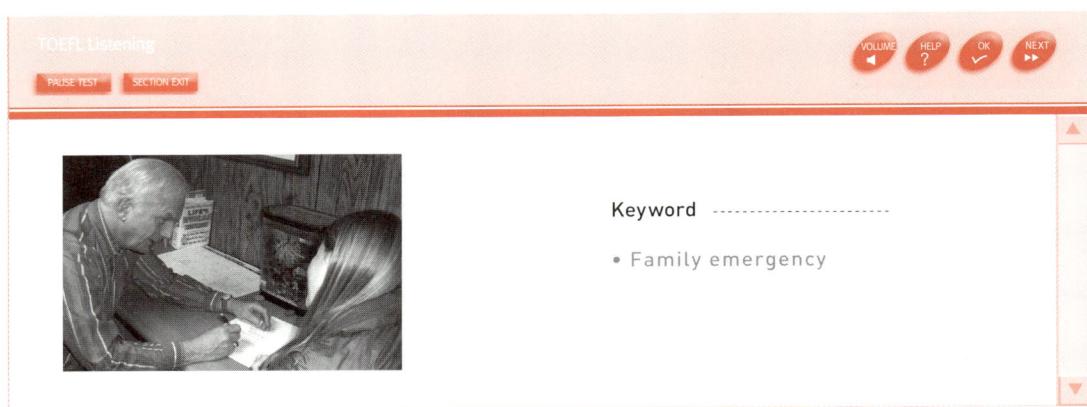

Keyword ----------------------------

• Family emergency

1 Why does the student want to talk to the professor?
- Ⓐ To get permission to be absent from this week's class
- Ⓑ To hand in a homework assignment for this week's class
- Ⓒ To ask the exact guideline for this week's homework assignment
- Ⓓ To use a printer to print out her homework for this week's class

2 What does the professor say about the woman's homework?
- Ⓐ She can turn the homework in only during class.
- Ⓑ She needs to improve her analysis in order to write a better paper.
- Ⓒ Her homework assignment does not fulfill the page number requirement.
- Ⓓ It does not meet the assignment requirement being over ten pages.

3 Listen again to part of the conversation. Then answer the question.
Why does the professor say this: 🎧
- Ⓐ To express his condolences to the woman about her loss
- Ⓑ To tell the woman to bring in her homework as soon as possible
- Ⓒ To turn the topic from the woman's family emergency to her homework
- Ⓓ To avoid an uncomfortable topic for both the professor and the student

Passage 2 Listen to part of a conversation between a student and a housing officer. 🎧

Keyword ----------------------

- Dorm room phone
- Static and noise

1 **What can be inferred about the man?**

(A) He lives in a studio in the dormitory with a roommate.

(B) He has moved into the dorm room five months ago.

(C) He does not like paying a visit to the housing office.

(D) He switched to a cordless phone after using a cell phone.

2 **Why does the man mention his roommate?**

(A) To prove that the problem is not because of his telephone

(B) To demonstrate the problem he and his roommate are having

(C) To explain the reason for the problem he is experiencing

(D) To change the topic from his telephone to his roommate

3 **Listen again to part of the conversation. Then answer the question. What does the man mean when he says this:** 🎧

(A) He is certain that the problem he is having with his telephone is not a big one.

(B) He wants the telephone problem to be fixed as soon as possible.

(C) He thinks that he can fix the problem without the help from the technician.

(D) He wishes that he does not have to spend a lot of money on fixing the problem.

Passage 3

Listen to part of a conversation between a student and an Athletic Center employee. 🎧

Keyword ----------------------

• Athletic center
• Rock climbing facility

1 What can be inferred about the woman's friend?

   Ⓐ She will probably use other facilities from the Athletic Center.

   Ⓑ She is likely to be a sports player from another university.

   Ⓒ She is likely to use the Athletic Center's rock climbing facility more than once.

   Ⓓ She will not use the Athletic Center's facility because the daily fee is too high.

2 What does the man say about the university students' Athletic Center use?

   Ⓐ They do not have to pay for the use of the facility separately because they already pay it along with the tuition.

   Ⓑ The Athletic Center's yearly fee for the university students is high.

   Ⓒ The yearly membership is cheaper than monthly membership.

   Ⓓ The university students have to pay $8.99 whenever they use the facility.

3 Listen again to part of the conversation. Then answer the question.
Why does the woman say this: 🎧

   Ⓐ To brag about her advantageous position to the man

   Ⓑ To refute the man's comments about the daily fee

   Ⓒ To provide evidence that she is a student of the university

   Ⓓ To confess her past mistakes to the man

Listen to part of a conversation between a student and an academic advisor. 🎧

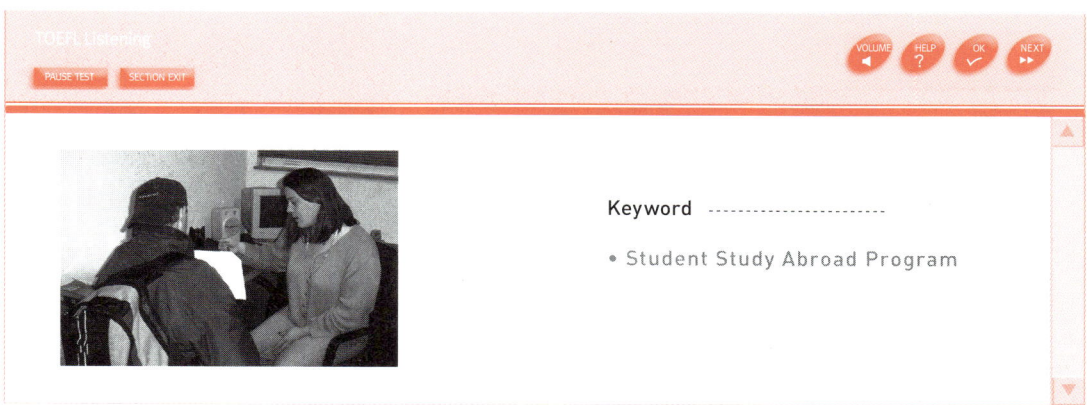

Keyword -----------------------

• Student Study Abroad Program

1 How is the information in the conversation organized?

- (A) From the student's most favorite choice of country to the least
- (B) From the most expensive program to the least
- (C) From the most famous history education program to the least
- (D) From the least populated country to the most

2 Why does the academic advisor mention AP French?

- (A) To recommend the student to choose a better French college
- (B) To find out whether the student is qualified for the French college
- (C) To find out the student's academic ability to learn French language
- (D) To persuade the student to take a class before he goes to a French college

3 Listen again to part of the conversation. Then answer the question. Why does the academic advisor say this: 🎧

- (A) To convince the man to go to a college in Spain
- (B) To emphasize the importance of making a good choice
- (C) To explain why she liked studying in an English college
- (D) To finish what she was saying and change the subject

Passage 5

Listen to part of a conversation between a student and a housing service employee. 🎧

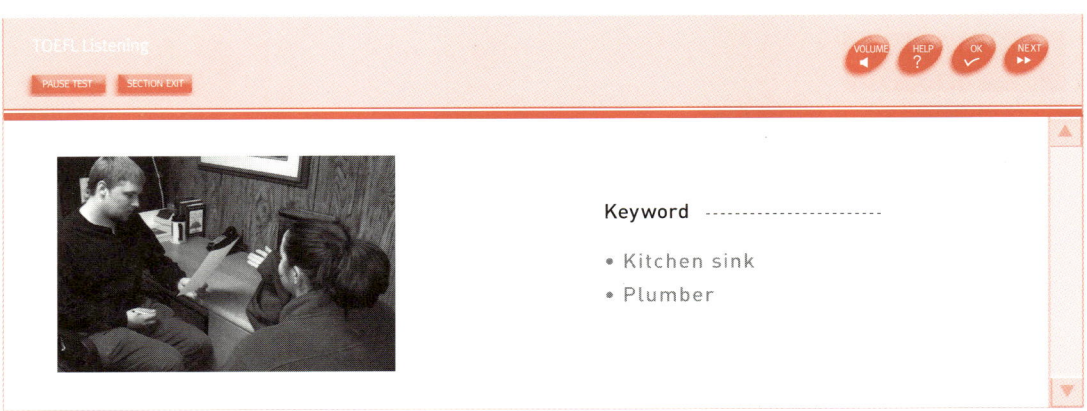

1. **Why does the woman want to talk with the man?**
   - (A) To request for a plumber to fix her kitchen sink
   - (B) To rearrange the appointment with the plumber
   - (C) To inform the man that she will be gone for a few days
   - (D) To explain the problems she is having with her kitchen sink

2. **What does the man say about the plumber?**
   - (A) The plumber will be on a vacation to New York for three weeks.
   - (B) The plumber does not allow re-scheduling the appointment.
   - (C) The plumber has been employed at the school for a long time.
   - (D) The plumber would not do a good job if she changed the schedule.

3. **Listen again to part of the conversation. Then answer the question. What does the woman mean when she says this:** 🎧
   - (A) The interview will be rearranged to another day.
   - (B) The interview is too important to be missed.
   - (C) She does not want to take the interview in New York.
   - (D) She does not have enough money to go to the interview.

4 What kind of problem does the woman have with her kitchen sink?

Ⓐ Her kitchen sink does not let the water drain.

Ⓑ Her kitchen sink does not pour out hot water.

Ⓒ The grater does not work to dispose leftover food.

Ⓓ A screw in the pipe went loose and the water leaks.

5 What can be inferred about the woman?

Ⓐ She likes to order people around.

Ⓑ She is excessively clean and fastidious.

Ⓒ She does not take good care of her utensils.

Ⓓ She does not let strangers in an empty house.

Vocabulary

✔ 박스에 체크 표기를 하며 주요 단어를 학습하시오.

☐ **turn in** 제출하다
☐ **occasion** 경우, 때, 특별한 일
☐ **be in a critical condition** 중태에 빠지다
☐ **right away** 곧, 즉시
☐ **pass away** 사망하다
☐ **session** 회의; 기간; 수업, 강습
☐ **reference** 참고 자료
☐ **refer to~** ~을 참고하다
☐ **pass out** 나눠주다
☐ **static** (수신기의) 잡음; 정전기
☐ **cordless** 코드가 없는, 무선의
☐ **phone jack** 전화 플러그를 꽂는 장치
☐ **the lines are crossed** 혼선이 되다
☐ **technician** 기술자, 전문가
☐ **detect** 발견하다, 인지하다
☐ **arrange** 조절하다, 준비하다
☐ **bill** 고지서
☐ **facility** 시설, 설비
☐ **reservation** 예약

☐ **inconvenient** 불편한
☐ **exception** 예외
☐ **usable** 사용할 수 있는
☐ **fee** 요금
☐ **treadmill** 런닝머신
☐ **abroad** 해외의
☐ **major** 전공
☐ **qualification** 자격(요건)
☐ **provide** 제공하다
☐ **proficiency** 실력, 능숙
☐ **intimidate** 겁주다, 협박하다
☐ **be up to~** ~에게 달려있다
☐ **expense** 비용
☐ **consider** 고려하다
☐ **plumber** 배관공
☐ **postpone** 연기하다, 뒤로 미루다
☐ **packed** 꽉 찬
☐ **permission** 허락
☐ **clog** (관, 파이프 등을) 막다

Vocabulary Test

✏️ 올바른 단어를 골라 문장을 완성하시오.

1 Stephen is having a problem with his car — sometimes his car won't start at all. He should take the car to a _____ as soon as possible.

(A) technician   (B) session   (C) occasion   (D) facility

2 I'm _____(-d/ed) by Professor Jackson — I always get terrified whenever he looks at me in class.

(A) pass away   (B) postpone   (C) pack   (D) intimidate

3 If you want to donate your old clothes to UNICEF, at least bring them something _____; not old rags like these.

(A) cordless   (B) exception   (C) proficient   (D) usable

4 I can't make _____(s) regarding the due date for the term paper. Other students will submit their paper on Wednesday and so will you.

(A) exception   (B) qualification   (C) occasion   (D) static

5 The drain got completely _____(-d/ed) and the water won't go down. What can I do?

(A) refer   (B) criticize   (C) clog   (D) intimidate

6 There used to be lots of educational _____(s) around here but all the schools had to close because the population decreased over the past few decades.

(A) static   (B) cordless   (C) treadmill   (D) facility

7 This is a special _____; it's my grandparents' 50th anniversary!

(A) occasion   (B) phone jack   (C) treadmill   (D) exception

8 Registration for classes was supposed to start from Monday but has been _____(-d/ed) until Wednesday due to the system failure.

(A) clog   (B) refer   (C) postpone   (D) usable

Part 3

iBT Actual Test

Set 1

Set 1

Listen to part of a conversation between a student and a student counselor.

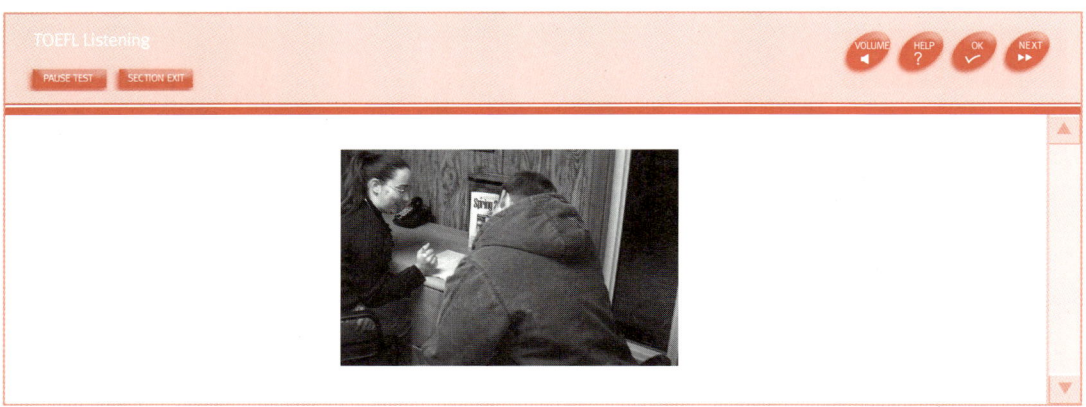

1   Why does the man want to talk with the woman?

    Ⓐ To get information on an on-campus volunteer job

    Ⓑ To get confirmation to teach at the International House

    Ⓒ To request information on ISC's English chatting meeting

    Ⓓ To get a part-time job as an English instructor abroad

2   What can be inferred about the man?

    Ⓐ He wants a part-time job that pays him well.

    Ⓑ He lives with a roommate who is an English teacher for ESL students.

    Ⓒ He wants to build his career in the field of English teaching.

    Ⓓ He has no experience in teaching an ESL class.

3   Listen again to part of the conversation. Then answer the question. How does the woman feel when she says this: 🎧

    Ⓐ She is annoyed because the printer is out of order.

    Ⓑ She is reluctant to read the job description for the man.

    Ⓒ She is excited to know that the man is interested in the job.

    Ⓓ She is irritated because the man is being rude to her.

4 How does the man feel about the job at the International House?

   Ⓐ He thinks the job will not help him stand out in his resume.

   Ⓑ He does not want to teach a small class with only five students.

   Ⓒ He does not want a job that does not help him financially.

   Ⓓ He thinks the teaching hours are too long and demanding for him.

5 What is the man most likely to do next?

   Ⓐ He will talk about the job with his roommate.

   Ⓑ He will go to ISC and register at the counter.

   Ⓒ He will receive the name list of the group members.

   Ⓓ He will notify the ISC counter that he will be the leader.

Passage 2
Listen to part of a discussion in an art history class. The professor is discussing Leonardo da Vinci.

1 **What is the discussion mainly about?**

(A) Several of Leonardo da Vinci's famous masterpieces

(B) Some artistic techniques used in Leonardo da Vinci's drawings

(C) Stylistic innovation in Leonardo da Vinci's *The Last Supper*

(D) Verrocchio's personal influence on Leonardo da Vinci's drawing technique

2 **Which of the following were mentioned as Leonardo da Vinci's drawings?**

Click on 3 answers.

(A) *Madonna with Child*

(B) *Mona Lisa*

(C) *The Baptism of Christ*

(D) *The Last Supper*

(E) *The Vitruvian Man*

3 **What can be said about Leonardo da Vinci's *The Last Supper*?**

(A) The 12 apostles are described as individual figures.

(B) The painting was finished by Verrocchio, not by da Vinci.

(C) It depicts the artist's innovative style different from his teacher's.

(D) It was drawn in da Vinci's early years as a pupil of Verrocchio.

4 Why does the professor mention Verrocchio?

(A) To digress from the main topic of the discussion

(B) To explain Verrocchio's initial influence on da Vinci

(C) To provide da Vinci's personal background information

(D) To compare Verrocchio's and da Vinci's artistic style

5 Listen again to part of the discussion. Then answer the question. Why does the professor say this: ∩

(A) To change the subject from sfumato to chiaroscuro

(B) To ask an interesting question to the students

(C) To comment about a common mistake made by art historians

(D) To provide a controversial subject among art historians and critics

6 The professor explains sfumato and chiaroscuro. Indicate whether each sentence below describes sfumato or chiaroscuro.

Click in the correct box.

	sfumato	chiaroscuro
It means "lightdark" in Italian.		
Its root word means "smoke" in Italian.		
It uses sharp contrast of light and shadow.		
It uses infinite transitions between color areas.		
It contributes to the famous question of Mona Lisa's smile.		

Passage 3 Listen to part of a lecture in a marine biology class. The professor is discussing life in the deep sea.

1 What is the main topic of the lecture?

    Ⓐ Marine animals that live in the photic zone by photosynthesis

    Ⓑ The difficulties humans encounter when exploring the deep sea

    Ⓒ The vertical division of the ocean and sea creatures of the deep sea

    Ⓓ New technology available for exploring the deep ocean realm

2 According to the professor, why does the epipelagic zone have a large concentration of plants and animals?

    Ⓐ Because it receives more light than any other zones

    Ⓑ Because many phytoplanktons live in this zone

    Ⓒ Because the water of the epipelagic zone is warmer than the other zones

    Ⓓ Because it provides better environment for animals to chemosynthesize

3 What does the professor say about deep sea animals when they are taken out of the water?

    Ⓐ Their body will emit faint light from chemical reaction.

    Ⓑ Their body will expand and explode due to lack of pressure.

    Ⓒ They will die immediately when exposed to excessive sunlight.

    Ⓓ Their body will shrink in order to adjust to less pressure.

4   Which of the following is true about the aphotic zone?
    (A) Tuna and porpoises can be found in the aphotic zone.
    (B) Some chemosynthetic plants may be found in the aphotic zone.
    (C) The food chains of the aphotic zone usually start with phytoplankton.
    (D) Many animals mainly rely on chemosynthesis rather than photosynthesis.

5   Why does the professor mention marine snow?
    (A) To describe a unique phenomenon of the deep sea
    (B) To explain unique hunting skills of some photic zone creatures
    (C) To comment on the affluent living condition of the deep sea
    (D) To explain a possible food source of some aphotic zone creatures

6   How does the professor organize the lecture?
    (A) By providing examples of animals and plants that live in the parts of the ocean
    (B) By comparing life and living conditions of the epipelagic zone and that of the mesopelagic zone
    (C) By explaining life and living conditions from the shallowest to the deepest zone of the ocean
    (D) By emphasizing the importance of technical development in order to explore life of the deep sea

Passage 4   Listen to part of a conversation between a student and a professor.

1 Why does the student want to talk with the professor?

- (A) To tell him why she was absent from yesterday's class
- (B) To ask him to summarize yesterday's lecture for her
- (C) To receive the handout he gave out in yesterday's class
- (D) To request his permission to be absent from the next class

2 What does the professor say about the technological development during the 1840's and the 1850's?

- (A) Americans imported machines from Europe and used them as they were.
- (B) The technological development in America was focused on agriculture.
- (C) The railroad growth played a crucial role for development in the travel industry.
- (D) Many European machines were adjusted by Americans according to their need.

3 According to the professor, why was the railroad used more often than canals to transport commercial goods in the 19th century America?

- (A) Because the railroad fare was cheaper than the canal fare
- (B) Because the railroad connected more cities than canals did
- (C) Because the railroad was faster and less subject to harsh weather
- (D) Because the railroad was safer from the attacks from Native Indians

4 Listen again to part of the conversation. Then answer the question. What does the professor mean when he says this: 🎧

    Ⓐ He believes that the woman read a wrong textbook.

    Ⓑ The woman has no knowledge to understand his lecture.

    Ⓒ The book does not deal with full particulars and details.

    Ⓓ The woman did not read the assigned reding thoroughly.

5 What can be inferred about the professor and his lectures?

    Ⓐ He is the author of the textbook.

    Ⓑ He is extremely proud of his lectures.

    Ⓒ He usually explains in detail at the lecture.

    Ⓓ He gives out much assignment to the students.

Passage 5   Listen to part of a lecture in a psychology class. The professor is
discussing cognitive development of infants.

1   What is the lecture mainly about?
   (A) Possible theories and basis of infants' mathematic skills
   (B) Difficulty most high school students undergo with learning math
   (C) The four sections of a person's mathematics learning phases
   (D) Cognitive development of learning linguistic skills and concepts

2   According to the lecture, why do most people think that children's ability to
   learn mathematics skills start from elementary school?
   (A) Because infants and preschoolers are too young to understand profound
       mathematic concepts
   (B) Because young children not attending school are usually uninterested in learning
       mathematics
   (C) Because infants cannot show their mathematic ability due to lack of appropriate
       demonstration skills
   (D) Because unlike some children who start learning math from preschool, most
       children start math classes in elementary school

3   Which of the following would Nativist psychologists probably agree with?
   (A) When shown the same picture repeatedly, infants lose interest in it.
   (B) Most 5-month-old babies have ability to display their math skills.
   (C) Ability to recognize number and space is innate in people.
   (D) Infants' math skills start to be fortified from the preschool phase.

4 According to the professor, what does the term subitizing mean?

- Ⓐ The ability to determine possible and impossible events based on logical thinking.
- Ⓑ The ability to perform addition, subtraction, and multiplication accurately and rapidly.
- Ⓒ The ability to perceive the number of present events without counting.
- Ⓓ Infants' math skills start to be fortified from the preschool phase.

5 Listen again to part of the lecture. Then answer the question. What does the professor imply when he says this: 🎧

- Ⓐ He is trying to look authoritative and haughty in front of the class.
- Ⓑ He thinks that the result of the experiment is surprising.
- Ⓒ He implies that he already knew the result of the experiment.
- Ⓓ He thinks that none of the students knows the result of the experiment.

6 The professor explains Karen Wynn's experiment on 5-month-old infants with Mickey Mouse dolls. Based on the information in the lecture, indicate the order of the given sentences.

Order	Sentence
First	
Second	
Third	
Fourth	

- Ⓐ A screen rolls up and hides a doll on a stage.
- Ⓑ A screen rolls down and shows a doll or three dolls on a stage.
- Ⓒ A doll is placed on a small stage in front of an infant.
- Ⓓ A hand holding a doll goes behind a screen and comes out empty-handed.

Passage 6

Listen to part of a discussion in an environmental studies class.

1   What is the discussion mainly about?

Ⓐ The life and behavior of polar bears in captivity

Ⓑ The distruction of the polar bear's habitat by human activity

Ⓒ The Arctic ecosystem which is in serious danger by global warming

Ⓓ The polar bear's physical condition which enables it to withstand cold

2   Why does the professor mention imperiled or threatened species?

Ⓐ To request the students to ponder over the current status of the polar bear

Ⓑ To demonstrate the reason for the decline in the number of the polar bear population

Ⓒ To provide a more accurate and suitable term according to the polar bear's status

Ⓓ To explain the differences between endangered species and imperiled or threatened species

3   Listen again to part of the discussion. Then answer the question.
How does the professor feel when she says this: 🎧

Ⓐ She feels frustrated because of the students' apathetic behavior.

Ⓑ She is slightly disappointed in the students' unpreparedness.

Ⓒ She is delighted at the students' ignorance on the subject.

Ⓓ She is indifferent towards the students' disobedience.

4 According to the professor, what physical feature of a polar bear makes it easier to withstand the extreme cold?   Click on 2 answers.

- (A) The translucent color of its fur
- (B) The thick layer of its bodyfat
- (C) The ability to run fast on land
- (D) The bulky fur all over its body

5 Which of the following is true about the effect of human activity on polar bears?

- (A) The global warming may melt the Arctic ice, the main habitat of polar bears.
- (B) The overhunting of polar bears by native Alaskans may harm the polar bear population.
- (C) The exploration for oil and gas in Greenland will seriously polute polar bears' habitat.
- (D) The overfishing in the Arctic region will gradually decrease the main food source of polar bears.

6 What will the professor probably discuss next?

- (A) Other human activities that threat polar bears' natural habitat
- (B) Another animal species that is posed danger by human activity
- (C) Native Alaskans and their hunting skills used over polar bears
- (D) The U.S. government's regulation on oil and gas exploration in the Arctic

Set 2

Set 2

Passage 1　Listen to part of a conversation between a student and a staff at the school transportation office.

1 **Why does the man want to talk to the woman?**

    Ⓐ He wants to know the driving direction to the airport.

    Ⓑ He wants to know how to get to the airport.

    Ⓒ He wants a time schedule for the airport shuttle bus.

    Ⓓ He wants to know the exact location of the airport.

2 **What does the man imply about taking a taxi to the airport?**

    Ⓐ He thinks that the taxi fare is too expensive for him.

    Ⓑ He thinks that it will take more time if he took the taxi.

    Ⓒ He prefers taking public transportation than taking the taxi.

    Ⓓ He does not like taking taxis because he thinks they are dangerous.

3 **Listen again to part of the conversation. Then answer the question. What does the man mean when he says this:** 🎧

    Ⓐ He usually does not like to wake up early.

    Ⓑ He always sweats a lot when he drives.

    Ⓒ It is not difficult for him to wake up early.

    Ⓓ He has problems with waking up in the morning.

4   How does the man feel about taking the public transportation?

(A) He would like to take the public transportation to the airport because it will cost him less.

(B) He feels that taking the public transportation might be better because he can enjoy the scenery.

(C) He prefers to take the airport shuttle bus, but is willing to take the public transportation as well.

(D) He prefers to take the airport shuttle bus although it takes more time to get to the airport than the public transportation.

5   Why does the woman recommend the man to arrive at the airport 2 hours before his flight?

(A) Because it is customary to arrive early at the airport

(B) Because the plane schedule might change unexpectedly

(C) Because more people have been using the airport lately

(D) Because the security at the airport has been intensified

Listen to part of a lecture in a literature class. The professor is discussing the history of Latin literature.

1 What is the main topic of the lecture?
   (A) Latin American poetry during the colonial period
   (B) Modernismo propagated in some European countries
   (C) Prestigious female writers from Latin American countries
   (D) Modernismo in Latin America and its greatest pioneer

2 Why does the professor mention Temple University in Philadelphia?
   (A) To digress from the topic of the lecture
   (B) To brag about the fact that she has been chosen a guest speaker
   (C) To announce the cancellation of the next class
   (D) To provide an example of a school that specializes in Latin literature

3 According to the lecture, what can be said about Modernismo in Latin America?
   (A) The Modernismo movement was confined to literature such as poetry and prose.
   (B) Modernismo made the Latin American literature more melodious and richer in vocabulary.
   (C) Spanish literature experienced revolution in versification before the introduction of Modernismo.
   (D) The Modernismo movement was introduced to the Latin America by romanticists such as Octavio Paz.

4 What was the initial response of the Latin American literary men on *Azul*...?

Ⓐ They were exhilarated to have finally found a revolutionary poet.

Ⓑ They felt extremely jealous of Dario's sophisticated linguistic skills.

Ⓒ They were apathetic because they thought Dario's work was mediocre.

Ⓓ They thought it was blasphemous for Dario to break from tradition.

5 According to the lecture, what subject matter did Dario adopt n his collection of poems, *Azul*...?   Click on 2 answers.

Ⓐ Imaginary world of fairies

Ⓑ Tales of heroes and dragons

Ⓒ Folklores of peasants and knights

Ⓓ Legendary stories of artists

6 Listen again to part of the lecture. Then answer the question. What does the professor mean when she says this: 🎧

Ⓐ Some popular Spanish love songs used parts of Dario's verses.

Ⓑ Dario also wrote songs for popular Spanish music artists.

Ⓒ Dario's love songs became one of the Spanish people's favorites.

Ⓓ Dario recorded love songs while he wrote poems and essays.

Passage 3   Listen to part of a discussion in a geology class.

1. What is the discussion mainly about?
   - (A) Plate tectonics and locations of volcanoes
   - (B) Historic examples of famous volcano eruptions
   - (C) Magma eruption and typical eruption types
   - (D) Definition and characteristics of lava and magma

2. According to the professor, why do vesicles form?
   - (A) When magma surrounding the vapor gas decompresses
   - (B) When magma cools and the vapor pressure decreases
   - (C) When balance between the gas and the surrounding rocks is equal
   - (D) When crystallization occurs and lessens magma's gas content

3. Listen again to part of the discussion. Then answer the question. Why does the student say this: 🎧
   - (A) Because she did not do her assigned reading
   - (B) Because she thought she gave a wrong answer
   - (C) Because she realized she used a word not encouraged to use
   - (D) Because she realized she interrupted the professor's lecture

4   What does the professor say about explosive eruptions?

    Ⓐ It causes relatively small danger compared to effusive eruption.

    Ⓑ It is extremely dangerous to humans and wildlife because of its tephra.

    Ⓒ Its lava moves very slowly after bursting out from Earth's fissure.

    Ⓓ It causes serious damage to manmade structures and the ecosystem.

5   Why does the professor mention the Kilauea volcano of Hawaii?

    Ⓐ To provide an example of one of the typical volcano eruptions

    Ⓑ To facilitate the students' understanding on magma eruption procedure

    Ⓒ To provide background information of the formation of Hawaiian islands

    Ⓓ To digress from the topic to explain his last trip to Hawaiian islands

6   The professor explains Plinian eruptions and Hawaiian eruptions. According to the information in the discussion, indicate whether each sentence below describes Plinian eruptions or Hawaiian eruptions.

Click in the correct box.

	Plinian	Hawaiian
It may produce wide lava lakes.		
It is under the category of effusive eruptions.		
Its lava moves extremely fast and destroys everything in its path.		
Its lava is relatively low in viscosity and gas content.		
It bursts out columns of smoke and ash high into the air.		

Listen to part of a conversation between a student and a university gym employee.

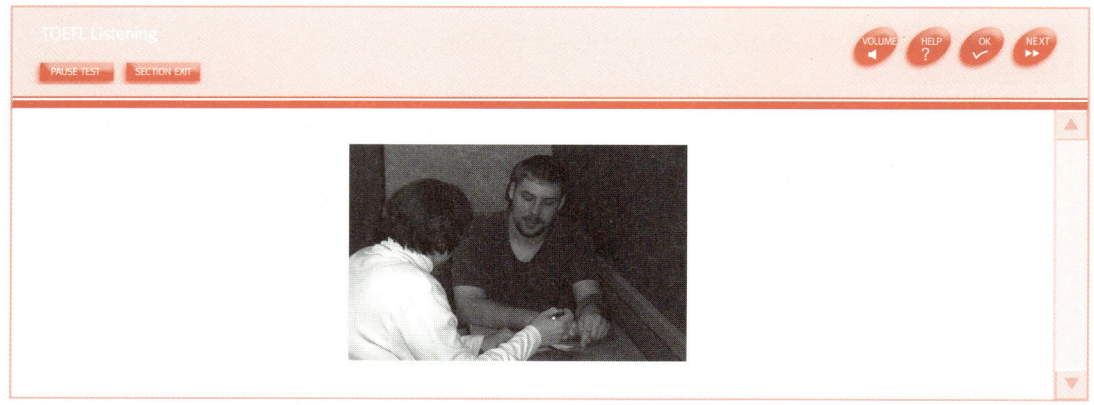

TOEFL Listening

PAUSE TEST   SECTION EXIT

VOLUME   HELP ?   OK ✓   NEXT ▶▶

1 Why does the woman want to join the gym?

    Ⓐ To take a swimming lesson

    Ⓑ To use the workout equipment

    Ⓒ To practice playing badminton

    Ⓓ To participate in a yoga class

2 What does the woman imply about her use of other gym equipment?

    Ⓐ She has no desire to use any of the gym equipments at all.

    Ⓑ She intends to use other equipments at the gym steadily.

    Ⓒ She will not use treadmills and cycles because they are too old.

    Ⓓ She prefers to use weight lifting equipments than cardio machines.

3 Listen again to part of the conversation. Then answer the question. How does the woman feel when she says this: 🎧

    Ⓐ She feels baffled at the man's arrogance.

    Ⓑ She is surprised to learn new information.

    Ⓒ She is frustrated at the man's untruthful remarks.

    Ⓓ She is angry because of the man's ignorance.

4   Why is the woman upset about the gym policy?

(A) Because she thinks the fee for the gym membership and other classes is too expensive for students

(B) Because the gym does not accept personal checks, cash, or money order but only receives credit cards

(C) Because she thinks it is unfair for people who intend to use the gym equipment but will not take other classes

(D) Because she thinks it is a waste of money when she will not use any of the gym equipments but the yoga class

5   What does the man say about the yoga class provided at the gym?

(A) It is difficult for novices to follow.

(B) It is somewhat expensive but affordable.

(C) It is taught by one of the best instructors.

(D) It provides classes four times a week for three months.

Passage 5 Listen to part of a discussion in a health science class. The professor is discussing anorexia.

1   What is the discussion mainly about?
   Ⓐ Possible reasons of eating disorder among teenage girls
   Ⓑ The physiological reasons for developing anorexia nervosa
   Ⓒ The symptoms and reasons for several types of eating disorder
   Ⓓ Possible treatments for anorexia and bulimia nervosa

2   Why does the professor show a picture of a model?
   Ⓐ To introduce the main topic visually
   Ⓑ To explain the potential danger of modeling
   Ⓒ To question students' knowledge of anorexia
   Ⓓ To end a topic and move onto another one

3   Listen again to part of the discussion. Then answer the question.
   How does the professor feel when she says this: 🎧
   Ⓐ She is disturbed because she thinks that the student is trying to disagree with her.
   Ⓑ She feels anxious because the student has asked her a question she does not have answer to.
   Ⓒ She is disappointed because the student does not remember what she had already mentioned.
   Ⓓ She feels confused because she thought she had already covered the answer for the student's question.

4   How does the professor explain medical consequences of anorexia?
  Ⓐ By referring to actual anorexics
  Ⓑ By providing several examples
  Ⓒ By giving precise definitions
  Ⓓ By contrasting it with symptoms of other diseases

5   What does the professor say about the reason for developing anorexia?

Click on 2 answers.

  Ⓐ Anorexia might develop from genes that regulate personality.
  Ⓑ Anorexia usually develops from peer pressure among young men.
  Ⓒ Anorexia might develop from lack of interest from family and friencs.
  Ⓓ Anorexia is closely related to thin images shown in the media.

6   According to the discussion, how is bulimia nervosa different from anorexia nervosa?
  Ⓐ Bulimia nervosa develops after an extremely strict dieting.
  Ⓑ Bulimia nervosa involves voracious overeating and regurgitating.
  Ⓒ Bulimia nervosa is more a psychological disorder than a medical one.
  Ⓓ Bulimia nervosa does not result in serious malfunction of the body.

Passage 6　　Listen to part of a discussion in a linguistics class.

1　What is the main topic of the discussion?

  Ⓐ The definition of superstrate and substrate languages

  Ⓑ The languages that were developed from European languages

  Ⓒ The formation of primitive languages from dominant languages

  Ⓓ The dominant language that was used among slaves in colonial times

2　According to the discussion, which of the following is required in order for a pidgin language to develop?　Click on 2 answers.

  Ⓐ Continuous, normal contact between two different language groups

  Ⓑ A need to communicate between two different language groups

  Ⓒ Deterioration of an original language which eventually becomes obsolete

  Ⓓ A need to strengthen the grammar structures of an original language

3　What is mentioned in the discussion about a creole language?

  Ⓐ It has very pristine and limited vocabulary.

  Ⓑ It is used as a mother tongue among certain generation.

  Ⓒ It creates its own vocabulary rather than borrow it.

  Ⓓ It takes its grammatical rule from another language.

4 What can be inferred about the lexifier language?

    Ⓐ Its users have socio-economic dominance over a society.

    Ⓑ It is usually used by a society with more population.

    Ⓒ It usually has large vocabulary but lacks complicated sentence structure.

    Ⓓ Its power over a society may become weak and it may become obsolete.

5 Listen again to part of the discussion. Then answer the question. Why does the professor say this: 🎧

    Ⓐ He is trying to encourage the student.

    Ⓑ He wants the student to end his presentation.

    Ⓒ He wants to comment on the student's presentation.

    Ⓓ He wants the student to move on to the next subject.

6 What will the students probably do next?

    Ⓐ Research the difficulties many creole speakers confront

    Ⓑ Watch a video clip of an interview with an AAVE speaking woman

    Ⓒ Form discussion groups and work on the questions on the screen

    Ⓓ Discuss the differences between creole language and AAVE

MEMO

MEMO

The Best Solution for TOEFL iBT

HOW
TO
TOEFL ®

iBT

120
LISTENING
정답 및 해설

넥서스

PART 1   LECTURE

1   Main Idea

오늘 수업에서는 개미의 의사 소통에 대해 다루어 보겠어요. 개미는 기본적으로 페로몬이라는 화학 물질을 통해서 의사 소통해요. 페로몬에 대해서는 많이 들어봤죠? 이성을 매혹시키기 위해 동물들이 사용하는 것이라고 들어봤을 거예요. 개미들은 같은 집단에서 사는 동료들이 먹이를 찾거나 사냥하러 가는 길을 찾도록 돕기 위해 페로몬을 사용해요. 예를 들어서 한 개미가 먹이를 찾았다고 합시다. 이 사냥꾼은 집에 돌아오는 길에 땅에 페로몬 흔적을 남겨요. 곧이어 다른 개미들이 이 흔적을 따라가게 되죠. 왔다 갔다 하면서 개미들은 이 흔적을 보다 강화시키게 되고, 먹이를 완전히 먹어치우거나 그들의 거처로 가져갈 때까지 다른 개미들을 유인해요. 먹이를 다 먹고 나면 페로몬 흔적은 더 이상 강화되지 않고 천천히 없어지게 되어요.

Strategy Focus

1. D   **2.** A   **3.** A   **4.** A

1. D

P(M): Today I will be talking about iconoclasm in medieval Europe. As you might have heard before, iconoclasm is destroying religious icons and other symbols or monuments set up for religious veneration. It can also be out of a political motivation. "Breaking the image," if you say it literally. In order to, uh, in order for you to understand this concept better, I think we should first talk about what an icon is. Icons, a word derived from the Greek word, eikones, are sacred images representing gods, goddesses, or saints.

오늘은 중세 유럽의 성상파괴에 대해 얘기해 보겠습니다. 이미 들어보았을 수도 있지만, 성상파괴는 종교적 숭배를 위해 세워진 우상, 상징물, 혹은 기념비를 파괴하는 행위입니다. 이것은 또한 정치적인 동기를 가질 수도 있습니다. 말 그대로 옮기면 "이미지를 파괴하다"라는 뜻이지요. 여러분이 이 개념을 좀 더 잘 이해하기 위해서는 우선 성상이 무엇인지에 대해 이야기 해 보아야 합니다. 그리스 단어 에이카네스에서 비롯된 단어인 아이콘(성상은 신이나 여신, 혹은 성자를 상징하는 신성한 이미지입니다.

2. A

P(W): One of the most important inventions in the 18th century was made by Alexander Graham Bell. Well, I guess you've all heard about him, or even read his biography, right? Bell, who was a Scottish scientist and inventor, was born on March 3, 1847. His family was associated with the teaching of elocution — you know, teaching someone to speak clearly and in an accent that's considered to be standard and acceptable... and, uh, after graduating high school at the age of 13, he started working as a student teacher of elocution and music at the Weston House Academy in Scotland. Well, it is somewhat odd or ironic to say that Bell is also called "the Father of the Deaf" if you think about the fact that he invented the telephone and was involved in teaching elocution... but it is also known that Bell had invented the telephone in order to communicate with his wife and mother, both deaf.

18세기의 가장 중요한 발명 중 하나는 알렉산더 그레이엄 벨에 의해 이루어졌습니다. 여러분은 모두 그에 대해 한번쯤은 들어봤거나 그의 자서전을 읽어보았겠죠? 벨은 스코틀랜드 태생의 과학자이자 발명가로써, 1847년 3월 3일에 태어났습니다. 그의 가족은 웅변술을 가르치는 일을 했습니다 – 즉, 사람들이 적절한 표준 억양을 사용해 명확하게 말하는 것을 가르치는 것이죠... 그리고 13살에 고등학교를 졸업한 후 그는 스코틀랜드의 웨스턴 하우스 아카데미에서 웅변 및 음악 조교로 일하기 시작했습니다. 벨이 전화기를 발명했으며 웅변술을 가르치는 일을 했다는 사실에 대해 생각해 보면, 그가 "귀머거리의 아버지"라고 불리는 것이 다소 아이러니하지만, 그가 귀머거리인 자신의 아내와 어머니와 의사 소통하기 위해 전화기를 발명했다는 것 또한 잘 알려져 있습니다.

3. A

P(M): Whether it's a craving or lack of options, fast food is sometimes unavoidable. It's fast, addictive, and cheaper than eating at fancy restaurants... plus, you don't have to tip, so no wonder so many people go to fast food restaurants. However, many people are just unaware of the potential dangers of fast food-high calorie as well as trans fat. Now, let's talk about this trans fat — what it is, what it does to our bodies, and whether it's okay to consume fast food chock-full of trans fat.

정말 먹고 싶어서이든 다른 먹을 거리가 없어서이든, 패스트푸드는 이따금 피할 수 없는 경우가 있어요. 빨리 먹을 수 있고 중독성이 있으며 호사로운 레스토랑에서 먹는 것보다 저렴하죠. 게다가 팁을 주지 않아도 되니 많은 사람들이 패스트푸드 레스토랑에 가는 이유를 알 만도 해요. 하지만 많은 사람들이 패스트푸드에 잠재되어 있는 위험을 모르고 있어요. 바로 높은 칼로리와 트랜스 지방인데요. 자. 이제 이 트랜스 지방에 대해 얘기해 봅시다. 트랜스 지방이 무엇인지, 우리 몸에 어떤 영향을 미치는지, 그리고 트랜스 지방이 가득 들어 있는 패스트푸드를 먹어도 괜찮은지 등에 대해서 말입니다.

4. A

P(W): Every year in the United States, tens of thousands of people are arrested for DUI — driving under the influence of alcohol. It's also expressed as drunk driving or drinking and driving. You know, you might think that you get charged for DUI only when you operate a motor vehicle, but sometimes you can also get charged when you ride a bicycle and hit a person, or any type of similar human-powered vehicle. Um, usually DUI offense consists of driving under the influence of alcohol, but it also includes, uh, driving under the influence of other drugs, or alcohol and other drugs combined. It doesn't matter if the drug is illegal or lawfully prescribed or just a simple over-the-counter medication.

매년 미국에서는 수만 명의 사람들이 음주 운전으로 체포됩니다. 음주 운전은 약물 복용 운전이라는 말로도 표현되는데요. 여러분은 자동차를 운전할 때에만 음주 운전으로 체포된다고 생각할지도 모르지만, 때로는 자전거 혹은 이와 유사한 인력을 사용하는 기타 운송 수단 등을 타다가 사람을 쳤을 경우에도 음주 운전으로 체포될 수 있습니다. 보통 음주 운전의 죄목은 알코올을 마시고 운전하는 것이지만, 다른 약을 먹은 경우나 술과 약을 동시에 먹었을 경우 또한 포함됩니다. 그 약이 불법이건 합법적으로 조제된 것이건, 혹은 단순히 약국에서 파는 약이건 상관없습니다.

Exercise

P.1	**1.** C	**2.** D	**3.** C
P.2	**1.** A	**2.** C	**3.** C
P.3	**1.** A	**2.** D	**3.** A
P.4	**1.** B	**2.** A	**3.** B, C
P.5	**1.** A	**2.** C	**3.** D
P.6	**1.** C	**2.** D	**3.** B
P.7	**1.** C	**2.** C	**3.** A, D
P.8	**1.** B	**2.** A	**3.** C, D
P.9	**1.** A	**2.** C	**3.** C
P.10	**1.** C	**2.** B	**3.** A
	4. D	**5.** D	**6.** B

1. C　　**2.** D　　**3.** C

P(M): Today, I'll be talking about scars. Many of you have had scars from falling down when you were kids, right? Or maybe, some of you might have a bandage on your finger from last night's cooking. Well, scars come from the biologic process of wound repair in the skin and other tissues of the body. So... well, we can say that scars are a normal part of the body's response to injury... a very natural thing, but most people feel uncomfortable with their appearance and want them to just go away. Now, I have a 17-year-old daughter, and when she was five years old, she fell down and had a scratch on her forehead. We thought it would go away soon, but the scar's still on her forehead, and she wants it removed... well, by a plastic surgery or by a scar remover. Well, speaking of which, scar removal treatment can take one of two forms, depending on the specific type of scar or blemish involved. We're gonna talk about that later today.

오늘은 흉터에 대해서 이야기해 보겠어요. 여러분은 어렸을 적에 넘어져 흉터가 생긴 적이 있죠? 혹은 어제 저녁에 요리를 하다가 다쳐서 손가락에 밴드를 붙인 사람도 있을 거예요. 흉터는 피부와 몸의 다른 조직에 생긴 상처를 치유하는 생리적 과정에서 생겨요. 흉터는 상처에 대한 몸의 정상적인 반응의 일부라고 할 수 있어요. 이것은 상당히 자연스러운 것인데, 많은 사람들은 흉터의 모양을 불편하게 여기고 없애고 싶어하죠. 저에게는 17살 난 딸이 있는데 5살 때 넘어져 이마에 상처가 생겼어요. 이 흉터가 금방 없어질 거라고 생각했지만 아직도 이마에 남아 있어요. 딸아이는 이것을 성형 수술이나 흉터 제거제를 사용해서 없애고 싶어해요. 아, 말이 나왔으니 말인데, 흉터 제거 시술은 흉터의 종류와 형태에 따라 두 가지 방법으로 진행되어요. 이에 대해서는 나중에 이야기해 보겠어요.

❶ **What is the topic of the lecture?**
　"Today, I'll be talking about scars"에서 오늘의 주제를 찾을 수 있다. 선택지 A, B와 D는 너무 좁은 범위를 다루고 있다.

❷ **According to the professor, what is a scar?**
　"Scars are a normal part of the body's response to injury"에서 답을 찾을 수 있다. 선택지 A는 "상처에서 흘러나오는 피"로 해석되기 때문에 답이 될 수 없으며, B는 "햇빛에 의한 피부 이상"이라고 했기 때문에 오답이다. 선택지 C는 "피부 이상으로 일어나는 불편함"이라고 했기 때문에 오답이다.

❸ Why does the professor mention his 17-year-old daughter?

교수는 자신의 17살 난 딸을 언급하면서 딸이 오래된 흉터를 없애고 싶어한다고 예를 들어 설명한다. 선택지 A는 강의와 관련 없으며, B는 너무 범위가 좁은 답안이다. D는 논리적으로 틀린 답안이다.

(Passage 2)

1. A   **2.** C   **3.** C

P(W): All right... so, today we're going to talk about black light. Has anybody heard about black lights, or know what they are or how they look like?

M: ❷ Um... are they... basically, uh, do they emit black light? I just don't understand, because... I mean, if you think about it, I've never seen any type of black light at all. If light is black, then we can't see in the dark, right?

P: Well, Peter, I think you're taking the term too literally. Well, black lights look just like incandescent light bulbs or normal fluorescent lamps, but they are not quite like those lights. There's some difference. If you switch a black light on, then white stuff such as your white clothes, teeth and other things glow in the dark while the bulb itself only emits faint purple light. You've seen this, right? Can you tell me where you've seen this type of light?

W: Oh, last time I went to a karaoke bar, my white shirt kind of glowed in the dark. I thought it was interesting, but I've never thought about it deeply.

P: That's right, Amy. Good example there. Uh, just like Amy said, you've probably seen this in clubs, science museums, amusement parks or even in your own bedrooms.

P: 자, 오늘은 비가시광선에 대해 알아봅시다. 혹시 비가시광선에 대해 들어보았거나, 그것이 무엇인지, 혹은 어떻게 생겼는지 아는 사람 있나요?

M: 어, 비가시광선이란 게 검은 빛을 내뿜는 건가요? 이해가 안 돼요, 왜냐면, 생각해 보면, 검은 빛이란 것을 한 번도 본 적이 없거든요. 만약에 빛이 검다면 어두운 곳에서는 전혀 볼 수 없는 게 아닌가요?

P: 글쎄요, 피터, 이 용어를 너무 글자 그대로 받아들이는 것 같네요. 비가시광선은 백열등 혹은 일반 형광등처럼 생겼지만, 이러한 불빛과는 조금 달라요, 약간의 차이가 있지요. 비가시광선을 켜면, 흰 옷이나 치아 등의 물체들이 어둠 속에서 빛을 발해요. 그렇지만 전구 자체는 희미한 보라색을 띠죠. 이것을 본 적이 있죠? 이러한 빛을 어디서 봤는지 얘기해 볼 사람 있나요?

W: 아, 지난번에 노래방에 갔을 때 제 하얀 셔츠가 어둠 속에서 빛났어요. 신기하다고 생각은 했는데 깊이 생각해 보지는 않았어요.

P: 맞아요, 에이미. 좋은 예네요. 에이미가 말한 것처럼, 여러분은 이 광선을 주로 클럽, 과학 박물관, 놀이동산이나 심지어 침실에서도 봤을 거예요.

❶ What does the professor mainly discuss?

교수의 처음 말 "today we're going to talk about black lights"에서 오늘의 주제를 찾을 수 있다. 나머지 선택지들은 너무 좁은 범위를 다루고 있다.

❷ What does the professor mean when she says this:

"Take the term too literally"란 너무 글자 그대로 해석한다는 뜻이다. 앞에서 학생이 검은 빛이라면 볼 수 없는 것이 아니냐고 묻자 교수는 글자 그대로 이해하지 말라고 한다. 선택지 A와 B는 답과는 관련이 없으며, "표면적 뜻 이면의 것을 생각해야 한다"는 선택지 C가 "항상 용어에 대해 깊이 생각해야 한다"는 D보다 더 나은 선택이다.

❸ What can be said about the professor?

"Has anybody heard about black lights, or know what they are or how they look like?"와 "Can you tell me where you've seen this type of light?" 등에서 교수는 학생들의 참여를 이끌어내기 위해 노력한다는 것을 알 수 있다. 제시된 지문만으로는 선택지 B를 알 수 없으며 선택지 A와 D 또한 틀린 선택이다.

(Passage 3)

1. A   **2.** D   **3.** A

P(M): Last week we discussed Emily Dickinson's life and her poetry. Now, let's turn our attention to Walt Whitman, one of the most influential and innovative American poets. He was born on May 31, 1819 into a working family in New York. The family lived in Brooklyn and Long Island during the 1820's and 1830's. Now, Whitman's father, Walt Whitman Sr., was a very stern man whom Whitman respected. However, Whitman had a closer kinship with his mother and depended on her as a pillar for emotional strength. Well, Whitman is proclaimed the "greatest of all American poets" by many foreign critics. Uh... who... who can tell me one of his most famous works? Yes, Patricia?

W: Uh, I read the collection of his poems, *Leaves of Grass.*

P: Okay, uh, can you tell me what you felt when you read one of the poems in that collection?

W: Um... I, uh... I did read the collection, but I don't remember the poems in particular.

P: That's okay, Patricia. ❸ Well, at least, from now on when you read a famous collection of poems, you might want to research first and find out which one of the poems is the most famous, and try to focus on that poem, all right? <u>Okay. Uh... all right, let's go back to *Leaves of Grass*.</u> Uh, the most famous poem of this collection is *Song of Myself*.

P: 지난 시간까지 우리는 에밀리 디킨슨의 삶과 시에 대해 얘기했어요. 이제 가장 영향력있고 혁신적인 미국 시인 중 한 명인 월트 휘트먼에 대해 살펴 보도록 합시다. 그는 1819년 5월 31일 뉴욕의 근로자 집안에서 태어났어요. 그의 가족은 1820에서 1830년대까지 브루클린과 롱아일랜드에서 살았어요. 휘트먼의 아버지인 월트 휘트먼 1세는 매우 엄격한 사람이었고, 휘트먼은 그를 존경했어요. 그렇지만 휘트먼은 그의 어머니와 더 친밀한 유대감이 있었고 감정적인 면에서 그녀에게 의지했어요. 많은 외국 비평가들은 휘트먼을 "전 미국 시인 중 가장 위대한 시인"이라고 칭송하는데요, 휘트먼의 유명한 작품에 대해 말해 줄 사람 있나요? 네, 패트리샤?

W: 음, 저는 휘트먼의 "풀잎"이라는 시집을 읽었어요.

P: 좋아요. 그 시집에 수록된 시들 중 하나를 읽은 소감을 말해볼까요?

W: 어... 시집을 읽기는 했는데, 딱히 기억나는 시는 없어요.

P: 괜찮아요, 패트리샤. 이제부터는 유명한 시집을 읽을 때 먼저 조사를 해서 그 중에서 어느 작품이 가장 유명한지 알아본 후에 그 시에 집중하도록 하세요, 알았죠? 좋습니다. 시집 "풀잎"으로 돌아갑시다. 이 시집에서 가장 유명한 시는 바로 "자아의 노래"라는 시예요.

❶ **What is the main purpose of the discussion?**
토론의 "목적"을 묻는 것 같지만, 결국 토론의 "주제"를 묻는 질문이다. "We've been discussing Emily Dickinson's life and her poetry until last class. Now, let's turn our attention to Walt Whitman"에서 오늘의 주제를 찾을 수 있다.

❷ **What does the professor say about the relationship between Whitman and his family?**
"Whitman had a closer kinship with his mother and depended on her as a pillar for emotional strength." 라는 부분에서 답을 찾을 수 있다.

❸ **Why does the professor say this:**
교수는 유명한 시집을 읽을 때는 먼저 조사를 하라고 학생에게 제안한 후, 휘트먼의 시집으로 돌아가자고 말하고 있다. 선택지 B는 지문에서 언급되지 않았으며, 교수는 학생의 나태함을 언급하거나 주제에 대해 잘 모르는 것을 꾸짖으려는 것이 아니므로 선택지 C와 D는 틀린 선택이다.

Passage 4

1. B   **2.** A   **3.** B, C

P(W): Today's class will focus on New York City's first subway. Just imagine the busy streets of New York in the mid-1800's... as you might have imagined, NYC didn't have any type of mass transportation for millions of people to use but horse drawn carriages. Any type of engine powered vehicles for city use had not been invented yet. It was a mess... you can easily imagine that, huh? All right, so... well, there was a big problem there... the population was growing and the city was expanding with no practical solution to the problem of transportation. But this one man... uh, Alfred Ely Beach, came up with two solutions: First, he suggested that the city build elevated roads so that extra traffic can all be placed up there. Second, he proposed that if the first solution was not plausible, the transportation should go underground. In 1849, he proposed to make a tunnel the entire length of Broadway, but... well, this wasn't designed for trains but for horses.

오늘은 뉴욕시 최초의 지하철에 대해 얘기해 봅시다. 1800년대 중반 뉴욕시의 분주한 거리를 상상해 보세요... 여러분이 상상한 바와 같이, 뉴욕에는 말이 끄는 마차를 제외하고는 수백만 명의 사람들이 사용할 대중교통 수단이 없었습니다. 도시에서 사용할 수 있는 엔진 차량은 아직 발명되지 않았었죠. 도시는 난리였습니다. 쉽게 상상이 가지요? 자, 그래서 그곳에는 큰 문제가 하나 있었는데요, 인구는 증가하고 있었고 도시는 교통수단에 대한 실질적인 해결책이 없는 상태에서 팽창하고 있었습니다. 하지만 알프레드 엘리 비치라는 사람 두 가지 해결 방안을 모색했습니다. 첫 번째로 그는 시에서 공중에 도로를 만들어 잉여 교통량이 이용할 수 있도록 할 것을 제안했습니다. 두 번째로 그는 첫 번째 해결책이 불가능한 경우, 교통량이 지하로 가야 한다고 제안했습니다. 1849년에 그는 브로드웨이 전체 길이의 터널을 만들자고 제안했는데, 이것은 전철이 아니라 말을 위한 것이었습니다.

❶ **What does the professor mainly discuss?**
"Today's class will focus on New York City's first subway"에서 오늘의 주제가 드러난다. 선택지 A, C, D는 너무 좁은 선택이다.

❷ **How does the professor make her point about the transportation situation of New York City in the mid-1800s?**
1800년대 중반의 뉴욕시의 교통 상황 문제를 설명하기 위해 교수는 말과 마차를 언급하며 그 당시의 교통 문제를 묘사한다. 자신의 경험과 비교하는 것이 아니므로 선택지 B는 틀렸으며, 뉴욕시 외에 다른 시의 교통 상황이 언급된 바가 없으므로 선택지 D 또한 틀렸다.

What did Alfred Beach propose for the transportation problem?

뉴욕시의 심각한 교통 문제를 해결하기 위해 알프레드 비치는 도로를 공중에 만들거나 지하에 만드는 것을 제안한다. 따라서 정답은 B와 C이다.

Passage 5

1. A   **2.** C   **3.** D

> **P(M):** A cultural movement, Dada or Dadaism began in Switzerland during World War I. It was a radical international movement in literature and art, initiated by a group of young artists and writers such as Ball, Arp, Hoddis and Tzara at the Cabaret Voltaire in Zurich, and the movement later split into an American, a French, and several German groups. It enjoyed its peak from 1916 to 1920 and it involved visual arts, literature, theatre, and graphic design. Well... Tzara's point of departure in Dadaism was "a disgust with all forms of modern civilization." In other words, Dadaism denied all forms of art and values of the past and pursued a complete break from tradition and the systematic destruction of culture and of civilization. When Dadaism faded after 1922, many Dadaists grew interested in surrealism. Now, I believe that if you took a glimpse of the famous art works of Dadaists of renown, you'll take a hold of what they sought after through art.
>
> 다다 혹은 다다이즘은 1차 세계대전 중 스위스에서 태동한 문화적 움직임입니다. 이는 문학과 예술 분야에서 일어난 급진적인 전 세계적 움직임으로 쥐리히의 카바레 볼테르에서 벨, 아프, 호디스와 짜라 등의 젊은 화가들과 작가들 사이에서 시작되었으며, 이후에는 미국, 프랑스, 그리고 몇몇 독일 집단으로 나뉘었습니다. 다다이즘은 1916년에서 1920년까지 성황을 이루었고 시각 예술, 문학, 연극, 그리고 그래픽 디자인 등을 포함하였습니다. 짜라는 다다이즘이 시작된 이유로 "현대 문명의 모든 형태에 대한 혐오감"을 꼽았습니다. 즉, 다다이즘은 과거의 모든 예술과 가치를 부정했고 전통으로부터의 완전한 탈피와 문화와 문명의 조직적인 파괴를 추구하였습니다. 다다이즘이 1922년 이후 점점 쇠퇴하면서, 많은 다다이스트들은 초현실주의에 관심을 돌리기 시작했습니다. 여러분들이 유명한 다다이스트들의 작품을 살펴본다면, 그들이 예술을 통해 무엇을 추구했는지 알 수 있을 것이라 생각됩니다.

❶ **What is the primary purpose of the lecture?**

강의는 다다이즘에 대한 설명으로, 선택지 A(다다이즘에 대한 이해를 돕기 위해)가 정답이 된다. 선택지 B와 C는 지문에 잠깐 언급된 것으로 정답이 되지 않으며, 선택지 D는 지문에서 언급된 바가 없다.

---

❷ **According to the lecture, what can be said about Dadaism?**

다다이즘에 대해 전반적으로 묻는 질문이다. 다다이즘이 1916년에서 1920년 사이에 전성기를 누렸고 1922년 이후 쇠퇴했지만 다른 예술 분야에 영향을 주었다는 부분에서 선택지 C가 정답임을 알 수 있다. 선택지 A, B와 D는 지문의 내용과 상반되는 내용이므로 틀린 선택이다.

❸ **What did many Dadaists grow interested in after Dada faded?**

다다이즘의 쇠퇴 이후 다다이스트들은 초현실주의에 눈을 돌리기 시작했다고 했으므로 정답은 D이다.

Passage 6

1. C   **2.** D   **3.** B

> **P(M):** All right, everyone. Before we continue, is there anybody who has a question?
>
> **M:** Yes, sir. Umm... I have one question.
>
> **P:** Yes, Tom.
>
> **M:** Um, it's from what you talked about last week about the Morse code, and uh... I did do the reading that you assigned last week, but I'm still a little bit confused.... The book said that the international Morse code is composed of six elements. Is that right, six? Because I've always thought that the Morse code was composed of only two elements, the dot and the line.
>
> **P:** You read the book correctly — six elements, yes. Uh, is it the number of the elements of the Morse code that you were confused about?
>
> **M:** Um, if you can, can you go over the Morse code very briefly... like, how it was invented and how it works and stuff?
>
> **P:** All right, then. Uh... you all know that the name Morse came from the name of the person who first developed an electric telegraph, right?
>
> **W:** Yeah, it was Samuel Morse.
>
> **P:** That's right. Uh, I also mentioned another person, Alfred Vail. Do you all remember that? Well, Morse and Vail's initial telegraph went into operation in 1844. It kind of works this way...
>
> **P:** 자, 여러분. 계속하기 전에, 질문 있는 사람 있나요?
>
> **M:** 네, 교수님. 질문이 하나 있습니다.
>
> **P:** 그래요, 톰.
>
> **M:** 지난주에 교수님께서 말씀하신 모르스 코드에 관한 것인데요. 지난주에 과제로 내 주신 부분을 읽었지만, 아직도 약간 헷갈려서요... 책에서는 국제 모르스 코드가 6개의 요소로 이뤄졌다고 했는데, 6개가 맞나요?

왜냐하면 전 모르스 코드는 점과 선, 오직 두 개로만 이뤄진 줄 알았거든요.

P: 정확하게 읽었어요 – 여섯 개가 맞아요. 모르스 코드를 구성하는 요소의 개수 때문에 헷갈렸던 건가요?

M: 혹시 괜찮다면 모르스 코드에 대해 간략하게 설명해 주실 수 있나요... 예를 들어 언제 개발되었고, 어떻게 작용하는지 등에 대해서요.

P: 좋아요. 모두들 모르스라는 이름이 전기 전보를 처음으로 개발한 사람의 이름에서 유래되었다는 건 알고 있겠지요?

W: 네, 사무엘 모르스였어요.

P: 맞아요. 또 다른 사람을 언급했었는데요, 알프레드 베일이라고 기억나지요? 모르스와 베일의 초기 전보는 1844년에 사용되기 시작했어요. 이것은 이런 방식으로 작동해요...

❶ What is the main topic of the discussion?

"Can you go over the Morse code in general real short... like, how it was invented and how it works and stuff?"라는 학생의 질문에서 답을 찾을 수 있다. 선택지 A, B, D는 지문에 잠깐 언급된 것이기 때문에 너무 범위가 좁은 선택이다.

❷ Why is the student confused about the Morse code?

학생은 지난주에 내준 숙제를 읽었다고 했으므로, 수업에 처음 참석하는 것이 아님을 알 수 있다. 따라서 선택지 A와 B는 오답이다. 모르스와 베일의 초기 전보에 대한 사항을 몰랐기 때문에 혼란한 것인지는 알 수 없으므로 C 또한 오답이다. 학생은 모르스 부호가 2개의 요소로 이루어진 줄 알았는데 책을 읽어보니 6개였다고 말하며, 이것에 대해 헷갈려 한다. 따라서 답은 D이다.

❸ What will the professor probably discuss next?

"Morse and Vail's initial telegraph went into operation in 1844. It kind of works this way..."라는 말을 통해 모르스와 베일의 초기 전보가 작동하는 방법에 대해 이어서 설명할 것임을 알 수 있다.

Passage 7

1. C   **2.** C   **3.** A, D

P(W): This week, we're talking about social insects. Can anybody tell me what they are?

W: Um, they are insects that form large, organized social structures.

P: That's correct, Lorraine. Can you tell me what kind of insects can be included in the social insects?

W: That would be... um, I guess, termites? Or bees?

P: Right again. Now, these insects form a society called a "colony" which typically has hundreds of thousands of members with one queen. A colony usually starts with one queen, and when another queen emerges, she has to leave the colony and start one of her own.

M: Professor, it doesn't seem logical for one queen to form a colony with thousands of members. How... how long do these colonies take to form a complete society, and how does the queen do that?

P: That's a good question. Well, we were supposed to talk about the type of insects that form these types of colonies, but before we go on, let's talk about the time and procedure of constructing a colony very briefly.

P: 이번 주에는 사회성 곤충에 대해 이야기 해 보겠어요. 이것이 어떤 곤충인지 얘기해 줄 사람 있나요?

W: 음, 그것은 대규모 조직 사회 구조를 형성하는 곤충이에요.

P: 맞아요, 로레인. 사회성 곤충에 어떤 종이 포함되는지 말해줄 수 있나요?

W: 음, 흰개미나 벌 아닌가요?

P: 맞아요. 자, 이 곤충들은 "군체"라는 집단을 형성하는데 이것은 여왕 한 마리와 수백 수천 마리의 무리로 구성되어요. 군체는 일반적으로 한 마리의 여왕에서 시작되는데, 다른 여왕이 태어날 경우에는 기존의 여왕은 독립하여 새로운 군체를 형성해야 하죠.

M: 교수님, 여왕 한 마리가 수천 마리의 무리와 군체를 형성한다는 것이 논리적이지 않은 것 같아요. 이런 군체가 완전한 사회로 형성되려면 얼마나 걸리나요? 그리고 여왕은 어떻게 그 일을 하나요?

P: 좋은 질문이에요. 이런 종류의 군체를 형성하는 곤충들에 대해 얘기할 예정이었지만, 더 나가기 전에 군체가 구성되는 시간과 절차에 대해 간단하게 알아보죠.

❶ What is the discussion mainly about?

교수는 social insects에 대한 정의로부터 시작하며 colony가 어떻게 이루어지는지를 설명하고 있다.

❷ What happens when a new queen emerges in an existing colony?

새로운 여왕이 태어날 경우 기존의 여왕은 독립하여 새로운 사회를 형성한다고 한다. 선택지 A, B와 D는 지문에 언급되지 않았으므로 정답이 아니다.

❸ Which of the following were mentioned as the example of social insects?

"That would be... um, I guess, termites? Or bees?"라는 학생의 말에서 정답을 찾을 수 있다.

1. B　　**2.** A　　**3.** C, D

P(W): You've all probably heard of the Empire State Building, right? It is a 102-story skyscraper in New York City. The American Society of Civil Engineers announced that it was one of the Seven Wonders of the Modern World. It was designed by Shreve, Lamb, and Harmon, and was finished in 1931 as the tallest building in NYC until the World Trade Center came along. Well... now that the World Trade Center was destroyed in the 9/11 attacks in 2001, the Empire State Building became the tallest building in NYC again, and the second tallest building in the States after the Sears Tower in Chicago.

여러분 모두 엠파이어 스테이트 빌딩에 대해 들어보았죠? 이 빌딩은 뉴욕 소재의 102층 마천루입니다. 미국 민간 건축협회에서는 이 빌딩을 현대 사회의 7대 불가사의 중 하나라고 선포했습니다. 이것은 슈레브, 렘, 하몬에 의해 고안되었으며 1931년에 완공되어 세계무역센터가 들어서기 전까지 뉴욕시에서 제일 높은 건물이었습니다. 세계무역센터가 2001년 911 사건 당시 무너지고 난 후, 엠파이어 스테이트 빌딩은 다시 뉴욕시에서 제일 높은 건물이 되었으며, 시카고의 시어스 타워 다음으로 미국에서 가장 높은 건물이 되었습니다.

❶ **What is the main topic of the lecture?**
전반적으로 엠파이어 스테이트 빌딩에 대해 설명하고 있다. 선택지 A는 지문에 언급된 바가 없으므로 정답이 아니며, 선택지 C와 D는 지문에 잠시 언급된 것이므로 지문의 주제가 될 수 없다.

❷ **According to the professor, what is the current tallest building in the United States?**
교수는 엠파이어 스테이트 빌딩이 시카고의 시어스 타워 다음으로 미국에서 두 번째로 높은 빌딩이라고 말한다. 따라서 미국에서 가장 높은 빌딩은 시카고의 시어스 타워가 된다.

❸ **Which of the following designers were mentioned in the lecture as the designers of the Empire State Building?**
"It was designed by Shreve, Lamb, and Harmon, and was finished in 1931"라는 교수의 말에서 정답이 C와 D임을 알 수 있다.

1. A　　**2.** C　　**3.** C

P(M): So, previously in class last week, we talked about Mohawks, indigenous people of North America, and their language. Today, we're gonna be talking about their history and their community. But before we go on, let's take a look at these pictures. Familiar, huh? The first picture is a young American male wearing a hairstyle that is widely known as a Mohawk or Mohican in Britain. The picture right next to it is the one of a Mohawk warrior in the Mohawk Nation flag — focus on the resemblance of their hairstyle, huh? The Mohawks wore a hairstyle like this picture... uh, they cut all their hair off except for a narrow strip down in the middle of the scalp, like many other indigenous tribes in the Great Lakes region. Not all Mohawk males wore this hairstyle... only warriors going to war used the style.
Now that we know where the Mohawk hairstyle came from, let's go back to our main topic of today.

지난주에는 북미의 토착민인 모하크족과 그들의 언어에 대해 얘기해 보았습니다. 오늘은 그들의 역사와 사회에 대해 얘기해 보겠습니다. 하지만 계속하기 전에, 이 사진을 봅시다. 낯이 익죠? 첫번째 사진은 젊은 미국 남성이 모하크, 혹은 영국에서는 모히칸이라 불리는 헤어스타일을 하고 있는 모습입니다. 그 옆의 사진은 모하크 부족의 깃발에 그려져 있는 모하크 전사의 그림입니다 — 이들 헤어스타일이 얼마나 유사한지 보세요. 모하크족은 이 사진에서 보이는 헤어스타일을 하고 지냈습니다... 5대호 부근의 많은 토착민들처럼 머리 가운데에 가느다랗게 머리카락 한 줄기만 남겨놓고 나머지는 모두 잘라냈죠. 모든 모하크족 남성이 이 헤어스타일을 한 것은 아니었습니다... 이것은 전쟁에 나가는 전사들만이 할 수 있었던 헤어스타일이었습니다.
이제 모하크 헤어스타일의 기원을 알았으니, 오늘의 주제로 돌아갑시다.

❶ **What is the lecture mainly about?**
지난주에 모하크 부족과 그들의 언어에 대해 살펴보았으므로 선택지 C는 정답이 아니며, "Today, we're gonna be talking about their history and their community"라는 교수의 말에서 정답이 A임을 알 수 있다. 선택지 B는 지문에 잠깐 언급됐을 뿐이며, 선택지 D는 언급된 바가 없으므로 정답이 아니다. 제시된 지문에서는 모하크 부족의 헤어스타일에 대해 이야기하지만, "let's go back to our main topic of today"라는 교수의 말에서 강의의 주제가 헤어스타일이 아니라 모하크 부족의 역사와 사회라는 것을 알 수 있다.

❷ **Why does the professor compare the pictures of an American male and a Mohawk warrior?**
교수는 두 사진을 보여주며 모하크 전사의 헤어스타일과 미국인의

모하크 헤어스타일이 유사하다는 것을 설명한다. 따라서 정답은 C 이다. 선택지 A는 너무 광범위한 선택이며, 선택지 B와 D는 강의 와 관련 없는 내용이다.

❸ Which member of the Mohawks wore the hairstyle mentioned by the professor?

"Not all Mohawk males wore this hairstyle... only warriors going to war used the style."라는 교수의 말에 서 정답이 C임을 알 수 있다.

Passage 10

1. C **2.** B **3.** A **4.** D **5.** D **6.** B

P(M): Okay, class. So far, we've been talking about mass extinction of various species about 65.5 million years ago. This was around at the end of the Cretaceous Period and the beginning of the Tertiary Period, and it is also known as the K-T extinction event. Many forms of life perished, most conspicuously dinosaurs, and, uh... about 50 to 80 percent of plant and animal species were wiped out from the Earth. Many possible causes of mass extinction have been proposed... you may have heard people saying that dinosaurs became extinct because an object from outer space collided with Earth, or even that there were a series of massive volcanic explosions and rapid climate change. Now, today, we're gonna talk about the Alvarez Hypothesis.

Luis Alvarez is a physicist who won the Nobel prize in 1968. In 1980, Alvarez, several other scientists, and a group of researchers led by them discovered that fossilized sedimentary layers found at the Cretaceous Tertiary boundary all over the world contained a concentration of iridium much more greater than usual. After the Cretaceous Period when massive, extraordinary extinction has taken place, the Tertiary Period began, in which mammals came to dominate on Earth. Can you guess what had happened back then? Well, Alvarez and team of scientists suggested that the dinosaurs had been wiped off by an impact event from a 10-kilometer-wide asteroid. One of the two facts supporting the theory is the relative abundance of iridium in many asteroids. You know... the asteroid hit the Earth and because the asteroid exploded, it caused the iridium in the asteroid to spread over the Earth during that period. You should know, my friends; iridium is very rare on the Earth's surface... you don't find it a lot on the surface but you can find

iridium easily in the Earth's center and in extraterrestrial objects such as asteroids and comets. Another fact that supports the theory is the similarity between the isotopic composition of iridium in asteroids and K-T layers, which is different from that of terrestrial iridium.

So... as I was saying... the asteroid hit the Earth. Have you ever seen the movie, the *Deep Impact*? You can see how an asteroid the size of a small town can inundate one third of a continent. The blast resulting from the impact 65.5 million years ago would have been... like, hundreds of millions of times more disastrous than the most powerful nuclear weapon ever detonated. It is safe to say that, um, it may have created a monstrous hurricane and thrown massive amounts of dust and vapor into the upper atmosphere. Also... there might have been global firestorms. Scientists found out that the oxygen content of the atmosphere was extremely high during the late Cretaceous Period by analyzing fluid inclusions in ancient amber, and this would have supported intense combustion. **❹ The gas and dust from the worldwide firestorm could have covered the atmosphere and blocked sunlight for months or even years... for God knows how long... and we all know what happens if we don't have sunlight, right?** Yes, it might have decreased photosynthesis and thus depleted food resources.

Now, let's think of the consequences here... long winter because of the blocked sunlight... and what else, ah, greenhouse gases might have raised the Earth's temperature for years. There might have been acid rains that might have ruined natural habitats, but recent research suggests this effect was relatively minor. However, even though consecutive studies of the K-T layer consistently displayed the excess of iridium, the Alvarez Hypothesis which explained that dinosaurs were exterminated by a huge asteroid remained quite controversial among many paleontologists and geologists for many years thereafter.

자, 여러분. 지금까지 우리는 6,550만 년 전에 발생한 다양한 종의 대량 멸종에 대해 얘기해 보았습니다. 이는 백악기 말, 제3기의 시작 즈음인데, 이 시기는 또한 K-T멸종이라고도 알려져 있습니다. 다양한 종의 생명이 사라졌는데, 이 중 가장 눈에 띄는 것은 공룡이며, 약 50에서 80퍼센트 의 식물과 동물종이 지구상에서 사라졌습니다. 대량 멸종의 원인에 대해 다양한 의견이 제시되었습니다. 우주에서 물체가 떨어져 지구와 충돌하 면서 공룡이 멸종되었다거나, 혹은 대량 화산 폭발과 그로 인한 기후 변 화로 인해 공룡이 멸종되었다는 얘기를 들어 보았을 겁니다. 자, 그럼 오늘은 알바레즈 가설에 대해 알아봅시다.

루이스 알바레즈는 1968년 노벨 물리학상 수상자입니다. 1980년도에 알바레즈와 몇몇 과학자들 및 연구진들은 백악기–제3기 시대에 전세계적으로 형성된 화석 지층의 이리듐 함유량이 정상보다 훨씬 더 높다는 것을 발견했습니다. 전례없는 대량의 멸종이 발생한 백악기 이후, 포유류가 지배하기 시작한 제3기가 시작되었습니다. 그 당시 무슨 일이 있었는지 추측할 수 있나요? 알바레즈와 다른 과학자들은 직경 10킬로미터의 대형 운석이 충돌하여 공룡들이 전멸되었다고 시사했습니다. 이 이론을 뒷받침하는 두 가지 증거 중 하나는 수많은 운석에 대량 포함된 이리듐입니다. 즉... 운석이 지구와 충돌하여 폭발하게 되면서 지구 곳곳에 이리듐을 퍼뜨린 것입니다. 자, 여러분, 이리듐이 지표면에 매우 드문 물질이라는 사실에 주목해야 합니다... 지표면엔 거의 없지만 지구의 중심과 운석이나 혜성과 같은 지구 밖의 물체에는 다량이 함유되어 있습니다. 이 이론을 뒷받침하는 또 다른 사실은 운석과 K–T 지층의 이리듐 동위원소가 갖는 유사성으로, 지구권 내의 이리듐과는 성분이 다릅니다.

자, 얘기하던 대로... 운석이 지구와 충돌했습니다. "딥임펙트"라는 영화를 본 적이 있나요? 작은 마을 크기의 운석이 대륙의 3분의 1을 초토화시킬 수 있다는 것을 볼 수 있습니다. 6,550만 년 전의 충돌로 인한 폭발은 가장 위력적인 핵폭탄보다 수백만 배 더 가공할 위력을 가진 것이었을 것입니다. 이는 아마도 대형 허리케인을 생성시키고 대량의 먼지와 수증기를 대기권 상층부로 올려 보냈을 것입니다. 또한, 전 세계적인 화재 폭풍도 발생했을 것입니다. 고대 석탄층의 액체 함유를 분석한 결과, 과학자들은 백악기 말에 대기 중의 산소 농도가 상당히 짙다는 것을 알게 되었는데, 이것이 격렬한 연소를 야기했을 것입니다. 전 세계적으로 발생한 화재 폭풍의 가스와 먼지는 대기권을 덮어 햇빛을 수 개월에서 수년간 차단시켰을 것입니다. 얼마나 오랫동안 그랬을지는 아무도 모릅니다. 그리고 햇빛이 없으면 어떻게 되는지 다들 아시죠? 네. 광합성을 감소시켜 음식 자원이 고갈되었을 수 있습니다.

자, 이제 결과에 대해서 생각해 봅시다... 햇빛 차단으로 인한 긴 겨울... 그리고 온실 가스 등이 지구의 기온을 수년간 상승시켰을 것입니다. 산성비가 생태계를 파괴했을 수도 있지만, 최근 연구 결과 이는 경미한 피해만을 야기했음을 알 수 있습니다. 그러나 비록 K–T지층에 대한 추가적인 연구 결과가 이리듐이 과다 포함되어 있다는 것을 꾸준히 보여주지만, 공룡이 거대 운석으로 인해 멸종했다고 설명하고 있는 알바레즈 가설은 많은 지질학자와 고생물학자 사이에 수년간 논란이 되었습니다.

❶ **What is the topic of the lecture?**

"Now, today, we're gonna talk about the Alvarez Hypothesis"라는 교수의 말에서 이 지문이 6,550만 년 전의 대량 멸종에 대한 가설을 소개하며 설명하고 있음을 알 수 있다. 선택지 A는 광범위한 선택이며 선택지 B와 D는 범위가 좁은 선택이다.

❷ **How does the professor explain the Alvarez Hypothesis?**

교수는 알바레즈 가설을 뒷받침하는 근거들을 설명하는데 그 중 하나가 바로 이리듐의 함량이다. 유명한 영화를 언급한 이유는 문제 3번에서 알 수 있으며 이 문제와는 관련이 없다. 알바레즈 가설 외에 언급된 가설이 없으므로 선택지 C는 답이 아니며, 알바레즈와 그의 연구팀의 배경(노벨상 수상)을 언급한 이유는 그의 가설을 설명하기 위해서가 아니라 알바레즈의 경력을 소개하기 위해서이다.

❸ **Why does the professor mention the movie, *Deep Impact*?**

교수가 "Have you ever seen the movie, the *Deep Impact*? You can see how an asteroid a size of a small town can inundate one third of a continent"라며 영화 제목을 언급한 이유는 지구와 운석이 충돌했을 경우의 결과를 시각적으로 설명하기 위해서이다. 따라서 정답은 A가 되며, 선택지 B는 답이 되지 않는다. 선택지 C와 D는 문제와 관련이 없다.

❹ **Why does the professor say this:**

"For God knows how long"이라는 표현은 "아무도 그 기간을 모른다"라는 표현이다. 따라서 선택지 A는 답이 아니며 이 표현만으로 교수의 주제에 대한 지식을 가늠할 수 없으므로 선택지 B 또한 정답에서 제외해야 한다. 선택지 C는 이 문제와 관련이 없다.

❺ **According to the lecture, what can be said about the Alvarez Hypothesis?**

알바레스는 1968년 노벨상 수상자이며 그의 가설은 1980년에 제기되었으므로 선택지 A는 틀린 답이다. 알바레스 가설이 향후 수년간 과학자들 사이에 논쟁을 불러일으켰다는 교수의 마지막 말에서 선택지 B 또한 틀렸음을 알 수 있으며, 이 가설이 다른 유명한 영화에 영감을 주었는지는 지문에서 알 수 없으므로 선택지 C도 틀린 답안이다. 지문 전체에서 알바레스 가설의 과학적 근거가 제시되어 있으므로 정답은 D이다.

❻ **How does the professor describe the impact of the asteroid collision on Earth 65.5 million years ago?**

6,550만 년 전의 운석의 충돌은 가장 위력적인 핵폭탄보다 훨씬 더 가공할 위력을 가졌다고 하는 부분에서 교수가 강력한 핵무기의 폭발과 운석의 지구 충돌을 비교해서 설명하고 있음을 알 수 있다. 지구와 운석의 충돌 과정을 설명하지 않으므로 선택지 C는 틀린 선택이며, 시각적 자료를 사용하지 않으므로 A 또한 정답이 아니다. 6,550만 년 이전의 지구와 운석의 충돌을 언급하지 않았으므로 선택지 D도 틀렸음을 알 수 있다.

Vocabulary Test

1. influential	**2.** extraterrestrial	**3.** conspicuous
4. indigenous	**5.** controversial	**6.** emit
7. literally	**8.** resemblance	**9.** c
10. a	**11.** d	**12.** b
13. a	**14.** d	**15.** c

2 Supporting Detail

당뇨병은 비록 전염병은 아니지만 마치 전염병처럼 확산되고 있습니다. 1980년도 이래로 미국에서의 당뇨병 발병율은 47퍼센트나 상승했는데, 이것은 다음 10년 동안 더욱 급격히 상승할 것으로 예상됩니다. 그 원인은 미국인들의 거의 절반, 특히 남성들이 당뇨가 발병하는 조건을 가지고 있거나 당뇨가 발병하기 직전 단계에 있기 때문입니다. 그리고 여러분들이 쉽게 상상할 수 있듯이 이는 심각한 결과를 낳습니다. 당뇨병은 심혈관 질환의 주된 원인이 되는데, 수명을 평균 13년이나 단축시킵니다. 일찍 사망하지 않는다고 해도 시력을 잃거나 신부전이 발생할 수도 있고, 발을 잃게 될 수도 있습니다.

Strategy Focus

1. B   **2.** D   **3.** A   **4.** C, D

1. B

P(M): Legal Assistants, also called paralegals, are employed in many parts of the field of law… let's say, uh, law firms, courts, government agencies, corporations, public and private agencies, financial institutions, insurance companies and real estate offices. Paralegal is a person who is qualified through education, training or work experience. Um… usually, a paralegal performs substantive legal work that requires knowledge of legal concepts, but they are not allowed to perform particular activities that only attorneys can carry out.

The tasks assigned to a paralegal are diverse and numerous, but, uh… the responsibilities of a paralegal actually varies according to the specialty area involved and the level of his or her education and experience. Typical tasks a paralegal performs under the supervision of an attorney include interviewing clients and witnesses, preparing, drafting and reviewing pleadings, subpoenas, wills, contracts, and other legal documents, and researching factual and legal issues. However, paralegals are not allowed to give legal advice, sign real documents, represent clients in a court of law, or set legal fees. These are all performed by an attorney.

Paralegal이라고도 불리는 변호사 보조원은 법의 여러 영역에서 일을 합니다. 예를 들어 법률회사나, 법정, 정부 기관, 회사, 공공 혹은 사설 기관, 재무 기관, 보험 회사 그리고 부동산 회사 등이지요. 변호사 보조원은 교육, 연수, 혹은 업무 경력 등을 통해서 자격을 얻은 사람입니다. 일반적으로 이들은 법적 지식이 있어야 하는 실질적인 일을 하지만 변호사만이 할 수 있는 특정 업무는

할 수 없게 되어 있습니다.

변호사 보조원에게 할당되는 일은 다양하고 많지만, 실제로 주어지는 일은 이들의 전문 영역, 교육 및 경력 등에 따라서 달라집니다. 변호사의 감독 아래 변호사 보조원이 일반적으로 하는 일은 고객과 목격자를 인터뷰하고 고소장, 소환장, 유언장, 계약서, 그리고 다른 법률 서류 등을 준비하고 작성하고 검토하는 것입니다. 하지만 변호사 보조원은 법적 조언을 준다거나 실제 서류에 서명하거나 법정에서 고객을 대변하거나 혹은 법률비용을 정하는 일 등은 할 수가 없습니다. 이러한 일들은 변호사만이 할 수 있습니다.

2. D

P(W): Now, let's talk about diabetes. Who can tell me the definition of diabetes? No one? Well, let me make it easier for you to understand it here — it's a disease of the hormone insulin. Insulin is secreted by your pancreas and it moves glucose from your bloodstream into your body cells. Uh, I hope you all know what glucose is… it's the form of sugar your body uses for energy, get it? All right. Um, as you might easily imagine, not all people have normal body function. When your cells start to become resistant to the effects of insulin, often due to excessive weight gain, then we've got a problem there. Consequently, you need more insulin in order to dispose of the same amount of glucose. Uh, let's put it this way to make it easier for you to understand: when you knock on the door but nobody answers, what do you do? Just turn away? Well… you would think that the person inside didn't hear it, so you'd bang on the door louder, right? Everyone follow? This condition, called insulin resistance, is the first stage of type-2 diabetes which may account for about 90 to 95 percent of all diagnosed cases of diabetes.

Over time, insulin resistance gets worse which forces your pancreas to pump out enormous amounts of insulin to allow glucose to pass from blood to cells. Your pancreas eventually has trouble keeping up and glucose builds up in the blood and spills into the urine. This chronic high blood sugar is also known as hyperglycemia… well, it's a defining marker of diabetes and it may cause many other calamities such as eye and kidney disease. If insulin resistance continues to increase, some of the insulin-producing beta cells inside your pancreas will stop working altogether, and once this happens, you're gonna have to get daily insulin injections for the rest of your life.

자, 이제 당뇨병에 대해 얘기해 봅시다. 당뇨병이 무엇인지 말해 줄 사람? 아무도 없어요? 여러분이 쉽게 이해할 수 있도록 설명할게요. 당뇨병은 인슐린 호르몬과 관련된 병입니다. 인슐린은 우리 몸의 췌장에서 분비되고 혈류에서 체세포로 포도당을 운반합니다. 포도당이 무엇인지는 다 알겠지요… 이것은 우리 몸이 에너지원으로 이용하는 당의 형태입니다. 이해하지요? 좋아요. 음,

여러분이 쉽게 이해할 수 있듯이, 모든 사람들의 몸이 정상적으로 기능하는 것은 아닙니다. 주로 과도한 체중 증가로 인해 몸의 세포가 인슐린의 작용에 저항력을 갖기 시작하면 문제가 생기게 됩니다. 결과적으로 같은 양의 포도당을 제거하기 위해 더 많은 양의 인슐린이 필요하게 됩니다. 더 쉽게 이해할 수 있도록 이렇게 표현해 보죠. 노크를 했는데 아무도 대답하지 않으면 여러분은 어떻게 하나요? 그냥 돌아가나요? 아마 안에 있는 사람이 노크를 듣지 못했다고 생각할 것이고 더 세게 문을 두드리겠죠? 모두들 이해되나요? 이러한 상태를 인슐린 저항이라고 부르는데, 이것이 제2형 당뇨병의 첫 단계입니다. 제2형 당뇨병은 모든 당뇨병 발병의 약 90에서 95퍼센트를 차지하지요.

시간이 지나면서 인슐린 저항은 심해지게 되고, 이것은 혈류에서 체세포로 포도당을 통과시키기 위해 췌장으로 하여금 엄청난 양의 인슐린을 생산하게 합니다. 결국 췌장에 문제가 생기게 되고 포도당이 혈류에 쌓여서 소변으로 흘러 들어가게 되지요. 이렇게 만성적으로 혈당이 높아지는 것을 고혈당증이라고 하는데, 이것은 당뇨병을 결정하는 지표이며 눈병과 신장병 등의 다른 질병들의 원인이 됩니다. 인슐린 저항이 계속해서 증가하게 되면 췌장에서 인슐린을 생산하는 베타 세포가 한꺼번에 작동을 멈추게 되고, 이러한 문제가 발생하게 되면 평생토록 매일 인슐린을 맞으며 살아야 합니다.

3. A

P(M): All right, so... um, let's start now. Uh, we've been talking about cost accounting for the last few weeks. There are at least four approaches to cost accounting and we've already covered three of them: Standard Cost Accounting, Activity-based Costing, and Marginal Costing. Today we'll talk about Throughput Accounting.

Throughput Accounting or TA was first proposed by Eliyahu Goldratt. It was proposed as an alternative to Cost Accounting, which is an organization's internal method used to measure efficiency. Well, theoretically, TA tries to eliminate bottlenecks within the organization that hinders the velocity at which products move through the organization, thereby improving profit performance. Goldratt thought that each organization has a goal or a mission and that its value would be increased by better decisions. What do you think the goal for a company is? Will?

M: Um, uh... I guess, increasing its profit?

P: Yes, that's right, increasing its profit now and in the future.

W: Does TA apply to non-profit organizations?

P: Of course, but those non-profit organizations should develop a goal that makes sense in their own cases. Okay, then, who can tell me what "throughput" in Throughput Accounting means? ... Nobody? Well, then, um, let me explain this first... measures of income and expense which TA uses: T or Throughput, I or Investment, and OE or Operating Expense.

P: 좋아요, 이제 시작합시다. 지금까지 몇 주 동안 원가 계산에 대해 얘기했었

는데요. 원가 계산에는 적어도 네 가지 접근법이 있고 이미 그 중 세 가지에 대해 얘기했지요. 표준원가계산, 활동기준원가계산, 그리고 한계원가입니다. 오늘은 현금창출회계에 대해 이야기해 봅시다.

TA라고도 불리는 현금창출회계는 엘리야후 골드랫에 의해 처음 제시되었어요. 이것은 원가 계산에 대한 대안으로 제시되었는데, 원가 계산이란 효율을 평가하기 위해 조직이 내적으로 사용하는 방법이에요. 이론적으로 보면 TA는 조직 내에서 상품이 움직이는 속도를 방해하는 병목 현상을 제거하려고 노력하는데요, 이렇게 함으로써 이윤 성취를 개선하려고 합니다. 골드랫은 각 조직들이 목표나 사명을 갖고 있고 보다 나은 결정에 의해 그 가치가 상승할 것이라고 생각했어요. 회사의 목표란 무엇일까요? 윌?

M: 음... 글쎄요, 이윤을 높이는 것이요?

P: 맞았어요. 현재와 미래의 이윤을 높이는 것이죠.

W: TA가 비영리 단체에도 적용이 되나요?

P: 물론이죠. 하지만 이러한 비영리 단체들은 그에 맞는 목표를 설정해야 해요. 좋아요, 그러면 누가 현금창출회계(Throughput Accounting)의 throughput이 무슨 뜻인지 말해 볼까요? 아무도 없어요? 그러면 이것 먼저 설명하죠... TA가 사용하는 수입과 비용의 측정법은 Throughput(작업처리량)을 나타내는 T, Investment(투자)를 나타내는 I, 그리고 Operating Expense(작업 비용)를 나타내는 OE예요.

4. C, D

P(W): BSE, an acronym for Bovine Spongiform Encephalopathy, is also known as the Mad Cow Disease. Many of you have probably heard about it — it's an ever-looming nightmare to the cattle industry. It's a slowly progressive, degenerative, fatal disease which affects the central nervous system of adult cattle. Well, if it only claims cattle's lives, you might say, what's the problem, then? The cattle are supposed to die anyways, right? Well, yes, if it only kills the cattle alone; but what it might also do is that it might affect the humans who eat beef from a cow that's been infected by Mad Cow Disease. In the 1980s and '90s, 180,000 livestock were infected by BSE in Britain which also claimed dozens of human lives.

Let's first talk about the cause of BSE. The exact cause of BSE is not known for sure, but scientists think that the likely cause is prion, an infectious form of a type of protein, which is normally found in animals. It kills the cow's brain cells, forming sponge-like holes in the brain. The cow that has BSE behaves strangely and eventually dies. Um, and then, there's a disease similar to BSE called Creutzfeldt-Jacob Disease or CJD that's found in people. When people eat contaminated beef products from BSE-affected cattle, a new variant form of CJD, or nvCJD, occurs.

소해면상 뇌증(Bovine Spongiform Encephalopathy)은 광우병으로도 잘 알려져 있습니다. 여러분은 이미 이것에 대해 들어본 적이 있을 것입니다 — 이 병은 쇠고기 산업에 도사리고 있는 악몽과도 같은 것이지요. 이것은 천천히 진행하는 치명적인 퇴행성 질병으로 소의 중앙 신경 체계에 영향을 미치

게 됩니다. 이 병이 소의 목숨만 앗아간다면 무슨 문제가 있냐고 말할 수도 있겠지요... 소는 어차피 죽는 것이니까요. 그렇죠? 물론 그렇습니다. 이 병이 소만 죽인다면 말이지요. 하지만 이 병은 광우병에 걸린 쇠고기를 먹은 사람에게도 영향을 줍니다. 1980년대와 90년대에 영국에서 18만 마리가 이 병에 걸렸는데, 이것은 또한 수십 명의 사람들의 목숨을 앗아갔습니다.

우선 광우병의 원인을 알아봅시다. 광우병의 정확한 원인은 확실히 알려지지는 않았지만, 과학자들은 일반적으로 동물에게서 발견되는 감염성 단백질의 형태인 프라이온이 아마 그 원인일 것이라고 생각합니다. 프라이온은 소의 뇌세포를 죽이는데, 뇌에 스펀지처럼 구멍이 생깁니다. 광우병에 걸린 소는 이상한 행동을 하며 결국에는 죽게 됩니다. 그리고 광우병과 비슷한 크로이츠펠트 야콥병, 혹은 CJD라고 불리는 병이 있는데, 이것은 사람에게서 발견됩니다. 사람이 광우병에 걸린 오염된 쇠고기를 먹으면, CJD의 변종, 즉 nvCJD가 발병하게 됩니다.

Exercise

	1.	2.	3.	4.	5.
P.1	1. A	2. B	3. D		
P.2	1. C	2. B	3. A		
P.3	1. D	2. C	3. D		
P.4	1. D	2. C	3. B, D		
P.5	1. B	2. A	3. C		
P.6	1. D	2. D	3. A		
P.7	1. C	2. D	3. A		
P.8	1. B	2. B	3. C		
P.9	1. A	2. B	3. D	4. C	5. D
P.10	1. C	2. A	3. A, C		

Passage 1

1. A **2.** B **3.** D

P(M): Well, when we learn how to write... how to express our ideas in full sentences, well, cohesive devices are highly crucial. They turn separate clauses, sentences and paragraphs into connected prose. They signal the relationships between ideas and they help you understand what the writer is trying to say. However, it has been found that English language students experience much problem when learning English because of these linking devices. Why is that? Well, have you ever wondered how to teach writing to a 5-year-old? What about a 10th-grade-student? What about ESL students? The method of teaching writing to these different groups is different from each other, and perhaps many ESL students are misleadingly taught that some of these cohesive devices can be used interchangeably. Now, here comes the confusion.

우리가 글을 쓰는 것을 배울 때, 즉, 우리의 생각을 완전한 문장으로 표현하는 법을 배울 때, 응집 장치가 매우 중요합니다. 이는 독립적인 절, 문장, 그리고 문단을 하나의 산문으로 바꿔줍니다. 이것은 아이디어간의 관계를 알리고 작가의 의도를 파악하게 도와줍니다. 하지만 영어를 배우는 학생들의 경우, 이러한 연결 장치로 인해 영어를 배우는 데 많은 어려움을 겪고 있다는 것이 밝혀졌습니다. 왜 그런 것일까요? 여러분은 5살짜리에게 어떻게 작문을 가르칠지 생각해 본 적이 있나요? 10학년 학생은 어떤가요? ESL 학생은 어떤가요? 각기 다른 집단의 학생들에게 작문을 가르치는 방법은 각각 서로 다른데, 아마 많은 ESL 학생들이 이러한 응집 장치가 호환되어 사용될 수 있다고 잘못 배우고 있을지도 모릅니다. 바로 여기서 혼란이 오는 것입니다.

❶ What does the professor mainly discuss?

주제가 말머리에 명확하게 제시되지 않는 경우에는 지문의 keyword를 찾아야 하는데, 교수는 "cohesive device"의 역할을 설명한 후, ESL 학생들이 이것을 쉽게 배우지 못하는 이유를 설명한다. 따라서 정답은 A이다. 이 지문은 미국의 ESL 학생들에 대해 설명하는 것이 아니므로 선택지 B는 정답에서 지워야 하며, 선택지 C와 D는 너무 좁은 범위를 다루고 있으므로 정답이 될 수 없다.

❷ According to the professor, what is a cohesive device?

전체적인 지문의 내용으로 보아 cohesive device란 생각을 언어로 표현할 때 사용하는 언어적 장치임을 알 수 있다. 따라서 "물질적 재료"라고 한 선택지 A는 정답이 될 수 없으며, "ESL 학생들이 배우기 쉬운 정신적으로 만들어지는 장치"라고 한 선택지 C 역시 틀린 답이다. 선택지 D는 지문의 내용과 상반된 내용을 다루고 있으므로 틀린 선택이다.

❸ What can be inferred about the reason why many English learners have problems with learning cohesive devices?

교수는 영어를 배우는 학생이 cohesive device를 습득하기 어려운 이유는 많은 cohesive device들이 서로 호환되어 오용되기 때문에 혼동스러워지기 때문이라고 설명한다. 따라서 정답은 선택지 D이다.

Passage 2

1. C **2.** B **3.** A

P(W): Let's imagine a situation here. You're biking up a hill, pedaling as hard as you can. You're running on a treadmill at a local gym, or you're lifting a 15-pound weight. Then you realize that your back is all wet and so is your face — yes, you sweat, or perspire. Your body works best when the body temperature is about 98.6 degrees Fahrenheit, or 37 degrees Celsius. We've talked about this last time, so you remember, right? Well, hopefully. Anyways, when your body heat increases more than that, your brain will automatically function to lower your body temperature by perspiration. The part of your brain that controls temperature is called the hypothalamus, and the special glands in your skin that makes sweat is called... well, sweat glands, obviously. Your sweat mainly consists of water and sodium chloride, which is basically table salt.

자, 이런 상황을 상상해 보죠. 여러분들이 자전거로 언덕을 전력 질주하고 있다고 칩시다. 인근 체육관에서 런닝머신을 뛰거나, 15파운드 무게의 아령을 들고 있다고 합시다. 곧 등이 땀에 젖어있고 얼굴도 마찬가지라는 것을 깨닫습니다 – 네, 땀을 흘리는 것이죠. 여러분의 몸은 체온이 화씨 98.6도 혹은 섭씨 37도일 때 기능을 가장 잘 발휘합니다. 이것은 지난번에 얘기했으니 기억하죠? 그렇길 바래요. 어쨌든 체온이 그 이상 올라가면, 땀을 흘려서 체온을 낮추기 위해 뇌가 자동으로 기능하게 됩니다. 체온을 조절하는 뇌의 부위는 연수라고 불리며, 땀을 생성하는 피부 조직은... 물론 땀샘이라고 불립니다. 땀은 주로 물과, 소디움 클로라이드, 즉 소금으로 이뤄져 있습니다.

❶ What is the main topic of the lecture?

교수는 땀을 흘릴 수 있는 조건, 발한하는 이유 및 땀의 구성분을 설명한다. 이러한 내용을 가장 종합적으로 담고 있는 선택지는 C이다. "체육관에서 운동하는 법"이라고 한 선택지 A는 정답이 아니며, 선택지 B와 D는 지문에서 잠시 언급된 제한적인 내용을 담고 있으므로 틀린 선택이다.

❷ According to the professor, why do people sweat?

"When your body heat increases more than that, your brain will automatically function to lower your body temperature by perspiration"라고 한 교수의 말에서 답을 찾을 수 있다. 정답은 B. "체온을 낮추기 위해서"이다.

❸ According to the professor, what does human sweat mainly consists of?

지문의 마지막에 정답이 나와 있다. 정답은 A. "water and sodium chloride"이다.

Passage 3

1. D **2.** C **3.** D

P(M): We've been talking about the English language for the last couple of weeks. Now, let's turn our attention to where English language got its form from... you know, the history of the English language. If you did your readings from last class, you would already know that English is actually one of the languages that were heavily influenced by other languages such as Latin, French, German, and so on. All right, who can give me an example of a common English word that was initially borrowed from... let's say, French?

W: Um, like, ballet, camouflage, entrepreneur, etiquette, rendezvous and so on?

P: Very good, Shauna. Well, most of you would already recognize that the words that Shauna just mentioned were borrowed from the French language. Then what about these words: crayon, debris, marinade, mortgage, nasal, publicity, soup, and velocity?

M: Well, aren't they just, uh, plain English words?

P: Many people think they are original English words, but actually, they are borrowed words from the French language as well.

W: Amazing!

P: Isn't it? Well, what about borrowed words from German? Clock, clown, hamburger, luck, school, tackle, swindle, even dollar.

W: Interesting, they're all German? Um, Professor Mitchell, then what other languages are there that the English language borrowed its words from?

P: Well, you've heard a lot of Spanish words used among Americans in normal everyday conversations, right? Like the words like... uh, salsa, alligator, guitar, and tuna are one of the most widely known Spanish loanwords. Or other words like alcohol, algebra, hazard, uh... mattress, satin, and zero came from Arabic.

M: Man, it seems like the English language isn't very original anymore.

P: You think so? Well, let's talk about that for the next... uh... thirty minutes or so. Well, the history of English is divided into three periods called Old English, Middle English, and Modern English. First, let's talk about the earliest period. The Germanic language spoken in the southern part of the island of Britain before the Norman Conquest in 1066 is called Old English. Although it is quite different from English in sound and appearance, the Germanic language is widely considered the ancestor of the Modern English spoken today. Let's talk about this first.

P: 지난 몇 주간 영어에 대해 이야기를 해 보았는데요, 이제 영어가 그 형태를 어디서 갖게 됐는지 살펴봅시다... 영어의 역사 말입니다. 저번 시간에 내준 분량을 읽었다면 영어가 라틴어, 불어, 독일어 등의 여러 언어

에서 크게 영향을 받은 언어 중 하나라는 것을 이미 알고 있을 거예요. 자, 그렇다면 예를 들어 프랑스어에서 차용되서 자주 쓰이는 영어 단어의 예를 들어 볼 사람?

W: 발레, 위장, 기업가, 에티켓, 랑데부 같은 단어들이 있어요.

P: 좋아요, 셔나. 셔나가 방금 얘기한 단어들이 프랑스어에서 차용된 단어들이라는 걸 여러분들 대부분은 알고 있겠죠. 그렇다면 크레용, 파편, 매리네이드, 저당, 비음, 광고, 수프, 그리고 속도 같은 단어들은 어떨까요?

M: 그 단어들은 그냥 단순한 영어 단어 아닌가요?

P: 많은 사람들이 이 단어들이 원래 영어 단어라고 생각하지만, 사실은 이 단어 역시 프랑스어에서 빌려온 차용어랍니다.

W: 놀랍네요!

P: 그렇죠? 자, 그러면 독일어에서 온 차용어로는 무엇이 있을까요? 시계, 어릿광대, 햄버거, 운, 학교, 태클, 사기, 심지어 달러라는 단어도 있어요.

W: 흥미롭네요. 그 단어들이 전부 독일어란 말씀이시죠? 미첼 교수님, 그렇다면 영어는 또 어떤 언어의 단어를 차용했나요?

P: 미국인들이 일상 생활 회화에서 스페인어를 많이 사용하는 걸 들어봤을 거예요, 그렇죠? 살사, 악어, 기타, 그리고 참치라는 단어들이 널리 알려진 스페인어 차용어예요. 또한 알코올, 대수학, 위험, 매트리스, 새틴, 그리고 제로라는 단어들은 아랍어에서 온 말이죠.

M: 그렇군요. 영어라는 언어가 그다지 독창적인 것 같지는 않네요.

P: 그렇게 생각되나요? 그렇다면 지금부터 한 30분 동안 이것에 대해 얘기해 봅시다. 영어의 역사는 고대 영어, 중세 영어, 그리고 현대 영어의 세 시기로 나뉘어요. 우선 초기 영어에 대해 얘기해 보죠. 1066년 노르망 정복 전 영국 섬의 남부에서 사용된 독일어 형식의 언어를 고대 영어라고 해요. 영어와는 소리 및 형태에서 꽤 차이가 나지만, 이 독일어 형식의 언어는 오늘날 사용되는 현대 영어의 원형으로 널리 인정되고 있어요. 이것에 대해 먼저 얘기해 봅시다.

❶ **What is the main topic of the discussion?**
지문 초반의 교수의 말에서 오늘의 토론은 영어의 역사, 즉 영어가 어떻게 현재의 형태를 갖게 되었는지에 대해 이야기할 것임을 알 수 있다. 또한 영어에 영향을 주게 된 많은 외국어들(프랑스어, 독일어, 스페인어 등)에 대해서도 언급한다. 따라서 정답은 D이다. 선택지 A는 너무 광범위하면서도 언급되지 않은 내용을 담고 있다. 선택지 B는 너무 좁은 내용을 담고 있으며 선택지 C는 지문 내용에서 언급되지 않았기 때문에 답이 될 수 없다.

❷ **According to the discussion, which of the following statements is NOT true?**
지문에서 "crayon, mortgage, publicity" 등의 단어들은 프랑스어의 차용어라고 했으므로 정답은 C이다.

❸ **What will the professor probably discuss next?**
강의의 마지막에서 교수는 고대 영어와 현대 영어의 발음과 형태가 서로 다르다며 먼저 이것에 대해 논해보자고 한다. 따라서 고대 영어와 현대 영어의 발음과 형태상의 차이점에 대해 이어서 설명할 것임을 알 수 있다.

Passage 4

1. D   **2.** C   **3.** B, D

P(W): Then, how would you know that this masterpiece, which, if you see it with your bare eyes, bears exactly identical features of the painter, is the real production of the painter? What if you examined the art piece and concluded that it was a forgery, a scam, but later it proves to be the original piece of the master? Well, here's where science interferes... ranging from polarizing light microscopy to infrared X-ray reflectography. Advances in scientific techniques started to help answering many of the old questions and solve quandaries in the world of art: "Is this piece fake or real? Was the piece of art actually drawn by the artist himself or other forgers with masterful skills?"

Well, until the 1950s, in order to find out whether a debated work was authentic or forged, people had to rely on literature searches and careful examination using conventional magnification. Now, scientists and art historians use scientific analysis to pin-point the age of a painting by looking at various factors, thereby uncovering the authenticity of the painting. For example, when scientists tried to distinguish the work of a Dutch artist Vermeer, *Young Woman Seated at the Virginals*, they found out that the pigment lapis lazuli, which produces a beautiful pure blue color, was used in the drawing. Um, lapis lazuli was a brightly-colored semiprecious stone and it was very expensive. During the 17th century, artists generally used it in a prominent way in painting, you know, such as when, um, coloring a woman's clothing or something like that. But Vermeer used lapis lazuli on chairs or in the background as well. Another thing that they've found in Vermeer's painting was by using X-ray examination of the canvas. It turned out that the warp and weft of the canvas of the painting matched the canvas used in another famous Vermeer painting, *The Lacemaker*. This revealed that the canvas cloth used for both paintings were from the same cloth.

그렇다면 육안으로 봤을 때엔 그 작가의 특징을 그대로 가지고 있는 이 작품이 진품인지를 어떻게 알 수 있을까요? 만약 작품을 검사하고 이것이 위조품이며 사기라고 결론지었지만 나중에 원본이라는 것이 밝혀진다면 어떻게 될까요? 여기서 바로 과학이 개입됩니다. 광학 편광법에서 엑스레이 반사 검사까지 그 범위는 다양하지요. 과학 기술의 진보는 예술 세계에서 오랫동안 존재한 질문에 답하는 데 도움을 주기 시작했습니다. 바로 이것입니다. "이 작품은 가짜인가 진짜인가? 이 예술 작품이 작가 본인의 것인가 아니면 모조 솜씨가 뛰어난 위조자의 모조품인가?" 1950년대까지는 논란이 되는 작품이 진품인지 모조품인지 알아내기 위해 사람들은 문서를 조사하고 기존의 돋보기를 이용하여 면밀하게 검사하는 방법에 의존할 수 밖에 없었습니다. 오늘날 과학자들과 미술사가들은 과학적 검사를 사용하여 다양한 요소를 살펴봄으로써 작품의 정확한 제작 시기를 알아내고, 이를 통해 작품의 진위 여부를 확인합니다. 예를 들어 과학자들이 네덜란드 화가인 베르메르의 작품 "버지널 앞의 소녀"를 조사했을 때, 그들은 아름다운 천연 파란색을 내는 청금석의 색소가 그림에 사용되었다는 것을 알아냈습니다. 청금석은 밝은 색의 준보석이었고 매우 비쌌습니다. 17세기에 미술가들은 일반적으로 이것을 그림의 두드러진 곳에 사용했는데, 가령 여인의 옷을 그릴 때 등입니다. 그러나 베르메르는 청금석 색소를 의자와 배경에도 썼습니다. 그들은 또한 캔버스에 엑스레이를 사용하여 또 다른 사실을 알게되었습니다. 캔버스의 날실과 씨실이 베르메르의 다른 유명한 작품인 "레이스 짜는 여인"의 것과 같다는 것이 밝혀졌습니다. 이것은 두 작품이 같은 천에 그린 것이라는 것을 드러냈습니다.

❶ **What does the professor mainly discuss?**

지문의 첫머리에서 교수는 작품의 진위 여부를 어떻게 가려내는지 질문을 던진 후, 작품의 진위를 가려내기 위해 오늘날 사용되는 기술들을 설명한다. 따라서 정답은 D가 되며, 선택지 A와 B는 너무 좁은 내용을 담고 있기 때문에 답이 될 수 없다. 베르메르의 작품이 언급된 이유는 작품의 진위를 가려낼 때 사용되는 기술을 설명하기 위해 언급된 것일 뿐이므로 베르메르와 그의 작품이 전체 지문의 주제는 아니다.

❷ **What aspect of a painting do scientists and art historians try to discover in order to verify its authenticity?**

작품의 진위 여부를 가려내기 위해 과학자들과 미술사가들은 작품의 색소를 분석하고 캔버스의 엑스레이를 찍는데, 그 이유는 사용된 재료가 미술가의 시대와 맞는지를 알기 위해서이다. 따라서 답은 C이다.

❸ **According to the professor, what was mentioned as the method to distinguish the authenticity of *Young Woman Seated at the Virginals*?**

두번째 문단에서 보면, 사용된 색소를 분석하고 엑스레이 분석을 통해 진위 여부를 가려냈다고 한다. 따라서 답은 선택지 B와 D이다.

1. B   **2.** A   **3.** C

P(M): Also known as the purple Kansas coneflower, Echinacea once grew all over the American plains. Native Americans used the flower as a remedy for ailments, such as colds, flu, and infections. They were so heavily dependent on the healing power of the flower that they even used it to heal wounds and to treat bee stings and rattlesnake bites. It has long been valued in Europe and is particularly popular in Germany, where it's used for a variety of ailments. A new generation of Americans is also beginning to realize its benefits, so much so that it's now the best-selling herb on the US medicinal herb market.

It is believed that Echinacea stimulates the overall activity of the cells that fight infection. Whereas antibiotics attack the bacteria itself, Echinacea enhances the fighting ability of our immune cells so that they can attack bacteria, viruses, and abnormal cells more efficiently.

Much research has been done into Echinacea, and, according to a study from 2002, when a group of women was given Echinacea over the course of six weeks, they began to show improvements in overall physical and emotional health after just four weeks.

보라색 캔자스 꽃으로도 알려진 에키나세아는 한때 미국 평원 전지역에서 자랐어요. 미국 원주민들은 이 꽃을 감기, 독감, 염증의 치료제로 사용했어요. 그들은 이것의 치유력을 전적으로 믿어서 상처를 치료하고 심지어 벌에 쏘이거나 뱀에 물린 것을 치유하기 위해서도 이것을 사용했죠. 유럽에서는 그 가치를 오래전에 인정받았는데, 특히 독일에서 인기가 많고 여러 종류의 병에 사용되고 있어요. 미국의 신세대들도 이 효과를 믿기 시작해서, 요즘 미국 약재 시장에서 가장 많이 팔리는 제품이 되었어요.

에키나세아는 염증에 대항하는 세포의 전반적인 활동을 자극하는 것으로 알려져 있어요. 항생제가 박테리아 자체를 공격하는 것에 비해, 에키나세아는 우리의 면역 세포의 저항력을 강화시켜서 박테리아, 바이러스, 비정상 세포를 보다 효과적으로 공격할 수 있도록 해요.

에키나세아에 대해 많은 연구가 이뤄졌고, 2002년 연구에 의하면 여성 집단에게 6주간 에키나세아를 복용하도록 했을 때 4주만에 신체적, 감정적 건강이 전반적으로 개선되었다고 해요.

❶ **What is the lecture mainly about?**

교수는 먼저 에키나세아가 과거에 사용된 예를 언급하며 이것이 현재 약재로 사용되고 있다고 소개한다. 따라서 답은 B이다. 선택지 A와 D는 지문에서 잠시 언급된 것으로 전체적인 주제가 될 수 없으며, 선택지 C는 지문의 내용과 상반된 내용이다.

❷ **What did Native Americans use Echinacea for?**

미국 원주민들은 에키나세아를 감기, 독감, 염증의 치료제로 사용했다고 했으므로 정답은 A이다.

❸ **According to the lecture, how does Echinacea heal diseases?**

에키나세아는 박테리아 자체를 공격하는 것이 아니라 인체의 면역 세포를 강화시켜 질병을 치유한다고 했다. 선택지 A는 항생제의 역할을 설명한 것이다. 선택지 B의 내용은 지문에 언급된 바가 없으며 선택지 D는 위 내용과 상반되는 내용이다.

Passage 6

1. D **2.** D **3.** A

P(W): Dixieland is a name of an early style of jazz which started in New Orleans, Louisiana at the start of the 20th century and spread to Chicago, New York, Kansas City, and across the Midwest to California. It is usually considered as the first type of jazz, and it was quite popular among the general public for a time being. Dixieland jazz is also known as traditional jazz or New Orleans jazz. Its name came from the band, Original Dixieland Jazz Band, the first band ever to make a jazz recording in 1917. Common instruments used in a Dixieland-jazz style group included trumpet, cornet, clarinet, trombone, saxophone, banjo, piano, drums, string base, and tuba.

딕시랜드는 루이지애나 주의 뉴올리언스에서 시작된 재즈의 초기 형태를 나타내는 이름입니다. 이것은 20세기 초에 시작되어 시카고, 뉴욕, 캔자스시티, 그리고 캘리포니아 중서부로 확산되었습니다. 딕시랜드는 일반적으로 재즈의 최초 형태로 여겨지고, 대중에게 한동안 상당히 인기가 있었습니다. 딕시랜드 재즈는 전통 재즈 혹은 뉴올리언스 재즈로도 알려져 있습니다. 이 이름은 1917년 최초로 재즈 녹음을 한 첫 밴드인 Original Dixieland Jass Band라는 이름에서 유래했습니다. 딕시랜드 재즈 스타일의 그룹에서 사용한 일반적인 악기로는 트럼펫, 코넷, 클라리넷, 트롬본, 색소폰, 밴조, 피아노, 드럼, 현악 베이스 및 튜바가 있습니다.

❶ **What is the topic of the lecture?**

교수는 딕시랜드 재즈에 대해 소개하며 이것이 어디에서 유래되었는지도 언급한다. 선택지 A와 B의 내용은 지문에 잠시 언급된 것으로, 주제라고 보기는 힘들다. 선택지 C의 내용은 지문에 언급되어 있지 않다. 따라서 가장 좋은 답은 선택지 D이다.

❷ **What is NOT true about Dixieland?**

"Dixieland jazz is also known as traditional jazz or New Orleans jazz"에서 선택지 A는 맞는 선택이며, "spread to Chicago, New York, Kansas City, and across the Midwest to California"에서 B 역시 맞는 선택임을 알 수 있다. "It is usually considered as the first type of jazz"를

보면 선택지 C 역시 맞는 선택이다. 지문에서 딕시랜드는 20세기 초반에 시작되었다고 했기 때문에 선택지 D가 틀렸음을 알 수 있다.

❸ **According to the lecture, where did Dixieland get its name from?**

지문에서는 딕시랜드의 이름이 그 당시의 유명한 재즈 밴드의 이름(Original Dixieland Jass Band)에서 유래했다고 하며, 이 밴드가 최초로 재즈 녹음을 한 밴드라고 했으므로 선택지 A가 정답이다.

Passage 7

1. C **2.** D **3.** A

P(M): Okay. Um, I hope that you have all read John Bunyan's book, *The Pilgrim's Progress*. I gave you a month, so I believe you've all read it.... So, let's talk about Bunyan and his book before we delve more deeply into this masterpiece. Well, first of all, Bunyan was born in the parish of Elstow, England. He was the most famous of the Puritan writers and preachers. Of his many other books, he is most well-known for *The Pilgrim's Progress*, which is arguably one of the most famous Christian books in history. Well, Bunyan wrote this book when he was imprisoned for preaching without a license. Some people also argue that he went to jail because he was a Baptist... people who refused to worship in the Anglican church were called nonconformists and were sent to jail back then.

Uh... all right. Here's an interesting fact about back then... the established church in England was the Anglican Church, and people who belonged to that church were called establishmentarians. Um, it gets a little bit confusing here... let me write this down for you so you know how to pronounce it better... um, you don't have to memorize this or write it down... but... um... well, so, here we go... people who opposed the state church, like Bunyan, were called disestablishmentarians. Getting longer and longer, huh? Giving us our favorite long word... and, un, people opposed to disestablishmentarians were called antidisestablishmentarians. Well, it's not that confusing once you get the idea...

All right, let's get back to our topic, shall we? Okay. Um, the first part of this book was published in London in 1678 and the second in 1684. Its full title is *The Pilgrim's Progress from This World to That Which is to Come*. It... it's basically an allegory. Allegory was first invented by Greeks and then adopted by Christians later.

좋습니다. 자, 여러분 모두 존 버니언의 저서 "천로역정"을 읽었기 바랍니다. 한 달을 주었으니, 모두 읽었으리라 믿습니다. 이제 이 걸작에 대해 더 상세하게 알아 보기 전에 버니언과 그의 책에 대해 얘기해 봅시다. 우선, 버니언은 영국 엘스토우 교구에서 태어났습니다. 그는 청교도 저자와 설교자 중에 가장 유명했던 사람입니다. 그는 많은 저서 중, "천로역정"으로 가장 유명한데, 이는 논란의 여지는 있지만 역사상 가장 유명한 기독교 저서 중 하나라고 할 수 있습니다. 버니언은 면허 없이 설교했다는 이유로 옥에 갇혀 있는 동안 이 책을 썼습니다. 어떤 이들은 버니언이 침례교도였기 때문에 감옥에 갔다고도 하는데요, 그 당시에 영국 국교를 믿기를 거부한 사람들은 불순응주의자라고 불렸고, 옥에 갇혔습니다.

자, 그 당시의 상황에 대해 재미있는 사실이 있습니다. 영국의 국교는 성공회였는데, 성공회에 속한 사람들을 국교 신봉자라고 불렀습니다. 자, 여기서부터 조금씩 복잡해지기 시작하는데요, 발음을 더 쉽게 하기 위해 칠판에 적겠습니다. 이것을 외우거나 받아 적을 필요는 없어요. 자... 됐습니다. 버니언과 같이 성공회에 반대한 사람들을 국교제도 폐지론자라고 불렀습니다. 자, 단어가 점점 더 길어지죠? 그리고 국교제도 폐지론자들을 반대한 사람들을 반(反)국교제도 폐지론자라고 했습니다. 일단 핵심 아이디어만 파악하면 그다지 어렵지 않아요.

자, 그럼 이제 주제로 돌아갑시다. 이 책의 처음 부분은 런던에서 1678년에, 그리고 다음 부분은 1684년에 출판됐습니다. 전체 제목은 The Pilgrim's Progress from This World to That Which is to Come입니다. 이 책은 기본적으로 우화입니다. 우화는 그리스인들이 처음 만들었는데, 나중에 기독교인들이 차용했습니다.

❶ **What is the main topic of the lecture?**

교수는 전체적으로 존 버니언의 삶과 그의 저서 "천로역정"에 대해 설명하고 있다. 선택지 A는 너무 좁은 선택이며, 선택지 B와 D는 지문에 언급된 바가 없으므로 선택지 C가 올바른 답이다.

❷ **Why does the professor mention establishmentarians?**

Establishmentarian과 그와 관련된 몇 개의 용어들을 설명하고 나서, 교수는 "All right, let's get back to our topic, shall we?"라고 말함으로써 방금 한 얘기들이 그다지 중요한 내용이 아님을 암시하고 있다. 또한 용어들을 칠판에 적을 때 받아 적지 않아도 된다고 말한 것을 통해, 교수가 이 용어들을 언급한 이유가 주제에서 잠시 벗어나 다른 이야기를 하기 위해서라는 것을 알 수 있다. 따라서 정답은 D이다.

❸ **How does the professor feel about The Pilgrim's Progress?**

"He is most well-known for The Pilgrim's Progress, which is arguably the most famous Christian books in history"라고 한 부분에서, 어느 정도 논쟁은 있을 수 있지만 교수는 "천로역정"이 가장 유명한 기독교 저서 중 하나라고 생각하는 것을 엿볼 수 있다. 따라서 정답은 A이다. 교수가 이 책이 청교도에 의해 쓰여졌다는 것에 대해 무관심하게 생각하는지는 알 수 없으므로 선택지 B는 정답이 아니며, 선택지 C는 지문에서 알기 힘들기 때문에 답이 아니다. 어려운 우화가 사용되었다는 것에 대해서도 열정적으로 생각하는지는 지문만으로는 알 수 없으므로 D 역시 오답이다.

Passage 8

1. B   **2.** B   **3.** C

P(W): All right, let's go on with our topic today. Stephen, can you tell me what osteoporosis is?

M: Um, it's a disease in your bone...

P: Yes, go on.

M: Uh, the density of your bone is somehow very low because... I guess, like, you don't have as much calcium as you should have in your bone? So you break your bones a lot?

P: Well, Stephen, you do have the idea, so why stutter? Be more confident from now on. Well, as Stephen has just said; yes, osteoporosis is a disease in which bone mineral density or BMD is reduced, bone microarchitecture is disrupted, and the variety and amount of non-collagenous proteins in the bone is altered. In other words, there's an imbalance between bone resorption and bone formation — either bone resorption is disproportionate or bone formation is diminished. When you have osteoporosis, you end up with a literally porous bone that kind of looks like a sponge. Let's see the picture here... the one on the left is a picture of a normal bone, and the one on the right is the one with osteoporosis. See the difference?

W: Oh, now I get it. It looks like the bone with osteoporosis is very feeble and weak.

P: That's right. Normal bones are composed of protein, collagen, and calcium, but bones with osteoporosis can easily be fractured with only a minor fall or injury. They can be cracked as in a hip fracture or can be collapsed. Common areas of osteoporosis-related bone fractures include the spine, hips, and wrists, although almost anywhere in the bone area can be influenced by osteoporosis.

W: Well, why do you have osteoporosis anyways? Is there any way to prevent it?

P: Well, let me tell you this first — as people get older and grow feebler, the amount of bone in their body decreases slowly but constantly. Usually, though, women are more susceptible to osteoporosis since they don't develop as much bone as they should while they are young. Also, the rate of bone loss in women is greater than in men, especially when they become pregnant and breast-feed their babies if they do not have a sufficient intake of calcium. Post menopausal women have the most serious risk of osteoporosis because estrogen deficiency following menopause will cause a rapid reduction in BMD. Interestingly, sedentary lifestyle that we have nowadays might also increase osteoporosis.

P: 좋아요. 그럼 오늘의 주제로 넘어갑시다. 스티븐, 골다공증이 무엇인지 말해 보겠어요?

M: 어, 골다공증은 뼈에 생기는 질병인데…

P: 네, 계속해 보세요.

M: 어, 그러니까 뼈의 밀도가 매우 낮은데, 제 생각에는 뼈에 있어야 할 만큼의 칼슘이 없어서가 아닐까요? 그래서 뼈가 자주 부러지고요.

P: 스티븐, 대충 감은 잡았는데 왜 머뭇거리나요? 앞으로는 좀 더 자신감을 가지세요. 스티븐이 방금 얘기한대로, 골다공증은 뼈의 구성 성분, 즉 BMD가 줄어들고, 미세 구조가 파괴되며, 비콜라겐성 단백질의 양과 종류가 변경되는 질병이에요. 다시 말해 뼈의 흡수와 형성이 불균형을 이루는 것이죠. 뼈의 흡수 작용이 불균형을 이루거나 뼈의 형성이 감소되거나 둘 중 하나예요. 골다공증에 걸리게 되면 마치 스펀지처럼 말 그대로 뼈에 구멍이 숭숭 뚫리게 돼요. 여기 사진을 봅시다. 왼쪽 사진이 정상적인 뼈이고 오른쪽이 골다공증에 걸린 뼈예요. 차이점이 보이지요?

W: 아, 이제 알겠어요. 골다공증이 있는 뼈가 굉장히 약해 보여요.

P: 맞아요. 정상적인 뼈는 단백질과 콜라겐, 그리고 칼슘으로 구성되어 있지만 골다공증에 걸린 뼈는 살짝 넘어지거나 부상을 당해도 쉽게 부러져요. 골반뼈가 부러지는 식으로 쪼개지거나 함몰되는 경우가 있어요. 골다공증과 관련해 골절되기 쉬운 부위로는 척추뼈, 엉덩이뼈, 그리고 손목 등이 있지만, 대부분의 뼈가 골다공증의 영향을 받을 수 있어요.

W: 그런데 골다공증은 왜 걸리나요? 예방할 수 있는 방법은 없나요?

P: 이 얘기를 먼저 해 줄게요 – 사람이 나이가 들고 약해지면서 몸의 뼈의 밀도는 점차적으로 일정하게 낮아져요. 하지만 일반적으로 여성이 더 쉽게 골다공증에 걸리는데요, 그 이유는 어린 시절에 뼈가 적절하게 발달되지 않기 때문이에요. 또한 남성들보다 여성이 뼈 손실율이 높은데, 특히 여성이 임신을 하고 아기에게 수유하면서 칼슘 섭취가 부족한 경우에 더 그렇죠. 폐경기 여성들은 골다공증에 걸릴 위험이 더욱 높은데, 그 이유는 폐경 이후의 에스트로겐 감소가 BMD의 급격한 감소를 야기하기 때문이에요. 흥미롭게도 우리의 현재 생활 습관인 좌식 생활로 인해 골다공증의 위험이 높아질 수도 있어요.

❶ **What is the discussion mainly about?**
교수는 먼저 골다공증의 정의를 묻고 골다공증에 관련된 전반적인 설명을 이어나간다. 따라서 정답은 B이다. 선택지 A와 C. 그리고 D는 지문에 잠시 언급된 내용만을 다루고 있을 뿐, 전체적인 지문의 주제가 될 수 없다.

❷ **Why does the professor mention a sponge during her speech?**
교수는 "골다공증에 걸리게 되면 마치 스펀지처럼 뼈에 구멍이 숭숭 뚫린다"고 말하며 학생들이 골다공증에 걸린 뼈를 더 쉽게 이해할 수 있도록 스펀지와 비교한다. 선택지 A는 논리적으로 틀렸으며 선택지 C는 "스펀지가 만들어지는 과정을 묘사함으로써"라는

부분이 토론의 내용과 맞지 않으므로 답이 되지 않는다. 교수는 스펀지가 어떻게 부서지는지 설명한 것이 아니므로 선택지 D 또한 틀린 선택이다.

❸ **Why is a woman in her menopause more susceptible to osteoporosis?**
교수는 폐경 이후의 여성들에게는 폐경 이후의 에스트로겐 감소로 인해 BMD가 급격하게 감소하기 때문에 골다공증이 올 수가 있다고 설명한다. 따라서 정답은 선택지 C이다.

(Passage 9)

1. A   **2.** B   **3.** D   **4.** C   **5.** D

P(W): So, class, let's take a look at this sentence: "Buffalo buffalo Buffalo buffalo buffalo buffalo Buffalo buffalo." Well, what do you think?

M: Well, ma'am, I, I just think that… it's just a repetition of the same word… like, how many times have you used the word, buffalo? I don't know… it just doesn't make sense to me at all.

P: ❹ Well, I'm sorry to say this, but the sentence I just mentioned is a grammatically correct sentence. Okay, then let's take a look at this picture. In the sentence, the first, third, and the seventh Buffalo are capitalized. Does this ring any bell? Anyone?

W: Oh, oh, um, there's a city named Buffalo in New York!

P: Good job, Cindy. Let's consider this the first definition of buffalo, and let's just refer to this as "A." What's the first thing you think of when you hear the word, "buffalo?"

W: Well, it's a name of an animal.

P: Well done again. This is actually in the plural form, which is equivalent to buffaloes, used in order to avoid articles. That's our second definition, which we will call, "B." The third definition of buffalo is a verb, meaning to confuse, intimidate, or to deceive, which we will call, "C." Interesting, isn't it? Does anyone not understand thus far? No? Okay, so, if we break this sentence down… "Buffalo buffalo" means, you know, the buffaloes that live in the city, Buffalo. Next three buffaloes, "Buffalo buffalo buffalo" means "who other buffaloes in the city intimidate." Got it?

M: It is extremely confusing.

P: Well, we're almost there. And the next three buffaloes, "buffalo Buffalo buffalo" means…

W: Um, "intimidate other buffaloes in the city of

Buffalo?"

P: That is correct. So, if we translate the whole sentence, you get this sentence: "Bison from Buffalo, New York, who are intimidated by other bison in their community, also intimidate other bison in their community."

W: Oh, I got it now. At least when I stare at this sentence for a long time enough. Um, why are there sentences like these? Are these just some sort of pranks?

P: Quite unlikely. Actually, people use these types of sentences in order to show how homonyms and homophones can be used to created complicated sentence structure. Maybe you're more used to this sentence: "Don't trouble trouble until trouble troubles you."

M: Um... professor, I still don't seem to get this. Can you explain the construct of the buffalo sentence once again?

P: Maybe it would be better if I replaced all instances of the animal buffalo with "people," and the verb buffalo with "intimidate." So, the result should be as follows: "Buffalo people Buffalo people intimidate intimidate Buffalo people." Get it? Buffalo people that Buffalo people intimidate also happen to intimidate Buffalo people.

P: 자, 여러분, 이 문장을 봅시다: "Buffalo buffalo Buffalo buffalo buffalo buffalo Buffalo buffalo." 어떤가요?

M: 글쎄요... 그냥 같은 단어를 반복해서 나열하는 것 같은데요... 버팔로라는 단어를 몇 번 썼냐는 것인가요? 모르겠어요... 전혀 이해가 안되는데요.

P: 이런 말을 해서 미안하지만, 제가 방금 말한 문장은 문법상 오류가 없어요. 좋아요, 그럼 이 그림을 봅시다. 문장에서 첫번째, 세번째, 그리고 일곱번째 버팔로는 대문자로 되어있죠. 뭔가 떠오르는 게 있는 사람 있나요?

W: 음, 뉴욕에 버팔로시가 있어요!

P: 좋았어요. 신디. 이것을 버팔로의 일차 정의로 하고, "A"라고 정합시다. 버팔로라는 단어를 들으면 제일 먼저 무엇이 떠오르나요?

W: 음, 그건 동물의 이름이에요.

P: 맞았어요. 이는 주로 복수형이고 buffaloes와 동급으로, 관사를 피하기 위해 사용되어요. 이것을 두 번째 정의, "B"라고 부릅시다. 버팔로의 세 번째 정의는 동사인데, 혼동하다, 협박하다, 속이다라는 뜻으로 사용되어요. 이것을 "C"라고 합시다. 흥미롭죠? 지금까지 다 이해되나요? 안되나요? 자, 이제 이 문장을 풀어보면 "Buffalo buffalo"는 버팔로시에 사는 버팔로란 뜻입니다. 다음 세 버팔로는 "Buffalo buffalo buffalo," 즉 "버팔로시의 다른 버팔로가 협박하다"란 뜻입니다. 이해되죠?

M: 매우 헷갈리는데요.

P: 자, 이제 거의 다 됐어요. 마지막 세 버팔로 "buffalo Buffalo buffalo"의 뜻은...

W: 음, "버팔로 시의 다른 버팔로들을 협박한다?"

P: 맞아요. 그러니까 전체 문장을 번역하면, 이런 문장이 나오죠: "들소 사회에서 협박받는 뉴욕 버팔로시의 들소는 집단 내의 다른 들소를 협박한다."

W: 이제 알겠네요. 최소한 오랫동안 이 문장을 보면 말이죠. 이런 문장이 왜 있는 건가요? 그냥 장난인가요?

P: 아니에요. 사실 사람들은 동음이의어와 이형 동음이의어가 복잡한 문장 구조를 만들 수 있다는 것을 보여주기 위해서 이런 문장들을 사용해요. 여러분은 아마 이 문장에 더 익숙할 거예요 – "문제가 당신에게 문제가 되기 전에 문제를 문제삼지 마라."

M: 교수님, 전 아직도 이해가 안돼요. 버팔로 문장의 구조를 다시 설명해 주시겠어요?

P: 동물을 나타내는 버팔로를 전부 "사람들"로 바꾸고 동사형 버팔로를 "협박하다"로 바꿔보면 이해하기 쉬울 거예요. 자, 그러면 결과는 이렇게 되죠: "버팔로 사람이 협박하는 버팔로 사람은 버팔로 사람을 협박한다." 알겠죠? 버팔로시에 사는 사람들이 협박하는 버팔로 사람들은 또한 다른 버팔로 사람들을 협박한다는 뜻이죠.

❶ What is the topic of the discussion?

교수는 문장을 제시하고 분석함으로써 동음이의어와 동의이음어의 사용이 얼마나 복잡한 구조를 만들어내는지를 설명한다. 따라서 답은 A이다.

❷ According to the professor, what is the capitalized Buffalo?

대문자로 사용된 "Buffalo"가 무엇이냐는 교수의 질문에 여학생이 "there's a city named Buffalo in New York"라고 대답하는 부분에서 정답이 B임을 알 수 있다.

❸ What can be inferred about homonyms and homophones?

선택지 A와 B는 토론의 내용과 상반된 주장을 하고 있기 때문에 틀린 선택이며, 특히 선택지 B처럼 "always" 등의 단어가 포함된 선택지는 강의에 그렇게 설명되어 있지 않는 이상 대부분 틀린 선택이라고 볼 수 있다. 선택지 C 또한 교수의 설명과 상반되는 내용이므로 틀린 선택이다.

❹ What does the professor want to know when she says this:

"Ring a bell"은 "무언가를 생각나게 하다"라는 뜻으로, 교수는 "내가 방금 준 힌트로 뭐 생각나는 것 없습니까?"라고 묻고 있다. 따라서 정답은 C이다.

❺ Why did the professor mention the sentence, "Don't trouble trouble until trouble troubles you"?

교수는 동음이의어와 동의이음어가 복잡한 문장 구조를 만들어낼 수 있다면서 학생들이 더 익숙해 할 만한 문장을 예로 제시한다. 따라서 정답은 D이다.

1. C   **2.** A   **3.** A, C

P(M): Muhammad Yunus was born in 1940 in a small town in Bangladesh. He earned his bachelor's degree and master's degree from Dhaka University and his Ph.D. in economics from Vanderbilt University in 1969. From 1969 to 1972, he worked as an assistant professor of economics at Middle Tennessee State University but moved back to Bangladesh, where he joined the faculty at Chittagong University as an economics professor.

In 1974, a terrible famine struck the country which swept away over a million people. It was generally believed that the famine came from natural disasters such as cyclones, droughts and floods in the early 1970s. Also, various local and internationally influenced socio-political factors following the Bangladesh Liberation War in 1971 were blamed for the national adversity. Yunus was greatly inspired by this famine and started making a small loan of about $27 to a group of 42 families who lived near Chittagong University so that they could create small items such as bamboo furniture to sell and start making money and avoid debt. Oh, before we move on, let's talk about the situation before he started the small loan program. Um, poor people had to take out usurious loans to buy bamboo to make furniture out of it. They sold these items they made to the moneylenders so that they can repay them. Their net profit was about 5 Bangladeshi taka which was about only 2 cents in US dollar. Would you think this is enough to support the family? Of course not. Just think about it... you spend the whole day making a piece of furniture out of bamboo and you only make two cents, but your interest rate is higher than what you make! What was more dejecting was the attitude of traditional banks... well, they weren't very interested in making very small loans at low interest rates to these poor people.

So, what Muhammad Yunus came up with was the concept of microcredit loan, which is defined as any program that extends small loans, anywhere between $30 to $200, to very poor people for self-employment projects that generate income, or entrepreneurs too poor to qualify for traditional bank loans. For example, let's say that there's one family who used to make bamboo furniture borrowing money with a very high interest rate.

Instead of taking out usurious loans, the family lends $20 with a low interest rate, makes bamboo furniture out of it and sells them at a market, making some more money with which they can pay the loan back along with the interest rate. Yunus founded a bank called the "Grameen Bank" in 1976 which has helped countless poor people in his country as well as inspired similar programs all over the world. He and his bank were jointly awarded the Nobel Peace Prize in 2006.

무하마드 유누스는 방글라데시의 작은 마을에서 1940년에 태어났습니다. 그는 다카 대학에서 학사 학위와 석사 학위를 취득했고 1969년에 밴더빌트 대학에서 경제학 박사 학위를 취득했습니다. 1969년에서 1972년 사이에 그는 중부 테네시 대학에서 경제학 조교수로 일했으며 방글라데시로 돌아와 치타공 대학에서 경제학 교수로 재직했습니다.

1974년도에 심각한 기아가 방글라데시를 덮쳐 수백만 명의 목숨을 앗아갔습니다. 1970년대 초반에 발생한 태풍, 가뭄과 홍수 등의 자연 재해가 기아의 원인이라고 여겨졌습니다. 또한 방글라데시의 1971년 독립 전쟁 이후 발생한 다양한 내적, 국제적 영향을 받은 정치 사회적 요소가 내부적 재난의 원인이라는 비난을 받았습니다. 유누스는 이 기간에 크게 영향을 받고 치타공 대학 주변의 마른 두 가구에게 27달러를 빌려주어 대나무 가구 같은 작은 물건들을 만들어 빚을 지지 않고 가게를 꾸릴 수 있게 했습니다. 아, 더 나가기 전에, 그가 소액 대출 프로그램을 시작하기 전의 상황에 대해 알아봅시다. 가난한 사람들은 대나무 가구를 만들기 위해 고리대금을 얻어야 했습니다. 이들은 돈을 갚기 위해 직접 만든 대나무 가구를 업자들에게 팔았습니다. 이들의 순익은 미화로 2센트, 방글라데시에서는 5타카였습니다. 이것이 가족을 부양하기에 충분할까요? 물론 아니었습니다. 생각해 보세요... 하루 종일 대나무로 가구를 만들어 2센트를 벌지만, 이율이 버는 돈보다 높다니! 더욱 참담했던 것은 기존 은행의 태도였습니다. 이들은 가난한 사람들에게 낮은 이율로 소액을 대출하는 것에 관심이 없었습니다.

그래서 무하마드 유누스가 생각해 낸 것이 바로 소규모 대출인데요, 이것은 30에서 200달러 정도의 금액을 매우 가난하거나 일반 은행 대출 자격이 안 되는 기업가들에게 대출해 주어, 자가 고용 계획을 통해 소득을 창출할 수 있도록 하는 프로그램을 뜻합니다. 예를 들어, 매우 높은 이율에 돈을 빌려 대나무로 가구를 제조하는 가족이 있다고 합시다. 고리대금을 얻는 것 대신, 이 가족은 20달러를 저금리에 대출받아 가구를 만들고 시장에 팔아 돈을 벌 수 있고, 이것으로 이자를 포함하여 대출금을 갚을 수 있습니다. 유누스는 1976년도에 방글라데시의 수많은 가난한 이들에게 도움을 준 그라민 은행을 설립했고, 이는 전 세계적으로 비슷한 프로그램을 양산했습니다. 그와 그의 은행은 2006년도에 노벨 평화상을 공동 수상했습니다.

❶ What is the professor mainly discussing?
교수는 먼저 무하마드 유누스의 개인적인 삶을 짤막하게 소개하고 이어서 그가 그라민 은행을 설립하게 된 배경을 설명한다. 따라서 전체적인 주제를 가장 잘 설명한 선택지 C가 정답이 된다. 선택지 A와 B는 너무 제한적인 내용만을 담고 있으므로 주제라고 할 수 없으며, 이 강의는 유누스가 소규모 대출의 개념을 만들고 그라민 은행을 어떻게 설립하게 되었는지에 대한 전체적인 내용을 담고 있기 때문에, 단지 "소규모 대출 개념의 설립"이라는 선택지 D 역시 답이 될 수 없다.

❷ According to the professor, what is the concept of microcredit loan?

"Any program that extends small loans, anywhere between $30 to $200, to very poor people for self-employment projects that generate income, or entrepreneurs too poor to qualify for traditional bank loans"에서 알 수 있듯 가난한 사람들이나 사업가들에게 매우 낮은 이자로 소액 대출을 해주는 프로그램이다.

❸ What were mentioned as the reasons for chronic poverty in Bangladesh?

방글라데시에서의 고질적인 가난의 문제로 교수는 "고리대금"과 "이자를 갚을 수도 없을 정도로 너무 적은 소득"을 꼽는다.

Vocabulary Test

1. remedy	**2.** repetition	**3.** authentic
4. drought	**5.** abnormal	**6.** immune
7. problematic	**8.** imprison	**9.** b
10. b	**11.** d	**12.** a
13. c	**14.** b	**15.** a

3 Organization

Sample

그리고 저는 이 질병을 잘 이해하지 못하는 사람들을 많이 봤어요. 사람들은 심장마비와 발작을 종종 혼동해요. 그래서 올바르게 대처해서 목숨을 구할 수 있는 소중한 기회를 놓치게 되죠. 우선 심장마비는 심장 일부로 가는 혈액이 막혔을 때 발생하는데, 이때 심장 조직이 손상되어요. 심장마비는 전 세계적으로 남녀를 불문하고 가장 높은 사망 원인인데, 증상으로는 극심한 흉통과 자율 신경계의 이상이 있어요. 그러니까… 환자가 창백해지고, 속이 울렁거리고 땀을 흘리죠. 반면에 발작은 뇌에 일시적으로 발생하는 비정상적 전기 생리학적 이상이에요. 근육이 갑자기 무의식적으로 경련을 일으키거나 몸의 일부가 마비될 때 발작을 의심할 수 있어요. 이러한 증상을 보이는 사람은 의식을 잃고 쓰러지고 심한 경련을 일으킬 수 있어요.

Strategy Focus

1. B **2.** D **3.** A **4.** A

1. B

P(M): Omega-3 fatty acids play a wide role in a range of key body processes, from regulating blood pressure and blood clotting to boosting immunity and fighting against inflammation associated with psoriasis, Crohn's disease, and rheumatoid arthritis. They also play a vital role in the development of a baby's eyes and brain both before birth and during childhood. Present in oily fish like salmon and sardines as well as walnuts, flaxseeds, and dark green vegetables, it's often hard to get all the omega-3 fatty acids you need on a regular basis through diet alone. Two types of omega-3 supplements, eicosapentaenoic acid or EPA and docosahexaenoic acid or DHA, come from fish oil supplements, while flaxseeds contain alphalinolenic acid or ALA. Well, it's best to take omega-3 supplements with meals, and to not buy them in bulk, since they can go rancid. Storing these supplements in the refrigerator will help preserve their shelf life.

오메가-3 지방산은 우리 몸의 주요 작용에서 다양한 역할을 맡는데, 혈압과 응혈을 조절하고 면역성을 높이고 건선, 크론씨병, 그리고 류머티스 관절염과 관련된 염증에 대항하는 등의 역할을 합니다. 또한 출생 전 및 유아기에 영아의 눈과 뇌의 발달에도 중요한 역할을 합니다. 오메가-3 지방산은 연어과 정어리 같은 지방이 많은 생선과 호두, 아마씨, 그리고 짙은 녹색 야채에 들어있지만 식단만으로 우리가 주기적으로 필요로 하는 양을 얻는 종종 쉽지 않습니다. EPA라고도 불리는 에이코사펜타에노산과 DHA라고 불리는 도코사헥사에노산 등 두 종류의 오메가-3 지방산은 생선 지방에 있는 반면, 아마씨는 ALA라고 불리는 알파리놀레닉산을 함유하고 있습니다. 오메가-3 지방산은 음식을 통해 섭취하는 것이 좋으며, 상할 수 있으므로 이 음식들은 한꺼번에 대량으로 사지 않는 편이 좋습니다. 이러한 음식들을 냉장 보관하는 것이 좀 더 오래 저장하는 방법입니다.

2. D

P(W): And so, this is basically what Bode's Law is. Uh, actually, it isn't really a scientific law... it doesn't, um, tell you how to predict gravitation mathematically or anything of that sort, but, um, it's attempting a pattern in the spacing of planets. Now, let's move on to the asteroid, Ceres. When was Ceres discovered?

M: Um... I remember it was some time in the 1800s.

P: Yes, 1801, to be exact. It was the first asteroid ever detected. Who can tell me how big this asteroid is?

W: It was as big as the state of Texas... about 580 miles across.

P: That's correct. So, in 1801, an astronomer named Guiseppe Piazzi, who was also a monk in Sicily, first identified this enormous rock which wasn't one of the planets, their moons or a star.

P: 자, 이것이 바로 보데의 법칙의 기본적인 내용이에요. 이것은 사실 과학적 법칙은 아니에요. 중력을 산술적으로 예측하는 방법을 가르쳐 주거나 하지는 않지만, 행성간의 간격에서 나타나는 패턴을 예측하려고 하죠. 자, 그럼 이제 소행성 세레에 대해 알아보겠어요. 세레스가 언제 발견됐죠?

M: 음. 1800년대 쯤이었던 것 같아요.

P: 네. 정확히 말하면 1801년도예요. 이것은 최초로 발견된 소행성이었지요. 이 소행성의 크기를 말해줄 사람?

W: 텍사스 주 만해요... 직경이 약 580마일이죠.

P: 맞았어요. 1801년도에 시실리의 수도승이자 천문학자였던 쥬세페 피아치가 행성도, 행성의 달도, 또한 별도 아닌 이 거대한 돌을 처음으로 찾아냈어요.

3. A

P(M): OK, let's get going. In today's class, we'll be discussing the first adventure comic strips. What cartoon characters can you think of in terms of adventure?

M: Oh, my favorite adventure cartoon character used to be *Tarzan*.

P: Okay. Interestingly enough, *Tarzan* was the first adventurous comic character who appeared in 1929. *Tarzan* was drawn by a man named Harold Foster who also created the character, Prince Valiant. Foster was a Canadian-American who was working as an illustrator before getting involved with *Tarzan*, an adaptation of the novels of Edgar Rice Burrough. When he first started working on *Tarzan*, he actually hated the character and soon grew tired of adaptation. Craving to create a character of his own, he proposed this to William Hearst, the legendary newspaper tycoon, who

enthusiastically approved the idea and gave Foster the ownership of the strip if he could start the series. Oh, I almost forgot... when *Tarzan* appeared in the newspaper in 1929, another adventure comic strip appeared as well. Its name was *Buck Rogers*.

Well, I could say that those were the golden years of the adventure comic strip. After *Tarzan* and *Buck Rogers*, more adventure comics started to appear: *Flash Gordon, Phantom, Tim Taylor, Jungle Jim,* and *Brick Bradford*.

P: 자. 계속합시다. 오늘 시간에는 최초의 모험 만화에 대해 논의해보겠어요. 모험이라는 관점에서 어떤 만화 캐릭터가 생각나죠?

M: 아, 제가 제일 좋아하는 모험 만화 캐릭터는 "타잔"이었어요.

P: 좋아요. 흥미롭게도 "타잔"은 1929년도에 처음으로 출현한 모험 만화 캐릭터였어요. "타잔"은 해롤드 포스터라는 사람이 그렸는데, 이 사람은 프린스 밸리언트라는 캐릭터도 창조한 사람이었지요. 포스터는 캐나다 태생의 미국인으로 에드가 라이스 버로우의 소설을 각색한 "타잔"과 관련되기 전에 일러스트레이터로 활동했어요. 그가 처음 "타잔"을 작업할 때, 그는 사실 이 캐릭터를 싫어했고 곧 각색에 싫증을 느꼈어요. 자신만의 캐릭터를 만들고 싶어한 그는 신문 업계의 전설적인 거물인 윌리엄 허스트에게 이 제안을 했고, 허스트는 이에 적극 찬성했어요. 그리고 그는 포스터에게 새로운 시리즈를 만들수 있으면 만화의 소유권을 허락한다고 했죠. 아, 깜빡할 뻔 했네요... 1929년도에 "타잔"이 신문에 처음 실렸을 때. "벅 로저스"라는 새로운 모험 만화도 신문에 등장했어요.

이때가 모험 만화의 황금기라고 할 수 있어요. "타잔"과 "벅 로저스" 이후로 "플래쉬 고든". "팬텀". "팀 테일러". "정글짐" 그리고 "브릭 브래드포드" 등 많은 모험 만화가 등장하기 시작했어요.

4. A

P(W): Okay, let's, uh, let's move on. Okay, um, let me tell you an example of this... um, let's see... let's say that Janet has a CD player which she doesn't wish to use anymore. She's tired of it and she doesn't like the color. Instead, she wants to buy an MP3 player, but she can't afford it. Now, Jeremy here has an old MP3 player which he's been using for about a year. He got a newer version for his birthday, and wants to get rid of his old one. Janet tells Jeremy her story and Jeremy proposes a trade. What am I talking about?

M: About barter?

P: That's right. Um... maybe, a more modern version of barter, but yes, since no money-exchange was involved and the things they exchanged were... well, goods. So, now, you can all guess what condition should be met in order for some action to be called barter, right? Barter is a non-monetary exchange of goods and/or services between two or more parties. That is not to say that barters do not exist in a monetary system. Societies with a monetary system can use the barter system, especially in economies suffering from a very unstable currency, such as those under hyperinflation.

P: 자, 계속하도록 합시다. 좋아요. 이것에 대한 예를 하나 들어보죠... 어디보자... 자넷이 이제 더 이상 쓰고 싶지 않은 CD 플레이어를 갖고 있다고 해 봅시다. 그녀는 그 CD 플레이어에 싫증이 났고 색도 맘에 안 듭니다. 그녀는 CD 플레이어 대신 MP3 플레이어를 사고 싶지만, 돈이 없습니다. 자, 제레미에게는 1년 정도 사용한 낡은 MP3 플레이어가 있습니다. 그는 생일 선물로 새로 나온 버전의 MP3 플레이어를 받아서 낡은 것은 없애고 싶어하죠. 자넷이 제레미에게 자신의 얘기를 하고 제레미는 거래를 하자고 제안합니다. 제가 무엇에 대해 이야기를 하고 있는 건가요?

M: 물물교환이요?

P: 맞아요. 음, 좀 더 현대적인 의미의 물물교환이지만, 맞아요. 왜냐하면 돈을 교환하지 않았고, 이들이 교환한 것이... 물건이었기 때문이에요. 자, 그러면 이제 어떠한 행위가 물물교환이 되기 위해 필요한 조건이 무엇인지 다들 맞출 수 있겠죠? 물물교환이란 돈이 관련되지 않는 양방 또는 그 이상간의 물품 및 서비스의 교환이에요.

그렇다고 해서 물물교환이 화폐 제도에서는 존재하지 않는다는 뜻은 아니에요. 화폐 제도가 있는 사회 또한 물물교환을 사용할 수 있는데, 특히 통화 가치가 굉장히 불안한 사회, 가령 초인플레이션을 겪고 있는 곳에서 사용 가능하죠.

Exercise

P.1	1. D	2. A, D	3. C
P.2	1. A	2. A, C	3. A
P.3	1. D	2. A, B	3. D
P.4	1. A	2. B	3. B
	4. C	5. B, D, E	
P.5	1. C	2. C	3. B, C
P.6	1. C	2. C	3. B
	4. B	5. 참조	
P.7	1. C	2. A, B	3. C
	4. B	5. A, B, E	6. D
P.8	1. D	2. C, D, E	3. A
	4. D	5. C, D	
P.9	1. B	2. A	3. C
	4. B, D	5. C	
P.10	1. D	2. B, C, D	3. B

(Passage 1)

1. D   **2.** A, D   **3.** C

P(W): All right, uh... let's start for now. Um, today, we're gonna talk about guerrilla warfare. Well, guerrilla warfare is basically a political war because it is a necessary part of a revolution. The operations of guerrilla warfare far exceed the

concept of conventional warfare which is usually limited to territorial warfare. This is because the guerrilla warfare tries to penetrate the political entity itself. Um, let's not confuse guerrilla warfare with war operations by a regular force or a defensive maneuver to avoid battle; instead, you should understand that guerrilla warfares bear the character of a resistance movement.

Now, let's discuss some guerrilla tactics that should be considered. Guerrilla tactics heavily involve intelligence, ambush, deception, sabotage, and espionage — in other words, you shouldn't be a guerrilla unless you're willing to deceive the enemy and send spies to their camp. When guerrilla warfare is conducted in, let's say, an unfamiliar foreign terrain, it can be quite successful. Well, for the guerrillas, that is. You can see an example from the Vietnam War. Um, in order to conduct guerrilla warfare successfully and efficiently, some essential equipment is necessary: a weapon, naturally, um, a sleeping bag or wool blanket to keep a soldier warm at night, a backpack, good boots, a hammock, and an ammo belt. A mosquito net might come in handy especially during the warm seasons.

자, 이제 시작합시다. 오늘은 게릴라전에 대해 이야기해 보겠어요. 게릴라전은 기본적으로 정치적 전쟁인데요. 그 이유는 게릴라전이 혁명에 필요한 부분이기 때문이에요. 게릴라전의 작전은 주로 영토 전쟁에 국한되는 전형적인 전쟁의 개념을 탈피하게 되는데, 그 이유는 이것이 정치적 본질 자체를 침투하려고 하기 때문이에요. 게릴라전을 일반 군대에 의한 군사 작전이나, 전쟁을 피하기 위한 수비적 작전 행동과는 혼동하지 않길 바래요. 게릴라전은 오히려 저항 세력의 특징을 갖는다는 것을 이해해야 해요.

이제 고려해야 할 몇 가지 게릴라 작전에 대해 알아보죠. 게릴라 작전은 정보, 매복, 속임수, 파괴, 그리고 정탐 등과 관련되는데, 한 마디로 적군을 속이고 적의 진영에 스파이를 보낼 준비가 되어 있지 않다면 게릴라가 되면 안되겠지요. 게릴라전이 예를 들어 낯선 지형에서 개시될 경우에는 매우 성공적일 수 있어요. 물론 게릴라에게 성공적이라는 거지요. 베트남 전쟁에서 그 예를 찾을 수 있어요. 게릴라전을 성공적이고 효율적으로 수행하려면 몇 가지 기본적 장비가 필요한데요. 당연히 무기가 필요하겠고, 밤을 따뜻하게 나기 위한 침낭이나 모포, 배낭, 튼튼한 부츠, 해먹, 그리고 탄창 등이 있어야 하겠죠. 특히 따뜻한 계절에는 모기장이 유용할 수 있어요.

❶ **Why does the professor mention the Vietnam War?**

교수는 낯선 지형에서 전개되는 게릴라전이 성공적임을 설명하며 베트남 전쟁이 그 예라고 설명한다. 따라서 답은 D이다.

❷ **What were mentioned in the lecture as the equipment a guerrilla soldier should carry?**

게릴라 병사가 지녀야 할 도구로는 "a weapon, a sleeping bag or wool blanket, a backpack, good boots, a hammock, an ammo belt, a mosquito net" 등이 언급되었으므로, 정답이 선택지 A와 D임을 알 수 있다.

❸ **How does the professor organize the lecture?**

교수는 먼저 게릴라전의 정의를 설명하고 작전 및 필요한 도구 등을 설명한다. 따라서 정답은 C이다. 교수는 게릴라전과 다른 용어를 비교하지 않으므로 선택지 A는 정답이 될 수 없으며, 게릴라전에 필요한 기본적 도구들을 설명했을 뿐, 가장 중요한 도구라는 얘기는 없으므로 선택지 B 또한 답이 아니다. 게릴라전의 예는 베트남 전쟁 하나만 들었을 뿐이며, 그 또한 낯선 지형에서 전개되는 것에 대한 예를 든 것일 뿐이므로 선택지 D 또한 지워야 한다.

Passage 2

1. A   **2.** A, C   **3.** A

P(M): The first astronauts were selected in 1959 — it was even before human spaceflight operations began. **❶ NASA recruited their first astronauts from the military — it basically required the military to provide them with a list of personnel who met NASA's qualifications. Seven men were selected as the first American astronauts after a highly rigid screening, and what do you know, they all happened to be pilots.** They were called the "Original Seven." After these men were selected, NASA went on to recruit 18 more groups of astronauts. Candidates for astronauts should have at least a bachelor's degree but many of them are specialists or educators in the field of engineering, biology, or physics such as doctors, schoolteachers, scientists, engineers, pilots, or military personnel. The standard for selecting astronauts is highly rigid — among thousands of applicants all over the country, NASA has only chosen 321 people for astronauts until now since the "Original Seven."

최초의 우주 비행사는 1959년에 선발되었는데, 이것은 인간의 우주 비행 계획이 진행되기도 전이었어요. 미국 항공우주국인 NASA는 첫 우주 비행사를 군에서 선발했어요 – 쉽게 말해 NASA의 지원 요건에 맞는 대원의 명단을 제공하도록 요구했죠. 엄격한 선발을 통해 7명이 미국의 첫 우주 비행사로 선정되었는데, 우연히도 이들은 모두 조종사였어요. 이들은 "최초의 7인"으로 불렸어요. 이들이 선택된 후, NASA는 18개의 우주 비행사 그룹을 추가 선발했어요. 우주 비행사 후보들은 최소한 학사 학위가 있어야 하지만, 많은 이들이 공학, 생물학, 혹은 물리학의 전문가 혹은 교육자로, 의사, 교사, 과학자, 공학자, 조종사, 그리고 군 관계자들

이에요. 우주 비행사를 선발하는 기준은 매우 엄격해요 – 전국의 수천 명의 후보들 중, NASA는 "최초의 7인" 이후로 현재까지 단 321명만을 선발했어요.

❶ **What does the professor imply when he says this:**

"What do you know"라는 표현은 "네가 무엇을 알겠느냐"라는 뜻이 아니라 무언가에 놀랐거나 새로운 소식 등을 접했을 때 놀랐다는 감정을 나타낼 때 사용된다. "happened to be"라는 표현은 "우연히 ~이다"라는 뜻을 내포하고 있으므로, "우연히 7명의 우주 비행사 모두 전직 파일럿이었다"는 선택지 A가 정답이 된다. 선택지 B는 강의의 내용과 상반되는 억지스러운 내용이므로 답이 될 수 없다. 선택지 C는 강의 내용만으로는 알 수 없는 내용이다.

❷ **What were mentioned in the lecture as the former occupation of astronauts recruited by NASA?**

"Many candidates include doctors, schoolteachers, scientist, engineers, pilots, or military personnel"라는 교수의 말에서 답을 알 수 있다.

❸ **In what order does the professor explain the recruit of astronauts by NASA?**

교수는 먼저 최초의 우주 비행사 선발에 대해 설명하고 점차 최근의 예로 옮겨간다. 따라서 선택지 A가 정답이 된다. 가장 유명하고 덜 유명한 얘기를 하는지는 알 수 없으므로 선택지 B는 답이 될 수 없으며, 가장 정확한 예가 무엇인지 역시 알 수 없기 때문에 선택지 C 또한 틀린 선택이다. 마찬가지로 가장 중요한 일에 대해서도 언급된 바가 없으므로 선택지 D 역시 답이 될 수 없다.

Passage 3

1. D   **2.** A, B   **3.** D

P(W): Except for the computer-related operations, the main system of mathematical notation today used everywhere else is the decimal system. This is a base-10 system, in which the quantity represented by any of the ten symbols used... uh, from zero to nine, um, depends on its position in the number. However, most modern computer systems operate using binary logic, using only two digits, zero and one. For example, the number three in decimal notation would be one-one (11) in binary system, one-zero-one (101) for five, and, um, one-double-zero-one (1001) for nine. Naturally, because the binary system only uses two numbers, it is complicated and, well, it gets longer to express a particular number, so we don't use this system in ordinary life but when it comes to computers, the situation is different because of the greater simplicity of the binary system in computer applications.

M: Professor Williams, then, what's the difference between bit and byte? I've heard these terms a lot, but I never got to understand what they are.

P: Well, that's a good question, Billy. Let me put it this way... another name for binary digit is bit — the smallest unit of information in the digital world. Got it? The term bit was first introduced by John Tukey, an American statistician and early computer scientist. He used the term in 1946, as an abbreviation of the term binary digit. Bits are usually combined into larger units called bytes, and eight bits equal one byte.

P: 컴퓨터 관련 작업을 제외한 기타 모든 분야에서 오늘날 널리 쓰이는 수학 표기법의 주 시스템은 십진법이에요. 이것은 0에서 9까지의 10개의 기호로 표시된 양이 숫자의 위치에 의해 결정되는 10단위 시스템이에요. 그렇지만 오늘날 대부분의 컴퓨터는 이진법, 즉 0과 1 두 개만을 사용해요. 예를 들어 십진법의 3은 이진법에서는 11로 표기되고, 5는 101, 그리고 9는 1001로 표기되어요. 이진법은 두가지 숫자만 사용하기 때문에 당연히 복잡하고 특정 숫자를 표시할 때 길이가 길어져요. 그래서 일상 생활에서는 이 시스템을 사용하지 않아요. 그렇지만 컴퓨터 적용에 있어서는 이진법이 보다 간단하기 때문에 상황이 다르죠.

M: 윌리엄스 교수님. 그러면 비트와 바이트의 차이점은 무엇인가요? 이 용어를 많이 들어봤지만 뭔지 잘 모르겠어요.

P: 좋은 질문이에요. 빌리. 이렇게 설명해 보죠... 이진수의 다른 이름이 바로 비트인데요, 이것은 디지털 세계에서 사용되는 가장 작은 정보 단위예요. 이해되나요? 비트란 단어는 미국의 통계학자이며 초기의 컴퓨터 과학자인 존 튜키가 처음 소개했어요. 그는 1946년에 바이너리 디짓(binary digit), 즉 이진 숫자라는 단어의 생략형으로 이 비트라는 단어를 사용했어요. 비트는 보통 바이트라는 더 큰 단위로 합쳐지고, 8비트가 1 바이트가 되죠.

❶ According to the professor, why is binary system used for computer systems?

컴퓨터 적용에 있어서는 두 개의 숫자만을 사용하는 이진법이 보다 간단하기 때문에 널리 쓰인다고 했으므로 정답은 D이다.

❷ Which of the following are true about bit and byte?

"Another name for binary digit is bit—the smallest unit of information in a digital world"라는 교수의 말에서 선택지 A가 맞는 정보임을 알 수 있고, "eight bits equal one byte"에서 선택지 B 또한 맞는 정보임을 알 수 있다. 비트라는 단어는 바이너리 디짓(binary digit)의 약어이며, 존 튜키가 처음 사용했으므로 선택지 C와 D는 틀린 선택이다.

❸ Why does the professor mention 11, 101, and 1001?

"For example, the number three in decimal notation would be one-one (11) in binary system, one-zero-one (101) for five, and, um, one-double-zero-one

(1001) for nine"이라는 교수의 말에서 정답을 찾을 수 있는데, 즉 십진법 숫자가 이진법 숫자로 어떻게 표기되는지를 설명하기 위해 든 예이다. 따라서 정답은 선택지 D이다.

⎯⎯⎯⎯(Passage 4)⎯⎯⎯⎯⎯⎯⎯⎯⎯⎯⎯⎯⎯⎯

1. A   **2.** B   **3.** B   **4.** C   **5.** B, D, E

P(M): So, like I said, if there's no choice for you but going to a fast food restaurant, you should at least remember this: smaller is always better. You can get a small batch of french fries instead of a big one, or one beef patty rather than two. This rule goes for pizzas as well. A single slice of cheese pizza can have up to 600 calories. So why not share the pizza with someone and have a small salad?

M: 600 calories for a slice of pizza? I never thought about calories when I ate... um, professor, how many calories do you need a day?

P: Well, Matthew... it kind of depends on the age and sex... and uh, it varies according to the person's lifestyle and other factors, let's say... uh, like I said, the age and sex... and uh, height and weight, your basic level of daily activity... you know, whether you're an athletic person, an office worker who sits in front of the desk all day, or a construction worker... well, you guys, I was supposed to talk about this next week, but since it was brought up now, let's talk about it briefly. We'll go over this more thoroughly next class, all right? Like I said, factors that affect the daily calorie intake include all the things that I just mentioned... I'm not gonna go over it now since I already talked about it... Well, about the, uh, recommended personal daily calorie intake... well, the UK Department of Health estimates that women should take 1940 calories a day, and men, about 2250. In order for you to lose weight, however, uh, let's say, 2 pounds a week, you should take 1000 less calories a day. That's extremely hard since a slice of pizza can go up to 600 calories. I don't think I can live with only two slices of pizza a day.
❹ Okay, let's go back to our topic. Uh... where was I?

W: Um, you were talking about smaller is always better when you go to a fastfood restaurant.

P: Oh, that's right. Thank you, Kirstin. Another rule you should bear in mind is that you should always consider the alternative. All right, so... when you go to your favorite pizza place, the options are endless, right? You can cut down a lot of calories if you load your pizza with veggies and extra tomato sauce instead of a variety of meats and extra cheese. Tomato sauce is low in calories... that's a surprise, huh? And you all know that veggies provide fiber and vitamins. Also, damage control is easy if you order thin-crust.

Okay, and another rule: don't be fooled by a commonly accepted notion. Somehow, people seem to think that fish or chicken options are generally better than red meat, but that's not always the case. A fried piece of fish is going to have more fat and calories than a grilled burger. Even white meat isn't healthy if it's battered and fried.

P: 그러니까 얘기했듯이 패스트푸드 레스토랑에 가는 것 외에 다른 선택의 여지가 없을 때에는 적어도 이 정도는 기억합시다. 적게 먹는 것이 언제나 낫다는 것을 말입니다. 라지 사이즈의 감자 튀김보다는 작은 사이즈를 먹을 수 있고, 고기 패티도 두 개 보다는 한 개를 먹으면 됩니다. 이 법칙은 피자를 먹을 때에도 해당되는데요, 치즈 피자 한 조각이 600 칼로리까지 올라갈 수 있습니다. 그러니까 피자를 나누어 먹고 작은 샐러드를 먹는 건 어떨까요?

M: 피자 한 조각에 600 칼로리라고요? 저는 음식을 먹을 때 칼로리에 대해서 생각해 본 적이 없는데요... 교수님, 그러면 하루에 몇 칼로리가 필요한가요?

P: 글쎄요. 매튜... 그건 나이와 성별에 따라 달라요... 그 사람의 생활 습관과 다른 요인들, 예를 들어 방금 얘기한 것처럼 나이와 성별, 그리고 키와 몸무게, 하루의 기본 활동량 등에 따라 차이가 나죠. 예를 들어 여러분이 활동적인 사람인지 아닌지, 책상 앞에 하루종일 앉아 있는 사무직인지, 아니면 공사장에서 일하는 사람이던지 말이죠. 여러분, 이 얘기는 원래 다음 주 수업시간에 하려고 했는데 지금 얘기가 나왔으니 간단하게 설명하고 넘어가도록 하죠. 다음 시간에 더 자세하게 살펴 보도록 할게요.

얘기했듯이 하루 칼로리 섭취량에 영향을 주는 요인들은 방금 언급한 것들을 전부 포함해요. 이미 얘기했으니 다시 언급하진 않을게요. 1인당 칼로리 섭취 권장량에 대해서 말하자면, 영국 보건국에서는 여성은 하루에 1940 칼로리를, 남성은 2250 칼로리를 섭취해야 한다고 해요. 하지만 예를 들어 일주일에 2파운드씩 살을 빼기 위해서는 하루에 1000 칼로리씩 덜 섭취해야 하겠죠. 피자 한 조각에 600 칼로리까지 나갈 수도 있는 상황에서 이렇게 먹는 것은 매우 힘들어요. 전 피자 두 조각만 가지고 하루를 버틸 자신이 없거든요.

자, 그럼 아까 얘기하던 주제로 돌아갑시다. 음... 어디까지 얘기했었죠?

W: 패스트푸드 레스토랑에 가면 항상 적게 먹는 것이 낫다고 하셨어요.

P: 아, 맞아요. 고마워요. 커스틴. 기억해야 할 또 다른 법칙은 항상 대안을 생각해야 한다는 거에요. 제일 좋아하는 피자 가게에 가면 선택할 수 있는 메뉴가 너무나도 다양하죠? 피자 토핑으로 다양한 고기를 넣거나 치즈를 추가하는 것보다는 야채와 토마토 소스를 더 넣는 것이 칼로리를 많이 줄일 수 있어요. 토마토 소스는 칼로리가 낮거든요, 의외죠? 그리고 여러분 모두 야채가 식이섬유와 비타민을 제공한다는 것은 알고 있

을 거예요. 또한 얇은 크러스트를 주문하면 피해가 덜하죠.
좋아요. 그리고 또 다른 법칙이 있는데요, 일반적인 견해에 속아 넘어가지 말자는 거에요. 왜 그런지는 모르겠지만, 사람들은 생선이나 닭고기 음식을 선택하는 것이 붉은 고기를 먹는 것보다 일반적으로 낫다고 생각하는데, 항상 그런 것은 아니거든요. 튀긴 생선은 구운 버거보다 지방도 많고 칼로리도 더 많아요. 심지어 흰 살고기도 반죽을 입히고 튀기면 몸에 좋지 않지요.

❶ **What is the main topic of the discussion?**

교수는 패스트푸드 레스토랑에 가서 선택의 여지가 적을 때 칼로리를 줄이는 방법을 소개하는데, 적게 먹는 것과 대안을 생각하는 것이다. 따라서 정답은 선택지 A이다. 중간에 학생이 하루에 필요한 칼로리 양을 묻고 교수는 그에 대해 설명하지만, 다시 오늘의 주제로 돌아가자고 했으므로 선택지 B는 답이 아님을 알 수 있다. 선택지 C와 D는 내용과 관련 없는 선택이다.

❷ **What does the professor say about ordering food at a fastfood restaurant?**

교수는 구운 버거보다 튀긴 생선이 안좋다고 했기 때문에 선택지 A는 답이 아니며, 피자를 시킬 때에는 야채 토핑을 시키라고 했으므로 아예 피자를 시키지 말라는 선택지 C 역시 오답이다. 또한 교수는 적은 양의 감자 튀김과 두 개의 고기 패티보다는 한 개가 낫다고 했으므로 D 역시 답이 아니다. 따라서 정답은 선택지 B이다.

❸ **Why does the professor mention the UK Department of Health and the recommended daily calorie intake?**

하루 칼로리 섭취 권장량을 제시한 기관의 이름을 제공함으로써 그 정보에 대한 신뢰도와 권위를 높일 수 있으므로 정답은 선택지 B이다. 하루 권장 칼로리를 제시한 기관의 이름을 언급한 것이 직접적으로 주제에서 벗어난 것은 아니므로 선택지 A는 답이 될 수 없다. 칼로리를 산출하기 위해 기관의 이름을 예를 들어 설명한 것도 아니므로 선택지 C 역시 틀린 선택이며, 선택지 D는 지문에서 제시된 적이 없다.

❹ **Why does the professor say this:**

"Where was I?"는 "내가 어디에 갔었지?"라는 뜻도 되지만, 여기에서는 문맥상 교수가 앞서 무엇을 설명했는지 잊어버린 것으로 해석해야 한다. 따라서 선택지 A가 아닌 C가 정답이 된다. 선택지 B의 경우 지문을 통해서는 알 수 없으므로 정답이 될 수 없다. 교수는 "Let's go back to our topic"이라고 함으로써 질문이 아닌 오늘의 주제로 돌아가고자 한다는 것을 나타낸다. 따라서 선택지 D도 오답이다.

❺ **What were mentioned in the discussion as the factor that affects the personal daily calorie intake?**

"It varies according to the person's lifestyle and other factors, let's say... uh, like I said, the age and sex... uh, height and weight, your basic level of daily activity"에서 정답을 찾을 수 있다.

1. C **2.** C **3.** B, C

P(M): The brain is an incredibly complex masterpiece of creation. With much of its function beyond our understanding, the brain is still shrouded in mystery. However, cutting-edge research is proving that despite this mystery, like any other part of the body, the brain benefits from the age-old tenets of good health. I hope you are all aware of the fact that the brain needs plenty of exercise and the right nutrition to stay in a state of youthful, peak-performing health. Well, science continues to discover how certain exercises and nutrients can benefit our brains. One widely researched discovery which appears to have a significant effect on brain health is phosphatidylserine, or PS for short... ❶ **Okay, let me write this down for you... here you go... well, I'll give you some time later, so let's focus on the lecture here first, all right?** Okay, so... um, as I was saying... PS was initially known for its role in supporting brain function, but subsequent research has revealed a myriad of additional benefits for both body and mind—hinting that people can achieve optimal brain health well into their golden years.

뇌는 매우 복잡한 창조의 걸작입니다. 우리는 아직 뇌의 많은 기능에 대해 이해하지 못하고 있기 때문에, 뇌는 여전히 베일에 가려져 있습니다. 그렇지만 최첨단 연구에 의하면 이렇게 알려지지 않은 부분이 많음에도 불구하고 우리 몸의 다른 기관과 마찬가지로 뇌 또한 건강을 유지하는 기본적인 지침으로부터 이익을 얻는다고 합니다. 여러분 모두 뇌가 젊고 활발하게 활동하는 건강한 상태를 유지하기 위해서 충분한 운동과 적절한 영양을 필요로 한다는 것을 알고 있을 것입니다. 과학은 특정 운동과 영양이 어떠한 면에서 뇌에 긍정적인 영향을 미칠 수 있는지를 지속적으로 밝혀내고 있습니다. 뇌 건강에 상당한 영향을 주는 것으로 보이며, 광범위하게 연구된 물질이 바로 포스파티딜세린, 약자로 PS라는 물질입니다. 자, 여러분을 위해 적어 드리죠... 나중에 시간을 줄테니 지금은 우선 강의에 집중합시다, 알았죠? 자... 아까 말씀드렸듯이, PS는 원래 뇌의 기능을 뒷받침하는 역할로 알려졌지만, 이후의 연구 결과에 따르면 이는 신체 및 정신 건강에 여러가지 긍정적인 영향을 미친다는 것이 밝혀졌습니다. 이는 즉, 사람이 노년기까지 뇌 건강을 최적의 상태로 유지할 수 있다는 것을 알려주는 것이었습니다.

❶ **What does the professor mean when he says this:**

교수는 용어를 받아 적을 시간을 나중에 줄테니 강의를 잘 들으라고 말한다. 따라서 선택지 A, B와 D는 정답이 될 수 없다.

❷ **Why does the professor mention phosphatidylserine?**

"One widely researched discovery which appears to have a significant effect on brain health is phosphatidylserine, or PS for short"라는 교수의 말에서 정답이 C임을 알 수 있다.

❸ **According to the lecture, how does the brain maintain optimal health?**

"The brain needs plenty of exercise and the right nutrition to stay in a state of youthful, peak-performing health"라는 교수의 말에서 정답을 찾을 수 있다. 주기적으로 다이어트를 하거나 충분한 휴식을 취하는 것이 뇌 건강에 도움이 된다고는 언급되지 않았다.

1. C **2.** C **3.** B **4.** B **5.** 참조

	In wilderness	In captivity
Male pandas cannot learn how to mate from other pandas' behaviors.		✔
Male pandas compete for a female during mating season.	✔	
Female pandas give birth every two years for about 15 years.	✔	
The mother panda and the cub are separated six months after birth.		✔
Male pandas and female pandas live in different domains until the female is fertile.		✔

P(W): On September 6, 2006, a cub of a 9-year-old giant panda was born. This little cub, however, was only the fifth giant panda cub born in the United States since 1990. The number seems... a little bit low, since four zoos in the U.S. host breeding pairs of pandas. Why is it this way? Is it the breeding programs that's making the birthrate so low for giant pandas? Well, veterinarians and researchers say that they've not always had much success with breeding giant pandas. In captivity, many male pandas appear simply uninterested in mating or don't know how to mate.

M: What about those that are not kept in captivity? I heard that giant pandas are endangered species and not many of them exist in the wild.

P: Well, researchers thought so, at least in the beginning. You see, the first pair of pandas to live in the United States, Ling-Ling and Hsing-Hsing, tried to mate for 10 years in vain. When they eventually learned how to mate, they had five cubs, but... it's a pity that none of the five cubs actually survived to become adults. See, so scientists initially thought that this failure to mate was the same in the wild, but later, they found out that several male pandas actually compete for each female during mating season which is from March to April. The dominant male can even mate with the female several times. Younger male pandas learn from this process about mating. Actually, wild giant pandas usually give birth every two years for about 15 years, although, that isn't a very high number of reproduction rate.

W: Then is it different for pandas in zoos because they don't have any other pandas to teach them how to mate?

P: That might be one of the most compelling explanations. You see, zoos outside of China generally have one or two breeding panda pairs. You know what this means — there's no competition among male pandas for females. Also, males and females usually live in different cages until the female is fertile. The gestation period for wild female pandas is about three to five months, and after they give birth, they care for their young for about a year and a half. They are not fertile during that time. So, zoos, hoping that the mother panda is able to conceive again earlier than expected, separate the cubs from their mothers when they become six months old. However, some scientists believe that this might cause behavior problems, including pandas' reluctance to breed. ❹ Plus, a female panda can only conceive during a very short period of time... she is fertile for 24 to 36 hours a year, so that's another factor that contributes to the low reproduction rate of giant pandas.

M: Did you say a year? 24 to 36 hours a year?

P: Yes, I did. That's pretty short, if you think about it in terms of human beings...

W: That's incredible. Um, then, is there any other method incorporated by zoos in order to increase the reproduction rate?

P: Actually, yes, thanks to the development of scientific skills. Now, zookeepers could conduct hormone tests in females in order to determine whether they're ovulating or not. They also understand the pandas' behavior patterns better, and have more reliable artificial insemination procedures.

P: 2006년 9월 6일, 9살 난 자이언트 팬더곰의 새끼가 태어났습니다. 하지만 이 작은 새끼 팬더는 미국에서 1990년 이래로 태어난 다섯번째 자이언트 새끼 팬더에 불과했습니다. 태어난 새끼의 숫자가 다소 낮아 보이는데요, 특히 팬더를 사육하는 동물원 시설이 미국의 경우 4개나 된다는 점에서 볼 때 더욱 그렇죠. 왜 이런 일이 벌어지는 걸까요? 사육 프로그램이 자이언트 팬더의 출생율을 낮추는 것일까요? 수의사와 연구자들은 자이언트 팬더의 사육은 지금껏 그다지 성공적이지 않았다고 합니다. 갇혀 있는 상태에서, 많은 수컷 팬더들은 교미에 관심이 없거나 할 줄을 모르는 것 같다고 합니다.

M: 사육되지 않는 팬더들은 어떤가요? 팬더는 멸종 위험에 처한 동물이고 야생에서도 수가 적다고 들었어요.

P: 음. 연구자들도 최소한 처음엔 그렇게 생각했습니다. 미국에서 처음 살았던 팬더곰 부부 링링과 싱싱은 10년간 교미를 하려고 노력했지만 실패하였죠. 그들이 교미하는 방법을 결국 알아낸 후 다섯 마리의 새끼를 낳았지만, 안타깝게도 이 다섯 마리 전부 완전히 성장하기 전에 죽어버렸습니다. 그래서 과학자들은 처음에 이처럼 교미에 실패하는 것이 야생에서도 마찬가지일 것이라고 생각했지만, 후에 여러 마리의 수컷 팬더들이 교미 기간, 즉 3월에서 4월 사이에 실제로 암컷 팬더들을 두고 서로 경쟁한다는 것을 알게 되었습니다. 경쟁에서 이긴 수컷은 암컷과 심지어 여러 차례 교미할 수 있죠. 어린 수컷 팬더는 이 과정에서 교미를 배웁니다. 실제로, 야생 자이언트 팬더는 15년동안 매 2년마다 새끼를 낳지만, 이것도 그다지 높은 번식율은 아니죠.

W: 그럼 동물원의 팬더의 번식률이 다른 이유는 교미 방법을 가르쳐 줄 다른 팬더들이 없어서인가요?

P: 아마 그것이 가장 유력한 설명 중 하나가 아닐까 생각됩니다. 중국 외의 동물원들은 주로 한 두쌍의 번식을 위한 팬더를 보유하고 있습니다. 이것이 무엇을 의미하는지 아시겠죠. 즉, 수컷들 사이에 암컷을 위한 경쟁이 없다는 것입니다. 또한, 수컷과 암컷들은 주로 암컷이 새끼를 낳을 수 있을 정도로 성숙하기 전까지 서로 다른 우리에서 자랍니다. 야생 팬더의 임신 기간은 대략 3~5개월이고 새끼를 낳은 후 돌보는 기간은 대략 1년 반입니다. 그 기간 동안에는 임신을 할 수가 없죠. 그래서 동물원들은 좀더 빨리 다시 새끼를 갖게끔 하기 위해 새끼가 생후 6개월이 지나면 어미와 격리시킵니다. 그러나 일부 과학자들은 이것이 팬더곰들의 행동 장애, 즉 번식을 꺼려하는 행동 등을 유발시킬 수 있다고 생각합니다. 게다가 암컷 팬더가 새끼를 가질 수 있는 시간이 아주 짧습니다. 1년에 겨우 24~36시간 동안에만 새끼를 가질 수 있기 때문에, 이것 또한 자이언트 팬더의 낮은 번식율의 한가지 원인이기도 합니다.

M: 1년이라고 하셨나요? 1년에 24에서 36시간이요?

P: 네, 맞습니다. 사람과 비교해서 생각하면 매우 짧은 시간이지요...

W: 놀랍네요. 그렇다면 번식율을 높이기 위해 동물원이 시도하는 다른 방법들이 있나요?

P: 물론 있습니다. 과학 기술의 진보 덕분이지요. 요즘에는 동물원의 사육사들이 암컷에게 호르몬 실험을 해서 이들이 배란을 하는지를 알아볼 수 있습니다. 그들은 또한 팬더의 행동 유형을 더 잘 이해하고 있고, 보다 신뢰성이 높은 인공 수정 과정을 보유하고 있습니다.

❶ **What is the discussion mainly about?**

강의의 초반에서 교수는 "In captivity, many male pandas appear simply uninterested in mating or don't know how to mate"라고 말하며 오늘의 주제를 제시한다. 중간에 야생 팬더의 번식을 언급하기도 하지만, 이것은 야생 팬더의 번식과

동물원 팬더의 번식을 비교하기 위해 언급된 것일 뿐, 다시 동물원 팬더의 번식 내용으로 돌아간다. 따라서 정답은 C이다. 나머지 선택지들은 지문에서 잠시 언급된 제한적인 내용을 담고 있기 때문에 주제가 될 수 없다.

❷ Why does the professor mention the cub of a 9-year-old giant panda that was born on September 6, 2006?

이 자이언트 팬더의 새끼를 언급한 이유는 오늘의 주제를 소개하기 위해서이기도 하지만, 야생의 상태가 아닌 사육되는 팬더의 번식률이 매우 낮다는 것을 보여주기 위해서이기도 하다. 따라서 가장 근접한 답은 선택지 C이다. 선택지 A와 D는 지문과 관련이 없으며, 교수는 미국 내의 팬더곰 번식 프로그램이 비효율적이라고 직접적으로 비판한 적이 없으므로 선택지 B 역시 답이 될 수 없다.

❸ According to the professor, why is the reproduction rate of giant pandas in zoos so low?

"Then is it different in pandas in zoos because they don't have any other pandas to teach them how to mate?"라는 학생의 질문에 대한 교수의 답, "That might be one of the most compelling explanations"에서 정답을 찾을 수 있다.

❹ Why does the student say this:

암컷 팬더곰의 가임기가 일년에 24~36시간 밖에 안된다는 교수의 말에 믿을 수 없다고 하는 학생의 반응과 말투에서 답을 알 수 있다. 반 학생들 앞에서 돋보이기 위해 이 말을 한 것이 아니므로 선택지 A는 오답이며 교수의 말에 반대하는 것도 아니므로 C 역시 오답이다. 새로운 정보를 제공한 것이 아니므로 선택지 D 역시 지워야 한다.

❺ Based on the information in the discussion, indicate whether each sentence below describes giant pandas in the wild or in captivity.

야생 상태의 수컷 팬더는 번식 기간에 다른 수컷들과 경쟁을 하며, 암컷 팬더는 15년동안 2년마다 새끼를 낳는다. 사육 상태의 수컷 팬더는 다른 팬더에게서 번식 행태를 배울 수 없으며, 새끼는 태어난 지 6개월 만에 어미와 분리된다. 또한 동물원에서는 암컷이 새끼를 낳을 수 있을 정도로 자랄 때까지 암컷과 수컷을 분리시킨다.

Passage 7

1. C   **2.** A, B   **3.** C   **4.** B   **5.** A, B, E   **6.** D

P(M): Okay, before we move on to the definition of cataracts, who can tell me what a cataract is?

W: Um, I always thought that cataract is a film over the eye and is caused by overusing the eyes.

M: And it spreads from one eye to the other, no?

P: Well, what you have just mentioned are several of the many misconceptions about cataract that many people generally hold. Cataract is not a film over the eye, it's not caused by overusing the eyes, and it doesn't spread from one eye to the other. A cataract is actually a clouding of the lens of the eye which is clear in normal cases. It might be easier if you think of a window that's frosted or yellowed, got the idea?

M: If my vision is blurred, professor, then does it mean I have cataracts? Because that happens to me sometimes.

P: Good question, Jimmy. Let me talk about the common symptoms of cataract first. They include, um, a painless blurring of vision, sensitivity to light, not being able to see clear at night, double vision in one eye, needing brighter light to read, and fading or yellowing of colors. Usually, the presence of a cataract can be detected by an ophthalmologist through a thorough eye examination. The eye doctor can also find out other conditions that may be causing blurred vision or other eye problems.

W: Then, what causes cataracts? Is there anything we can do to prevent it?

P: Well, the most common type of cataract is related to aging of the eye. Cataracts can develop from a variety of reasons, including family history, medical problems such as diabetes, an injury to the eye, long-term ultraviolet exposure, medications, or previous eye surgery. So, you may want to avoid taking unsafe medication such as steroids and try to protect your eyes from being exposed to the sun directly on very sunny days.

M: How long does it take to develop?

P: Well, it really depends on the individual — you know, it may even be different between the two eyes of a same person. Most age-related cataracts develop slowly but gradually over a period of years. However, some people... say, younger people and those with diabetes, may have cataracts that progress rapidly over a short period of time. Therefore, it's extremely difficult to predict exactly how fast cataracts will develop in any given person.

P: 자, 백내장의 정의에 대해 알아보기 전에, 백내장이 무엇인지 말해 볼 사람 있나요?

W: 음, 저는 백내장이 눈을 많이 써서 눈에 얇은 막이 덮이는 거라고 알고 있는데요.

M: 그리고 한쪽 눈에서 다른 쪽 눈으로 번지지 않나요?

P: 자, 방금 여러분들이 얘기한 것은 많은 사람들이 일반적으로 백내장에 대해 오해하고 있는 여러 가지 개념들 중 일부예요. 백내장은 눈에 덮이는 얇은 막도 아니고, 눈을 많이 써서 생기는 것도 아니에요. 그리고 한쪽 눈에서 다른 쪽 눈으로 번지지도 않아요. 백내장은 일반적으로 맑은 눈의 렌즈가 흐려지는 거예요. 서리가 끼거나 먼지가 낀 창문을 생각해 보면 더 쉬울 거예요. 이해되나요?

M: 교수님, 시력이 흐려지면 백내장이 있다는 뜻인가요? 제가 이따금 그러거든요.

P: 좋은 질문이에요, 지미. 백내장의 흔한 증상부터 먼저 얘기해 보죠. 증상으로는 보통 통증없는 시야의 흐림, 빛에 대한 민감성, 야간시력의 저하, 한쪽 눈의 겹침 현상, 책을 읽을 때 더 밝은 빛이 필요한 것, 그리고 색감이 흐려지거나 노란빛으로 보이는 것 등이 있어요. 일반적으로 안과 의사의 철저한 검사를 통해 백내장이 있는지 확인할 수 있어요. 안과 의사는 또한 시야가 흐려지는 등의 기타 눈과 관련된 문제를 야기하는 다른 질환이 있는지 확인할 수 있죠.

W: 그럼 백내장의 원인은 무엇인가요? 예방할 수 있는 방법이 있나요?

P: 가장 흔한 종류의 백내장은 눈의 노화와 관련이 있어요. 백내장은 여러 원인이 있는데 가족력, 당뇨병 같은 의학적 문제, 눈의 부상, 자외선에의 장시간 노출, 약 복용, 혹은 과거에 했던 눈 수술 등이 있죠. 따라서 스테로이드 같은 위험한 약은 피하고, 맑은 날 햇빛에 눈이 장기간 직접적으로 노출되는 것을 방지하는 것이 좋아요.

M: 발병은 얼마나 걸리나요?

P: 음, 그건 개인에 따라 달라요 – 심지어 한 사람의 양쪽 눈이 각기 다른 경우도 있죠. 대부분의 노화 관련 백내장은 오랜 기간에 걸쳐 서서히 진행돼요. 하지만 젊은 사람들이나 당뇨병 환자의 경우에는 백내장이 짧은 기간 내에 빠른 속도로 진행될 수 있어요. 그렇기 때문에 백내장이 특정인에게 얼마나 빨리 진행될 것인지 예측하기란 매우 어려워요.

❶ What is the possible subject of the discussion?

교수는 백내장의 정의를 내리기 전에 먼저 백내장이 무엇인지를 설명하고 증상, 원인, 그리고 예방법 등을 언급한다. 따라서 이 지문을 가장 잘 요약한 정답은 선택지 C이다.

❷ What were mentioned as the common misconceptions about cataract?

교수는 "Cataract is not a film over the eye, it's not caused by overusing the eyes, and it doesn't spread from one eye to the other"라고 하면서 백내장에 대한 가장 흔한 오해에 대해 설명한다. 따라서 정답은 선택지 A와 B이다.

❸ Why does the professor mention a frosted window?

"It might be easier if you think of a window that's frosted or yellowed, got the idea?"에서 답을 찾을 수 있다. 이 지문은 당뇨병과는 관련이 없으므로 선택지 A는 지워야 하며, 서리가 낀 창문이 백내장의 주요 원인은 아니므로 선택지 B 역시 지워야 한다. 선택지 D는 본문의 내용과 관련이 없다.

❹ According to the professor, who is most likely to develop cataract?

"The most common type of cataract is related to

aging of the eye"라는 교수의 말에서 일단 고령의 사람이 백내장에 가장 잘 걸릴 수 있다는 것을 알 수 있으며, "Family history, medical problems such as diabetes, an injury to the eye, long-term ultraviolet exposure, medications, or previous eye surgery"의 내용을 보아, 눈 수술 경험이 있는 고령자, 즉 선택지 B가 백내장에 걸렸을 가능성이 가장 높음을 알 수 있다. 선택지 A 역시 백내장이 있을 가능성이 있지만 B보다는 낮으므로 B가 더 나은 선택이다. 나병 (leprosy)과 한쪽 눈을 사고로 잃은 것에 대한 언급은 본문에 없으므로 선택지 C와 D는 옳은 선택이 아니다.

❺ What were mentioned as the common symptoms of cataract?

"Let me talk about the common symptoms of cataract here first. They include, um, a painless blurring of vision, glare or light sensitivity, poor night vision, double vision in one eye, needing brighter light to read, and fading or yellowing of colors"에서 정답을 찾을 수 있다.

❻ According to the professor, how long does it take to develop cataract?

교수에 따르면 백내장의 발병 기간은 사람마다 다르기 때문에 정확하게 예측하기란 불가능하다. 따라서 정답은 D이다.

(**Passage 8**)

1. D　　**2.** C, D, E　　**3.** A　　**4.** D　　**5.** C, D

P(W): Let's imagine a situation here — you went on a camping trip to a far away mountain with some of your closest friends, let's say, for a month. What would you first think of to carry with you? You'd have no access to markets or grocery stores. Well, you'd most likely take lots of food and basic ingredients, of course, along with some kitchen utensils, such as... uh, frying pan, a pot, or a wok, not to mention paper plates, paper towel, plastic forks and knives, spoons, um, what else... well, you get the idea, right? Also, you'd want to make sure that you store your food properly, so you would probably take lots of canned or dried food that's nonperishable, easier to eat, and take up less space. When you finish camping and are about to come back home, you'd need a big garbage bag to clean up all your mess.

Well, that's basically the same with astronauts who live in space for months, sometimes up to years. There are different ways to cook food in space according to what type of food it is — you can eat some types of food in their natural form, such as cookies, brownies, or fruit, but sometimes you need to add water for food such as spaghetti and macaroni and cheese. Some food is cooked in the oven which is already provided in the space shuttle; however, there's no refrigerator in the shuttle. So how do they keep food from spoiling? Well, in order for it to last long, space food must be stored in special packages and prepared properly.

Here's an interesting fact about food in space — about 50 percent of the food being consumed in space, especially on the International Space Station, is packaged and supplied by the United States, with the rest by Russia. Russians mainly use cans for packaging their food but the US uses retort pouches for most thermostabilized entrees. Another thing to consider about food consumed in space is crumbs from cookies or crackers. Because the air quality in the shuttle is directly dependent upon the amount of contamination that's released into the cabin during flight, food that produces lots of crumbs can be a big contributor to pollution. Thus, cookies are prepared as bite-size so that astronauts don't spread crumbs all over the place.

이런 상황을 한 번 생각해 봅시다. 예를 들어 여러분이 친한 친구들과 함께 먼 곳에 있는 산으로 한 달간 캠핑을 갔다고 합시다. 제일 먼저 무엇을 가져가야겠다고 생각할까요? 마켓이나 식료품점에는 갈 수 없는 상황입니다. 아마 많은 음식과 기본 재료, 그리고 몇 가지 주방 기구, 가령 프라이팬, 냄비, 혹은 조리용 팬을 가져갈 것입니다. 이 밖에도 종이 접시, 페이퍼 타올, 플라스틱 포크와 나이프, 숟가락 등도 가져가겠죠, 무슨 말인지 아시겠죠? 또한 음식을 알맞게 저장해야 하니까 깡통 음식이나 마른 음식 등 상하지 않고, 먹기 쉽고, 공간을 적게 차지하는 것을 많이 가져갈 것입니다. 캠핑을 끝내고 집에 올 때 쓰레기를 치울 큰 쓰레기 봉지도 필요하겠죠.

자, 이것은 우주에서 몇 달, 심지어 몇 년간 생활하는 우주 비행사들에게도 마찬가지입니다. 우주 음식은 종류에 따라 조리하는 방법도 여러가지입니다 – 과자, 케익, 과일과 같은 일부 음식은 원상태 그대로 먹을 수 있지만, 스파게티나 마카로니와 치즈와 같은 음식에는 종종 물을 타야 하죠. 일부 음식은 우주 왕복선에 내장되어 있는 오븐에서 굽지만, 냉장고는 내장되어 있지 않습니다. 그렇다면 음식이 상하는 것을 어떻게 막을까요? 우주 음식을 오래 보존하기 위해서는 특수 포장하여 올바르게 준비해야 합니다.

우주에서 먹는 음식에 대해 흥미로운 사실 한 가지를 알려드리죠 – 우주에서, 특히 국제 우주 정거장에서 소비되는 음식의 50%는 미국에서 포장 및 공급되고 나머지는 러시아가 제공합니다. 러시아는 음식 저장을 위해 주로 깡통을 사용하지만 미국은 대부분의 열 안정화된 주식을 레토르트 용기에 포장합니다. 우주에서 먹는 음식에 있어 고려해야 하는 또 다른 문제는 쿠키나 크래커의 부스러기입니다. 우주선 내의 공기 질이 비행 도중 선실 내로 방출되는 오염량에 따라 직접적으로 좌우되기 때문에, 부스러기를 많이 만들어 내는 음식은 오염의 주 원인이 됩니다. 따라서 과자는 한 입 크기로 만들어져 우주 비행사들이 사방에 부스러기를 흘리는 것을 방지합니다.

❶ What is the lecture mainly about?

교수는 우주에서 생활하는 우주 비행사들이 먹는 음식에 대해 설명하면서 우주 음식을 제공하는 국가와 용기, 그리고 준비시 주의점 등을 설명한다. 이러한 내용을 가장 잘 담고 있는 선택지는 D이다. 선택지 A는 강의의 초반에서만 설명된 제한된 내용이며, 선택지 B는 강의의 내용과 관련이 없다. 선택지 C 또한 제한된 내용을 담고 있으므로 정답이 아니다.

❷ What are mentioned in the lecture as the necessity for a long-term camping trip?

"Frying pan, a pot, a wok... lots of paper plates, paper towel, plastic forks and knives, spoons"에서 정답을 찾을 수 있다.

❸ Why does the professor mention canned food or dried food that is nonperishable when going camping?

교수는 오랜 기간 캠핑을 갈 때 챙겨가야 할 음식을 언급하며 우주에서 오랜 기간 생활하는 우주 비행사들도 이와 마찬가지라고 말한다. 따라서 "우주에서 필요한 음식이 어떤 것인지 설명하기 위해서"라고 한 선택지 A가 정답이다. 선택지 B와 D는 강의의 내용과 관련이 없으며, "우주에서 소비되는 건조 음식이나 깡통 음식의 제조자를 설명"하는 것과 캠핑갈 때 이러한 음식을 가져가는 것은 직접적인 관련이 없다.

❹ How does the professor organize the lecture?

교수는 먼저 캠핑에 대한 예를 제시하고 이것이 우주에서 생활하는 것과 비슷하다며 그 둘을 비교한 후, 우주 음식에 대한 중요한 사항을 설명한다. 연대기적으로 설명하는 것이 아니므로 선택지 A는 틀린 선택이며, 강의 전체에 걸쳐 우주 음식의 예를 드는 것은 아니므로 선택지 B 역시 정답이 아니다. 선택지 C는 강의의 후반부에 잠시 언급된 내용이므로 정답이 아니다. 가장 좋은 답은 선택지 D이다.

❺ What are mentioned in the lecture about space food?

"There are different ways to cook space food according to what type of food it is—you can eat some types of food in their natural form, such as cookies, brownies, or fruit"라는 교수의 말에서 선택지 A는 틀렸음을 알 수 있다. 우주 음식은 레토르트 용기와 캔 용기에 담겨 제공된다고 했으므로 선택지 B 역시 틀렸다. 러시아와 미국이 우주 음식을 각각 절반씩 제공한다고 했으며, 과자나 케익, 과일은 원상태로 먹을 수 있다고 했으므로 정답은 C, D이다.

1. B   **2.** A   **3.** C   **4.** B, D   **5.** C

P(M): All right, let's begin. Oh, uh, before we start, I'm going to have to tell you this first... um, I have a meeting with my accountant next Monday so I'll have to leave early, like, an hour earlier. ❸ Um, I'll make up for the missed time next class... that's, uh, Thursday, right? Yes, yes, Thursday... so be advised that we'll be having a shorter class next Monday and a little bit longer class on Thursday.

Okay, then. Um, today, we're gonna talk about the Ozone Layer and its function, and... some recent environmental issues involved with the Layer. Um, ozone occurs naturally in the Earth's atmosphere through a multi-step chemical process that requires sunlight. The Ozone Layer exists in the stratosphere, where 90 percent of the Earth's ozone resides. What Ozone Layer does, basically, is that it absorbs about 97 to 99 percent of the sun's harmful rays such as ultraviolet light which is potentially damaging to life on Earth. To be more exact, the Layer filters out the shorter wavelengths of ultraviolet light from the sun. If, um, a living thing is exposed to this light, it can develop cancer, genetic damage, eye damage, and it can pose serious danger to marine life.

However, because of recent environment pollution and, uh, increase in greenhouse gas, the Layer has been found thinning every year. You guys have heard about this countless times, right? Since it is highly essential for humankind to survive, not to mention plants and animals, NASA and other organizations have been trying to study the Ozone Layer and measure ozone in the Earth's atmosphere. NASA built a satellite that weighs approximately 6,500 pounds that's called Aura satellite. This state-of-the-art spacecraft carries four high-tech instruments that scan the globe from more than 700 kilometers above the Earth. Um, the four instruments include two radiometers and two spectrometers that each looks down on Earth from a different angle.

좋아요, 시작합시다. 아, 시작하기 전에 이것 먼저 얘기를 해야겠네요... 다음 주 월요일에 회계사와 미팅이 있어서 수업을 조금 일찍 끝내야 할 것 같습니다. 한 시간 정도 말이지요. 이 한 시간은 그 다음 시간에 보충 강의를 하겠습니다. 목요일 맞죠? 네, 목요일에... 그러니까 다음 주 월요일은 수업을 좀 짧게 하고 목요일엔 좀 길게 수업할 거라고 미리 알고들 계세요.

자, 그럼 시작합시다. 오늘은 오존층과 오존층의 기능, 그리고 오존층과 관련한 최근의 환경 문제 등에 대해서 얘기해 보겠습니다. 오존은 햇빛을 필요로 하는 다단계적 화학 작용을 통해 지구의 대기에 생성됩니다. 오존층은 지구의 90%의 오존이 위치한 성층권에서 생성됩니다. 오존층의 기본적 역할은 태양의 유해한 광선의 97에서 99%를 차단하는 건데요, 이러한 광선은 지구의 생명에 잠재적으로 해를 끼치는 자외선 같은 것을 말합니다. 더 정확히 말하자면, 오존층은 태양에서 오는 자외선의 짧은 파장을 여과합니다. 만약 생물이 이 빛에 노출되면 암에 걸리거나 유전적 손상, 시력 손상 등이 생길 수 있고 해저 생물에도 큰 위험을 끼칠 수 있습니다.

그렇지만 근래의 환경 오염과 온실 가스의 증가로 인해 매년 오존층이 얇아지고 있습니다. 이 얘기는 수도 없이 들어봤겠죠? 인류 뿐 아니라 동식물의 생존을 위해 오존층이 매우 중요하기 때문에, NASA와 다른 기관들은 오존층을 연구하고 지구 기층의 오존을 측정해 왔습니다. NASA는 오라 인공 위성이라는 약 6500 파운드 무게의 인공 위성을 제작했습니다. 이 최첨단 우주선은 4개의 첨단 기계를 탑재하고 있는데, 이 기계로 700 킬로미터 상공에서도 지구를 측정할 수 있습니다. 이 4개의 기계는 2개의 방사선 측정기와 2개의 분광계인데, 각각 다른 각도에서 지구를 측정합니다.

❶ **What is the lecture mainly about?**

교수는 먼저 오존층과 오존층의 기능에 대해 설명하고, 오존층과 관련된 환경 문제를 간단하게 설명한다. 따라서 강의의 전반적인 주제를 가장 잘 담고 있는 답은 선택지 B이다. 오존층의 성분과 NASA의 위성은 강의에서 잠시 언급된 것이므로 오답이며, 오존층의 외형에 대해서는 강의에서 언급된 바가 없다.

❷ **Why does the professor mention the meeting with his accountant?**

다음 주 수업 시간에 변경이 생기는 이유는 교수가 회계사와 만나야 하기 때문이다. 따라서 정답은 A이다. 교수가 회계학에 관심이 있어서 이를 언급한 것은 아니므로 선택지 B는 틀렸으며, 오늘 수업에 늦은 것이 아니므로 선택지 C 또한 오답이다. 다음 주 월요일에 수업이 일찍 끝나는 것이지, 쪽지 시험을 보겠다고 한 것이 아니므로 D 역시 지워야 한다.

❸ **Why does the professor say this:**

교수는 다음 주 월요일에 수업을 일찍 끝내야 하며 언제 보충 강의를 할 것인지에 대한 안내를 먼저 한 다음, 강의를 시작한다. 다시 듣는 부분은 교수가 안내를 끝내고 수업을 시작할 것임을 알려주는 표현이므로 정답은 C이다.

❹ **What are mentioned in the lecture about the Ozone Layer?**

"Ozone occurs naturally in the Earth's atmosphere through a multi-step chemical processes that requires sunlight"에서 선택지 A가 잘못된 내용임을 알 수 있고, "The Ozone Layer exists in the stratosphere, where 90 percent of the Earth's ozone resides"에서 선택지 B는 맞는 내용임을 알 수 있다. 오존층은 유해한 태양 광선을 97~99% 차단한다고 했으므로 선택지 C는 오답이며, "Because of recent environment po lution and increase in greenhouse gas, the Layer has been found thinning every year"라는 교수의 말에서 선택지 D는 맞는 내용임을 알 수 있다.

❺ **According to the lecture, what will probably happen if a living creature is exposed directly to the shorter wavelengths of ultraviolet light from the sun?**

교수는 태양에서 오는 자외선의 짧은 파장에 생물이 노출되면 암에 걸릴 수도 있고 유전적 손상, 시력 손상 등이 생길 수도 있다고 하며 해저 생물에도 큰 위험을 끼칠 수 있다고 한다. 시력 손상만 생기는 것이 아니기 때문에 선택지 A는 오답이며, 해저 생물에게만 위험을 끼치는 것이 아니라 생물 전체에 위험을 가할 수 있기 때문에 B 역시 틀렸다. 더 많은 새끼를 낳는다는 말은 언급된 바가 없으므로 D 역시 오답이다.

Passage 10

1. D **2.** B, C, D **3.** B

P(M): Another type of social insect is the bee. There are about 400 different species of social bees, including but not limited to bumblebees, stingless bees, and honeybees. Today, let's talk about honeybees and their society. Honeybees are commonly raised for production of honey and wax in many parts of the world. They build nests, or combs, as we usually call them, made out of wax which is secreted by glands in the abdomen. Hives are usually boxes provided by beekeepers.

There are three castes in a typical bee Colóny: the queen, many thousands of workers, and a few hundred drones. The queen produces all the eggs which are attended by workers who are sexually undeveloped females. The workers' job is to gather nectar, make and store honey, build the cells in their nest, clean and ventilate, and protect the hive. They also feed and take care of the queen and the larvae. Drones are fertile males who impregnate the queen during the mating season. What drones do... well, I think I just answered my question right now. We don't have much to talk about regarding the drones.

Um, you'd all know that bees have stings... um, they are located at the tip of the female bee's abdomen, and are usually strong and sharp, connected to the poison glands. The queen bee also has a sting but hers is smooth and can be withdrawn easily so she only uses it for rival queens. The worker bee's sting, on the other hand, is barbed at the end and cannot be withdrawn without tearing the body of the bee, which causes it to die.

또 다른 종류의 사회성 곤충은 바로 벌입니다. 약 400여 종의 사회적 벌은 뒹벌, 침 없는 벌, 그리고 꿀벌 외에도 다양합니다. 오늘은 꿀벌과 그 사회에 대해 봅시다. 꿀벌은 일반적으로 꿀과 밀랍을 만들기 위해 세계 각지에서 양식됩니다. 그들은 우리가 흔히 벌집이라고 부르는 둥지를 짓는데, 이는 복부의 분비기관에서 나오는 밀랍으로 만들어 집니다. 꿀벌통은 주로 양봉자가 제공하는 상자입니다.

일반적인 꿀벌 집단은 여왕, 수천 마리의 일벌, 그리고 수백 마리의 수벌의 세 계급으로 구성됩니다. 여왕은 알을 생산하는데, 이는 성적으로 분화하지 않은 암컷인 일벌이 돌보게 됩니다. 일벌의 임무는 꽃에서 꿀물을 모아 꿀을 만들고 저장하고, 벌집의 방을 만들고, 오물을 치우고 집을 환기시키며, 벌집을 보호하는 것입니다. 이들은 또한 여왕과 유충을 돌봅니다. 수벌은 짝짓기 기간 동안 여왕벌을 수임시키는 번식력이 있는 수컷입니다. 수벌이 하는 일은... 글쎄요, 방금 제 질문에 제가 답한 것 같네요. 수벌에 대해서는 얘기할 만한 것은 별로 없어요.

자, 여러분 모두 벌이 침을 갖고 있다는 것을 알고 있을 것입니다. 침은 암벌의 배 끝에 있는데 일반적으로 튼튼하고 날카로우며 독침선과 연결되어 있습니다. 여왕벌 또한 침이 있지만 이는 둥글고 빼내기 쉽기 때문에 주로 라이벌 여왕벌에게만 사용합니다. 반면, 일벌의 침은 끝에 가시가 있고, 빼내는 과정에서 벌의 몸을 찢어 죽게 만듭니다.

❶ **What does the professor say about the queen bee?**

여왕벌은 수벌에 의해 수임되므로 선택지 A는 정답이 아니며, 알을 낳긴 하지만 꿀을 만들고 벌집을 보호하는 것은 일벌이므로 B 역시 오답이다. 선택지 C는 일벌에 대한 설명이다. 강의에서 여왕벌은 라이벌 여왕벌을 쫓아내기 위해 침을 사용한다는 것을 추론할 수 있으므로 정답은 D이다.

❷ **Which of the following are the jobs of the worker bees?**

"The workers' job is to gather nectar, make and store honey, build the cells in their nest, clean and ventilate, and protect the hive. They also feed and take care of the queen and the larvae"라고 한 부분에서 정답을 찾을 수 있다. A는 여왕벌의 일이며 E는 수벌의 일이다.

❸ **How does the professor organize the lecture on the caste of a typical bee colony?**

교수는 꿀벌 집단의 세 계급에 대해 설명하며 각 계급별로 행하는 임무를 설명한다. 따라서 꿀벌 집단의 계급별 임무를 설명한 선택지 B가 정답이 된다. 어느 정보가 가장 중요한지는 알 수 없으므로 선택지 A는 바른 답이 아니며, 외국의 연구를 언급한 적 또한 없으므로 C도 틀린 답이다. 비사회성 벌에 대한 언급 역시 없으므로 선택지 D도 오답이다.

Vocabulary Test

1. absorb **2.** overuse **3.** medication
4. optimal **5.** withdraw **6.** countless
7. dominant **8.** drone **9.** a
10. c **11.** d **12.** b
13. d **14.** a **15.** b

4 Content

P: 자, 이제 시작합시다. 오늘은 신용 점수의 개념과 계산 방법에 대해 이야기 해 보겠습니다. 우선 신용 점수란 무엇인가요? 이것이 무엇인지 말해 줄 사람 있나요? 네, 톰?

M: 음. 신용 점수란 특정 시기에 소비자가 갖는 신용 위험을 나타내는 숫자인 것 같아요.

P: 맞아요. 누구나 신용 점수를 가지고 있어요. 최소한 미국에서 신용 기록을 갖고 있으면 말이죠. 자, 그럼 일반적인 신용 점수의 범위를 살펴봅시다. 이론적으로 신용 점수의 범위는 375에서 900사이인데, 375는 신용 점수가 낮다는 것을 의미해요. 그렇지만 미국의 평균 신용 점수는 680 정도예요.

W: 음. 신용 전수는 왜 375에서 900사이인가요? 예를 들어서 00나 1에서 시작하고, 100에서 끝날 수도 있을 텐데요.

Strategy Focus

1. C   **2.** D   **3.** D   **4.** A

1. C

P(W): Now, do you remember Hurricane Katrina that struck New Orleans, Louisiana in August, 2005? It devastated the region and left thousands homeless. So, what are some of the causes of this destructive force of nature known as a hurricane?

Well, let me first tell you that the term hurricane is used for the types of storms in the eastern and gulf coasts of the United States, Mexico, Central America and the Caribbean... uh, during the hurricane season, which is typically between early June and late November. Um, in other parts of the world, the same types of storms are called typhoons or cyclones. The... uh, the low-pressure systems that develop in the tropics are called tropical cyclones. The name changes to tropical storm once the tropical cyclone reaches winds of at least 17 meters per second. Uh, if winds reach 33 meters per second, then you call it a hurricane.

Speaking of hurricanes forming in the tropics... they usually form in tropical regions with warm water... uh, at least 80 degrees Fahrenheit... that's about 27 degrees Celsius... Also, moist air and converging equatorial winds are involved in forming of hurricanes.

2005년 8월에 미국 루이지애나 주의 뉴올리언스를 강타한 허리케인 카트리나를 기억하나요? 이 허리케인은 그 지역을 초토화시키고 수천 명의 집을 앗아갔습니다. 그렇다면 허리케인이라는 파괴적인 자연의 힘이 발생하는 원인은 무엇일까요?

우선, 허리케인이라는 용어는 미국의 동해안과 걸프만, 멕시코, 중앙 아메리카와 카리브해 등에서 발생하는 폭풍의 종류를 일컫는 것입니다. 허리케인은 보통 6월 초에서 11월 말까지인 허리케인 시즌에 발생합니다. 세계의 다른 지역에서는 이와 똑같은 폭풍이 태풍이나 사이클론이라고 불립니다. 열대 지역에서 발생하는 저기압 시스템은 열대 사이클론이라고 불리며, 풍속이 최소 초속 17미터에 이르게 되면 열대 사이클론의 이름이 열대 폭풍으로 바뀝니다. 풍속이 초속 33미터에 이르게 되면 이것을 허리케인이라고 부르게 됩니다.

열대 지역에서 발생하는 허리케인에 대해 잠시 언급하자면... 이 허리케인은 주로 따뜻한 바다가 있고, 기온이 화씨 80도 혹은 섭씨 27도 정도인 열대 지역에서 발생합니다. 또한 습한 대기와 적도풍이 수렴하는 것도 허리케인의 발생에 영향을 미칩니다.

2. D

P(M): In United States history, the story of the Native Americans is very tragic. Their land was taken over by the white settlers and thousands were slaughtered because of various reasons, misunderstanding of their culture being one of those reasons. Ironically, the U.S. government turned to Navajos for help during World War II.

There is no doubt that communication is highly essential at any war and World War II was no different. You should know when and where to attack or whether to retreat or not in order to win the battle or at least survive from it. So codes were widely used, but unfortunately, these codes were frequently broken. Now here's where the Navajos take part in the war. In 1942, a man named Philip Johnston, the son of a Protestant missionary who spent most of his childhood on a Navajo reservation, came up with a code which was based on the Navajo language. Since he spent a significant part of his childhood with Navajo children and learned the language, he thought that a code based on their language, which was completely unknown to outsiders of the Navajo tribe, might be unbreakable by an enemy. The U.S. Marine Corps thought this was a pretty good idea and started a pilot program which proved to be highly successful and they started to recruit more Navajo Code Talkers. Some of the examples these Code Talkers developed are lo-tso meaning "whale" for "battleship," beh-na-ali-tsosie meaning "slant eye" for "Japan," and tas-chizzie which means "swallow" in Navajo, which stands for "torpedo plane."

미국 역사에서 아메리카 원주민의 이야기는 매우 비극적이에요. 백인 식민자들에게 그들의 땅을 빼앗겼고 여러 가지 이유 때문에 수천 명이 학살당했는데, 그들의 문화에 대한 오해가 그 이유 중 하나였어요. 아이러니하게도 미국 정부는 제2차 세계대전 당시에 아메리카 원주민인 나바호 부족에게 도움을 요청했죠.

어떠한 전쟁에서든지 의사 소통이 매우 중요한 위치를 차지한다는 것은 의심의 여지가 없어요. 제2차 세계대전도 예외는 아니었죠. 전투에서 이기거나 적어도 살아남기 위해서는 언제 어디를 공격해야 하는지, 혹은 퇴각해야 하는지 말아야 하는지 등을 알아야 해요. 그래서 암호가 널리 사용됐지만 안타깝게도 이러한 암호들은 금방 해독이 되곤 했죠. 자, 이때 바로 나바호 원주민들이 전쟁에 참여하게 되었어요. 1942년에 개신교 선교사의 아들이자 어린 시절의 대부분을 나바호 원주민 보호구역에서 자란 필립 존스턴이라는 사람이 나바호 언어에 바탕을 둔 암호를 생각해 냈어요. 그는 나바호 어린이들과 함께 자라고 그들의 언어와 문화를 알고 있었기 때문에 부족이 아닌 외부인에게는 전혀 알려지지 않은 나바호 언어를 바탕으로 하는 암호는 적군에게 해독되지 않을 것이라고 생각했어요. 미 해군은 이것이 상당히 좋은 아이디어라고 생각했고 실험 프로그램을 실시했는데, 결과가 상당히 성공적이었죠. 그래서 미 해군은 나바호 암호가들을 더 많이 고용하기 시작했어요. 이 암호가들이 만들어 낸 암호를 예로 들어보면, "전함"이라는 단어는 나바호 언어로 "고래"를 뜻하는 라초라는 단어가 사용되었고, "일본"은 "찢어진 눈"을 뜻하는 베나알리초시라는 단어가, 그리고 "뇌격기"는 "제비"를 뜻하는 타스치라는 단어가 사용되었어요.

3. D

P(M): OK, let's, uh, let's start. Um... today, we're going to talk about Christian Symbolism. Um, Christian Symbolism, basically, is the use of actions or objects to symbolize the truths of the Christian faith. It reminds the people of those truths and emphasizes the spiritual connection with the underlying truth or act. Now, who can tell me what the most important symbols in the Christian Churches are?

W: Um, they're the sacraments.

P: Okay, and what are they?

W: Um, they are like, rites... well, the sacraments of the Protestant church are baptism and the Lord's Supper, and those of the Roman Catholic and Greek Orthodox churches are confirmation, the Eucharist, matrimony, and, um, extreme unction.

P: Very good, Chrissy. I guess you did your assignment. Okay, so, in communion, the bread and wine symbolize the broken body and shed blood of Jesus. And, baptism symbolizes...?

M: Um, the cleansing of the sinner by God and the Holy Spirit?

P: Thank you, Jesse. Baptism, especially where baptism is by total immersion into water, is symbolic of the spiritual death and recreation of the baptized person. Now, let's take a look at the handout on the Eucharist from last week.

P: 자, 이제 시작합시다. 오늘은 기독교적 상징주의에 대해 얘기해 보겠어요. 기독교적 상징주의란 기본적으로 기독교 신앙의 진실을 형상화하기 위해 사용하는 행동이나 사물입니다. 이는 사람들에게 진실을 환기시키고 잠재적인 진실이나 행동과의 영적인 연관성을 강조해 줍니다. 자, 그러면 기독교의 가장 중요한 상징이 무엇인지 말해줄 사람 있나요?

W: 음, 가장 중요한 상징은 성례전이에요.

P: 좋아요. 그게 무엇이죠?

W: 음, 그건... 일종의 의례 같은 거예요... 개신교의 성례전은 세례식과 성만찬이고, 로마 카톨릭과 그리스 정교회의 성례전은 고해 성사, 성체 성사, 혼인, 그리고 종부 성사예요.

P: 잘 했어요. 크리시. 숙제를 했나 보군요. 좋아요. 성찬식에서 빵과 포도주는 예수의 상한 몸과 흘린 피를 뜻해요. 그러면 세례는 무엇을 상징하나요?

M: 음, 하나님과 성령에 의해 죄를 씻는 것이요?

P: 고마워요. 제시. 세례, 특히 몸을 완전히 물에 담그는 것은 세례받은 이의 영적 죽음과 재부활을 상징해요. 자, 이제 지난주에 나눠준 성체 성사에 관한 프린트물을 봅시다.

4. A

P(M): All right. Another ancient Greek philosopher we're gonna discuss is Aristotle and his ethical theory. He was interested in human happiness — you know, how to be happy and what happiness is — and his philosophy is called eudemonia.

Before we move further, I'd like to define a couple of technical terms: extrinsic value and intrinsic value. The word extrinsic refers to something outside — so the term extrinsic value means anything that derives its value from something outside, basically something you can touch or see. Money has extrinsic value. This hat I bought yesterday has extrinsic value. All those things we desire and hold to be valuable for themselves alone. Well, and then, something that is not extrinsic is intrinsic. When something is valuable in itself or for its own sake, it has an intrinsic value. A 10-year-old teddy bear which is shaggy and worn out might have the extrinsic value of, say, fifty cents if you sold it at your garage sale, but for a little girl who has been its owner for ten years, the intrinsic value might be priceless.

자. 우리가 토의할 또 다른 그리스 철학자는 아리스토텔레스와 그의 윤리론이에요. 여러분도 알듯이 그는 인간의 기쁨. 즉. 어떻게 하면 기쁘게 되는지와 기쁨이 무엇인지 등에 대해 관심이 있었어요. 그의 철학은 복리라고 불려요.

더 나아가기 전에, 내적 가치와 외적 가치라는 두 가지 전문 용어의 뜻을 정의해 보았으면 해요. 외적이라는 말은 바깥을 뜻하기 때문에 외적 가치는 외부에서 가치를 가져오는 것을 말해요... 한마디로 보거나 만질 수 있는 것이죠. 돈은 외적 가치를 가지고 있어요. 제가 어제 산 이 모자도 외적 가치가 있어요. 우리가 열망하고, 그것 자체가 가치가 있다고 생각하는 것들이죠. 자, 그렇다면 외적이 아닌 것이 바로 내적인 것인데요. 어떤 것이 스스로 가치있을 경우, 혹은 스스로를 위해 가치가 있는 경우에는 내적 가치가 있어요. 10년 된 지저분하고 낡은 곰인형은 차고 세일에서 팔면 가령 50센트의 외적 가치 밖에 없을지라도 그것을 10년간 소유한 소녀에게 갖는 내적 가치는 값으로 따질 수 없겠죠.

Exercise

P.1	1. B	2. C	3. C	4. A	5. D
P.2	1. A	2. A, C	3. C	4. 참조	
P.3	1. C	2. D	3. D		
P.4	1. C	2. A	3. A	4. 참조	5. D
P.5	1. C	2. 참조			
P.6	1. B	2. 참조			
P.7	1. B	2. B	3. 참조	4. D	
P.8	1. A	2. C	3. C	4. 참조	5. B
P.9	1. B	2. D	3. A	4. C	5. 참조
P.10	1. C	2. B	3. D	4. 참조	5. C

Passage 1

1. B   **2.** C   **3.** C   **4.** A   **5.** D

P(M): Let's say... um... oh, okay. Let's say it's your mother's birthday and you went to a big shopping mall with your friend to buy a gift for her. You've got some money in your pocket, about five hundred dollars and you can spare two hundred for your own, but you don't have anything particular in mind to buy for yourself. Now, you want to buy her a nice scarf so you go to the ladies' clothing section. When you come out of the mall, you not only have a shopping bag for your mom's birthday present but also several other bags for your own. Now, what am I talking about?

W: Oh, that's an example of an impulsive purchase. I do that a lot myself.

P: I believe many of us here do this quite often, no? Yes, this is what we call an impulse buying or impulse purchase, an unplanned or spontaneous purchase. This is considered quite important in the marketing business — recent tests reveal that impulse purchases represent almost 40 percent of all the money spent on e-commerce sites. Um... there are four models of impulse purchase, but today, let's talk about two of them: pure impulse purchase and reminder impulse purchase. Pure impulse purchase is when you buy something out of your ordinary habit of purchasing, and, um, reminder impulse purchase occurs when you remember the need for an essential item on seeing it in the shop or when you remember a commercial you saw on television in the past. Usually, people who buy stuff out of impulse end up regretting it afterwards.

P: 자, 예를 들어서... 좋아요. 어머니의 생일이라서 선물을 사기 위해 친구와 함께 큰 백화점에 갔다고 칩시다. 주머니에 약 500달러 정도를 가지고 있고 자신을 위해 200달러는 쓸 수 있지만, 딱히 사고 싶은 것은 없습니다. 자, 어머니에게 예쁜 스카프를 사드리고 싶어서 숙녀복 코너에 갑니다. 백화점에서 나올 때, 어머니의 선물이 담긴 쇼핑백 말고도 자신의 것이 담긴 다른 쇼핑백들도 들고 있습니다. 내가 지금 무슨 얘기를 하고 있는 걸까요?

W: 충동 구매에 대한 예시네요. 저도 충동 구매를 자주 해요.

P: 우리 모두 자주 그럴 것 같은데요, 그렇죠? 맞습니다. 이것을 충동 구매, 즉 계획 없이 충동적으로 일어나는 구매라고 부릅니다. 이는 마케팅 업계에서 매우 중요하게 여겨집니다. 최근 실험에서 충동 구매가 인터넷 사이트 판매의 40%를 차지한다고 나타났습니다. 음... 충동 구매에는 네 가지 모델이 있지만, 오늘은 그 중 두 가지만 살펴 보죠. 바로 순수 충동 구매와 기억 충동 구매입니다. 순수 충동 구매는 자신의 일상적인 구매 습관에 따라 무언가를 구매하는 것이고, 기억 충동 구매는 필요했던 물품을 가게에서 봤을 때, 혹은 그에 대한 광고를 과거에 봤다가 갑자기 기억이 났을 때 제품을 사는 것을 말합니다. 일반적으로, 충동적으로 물건을 구매한 사람들은 나중에 후회를 하게 됩니다.

❶ What is the topic of the discussion?

토론의 주제는 충동 구매이며, 교수는 충동 구매의 네 가지 모델 중 두 가지에 대해 설명한다. 따라서 정답은 B이다. 선택지 A와 D는 제한적인 내용만을 담고 있으며, 이와 반대로 선택지 C는 너무 광범위한 선택이다.

❷ Why does the professor mention your mother's birthday?

교수는 어머니의 생일 선물을 사러 갔다가 충동 구매를 하게 되는 예를 들어 오늘의 주제를 소개하고 있다. 토론의 주제를 바꾸거나 주제와 무관한 이야기를 하는 것이 아니며 토론을 마무리 지으려는 것도 아니다.

❸ According to the discussion, which of the following statements is NOT true about impulse purchase?

교수는 "There are four models of impulse purchase"라고 했으므로 선택지 A는 맞는 내용이며, 충동 구매는 "Unplanned or spontaneous purchase"라고 했으므로 선택지 B 역시 맞는 내용이다. 온라인 쇼핑에 대한 언급이 되어 있지만, 충동 구매가 온라인 쇼핑을 할 때에만 일어난다는 말은 없으므로 정답은 C이다. "Reminder impulse purchase occurs when you remember the need for an essential item on seeing it in the shop"라는 부분에서 선택지 D가 토론의 내용과 맞는 것임을 알 수 있다.

❹ What does the professor say about impulse purchase on e-commerce sites?

최근 실험에서 충동 구매가 인터넷 사이트 판매의 40 퍼센트를 차지한다고 한 교수의 말에서 정답을 알 수 있다. 기타 선택지들의 내용은 강의에서 언급된 바가 없다.

❺ What will the professor discuss during the next class?

"충동 구매에는 네 가지 모델이 있지만 오늘은 두 가지만 얘기해 보자"는 교수의 말에서 힌트를 찾을 수 있다. 오늘 수업에서는 충동 구매의 두 가지 모델(즉, 순수 충동 구매와 기억 충동 구매)만 설명하고 다음 시간에 나머지 두 개의 모델에 대해 설명할 것임을 알 수 있다. 따라서 정답은 선택지 D이다.

Passage 2

1. A **2.** A, C **3.** C **4.** 참조

	Order
Yellowstone and other parks instituted a national fire management plan.	5
People thought that the wildfire was a destructive force—one to be mastered.	2
There was a series of wildfire across much of the ecosystem.	1
Ecologists recognized that fire was a primary agent of change in many ecosystems, including the arid mountainous western United States.	3
National parks and forests began to experiment with controlled fires.	4

P(M): All right, now... let's move on to our next topic — fire management. First, um... ❶ **have any of you ever been to Yellowstone National Park? Well, it's America's first national park located in Wyoming, Montana, and Idaho which was established in 1872.** It is home to various wild animals including grizzly bears, wolves, bison, and elk. The Old Faithful Geyser preserved in the park and other geysers and hot springs... um, and the Grand Canyon of the Yellowstone are a few of the most famous tour sites within the park.

Uh, before the European settlers arrived in the U.S. in the 1700's, there was a series of wildfire across much of the ecosystem. Well, what do we think of when we first hear that there's a wildfire in a national park? Most of us would think that it would destroy the ecosystem and the natural habitat of many animals... um, wipe out the forest which has been created throughout a very long period of time. This viewpoint was the mainstream throughout much of the 20th century. Park managers as well as visitors and other authorities alike have continued to hold the belief that the wildfire was a destructive force, one that was to be conquered. However, by the 1940's, ecologists found out that fire was actually a primary agent of change in many ecosystems. So, based on this belief,

national parks and forests started experimenting with controlled fire in the 50's and 60's, and by the 1970's, other parks along with Yellowstone had instituted a natural fire management plan, thereby approving the procedure of lightning-caused fire changing and affecting wildland succession.

자, 이제 다음 주제인 화재 관리로 넘어갑시다. 우선 여러분 중에 옐로스톤 국립 공원에 가 본 적이 있는 사람 있나요? 와이오밍주, 몬타나주, 그리고 아이다호주에 걸쳐 위치한 미국의 첫 국립 공원인 옐로스톤 국립 공원은 1872년에 설립되었습니다. 이곳은 회색곰, 늑대, 들소와 엘크를 포함한 다양한 야생 동물의 서식지이기도 하죠. 공원 내에 보존되어 있는 올드 페이스풀 간헐천 외에도 다른 간헐천들과 온천들, 그리고 옐로스톤의 그랜드 캐년 등은 공원 내의 유명한 관광지들 중 일부일 뿐입니다.

1700년대에 유럽 정착민들이 미국에 도착하기 전에, 옐로스톤의 전 생태계에 걸쳐 산불이 여러 번 발생했습니다. 국립 공원에서 불이 났다고 하면 우리는 제일 먼저 무슨 생각을 하나요? 우리 대부분은 산불이 생태계와 동물의 서식지를 파괴할 것이라고 생각하겠죠. 어, 그러니까... 오랜 기간에 걸쳐 생긴 숲을 없애버릴 것이라고 생각할 겁니다. 20세기에는 이러한 관점이 주를 이루었습니다. 공원 관리자와 방문자들, 그리고 다른 공공 기관 역시 산불이 파괴적인 것이며, 우리가 정복해야 할 대상이라고 생각했습니다. 그렇지만 1940년대에 들어 생태학자들은 산불이 실제로는 많은 생태계의 변화를 주도하는 역할을 했다는 것을 알게 되었습니다. 이러한 생각을 바탕으로 50년대와 60년대에는 국립 공원과 숲에서 통제된 산불을 사용해 실험을 하기 시작했고, 1970년대에 이르러서는 옐로스톤을 포함한 다른 공원들이 황무지 천이(遷移)에 영향을 주기 위해 번갯불로 인한 화재를 허용하는 자연 화재 관리 계획을 실행하게 되었습니다.

❶ Why does the professor say this:

이 강의의 주제는 화재 관리인데, 교수는 특히 옐로스톤 국립 공원의 화재 관리 방식에 대해 설명한다. 교수가 이 말을 한 이유는 실제로 학생들 중 몇 명이 옐로스톤 국립 공원에 가 봤는지 알아 보고자 하는 것보다는 학생들의 주목을 끌어 강의의 주제를 효과적으로 소개하기 위해서라고 할 수 있으므로 정답은 A이다. 옐로스톤 국립 공원으로 체험 학습을 나갈 것이었는지 강의에서 알 수 없으므로 선택지 C는 틀린 선택이며, 선택지 D는 강의의 내용과 관련이 없다.

❷ Which of the following was mentioned in the lecture as one of the most famous tour sites within Yellowstone National Park?

"The Old Faithful Geyser preserved in the park and other geysers and hot springs... um, and the Grand Canyon of the Yellowstone are a few of the most famous tour sites within the park"라는 교수의 말에서 정답을 찾을 수 있다.

❸ What does the professor think about wildfires in national parks?

산불에 대해 부정적이었던 시각을 소개하면서 교수는 "However, by the 1940's, ecologists found out that fire was a

primary agent of change in many ecosystems"라고 하
며 긍정적인 측면이 있다고 얘기한다. 따라서 선택지 A는 답이 아
니며, 선택지 B는 너무 극단적인 내용이므로 오답이다. 주어진 강
의 내용만으로 교수가 통제된 산불에 반대하는지의 여부를 알 수
없으므로 선택지 D 역시 오답이다.

④ The professor discusses Yellowstone National Park and wildfires. Put in the sentences below in the order they occurred.

먼저 옐로스톤의 생태계 전반에 걸쳐 산불이 일어났으며, 20세기
전반에 걸쳐 산불에 대한 부정적인 생각이 주류를 이루었다. 그러
나 1940년대에 들어 산불이 생태계를 변화시키는 힘이라는 다른
시각이 고개를 들기 시작했고 50년대와 60년대에 걸쳐 국립 공원
과 숲 등에서 통제된 산불을 실험하기 시작했으며 1970년대에 들
어 옐로스톤을 포함한 다른 국립 공원들이 자연 화재 관리 계획을
만들었다.

Passage 3

1. C **2.** D **3.** D

P(W): Okay, then how much sodium do you need in a day? Well, um... the official daily recommended intake of sodium is 1,500 milligrams, 1,300 after age 50. Some evidence, however, suggests that we might be better off with 1,200 milligrams a day. Either way, you're more likely to get eaten by a shark than to suffer from a sodium deficiency. The majority of Americans get way too much, you know, around 4,000 milligrams a day, which is 2,500 milligrams over the upper limit! The Center for Science in the Public Interest, a consumer watchdog group, has actually sued the FDA for labeling sodium a generally safe nutrient, claiming excessive amounts lead to 150,000 deaths a year from heart attacks and strokes. While the suit seems a little bit over-the-top, we cannot deny the fact that sodium is a major contributor to hypertension. Also, high intake of sodium may cause calcium to be leached from the bones. Considering how much salt is dumped into food — even cookies, bread, cereal, and soda — it's hard to avoid sodium. But let's not lose hope, for there is a way to avoid excessive sodium intake.

좋아요. 그러면 하루에 나트륨이 얼마나 필요할까요? 음, 나트륨의 공식
일일 권장량은 1,500 밀리그램이고, 50세 이후로는 1,300 밀리그램이에
요. 그렇지만 일부 증거에 의하면 하루에 1,200 밀리그램만 섭취하는 것
이 낫다고 해요. 어쨌든 나트륨 결핍이 되는 것보다 상어에게 먹힐 확률
이 더 높을 거예요. 여러분도 알겠지만 미국인들 대부분은 나트륨을 너무
많이 섭취해요. 한계치를 2,500 밀리그램이나 초과한 4,000 밀리그램을
하루에 섭취하죠. 소비자 감시 단체인 공공 이익을 위한 과학 센터에서는

나트륨 과다 섭취로 인해 연간 15만 명이 심장마비와 고혈압으로 사망
한다고 주장하며, 나트륨을 일반적으로 안전한 영양소라 표기한 것에 대
해 미국 식품안정청을 실제로 고소했어요. 고소를 한 것이 다소 과했을
지 모르지만, 나트륨이 고혈압의 주요 원인이라는 점을 부정할 수는 없
어요. 또한 나트륨의 과다 섭취는 뼈에서 칼슘이 빠져나가게 할 수도 있
어요. 음식에, 심지어 과자, 빵, 시리얼, 그리고 소다 등에 얼마나 많은 양
의 소금이 들어가는지를 생각해 볼 때, 나트륨을 섭취하지 않기란 힘들
어요. 하지만 나트륨 과다 섭취를 피할 수 있는 길이 있으니까 희망을 버
리지는 말도록 합시다.

① What does the professor say about sodium intake?

"나트륨의 과다 섭취는 뼈에서 칼슘이 빠져나가게 할 수 있다"는
교수의 말에서 정답(선택지 C)을 알 수 있다. 미국인들 대부분은
하루에 약 4,000 밀리그램의 나트륨을 섭취하며 나트륨의 공식
일일 권장량은 1,500 밀리그램이다. 따라서 선택지 A와 B는 오
답이며, 선택지 D는 강의에서 언급된 바가 없다.

② What can be inferred about the content of sodium in food?

"음식에, 심지어 과자, 빵, 시리얼, 그리고 소다 등에 얼마나 많은
양의 소금이 들어가는지를 생각해 볼 때, 나트륨을 섭취하지 않기
란 힘들다"는 교수의 설명에서 볼 때, 과자, 빵, 시리얼과 소다 등의
음식은 사람들이 일반적으로 나트륨이 적게 들어가는 음식이라고
생각하지만, 실제로는 나트륨 함량이 높다는 것을 유추할 수 있다.
따라서 정답은 선택지 D이다.

③ What will the professor probably discuss next?

교수는 먼저 나트륨의 일일 권장량을 소개하며 대부분의 미국인이
한계치를 넘어 소비한다고 설명한다. 지문 마지막에서 나트륨 과
다 섭취를 피할 수 있는 길이 있다고 말함으로써 앞으로 나트륨 과
다 섭취를 피할 수 있는 방법에 대해 설명할 것임을 암시한다. 따
라서 정답은 D이다. 선택지 A, B와 C의 내용은 지문에서 찾을 수
없다.

1. C   **2.** A   **3.** A   **4.** 참조   **5.** D

	Order
Christian Dior opened an art gallery on rue de la Boetie with his friend, Jacques Bonjean.	2
Christian Dior's mother and brother died.	3
Christian Dior was born in Grenville, France.	1
Christian Dior started working for Robert Piguet at his fashion house as a designer.	4
Christian Dior presented his first collection.	5

P(M): Now, let's go on to Dior. One of the best known designers, Christian Dior was born in the town of Grenville on the French coast in 1905. ❷ **His family owned a fertilizer company, so, I guess he was born with a silver spoon in his mouth.** He spent most of his time in museums and galleries when growing up; however, instead of studying art, he majored in Political Science at the Ecole des Sciences Politiques. He did his compulsory military service for two years in the French Army, and opened an art gallery on rue de la Boetie with his friend, Jacques Bonjean in 1928.

Well, the early 1930's wasn't very friendly to the U.S. as it was to Dior: When the U.S. was undergoing its worst depression in history, Dior had to undergo his, with his mother and brother passing away in 1931 and his family experiencing extreme financial crisis. His father's company declared bankruptcy and Dior contracted tuberculosis. When he returned to France after a visit to the Soviet Union, he found that his partner Bonjean had also become bankrupt. Because of his illness, Dior had to leave Paris for a year, but returned in 1935 and started to do some sketches for dresses and hats. He started to sell his sketches some of which were purchased by Milliner Agnes and Robert Piguet. Later, some of his sketches sold to Piguet were published in *Le Figaro*. Dior started working for Piguet in 1938 at his fashion house as a designer, and in 1941, he joined Lucien Lelong until 1946. Afterwards, he took up Marcel Boussac's salon and presented his first collection in 1947 with the revolutionary new look — beautiful, feminine clothes with soft rounded shapes, full, wide, flowing skirts, constricted waist, narrow shoulders, and hemlines below the knee. Actually, women of that time were sick and tired of the severity of the wartime dresses... the shabby, worn-out clothes made with the minimum of material with wide shoulders that looked like the army uniforms. His show was a huge success and his design began to be called the New Look all over the world. Dior's New Look is considered to have revolutionized women's dress and reestablished Paris as the center of the fashion world after World War II, which we'll be discussing in a while.

이제 디올로 넘어갑시다. 세계적으로 유명한 디자이너 중 한 명인 크리스찬 디올은 프랑스 해안의 그랜빌 마을에서 1905년에 태어났습니다. 가족이 비료 공장을 소유하고 있었으니, 그는 무척 부유한 집안에서 태어난 것이었죠. 그는 성장기의 대부분을 박물관과 갤러리에서 보냈지만, 미술을 공부하는 대신 Ecole des Sciences Politiques(정치과학 대학교)에서 정치 과학을 전공했습니다. 프랑스 군에서 2년 간의 의무 복무를 마치고, 자신의 친구인 쟈끄 봉장과 함께 1928년 뵈띠가(街)에 미술 갤러리를 열었습니다.

1930년 초기는 미국과 디올에게 호의적이지 않았습니다. 미국이 역사상 최악의 공황을 겪을 때, 디올 역시 공황을 겪었습니다. 그는 1931년도에 어머니와 형제를 잃었고, 가족이 심각한 재정 위기를 겪었습니다. 그의 아버지의 회사는 파산했고 디올 자신은 결핵에 걸렸습니다. 소련 방문을 마치고 프랑스로 돌아왔을 때 그는 동업자인 봉장 역시 파산한 것을 알게 되었습니다. 병으로 인해 디올은 파리를 1년 간 떠나야 했지만, 1935년에 돌아와 드레스와 모자 스케치를 시작했습니다. 그는 자신의 스케치를 판매하기 시작했는데 모자 상인인 아녜스와 로베르 피케가 그 중 몇 장을 구입했습니다. 후에, 피케에게 팔린 그림 몇 장이 "르 휘가로"지에 실렸습니다. 디올은 1938년에 피케의 양장점에서 디자이너로 일하기 시작했고, 1941년부터 1946년까지 루시엥 르롱 밑에서 일했습니다. 이후, 그는 마르셀 부삭의 살롱을 인수했고 1947년도에 자신의 최초 컬렉션을 통해 새롭고 파격적인 패션을 선보였습니다. 그의 컬렉션은 부드러운 곡선, 크고 넓으며 나풀대는 치마, 잘록한 허리, 좁은 어깨, 그리고 무릎 아래의 치마선의 아름답고 여성스러운 옷들로 이루어졌습니다. 사실, 그 당시의 여성들은 전시의 엄숙한 타입의 드레스에 질린 상태였습니다. 이는 허름하고 최소한의 소재로 만들어진 옷으로, 넓은 어깨가 마치 군복처럼 보였습니다. 디올의 쇼는 대성공이었고 그의 디자인은 세계적으로 "뉴 룩"이라고 불리게 되었습니다. 디올의 뉴 룩은 여성 드레스의 혁명을 가져왔다고 여겨지며 제2차 세계대전 이후로 파리는 다시 한번 패션의 중심지로 자리잡게 되었습니다. 잠시 후 이것에 대해 얘기해 보도록 하겠습니다.

❶ **What is the subject of the lecture?**

이 강의에서 교수는 크리스찬 디올의 전반적인 생애에 대해 다루고 있는데, 특히 그의 디자이너로서의 삶을 소개한다. 이러한 내용을 가장 잘 표현한 선택지는 C이다. 강의는 살롱 주인보다는 디자이너로서의 디올을 다루고 있으므로 A는 적절한 선택이 아니며, 디올이 군대에 입대한 얘기는 잠시 언급되므로 B 역시 바른 선택이 아니다. 선택지 D 역시 강의의 내용상 크게 관련 없는 쟈끄 봉장을 언급했기 때문에 틀린 답이다.

❷ **What does the professor mean when he says this:**

"Be born with a silver spoon in one's mouth"라는 표현은 "부유한 집안에서 태어나다"라는 뜻이며, "silver spoon"은

비유적으로 "상속받은 부"를 뜻한다. 따라서 정답은 A이며, "His family owned a fertilizer company"라는 부분에서도 이 표현의 뜻을 유추할 수 있다.

❸ **According to the lecture, what can be said about Dior and his New Look?**

군복처럼 딱딱한 의복에 식상해 있던 당시 여성들에게 나풀거리는 치마와 잘록한 허리 등의 여성스러운 디자인을 선보인 디올의 "뉴 룩"은 큰 환영을 받았다. 따라서 정답은 A이다. 디올이 뉴 룩을 만들게 된 계기가 소련 방문에 의한 것인지 직접적으로 지문에서 알 수 없으므로 B는 답이라고 할 수 없으며, 재료를 적게 쓰는 디자인은 당시의 전시 의복이므로 선택지 C 역시 정답이라고 볼 수 없다. 디올의 새로운 패션은 큰 성공을 이뤘으므로 D 역시 올바른 선택이 아니다.

❹ **Based on the information in the lecture, indicate the order of the following sentences.**

강의는 크리스챤 디올의 출생부터 시작하여 친구인 봉장과 미술 갤러리를 열었다고 소개한다. 그 후, 디올은 어머니와 형제를 잃고 결핵을 앓지만 로베르 피케의 패션 가게에서 디자이너로 일하게 되고 자신의 첫 컬렉션을 성공적으로 치뤄내게 된다.

❺ **What will the professor probably discuss next?**

"Dior's New Look revolutionized women's dress and reestablished Paris as the center of the fashion world after World War II, which we'll be discussing in a while"라는 교수의 말에서 정답을 찾을 수 있다.

(Passage 5)

1. C   **2.** 참조

	Buddhism	Islam
the Bodhi Tree	✓	
Mecca		✓
Bodh Gaya	✓	
Kandy	✓	
Medina		✓

P(W): Most religions and various groups that exist on Earth have their own holy places or cities. This means that there may be thousands of holy places out there since it is estimated that there exists about 4,300 different religious groups, including very small, unknown groups in Africa. However, you can name some of the most well-known places of the several major religions in the world. Well, in Buddhism, Bodh Gaya is considered sacred. It is said that Siddhartha Gautama who later became the Buddha attained unsurpassed, supreme Enlightenment there. The Bodhi Tree is also considered as one of the sacred places in Buddhism. The Buddha sat under this tree after his Enlightenment for seven days, meditating without moving from his seat. Another religious place of Buddhism is Kandy in Sri Lanka where the Esala Peraherea festival takes place.

Okay, let's move on to the Muslim holy cities. Um, I believe you've all heard about Mecca, right? It's located in Saudi Arabia and is considered as the holiest place for Muslims all over the world. Muhammad was born in Mecca, and Muslims bow to pray five times a day towards this place. All Muslims must go on a haji to Mecca. Um, haji is basically the pilgrimage which they should make, at least once in their lifetime if they are financially and physically able. Um, what else... yes, Medina. This city is where Muhammad went to when he could not find support for his ideas in Mecca. He received a warm welcome in Medina and spent some important time there, so this place has become a holy place. Medina was the capital of the Muslim empire until 661, when the capital was moved to Damascus. Oh, and the Mosque of Muhammad is located in the eastern part of the city. The Mosque contains the tomb of Muhammad, his daughter, Fatimah, and the second caliph, Umar, whom we will be talking about shortly.

지구상에 존재하는 많은 종교와 다양한 집단들은 그들만의 성지를 가지고 있습니다. 이것은 즉, 세상에 수 천 개의 성지가 존재한다는 것을 뜻합니다. 왜냐하면 아프리카의 가장 작은 종교를 포함하여 약 4,300개의 서로 다른 종교 집단이 있다고 예측되기 때문입니다. 그렇지만 세상의 주요 종교들의 가장 널리 알려진 성지 몇 곳은 얘기할 수 있을 것입니다. 불교에서는 보드가야를 성지로 여깁니다. 후에 부처가 된 고타마 싯다르타가 이곳에서 궁극의 깨달음을 얻었다고 알려져 있습니다. 보리수 또한 불교의 성지로 여겨집니다. 부처가 깨달음을 얻은 후 이 나무 아래에서 7일 간 앉아 움직이지 않고 명상을 했다고 합니다. 불교의 또 다른 성지는 에살라 페라헤라 축제가 열리는 스리랑카의 칸디라는 곳입니다.

좋습니다. 이제 이슬람 성지로 넘어가도록 하죠. 여러분 모두 메카에 대해서는 들어봤죠? 메카는 사우디 아라비아에 위치해 있으며 전 세계의 이슬람 교도들에게 가장 성스러운 곳으로 여겨집니다. 무하마드는 메카에서 태어났고, 이슬람 교도들은 매일 다섯번씩 이곳을 향해 절을 합니다. 모든 이슬람 교도들은 메카로 하지를 가야 합니다. 하지란 재정적, 육체적인 면에서 능력이 되는 모든 이슬람 교도들이 일생에 한 번은 행해야 하는 순례입니다. 그리고... 네, 메디나가 있죠. 이곳은 무하마드가 메카에서 자신의 아이디어에 대한 지지를 받지 못하자 찾아 나선 도시입니다. 그가 메디나에서 환대를 받고 중요한 시간을 보냈기 때문에 이곳이 성지가 되었습니다. 메디나는 또한 661년까지 다마스쿠스로 천도하기 전에 이슬람 제국의 수도였습니다. 그리고 무하마드의 모스크는 메디나 시의 동쪽에 위치해 있습니다. 이 모스크에는 무하마드의 무덤과 그의 딸 파티마와 두번째 칼리프인 우마르가 잠든 무덤이 있습니다. 이들에 대해서는 곧 얘기해 보도록 하겠습니다.

❶ What does the professor mainly discuss?

교수는 "Most religions and various groups that exist on Earth have their own holy places or cities"라며 강의를 시작하며 주요 종교들(불교와 이슬람)의 성지를 설명한다. 불교와 이슬람교의 근원을 설명한 것이 아니므로 선택지 A는 틀린 선택이며, 불교의 성지 역시 설명했기 때문에 선택지 B 역시 옳은 답이 아니다. 부처와 무하마드는 불교와 이슬람교를 설명할 때 언급되었을 뿐, 강의의 전체적인 주제는 아니다.

❷ Based on the information in the lecture, indicate whether each statement below is the sacred place of pure Buddhism or of Islam.

불교의 성지로는 보드가야와 보리수, 칸디가 언급되었으며, 이슬람의 성지로는 메카와 메디나가 언급되었다.

Passage 6

1. B   2. 참조

	Yes	No
The museum is located in the Jefferson Medical College.		✓
The museum's collections include preserves of medical oddities, antique medical equipment and biological specimens.	✓	
Only medical doctors are allowed to visit the museum.		✓
Thomas Dent Mütter played a significant role in establishing the museum in both financial and collectional ways.	✓	
One of the museum's boasted collection items is the mummy of the world-famous Siamese Twins, Chang and Eng Bunker.		✓

P(M): When your friend asks you to go to a museum with her, you'd probably think of going to an art museum or at least a museum that has lots of weird stuff. There are so many different types of museum in this world — wax museums, money museums, museums that display various types of robots, tea, all kinds of dead animals, historical features, or teddy bears. The Mütter Museum in Philadelphia is... well, weird, in that it is a museum of medical oddities, antique medical equipment and biological specimens. It's, uh, located in the College of Physicians of Philadelphia, and they say that most visitors are current doctors but many curious minds visit there as well.

Um, in 1858, a retired Professor of Surgery at Jefferson Medical College, Thomas Dent Mütter, presented his personal collection of unique anatomic and pathological materials to the College of Physicians of Philadelphia. The school already had a large collection of such objects since 1849, but Mütter's contribution boosted up the growth of the museum's financial status and collection. The museum owns a large collection of skulls and unique specimens, including the plaster cast of the torso of world-famous Siamese Twins, Chang and Eng Bunker, and their conjoined livers, preserved body of the "Soap Lady", collection of 2,000 objects extracted from people's throats, tallest skeleton on display in North America, the part of the brain of Charles Guiteau who killed President Garfield, and so on.

여러분의 친구가 박물관에 가자고 하면, 여러분은 아마도 미술관이나 최소한 이상한 것이 많이 있는 박물관을 생각하겠죠. 세상엔 정말 여러 종류의 박물관이 있어요 – 왁스 박물관, 화폐 박물관, 각종 로봇을 전시하는 박물관, 차, 동물의 사체, 역사적 유물, 혹은 곰인형 박물관까지 말이죠. 필라델피아의 뮤터 박물관은 의학적 특이물, 고전 의료기기와 생물학적 표본이 있다는 점에서 상당히 독특해요. 이 박물관은 필라델피아 내과 의대 안에 위치하는데, 대부분의 방문객이 현직 의사이지만 호기심에 찾는 이들도 많아요.

1858년에 제퍼슨 의대의 은퇴한 외과 교수인 토마스 뮤터가 개인적으로 수집한 독특한 해부학 자료와 병리학 자료들을 필라델피아 내과 의대에 기증했어요. 이 학교는 이미 1849년부터 이러한 자료를 수집해 왔는데요. 뮤터의 기부가 박물관의 재정 상태와 전시물에 큰 성장을 가져왔죠. 이 박물관에는 해골과 독특한 표본이 많은데, 세계적으로 유명한 삼 쌍둥이인 창과 엥 벙커의 상체와 그들의 붙은 간의 석고 표본, "비누 아가씨"의 보존체, 사람의 목구멍에서 추출된 2,000가지의 물체와 북미 전시 유골 중 최장신의 뼈, 가필드 대통령을 죽인 찰스 괴테의 뇌의 일부 등이 있어요.

❶ Why does the professor mention wax and money museums?

교수는 왁스 박물관, 화폐 박물관 등 여러 종류의 박물관을 예를 들고 있다. 따라서 정답은 B이다. 선택지 A는 지문과 관련이 없으며, 교수는 뮤터 박물관에 대한 수업을 시작하기 위해 여러 종류의 박물관을 언급한 것이므로 선택지 C 역시 틀린 선택이다. 교수가 박물관을 건립했다는 내용은 지문에 언급된 바가 없으므로 D 역시 오답이다.

❷ Based on the information in the lecture, indicate whether the following statements are information about the Mütter Museum.

뮤터 박물관은 필라델피아 내과 의대 내에 위치하므로 첫 문장은 틀렸으며, "It is a museum of medical oddities, antique medical equipment and biological specimens"라는 부분에서 두번째 문장의 내용이 맞는 것임을 알 수 있다. "Most visitors are current doctors but many curious minds visit there as well"라는 부분에서 세번째 문장이 틀렸음을 알 수 있다. "Mütter's contribution boosted up the growth of the museum's financial status and collection"에서

네번째 문장의 내용은 올바른 것임을 알 수 있다. 뮤터 박물관이 자랑하는 표본은 삼 쌍둥이의 상체 석고 표본이지 미이라가 아니므로 다섯 번째 문장은 틀렸다.

1. B　　**2.** B　　**3.** 참조　　**4.** D

	True	False
The basic ingredients for making beer are barley, yeast, sugar, and alcohol.		✔
In order to make beer, a brewer should only mix two of the four basic ingredients.		✔
In the Middle Ages, it was safer to drink beer than to drink water because of poor sanitation and close quarters.	✔	
Lager was first brewed in Germany in the 1400's.	✔	
The Prohibition on beer lasted from 1920 to 1933 which kicked many small breweries out of business.	✔	

P(M): You guys like to drink beer a lot, right? Well, I myself am a huge beer fan — when I sit on my couch watching football on Sunday afternoons, I just can't do without a can of good lager. But have you ever thought about how beer is made? Let's talk about beer brewing today. There are four basic ingredients to make beer. Who knows what they are?

M: ❷ Oh, they are barley, water, hops and yeast. That's easy.

P: That's right. I guess you're a beer lover yourself, aren't you, Steve?

M: Yeah, I drink it every Friday night when I go out to a movie or a party.

P: Uh-huh, I don't blame you. Well, these are the four simple ingredients, but brewers don't just mix the right amount of ingredients to make beer — there's actually something more to it. A complex series of biochemical reactions are involved here to convert barley to fermentable sugars, to allow yeast to live and multiply, and to convert those sugars to alcohol.

But before we delve into the making of beer, let's briefly discuss the history of beer. People have been brewing beer for thousands of years, possibly... and it became a staple in the Middle Ages when people lived in cities where it was difficult to find clean water because of close quarters and poor sanitation. You know... because of the alcohol in beer, it was safer to drink beer than to drink dirty water from the streets. In the 1400's, Germans began to brew beer which was fermented in the winter with a different type of yeast. This beer, which happens to be my favorite type, was called a lager. This type of beer is pretty much dominant in the U.S. today because of the Prohibition.

Well, let's talk a little bit more about the Prohibition and lager in the United States. Starting in 1920, the production of alcoholic beverages in the United States was prohibited by a constitutional amendment. It lasted for 13 years. The Prohibition forced most breweries, thousands of which enjoyed their heyday before Prohibition, out of business, and only the largest breweries survived when the laws were repealed in 1933. During World War II, you know, everything was short — food, supplies, everything including the work force because many men were sent overseas. And so, breweries began to brew a lighter style of lager that is very common today. Since the late 1980's and the early 1990's, small regional breweries managed to come back in business, increasing the variety of beer in the United States.

P: 맥주 많이들 좋아하죠? 저도 맥주를 정말 좋아해요 – 일요일 오후 소파에 앉아 풋볼 경기를 볼 때면, 맛있는 라거 없인 안 되겠더라고요. 그렇지만 맥주가 어떻게 만들어지는지 생각해 본 적이 있나요? 오늘은 맥주 생산에 대해 얘기해 보죠. 맥주의 주 원료는 네 가지가 있는데, 무엇인지 아는 사람이 있나요?

M: 보리, 물, 홉과 효모입니다. 쉽네요.

P: 맞아요. 맥주를 좋아하나 보죠, 스티브?

M: 네, 매주 금요일 밤에 영화를 보러 가거나 파티에 갈 때 맥주를 마셔요.

P: 네, 그럴만 하죠. 자, 이것이 네 가지 기본 원료이지만, 양조자들이 맥주를 만들 때 적정량을 단순히 섞기만 하는 건 아니에요 – 실제 양조에는 그 이상의 것이 있답니다. 복잡한 미생물 반응을 통해 보리가 발효 가능한 설탕으로 재생되고, 효모가 번식되고, 이 설탕이 알코올로 바뀌어요. 맥주 생산에 대해 더 자세하게 이야기하기 전에, 맥주의 역사에 대해 간략하게 알아보도록 하죠. 사람들은 수천 년 이상 맥주를 만들어 왔어요. 그리고 중세 시대 도시의 밀집한 주택 환경과 열악한 배수 환경으로 인해 깨끗한 물을 찾기 힘든 사람들에게 맥주는 주식이 되었어요. 그러니까... 맥주에 있는 알코올 때문에 길거리에서 더러운 물을 마시는 것보다는 맥주를 마시는 것이 더 안전했지요. 1400년대에 독일에서는 다른 종류의 효모를 사용해서 겨울에 발효되는 새로운 종류의 맥주가 생산되기 시작했어요. 제가 제일 좋아하는 종류인 이 맥주는 라거라고 불렸어요. 이 맥주는 알코올 금지법 때문에 오늘날 미국에서 주를 이루고 있어요.

미국의 알코올 금지법과 라거에 대해 조금 더 이야기를 해 보죠. 1920년부터 미국의 알코올 음료 제조는 헌법 제정으로 인해 금지됐었어요. 이것이 13년 간 계속되었죠. 이 금지령은 그동안 성황을 이루던 수천 개의 양조장을 파산하게 만들었고, 1933년에 법률이 폐지될 때까지 대형 양조장만이 살아남았어요. 제2차 세계대전 중에는 음식, 물자, 심지어 노동력까지 해외로 나갔기 때문에 모든 것이 부족했어요. 그래서 양조장은 오늘날 일반적으로 마시는 알코올 성분이 적은 라거를 만들기 시작했죠. 1980년 후반과 1990년 초반 이래로 지방의 소규모 양조장들이 다시 사업을 시작하면서 미국에서 판매되는 맥주의 종류가 다양해지기 시작했어요.

❶ Why does the professor mention watching football on Sunday afternoons?

교수는 일요일 오후 풋볼 경기를 보면서 맥주를 마신다고 언급하며, 오늘의 주제인 맥주 생산을 소개한다. 전혀 무관한 이야기를 하는 것이라기 보다는 오늘의 주제를 효과적으로 소개하기 위해 언급한 것이므로 A보다 B가 답으로 적절하다. 강의를 하다 다른 이야기를 하는 것도 아니므로 선택지 C 역시 틀렸다. 강의는 맥주와 풋볼의 관계에 대한 것이 아니므로 선택지 D도 바른 선택이 아니다.

❷ Why does the professor say this:

애주가인 교수는 영화를 보거나 파티를 할 때 맥주를 즐겨 마시는 학생을 탓하지 않는다고 한다. 이는 즉, 학생과 공감을 하고 있다는 것을 뜻하는 것으로 정답은 B이다. 학생이 거짓말을 하고 있다고 생각하는지의 여부는 지문 내용상 알 수 없으므로 선택지 A는 틀린 것이며, 교수가 많은 학생들이 금요일 밤에 영화를 보거나 파티를 하는 것을 아는지의 여부도 알 수 없으므로 선택지 C 역시 틀린 선택이다. 선택지 D 역시 지문의 내용상 알 수 없는 내용이다.

❸ Based on the information in the discussion, indicate whether the following statements about beer and history about beer are true or false.

맥주 제조의 원료는 "barley, water, hops and yeast"이라고 했으므로 처음 문장은 틀린 내용이며 맥주 제조를 위해 네 가지의 원료 중 두 가지만 사용해도 된다는 말은 언급된 적이 없으므로 두 번째 문장 역시 틀렸다. 중세 시대에는 위생이 좋지 않았기 때문에 물을 마시는 것보다는 맥주를 마시는 것이 더 안전했다고 했으므로 세 번째 문장은 맞는 내용임을 알 수 있으며 라거는 1400년대에 독일에서 양조됐다고 했으므로 네 번째 문장 역시 맞는 내용이다. 1920년부터 13년간(1933년까지) 지속된 금주령 때문에 수천 개의 양조장이 파산했다는 내용에서 볼 때 마지막 문장도 맞는 내용이다.

❹ What does the professor say about the reason for beer being more important than water in the Middle Ages?

"Because of the alcohol in beer, it was safer to drink beer than to drink dirty water on the streets"라는 부분에서 정답을 찾을 수 있다. 깨끗한 물을 찾기 어려웠던 중세 시대에 물보다 맥주가 더 중요했던 이유는 위생상 더 안전했기 때문인데, 이는 맥주에 들어있는 알코올 때문이었다.

1. A   **2.** C   **3.** C   **4.** 참조   **5.** B

	déjà vu	jamais vu
It means "already seen" in French language.	✔	
It means "never seen" in French language.		✔
According to some researchers, it has three different types.	✔	
This term was first used by Emile Boirac, a French psychic researcher.	✔	
It describes any familiar situation which is not recognized by the observer.		✔

P(W): All right, now... today, we're going to talk about déjà vu, French for "already seen." It's also called paramnesia which refers to a distortion of memory where fantasy and objective experience are often confused. You've probably experienced this quite frequently... for example, when you first visit your friend's neighborhood but you have this uncanny, strange, and eerie feeling that you've been there before, or when you met a person for the first time but it feels like you've met him or her from somewhere else, and so on. Got it? So, if I explain this easier, déjà vu is the experience of an overwhelming sense of familiarity with something that should not be familiar at all.

The term, déjà vu, was coined by Emile Boirac, a French psychic researcher, in his book, *The Future of Psychic Sciences*. Well, the phenomenon is rather complex, and many different theories try to explain why déjà vu happens. Recent studies indicate that about 70 percent of people have experienced this phenomenon, especially more often among young people between the ages of 15 to 25. However, as you could easily imagine, déjà vu is extremely difficult to be ignited in a laboratory setting, so researchers had to rely heavily on a few empirical findings.

Like I just mentioned, because most theories related with déjà vu are speculative at best, there are tons of theories about this phenomenon. For example, psychoanalysts believe that déjà vu has to do with wish fulfillment — that a person experiencing déjà vu is expressing his wish to repeat his past experience but with a more satisfactory outcome. Meanwhile, parapsychologists maintain that it's a fleeting glimpse of some past life.

Researchers suggest that there are three types of déjà vu: déjà vecu, which is basically the same with déjà vu, déjà senti meaning "already felt", and déjà visité which means "already visited." We'll talk about these three types of déjà vu in a bit, but let's first talk about jamais vu before we move on... uh, it's another related phenomenon meaning "never seen." This one is used to describe the experience of not recognizing a familiar situation. For instance, when a person has a feeling that he has never seen the scenery he's looking at or never heard of a word which is, actually, a pretty familiar word, then you call that phenomenon jamais vu. So, it might be safe to say that this phenomenon is quite the opposite of déjà vu. Now, back to déjà vu.

자, 오늘은 데자부에 대해서 얘기해 보겠어요. 데자부란 프랑스어로 "이미 본"이란 뜻인데, 이는 상상과 객관적 경험이 종종 혼동되는 기억의 왜곡을 뜻하는 기억 착오라고도 불려요. 여러분도 이 현상을 자주 경험해 봤을 거예요... 예를 들어서, 친구가 사는 동네를 처음으로 방문했는데 그곳에 예전에 왔었던 것 같은 섬뜩하고 이상한 느낌이 든다던가, 아니면 어떤 사람을 처음 만났는데 그 사람을 다른 곳에서 예전에 만났던 것 같은, 그런 느낌이 들 때 말이죠. 이해되죠? 좀 더 쉽게 설명하자면, 데자부란 익숙한 느낌이 들 수 없는 것에 대해 그러한 느낌이 압도적으로 드는 경험을 말해요..

데자부라는 용어는 프랑스의 심령학자인 에밀 보아락이 그의 책 "심령 감각의 미래"에서 처음 사용했어요. 이 현상은 상당히 복잡하고 이 현상이 왜 일어나는가에 대한 다양한 이론들이 많이 있죠. 최근의 연구들에 의하면 약 70퍼센트에 달하는 사람들이 이 현상을 체험했다고 하는데요, 특히 15세에서 25세 사이의 젊은이들에게서 더 자주 나타났다고 해요. 하지만 여러분이 쉽게 상상할 수 있듯이, 데자부 현상을 실험 환경에서 유도하기란 매우 어렵기 때문에 연구진들은 소수의 경험에 의존해야 했죠.

앞서 말했듯이 데자부와 관련된 대부분의 이론들이 잘 해야 추론적인 것이기 때문에 이 현상에 대한 수많은 이론들이 나와 있어요. 예를 들어, 정신분석학자들은 데자부가 희망하는 바를 성취하는 것과 관련이 있다고 생각하는데요, 데자부를 경험하는 사람은 자신의 과거 경험을 반복해서 경험하고자 하는 희망을 표현하는 것이라고 해요. 하지만 조금 더 만족스러운 결과로 끝나기를 바라는 것이죠. 반면에 초심리학자들은 데자부가 자신의 전생을 아주 잠깐동안 보는 것이라고 생각해요.

연구자들은 데자부에는 세 가지 종류가 있다고 하는데요, 데자부와 기본적으로 유사한 기체험감(déjà vecu), "이미 느껴진"을 뜻하는 기지각감(déjà senti), 그리고 "이미 방문된"을 뜻하는 기방문감(déjà visite) 등이에요. 잠시 후에 이 세 가지 종류의 데자부에 대해 이야기 해 보도록 할 텐데, 우선은 미시감(jamais vu)에 대해 살펴보죠. 이것은 "전혀 보지 못한"이라는 뜻을 갖는 관련된 현상이에요. 이것은 익숙한 상황을 인지하지 못하는 경험을 설명하기 위해 사용되는 말인데요, 예를 들어 어떤 사람이 자신이 보는 풍경을 한번도 보지 못했다는 느낌을 가지고 있거나, 아니면 실제로는 아주 익숙한 단어임에도 불구하고 한번도 들어보지 못했다는 느낌을 갖는다면 그 현상을 미시감이라고 불러요. 이 현상은 데자부와 반대되는 현상이라고 할 수 있겠죠. 자, 다시 데자부로 갑시다.

❶ What does the professor mainly discuss?

교수는 먼저 데자부의 정의와 뜻, 그리고 그 현상에 대한 전반적인 설명을 하며 지문의 마지막에서 jamais vu와 비교한다. 따라서 선택지 A가 가장 좋은 답안이다. 선택지 B, C, D는 제한적인 내용을 담고 있다.

❷ Why does the professor mention visiting your friend's neighborhood?

데자부를 경험할 때의 느낌을 설명하기 위해 친구의 동네를 방문했을 때의 예를 들고 있으므로 정답은 C이다. 주제를 바꾸거나 주제와 관련없는 이야기를 하는 것이 아니므로 선택지 A와 B는 틀린 답안이며, jamais vu는 지문의 마지막에 언급하므로 선택지 D 역시 오답이다.

❸ What can be inferred about déjà vu?

데자부는 실험실에서 필요할 때마다 불러 일으킬 수 있는 것이 아니기 때문에, 이따금 발생하는 경험에 의존해 연구해야 한다는 고충이 있다. 따라서 선택지 C가 정답으로 가장 적절하다.

❹ Based on the information in the lecture, indicate whether each sentence below describes déjà vu or jamais vu.

데자부는 "이미 본"이라는 뜻이며 jamais vu는 "전혀 보지 못한"이라는 뜻이다. 데자부에는 세가지 종류가 있으며 에밀 보아락에 의해 처음 사용되었다. 이미 경험한 느낌을 받는 데자부에 반해, jamais vu는 익숙한 상황이지만 그것을 인지하지 못하는 상황을 뜻한다.

❺ What will the professor probably discuss next?

교수는 "We'll talk about these three types of déjà vu in a bit, but let's talk about jamais vu first before we move on"이라고 하며, 잠시 후에 세 가지 종류의 데자부에 대해 설명할 것이지만 먼저 jamais vu에 대해 설명하겠다고 한다. Jamais vu에 대한 설명이 끝나자, 교수는 "Now, back to déjà vu"라고 하며 원래의 주제인 데자부로 돌아가자고 한다. 따라서 정답은 선택지 B이다.

1. B **2.** D **3.** A **4.** C **5.** 참조

	True	False
Rugova was elected as President of Kosovo by the first referendum in June, 1999.		✓
Slobodan Milosevic, the Serbian leader, eradicated autonomy of Kosovo within the former Yugoslavia and brought it under the direct control of Belgrade.	✓	
The Kosovo Liberation Army (KLA) attacked on Serbian civilians and security personnel simultaneously in several parts of Kosovo.	✓	
A so-called ethnic cleansing campaign was conducted by Kosovar Albanians against Serbs.		✓
NATO carried on a bombing campaign because a peace agreement could not be reached.		✓

P(M): We've been talking about ethnic warfare for the last couple of weeks. Today, let's move on to Kosovo which lies in southern Serbia. It has a mixed population of which the majority consists of ethnic Albanians. Until 1989, Kosovo had a high degree of autonomy within the former Yugoslavia, but Serbian leader Slobodan Milosevic changed the situation — he removed the autonomy and brought it under the direct control of Belgrade, the Serbian capital, to which, of course, the Kosovar Albanians seriously opposed. The Albanian nationalism and separatism in response to persecution was constantly growing which led to increasing ethnic tensions between the Serbs and Albanians. As a result, um, the Albanians started to lose jobs... about 115,000 were left jobless. They did fight for their freedom — in 1991, the Democratic League of Kosovo, an Albanian political party led by Ibrahim Rugova decided to resist peacefully, but they ended up organizing a referendum on independence for Kosovo. Rugova was elected as President of Kosovo by a second referendum in May, 1992. However, the Serbian government declared that both referendums were illegal and thus their results null.

Rugova's policy against the Serbian repression was passive and this agitated and radicalized many Albanians. On April 22, 1996, in several parts of Kosovo, four attacks on Serbian civilians and security personnel were carried out at the same time, which was the responsibility of an unknown organization called the "Kosovo Liberation Army" or KLA. Most Albanians viewed the KLA as legitimate and as... well, "freedom fighters," but as you can easily imagine, the Serbian government wasn't very happy about this and saw it as a group of terrorists.

In the 1998 open conflict between Serbian militay and polices of Kosovar Albanian forces, over 1500 Kosovar Albanians died and 400,000 people were forced to leave their homes. Tens of thousands of people were out in the woods, without clothing or shelter. Winter was approaching. Villages and crops were destroyed. A so-called ethnic cleansing had begun, and by the beginning of April, 1999, this campaign of ethnic cleansing had resulted in 226,000 refugees in Albania, 125,000 in the former Yugoslav Republic of Macedonia, and 33,000 in Montenegro. A peace plan was desperate, and on October 12, 1998, the Kosovo Verification Agreement was reached. NATO and other international organizations tried to persuade Milosevic to permit NATO peacekeeping troops to enter Kosovo; however, those attempts failed.

Hence, from March 24 to June 11, 1999, NATO's bombing campaign lasted. The campaign, which was initially designed to demolish Serbian air defenses and high-value military targets, didn't go very well at first because of adverse weather and Milosevic's extreme will to exist. While the bombing continued, the ethnic cleansing reached its peak, and an estimate of 1.5 million people, that is, about 90 percent of the population of Kosovo, had been expelled from their homes by the end of May. About 225,000 Kosovar men were believed to be missing, and at least 5,000 had been executed.

우리는 지난 몇 주간 민족 전쟁에 대해 얘기했습니다. 오늘은 세르비아 남부에 위치한 코소보에 대해 알아보겠습니다. 이 지역에는 여러 인종이 섞여있는데 그들 중 대다수가 알바니아계입니다. 1989년까지 코소보는 전 유고슬라비아 영내에서 강한 자치권이 있었지만, 세르비아의 지도자인 슬로보단 밀로셰비치가 이 상황을 바꾸어 놓았습니다. 그는 이 지역의 자치권을 없애고 세르비아 수도인 베오그라드의 직속령으로 바꾸었는데, 이것은 물론 알바니계 코소보인들의 강한 반발을 불러일으켰습니다. 박해에 저항한 알바니아인의 국수주의와 분리주의는 계속 증가했으며, 이것은 세르비아인과 알바니아인 사이에 긴장을 가중시켰습니다. 그 결과, 알바니아인은 직장을 잃기 시작했습니다. 무려 115,000명이 실업자가 되었죠. 그들은 자유를 위해 투쟁했습니다. 1991년에 이브라힘 루고바가 이끄는 알바니아의 정당인 코소보 민주 의회가 평화적으로 대항하기로 결심했지만, 결국 코소보 독립을 위해 국민 투표를 준비하게 되었

습니다. 루고바가 1992년 5월 두 번째 국민 투표에 의해 코소보의 대통령으로 선출됐습니다. 그렇지만 세르비아 정부는 두 번의 국민 투표 모두가 불법이며 그 결과 역시 모두 무효라고 선언했습니다.

세르비아 독재에 대한 루고바의 정책은 수동적이었고 이는 많은 알바니아인을 격분시키고 극단화시켰습니다. 1996년 4월 22일, 코소보의 몇몇 지역에서 동시 다발적으로 세르비아 민간인과 경비인들에게 네 차례의 공격이 행해졌으며 이는 "코소보 민간 해방군", 혹은 KLA라 불리는 알려지지 않은 단체의 소행이었습니다. 대부분의 알바니아인들은 코소보 민간 해방군을 합법적이라고 보았으며, "자유투사"라고 간주했지만, 쉽게 상상할 수 있듯이 세르비아 정부는 이를 좋게 보지 않았고 테러리스트로 규정했죠.

1998년 세르비아 군대와 경찰과 알바니아 세력간에 전투가 벌어져 1,500명 이상의 알바니아계 코소보인들이 죽고 40만 명이 주거지역에서 쫓겨났습니다. 수만 명이 옷과 거처가 없이 겨울이 닥쳐오는 상황에서 숲에서 살아야만 했습니다. 마을과 양식은 파괴되었고, 소위 인종 청소라 불리는 것이 시행되어 알바니아에서만 22만 6천명의 피난민이, 전 유고슬라브 공화국에서는 약 12만 5천명, 그리고 몬테네그로에서 3만 3천명의 피난민이 발생했습니다. 평화 정책이 시급했으며, 1998년 10월 12일 코소보 분리 합의가 도출되었습니다. NATO와 다른 국제 조직들이 밀로세비치를 설득해 평화 유지군이 코소보로 진입할 수 있도록 하려고 했지만 수포로 돌아갔습니다.

이에 따라 1999년 3월 24일부터 6월 11일까지 나토 평화유지군의 폭격이 지속되었습니다. 이 작전은 세르비아 대공 방어력과 주요 군사시설을 초토화시키는 것이 초기 목적이었는데, 처음엔 기상 악화와 밀로세비치의 강력한 저항 의지로 인해 어려움을 겪었습니다. 폭격이 계속되는 동안 인종 청소는 극에 달해, 코소보 인구 전체의 90%인 약 150만 명의 주민들이 5월 말까지 모두 주거지에서 쫓겨났습니다. 약 22만 5천여 명의 코소보 남성이 실종되었으며, 최소한 5천명이 처형되었습니다.

① What does the professor mainly discuss?

"We've been talking about ethnic warfare for the last couple of weeks. Today, let's move on to Kosovo which lies in southern Serbia"라는 교수의 말에서, 이 강의는 남부 세르비아의 코소보에서 있었던 민족 전쟁에 대한 것임을 알 수 있다. 세르비아 전쟁이 전반적으로 어떻게 전개되었는지 설명하고 있으므로 이 내용을 가장 잘 담은 선택지는 B이다. 선택지 A는 너무 광범위한 내용이며, 반대로 선택지 C와 D는 제한적인 내용을 담고 있으므로 답이 될 수 없다.

② What can be inferred about the definition of ethnic cleansing?

강의에 따르면 인종 청소란 세르비아인에 의한 코소보 알바니아인의 추방과 학살을 뜻하는 것임을 알 수 있다. 선택지 A는 강의 내용과 관련이 없으며, 단순히 알바니아인을 직장에서 내쫓는 것만은 아니므로 선택지 B 역시 좋은 선택이 아니다. 선택지 C는 가해자와 피해자의 관계가 반대로 되어 있다.

③ In what order does the professor explain the warfare?

세르비아전에 대한 설명을 시간 순서대로 하고 있으므로 정답은 A이다.

④ According to the lecture, what can be inferred about the reason for NATO's bombing campaign?

"Attempts were made to persuade Milosevic to permit NATO peacekeeping troops to enter Kosovo, but it didn't go well. Hence, from March 24 to June 11, 1999, NATO's bombing campaign lasted"라는 교수의 말에서 정답을 찾을 수 있다. 즉, 외교적으로 나토 평화유지군을 코소보에 들여보내려고 한 노력이 수포로 돌아가서 공습을 선택했다는 이야기이다. 코소보 알바니아인들이 나토에게 공습을 요청했는지의 여부는 언급되어 있지 않으므로 A는 틀린 답안이며, 나토가 공습을 한 원인은 날씨와는 관련이 없으므로 B 역시 틀린 선택이다. 선택지 D는 강의의 내용에서 알 수 없는 내용이다.

⑤ Based on the information in the lecture, indicate whether the following sentences are true or false.

루고바는 1992년의 두 번째 국민 투표에서 대통령으로 선출되었기 때문에 처음 문장은 틀렸으며 밀로세비치가 코소보의 자치권을 없애고 베오그라드의 직속령으로 바꿨으므로 두 번째 문장은 맞는 내용이다. 코소보 민간 해방군이 서로 다른 지역에서 세르비아계 민간인과 경찰에게 공격을 가했으므로 세 번째 문장은 맞는 내용이며, 인종 청소는 세르비아인들이 코소보계 알바니아인에게 가행한 것이므로 네 번째 문장은 틀렸다. 평화 정책인 코소보 분리 합의가 도출되기는 했지만 밀로세비치의 강력한 저항으로 나토의 폭격이 거행된 것이므로 마지막 문장 역시 틀린 내용이다.

Passage 10

1. C **2.** B **3.** D **4.** 참조 **5.** C

	Church music	Secular music
Creating manuscript was available which still survives to the current time.	✔	
One type of this is known as Gregorian Chant.	✔	
It was played during times of celebration and festivities.		✔
It can be represented by the monophonic chant.	✔	
It was called "chivaree."		✔

P(M): For people who live in the world of technology, music is accessible and highly affordable, whether that be a piece of song of an independent rock group or a masterpiece of Bach, conducted by the most famous conductors out there. You can either go to the nearest store to buy a CD or just log on to the Internet and download or purchase a song or two. Well, it is extremely comfortable for us to enjoy music nowadays, but the situation was different during the Middle Ages. First of all, creating a musical manuscript itself was very expensive due to the expense of parchment, and too much time was spent in order for a scribe to reproduce a manuscript. So, you can easily conclude that only rich institutions such as the church and monasteries were able to create manuscripts which survived to the current time.

The early medieval music can be represented by chant, a monophonic song which is a sacred form of the Christian church. Chant developed in several parts of Europe such as Rome, Spain, Milan, Ireland, and Gaul. These chants were primarily used during the Mass and according to each region, different forms of chant developed. Around 1011 AD, the Roman Catholic Church standardized the chant which became known as Gregorian Chant.

W: Um, professor, then, do you mean that other people, like peasants and merchants... they didn't sing at all? I mean, people have been singing throughout history... I just don't think that ordinary people who weren't associated with the church sang Gregorian Chants and stuff.

P: Good question, Maria. Ordinary people of the Middle Ages did have their own music. Actually, music was an integral part of everyday life. Medieval music, or I should say, medieval secular music was especially popular during times of celebration and festivities such as weddings and birthdays. People played romantic lovers' music for weddings. This type of everyday, secular music was called "chiveree." The musicians would play buoyant, cheery, uplifting music with instruments such as recorders, horns, trumpets, whistles, bells, and drums. People danced and ate to the sound of traditional music during and between meal courses.

M: I'm confused... you said that only the rich institutions such as the church could create music manuscripts... that's how we can study medieval music, no? Then, how do we know how medieval secular music was like? I don't think the ordinary people could write musical manuscripts.

P: That was what I was about to explain. Before we go on to that, let's take a look at this video strip first.

P: 과학 기술의 세계에 사는 사람들에게 있어 음악은 이용하기 수월하고 가격도 저렴해요. 그것이 인디 락 그룹의 노래이건 유명한 지휘가가 지휘한 바흐의 걸작이건 말이죠. 가까운 가게로 가서 CD를 사거나 인터넷에 접속해서 노래를 다운로드 받거나 한두 곡 정도를 살 수도 있어요. 요

즘에는 음악을 즐기기가 매우 쉬워졌지만, 중세 시대에는 상황이 달랐어요. 우선, 악보를 만드는 것 자체가 종이에 드는 비용 때문에 매우 비쌌고, 사본 필경자가 악보를 베끼는 것도 시간이 오래 걸렸죠. 따라서 부유한 기관, 즉 교회와 수도원만이 현 시대까지 살아남은 악보를 만들 수 있었다는 결론을 내릴 수 있겠죠.

초기의 중세 음악은 성가, 즉 기독교의 성가의 유형인 단선율의 노래로 대표되어요. 성가는 로마, 스페인, 밀라노, 아일랜드, 그리고 갈리아 등의 유럽 몇몇 지역에서 발전했죠. 이러한 성가는 미사 시간 등에 주로 사용되었고, 각 지역에 따라 고유의 성가가 개발되었어요. 서기 1011년 경, 로마 카톨릭 교회는 미사와 성가를 표준화시켰는데, 이게 바로 그레고리안 성가예요.

W: 교수님, 그럼 다른 사람들, 즉 농민과 상인들은, 노래를 아예 안 했단 말씀이신가요? 선사시대 이래로 인간은 계속 노래를 했잖아요... 교회에 속해 있지 않은 평민들이 그레고리안 성가를 불렀다는 생각은 안 드는데요.

P: 좋은 질문이에요, 마리아. 중세 시대의 일반인들에게도 그들만의 음악이 있었죠. 사실, 음악은 일상의 주요 부분이었어요. 중세 음악, 혹은 중세 세속 음악은 특히 결혼과 생일 등의 축제 때 인기가 많았어요. 결혼식에서는 로맨틱한 연인들의 음악을 연주했는데, 이러한 일상적인 세속 음악을 "chivaree"라고 불렀어요. 음악가들은 경쾌하고, 즐겁고, 활동적인 음악을 리코더, 호른, 트럼펫, 호각, 벨, 그리고 드럼 등을 통해서 연주했어요. 사람들은 음악에 맞춰 춤을 추고 전통 음악에 맞춰 식사 시간에 음식을 먹곤 했죠.

M: 헷갈려요... 교회 같은 부유한 기관만이 악보를 만들 수 있다고 하셨는데... 그것으로 중세 음악을 연구하는 것 아닌가요? 그럼 중세 세속 음악이 어땠는지 어떻게 아는 건가요? 일반인이 악보를 만들 수는 없었을 텐데요.

P: 지금부터 그것에 대해 설명하려고 했어요. 그 내용으로 넘어가기 전에 먼저 이 비디오를 보도록 하죠.

❶ According to the professor, why was creating music manuscript difficult during the Middle Ages?

"Creating musical manuscript itself was very expensive due to the expense of parchment"라는 부분에서 정답 A를 찾을 수 있다. 음악이 단조로운 것과 악보를 만드는 것이 힘든 것과는 관련이 없으므로 B는 틀린 선택이며, 악보를 베끼는 사람을 찾는 것이 힘들다는 내용은 언급되지 않았으므로 C 역시 오답이다. 악보가 비밀스럽게 제작되었다는 내용 역시 언급되지 않았으므로 D 또한 틀린 답안이다.

❷ According to the discussion, when was medieval secular music played the most?

"Medieval secular music was especially popular during times of celebration and festivities such as weddings or birthdays"라는 말에서 정답을 찾을 수 있다.

❸ What can be inferred about medieval secular people and their music?

"Music was an integral part of everyday life"라는 교수의 말에서 선택지 A는 틀린 선택임을 알 수 있으며, 단조로운 음악은 chant이며, chivaree는 매우 경쾌하고 발랄한 음악이었다.

Chivaree는 상인들과 농민 모두가 즐겼던 음악이다. 선택지 D의 "standardized music"은 chant를 말하는 것으로, 올바른 내용을 담고 있다.

❹ **Based on the information in the discussion, indicate whether each sentence below describes church music or ordinary people's music.**

교회 음악은 악보가 제작되었으며 그레고리안 성가가 교회 음악의 한 종류이다. 교회 음악은 매우 단조로운 성가로 알려져 있다. 세속적 음악은 chivaree라고 불리우며, 축제 등의 시기에 특히 인기가 있었다.

❺ **What will the video strip probably be about?**

중세의 세속 음악이 어땠는지 현재 사람들이 어떻게 아느냐는 학생의 질문에 교수는 이제 막 그 얘기를 하려고 했다며 먼저 비디오를 보자고 한다. 따라서 교수는 앞으로 중세의 세속 음악이 악보 없이 현재까지 어떻게 전해지게 되었는지를 설명할 것이며 비디오에 그와 관련된 내용이 담겨져 있을 것임을 추측할 수 있으므로 가장 좋은 답은 C이다. 선택지 A는 이미 앞에서 설명된 내용이며, 선택지 B와 D는 교수가 앞으로 설명할 내용과는 관련이 없다.

Vocabulary Test

1. adverse	**2.** destructive	**3.** affordable
4. empirical	**5.** persecution	**6.** spontaneous
7. tension	**8.** severity	**9.** c
10. a	**11.** b	**12.** a
13. d	**14.** c	**15.** b

5 Stance

P: 에르난 코르테스의 지배하에 스페인 사람들이 1519년도에 처음 도착했을 때 아즈텍 문명은 전성기를 이루고 있었어요. 다른 피지배층 인디언 그룹들은 아즈텍의 통치에 반대했고 스페인 사람들과 동맹을 맺을 의사가 있었죠. 아즈텍 사람들은 스페인 사람들이 Quetzalcoatl신의 후예들이라고 믿었어요. Quetzalcoatl은 멕시코 Toltec의 전설적인 지도자이자 고대의 신성한 존재로, 수염이 있는 금발의 백인이라고 알려져 있었죠. 이것은 코르테스의 외모와 우연히도 일치했으O-요. 그래서 최후의 아즈텍 지도자인 목테주마 2세는 코르테스가 그들의 신의 화신이라고 생각했고 그를 받아들였어요. 코르테스는 이것을 아즈텍을 지배할 수 있는 좋은 기회라고 생각했죠.

W: 순진한 원주민들을 그렇게 교묘하게 다루다니 꽤 교활한 것 같아요.

Strategy Focus

1. B   **2.** A   **3.** C   **4.** C

1. B

P(M): Today, we'll talk about magazines. Who knows when the first American magazines appeared? Yes, Samuel?

M: Uh... I believe it appeared a half century after the first newspapers.

P: That's right; although, it took longer to establish a widespread readership. The first magazine in U.S. history was first published in Philadelphia on February 13, 1741 by Andrew Bradford, a printer who was born in London. However, it only lasted three months. **In 1893, which was about 152 years later, the first mass-circulation magazines started to appear and they only cost ten cents at the time. If you think about the fact that most magazines today cost well over several dollars... whoa.**

W: That really was cheap. Um, then, when was the magazine *Time* created?

P: That's a good question. It was introduced in 1923 by a man named Henry Luce. He was the first to invent the concept of the weekly news magazine. *Time* gradually carved out important niches along with its major competitor, *Newsweek*, with their in-depth analyses of national and international developments.

P: 오늘은 잡지에 대해 얘기해 봅시다. 미국의 첫번째 잡지가 언제 등장했는지 아는 사람? 네, 사무엘?

M: 음... 신문이 처음 등장한 지 50년 후에 등장한 것 같아요.

P: 맞았어요, 비록 독자층을 확보하기까지 한참 더 걸렸지만요. 미국 역사상 처음으로 등장한 잡지는 1741년 2월 13일, 필라델피아에서 앤드류 브래드포드 라는 영국 태생 인쇄업자에 의해 처음으로 발간됐어요. 하지만 이 잡지는 3개월 밖에 못갔죠. 152년 후 1893년에 처음으로 대량 유통되는 잡지가 출간되기 시작했는데, 그 당시에는 가격이 10센트 밖에 하지 않았어요. 요즘 잡지들이 몇 달러 이상 나간다는 걸 생각해 보면 놀랍죠...

W: 정말 저렴했네요. 음, 그렇다면 잡지 "타임지"는 언제 만들어졌나요?

P: 좋은 질문이에요. "타임지"는 1923년에 헨리 루스라는 사람에 의해 출간되었어요. 이 사람은 주간제 뉴스 잡지라는 개념을 처음으로 도입한 사람이었어요. "타임지"는 큰 라이벌인 "뉴스위크지"와 함께 국내외 사건들에 대한 심도 있는 분석으로 점차적으로 중요한 틈새 시장을 확보했어요.

2. A

P(W): Many of you might have experienced insomnia and seriously considered taking medication. Well, we all know that when a person is deprived of good sleep, he or she is likely to get extremely sensitive and pointy. But do you know that a good night's sleep also affects your heart health? Well, it's easy to understand that your heart is in danger when your blood carries elevated inflammation markers. Some scientists found out from an experiment that there's a connection between total sleep deprivation and an increase in white blood cells, interleukin-6 and C-reactive protein which induce inflammation. What's more surprising was that it can also happen with partial sleep deprivation. According to their study, blood pressure and heart rate increased in people who were denied sleep. Hypertension, uh... basically persistent high blood pressure, um, is one of the factors that can cause arterial plaques to rupture, and if the blood clots narrow a heart artery, you can lose your life.

But luckily, there is a relatively new solution available, and it has nothing to do with taking medication constantly. The cure for insomnia is cognitive behavioral therapy or CBT for short. A 2006 study revealed that it's as effective as a sedative in inducing sleep.

여러분들도 불면증으로 고생하고 약을 복용하는 것을 심각하게 고려해 본 적이 있을 텐데요. 사람이 잠을 못 자게 되면 매우 예민해지고 민감해진다는 것을 다들 알고 있을 거예요. 하지만 잠을 잘 자는 것이 심장 건강에도 영향을 미친다는 것은 알고 있나요? 혈액의 염증 표지가 높으면 심장이 위험하다는 것은 이해하기 쉽지요. 일부 과학자들은 실험을 통해 완전 불면증과 백혈구. 인터루킨-6, 그리고 염증을 유발하는 C-반응성 단백질의 증가 간에 연관이 있다는 것을 밝혀냈는데요. 더 놀라운 것은 불면증이 부분적으로만 발생해도 이러한 증상이 생길 수 있다는 거예요. 이들의 연구에 따르면 잠을 자지 못한 사람들의 혈압과 심박수가 상승한다고 하는데요. 만성적으로 혈압이 높은 현상인 고혈압은 동맥 플라크를 파열시킬 수 있는 원인들 중 하나이고, 만약 응고된 혈액이 심장 동맥을 좁게 만들면 목숨을 잃을 수도 있어요.

하지만 다행히도 비교적 새로운 해결 방법이 있는데, 이것은 지속적으로 약을 먹는 것과는 무관해요. 불면증을 치료할 수 있는 방법은 CBT라고도 불리는 인지행동치료예요. 2006년에 시행된 연구에 의하면 잠을 유발하는 데에 CBT가 안정제처럼 효과적이라고 해요.

3. C

P(M): The sod house, or soddy, is a house that has walls made of strips of sod laid horizontally in courses like bricks. Sod houses were commonly established on the western plains of the United States in the frontier days. Can you guess why people built houses from sod rather than log or brick? Nobody? Well, that's because standard building materials such as wood or stone usually couldn't be found in the prairie. Sod, however, which is from thickly-rooted prairie grass, was abundant there, and what do you know, prairie grass there was basically thicker and stronger than the grass that we use in gardens today.

The sod was turned by the plow and held together by roots. It was usually lifted in strips and cut in three-foot lengths, and these strips of sod were piled into walls. Um, the roofs usually had frame construction but builders employed various roofing methods. Um, typical sod house roofs were thatched or covered with sods, but had to be replaced after heavy rains. Although the thick layers of sod captured heat and were fire and wind-proof, the dwelling condition was... well, pretty damp and dark. Um, sod houses usually allowed only small window and door openings, so... I guess they permitted little sunlight... oh, and, uh, it was subject to dirt and insect infestations, so I don't think any of you would like to live in one of them even if they were extremely cheap.

잔디집이라고도 불리는 뗏집은 잔디의 줄기를 이용해서 벽을 만든 집인데, 마치 벽돌을 쌓아 올리듯 수평으로 잔디 줄기를 엮어 올립니다. 뗏집은 미국의 서부 개척시대에 흔히 지어졌습니다. 사람들이 왜 통나무나 벽돌 대신 잔디로 집을 지었는지 맞출 수 있나요? 아무도 없나요? 그 이유는 일반적으로 사용되는 건축 자재인 나무나 돌 등이 평야에서는 찾기 힘들었기 때문입니다. 하지만 그곳에는 뿌리가 빽빽하게 박힌 초원풀에서 나는 잔디가 많았고, 이것은 오늘날 우리의 정원에 있는 것보다 두껍고 튼튼했습니다.

잔디는 쟁기로 파내어 뿌리로 엮었습니다. 주로 긴 줄로 파내어 3피트 길이로 잘랐는데. 이와 같은 잔디줄을 겹겹이 쌓아 벽을 만들었습니다. 지붕은 대부분 틀이 있었지만 뗏집을 짓는 사람들은 다양한 방법으로 지붕을 만들었습니다. 일반적인 뗏집의 지붕은 이엉으로 이어지거나 잔디로 덮혔지만 큰 비가 온 후에는 이것을 갈아야만 했습니다. 비록 두꺼운 층의 잔디가 난방 효과 외에도 방화 및 방풍 효과가 있었지만 주거 상태 자체는 습하고 어두웠습니다. 뗏집에는 보통 작은 창문과 문을 설치하는 것만이 허용되었기 때문에, 햇빛이 거의 들지 않았을 것입니다... 그리고 먼지와 벌레도 많았습니다. 이 집이 아무리 값이 싸다고 해도, 여러분 중 이곳에서 살고 싶어할 사람은 아마 아무도 없을 거라 생각해요.

4. C

P(W): The Homestead Strike was one of the most bitterly fought labor disputes in U.S. history, and probably one of the most difficult adversities that Andrew Carnegie had experienced. You know what Carnegie is famous for, right? Steel baron. Yes, he had a steel company at Homestead, Pennsylvania. The workers working at the Carnegie Steel Company had a three-year contract which was set to expire on June 30, 1892. The workers belonged to the Amalgamated Association of Iron and Steel Workers. When this day was coming closer, Carnegie, who had often publicly expressed union sympathies, fled for Scotland, leaving Henry C. Frick, the company's general manager, with managing authority. Frick decided to cut the wages of the workers and break the union, but of course, the workers protested. The workers were laid off because of this protest. On June 30, the workers struck the company, and uh... on July 6, many of them were killed or wounded in an armed battle with Pinkerton detectives hired by Frick.

홈스테드 파업은 미국 역사상 가장 치열했던 노동 쟁의 중 하나였고, 아마도 앤드류 카네기가 경험한 가장 어려운 역경 중 하나였을 것입니다. 카네기가 무엇으로 유명한 줄 아시죠? 철강왕이라고 불렸던 그는 펜실베니아 홈스테드에 철강회사를 갖고 있었습니다. 카네기 철강회사에 다니고 있던 이 노동자들은 3년 계약직이었는데, 이 계약은 1892년 6월 30일에 만료될 예정이었습니다. 이 근로자들은 철강 노동자의 통합 협회에 소속되어 있었습니다. 계약 만료날이 다가오자 종종 공개적으로 조합에 호감을 표명했던 카네기는 스코틀랜드로 도주하며 회사의 부장인 헨리 프릭을 관리자로 앉혔습니다. 프릭은 근로자들의 급여를 깎고 조합을 해체시키려고 했지만, 당연히 근로자들은 반항했습니다. 근로자들은 이로 인해 해고되었습니다. 6월 30일에 근로자들은 공장을 습격했고 7월 6일 프릭이 고용한 핑커턴 사립 탐정들과의 교전에서 많은 사람들이 죽거나 다쳤습니다.

Exercise

P.1	1. C	2. A	3. B, C	4. B, C	5. D
P.2	1. A	2. C, D	3. B	4. C	5. D
P.3	1. C	2. B	3. D	4. B	5. A
P.4	1. D	2. B	3. C	4. B	5. D
P.5	1. C	2. B	3. D	4. A	5. A
P.6	1. D	2. B	3. C	4. A	5. D
P.7	1. B	2. D	3. A		
P.8	1. B	2. A	3. A	4. B	5. 참조
P.9	1. D	2. C	3. C		
	4. A	5. B	6. A		
P.10	1. A	2. B	3. B		
	4. B, D	5. C	6. A		

Passage 1

1. C   **2.** A   **3.** B, C   **4.** B, C   **5.** D

P(M): Um, much attention is paid to the economics of markets, of manufacturing and trade in the postmodern world. ❷ **However, public goods and services area do not attract much attention and there is no widely accepted term to refer to these goods and services that are consumed or held collectively.** Um, what example can you give me for this? Yes, Adam?

M: <u>Um, public parks, maybe?</u>

P: Yes, yes, sure, public parks can be one example.

W: What about public health care or energy... um, or transportation?

P: Very good. All those things can be considered as the commons, as some commentators have begun using recently. These days, however, we witness that these commons are in a state of crisis, simply because we don't know what to think about the economics of these systems, or... well, just think that they're not their own property. Now, let us talk more in depth about the commons. There are two domains here—the natural commons and the social commons. First, the natural commons. It includes free natural resources such as air, water, earth, sunlight, you name it. Not only that, it also includes the basis of all life on earth. On the other hand, the social commons includes our cultural heritage, such as our languages and cultures, human knowledge, and public services.

M: Professor, you just mentioned that those commons are on the verge of crisis... how's that? Are you focusing more on the natural commons than on the social commons?

P: Yes. Well, actually, I was just about to explain that. Let me give you an example, just to help you see the picture better. Deforestation. Degradation of water and earth. Depletion of many vital natural resources. Many countries rely heavily on their natural resources for their nation's economy such as oil, gas, coal, or lumber. Get the picture? Now, let's see the examples of these three countries who adopted new systems to manage the commons, especially, their forests — Indonesia, Malaysia, and Thailand.

P: 포스트모던 시대에서는 시장 경제, 즉 제조업과 무역에 많은 관심이 주목되어요. 그렇지만 공공 재화나 서비스 부문은 별 관심을 끌지 못하고,

집단적으로 소비되거나 소유되는 이러한 재화나 서비스를 통용해서 부를 만한 널리 알려진 용어가 없는 상태예요. 자, 이것에 대해 어떤 예를 들 수 있을까요? 네, 아담?

M: 음, 공원이요?

P: 네, 맞아요. 공원도 한 예가 될 수 있죠.

W: 복지 건강 시설이나 전력... 아니면 운송이요?

P: 맞았어요. 일부 논평가들은 최근에 이러한 것들을 공유지라고 부르기 시작했어요. 하지만 오늘날 우리는 이 공유지가 위기에 봉착한 것을 볼 수 있는데, 이는 간단히 말해 이런 시스템의 경제에 대해 어떻게 생각해야 하는지 모르거나, 혹은 이것이 본인의 재산이 아니라고 생각하기 때문에 발생하게 되는 것이에요. 자, 이제 공유지에 대해 더 깊이 들어가 봅시다. 여기엔 두가지 범위가 있는데요, 자연적 공유지와 사회적 공유지입니다. 첫째로, 자연적 공유지는 무료 천연자원, 즉 공기, 물, 대지, 태양 등을 포함해요. 뿐만 아니라 지구상 모든 생명의 근원도 포함하죠. 한편 사회적 공유지는 우리의 문화 유산, 즉 언어와 문화, 지식, 그리고 사회 제도를 포함해요.

M: 교수님, 방금 이런 것이 위기에 봉착했다고 하셨는데... 왜 그런 건가요? 사회적 공유지보다 자연적 공유지에 더 초점을 맞추신 건가요?

P: 맞아요. 실은 이제 막 그 얘기를 하려고 했어요. 좀 더 이해하기 쉽게 예를 들어보죠. 삼림 벌채, 물과 대지의 오염, 주요한 여러 천연자원의 고갈. 그리고 많은 나라들이 국가 경제를 위해 기름과 가스, 석탄 혹은 나무 등의 천연자원에 많이 의존해요. 이해되나요? 이제 공유지, 특히 삼림을 관리하기 위해 새로운 시스템을 도입한 세 나라 – 인도네시아, 말레이지아, 태국에 대해 알아보죠.

❶ What does the professor mainly discuss?

교수는 우선 공유지의 개념을 설명한 후, 이어서 공유지가 봉착한 위기에 대해 설명한다. 이러한 내용을 가장 잘 담고 있는 선택지는 C이다. 선택지 A, B, D는 지문에 잠시 언급된 내용만을 제한적으로 담고 있다.

❷ How does the student feel when he says this:

"Maybe?"라는 학생의 말에서 불분명한 태도를 엿볼 수 있다. 교수에게 대든다거나 질문을 받고 싶어하지 않는다고 생각할 수는 없으며, 선택지 D는 학생의 태도와 상반된 선택이다.

❸ Which of the following are the specific examples of social commons?

공유지에는 자연적 공유지와 사회적 공유지의 두 종류가 있는데, 사회적 공유지는 전반적인 문화 유산을 의미한다. 선택지 A(코끼리)는 동물이기 때문에 사회적 공유지에 해당되지 않으며, B(영어)는 언어이기 때문에 사회적 공유지가 된다. C(결혼식)는 문화 유산이라고 볼 수 있기에 사회적 공유지의 범위에 들며, D는 오히려 자연적 공유지에 속한다.

❹ According to the professor, which of the following pose danger on the commons?

교수는 특히 자연적 공유지의 위기에 대해 설명하는데 "Deforestation. Degradation of water and earth. Depletion of many vital natural resources. Many countries rely heavily on their natural resources for their nation's economy such as oil and gas, coal, or lumber"라고 한 부분에서 답을 찾을 수 있다. 따라서 선택지 B(공기를 오염시키는 자동차 매연)와 C(천연자원의 개척)가 정답이라고 볼 수 있다. 선택지 A(실업으로 인해 노동인력에서 퇴출되는 것)와 D(동물의 천적의 개체수 급증)는 이와 관련되었다고 보기 힘들다.

❺ What is the professor's attitude towards the commons?

교수는 많은 사람들이 공공 재화의 경제에 대해 잘 모르거나 자신의 소유가 아니라고 생각하기 때문에 공공 재화가 오늘날 위험에 처해 있다고 한다. 따라서 정답은 D이다. 선택지 A는 지문과 관련 없는 내용이며, 선택지 B는 오히려 "natural commons"라고 해야 교수의 입장과 맞게 된다. 선택지 C는 강의의 내용과 상반되는 내용이다.

Passage 2

1. A   **2.** C, D   **3.** B   **4.** C   **5.** D

P(W): In Cognitive Psychology, attention refers to ability to focus on a task and to concentrate, and to the allocations of processing resources. ❺ Selective attention is one of the different aspects of attention. It basically stems from this question: Can people attend to more than one thing at a time?

Um, let me give you an example. You enter a friend's house and the first thing you see in the room is the television... maybe your favorite football team is playing... and later you see a coffee table you didn't even notice. Well, I believe many of you have experienced something very similar — this is called selective attention. It's a theory of a state of consciousness which explains how people process information from only one aspect of a scene or environment while ignoring other aspects. It can be either conscious, like the example of your friend's television, or unconscious, like, when you see a bush of red flowers in a green prairie. Generally, after watching a scene, people think that they've captured every single aspect of it; however, in reality, they had only concentrated on the area in which they had the most interest or attention, having only a general glimpse or gist of the rest of the scene.

Well, then, why does this happen? One possible reason for this is that the brain capacity is limited, and it cannot process all of the available information simultaneously. But how do we explain people who do multiple tasks at the same time, say, driving a car? Aren't they steering the wheel, shifting the gear, applying the brakes once in a while, um, sometimes turning the radio on and off, talking with a passenger, and so on? Well, in this case, only one of those activities, such as watching the road or its traffic, receives the forefront of awareness, while other activities are achieved quite automatically.

인지 심리학에서 "주의"는 한 가지 일에 집중하는 능력과 정보 처리 자원을 분배하는 능력 등을 일컫습니다. 선택적 주의는 주의의 여러 분야 중 하나인데요, 기본적으로 다음과 같은 질문에서 파생됩니다 – 사람이 과연 동시에 한 가지 이상의 일을 할 수 있을까요?

자, 예를 들어봅시다. 여러분이 친구의 집에 들어가서 제일 먼저 본 것이 텔레비전이었던 경우를 생각해 봅시다... 아마도 텔레비전에서는 여러분이 제일 좋아하는 풋볼팀이 경기를 하고 있을지도 모릅니다... 그리고 나중에 처음에는 보지도 못했던 커피 테이블이 있다는 것을 알게 됩니다. 많은 분들이 이와 비슷한 경험을 해봤을 텐데요, 이것을 바로 선택적 주의라고 부릅니다. 이것은 의식의 현상에 대한 이론으로, 사람들이 한 장면에서 다른 부분은 무시하고 특정 부분과 관련된 정보만을 처리하는 것을 설명해 줍니다. 이것은 아까 언급한 친구의 텔레비전의 경우처럼 의식적일 수도 있고 초록색 초원에서 붉은 꽃 더미를 봤을 때처럼 무의식적일 수도 있습니다. 일반적으로 한 장면을 본 후 사람들은 그 장면의 모든 양상을 봤다고 생각하지만, 실제로는 자신이 가장 관심이 있고 흥미있어 하는 부분에만 집중한 것입니다. 즉, 나머지 장면은 일부, 혹은 핵심적인 부분만을 본 것에 지나지 않는 거지요.

그럼, 왜 이런 일이 일어나는 것일까요? 한 가지 가능한 이유는 뇌의 용량이 한정되어 있고 모든 정보를 동시에 다룰 수 없다는 것입니다. 그렇지만 운전처럼 여러 일을 동시에 하는 사람들은 어떻게 설명할 수 있을까요? 운전대를 돌리고, 기어를 바꾸고, 브레이크를 종종 밟는 동시에 이따금 라디오를 켜고 끄거나, 승객과 이야기를 나누지 않나요? 자, 이러한 경우에는 이 활동들 중 한 가지, 가령 길이나 교통량을 보는 것이 가장 우선적인 주의를 받고 다른 활동들은 상당히 자동적으로 이루어집니다.

❶ What is the possible subject of the lecture?

교수는 선택적 주의를 설명하면서 이러한 현상이 일어나는 이유를 설명하고 있으므로 강의와 가장 잘 맞는 제목은 선택지 A이다. 선택적 주의의 결과를 설명하는 것이 아니므로 B는 틀린 선택이며, 선택적 주의의 경과를 이야기 한 것도 아니므로 C 역시 틀린 선택이다. 선택지 D는 강의 내용과는 무관하다.

❷ Which of the following are examples of conscious selective attention?

Conscious selective attention이란 의식적으로 일어나는 선택적 주의를 말한다. 흰 야구공이 들어있는 박스에서 오렌지색 농구공을 더 잘 보거나, 은색 스포츠카 사이에서 빨간색 스포츠카를 보는 것은 무의식적 선택적 주의라고 할 수 있다. 바비 인형을 갖고 싶어하는 소녀가 장난감 가게의 선반에서 바비 인형을 발견한 C와, 다른 스포츠 경기를 방영하는 쇼윈도에서 농구 경기를 방영해 주는 것을 본 농구 선수를 언급한 D가 가장 좋은 답이다.

❸ Why does the professor mention your friend's television?

교수는 어려운 용어를 보다 쉽게 설명하기 위해 친구의 집에 놀러 갔을 때 가장 먼저 본 텔레비전에 대한 예시를 들고 있으므로 정답은 B이다. 선택지 A는 광범위한 내용을 다루고 있으며, C는 본문과 관련이 없는 내용이다. 교수는 unconscious selective attention에 대해 아직 언급하지 않았으므로 D 역시 맞는 답이라고 할 수 없다.

❹ According to the lecture, what is the most possible explanation for simultaneous multi-tasking?

한꺼번에 수행되는 여러 가지 일들 중 한 가지만이 가장 우선적인 주의를 받으며 다른 활동들은 비교적 자동적으로 이루어진다는 교수의 설명에서 정답을 찾을 수 있다.

❺ How does the professor feel when she says this:

교수는 선택적 주의라는 개념이 "Can people attend to more than one thing at a time?"이라는 질문에서 파생되었다고 한다. 따라서 이 내용과 상반된 선택지 A는 정답이 아니다. 또한, 교수 본인이 궁금하게 여기는 것이 아니므로 B 역시 틀린 답안이며, 본인이 선택적 주의 개념이 어디에서 파생되었는지 몰라서 학생들에게 미안해하는 것이 아니므로 C 역시 옳은 답이 될 수 없다.

Passage 3

1. C **2.** B **3.** D **4.** B **5.** A

P(W): When we look at the results of an 11-year study reported this June, drinking lots of coffee, about five to six cups a day, appeared to cut women's risk of developing diabetes. But most of the women in the study were drinking decaf coffee. So what's the secret here? It's the antioxidant, not the caffeine, in the brew that's beneficial.

W: Um, Dr. Johanssen, what exactly are antioxidants? Because I've read about them so much in health magazines and stuff, but they never tell us what it exactly is and what it does to our body.

P: Well, antioxidant is a chemical that reduces oxidative damage, or damage due to oxygen, such as that caused by free radicals. Does anybody know what free radicals are?

M: Kind of. Don't they attack molecules, and uh, kind of capture electrons and modify chemical structures and stuff?

P: Thank you, Mr. Robert, that's correct. ❹ From the word, antioxidant, the prefix "anti" means against or corrective in nature, and "oxidant" is commonly known as "free radicals." You know, we are exposed to free radicals from so many sources: pollution, the sun, stress, alcohol, smoking, and unhealthy eating. Free radicals produced by cell breakdown attack healthy cells. This sequence of events weakens our bodies and speeds up the aging process. It's also linked to multiple forms of cancer and heart disease. Now, antioxidants reduce the side effects of dangerous oxidants by binding with these harmful cells... this decreases their power to cause destruction. Antioxidants can also help cells repair sustained damage. They say that antioxidants may possibly reduce the risks of cancer and age-related macular degeneration or AMD — well, at least, antioxidants can slow the progression of AMD.

W: Well, where do we find antioxidants, then? Do we have to eat, like, pills and stuff?

P: That's a good question. Vitamin C, vitamin E, and beta carotene which is converted to vitamin A are some of the well-known antioxidants. All of these substances are known to counteract the damaging effects of oxidation. Antioxidant agents are found in foods, so try to consume more dark green leafy vegetables. Look for vegetables and fruits that have the richest colors — carrots, tomatoes, orange, red peppers, spinach, and so on.

M: Is it better to eat fruit raw than to cook it?

P: If you can, choose raw fruits and vegetables rather than cooked. You know, eating these foods raw will provide the highest concentration and best absorption of antioxidants. If you don't consume enough antioxidants through food, you could use dietary supplement formulas with antioxidants. Of course, the best way to stay healthy is to eat a balanced meal three times a day. You know, you should stay away from junk foods and increase physical activity. Avoid excessive intake of sugar and sodium. Remember, eating right, exercising, and taking proper care of yourselves are the ways to stay healthy.

P: 이번 6월에 발표된 11년짜리 연구 결과에 따르면 커피를 많이 마시는 것, 즉 하루에 5, 6잔을 마시는 것은 여성의 당뇨병 발병율을 낮추는 것으로 보인다고 해요. 그렇지만 연구에 참여한 여성의 대부분이 디카페인 커피를 마셨어요. 그렇다면 비결이 무엇일까요? 바로 커피에 있는 카페인이 아니라 항산화 물질이 유익한 것이에요.

W: 음, 요한센 박사님, 항산화 물질이 정확히 뭔가요? 건강 잡지 등에서 그것에 대해 많이 읽어는 봤지만, 그것이 정확히 무엇이고, 우리 몸에 어떤 작용을 하는지는 나와있지 않아서요.

P: 항산화 물질은 산성 피해, 즉 활성 산소로 인한 피해와 같은 산소로

인한 피해를 감소시키거나 줄여주는 역할을 하는 화학 성분이에요. 활성 산소가 무엇인지 아는 사람 있나요?

M: 조금요. 그것은 분자를 공격해서 전자를 포획하고 화학 구조를 변환시키지 않나요?

P: 고마워요. 로버트군, 정답이에요. 항산화 물질이라는 단어에서 접두사 "anti-(항)"는 자연 질서에 반한다는 뜻이고, "oxidant(산화물질)"는 일반적으로 "활성 산소"라고 알려져 있어요. 우리는 다양한 부분에서 활성 산소에 노출되어 있어요, 예를 들어 오염, 태양, 스트레스, 알코올, 담배, 그리고 건강에 해로운 식습관 등이 있죠. 세포 파괴로 인해 만들어지는 활성 산소는 건강한 세포를 공격해요. 이러한 일이 반복되면 우리의 몸을 약화시키고 노화를 촉진하죠. 또한 이것은 다양한 암과 심장병과도 연관이 있어요. 항산화 물질은 이러한 유해한 세포들과 결합하면서 위험한 활성 산소의 부작용을 줄여 주어요. 즉, 이 작용은 활성 산소의 파괴력을 줄이게 되죠. 항산화 물질은 또한 세포가 이미 입은 피해를 복구하는 데에도 도움을 주어요. 항산화 물질은 암과 노화와 관련된 시력 감퇴, 즉 AMD 발병률을 감소시킨다고 알려져 있는데요, 최소한 AMD의 진행을 늦출 수는 있다고 해요.

W: 그럼 항산화 물질을 어디서 구하나요? 약 같은 것을 먹어야 되는 건가요?

P: 좋은 질문이에요. 비타민 C, 비타민 E , 그리고 비타민 A로 전환되는 베타 카로틴이 잘 알려진 항산화 성분들이에요. 이러한 성분들은 모두 산화의 피해를 줄여준다고 알려져 있죠. 항산화 물질군은 음식에 포함되어 있으니까 잎이 많은 짙은 녹색 야채를 많이 드세요. 풍성한 색을 가진 과일과 야채, 즉 당근, 토마토, 오렌지, 붉은 고추, 시금치 등을 드세요.

M: 과일을 요리하는 것보다 생으로 먹는 게 더 나은가요?

P: 가능하다면 조리된 것보다 생과일과 야채를 드세요. 이러한 음식을 생으로 먹으면 고농축된 항산화 물질을 먹을 수 있고 흡수도 잘 되죠. 음식을 통해서 항산화 물질을 충분히 섭취하지 않으면, 항산화 물질이 포함된 영양제를 먹어도 돼요. 물론, 가장 건강에 좋은 것은 균형 잡힌 식사를 하루에 세 번 하는 것이에요. 몸에 나쁜 간식을 멀리 하고 신체 활동을 늘려야 해요. 설탕과 소금을 과하게 섭취하는 것은 피하세요. 명심하세요 – 잘 먹고, 운동하고 자신을 잘 돌보는 것이 바로 건강을 유지하는 방법이에요.

❶ **What is the discussion mainly about?**

교수는 항산화 물질의 작용과 그 종류, 그리고 그것이 포함된 식품 등에 대해 설명하고 있다. 선택지 A, B, D는 제한적인 내용을 다루고 있으므로 오답이다.

❷ **Why does the professor mention the 11-year study reported in June?**

"It's the antioxidant, not the caffeine, in the brew that's beneficial"라고 말하는 부분에서 답을 찾을 수 있다. 교수는 커피의 카페인이 아닌 항산화 물질이 여성의 당뇨병 발병률을 낮췄다고 하며 오늘의 주제인 항산화 물질을 소개하고 있으므로 정답은 B이다.

❸ **What does the professor say about antioxidant and free radicals?**

항산화 물질은 과일과 야채 등에 포함되어 있으며 영양제를 통해서도 섭취할 수 있다고 했으므로 선택지 A와 B는 오답이다. 활성 산소는 몸에 해로운 것이므로 선택지 C 역시 오답이다.

❹ Why does the professor say this:

교수는 "antioxidant"라는 단어를 생소하게 여길 수 있는 학생들을 위하여 이 단어가 반대를 뜻하는 "anti"와 활성 산소를 뜻하는 "oxidant"의 합성어임을 설명한 후, 항산화 물질이 우리 몸에 해로운 활성 산소를 공격한다고 설명하고 있다. 자신의 지식을 자랑하거나 활성 산소가 몸에 해로운 이유를 설명하기 위해 말한 것이 아니다.

❺ What is the professor's attitude towards dietary supplement formulas with antioxidants?

"If you don't consume enough antioxidants through food, you could use dietary supplement formulas with antioxidants. Of course, the best way to stay healthy is to eat balanced meals three times a day" 라고 하는 교수의 말에서, 교수는 항산화 물질이 들어있는 영양제를 먹는 것이 어느 정도 도움이 된다고 생각한다는 것을 알 수 있다. 이를 통해 선택지 C와 D는 오답임을 알 수 있으며, 하루 세 번 균형 잡힌 식사를 하는 것이 가장 좋다고 하는 것이지 영양제를 하루 세 번 먹어야 한다고 생각하는 것이 아니므로 선택지 B 역시 오답이다.

Passage 4

1. D　**2.** B　**3.** C　**4.** B　**5.** D

P(M): Okay, now, uh, let's start. Um, today, we're gonna talk about the feudal society and the life in medieval England, especially custom of getting married. Uh... in feudal society, which is about mid-11th century and on, peasants were owned by a lord of the manor. The lord would give a piece of his land to a peasant, who was also known as serf or villein, and he was bound to work for the lord in return. Because of this, permission for peasants to marry and thus bear legitimate children was a right bestowed on knights by their liege-lords. You see, according to the law back then, peasants and all their belongings, like their houses, clothings, and even food didn't belong to themselves.

Well, of course, peasants wedded holding a wedding ceremony which was a way of proclaiming that they would be bonded as husband and wife, and start a new family. Sometimes they married each other, but other times, they married other free people in order to gain freedom. And, uh, speaking of which... the newlyweds had to be quite lucky to expand their family because of the high mortality rate of an infant. Some say that due to bad weather and a typically poor diet, most European peasants only lived until they reached 27. ❸ So... it would be logical to think that people

of the Middle Ages got married way before they reached 27, huh? Actually, more than 3/4 were married before they reached 19 years old!

W: Wow... If I were born in the Middle Ages, I would have already been married by now!

P: Well, most likely. Actually, though, there were some women who didn't get married until they reached the age of 24.

W: Well, that's relieving.

P: I don't know about that for sure, especially if you think that most people didn't even make it to live past their thirties. Anyways, if we go back to our topic... Um... many medieval weddings among these lower classes were the result of romance or pregnancy or as with nobles, a matter of business. What I'm trying to say is that, like many of the upper class, peasants had arranged marriages very commonly.

P: 자, 이제 시작하죠. 오늘은 중세 영국의 봉건 사회와 그 생활상, 특히 결혼 풍습에 대해 이야기해 보겠어요. 봉건 사회는 11세기 중엽부터 시작해서 그 이후로 이어졌는데, 당시 소작농들은 모두 영주에게 속해 있었어요. 영주는 농노라고 알려진 소작농에게 경작할 땅을 주었고, 이들은 그 대가로 영주를 위해 일을 해야 했어요. 그렇기 때문에 영주들은 기사들에게 농노들의 결혼 및 합법적인 출산을 허락하는 권리를 수여했어요. 그 당시의 법에 의하면, 농노들의 소유물, 즉 집, 옷, 심지어는 음식까지도 그들의 것이 아니었어요.

물론 농노들은 그들이 남편과 아내로 맺어지고 새로운 가족을 시작하는 것을 알리는 결혼식을 행했어요. 때로는 농노들끼리 결혼했지만, 간혹 자유를 얻기 위해 다른 자유민들과 결혼하기도 했죠. 그리고 얘기가 나와서 말인데, 신혼 부부들은 높은 유아 사망률로 인해 가족을 늘리는 데에 상당한 운이 필요했어요. 어떤 이들은 악천후와 열악한 음식 때문에 대부분의 유럽 농노들이 27살까지 밖에 살지 못했다고 해요. 그러니까... 중세 시대의 사람들은 27살이 되기 전에 결혼을 했다고 생각하는 것이 논리적이겠죠? 사실 3/4 이상이 19살이 되기 전에 결혼했답니다!

W: 와... 제가 중세 시대에 태어났다면 지금쯤 벌써 결혼을 했겠네요!

P: 아마도 그랬겠죠. 하지만 24살이 되기 전까지 결혼을 하지 않은 여성들도 있었어요.

W: 좀 안심이 되는데요.

P: 글쎄요. 대부분 사람들이 30대까지도 살지 못했다는 걸 생각해 보면, 그건 잘 모르겠군요. 어쨌든 다시 주제로 돌아가면... 중세 시대의 낮은 계급들 간의 결혼 중 다수는 연애나 임신을 해서, 혹은 사업상 이루어졌어요. 무슨 말이냐면, 많은 높은 계급 사람들이 그랬던 것처럼, 소작농들 또한 중매 결혼을 많이 하기도 했다는 거예요.

❶ What is the discussion mainly about?

교수는 토론을 시작하면서 "Today, we're gonna talk about the feudal society and the life in the medieval England, especially custom of getting married"라고 하며 오늘의 주제를 직접적으로 제시한다.

❷ What can be inferred about the newlyweds in the feudal society?

"High mortality rate of the infant"를 통해 답을 추론할 수 있다. 즉, 당시 영국의 영아 사망률이 높았다는 것이므로 정답은 B이다.

❸ How does the student feel when she says this:

대부분의 중세 영국인들이 19살이 되기 이전에 결혼했다는 교수의 말에, 학생은 자신이 중세 시대에 태어났다면 벌써 결혼했을 것이라며 놀라움을 나타내고 있다. 이 내용과 선택지 A는 관련이 없으며, 교수의 권위에 도전하는 것이 아니므로 선택지 B도 오답이다. 자신이 19살이 넘었는데도 결혼하지 않았다는 것에 아쉬워하는 것이 아니기 때문에 D 역시 정답이 아니다.

❹ What does the professor say about the relationship between peasants and a lord of the manor?

당시 평민들과 그들의 모든 소유는 영주에게 속해 있었으며 평민들이 경작하는 땅 역시 영주의 소유였다는 교수의 말에서 정답을 알 수 있다. 나머지 선택지들은 강의에 언급된 바가 없다. 따라서 정답은 B이다.

❺ According to the professor, which of the following is true about medieval weddings?

귀족들과 마찬가지로 평민들도 중매 결혼을 했다는 교수의 말을 통해 정답을 알 수 있다. 평민들은 다른 자유민들과 결혼을 할 수 있었으며 평민들 3/4이 19살이 되기 전에 결혼을 했으므로 선택지 A와 B는 정답이 아니다. 선택지 C의 내용은 강의에 언급된 적이 없으므로 오답이다.

Passage 5

1. C   **2.** B   **3.** D   **4.** A   **5.** A

P(M): So, in speech act, the form of a directive... for example, saying "Close the window," and, uh, the form of persuasion, like, "Let's close the window, shall we?" express some level of difference in politeness. People would usually consider the form of persuasion more polite, right? Now, let's connect this politeness expressed in these speech acts with gender difference. Do men and women differ in the way they use particular speech acts to express politeness? What about compliments to denote politeness?

❺ Well, using a lot of compliments in your dialogue is one of the most obvious ways to express positive politeness. It tells the listener that you are interested in his or her concerns, wants, or needs. This is called the first positive politeness strategy. But first of all, let's all

consider this: what is a compliment anyways? Well, a compliment is an expression of praise, commendation or admiration, and it's also a formal act or expression of civility, respect, or regard. When Jane met John, she said, "Hi, John, you're looking good. Have you been working out?" The part, "you're looking good" is a direct compliment and the other part "have you been working out?" is an indirect compliment from which you can infer the inner meaning. You know, in western society, people who work out and have lean bodies are generally... well, complimented.

Then, why do people give compliments? Um, compliments are usually intended to make others feel good, of course. The primary function of a compliment is most obviously affective and social, rather than referential or informative. You don't say "Hey, nice suit" just to tell the person the fact he's wearing a nice suit, but to make the person feel better. This type of speech serves to increase or consolidate the solidarity between the speaker and the addressee.

Now, let's turn our attention to compliments and gender difference. An experiment conducted in New Zealand which studied naturally occurring compliments among women and men suggested that 68 percent of the compliments given were from women and 74 percent of compliments were given to women. By contrast, compliments between males were relatively rare. We can understand that, at least among that community in New Zealand, complimenting appears to be a speech behavior occurring much more frequently in interactions involving women than men.

자, 그래서 언어 행동에서는 "문을 닫아라"라고 말하는 명령문과 "문을 닫을까요"와 같은 청유형은 공손함을 표현하는 데에 있어 어느 정도의 차이를 나타냅니다. 사람들은 보통 청유형을 더 예의바르다고 생각하겠죠? 자, 그러면 이러한 언어 행동에서 표현되는 공손함을 성별 차이와 연결지어 생각해 봅시다. 남성과 여성이 공손함을 표현하기 위해 사용하는 특정 언어 행동은 서로 다를까요? 공손함을 나타내기 위한 칭찬은 어떨까요?

대화에서 칭찬을 많이 사용하는 것은 긍정적 공손함을 표현하기 위한 가장 분명한 방법 중 하나입니다. 칭찬은 듣는 사람으로 하여금 여러분이 그 사람의 걱정이나 욕구, 필요에 관심이 있다는 것을 말해주죠. 이것을 첫번째 긍정적 예의 전략이라고 합니다. 하지만 먼저 이것을 생각해 봅시다... 도대체 칭찬이란 무엇일까요? 칭찬이란 칭송, 추천, 감탄 등의 감정을 표현하는 것이며 겸손이나 존경, 호의를 표현하는 공식적인 행동 혹은 표현입니다. 제인이 존을 만났을 때 그녀는 "안녕, 존, 좋아보이네요 요즘 운동하세요?"라고 말했습니다. "좋아보이네요"라는 부분은 직접적 칭찬이고 "요즘 운동하세요?"라고 한 다른 부분은 속뜻을 추론할 수 있는 간접적 칭찬입니다. 여러분도 알고 있듯이 서구 사회에서는 운동을 하고 몸이 날씬한 사람들이.. 일반적으로 칭찬을 듣지요.

그렇다면 사람들은 왜 칭찬을 할까요? 물론 칭찬은 듣는 이의 기분을 좋게 하려는 의도가 있습니다. 칭찬의 가장 중요한 기능은 물론 참조적이거나 정보를 제공한다기보다는 대부분 감정적이고 사회적입니다. "양복 멋지네요"라는 말은 그 사람이 멋진 양복을 입고 있다는 사실을 알려주기 위해서 말한다기보다는 그 사람의 기분을 좋게 해 주기 위해 하는 것이죠. 이러한 종류의 언어는 말을 하는 사람과 듣는 사람 사이의 연대감을 높이거나 더 견고하게 해 줍니다.

그럼 이제 칭찬과 성별 차이로 가 봅시다. 뉴질랜드에서 남성들과 여성들 사이에서 자연스럽게 발생하는 칭찬을 연구한 실험에서는 68퍼센트의 칭찬이 여성으로부터 주어졌고 74퍼센트의 칭찬이 여성에게 주어졌다는 것이 드러났습니다. 반면에 남성들 간의 칭찬은 상대적으로 드물었습니다. 이를 통해 적어도 뉴질랜드의 그 사회에서는 칭찬이 남성들보다는 여성들 간의 대화에서 더욱 빈번하게 발생하는 언어 행동이라는 것을 알 수 있습니다.

❶ What is the lecture mainly about?

"Now, let's connect this politeness expressed in these speech acts with gender difference. Do men and women differ in the way they use particular speech acts to express politeness? What about compliments to denote politeness?"라는 교수의 말에서 오늘의 주제, 즉 "칭찬과 성별 차이"를 알 수 있다. 선택지 A는 제한적인 내용을 담고 있으며 B는 강의에서 직접적으로 언급된 바가 없다. 이 지문에서는 남녀의 칭찬하는 방식이 다르다는 내용을 담고 있을 뿐, 그 이유를 언급하지는 않는다.

❷ What is the professor's attitude towards compliment?

"This type of positively affective speech acts serves to increase or consolidate the solidarity between the speaker and the addressee"라는 교수의 말에서 답을 확인할 수 있다.

❸ According to the lecture, which of the following situations is an example of the first positive politeness strategy?

"The first positive politeness strategy"는 공손함을 표현하기 위해 대화에서 칭찬을 많이 사용하는 것이다. 이것과 관련된 선택지는 D이다. 목소리를 줄여서 말하는 것이나 자신이 말하는 것 보다 다른 사람의 말을 더 잘 들어주려고 노력하는 것, 혹은 경어를 사용하는 것과는 관련이 없다.

❹ What can be inferred from the result of an experiment in New Zealand?

실험의 결과로 봤을 때, 뉴질랜드의 여성들이 남성보다 다른 여성들에게 더 많은 칭찬을 했음을 알 수 있다. 따라서 선택지 A가 답이 되며, B와 D는 틀린 내용이다. 또한 이 실험은 뉴질랜드의 실험 대상자들이 어떠한 언어 행동을 하는지를 알 수 있을 뿐, 모든 사람에게 확대 적용될 수 있는 것이 아니므로 선택지 C는 잘못된 선택이다.

❺ Why does the professor say this:

본격적인 강의 내용을 소개하기 위해 교수는 다시 들려주는 부분을 말하며 학생들에게 지문의 하위 주제를 효과적으로 제시하고 있다. 따라서 정답은 A이며, 주제에서 직접적으로 벗어나는 것이 아니므로 B는 답이 될 수 없다. 또한, 학생들에게서 직접적인 답을 요구하는 질문이 아니므로 C 역시 틀린 선택이며, 본인이 잊어버린 용어를 다시 생각해 내려고 하는 것도 아니기 때문에 D도 틀린 선택이 된다.

Passage 6

1. D   **2.** B   **3.** C   **4.** A   **5.** D

P(W): For the last couple of weeks, we've been talking about the Spanish empire prior to 1492 and Christopher Columbus' voyage to the Americas. Now, let's talk about Christopher Columbus, the navigator and maritime explorer who is known to have "discovered" the Americas.

M: Um, professor, I'm a Spanish Literature major, and, uh, we're learning about the *Colón Diario* — the diary written by Cristóbal Colón. I realized that this person also navigated to the Americas in the 15th century... So, is there any relationship between Colón and Columbus?

P: That's an interesting question, Juan. Actually... well, you might actually laugh when I tell you this, but, uh... actually, Christopher Columbus is the incorrectly Latinized name of Don Cristobal Colón. So, what I mean is that Columbus and Colón... they're the same person. In Italian, his name becomes Cristoforo Colombo.

W: Um, what you just said, professor... that Columbus "discovered" the Americas... is he actually the first one to have discovered the Americas or are there other people or explorers who've traveled to the Americas before him?

P: Well, it is known that Vikings such as Leif Eriksson had visited North America five centuries earlier. One of the major reasons that Columbus is known widely to have discovered the Americas is that... well, Columbus was sponsored by the Catholic Monarchs of Aragon, Castile, and Leon in Spain. ❹ Columbus had voyaged through the Atlantic four times when national imperialism was growing among European countries and economic competition between developing nations that sought wealth from establishing trade routes and colonies was constantly rising. All of you are probably aware of what happened afterwards to the European countries and those countries that had fallen into the hands of the European nations as colonies. Interesting thing here is that Columbus reached the Americas in 1492 during his first voyage but never reached the mainlands until his third voyage in 1498. However, his first voyage is recognized as a significant event in history and some American countries and Spain and Italy celebrate Columbus Day.

M: Oh, that's also celebrated in the United States as well.

P: True, but recently, there has been a major shift in approach and interpretation here. People started raising questions about the original inhabitants in the Americas. The older understanding stated that the "discovery" of the Americas was a great triumph from which Columbus became a heroic figure. You know, accomplishing four long voyages, bringing immense material profit to Spain and other European countries, opening up a route of settlement to European countries, and so on. However, this point of view has changed recently — it focuses more on the destructive aspect of the European conquest and emphasizes the devastating impact on the slave trade and disastrous results, such as imported disease on the indigenous peoples, of the American continents and the Caribbean region.

P: 지난 몇 주간 1492년 이전의 스페인 제국과 콜롬버스의 아메리카로의 여행에 대해 알아 봤는데요. 이제 아메리카를 "발견"했다고 알려진 항해 사이자 해양 모험가인 크리스토퍼 콜롬버스에 대해 이야기 해 봅시다.

M: 교수님, 저는 스페인 문학 전공이고, 크리스토발 콜론이라는 사람이 쓴 일기라는 "콜론 일기"에 대해 공부하고 있어요. 이 사람도 15세기에 미국으로 항해를 했거든요... 그렇다면 콜론과 콜롬버스 사이에 어떤 연관이 있는 건가요?

P: 흥미로운 질문이네요. 후안. 이 얘기를 하면 웃을지 모르겠지만... 사실 크리스토퍼 콜롬버스는 돈 크리스토발 콜론이라는 이름이 잘못 라틴화된 이름이에요. 그러니까 콜롬버스와 콜론, 이 두 인물은 동일 인물이라는 거지요. 이탈리아어로 그의 이름은 크리스토포로 콜롬보라고 해요.

W: 음, 교수님, 방금 말씀하신 콜롬버스가 아메리카를 "발견"했다는 말씀이에요... 실제로 그가 처음 아메리카를 발견한 건가요, 아니면 다른 사람들이나 모험가들이 콜롬버스 이전에 미국에 간 적이 있나요?

P: 리프 에릭슨 같은 바이킹이 콜롬버스보다 5세기 이전에 북미를 방문했다고 알려져 있어요. 콜롬버스가 아메리카를 발견했다고 널리 알려져 있는 가장 큰 이유 중 하나는... 콜롬버스가 스페인의 아라곤, 카스티야와 레온의 카톨릭 군주에게 후원을 받았기 때문이에요. 콜롬버스는 교역 루트와 식민지 확보를 통해 부를 얻으려는 개발도상국들 간의 경제적 경쟁과 유럽 국가들 간의 국가적 제국주의가 과열되고 있던 시기에 4번에 걸쳐 대서양을 건너 아메리카로 항해했어요. 유럽의 여러 나라와 유럽의 식민지로 전락한 나라들이 그 후 어떻게 되었는지는 여러분 모두 이미

알고 있을 거예요. 여기서 흥미로운 것은 콜롬버스가 그의 첫 항해인 1492년에 아메리카 대륙에 도착했지만 1498년 그의 세번째 항해 전까지는 사실상 아메리카 본토에 도달하지 못했다는 거예요. 그렇지만 그의 첫 항해는 역사적으로 의미있는 날로 기억되고 있고, 미국령 몇몇 국가와 스페인, 이탈리아에서는 콜롬버스의 날을 기념하고 있죠.

M: 아, 미국에서도 이 날을 기리고 있어요.

P: 맞아요. 하지만 최근에는 이것에 대한 접근과 해석에 큰 변화가 있었어요. 사람들은 아메리카의 원주민들에 대해 의문을 가하기 시작했죠. 기존의 해석에 의하면 아메리카의 "발견"은 커다란 쾌거였고, 이를 통해 콜롬버스가 영웅이 되었다고 보고 있죠. 4번의 긴 여정을 완수하고, 스페인과 다른 유럽 국가들에게 거대한 물질적 이윤을 가져다 주고, 유럽 국가들에게 새로운 정착지로 가는 길을 열어주는 등 말이에요. 하지만 최근에는 이러한 관점이 변했어요. 유럽 항해의 파괴적인 면에 더 주목하고 노예 매매에 끼친 파괴적인 영향이나 카리브해 지역과 아메리카 대륙의 원주민들에게 들여온 노예 매매와 질병과 같은 파괴적인 영향을 강조하고 있어요.

❶ What is the main idea of the discussion?

교수는 먼저 크리스토퍼 콜롬버스에 대해 설명하며 그의 항해가 역사적으로 어떠한 의미가 있는지를 설명한다. 그의 아메리카 항해로 인해 새로운 교역의 시대가 열리게 되었으며 아메리카 대륙의 원주민들에게도 커다란 영향을 미치게 되었으므로 정답은 D이다. 선택지 A는 단순히 콜롬버스의 항해의 결과만을 이야기하고 있기 때문에 답으로는 적절하지 않으며 선택지 B는 제한된 내용을 담고 있고 C는 지문에서 언급되지 않았다.

❷ According to the professor, what can be said about Christopher Columbus?

콜롬버스에 대해 맞는 내용을 찾으면 되는 문제이다. "it is known that Vikings such as Leif Eriksson had visited North America five centuries earlier"라는 말에서 선택지 A는 답이 아니며, "Columbus reached the Americas in 1492 during his first voyage but never reached the main lands until his third voyage in 1498"에서 C 역시 답이 아님을 알 수 있다. "Columbus was sponsored by the Catholic Monarchs of Aragon, Castile, and Leon in Spain"라는 말에서 D도 틀린 선택임을 알 수 있다. 콜롬버스라는 이름은 돈 크리스토발 콜론이 잘못 라틴화된 이름이며 콜롬버스와 동일 인물이라는 교수의 말에서 B가 정답임을 알 수 있다.

❸ What is the professor's attitude towards Columbus Day?

교수의 맨 마지막 말 "However, this point of view has changed recently — it focuses more on the destructive aspect of the European conquest and emphasizes the devastating impact on the slave trade and disastrous results, such as imported disease on the indigenous peoples, of the American continents and the Caribbean region."에서 정답을 찾을 수 있다. 선택지 A와 B, 그리고 D는 교수의 말에서 언급된 바가 없다.

❹ Why does the professor say this:

교수는 유럽 국가들의 식민지로 전락한 나라들에게 어떠한 일이 일어났는지 모두 알 것이라고 말하면서, 학생들이 이 주제에 대해 이미 알고 있을 것이라고 생각하고 이에 대한 학생들의 지식을 확인한다. 따라서 정답은 선택지 A이다. 주제에서 학생들의 주의를 돌리려는 것이 아니며, 학생들의 주제에 대한 무지를 탓하려는 것 또한 아니다. 마찬가지로 학생들의 질문에 대해 내용을 덧붙이려는 것도 아니므로 D또한 오답이다.

❺ According to the professor, what can be inferred about the European conquest?

선택지 A는 오히려 강의의 내용과 상반된 내용이며, 선택지 B의 내용은 지문에서 언급된 바가 없다. 유럽의 아메리카 대륙 식민지화는 학문적 이유 때문에 시작된 것이 아니므로 C 또한 오답이다. 유럽 항해로 인해 카리브해 지역과 아메리카 원주민들은 질병과 노예 매매 등의 문제를 직면하게 되었으므로 정답은 D이다.

(Passage 7) ─────────

1. B   **2.** D   **3.** A

P(M): As you might already know from your reading, bowerbirds are known for their eccentric and extraordinary behavior of males — to build a bower to attract mates. A bower, described in a dictionary as "a shady leafy shelter or recess," is kind of like a part of the male bowerbird's courtship rituals. The bird not only builds a bower with twigs, coarse grass or thatches but also titivates it with decorative colorful objects such as flowers, feathers, stones, berries, shells and leaves. It's amazing how they decorate their bowers when you see that they also use artificial objects like small plastic caps, um, shiny, small pieces of glass or similar things. At mating time, the female has the right to choose the male bowerbird. She will go from bower to bower, watching the male conducting an often elaborate mating ritual. ❷ **She will carefully inspect the quality and the strength of the bower, which is usually up to three feet in height and several inches thick.** I guess this is too obvious if you consider the cruel law of nature — a female bowerbird wants to mate a strong and competent male bird for reproduction.

이미 책을 읽어서 알겠지만, 풍조새는 수컷의 별나고 독특한 행동, 즉 짝을 유혹하기 위해 정자(亭子)를 만드는 것으로 잘 알려져 있습니다. 정자의 사전적 의미는 "그늘지고 잎이 있는 은신처"인데요, 이는 풍조새의 짝짓기 의식의 일부입니다. 풍조새는 나뭇가지, 거친 풀 혹은 이엉으로 은신처를 만들 뿐만 아니라 꽃, 깃털, 돌, 열매, 껍질과 나뭇잎 등의 장식적인 화려한 색상의 물건들로 이것을 치장합니다. 놀랍게도 이들은 작은 플라스틱 뚜껑, 반짝거리는 작은 유리 조각이나 이와 비슷한 물건 등의 인공적인 물건들도 사용합니다. 짝짓기 시기에 암컷은 수컷을 선택할 권

리가 있습니다. 정자에서 정자로 다니면서, 수컷들의 화려한 짝짓기 의식을 지켜봅니다. 암컷은 조심스럽게 정자의 품질과 강도를 살펴보는데, 정자는 보통 높이가 3피트 정도 되고, 두께는 몇 인치 정도 됩니다. 자연의 무자비한 법칙을 생각해 보면 이것은 너무나도 당연하죠 – 암컷은 번식을 하기 위해 튼튼하고 경쟁력 있는 수컷을 원한다는 겁니다.

❶ According to the lecture, what can be said about bowerbirds?

풍조새가 정자를 만드는 것은 짝을 유혹하기 위한 수컷의 행동이므로 선택지 A는 틀린 선택이며, 짝을 선택하는 것은 암컷의 권한이기 때문에 C 역시 틀렸다. 짝을 유혹하기 위해 짝짓기 의식을 하는 것도 수컷이다. 수컷 풍조새는 다양한 재료를 사용해 정자를 짓는다고 했으므로 정답은 B이다.

❷ What does the professor mean when he says this:

"Reproduction"이란 번식을 뜻하는 것으로, 즉 암컷 풍조새는 번식을 하기 위해 튼튼하고 경쟁력 있는 수컷과 짝짓기 하기를 원한다는 뜻이다. 따라서 정답은 D이다. 선택지 C는 내용상 오히려 강의의 내용과 반대의 이야기를 하고 있다.

❸ What is the professor's attitude towards bowerbirds and their bowers?

"It's amazing how they decorate their bowers"라고 하는 교수의 말에서 힌트를 찾을 수 있다. 교수는 무관심한 태도를 보이지는 않으므로 선택지 B는 틀린 선택이고, 풍조새들은 정자를 꾸밀 때 인공적 재료만 사용하는 것은 아니기 때문에 C 역시 맞는 답이 아니다. 선택지 D는 강의 내용과 무관하다.

(Passage 8) ─────────

1. B   **2.** A   **3.** A   **4.** B   **5.** 참조

	Psycho	The Birds
It has no ending card that says, "The End."		✔
It has the structure which Fellini called a filmic poem.		✔
It was filmed in 1960.	✔	
The famous scene in this movie is the shower scene which effectively creates suspense.	✔	
It was based on the novel with the same title by Robert Bloch.	✔	

P(W): *The man who knew too much, The Lodger, Rebecca, Strangers on a Train, Vertigo, Dial M for Murder, Psycho,* and *The Birds.* What am I talking about?

W: Movies?

M: Oh, yeah, movies of Alfred Hitchcock!

P: That's right. Today, we're gonna talk about

Alfred Hitchcock and his career as a filmmaker. He is widely recognized as the master of the thriller genre, which I am confident to say that he virtually invented. He was also a clever technician who tactfully intermixed suspense, sex and humor. Over a span of six decades, he has directed more than fifty films. He started his career from the silent film era, witnessing the invention of talkies and the color motion film.

His films relied heavily on fear and fantasy but are also known for their humor which is quite amusing. Basically, he was not a director of horror films, with the exception of two films, *Psycho* and *The Birds*. He mostly made small polite thrillers that mainly intended to create suspense, not terror. However, his two horror films, *Psycho* and *The Birds*, all filmed in the 1960's, had a tremendous effect on Pop culture. The movie *Psycho* was filmed in 1960 which was based on the novel of the same name by Robert Bloch. Bloch's novel, in turn, was based on the crimes of Wisconsin serial killer Ed Gein. I won't go into detail about the story of the movie — I'm afraid I might spoil it if you haven't watched it yet. Anyways, let me just brief the synopsis of the film... don't worry, I won't tell you what happens at the end. Um, in the movie, a secretary named Marion Crane, who is hiding at a motel after embezzling from her employer, encounters Norman Bates. Bates, who is depicted as lonely and profoundly disturbed, runs the motel and takes care of his ailing mother. The scene in this movie is one of the best-known in movie history... does anybody know what it is?

M: I've already seen that movie before... it's the shower scene, right?

P: Correct. And how did you feel when you were watching it?

M: Oh, boy... um, I thought... um, I was literally struck by the suspense it created. Although it was a relatively short scene, I felt like it was going on forever!

P: I understand. Well, yes, the shower scene in this movie is described as one of the most frightening scenes in cinema history. Hitchcock deftly combined extreme close-ups and medium shots that created the suspense so effectively. Because of the combination of the close shots with the short duration between cuts, the sequence feels longer, more subjective, more uncontrolled, and

more violent. The music... the high-pitched violin music heightened the suspense as well. Because of this fact, several sequels and a remake of the movie were spawned, but none of them were seen as works of better quality or even of similar quality. All right. If we move on to *The Birds*... Kathy, have you ever watched this movie before? How about you, Mark?

M: I'm a huge fan of horror movies — I've watched most of Hitchcock's movies already.

W: Um, in my case... I don't like horror films that much, but I've seen previews of this movie on TV before, and I've read reviews about it as well. I basically know what happens in the movie.

P: Very well. Um... In this movie, basically, people are attacked by birds. We don't know why the birds attack humans... it's never explained in the movie... I guess this is the part where viewers' imagination gets involved. *The Birds* has a highly interesting structure which the Italian filmmaker Fellini called a filmic poem. You know, just as poems end abruptly, so does this movie, and this is why the movie has no ending credit that says "The End."

P: "나는 비밀을 알고 있다", "하숙인", "레베카", "열차 안의 낯선 자들", "현기증", "다이얼 M을 돌려라", "사이코", 그리고 "새". 제가 지금 무엇에 대해서 얘기하고 있는 거죠?

W: 영화요?

M: 아, 알프레드 히치콕의 영화예요!

P: 맞아요. 오늘은 알프레드 히치콕과 영화 제작자로서의 커리어에 대해 얘기해 보겠어요. 그는 스릴러 장르의 대부로 널리 알려져 있는데, 실질적으로 이 장르는 그가 창조했다고 해도 될 정도예요. 그는 또한 서스펜스, 성(性), 그리고 유머를 기술적으로 융화시킨 기발한 기술자였죠. 60년이라는 기간 동안 그는 50편 이상의 영화를 감독했어요. 그는 무성 영화 시대에 자신의 커리어를 시작했는데, 유성 영화와 컬러 필름의 산 증인이기도 했죠.

그의 영화는 공포와 환타지에 크게 의지하지만 익살스런 유머로도 유명해요. 기본적으로 그는 "사이코"와 "새"를 제외하고는 공포 영화의 감독은 아니었어요. 그는 적당한 강도의 스릴러를 만들기는 했는데, 이 경우 목적은 공포가 아니라 주로 서스펜스를 자아내는 것이었죠. 그렇지만 1960년대에 만들어진 두 편의 공포 영화, "사이코"와 "새"는 대중 문화에 엄청난 영향을 미쳤어요. 1960년도에 촬영된 "사이코"는 위스콘신의 연쇄 살인범 에드 게인을 바탕으로 한 로버트 블로크의 소설에 기초를 두었어요. 영화의 상세 설명은 생략할게요 – 아직 보지 않은 사람들에게는 스포일러가 될 테니까요. 어쨌든 간략하게 영화의 스토리만 얘기해 보죠... 걱정마세요. 결말은 얘기 안 할게요. 이 영화에서는 고용주로부터 돈을 횡령한 후 모텔에 숨어 지내는 마리온 크레인이라는 이름의 비서가 노먼 베이츠를 만나게 돼요. 외롭고 정신 장애를 안고 있는 노먼 베이츠는 이 모텔의 주인이고 병든 어머니를 돌보고 있지요. 이 영화에는 영화 역사상 가장 유명한 장면이 있는데요, 혹시 어느 장면인지 아는 사람 있나요?

M: 전 그 영화를 이미 봤어요. 샤워 장면이죠?

P: 그래요. 그 장면을 보면서 어떤 느낌이 들던가요?

M: 음…. 전… 그 장면에서 조성되는 서스펜스에 말 그대로 압도되었어요. 비교적 짧은 장면이었지만 영원히 끝나지 않을 것처럼 느껴졌어요!

P: 이해해요. 맞아요. 그 샤워 장면은 영화 역사상 가장 무서운 장면으로 기억되죠. 히치콕은 극도의 클로즈업과 중간 샷을 솜씨있게 조합해서 서스펜스를 효율적으로 창조했어요. 클로즈업 샷을 짧은 간격으로 보여주기 때문에 이 장면은 더 길고, 주관적이고, 통제가 되지 않고, 더욱 폭력적으로 느껴졌죠. 음악의 경우… 고음의 바이올린 음악이 서스펜스를 더욱 두드러지게 했어요. 이러한 사실 때문에 몇 편의 후속편들과 리메이크판 영화들이 나왔지만 원작의 수준을 능가하거나, 심지어 비슷하다고 여겨진 작품조차 없었어요. 좋아요. 그럼 "새"로 넘어가보죠… 캐시, 이 영화를 본 적이 있나요? 마크는 어때요?

M: 전 공포 영화의 광팬이거든요 – 히치콕의 영화는 이미 대부분 다 봤어요.

W: 저 같은 경우에는 공포 영화를 좋아하진 않지만, TV에서 예고편을 본 적이 있어요. 그리고 평론도 많이 읽어봤죠. 영화의 기본 줄거리는 알고 있어요.

P: 좋아요. 음… 이 영화에서는 한마디로 사람들이 새들에게 공격당해요. 왜 새들이 사람들을 공격하는지는 영화에서 밝혀지지 않아요… 바로 여기서 관람객들의 상상력이 동원되는 것이죠. "새"라는 영화는 이탈리아의 영화 제작자인 펠리니가 "영화적 시"라고 부른 매우 흥미로운 구성을 갖고 있어요. 시가 갑자기 끝나는 것처럼, 이 영화도 마찬가지죠. 그렇기 때문에 영화에 "끝"이라는 자막이 안 나오는 것이에요.

❶ **What is the discussion mainly about?**

교수는 알프레드 히치콕 감독과 그의 영화, 특히 그의 유일한 공포 영화인 "새"와 "사이코"에 대해 설명하고 있다. 선택지 A와 D는 지문에 잠깐 언급된 내용만을 다루고 있으므로 주제가 될 수 없으며, 영화평이 아니므로 C 역시 틀린 답이다.

❷ **What does the professor mention about Hitchcock and his movies?**

"He is widely ecognized as the master of the thriller genre, which I am comfident to say that he virtually invented"라는 교수의 말에서 A가 정답임을 알 수 있다. "새"라는 영화는 동명 소설을 영화화한 것이며, "he was not a director of horror films, with the exception of two films, *Psycho* and *The Birds*"라고 하는 부분에서 히치콕의 공포 영화는 단 두 편임을 알 수 있다. 또한 영화 역사상 가장 무서운 장면으로 알려진 샤워 장면은 "새"가 아니라 "사이코"에서 나온 것이므로 D 또한 오답이다.

❸ **Why does the professor mention the list of films directed by Alfred Hitchcock?**

교수는 강의의 첫머리에 "*The man who knew too much*, *The Lodger*, *Rebecca*, *Strangers on a Train*, *Vertigo*, *Dial M for Murder*, *Psycho*, and *The Birds*. What am I talking about?"이라고 말하며 오늘의 주제를 소개한다. 단순히 히치콕 감독이 여러 편의 영화를 찍었다는 것을 강조하려는 것

이 아니라 히치콕 감독의 영화와 작품에 대한 설명을 시작하려 한 것이다.

❹ **How did the student feel when he first saw the shower scene of the movie, *Psycho*?**

학생은 유명한 샤워 장면을 보면서 그 장면이 연출해 내는 서스펜스에 놀랐으며 그 장면이 계속될 것 같다는 느낌을 받았다고 했으므로 선택지 B가 정답이다.

❺ **Based on the information in the discussion, indicate whether each sentence below describes the movie *Psycho* or *The Birds*.**

영화 "싸이코"는 1960년에 촬영되었으며 효과적으로 서스펜스를 창출해내는 것으로 유명한 샤워 장면이 있다. 또한 이 영화는 로버트 블로크의 동명 소설을 원작으로 한 것이다. 영화 "새"의 마지막에는 "끝"이라는 엔딩 카드가 없으며, 이탈리아의 영화 제작자인 펠리니가 "영화적 시"라고 부른 구조를 가지고 있다.

⬭ **Passage 9**

1. D　　**2.** C　　**3.** C　　**4.** A　　**5.** B　　**6.** A

P(M): Okay, let's start our discussion today. Um… today, we're gonna talk about Stephen Hawking and his theory about black holes. It's quite confusing, but I believe it will challenge your minds, so… first, let's take a brief look at his life, and then, uh, dive into his theory. Well, okay. Um, Stephen Hawking was born on January 8, 1942. From the age of 11, he attended St. Albans School where he was a good student but wasn't exceptional. He was always interested in science, but decided to study mathematics at Oxford University — one year later, however, he changed his concentration to physics. He received his bachelor's degree in 1962 and moved to Trinity Hall, University of Cambridge to study theoretical astronomy and cosmology.

While at Trinity Hall, Hawking was struck by a disease known as Motor Neuron Disease or Lou Gehrig's disease, a degenerative brain disorder of which the only good feature is that it doesn't damage the mind… but he was rendered quadriplegic by this disease. However, as soon as the disease had stabilized, Hawking, with some help from his doctoral tutor, returned to working on his Ph.D. and married Jane Wilde in 1965. He… I guess most of you all know this from his media exposure, but, um, he is confined in a wheelchair and, uh, he could speak very slowly and certainly cannot write or scribble diagrams on the blackboard. When you consider the fact that he manages to do first-rate Theoretical Physics, you can see the quality of his mind despite all of these physical disadvantages.

All right, now, let's move on to his theory. The... um, his area of interest includes theoretical cosmology, quantum gravity, and black holes. ❻ **Um, has anybody read his book, *A Brief History of Time*? <u>Nobody? Hmm. Well, I suggest you all read it when you have some time</u>—when you think about the fact that this book stayed on the London Sunday Times bestseller list for a record-breaking 237 weeks, I'm sure you're all going to enjoy reading it.** Anyways, back to our topic... black holes.

Hawking is well-known for his theories about black holes. According to Hawking, after the Big Bang, primordial or mini black holes were formed. The absorbing power of the black hole is too immense that even light cannot escape it. Let's all take a look here... how black holes are created. First, a massive star starts to collapse when it exhausts its nuclear fuel. The star cannot live any longer because it can no longer counteract the inward pull of gravity. So, what happens here is that the gravitation compresses the star inward, allowing the star to dig deeper into the fabric of space time. Now the star remains barely visible since the gravity of the star's collapsing core makes it difficult for the light to escape. Do you follow me? Good. Then, the star passes through its event horizon and disappears from our universe, forming a singularity of infinite density — a black hole.

For almost three decades, Hawking has been concerned with whether or not black holes really consumed and destroyed everything that entered them. Actually, he made a bet with a fellow colleague — he said that they do so; however, later he announced in public that black holes do not in fact consume and destroy everything which enters it, but instead, will eventually spit everything in a mangled form.

자, 오늘의 토론을 시작합시다. 오늘은 스티븐 호킹과 블랙홀에 관한 그의 이론에 대해 이야기 해 보겠습니다. 조금 복잡하긴 하지만 여러분에게 도전 의식을 심어줄 거라 생각합니다. 자, 먼저 그의 삶에 대해 간략하게 알아본 후에, 그의 이론으로 넘어갑시다. 스티븐 호킹은 1942년 1월 8일에 태어났습니다. 그는 11살 때부터 세인트 알반스 스쿨에 재학했는데, 모범생이었지만 뛰어나진 않았다고 합니다. 그는 늘상 과학에 흥미를 갖

고 있었지만 옥스포드 대학에서 수학을 공부하기로 결심합니다. 그렇지만 1년 후 물리학으로 전공을 변경합니다. 1962년에 그는 학사 학위를 받고 캠브리지 대학의 트리니티 홀로 옮겨 천문학 이론과 우주학을 공부했습니다.

트리니티 홀에 있을 당시, 호킹은 루게릭 병이라고도 알려져 있는 퇴행성 뇌질환인 운동신경원 질환에 걸리게 되는데요. 이 병의 유일한 좋은 점은 적어도 정신만은 말짱하다는 것이지만 그는 이 병으로 인해 사지가 마비됩니다. 그렇지만 병이 안정되자마자 호킹은 박사 과정에 있는 개인 교사의 도움을 받아 박사 과정으로 돌아가고 1965년에 제인 와일드와 결혼을 합니다. 여러분도 모두 매스컴에서 호킹의 모습을 봐서 알겠지만, 그는 휠체어에 묶여 있습니다. 느리게 말을 할 수는 있지만 칠판에 글을 쓰거나 도표를 그리는 것은 전혀 할 수 없습니다. 이런 상태에서도 호킹이 제1급의 이론물리학을 할 수 있다는 사실을 볼 때, 신체적 결함에도 불구하고 그의 정신이 얼마나 뛰어난지를 알 수 있을 것입니다.

자, 그럼 이제 그의 이론으로 넘어갑시다. 그가 관심을 가지고 있는 분야로는 이론적 우주학, 양자 중력, 그리고 블랙홀이 있습니다. 그의 저서 "시간의 역사"를 읽어 본 사람 있나요? 아무도 없나요? 흠. 알겠습니다... 시간 나면 모두들 읽어보기 바래요. 이 책이 런던 썬데이 타임즈 베스트셀러 리스트에 전례 없이 237주 동안 올라 있었다는 것을 생각해 보면, 여러분 모두 재미있게 읽을 수 있을 겁니다. 어쨌거나 주제인 블랙홀로 되돌아 갑시다.

호킹은 블랙홀에 대한 자신의 이론으로 아주 유명합니다. 그에 의하면, 빅뱅 이후에 원시 블랙홀, 혹은 미니 블랙홀이 생성되었다고 합니다. 블랙홀의 흡입력은 너무나도 커서 심지어 빛마저도 빠져나오지 못합니다. 모두 여기를 봅시다... 블랙홀이 어떻게 생성되는지 말이죠. 먼저, 거대 행성이 핵연료를 다 소모하고 폭발하기 시작합니다. 이 별은 중력이 안으로 끌어당기는 힘에 맞설 수 없기 때문에 더 이상 지속될 수가 없는 것입니다. 이렇게 되면 중력이 별을 안쪽으로 밀게 되어 우주적 시간 안으로 더 깊이 파고 들어가게 됩니다. 이제 이 별은 부서지는 핵의 중력으로 인해 빛이 빠져나가기 어려워지고, 그 결과 거의 보이지 않을 정도가 됩니다. 제 말이 이해 되나요? 좋아요. 사상(事象: 블랙홀 바깥의 경계)의 지평선을 넘어가 우주에서 사라지게 되고 무한한 밀도를 가진 독자적 형태를 생성하게 됩니다. 즉 블랙홀이 되는 것이죠.

거의 30년 동안 호킹은 블랙홀이 실제로 안에 들어오는 모든 것들을 소모하고 파괴하는지 아닌지에 대해 관심이 있었습니다. 사실, 그는 동료 과학자와 내기를 했는데요, 호킹은 그렇다고 했지만 나중에 블랙홀은 내부로 들어오는 모든 것을 소모하고 파괴하지는 않고 모든 것을 망가진 형태로 결국 토해낸다고 공식적으로 발표했습니다.

❶ **What is the lecture mainly about?**

"Today, we're gonna talk about Stephen Hawking and his theory about black holes"에서 정답을 찾을 수 있다. 단순히 물리학자로서의 삶에 대해 설명한 것이 아니라, 블랙홀에 대한 그의 이론에 대해 논하고 있으므로 A보다는 D가 정답으로 적절하다.

❷ **What does the professor say about Lou Gehrig's disease?**

"Motor Neuron Disease or Lou Gehrig's disease which is a degenerative brain disorder of which the only good feature is that it doesn't damage the mind... but he was rendered quadriplegic by this disease"라는 교수의 말로 미루어 보아, 루게릭 병은 사지를 마비시키는 퇴행성 뇌질환이지만, 정신이 이상해지는 병은 아님을 알 수 있다. 보지도, 말하지도, 듣지도, 움직이지도 못하게 된다는 선택지 A는 틀린 선택이며, 신체가 아니라 정신만 마비시킨다는 내용의 B 역시 바른 답이 아니다. 또한 정신과 신체 모두 마비된다는 D 역시 오답이다.

❸ **How does the professor organize the lecture?**
교수는 스티븐 호킹의 삶에 대해 설명한 후, 블랙홀에 대한 그의 이론으로 넘어간다. 따라서 정답은 C이다. 호킹의 책은 중간에 잠시 언급된 것이므로 A는 바른 답이 아니며, 시간의 역순대로 강의를 구성한 것도 아니기 때문에 B 역시 틀린 답이다. 또한, 호킹의 이론을 다른 이론과 비교한 내용은 없으므로 D 역시 틀린 답이다.

❹ **What does the professor mention about black holes?**
블랙홀은 거대 행성의 폭발에서부터 시작되므로, 초신성에서 블랙홀이 생긴다는 선택지 C는 틀린 답이다. 마찬가지로 블랙홀은 눈에 거의 보이지 않으므로 B 역시 틀렸으며, 블랙홀은 빛조차 빠져나올 수 없을 정도로 거대한 질량을 가지고 있다고 했으므로 D도 틀린 답이다.

❺ **What can be inferred about Hawking's book, *A Brief History of Time*?**
호킹의 책이 픽션(소설)이라는 말은 언급되지 않았으므로 선택지 A는 옳은 답이 아니며, 시간 관리에 대한 책이 아니므로 이 분야의 역사에 신기록을 달성했다는 C 역시 틀린 내용이다. 또한 강의의 내용상, 인간의 시간 사용에 대한 역사를 다루고 있다고 보기 힘들기 때문에 D 역시 틀린 답이다. 런던 썬데이 타임즈 베스트셀러 리스트에 오랜 기간 올라 있었다는 내용으로 보아, 많은 이들에게 절찬받은 책이라는 것을 알 수 있다.

❻ **How does the professor feel when he says this:**
교수의 어투에서 유명한 책을 학생들 중 아무도 읽지 않았다는 것에 대해 어느 정도 실망했음을 읽을 수 있다. 교수의 말투로 미루어보아 이 책을 소개할 수 있는 기회가 주어졌음에 기뻐하는 것이 아님을 알 수 있으며, 이 책을 읽는 것이 숙제가 아니고 교수가 화를 내고 있다고 볼 수는 없으므로 선택지 B와 C는 오답이다. D에서와 같이 이 책을 읽지 않은 학생들에 대해 안타까워 한다기보다는 실망했다고 보는 것이 더 낫기 때문에 정답은 A가 된다.

Passage 10

1. A   **2.** B   **3.** B   **4.** B, D   **5.** C   **6.** A

P(W): Um, now... let's all settle down and start, shall we? All right. Uh... before we go on, uh, I'll pass this piece of paper... here you go, Johnny. Um, I told you in last class that you'll all be divided into groups of three, right? Well, I assigned all of you into five different groups, so look at the paper and, uh, check who's in your group. Now, what's

gonna happen is that, uh, at the end of this class, I'll give you five different topics on which you will do some research and prepare an oral presentation that will last 10 to 15 minutes. I'm gonna pass out the presentation guidelines together with the topics. Everybody got it?

Okay. So, uh... today, we're gonna talk about world's most venomous snakes. You know, I've, uh, ranked five different venomous snakes on my own, just to make this lecture interesting. Anyways, number five, the Tiger Snake. Um, Tiger Snakes are a common species in populated parts of Australia. These snakes are venomous and can grow up to 6.5 feet in length, but usually they're somewhere around 3.5 feet. Their colors and patterns also vary, ranging from light gray to brown or black with or without a banded pattern. So, just how venomous are these snakes? Well, Tiger Snakes can kill five men with one bite. That's amazing, huh? You want to be extremely cautious when you walk around forests or open grasslands in Australia.

Okay, moving on to the next snake... um, I ranked the Sea Snake as the fourth. They adapted to live in waters... uh, tropical waters from the Indian Ocean to the Pacific Ocean, but, um, they are particularly abundant in the Persian Gulf and the Bay of Bengal. Their tails look like a paddle and are useful for swimming. Other than this feature, they look pretty much like their land cousins. Most of the Sea Snakes are not actually very aggressive and usually will not bite humans unless they're extremely agitated or handled roughly. Their bites... extremely fatal.

Well, my number three is... it's getting more interesting... um, is the fastest snake on land... can you guess what it is? No? Well, I don't think you wanna meet this one especially on land... it's the Black Mamba. They can move at a rate up to 14 miles per hour and can grow up to 14 feet in length. You might think that the Black Mamba might be entirely black when you hear its name, but that's not true. Let's take a look at this picture. As you can see, the Black Mamba's body is not actually black, but it's somewhat brownish-gray with a light colored belly and brownish scales along its back. If you see the color of its mouth, you'll notice where it got its name from. The lining of its mouth is purple-black, see? These creatures usually live in South Africa and about 100 people are reported each year as victims. Um, the Black Mamba can kill 10 men with its venom from each bite and its bites were 100 percent fatal before antivenims were developed. Because of this fact, the Black Mambas are known to be invulnerable because not many animals can actually cause harm to them. Their venom can kill just about anything — the main threat for these reptiles is the destruction of their habitat. Any questions? ... Okay.

All right, now... if we go on to our next most venomous snake... um, this one has a very powerful venom which can kill 2.5 million mice or 125 men with the amount of venom from one strike. It's the Taipan snake, a snake which can be found in Australia's inland areas. They are known as Australia's deadliest and largest snake, since they can grow up to more than 8 feet in length! Well, these creatures are usually shy but when they're cornered, they'll fiercely defend themselves, moving quickly, often delivering several fatal bites. Their favorite prey are rats, but they also consume lizards and birds. Um, the snake will usually strike its prey very fast and draw back and wait for the poison to work on the prey. Their venom usually helps them digest because it will quickly melt the muscle of the prey. Uh... questions, so far?

All right, excellent. Now, the number one deadliest snake in the world... I am positive that all of you know this one: the Cobra. Uh, Cobras generally live in tropical and desert regions of Asia and Africa, and can grow up to 8.2 feet in length. Most of them are quite large. The King Cobra can grow up to 18 feet long and is the largest venomous snake in the world. Their usual preys are small rodents and birds, but they can also eat other snakes and sometimes humans... when they're attacked or provoked, of course. Uh, not all Cobra attacks are fatal... sometimes they do not inject venom when they bite. However, when they do inject venom, it can inject up to 6 teaspoons of extremely strong poison in your body. Although Cobra bites are known to be fatal in only about 10% of human cases, they should be treated as a potentially fatal injury and medical attention should be sought immediately. You never know whether the Cobra injected venom in your body, and if it did, most people die in about 30 minutes.

자, 이제 모두 자리 잡고 시작합시다. 좋아요. 시작하기 전에 이 종이를

돌릴게요. 여기 있어요, 조니. 지난 시간에 여러분들 모두 3명씩 조로 나눠질 거라고 얘기했지요? 전부 다섯 조로 나누었으니까 종이를 보고 자기 조에 누가 있는지 확인하세요. 자, 이렇게 하게 될 거예요. 오늘 수업이 끝나고 다섯 개의 다른 주제를 나눠줄 건데, 여러분은 그 주제에 대해 조사를 하고 10분에서 15분 정도의 구두 발표를 준비해야 해요. 발표 가이드라인은 나중에 주제와 함께 나눠줄게요. 모두 이해되죠?

좋아요. 자, 오늘은 세계에서 가장 독성이 강한 뱀에 대해 이야기 해 보겠어요. 강의를 더 재미있게 하기 위해 제가 직접 독사의 랭킹을 5위까지 만들어 봤어요. 어쨌든 5위는 바로 타이거 스네이크예요. 타이거 스네이크는 호주의 인구가 밀집한 지역에서 흔히 발견되는 종이에요. 이 뱀은 독성이 강하고 6.5피트까지 자랄 수 있지만 보통 3.5피트 정도의 길이에요. 색깔과 모양 또한 다양한데, 옅은 회색이나 갈색, 혹은 검은색도 있고 줄무늬가 있을 수도, 없을 수도 있어요. 그렇다면 이 뱀은 독성이 얼마나 강할까요? 타이거 스네이크는 한 번 물어서 5명의 성인 남성을 죽일 수도 있어요. 대단하죠? 호주의 숲이나 풀숲을 돌아다닐 때에는 정말 조심하는 게 좋아요.

좋아요, 다음 뱀으로 넘어가면... 물뱀이 4위를 차지했네요. 이들은 물에서 살 수 있도록 적응했는데, 인도양에서 태평양까지의 열대 지역의 수중에서 많이 서식하지만 페르시아만과 벵갈만에 특히 많이 서식해요. 이들의 꼬리는 노처럼 생겼고 헤엄칠 때 유용하게 쓰여요. 이 특징 외에는 물에 서식하는 다른 뱀들과 비슷하게 생겼어요. 대부분의 물뱀들은 사실 공격적이진 않고, 굉장히 화가 나거나 거칠게 다뤄지지 않는 한 사람들을 물지는 않아요. 이들이 한 번 물면 굉장히 치명적이죠.

자, 3위는... 점점 재미어지는데요. 물에서 가장 빠른 뱀이에요. 어떤 뱀인지 맞출 수 있나요? 모르겠어요? 이 뱀을 땅 위에서 만나고 싶지는 않을 거예요. 바로 블랙 맘바입니다. 이들은 최고 시속 14마일로 움직일 수 있고 길이는 14피트까지 자랄 수 있어요. 블랙 맘바라는 이름을 들으면 몸이 완전히 검은색일 것이라고 생각할 수도 있지만, 실제로는 그렇지 않아요. 이 사진을 보죠. 여기서 볼 수 있듯이 블랙 맘바의 몸은 실제로 검지는 않고 오히려 회갈색 몸에 밝은 색의 배를 가지고 있지요. 등에는 갈색 비늘이 있어요. 입의 색을 보면 블랙 맘바라는 이름이 어디서 왔는지 알 수 있을 거예요. 입가의 색깔이 자줏빛을 머금은 검은색이에요, 보이죠? 이들은 보통 남아프리카에 서식하고 매년 100명 정도가 블랙 맘바에 물려 죽는 것으로 발표되고 있어요. 블랙 맘바는 한 번 물 때마다 10명의 성인 남성을 죽일 수 있고, 사혈청이 개발되기 전까지는 100퍼센트 치명적이었어요. 이러한 사실 때문에 블랙 맘바는 천적이 없다고도 알려져 있는데, 사실상 블랙 맘바를 죽일 수 있는 동물은 많지 않거든요. 이들의 독은 무엇이든 죽일 수 있고 이들의 천적은 이들의 서식지 파괴예요. 질문 있나요? 좋아요.

다음 독사로 가 보면... 이 뱀은 한 번 물었을 때 나오는 독으로 250만 마리의 쥐, 혹은 125명의 성인 남성을 죽일 수 있는 매우 강력한 독을 가지고 있어요. 바로 호주의 내륙 지방에 사는 타이판 스네이크예요. 이들은 호주의 가장 치명적이고 또 가장 큰 뱀으로 알려져 있는데요. 8피트까지 자랄 수 있으니 그럴 만도 하죠. 이들은 보통 얌전하지만 구석에 몰렸을 때엔 맹렬히 자신을 보호하고 빨리 움직이며 생명에 위협을 가할 만큼 수차례 물 수도 있어요. 이들이 가장 좋아하는 먹이는 쥐이지만 작은 도마뱀이나 새도 먹어요. 이 뱀은 먹잇감을 굉장히 빠른 속도로 문 후, 뒤로 물러나 독이 퍼지기를 기다려요. 이들의 독은 먹잇감의 근육을 재빨리 녹이기 때문에 뱀으로 하여금 소화를 쉽게 할 수 있도록 도와주어요. 지금까지 질문 있나요?

좋습니다. 이제 세계에서 가장 독성이 강한 뱀을 알아봅시다. 이 뱀은 모

두들 알고 있을 것 같은데요, 바로 코브라입니다. 코브라는 일반적으로 아시아와· 아프리카의 열대, 사막 지역에 서식하고 8.2피트까지 자랄 수 있어요. 대부분의 코브라는 상당히 크지요. 킹코브라는 18피트까지 자랄 수 있고 세상에서 가장 큰 독사예요. 이들이 보통 사냥하는 것은 작은 설치류와 새이지만, 다른 뱀을 먹기도 하고 가끔씩은 사람도 먹는데요 물론 공격을 당했거나 자극됐을 때 그렇죠. 코브라의 모든 공격이 다 치명적인 건 아니에요... 가끔은 물었을 때 독을 주입하지 않을 수도 있거든요. 하지만 코브라가 독액을 주입하게 되면 몸에 6 티스푼 정도까지의 치명적인 독을 주입시킬 수 있어요 인간의 경우 코브라가 무는 것이 약 10퍼센트의 사망률을 가지고 있지만, 잠재적으로 치명적인 상처로 다루어져야 하고 곧바로 응급조치를 취해야 합니다. 코브라가 몸에 독을 주입했는지 알 수가 없고, 만약 그랬다면 대부분의 사람들은 30분 이내에 사망하기 때문이에요.

❶ How does the professor organize the lecture?

가장 독성이 강한 독사들을 소개하는데 보다 흥미롭게 하기 위해 독사의 순위를 매겨서 5위부터 1위까지 차례대로 소개하고 있으므로 정답은 A이다.

❷ What does the professor say about Tiger Snakes?

"호주의 숲이나 풀숲을 돌아다닐 때에는 주의하는 게 좋다"는 교수의 말에서 정답을 찾을 수 있다. 타이거 스네이크는 아프리카가 아니라 호주에 주로 서식하므로 선택지 A는 오답이며, 지상에서 가장 속도가 빠른 뱀은 블랙 맘바이므로 C 또한 오답이다. 선택지 D의 내용은 강의에서 언급된 바가 없다.

❸ According to the professor, why do most venomous snakes attack people?

"Most of Sea Snakes are not actually very aggressive and usually will not bite humans unless they're extremely agitated or handled roughly" 와 "Their usual preys are small rodents and birds, but they can also eat other snakes and sometimes humans... when they're attacked or provoked, of course"에서 알 수 있듯 대부분의 독사들이 사람을 공격하는 이유는 자신이 궁지에 몰렸거나 먼저 공격을 당했을 때임을 알 수 있다. 따라서 정답은 B이다. 강의의 내용상 대부분의 독사는 작은 새나 동물을 먹고 살기 때문에 선택지 A는 틀렸으며 삼림 벌채에 대한 내용이나 밀렵에 대한 이야기는 나오지 않았으므로 C와 D 또한 오답이다.

❹ Which of the following is true about the Black Mamba?

블랙 맘바는 육지에서 시속 14마일의 속도로 움직이며 그 이름은 몸의 색깔이 아니라 입의 색깔에서 붙여진 것이라고 했다. 사혈청이 개발되기 전에는 블랙 맘바에게 물리면 치사량이 100퍼센트였으며 블랙 맘바의 독이 워낙 치명적이기 때문에 사실상 이 뱀을 죽일 수 있는 동물은 없다고 했다. 따라서 정답은 B와 D이다.

❺ Why does the professor pass the piece of paper to the students at the beginning of the lecture?

교수는 강의를 시작하기 전에 학생들에게 종이를 나눠주면서 본인이 어느 조에 속해있는지 확인하라고 했으므로 정답은 C이다. 학생들의 출결 사항을 체크하는 것이 아니므로 선택지 A는 틀렸으며, 학생들의 발표 주제와 가이드라인은 수업이 끝나고 나눠줄 것이므로 B와 D 역시 틀린 답이다.

❻ What is the professor's attitude towards Cobra bites on people?

코브라가 사람을 물 때 항상 독을 뿜는 것은 아니지만 물렸을 경우 곧바로 응급조치를 취해야 한다고 했으므로 정답은 A가 된다.

Vocabulary Test

1. stabilize	**2.** embezzle	**3.** scale
4. modify	**5.** primordial	**6.** deforestation
7. disorder	**8.** invulnerable	**9.** d
10. a	**11.** c	**12.** b
13. a	**14.** b	**15.** d

6 Function

Sample

개미들의 몸은 다른 곤충들과 마찬가지로 외골격이에요. 내골격인 인간이나 다른 척추 동물과는 달리 개미들은 보호용 외골격으로 둘러싸여 있어요. 개미와 유대류와 같은 작은 척추 동물간에는 몇 가지 차이점이 있어요. 우선 개미들에게는 폐가 없어요. 그렇다면 이들은 어떻게 숨을 쉴까요? 산소는 이들의 외골격에 있는 작은 숨구멍을 통과해요. 이산화탄소 역시 같은 숨구멍을 통해서 이들의 몸에서 배출되죠. 게다가 개미들에게는 심장이 없어요. 이들에게는 무색의 혈액인 혈액림프가 있는데, 이것이 긴 관을 따라서 몸 안에 흐르고 있어요. 다들 이해했나요?

Strategy Focus

1. B **2.** A **3.** C **4.** D

1. B

P(M): Many of you confuse baseball and softball. Well, we all know that the balls used in baseball games are small and hard. Nine players play for a team, and the pitcher usually throws the ball over-hand. **Well, then, what about softball? You can easily tell what kind of balls softball players use, judging from the name itself, right?**

많은 분들이 야구와 소프트볼을 헷갈려 하는데요. 야구에서 사용되는 공은 작고 단단하다는 것을 우리는 모두 알고 있습니다. 아홉 명의 선수가 한 팀에서 뛰고, 투수는 주로 공을 어깨 너머로 던집니다. 그렇다면 소프트볼은 어떨까요? 소프트볼 선수들이 어떤 공을 사용하는지는 이름만으로도 알 수 있겠죠?

2. A

P(W): Now, let's move on to Australopithecus, since we've been talking about these very old people. Australopithecus, also called southern ape, lived in Africa. I believe you've all done your readings for today's class... who can tell me about Lucy? Mark?

M: Um... is she one of our classmates? I don't think I met her before.

P: That's okay, Mark. Well, now that you know reading your assigned books is crucial for your next class, I believe you'll answer my questions better next time. Well, for your information, Lucy was a complete Australopithecus found in Ethiopia in 1974.

P: 자, 지금까지 선사 시대 사람들에 대해 이야기 해 보았으니까, 이제 오스트랄로피테쿠스에 대해 얘기해 보도록 합시다. 남부 유인원이라고도 불리는 오스트랄로피테쿠스는 아프리카에 살았어요. 모두들 오늘 수업 분량을 읽어 왔겠죠... 루시에 대해 얘기해 볼 사람 있나요? 마크?

M: 음... 우리 반 학생인가요? 저는 그녀를 만나본 적이 없는 것 같은데요.

P: 괜찮아요, 마크. 이제 숙제로 내 준 책을 읽는 것이 다음 시간을 위해 중요하다는 것을 알았을 테니, 다음 시간엔 더 잘 대답할 수 있으리라 믿어요. 참고로 루시는 1974년 에티오피아에서 발견된 완전한 오스트랄로피테쿠스에요.

3. C

P(M): This month is the American Indian Heritage month. **As we've been talking about for the last couple of weeks, there has been much controversy among anthropologists about the name, American Indian.** As you'd already know since grade school, Indian was the name Christopher Columbus applied to the people he encountered when he arrived in... you know, what he believed was the Indies. You can easily imagine what Indies was, right? It was the medieval name for Asia, yes. Well, so... the term Native American was introduced in the 1960s and it was used to eliminate confusion between the indigenous people of the Americas and the indigenous people of India. The term American Indian was also used for that purpose; however, it raised other problems. You see, some people began to think that the word Indian in any form was... well, derogatory.

이번 달은 아메리카 인디언 역사의 달입니다. 지난 몇 주간 얘기했듯이, 아메리카 인디언이라는 이름에 대해서 인류학자들 사이에 논쟁이 많았습니다. 초등학교 때부터 알고 있는 것이겠지만, 인디언은 크리스토퍼 콜럼버스가 자신이 인디즈라고 믿었던 곳에 상륙해 원주민을 만난 후 붙여준 이름입니다. 인디즈라는 이름이 무엇이었는지 쉽게 상상이 가시죠? 네, 바로 아시아를 가리키는 중세 이름이었습니다. 자, 그래서... 아메리카 원주민이라는 이름이 1960년대에 도입되었고 이것은 미국의 토착민과 인도의 토착민 사이의 혼란을 제거하기 위해 사용되었습니다. 아메리카 인디언이란 단어 또한 이러한 목적을 위해 사용되었지만, 이것은 다른 여러 가지 문제를 야기했습니다. 몇몇 사람들은 인디언이란 말이 얕잡아 보는 표현이라고 생각하기 시작했습니다.

4. D

P(W): As you might already know, there are countless universities and colleges that adopted the name of their founders or benefactors, such as... let's see... oh, I guess you'd all know this college for sure: Harvard University. Well, it's not only the oldest institution of higher learning in the United States — it celebrated its 350th anniversary back in 1986 — but also one of the most prestigious universities in the world. So when was it established? You do the math. Anyways, it was established by vote of the Great and General Court of the Massachusetts Bay Colony. The college got is name after a young minister named John Harvard of Charlestown, who left his library and half his estate to the institution upon his death in 1638.

여러분이 이미 알고 있을 수 있겠지만, 창시자 혹은 기부자의 이름을 따서 이름을 지은 대학들이 셀 수 없이 많아요. 예를 들어서... 아, 모두들 하버드 대학은 알고 있겠지요. 하버드는 미국의 가장 오래된 고등 교육기관일 뿐 아니라 – 1986년도에 350회 창립 기념일 행사가 있었죠 – 세계 유수의 대학 중 하나이기도 합니다. 그렇다면 하버드는 언제 설립된 것일까요? 계산해 보세요. 어쨌든 이 학교는 Massachusetts Bay Colony의 의회 투표에 의해 설립되었어요. 하버드 대학은 찰스톤의 존 하버드라는 젊은 목사의 이름을 땄는데, 그는 1638년도에 사망하면서 자신의 재산 절반과 도서관을 하버드 대학에 기부했어요.

Exercise

P.1	1. D	2. D	3. A				
P.2	1. D	2. A, C	3. D				
P.3	1. C	2. D	3. B				
P.4	1. A	2. A, C	3. D	4. A	5. B		
P.5	1. C	2. A	3. B				
P.6	1. A	2. D	3. B				
P.7	1. B	2. A, C	3. D				
	4. D	5. C	6. A				
P.8	1. B	2. A	3. C				
	4. A	5. C	6. D				
P.9	1. D	2. B	3. B, D				
	4. C	5. A	6. A				
P.10	1. A	2. D	3. A	4. B	5. 참조		

Passage 1

1. D   2. D   3. A

P(W): Dr. Jane Goodall is an English primatologist, ethologist and anthropologist. She's best known for conducting a 45-year-study of chimpanzee's social and family life. In July, 1960, Goodall began studying chimpanzees of Gombe Stream National Park in Tanzania. She established the Jane Goodall Institute in 1977, which serves as a protector of chimpanzees and their habitats. ❸ **Goodall devoted all her life for not only studying chimpanzees but also protecting them from reckless poaching and preserving their habitat. No wonder she's also known as the "chimp lady."**

제인 구달 박사는 영국의 영장류학자, 행동학자이자 인류학자입니다. 그녀는 침팬지의 사회와 가족 생활에 대해 45년간 연구를 실시한 것으로 잘 알려져 있습니다. 1960년 7월에 구달은 탄자니아의 감비 지류 국립공원의 침팬지를 연구하기 시작했습니다. 1977년에는 제인 구달 재단을 설립해 침팬지의 보호와 서식지 보호에 앞장섰습니다. 구달은 침팬지를 연구하는 것 뿐만 아니라 무분별한 밀렵으로부터 그들을 보호하고, 그들의

서식지를 보존하는 데 자신의 삶을 바쳤습니다. 그녀가 "침팬지 여인"이라고 알려진 것도 놀랄만한 일은 아니죠.

❶ **What is the main topic of the lecture?**

교수는 야생 침팬지의 생태를 연구하고 보호한 제인 구달의 삶을 간략하게 소개하고 있다. 선택지 A는 강의에서 알 수 없으며, B와 C는 강의에서 잠시 언급된 것일 뿐이므로 강의의 주제가 될 수 없다.

❷ **What can be inferred about wild chimpanzees before the establishment of the Jane Goodall Institute?**

제인 구달 재단이 설립된 이유는 침팬지와 그들의 서식지를 보호하기 위해서이다. 따라서 이 재단이 설립되기 이전의 야생 침팬지들은 무분별한 밀렵과 서식지 파괴 등으로부터 고통받고 있었음을 알 수 있다. 정답은 선택지 D이다.

❸ **What does the professor mean when she says this:**

"No wonder"이란 표현은 "어쩐지 ∼이더라" 혹은 "그럼 그렇지"라는 뉘앙스를 담고 있다. 따라서 다시 들려준 문장은 "그녀가 침팬지 여인으로 알려진 것에 대한 이유가 있었다"는 뜻인데, 그 이유는 구달이 침팬지들의 보호자로 활약했기 때문이었다. 정답은 선택지 A이며, 선택지 B, C, D는 본문의 내용으로는 알 수 없다.

Passage 2

1. D   2. A, C   3. D

P(M): ❸ **More than 34 million Americans rely on contact lenses to correct their vision. It's easy, it's convenient... you don't have to wear heavy glasses anymore... you experience total freedom from wearing glasses.** But how many of you are aware of the consequences of misusing contact lenses? One of the dire consequences may be fusarium keratitis, a microbial infection of the cornea. According to one study released by the Center for Disease Control and Prevention, 106 cases of the infection were reported in 2006 and 95 percent of the infected wore contact lenses. This disease can lead to permanent vision loss if you don't know the adequate use of contact lenses. Doctors recommend taking out the lenses before your eyes get irritated or when the vision is blurred. Ignoring the warning signs can lead to serious problems. You should also be sure to replace your lenses before they expire.

3천 4백만 명 이상의 미국인들이 시력 교정을 위해 콘택트 렌즈를 사용합니다. 콘택트 렌즈는 쉽고, 편리합니다... 무거운 안경을 쓸 필요가 없죠. 안경을 쓰는 것으로부터 완전히 해방되게 됩니다. 그렇지만 콘택트 렌즈를 잘못 썼을 때의 부작용에 대해 아는 분은 몇 명이나 되나요? 콘택트

렌즈의 무서운 부작용 중 하나는 각막염인데, 이것은 각막이 미생물로 인해 감염되는 것입니다. 질병 관리 예방 센터에서 출시한 연구 중 하나에 의하면, 2006년도에 106건의 감염이 보고되었고, 그 중 95퍼센트 이상이 콘택트 렌즈로 인한 것이었습니다. 이 질병은 렌즈를 올바르게 사용하지 않을 경우 영구 시력 감퇴로 이어질 수 있습니다. 의사들은 눈이 따가워지거나 시야가 흐릿해지기 전에 렌즈를 뺄 것을 권장합니다. 경고 사인을 무시하는 것은 심각한 문제를 야기할 수 있습니다. 또한 렌즈 유효 기간이 다하기 전에 반드시 교체해야 합니다.

❶ What is the topic of the lecture?

교수는 콘택트 렌즈의 오용으로 인한 부작용과 이로 인한 질병의 예방법 등을 설명한다. 선택지 A와 C는 강의에서 잠시 언급된 것이므로 주제가 될 수 없으며, 선택지 B는 강의에 언급된 바가 없다.

❷ According to the lecture, which of the following are the ways to prevent fusarium keratitis?

"Doctors recommend taking out your lenses before your eyes get irritated or when the vision is blurred" 와 "You should also be sure to replace your lenses before they expire"에서 정답을 찾을 수 있다.

❸ Why does the professor say this:

콘택트 렌즈를 착용할 때의 편안함과 안경으로부터의 해방감 등을 설명하면서 콘택트 렌즈를 사용하는 이유를 설명한다. 콘택트 렌즈 오용의 부작용을 설명하는 것이지 렌즈를 꼈을 때의 좋은 점을 부각시키거나 콘택트 렌즈를 많이 팔려고 하는 것이 아니며, 학생들에게 렌즈를 더 자주 끼라고 권유하는 것은 아니다. 따라서 정답은 D이다.

(Passage 3)

1. C   **2.** D   **3.** B

P(M): During the Middle Ages, people didn't take baths or showers as frequently as we do today — they took their yearly bath in May and this was why most people got married in June. They might have thought they still smelled pretty okay by June because they took a bath last month, right? However, they started to smell, of course, so brides carried a bouquet of flowers to conceal the body odor and this is where the tradition of carrying a wedding bouquet came from. **❷ Well, this, at least, is what many people believed. Actually, people who lived in the medieval era weren't as ignorant as it was described here.** You see, um, in the agricultural communities of medieval England, people usually got married in October, November and January when the harvest was over and the time for planting had not yet arrived. There were also summer weddings which

coincided with annual festivals. People enjoyed good weather and fresh flowers as well as the arrival of new crops for wedding ceremonies in June. Actually, the tradition of using flowers in wedding ceremonies goes back to ancient times.

❸ Now, let's turn our attention to "yearly baths." It's quite disturbing that many people consistently hold onto this false belief... actually, most medieval people did wash themselves on a regular basis. They even used soaps... probably a lot different from the ones that we use these days, of course. Public bathhouses were also common; however, they were secretly used by prostitutes as well, so the outward purpose of public bathhouses was often secondary.

중세 시대의 사람들은 오늘날 우리처럼 자주 목욕을 하거나 샤워를 하지 않았습니다. 그들은 연중 목욕을 5월에 했고 이것이 바로 대부분의 사람들이 6월에 결혼을 했던 이유입니다. 그들은 지난 달에 목욕을 했기 때문에 6월에는 냄새가 별로 나지 않는다고 생각했을지도 모릅니다. 그렇지만 물론 이들에게는 냄새가 나기 시작했기 때문에 신부들이 부케를 들어 체취를 없앴는데, 이것이 바로 결혼 부케의 유래입니다. 최소한 이것이 많은 사람들이 믿었던 속설이었는데요, 사실 중세 시대의 사람들은 방금 설명한 것처럼 그렇게 무지하지는 않았습니다. 중세 농경 시대의 영국에서는 추수가 끝나고 모내기가 시작되기 전인 10월, 11월, 그리고 1월에 주로 결혼을 했습니다. 또한 연례 축제가 있는 여름에 결혼을 하기도 했습니다. 6월의 결혼식에서 사람들은 화창한 날씨와 신선한 꽃, 그리고 햇곡식을 즐겼습니다. 결혼식에서 꽃을 사용하는 전통은 실제로는 고대 시대로 거슬러 올라갑니다.

자, 그럼 이제 "연례 목욕"에 대해 알아봅시다. 많은 사람들이 이 잘못된 속설을 믿고 있다는 것이 마음에 걸리는데요. 대부분의 중세 사람들은 실제로 규칙적으로 몸을 씻었습니다. 심지어 비누도 사용했습니다. 물론 오늘날 우리가 사용하는 것과는 많이 다르겠지만요. 공중 목욕탕도 흔했는데, 이곳은 창부들에 의해서도 은밀하게 사용되었기 때문에, 표면적인 용도는 종종 부차적인 것이기도 했습니다.

❶ What is the lecture mainly about?

교수는 먼저 많은 이들이 잘못 알고 있는 중세 시대의 목욕 풍습에 대한 속설을 소개하면서 이것이 잘못된 것임을 설명한다. 선택지 A는 강의에 언급된 바가 없으며, 중세 사람들의 위생 관념을 설명하는 것이지 축제를 설명하는 것이 아니므로 선택지 B는 강의와 관련이 없다. 선택지 D 또한 강의와 관련이 없는 내용이다.

❷ What is the professor about to explain when he says this:

교수는 중세 사람들은 여기에 묘사된 것처럼 위생에 무지하지는 않았다고 말하면서 앞으로 중세 사람들의 위생 관념에 대해 설명할 것임을 시사한다. 선택지 A는 교수의 주장과 상반된 내용이므로 정답이 아니며, 선택지 B는 일반 사람들이 갖고 있는 통념과 관련된 내용이므로 정답이 될 수 없다. 강의에 따르면 중세 사람들이 위생에 대해 무지하지는 않았으므로 C 역시 틀린 선택이다.

❸ Why does the professor say this:

많은 사람들이 잘못된 통념을 가지고 있는 것에 대한 불편함을 드러내며 이에 대한 올바른 정보를 제공한다. 선택지 A와 D는 강의의 내용과 관련이 없으며, 화를 내는 것이 아니므로 C 역시 오답이다.

Passage 4

1. A　　**2.** A, C　　**3.** D　　**4.** A　　**5.** B

P(M): All right, now... if we could all be seated... okay. Um, today, we're gonna talk about conservation and research of wildlife in national parks. Uh... before we go on... I'd like to turn all your attention to this picture here... what do you think this picture is about?

W: Uh... I see an elephant and two men.. but the elephant looks like it's dead or something. Um, is that a picture depicting poaching?

P: Exactly. What you see in this picture shows two men harvesting an elephant's ivory tusks. Of course, we do not know for sure who killed this elephant just by looking at this picture, but... uh, we can only guess that those men actually hunted and killed the animal.

M: That's so sad.

P: It is. Well, if we take a look at another picture here... it's a picture of elephant carcasses left by poachers who stripped away their ivory tusks in Garamba National Park in 2004.

W: ❹ What I don't get is, professor, um, usually people think that national parks are safe for animals, right? Like, national parks are designated places where poachings and huntings are not allowed.

P: That's why they call it illegal. Actually, illegal acts of trophy trades and poaching are constantly and increasingly threatening wildlife within protected areas. Many argue that enforcement within protected areas should be reinforced in order to preserve wildlife. In Serengeti National Park in Tanzania, one of Africa's most pristine preserves, about $2 million is spent annually for enforcement patrols, and recent study shows that wildlife population in that area has increased thanks to 10 to 20 patrols a day.

But in other places such as the Garamba National Park in the Democratic Republic of Congo along the border of Sudan, circumstances are much more dire. This World Heritage Site is under siege by poachers who are killing animals like the elephant and the last 30 northern white rhinos, and... well, even park rangers.

P: 자, 이제 모두 자리에 앉읍시다. 좋아요. 오늘은 국립공원 내에서 이루어지고 있는 야생 동물에 대한 보호 활동과 연구에 대해 얘기해 보겠어요. 계속하기 전에 모두 이 사진에 주목합시다. 이 사진이 무엇에 관한 걸까요?

W: 사진에 코끼리와 두 남자가 있는데요... 하지만 코끼리는 죽은 것 같아요. 음, 혹시 밀렵을 묘사하는 사진이 아닌가요?

P: 맞아요. 여러분이 보는 이 사진에는 두 남자가 코끼리의 상아 엄니를 가져가는 장면이 담겨 있어요. 물론 이 사진만으로는 누가 이 코끼리를 죽였는지 정확하게 알 수 없지만, 이 남자들이 실제로 코끼리를 사냥해서 죽였다고 추측할 수 있죠.

M: 슬픈 일이네요.

P: 그렇지요. 다른 사진을 하나 더 보면... 이것은 2004년 가람바 국립공원에서 밀렵꾼들에게 상아 엄니를 빼앗긴 코끼리들의 사체 사진이에요.

W: 교수님, 이해가 안되는 것이 있는데요. 보통 사람들은 국립공원이 동물들에게 안전한 곳이라고 생각하지 않나요? 국립공원은 밀렵이나 사냥이 금지된 지정구역이잖아요.

P: 그렇기 때문에 "불법"이라는 말을 쓰는 거예요. 사실 보호 구역 내의 야생 생태는 불법 전리품 무역과 밀렵으로부터 지속적인 위험을 받고 있고 있고, 이러한 위험은 점점 증가하고 있어요. 많은 이들이 야생 동물들을 보호하기 위해 보호 구역 내의 단속을 강화해야 한다고 언성을 높이고 있죠. 아프리카에서 가장 잘 보존된 급렵지구 중 하나인 탄자니아의 세렝게티 국립공원은 매년 순찰을 위해 2백만 달러를 사용하고 있어요. 그리고 연구 결과 하루 10, 20번의 순찰 덕분에 야생 개체수가 증가했다고 해요.

하지만 수단과 국경을 같이 하는 콩고의 가람바 국립공원과 같은 다른 곳에서는 상황이 훨씬 더 심각해요. 이 세계 유산 지역은 코끼리와 30마리 밖에 안 남은 북부 흰코끼리와 같은 동물들을 죽이고 심지어 공원의 순찰대원들까지 죽이는 밀렵꾼들에게 포위당해 있어요.

---

❶ What is the discussion mainly about?

이 강의는 국립공원 내에서 이루어지고 있는 야생동물에 대한 보호 활동과 연구에 대한 것이므로 정답은 A이다. 선택지 B와 C는 강의에서 언급되지 않았으며, D는 잠깐 언급된 제한적인 내용이므로 오답이다.

❷ According to the discussion, which of the following poses a threat to wildlife within protected areas?

"Illegal acts of trophy trades and poaching are constantly and increasingly threatening wildlife within protected areas"라는 교수의 말에서 정답을 찾을 수 있다.

❸ Why does the professor show pictures of elephant poaching at the beginning of the class?

교수는 수업 초반에 밀렵된 코끼리의 사진을 보여주면서 강의의 주제를 소개한다. 불법적인 밀렵과 사냥이라는 오늘의 주제를 시각적으로 더 효과적으로 소개하기 위해서이지, 단순히 인간의 폭력적인 본성을 보여주기 위해서라고 보기는 힘들기 때문에 선택지 A는 정답이 아니다. 학생들에게 충격을 주려고 한다는 내용의 선택지 B는 너무 극단적인 선택이며, 지난 시간에 밀렵 사진을 보여주겠다고 약속했는지의 여부는 확인할 수 없으므로 선택지 C 역시 지워야 한다.

❹ Why does the professor say this:

교수는 밀렵이나 사냥이 금지된 보호 구역에서 이러한 행위가 벌어지는 이유를 묻는 학생에게 그래서 "불법"이라는 단어가 붙는 것이라고 설명한다. 학생의 질문에 대한 답을 한 것이므로 정답은 선택지 A이다.

❺ What does the professor say about the conservation program of Serengeti National Park in Tanzania?

"아프리카에서 가장 잘 보존된 금렵지구 중 하나인 탄자니아의 세렝게티 국립공원은 매년 순찰을 위해 2백만 달러를 사용하고 있으며, 연구 결과 하루 10, 20번의 순찰 덕분에 야생 개체수가 증가했다"는 교수의 말에서 정답(선택지 B)을 찾을 수 있다. 세렝게티 국립공원에서 밀렵이 완전히 없어졌다는 말은 없으므로 선택지 D는 오답이다.

Passage 5

1. C **2.** A **3.** B

P(W): The first Barbie doll was patented in 1958 by Mattel, a company founded by Ruth and Elliot Handler and their partner, Harold Mattson. Ruth and Elliot were married and had two children: Barbie and Ken. When Ruth Handler paid a visit to Europe in the mid 50's, she purchased a German Lilli doll which inspired her to come up with the design of Barbie. Mattel, whose name came from Matt of Mattson and El of Elliot, hired a fashion designer Charlotte Johnson and had her create the wardrobe for Barbie. Barbie doll made her way to New York Toy Show in 1959 but received a mild reception from toy buyers... you know, she was shaped differently from traditional typical dolls that were sold back then: she had long limbs, was svelte and in shape, beautiful and only 11.5 inches tall. But the public welcomed these newly designed dolls. They saw the gorgeous Barbie on the shelves of toy stores and by 1960, the demand for Barbie dolls surged up. Within ten years, the public purchased $500 million worth of Barbie products.

Well, speaking of Barbie products, she had an infinite line of wardrobe which fascinated the public who were fed up with paper fashion dolls.

❸ In 1960, Barbie's boyfriend, Ken, was created. Now you know where Mattel got the names for their popular dolls, right? Well, Barbie not only has a boyfriend but also has siblings: a younger sister Skipper who was created in 1964, twin sister and brother Tutti and Todd, and younger sisters Stacie and Kelly. Barbie, Ken and the siblings also have countless other friends and cousins. Many designers contributed to the Modern Barbie Era which started in 1977, and here are a few of them: Christian Dior, Anne Klein, Ralph Lauren, Calvin Klein, Carol Spencer, and Bob Mackie.

최초의 첫 바비 인형은 1958년 루스와 엘리엇 핸들러, 그리고 파트너인 해롤드 맷슨이 설립한 마텔사에서 제작되었습니다. 루스와 엘리엇은 부부였고 두 아이를 두었는데 이들의 이름은 바비와 켄이었습니다. 루스 핸들러는 50년대 중반에 유럽을 방문했을 때 구입한 독일의 릴리 인형으로부터 바비 디자인의 영감을 받게 되었습니다. 마텔이라는 이름은 맷슨의 매트와 엘리엇의 엘에서 따왔는데, 이들은 샬롯 존슨이라는 디자이너를 고용해 바비의 옷을 디자인하게 했습니다. 바비 인형은 1959년 뉴욕의 장난감 전시회에 출품되었지만 장난감업자들에게 큰 호응을 얻지는 못했습니다... 그 당시의 전통적 인형들과는 전혀 다른 디자인이었기 때문이었습니다. 그녀는 긴 팔다리와 가는 체형을 가지고 있었고, 아름다웠으며 키가 겨우 11.5인치밖에 되지 않았습니다. 그렇지만 대중은 이 새로운 디자인의 인형을 환영했습니다. 일반 대중은 장난감 가게에 진열되어 있는 아름다운 바비 인형을 보았고, 1960년에 이르러 바비 인형에 대한 수요가 급증했습니다. 10년 이내에 일반 대중들은 5억 달러 어치의 바비 제품을 구입했습니다.

바비 제품 얘기가 나와서 말인데, 그녀는 종이 인형에 질린 사람들을 매혹시킬만큼 방대한 옷가지들을 갖고 있었습니다. 1960년도에는 바비의 남자친구 켄이 탄생했습니다. 마텔이 유명한 이 인형들의 이름을 어디서 가져왔는지 이제 아시겠죠? 바비는 남자친구 뿐 아니라 형제, 자매도 있습니다. 1964년 여동생 스키퍼가 태어났고, 쌍둥이 남매 투티와 토드, 그리고 여동생 스테이시와 켈리도 있습니다. 바비, 켄 그리고 동생들은 많은 친구와 사촌들이 있습니다. 많은 디자이너들이 1977년에 시작된 현대 바비 시대에 공헌했는데요, 크리스챤 디올, 앤 클라인, 랄프 로렌, 캘빈 클라인, 캐롤 스펜서, 그리고 밥 맥키 등이 이들의 일부입니다.

❶ What is the topic of the lecture?

바비 인형과 마텔사의 탄생 과정을 언급한 후에 바비 인형이 미국에서 얻은 인기에 대해 설명하고 있으므로 정답은 C가 된다. 선택지 A는 제한적인 내용을 다루고 있으며 선택지 B와 D는 이 강의와는 직접적인 연관이 없다.

❷ What is true about the Barbie doll and its creators?

마텔사는 부부인 루스와 엘리엇 핸들러에 의해서 설립되었다. 물론 파트너가 있었지만 기본적으로 가족 회사(family company)라고 해도 무방하다. 루스 핸들러는 독일의 릴리 인형에게서 영감을 받아 바비 인형을 만들었으며 핸들러 부부와 맷슨이 회사 경영에 대해 서로 이견을 가지고 있었다는 이야기는 언급된 바가 없으므로 선택지 B와 C는 틀린 선택이다. 또한 바비 인형은 처음 출품되었을 때 장난감 바이어들로부터는 큰 호응을 얻지 못하다가 대중에게서 인기를 얻기 시작했으므로 D 역시 틀린 답이다.

❸ Why does the professor say this:

루스와 엘리엇 핸들러 부부에게는 바비와 켄이라는 이름의 자녀가 있었는데, 이 부부가 설립한 마텔사에서 출시한 인형의 이름 역시 바비와 켄이었다. 따라서 교수는 마텔이 바비와 켄 인형의 이름을 핸들러 부부의 자녀 이름에서 따왔다는 것을 확인하고 있다. 정답은 B이다.

Passage 6

1. A **2.** D **3.** B

P(M): One of the most influential psychologists might be B. F. Skinner, the American-born psychologist who proposed staunch behaviorism. According to Skinner, man learns language by rote learning and repetition. **❷ When a particular response is reinforced, it becomes habitual or conditioned. Therefore, children produce linguistic responses that are positively or negatively reinforced. When a child says "want cookie" instead of saying "Please give me some cookie," and her mother gives her a cookie, her utterance is positively reinforced, and if this is repeated, it is conditioned.** So, I guess it's safe to say that Skinner assumed that a human was a mere complex machine or a slightly more developed version of the lower animal, not having free will to experiment his or her linguistic ability and consequently not being responsible for what he or she does.

Skinner is also known for his laboratory apparatus called the "Skinner's box" which was used to conduct and record the results of operant conditioning experiments with animals such as rats. This box has a pedal or a lever on one wall that, when pressed, makes a food pellet fall into the cage. So if the rat — or whatever is in the cage — accidentally presses the lever while bouncing around the cage or something, gets to have a treat. Its behavior is reinforced, and in no time, the rat keeps pressing on the lever, hoarding piles of food pellets in the corner of the cage. This might remind some of you of Pavlov and his dog... but Pavlov was concerned with respondent behavior — uh, behavior that is elicited by a preceding stimulus. Uh, Skinner, on the other hand, tried to account for most of human learning and behavior.

가장 영향력있는 심리학자 중 한 명은 미국 태생의 스키너라고 할 수 있는데, 그는 행동주의의 창시자입니다. 스키너에 의하면 인간은 암기와

반복을 통해 언어를 학습한다고 합니다. 특정 반응이 강화되면, 이는 습관되거나 조건화됩니다. 그래서 아이들은 긍정적 혹은 부정적으로 강화된 언어적 반응을 보이게 됩니다. 아이가 "과자 주세요"라는 말 대신 "과자 줘"라고 말을 하고 엄마가 과자를 주면, 아이의 발언은 긍정적으로 강화되는 것이고, 이것이 반복되면 조건화되는 것입니다. 따라서 스키너는 인간을 단순히 복잡한 기계 혹은 하류 동물의 진화된 모델이라고 생각했고, 자신의 언어적 능력을 실험해 볼 자유 의지가 없었으며 그 결과 자신의 행동에 대한 책임감이 없다고 생각했습니다. 스키너는 또한 "스키너 상자"라는 실험 기구로 유명한데 이는 쥐 등의 동물을 대상으로 자발적 조건부 실험을 실시하고 결과를 얻는데 쓰인 기구입니다. 이 상자는 벽에 페달이나 손잡이가 있어, 이것을 누르면 음식 덩어리가 우리 안에 떨어집니다. 즉, 쥐 혹은 우리 안에 있는 동물은 우리 안을 사방으로 돌아다니다 우연히 손잡이를 밟게 되고 간식을 얻게 되는 것입니다. 이 행동은 강화되게 되고, 곧 쥐는 손잡이를 계속 밟아 우리 구석에 음식을 쌓아놓게 됩니다. 이 얘기를 들으면 파블로프와 그의 개에 대해 생각나는 사람이 있을 텐데요... 파블로프는 반응적 행동에 주목했습니다 – 선행적 자극에 이끌린 행동 말이죠. 그렇지만 스키너는 이와는 반대로 인간의 학습과 행동을 설명하고자 했습니다.

❶ What is the lecture mainly about?

인간의 언어 학습과 태도에 대해 연구한 미국 태생의 행동주의 심리학자 B. F. Skinner에 대해 설명하고 있으므로 정답은 A이다. 선택지 B와 D는 너무 제한적인 내용을 다루고 있으며, 이와 반대로 C는 너무 광범위한 내용을 다루고 있으므로 정답이 될 수 없다.

❷ Why does the professor say this:

인간의 언어 습득에 대한 스키너의 이론을 이해하는데 도움을 주기 위해 예를 들고 있는 것이므로 정답은 D이다.

❸ What can be inferred about Skinner?

교수는 파블로프가 반응적 행동에 더 무게를 두었다고 말하며 이와는 반대로 스키너는 인간의 학습과 행동에 중점을 두었다고 말한다. 따라서 스키너와 파블로프 모두 반응적 행동에 관심이 있었다고 하는 선택지 A는 잘못된 것이며, 선택지 B가 정답이 된다. 파블로프가 스키너의 강화 전략을 사용했다는 언급은 없으므로 C는 틀린 선택이며, 선택지 D에 대해서는 지문만으로는 알 수 없다.

Passage 7

1. B **2.** A, C **3.** D **4.** D **5.** C **6.** A

P(W): Angkor Wat... you see the temples in the slide picture over here... is the prime examplification of the classical style of Khmer architecture. Khmer architects mainly used sandstone and laterite and brick as the main building material. **❺ The Khmer architecture — the Angkor Wat style — was a unique style of building. As in many other aspects of their culture, the Cambodians were heavily influenced by Indian methods of architecture.** All right, now, let's go deeper into our topic for today.

Let's first talk about the religions the Khmer architecture had influence from. Who can tell me what kind of religion the Cambodians have? Sean?

M: Um, I guess... the Hindu religion?

P: All right. Yes, the Hindu. Uh, it played a vital role in the development of the Khmer temple. The religion was established in Cambodia some time between the second and the third century which was at the time of the beginning of the Funan kingdom. The Cambodians built temples to worship Hindu gods. But some time in the first part of the 9th century.. uh, from the year 800 to 850 AD, a king named Jayavarman II introduced the cult of devaraja into the country and established the king as a representative of the Hindu god Siva or a god-king. ❻ **From then on, people began to build temples to honor both the god and the king.** <u>Everyone follow me?</u> All right. Following the erection of these temples, new kings began to build his own temple which, basically, became his tomb on his death.

Okay..., now back to our topic. Uh, if you take a look at this picture here... I already mentioned that Khmer architects used sandstone to build the temple, right? Well, originally, all buildings in Cambodia were made of wood — including temples as well. Of course, none of these buildings have survived until today. Um, from early Funan times, which was from the 2nd through the 7th century, Cambodians manufactured bricks of a high quality; however, stones were not abundant. Temples that were built around the sixth century were... well, let's just think of it as a single brick tower with only one door and a small room that kept the statue of the Khmer god, usually Siva or Vishnu.

Now, here's where laterite and sandstone play a role. These materials were used between the 9th and 13th centuries as chief building materials. Um, laterite... well, since we're not geologists here, so I'd better make it easier for you guys... um, laterite is a soft red stone which can be cut easily but becomes hardened when dried in the sun. They are cut in blocks and used as brick for house building. Thus, the Khmers used this extremely hard material for strong foundations and city walls.

M: Um, professor, you just mentioned that, uh, the laterite was extremely hard when it was dried in the sun, right? That's why it was used for building material.

P: That's correct.

M: What I don't understand is... uh, if the material was very hard, then how could the Khmers carve decorative patterns in the temple walls?

P: That is a very good question, Lindsay. Well, actually, I was just about to explain about sandstone, which could be more easily carved.

M: Oh.

P: So, you got the idea? The Khmers used laterite in order to build a strong foundation, and used sandstone for outer wall decoration. Sandstone was more available and accessible in the Kingdom of Chenla which came after the fall of Funan. Thousands of tons of rocks had to be brought from faraway quarries to which the Kingdom of Chenla had easy access.

P: 앙코르와트... 여기 슬라이드에서 보면 신전 사진들을 볼 수 있는데요... 이는 크메르 건축의 전형적인 예로 볼 수 있어요. 크메르 건축가들은 주 건축 자재로 사암과 라테라이트, 그리고 벽돌을 사용했어요. 크메르 건축 혹은 앙코르와트 양식은 세계의 위대한 종교적 유물의 건축에 전성기를 가져온 매우 독특한 양식이었죠. 문화의 여러 가지 다른 부분들과 마찬가지로 캄보디아인들은 인도 건축 양식으로부터 큰 영향을 받았어요. 좋아요. 이제 오늘의 주제에 대해 더 상세하게 이야기 해 봅시다. 우선 크메르 건축에게 영향을 미친 종교들에 대해 이야기 해 보죠. 캄보디아인들의 종교에 대해 말해 볼 사람? 션?

M: 힌두교인가요?

P: 네, 맞아요. 크메르 신전의 발달에 중요한 역할을 맡은 힌두교는 2세기와 3세기 사이에 캄보디아에 정착했는데, 이 시기는 푸난 왕국이 시작될 무렵이었어요. 캄보디아인들은 힌두교 신들을 기리기 위해 신전을 만들었어요. 하지만 9세기 초반 경에... 아, 기원후 약 800에서 850년 정도 즘에 자야바르만 2세라는 왕이 데바라자라는 종교를 캄보디아에 들여왔고 왕을 힌두교의 신, 시바의 대변인 혹은 왕신이라고 받들었죠. 그 이후로 사람들은 신과 왕 둘 다를 기리기 위해 신전을 짓기 시작했어요. 모두 이해되죠? 좋아요. 이 신전들을 지은 후 새로운 왕들은 자신을 위한 새로운 신전을 지었는데, 이 신전들은 기본적으로 사후에 자신의 무덤이 되었어요.

좋아요. 이제 오늘의 주제로 돌아갑시다. 여기 이 사진을 보면... 이미 크메르 건축에서는 신전을 짓기 위해 사암을 사용했다고 얘기했죠? 원래 캄보디아의 신전을 포함한 모든 건축물은 목재로 만들어졌어요. 물론, 이들 중 현재까지 보존된 것은 아무것도 없어요. 2세기에서 7세기까지였던 후난 시대 초기에서부터 캄보디아인들은 우수한 벽돌을 만들었지만 돌이 많지 않았어요. 6세기 경에 만들어진 신전들은 문이 단 한 개 밖에 없는 벽돌로 만들어진 타워였고, 크메르 신 시바나 비슈누의 조각상이 모셔진 작은 방이 있었지요.

자, 여기에서 라테라이트와 사암이 중요한 역할을 하게 되어요. 이 자재들은 9세기와 13세기에 주요 건축 자재로 사용됐어요. 라테라이트는... 우리는 지질학자가 아니니까 쉽게 설명할게요. 라테라이트는 부드러운 붉은 돌인데, 쉽게 잘라지지만 햇볕에서 말리면 단단해져요. 이것은 불럭으로 잘라져 집을 지을 때 벽돌로 사용되죠. 그래서 크메르인들은 이 단단한 자재를 건물의 강한 토대와 도시 벽을 짓는 데 사용했어요.

W: 교수님, 방금 라테라이트가 햇볕에서 말리면 단단해진다고 하셨잖아요. 그래서 건축 자재로 사용된다고요.

P: 네, 맞아요.

W: 제가 이해가 안 되는 부분은, 만약에 그 자재가 그렇게 단단하다면 크메르인들이 어떻게 신전 벽에 장식문양을 새겼을까요?

P: 아주 좋은 질문이에요, 린지. 사실 사암에 대해 막 설명하려고 하던 참이었어요. 사암은 더 쉽게 조각을 낼 수 있거든요.

W: 아, 그렇군요.

P: 그럼 이해가 되지요? 크메르인들은 강한 토대를 짓기 위해 라테라이트를 사용했고 벽면에 문양을 새기기 위해 사암을 사용했어요. 사암은 푸난 왕국 이후에 설립된 첸라 왕국에서 쉽게 얻을 수 있었어요. 첸라 왕국은 수천 간 톤의 돌을 채석장에서 가져왔고 이를 쉽게 확보할 수 있었어요.

❶ **What does the professor mainly discuss?**

크메르 건축에 대해 설명하고 있는데, 교수는 먼저 크메르 건축에 영향을 준 종교를 언급하지만, 이것은 주제인 건축 자재로 들어가기 전에 잠시 언급된 것일 뿐이다. 따라서 정답은 B이다.

❷ **According to the professor, which of the following building materials did Khmer architects mainly use?**

"Khmer architects mainly used sandstone and laterite and brick as the main building material"에서 정답을 알 수 있다.

❸ **According to the professor, what is Devaraja?**

Devaraja는 왕을 힌두교의 신, 시바의 대변인이거나 왕신이라고 추앙한 종교라고 하였다. 따라서 정답은 D이다.

❹ **Why does the professor mention King Jayavarman II?**

자야바르만 2세가 데바라자라는 이름의 종교를 캄보디아에 들여왔고, 이로써 신과 왕 둘 다를 기리기 위해 신전을 짓기 시작한 것이 크메르 건축의 발달에 중요한 역할을 했다. 따라서 정답은 D이다.

❺ **What does the professor imply when she says this:**

"Like many other aspects of their culture"이라는 교수의 말에서 캄보디아 문화의 다른 부분도 인도의 영향을 받았다는 것을 알 수 있으므로 선택지 C가 답이 된다. 선택지 A는 강의의 내용과 관련이 없으며, 캄보디아 문화가 인도 문화의 영향만 받았다는 것은 알 수 없으므로 B도 틀린 선택이다. 앙코르와트가 인도 건축 방식으로 지어진 최초의 신전인지는 알 수 없으므로 D 역시 틀린 답이다.

❻ **Why does the professor say this:**

"Everyone follow me?"란 "이해되나요?"라는 뜻으로 학생들이 자신의 설명을 이해하고 있는 것인지 묻고 있다.

Passage 8

1. B   **2.** A   **3.** C   **4.** A   **5.** C   **6.** D

P(M): Across astronomical distances, gravity is the most important and significant of the fundamental forces of physics; however, astronomers found that there somehow is a discordance between their calculations and observations. So, in order to fill up this gap, a new kind of idea was proposed: dark matter. Maybe you might think of that dark force... you know, like Darth Vader fighting with the Jedi knights in *Star Wars* or something like that. No, no, no, uh, it, it has nothing to do with the bad guys fighting to destroy the world or conquer the Universe or something... ❸ **The... uh, dark matter is an undetected matter which basically is something that cannot be detected from the light which it emits. In other words, it fails to give off light.**

W: Does that mean that it's literally dark? Like... uh, you can't see it with bare eyes?

P: Pretty much, yeah.

M: Then how'd the scientists come to believe that dark matter exists?

P: Good question. Well, the presence of dark matter is indirectly inferred from the motions of astronomical objects, such as stellar, galactic, or galaxy clusters or superclusters.

W: Uh... I don't get it. Uh... do you mean that scientists know that dark matter exists only by observing gravitational effects?

P: That's good, Trish. Yes, gravitational effects on visible matter. Uh, let's, uh, let's go back to the question of how much matter is in the Universe before we move further. Uh, we can estimate the Universe's mass based on our understanding of it such as... well, how fast the Universe is expanding and stuff. A more direct way of answering the question is by looking through the telescope and trying to find out just how much matter we can see, right?

However, like I mentioned, there's a discordance between the scientists' calculations and observations. Let's make this clearer for you. Uh, in order to estimate the total mass of a group of galaxies, scientists measured their brightness. However, they found out that their computed number of the total mass of a region was much more higher than it was originally expected from observation-according to their computation, there was supposed to be some type of mass in that region but they couldn't see anything. Do you all follow me? ... Good. So scientists came up with the idea of dark matter in the Universe.

M: ❻ So, simply put, there should be much more matter than we can actually see, but there's nothing that can be seen with our bare eyes, so scientists thought that there would be... well, an invisible matter that has mass, right?

P: That's right. Anything that has mass must have gravity. According to Einstein's theory of relativity, gravity distorts space and therefore light. This process is called gravitational lensing. So if we look at distant galaxies, our view should be distorted by the dark matter which, according to our prediction, lies between them and us. For example, a circular galaxy would look eliptical and so on.

P: 우주적 거리에 있어 중력은 물리학의 가장 중요하고 유의미한 근본적인 힘입니다. 그렇지만 천문학자들은 어떠한 이유에서인지 모르지만 그들의 계산과 관측 사이에 불일치가 있음을 알아냈습니다. 그래서 이 차이를 메우기 위해 새로운 제안이 거론됐습니다. 이것이 바로 암흑 물질이라는 것입니다. 암흑 물질이라고 하니까, 암흑의 힘이라고 생각하는 사람도 있을 겁니다. 가령, 다스베이더가 "스타워즈" 영화에서 제다이 기사랑 싸우는 것 같은 것을요. 아뇨, 아뇨, 이것은 세계를 파괴하고 우주를 지배하려는 악당과는 아무 상관없습니다. 이 암흑 물질은 이것이 발산하는 빛으로는 감지할 수 없는 물질입니다. 즉, 암흑 물질은 빛을 방출하지 않는 것이죠.

W: 암흑 물질이 정말 말 그대로 어둡다는 말인가요? 맨 눈으로는 볼 수 없나요?

P: 그런 셈이죠.

M: 그러면 과학자들은 암흑 물질이 있다는 것을 어떻게 알죠?

P: 좋은 질문이에요. 암흑 물질의 존재는 항성, 은하계, 은하 성단 또는 초은하 집단과 같은 우주 물체의 움직임을 통해 간접적으로 추론하는 것이에요.

W: 이해가 안돼요. 그렇다면 과학자들이 중력 효과를 관측하는 것을 통해서만 암흑 물질이 존재한다는 것을 알 수 있다는 말씀이신가요?

P: 대답 잘 했어요, 트리시. 네, 보이는 물질에 대한 중력 효과에 의해서죠. 어, 더 나가기 전에 우주에 얼마나 많은 물질이 있는가에 대한 질문으로 돌아가 봅시다. 우주의 물질은 우리가 우주에 대해 얼마나 이해를 하고 있는가, 예를 들어서 우주가 얼마나 빨리 팽창하는가 등과 같은 것을 통해서 추측할 수 있어요. 이 질문에 더 직접적인 답을 얻기 위해서는 망원경을 통해서 관측하고 우리가 볼 수 있는 물질이 어느 정도인가를 확인해야 할 거예요, 이해되죠?

하지만 방금 언급했듯이 과학자들의 계산과 관측 사이에 불일치하는 부분이 있어요. 더 쉽게 설명할게요. 은하계의 총 질량을 측정하기 위해 과학자들은 그들의 밝기를 측정해요. 하지만 특정 지역의 총 질량을 계산한 결과, 관측을 통해 예측했던 것보다 훨씬 더 밝다는 것을 알게 되었어

요. 이들의 계산에 따르면 그 지역에 무엇인가 질량이 있는 것이 있어야 했지만 아무것도 보이지 않았죠. 이해되나요? 좋아요. 따라서 과학자들은 이를 통해 우주에 존재하는 암흑 물질을 생각해 낸 거죠.

M: 그러니까 간단히 말하면, 우리가 실제 보는 것보다 더 많은 물질이 있어야 하는데 육안으로는 아무것도 보이지 않았고, 그래서 과학자들이 질량이 있는 보이지 않는 물질이 있을 것이란 생각을 하게 됐다는 말씀이시죠?

P: 맞아요. 질량이 있는 모든 것은 중력이 있어야 해요. 아인슈타인의 상대성 이론에 의하면 중력은 공간과 빛을 왜곡시키죠. 이 과정을 중력 렌즈 효과라고 해요. 그래서 우리가 멀리 있는 은하계를 바라보면 시야가 암흑 물질에 의해 왜곡되는데요, 예측에 따르면 이 암흑 물질은 은하계와 우리 사이에 있는 것이에요. 예를 들어 구형 은하가 타원형으로 보인다거나 하는 것 말이지요.

❶ **What is the main purpose of the discussion?**

과학계에 새로 제안된 암흑 물질에 대해 언급하며 이에 대해 설명하고 있으므로 가장 좋은 답은 B이다. 중력에 대해 학생들이 이해하는지를 묻는 지문이 아니므로 선택지 A는 틀린 선택이며, 영화 스타워즈는 지문에 잠시 언급되었을 뿐, 지문의 주제와는 직접적인 관련이 없으므로 C 역시 틀린 답이다. 학생들에게 숙제를 내주는 것은 지문에 언급되지 않았으며, 이것이 주제가 될 수는 없으므로 선택지 D 역시 틀린 답이다.

❷ **According to the professor, which of the following is true about dark matter?**

"Dark matter is an undetected matter which basically is something that cannot be detected from the light which it emits"라고 하는 부분에서 선택지 A는 맞는 내용임을 알 수 있다. 암흑 물질 때문에 영화 "스타워즈"가 만들어졌는지의 여부는 지문에서 알 수 없으며, 암흑 물질은 과학자들의 계산에 의해 존재여부가 알려진 것이므로 선택지 B와 C는 틀린 선택이다. 선택지 D는 강의의 내용과 상반되므로 답이 될 수 없다.

❸ **Why does the professor say this:**

교수는 암흑 물질이란 그 물질 자체에서 방출되는 빛으로 관측할 수 없는 것이라고 말하며, 다른 말로 말하면 이 물질은 빛을 방출하지 않는다고 설명한다. 바로 전 조금 어렵게 설명한 내용을 쉽고 명쾌하게 정리한 것이다. 따라서 정답은 선택지 C이다.

❹ **According to the professor, which of the following explains gravitational lensing?**

Gravitational lensing이란 중력이 공간과 빛을 왜곡시키는 과정이다. 따라서 정답은 선택지 A이다.

❺ **Why does the professor mention Darth Vader and Jedi knights from the movie, *Star Wars*?**

교수는 물리학에서의 "dark matter"이라는 용어를 제시한 뒤, 학생들에게 영화 "스타워즈"에서 나오는 "dark force"와 혼동하지 말라며 우스갯소리를 하는데, 학생들의 암흑 물질에 대한 이해를 돕기 위해 다스베이더와 제다이 기사를 언급했다고 보는 것이 좋다. 선택지 A, B, 그리고 D는 지문의 내용과 관련이 없다.

Why does the student say this:

학생은 교수의 설명을 쉽고 간단하게 요약함으로써 자신이 이해하고 있는 내용을 정리하고 있다. 따라서 정답은 D이다. 교수가 몰랐던 정보를 새로 제시한 것이 아니므로 A는 잘못된 선택이며, 자신의 지식을 자랑하거나 교수의 설명에 이의를 제기하는 것도 아니므로 B와 C 역시 답이 될 수 없다.

Passage 9

1. D **2.** B **3.** B, D **4.** C **5.** A **6.** A

P(W): Many people have pets these days — dogs, cats, birds, uh, monkeys, or even amphibians or reptiles such as frogs or snakes. They are considered as not only just pets that you keep at home just because your kids wanted them or you need a housekeeper from burglars, but as a member of their family or even companions. The most popular animals as pets might be dogs and cats... you know, it's easier to keep them since there are tons of dogs-and-cats-related information out there, and, by coincidence, your favorite vet specializes in only dogs and cats. Well, whatever the reason is, people keep pets, but they also keep some incorrect information about their pets. I don't know where they get this from, but... let's just call that wrongful information about cats and dogs myths. So, today, we'll be talking about these myths about dogs and cats. Anaka, why do you think dogs wag their tail?

W: Well, because they're glad to see a person, or their master, right?

P: Well, that is true, in part, at least. A dog that waggles its tail indicates that it is happy, but it's usually reserved for living things. You know, a dog would wag its tail for a person, another dog, a cat, a horse, a passing mouse, a flying moth... anything that's living and moving. If the dog is alone, it simply wouldn't wag its tail. But you should be aware that dogs wag their tail also when they're agitated, tense, anxious, annoyed, or ready to fight. So you wanna make sure you know if the tail-wagging dog is happy or is angry at you.

M: Wow, I didn't know that at all. Um, what about bones? Dogs usually like bones... can we give them any bones left over?

P: Actually, that's another dog-and-cat-related myth that might pose considerable danger to your pet if you don't know exactly. Well, dogs do love bones, yes. But you must be aware what kind of bone you give her... not all bones are good for your dog. ❷ Many bones, for example, small bones like those from chicken, can splinter or crack easily when chewed and cause dogs to choke. You'd rather offer a nylon bone or rawhide instead. <u>Okay, let's move on... what about dogs who jump around the yard when it snows? Can dogs see snowfalls? What colors can they see?</u>

M: Black and white?

P: There you go, another myth.

W: Really? Do you mean that dogs can see colors?

P: Well, not the way we do, but they do see colors. Dogs are like people with red and green color blindness — they only have receptors for bluish and greenish shades, not for reddish ones.

M: That's very interesting. What about cats?

P: Well, if you see those Disney cartoons, cats drink milk, right?

W: Oh, is that another myth? Can't they drink milk?

P: Well, although milk is highly healthy for humans, cats shouldn't be allowed to drink too much milk. Too much milk can cause problems such as diarrhea, so they should be fed in small quantities. Animal experts say that most cats like milk, but they don't need it if properly nourished. Oh, and, uh, there's another interesting urban myth about cats... I wonder if you've ever heard about it, but, um, this myth says that cats will lie on a baby's chest and suck their breath.

M: I've never heard that before! But I can easily see that it's just a myth... cats are just animals, not powerful sorcerers or something.

P: That's true, but some young mothers have qualms about keeping cats as pets when they hear somebody mention this information. However, cats are usually harmless unless they actually sit atop a baby's chest. You see, cats are said to be attracted to babies and like to lie by them. Therefore, mothers with newborns should make sure to keep the cat out of the baby's room when the baby is sleeping alone.

P: 오늘날 많은 사람들이 애완 동물을 키워요 – 개, 고양이, 새, 원숭이, 심지어 개구리나 뱀과 같은 양서류나 파충류도 키우지요. 이 애완 동물들은 자녀들이 원해서, 혹은 도둑으로부터 집을 지키게 하기 위해서 키우는 동물로써 여겨질 뿐만 아니라 가족의 일원, 혹은 심지어 동반자로 여겨지죠. 애완 동물로 가장 인기 있는 동물이 개나 고양이일 것 같은데요, 개와 고양이에 대한 정보가 굉장히 많기 때문에 키우기 쉽고, 우연하게도 여러분이 가장 좋아하는 수의사가 개와 고양이만을 전문으로 보죠. 이유야 어떻든, 사람들은 애완 동물을 키우지만, 애완 동물에 대한 잘못

된 정보를 가지고 있어요. 어디서 이런 정보를 얻는 것인지는 모르겠지만, 개와 고양이에 대한 이런 잘못된 정보를 일단은 "속설"이라고 해 보죠. 자, 오늘은 이러한 개와 고양이에 관한 속설에 대해 얘기해 보겠어요. 아니카, 개는 왜 꼬리를 흔들까요?

W: 사람이나 주인을 보니 반가워서 아닐까요?

P: 그 말도 일부는 맞아요. 꼬리를 흔드는 개는 기쁘다는 감정을 나타내지만, 이것은 보통 살아 있는 생물에게만 행하는 행동이에요. 개는 사람, 다른 개, 고양이나 말, 지나가는 쥐, 날아가는 나방 등, 살아 있고 움직이는 모든 것에 대해 이런 행동을 하죠. 개가 혼자 있으면 꼬리를 흔들지 않아요. 그렇지만 개는 흥분하거나, 긴장하거나, 불안하거나, 화났을 때, 싸울 준비가 되어 있을 때에도 꼬리를 흔든다는 사실을 알고 있어야 해요. 그러니까 꼬리를 흔드는 개가 있으면 기분이 좋은 것인지 화가 난 것인지 확실히 알아야 하겠죠.

M: 와, 전혀 몰랐어요. 그럼 뼈는요? 개는 뼈를 좋아하잖아요... 먹다 남은 뼈는 아무 것이나 주어도 되나요?

P: 실은 바로 그것도 잘 모르면 애완 동물에게 위험할 수 있는 속설 중 하나예요. 개들이 뼈를 좋아하긴 하지요. 그렇지만 어떤 뼈를 주어도 되는지 알아야 해요. 모든 뼈가 개에게 좋은 것은 아니거든요. 뼈들 중에는 작은 닭뼈처럼 씹으면 조각이 나거나 쉽게 깨져서 개를 질식시킬 수 있는 것이 많아요. 차라리 나일론 뼈나 생가죽을 주는 것이 낫죠. 자, 계속합시다... 눈이 오면 마당을 뛰어다니는 개는 어떤가요? 개가 눈을 볼 수 있을까요? 개는 어떤 색을 볼 수 있을까요?

M: 흑백이요?

P: 자, 그게 바로 또 다른 속설이에요.

W: 정말요? 그럼 개도 색을 볼 수 있다는 말씀이신가요?

P: 우리가 보는 것처럼은 아니지만 색을 볼 수 있어요. 개는 적록 색맹이 있는 사람과 같아요. 이들은 파란색이나 초록색은 보지만 적색은 못 보지요.

M: 정말 흥미롭네요. 그럼 고양이는요?

P: 디즈니 만화를 보면 고양이는 우유를 마시잖아요. 그렇죠?

W: 그것도 또 다른 속설인가요? 고양이는 우유를 못 마시나요?

P: 우유가 인간에게는 이롭지만, 고양이는 우유를 너무 많이 마시면 안 돼요. 우유를 너무 많이 마시면 설사와 같은 문제를 유발하기 때문에 적은 양을 줘야 해요. 동물 전문가들은 대부분의 고양이가 우유를 좋아하지만 먹이만 제대로 주면 우유는 필요 없다고 해요. 아, 그리고 고양이에 대한 재미있는 속설이 또 있어요. 들어봤는지 모르겠지만, 이 속설에 의하면 고양이는 아기의 가슴에 앉아 숨을 빨아먹는다고 해요.

M: 그건 한번도 못들어 봤어요. 하지만 그 이야기는 확실히 속설일 뿐이라는 건 알겠어요... 고양이는 동물이지, 마법사는 아니잖아요.

P: 맞아요, 하지만 어떤 젊은 아기 엄마은 이런 얘기를 들으면 고양이를 애완 동물로 두는 것에 대해 불편함을 느끼죠. 그렇지만 고양이가 실제로 아기의 가슴 위에 앉지 않는 한 대부분 안전해요. 고양이는 아기를 좋아하고 아기 옆에 눕는 것을 좋아한다는군요. 그렇기 때문에 신생아를 둔 엄마은 아기가 혼자 자고 있을 때 고양이가 아기 방 안에 있지 못하게 해야 해요.

❶ **What is the main topic of the discussion?**

교수는 많은 사람들이 애완 동물로 개와 고양이를 키우지만 이들

에 대해 잘 모르고 있다고 말하며, 잘못된 속설들에 대해 설명할 것이라고 한다. 따라서 정답은 D이다.

❷ **Why does the professor say this:**

"Let's move on"이라는 표현은 "다음으로 넘어가자"라는 뜻이다. 즉, 교수는 곧이어 많은 사람들이 잘못 알고 있는 개에 대한 또 다른 상식(개가 어떤 색깔을 볼 수 있는지)에 대해 설명할 것임을 알 수 있다. 따라서 정답은 B이다.

❸ **According to the professor, what kind of color receptors do dogs have?**

"They only have receptors for bluish and greenish shades, not for reddish ones"이라는 교수의 말에서 정답을 찾을 수 있다.

❹ **According to the professor, what does a dog wagging its tail indicate?**

개는 기분이 좋을 때, 살아있고 움직이는 것을 봤을 때, 혹은 화가 났거나 싸울 준비가 되어 있을 때 꼬리를 흔든다고 했으므로 가장 좋은 답은 선택지 C이다.

❺ **Why shouldn't cats be allowed to drink too much milk?**

"Too much milk can cause problems such as diarrhea, so they should be fed in small quantities"라는 설명에서 답을 찾을 수 있다.

❻ **What does the professor say about the source of myths about dogs and cats?**

"I don't know where they get this from, but... let's just call that wrongful information about cats and dogs myths"라고 하는 교수의 말에서 정답을 찾을 수 있다. 즉, 교수는 사람들이 개와 고양이에 대한 잘못된 정보를 어디에서 갖게 되는지 모른다고 말하고 있으므로 정답은 A이다.

Passage 10

1. A   **2.** D   **3.** A   **4.** B   **5.** 참조

	Social phobia	Specific phobia
Obesophobia (fear of gaining weight)	✓	
Arsonphobia (fear of fire)		✓
Homophobia (fear of blood)		✓
Psellismophobia (fear of stuttering)	✓	
Muriphobia (fear of mice)		✓

P(M): Okay, so, as I was saying, there are various types of phobias. But before we go on, what is a phobia?

W: It's a strong, persistent fear of things or situations, such as claustrophobia which is fear of confined places, bacteriophobia, fear of bacteria, and so on.

P: ❷ That's right. And how many types of phobia do you think there are?

M: I've heard of several phobias, so, maybe about a dozen?

P: Actually, there are hundreds of phobias out there.

W: Hundreds? Did you say hundreds?

P: Yes, I did. You see, people can be afraid of so many things like insects or mice, situations like being alone, you know... Most common phobias might be claustrophobia, bacteriophobia, acrophobia which is fear of heights, agoraphobia which is a fear of open spaces or leaving a safe place, xenophobia, fear of strangers or the unknown, etcetera, etcetera, etcetera. But have you ever heard about fear of eggs? Fear of garlic, or fear of eyes or hands? What about fear of opinions? Fear of peanut butter sticking to your palate? Fear of flutes?

M: ❸ Oh, my... if I ever had that fear of flutes, I don't know what musical instrument I'd be playing right now... I don't think I'll ever be in the school orchestra!

W: That's funny. Um, can you tell us more about these phobias... why they happen, and... I mean, why do people fear certain stuff, situations, or activities?

P: That's a good question, Angelina. Before I move on to that, I think I should explain this first. Most phobias can be classified into three categories: social phobias, specific phobias, and agoraphobia, which are all subgroups of anxiety disorder. First of all, social phobias, anxiety disorder in other words, involve fear against other people or social situations. People with social phobias have performance anxiety or think that other people are watching, staring or judging them, although they know that's not true. The second category, specific phobias, describes intense fears of specific panic triggers, such as spiders, dogs, cats, confined spaces, uh, specific insects, water, flying, heights, or even eggs or policemen. Usually, people with these phobias tend to avoid the entity they fear. For example, Alfred Hitchcock, the famous movie producer and filmmaker, had fear for eggs which is called the ovophobia and also fear of the police. He said he had never tasted eggs and didn't get a driver's license in fear of getting pulled over by the police. Well, the last one in the three categories,

agoraphobia, which literally means "fear of open spaces," is not only a fear for open spaces but also for being in places where the person cannot escape from or where help cannot be reached easily in case of unexpected panic attacks or panic-like symptoms. These people do not want to develop panic attacks, so they tend to stay in familiar or safer places like their home. It is the only phobia regularly treated as a medical condition.

Well, many phobias, especially specific phobias, can be obtained by a specific triggering event, usually a traumatic experience at an early age. For example, you can get an apiphobia if you were stung by many bees when you were eight. Or you can get an arachnophobia, fear of spiders, when you were bitten by a big spider or something like that. However, the reason for getting other types of phobias is slightly different. Researchers believe that a complex combination of a small structure in the brain called the amygdale, past experiences, and observational learning of others being publicly humiliated might provoke social phobias, while agoraphobia is related with panic disorder or other phobias.

P: 자, 아까 얘기하던 대로... 공포증에는 여러 종류가 있어요. 더 나가기 전에, 공포증이란 무엇이죠?

W: 사물이나 상황에 대한 강한 공포예요. 예를 들어서 밀실 공포증은 좁은 공간에 대한 두려움이고 세균 오염 공포증은 박테리아에 대한 두려움이죠.

P: 맞아요. 그럼 공포증에는 몇 가지 종류가 있는지 아시나요?

M: 몇 가지 공포증에 대해 들어봤으니까, 한 열두어 개 정도 있지 않나요?

P: 실은 공포증은 수백 가지 종류가 있어요.

W: 수백이요? 수백이라고 하셨나요?

P: 네. 사람은 곤충이나 쥐, 혼자 있는 상황 등 많은 것에 대해 두려움을 가질 수 있어요. 가장 흔한 것으로는 밀실 공포증, 세균 오염 공포증, 높은 곳을 두려워하는 고소 공포증, 안전한 곳을 떠나는 것이나 열려 있는 공간을 무서워하는 광장 공포증, 낯선 것을 두려워하는 외국인 공포증 등이 있지요. 그런데 여러분은 달걀 공포증에 대해 들어본 적은 있나요? 마늘에 대한 공포, 눈이나 손에 대한 공포는요? 의견에 대한 공포는 어떤가요? 땅콩 버터가 입천장에 붙는 것을 두려워 하는 것은요? 혹은 플룻에 대한 공포는요?

M: 이런... 만약 플룻에 대한 공포가 있었다면, 제가 지금 어떤 악기를 다루고 있을지 상상이 안 가네요... 교내 오케스트라에 가입도 못 하겠네요!

W: 재밌네요. 이런 공포증에 대해 더 알려주실 수 있나요... 왜 발생하는지, 왜 사람들이 물체, 상황, 활동 등을 무서워하는 건가요?

P: 좋은 질문이에요. 안젤리나. 그것에 대해 설명하기 전에 이것을 먼저 설명해야겠네요. 대부분의 공포증은 세 가지로 분류할 수 있어요. 사회 공포증, 특정 공포증, 그리고 광장 공포증으로 모두 정서 불안의 하위 그

룹이에요. 우선, 사회 공포증은 다른 말로 불안 장애라고 하는데, 타인이나 사회적 상황에 대한 두려움을 의미해요. 사회 공포증이 있는 사람들은 무대 공포증이 있거나 다른 사람들이 자신을 바라보거나 판단하고 있다고 생각해요. 비록 이것이 사실이 아니라는 것을 알면서도 말이죠. 두번째 항목인 특정 공포증은 거미, 개, 엘리베이터, 물, 비행, 특정 질병, 높이, 심지어 달걀 등의 특정 공포 유발물에 대한 강한 공포감을 뜻해요. 이런 공포증을 가진 사람들은 대부분 자신의 공포 대상을 기피하는 경향이 있죠. 예를 들어, 유명한 영화 제작자이자 영화 감독이었던 알프레드 히치콕은 달걀 공포증이 있었고 경찰 또한 무서워했어요. 그는 계란을 먹은 적도 없고 차를 타고 가다가 경찰이 차를 길가에 세울까봐 운전 면허도 없었죠. 세가지 종류의 공포증 중 마지막인 광장 공포증은 말 그대로 해석하면 "넓은 공간에 대한 두려움"이에요. 이것은 넓은 공간에 대한 두려움 뿐만 아니라 쉽게 탈출할 수 없거나 예상치 않았던 공포감이 생기거나 증상이 나타났을 때 쉽게 도움을 받을 수 없는 공간에 대한 두려움을 포함해요. 이 사람들은 패닉 상태에 빠지는 것을 원하지 않기 때문에 집과 같은 익숙하고 안전한 곳에만 있는 경향이 있어요. 이 공포증은 의료 치료를 주기적으로 받는 유일한 공포증이에요.

많은 공포증, 특히 특정 공포증은 특정한 유발 상황, 일반적으로 어렸을 때의 정신적 충격이 큰 경험이 원인이 되어요. 예를 들어 8살 때 벌에 여러 번 쏘인 경우에는 벌 공포증이 생길 수 있고, 큰 거미에게 물렸을 경우에는 거미 공포증이 생길 수 있어요. 그렇지만 다른 종류의 공포증이 생기는 이유는 이것과는 조금 달라요. 연구자들은 뇌에 있는 작은 부분인 편도와 과거의 경험, 타인이 공개적으로 창피를 당하는 것을 본 것이 복합적으로 작용하여 사회 공포증을 유발할 수 있어요. 반면 광장 공포증은 패닉증 혹은 다른 공포증과 관련이 있어요.

❶ What is the main topic of the discussion?

교수는 공포증의 정의부터 시작해서 그 종류와 세 가지 하위 그룹에 대해 설명하고 있으므로 답은 A이다.

❷ Why does the student say this:

실제로는 수백 가지의 공포증이 있다는 교수의 설명에 여학생은 놀라면서 자신이 제대로 들었는지를 확인한다. 따라서 정답은 D이다. 교수의 말에 반박하거나 교수의 말을 듣지 못해서 하는 말이 아니며, 공포증에 대한 자신의 지식을 자랑하려는 것 또한 아니므로 나머지 선택지들은 답이 될 수 없다.

❸ What does the student imply when he says this:

교수가 플룻 공포증을 언급하자, 만약 자신이 플룻 공포증이 있다면 교내 오케스트라에서 어떤 악기를 연주할지 상상할 수 없다는 학생의 말에서, 현재 학생이 교내 오케스트라에서 플룻을 연주하고 있음을 추측할 수 있다. 따라서 정답은 A이다.

❹ According to the professor, why do certain people develop specific phobias?

"Many phobias, especially specific phobias, can be obtained by a specific triggering event, usually a traumatic experience at an early age"라는 교수의 말에서 답을 찾을 수 있다. 선택지 A는 사회 공포증과 광장 공포증에 대한 설명이며, C는 사회 공포증에 대한 설명이다. D는 지문의 내용과 관련이 없다.

❺ Based on the information in the discussion, indicate whether each phobia below is an example of social phobia or specific phobia.

사회 공포증은 타인의 비난에 대한 공포증으로서, obesophobia(비만 공포증)와 psellismophobia(말더듬 공포증) 등이 이에 해당한다. 반면, 특정 공포증은 어린 시절 특정 대상에 대한 정신적인 충격을 받았을 때 생기는 것으로 arsonphobia(불 공포증), homophobia(피 공포증) 그리고 muriphobia(쥐 공포증) 등이 그것이다.

Vocabulary Test

1. inspire	**2.** nourish	**3.** distort
4. repetition	**5.** infinite	**6.** trigger
7. ignorant	**8.** concide	**9.** b
10. d	**11.** a	**12.** c
13. b	**14.** d	**15.** a

PART 2 — Conversation

1 Main Idea

Sample

W: 안녕하세요. 제 학생 보험에 대해 문의드릴 게 있어요.

M: 네. 무엇을 도와드릴까요?

W: 이 회사에 학생 보험을 들었는데... 두 달 전에 자동차 사고가 나서 응급실에 갔거든요. 응급실쪽에 학생 보험이 있다고 말을 했는데 엄청난 금액의 청구서를 보냈어요. 보험이 적용이 되지 않은 것 같아서... 어떻게 된 것인지 알아보려고요.

M: 아. 그런 경우라면 고객 서비스 부서로 가셔야 해요. 여긴 계약 서비스 부서거든요.

W: 알아요. 그쪽에 이미 갔었는데, 이쪽으로 가라고 했어요.

M: 알겠습니다. 성함과 계약 번호를 알려주시겠어요?

W: 네. 시에나 밀러이고, 계약 번호는 PWL2643475예요.

Strategy Focus

1. C **2.** A **3.** D **4.** B

1. C

M: Hey, Laurie! What's up?

W: Oh, hey, Will! Nothing much. How are you?

M: I'm okay, just a little bit busy with my midterm.

W: Oh, your midterms aren't over yet?

M: Well, you know Professor Stevenson — I don't think he ever wants us to take a break earlier than any of the other students!

W: I know what you mean. Oh, by the way, have you heard about that job fair at the end of this month?

M: Yeah, I'm so excited. After my midterms are over, I'm gonna start working on my resume.

W: I'm already working on mine. Hey, if you ever need any help with your resume, just call me any time — I bought that Resume Maker from Microsoft last week.

M: Oh, boy, you did? How much is it, is it like a hundred bucks?

W: Close, but not quite. It was fifty-something-ish. I'm not so sure. Don't worry, I won't charge you, though... Anyways, um, did you hear that you're supposed to pre-register to enter that job fair?

M: Really? I didn't know that. How do I do it?

W: You're supposed to log on to their Internet website... if you see on the top left, there's gonna be a tab that says "October Job Fair." Everything's okay, but then, they charge you, like, twenty bucks or something.

M: Gosh, that's a total rip-off!

M: 어이, 로리! 잘 지내?

W: 안녕, 윌! 별 것 없어. 넌 어때?

M: 나도 그럭저럭 지내. 중간고사 때문에 좀 바쁘지만.

W: 아직 중간고사가 안 끝났어?

M: 스티븐슨 교수님이 어떠신지 알잖아 – 다른 학생들보다 일찍 쉬는 걸 바라지 않으시나봐!

W: 무슨 말인지 이해해. 아. 그나저나 이번 달 말에 열리는 취업 박람회 얘기 들었니?

M: 응. 정말 기대돼. 중간고사가 끝난 후에 이력서 작성을 시작하려고 하거든.

W: 난 이미 쓰고 있어. 혹시 이력서 쓰는 데 도움이 필요하면 언제든지 얘기해. 지난 주에 마이크로소프트사의 이력서 작성 프로그램을 샀거든.

M: 그래? 얼만데. 100 달러 정도 되니?

W: 비슷하긴 한데, 그 가격은 아니야. 대충 50 몇 달러 정도였어. 확실하지 않아. 걱정마, 돈 안 받을게... 어쨌든, 취업 박람회에 가려면 미리 등록해야 되는 건 알고 있어?

M: 그래? 그건 몰랐네. 어떻게 해야 되는데?

W: 그쪽 인터넷 웹사이트에 접속해서... 상단 왼쪽에 보면, "10월 취업 박람회"라는 탭이 있어. 다 괜찮은데 20달러 정도 내야 해.

M: 이런. 완전 갈취잖아!

2. A

W: Hi, Chris! Where are you headed to?

M: Hello, Moesha. I'm going to the library to drop these books off. Oh, by the way, thank goodness I ran into you... I believe that you took Dr. Pico's Criminal Law class, right?

W: Yeah, I took her class last semester. Why?

M: Gee... you see, um, this is embarrassing, but... I... happened to get a C on my first exam last week, and I can't afford another C on my report card — it's gonna ruin my GPA. I mean, I'm already having a difficult time with other subjects, but this Crim Law's getting on my nerves. I just can't seem to understand what's going on with all those legal terms and conditions...

W: Whoa, whoa, whoa, easy there, Chris. Well, I had some hard time studying Crim Law myself, but I think I can give you some help there. What do you say we meet this Friday so that I can tutor you?

W: 안녕, 크리스! 어디 가고 있어?

M: 안녕, 모에샤. 이 책들을 반납하러 도서관에 가는 길이야. 아, 참, 널 만나서 정말 다행이다... 피코 박사님의 형법 강의 들은 적 있지?

W: 응, 저번 학기에 들었어. 왜?

M: 음... 있잖아, 이런 얘기 하기 부끄럽지만... 지난 주 첫 시험에서 C를 받았 거든. 성적표에 C가 더 이상 있어선 안 되는데... 내 GPA를 망칠 거야. 이미 다른 과목 때문에 고생하고 있는데, 이 형법 강의 때문에 정말 짜증나. 법률 용어랑 조건 등에 대해서 전혀 이해를 못 하겠어.

W: 이런 이런, 잠깐만, 크리스, 나도 물론 형법 때문에 고생하긴 했지만, 도와줄 수 있을 것 같아. 이번 금요일에 만나서 널 개인지도 해 주면 어떨까?

3. D

M: Hi. Can I help you?

W: Um, yeah, I'm having a bit of a problem with my new roommate.

M: What seems to be the problem?

W: Um... she's my classmate as well, so I don't want words spreading around... but she's just so lazy. She never does her own dishes, and at first, she said she was sorry and that she'd make sure she wouldn't leave her dirty dishes on the table.

M: Right. But?

W: But she just went back to her own self and started... well, not doing her dishes anymore, again!

M: I can see that you're pretty upset with your roommate. So, I guess you'd prefer to switch your roommate, right?

W: Well, yeah, if that's possible.

M: Actually, we advise that you and your roommate have a meeting with one of our residence advisors. We're gonna give you some more time to try to work things out. If we decide that the difference is irreconcilable, we'll take a step to accommodate you in a different room. Select a date and time you and your roommate are both available and inform it to me by e-mail. We'll arrange a meeting for you two.

M: 안녕하세요, 도와드릴까요?

W: 네, 제 새 룸메이트와 문제가 좀 있어요.

M: 무슨 문제인데요?

W: 어, 제 룸메이트는 저랑 같은 수업을 듣기도 해서 소문이 나는 건 싫지만... 그 애는 너무 게을러요. 자기 설거지를 한번도 안하는데, 처음에는 미안하다 면서 식탁에 지저분한 접시를 놔두지 않겠다고 했어요.

M: 네, 그런데요?

W: 그런데 다시 원래대로 돌아가서 설거지를 안하기 시작했어요!

M: 룸메이트 때문에 마음이 상하신 것 같네요. 룸메이트를 바꾸고 싶으시겠 네요. 그렇죠?

W: 네, 가능하다면요.

M: 우선은 룸메이트와 함께 저희쪽 주거 상담자와 만나 보시기를 권해 드릴 게요. 문제를 해결할 시간을 좀 더 드리는 거죠. 도저히 해결될 수 없다고 판 단되면 다른 방으로 옮겨드릴 거예요. 학생과 룸메이트 둘 다 가능한 날짜와 시간을 정해서 저한테 이메일로 보내주세요. 두 분을 위해 상담 일정을 잡아 드릴게요.

4. B

M: Hello, Professor Keaton. I heard you wanted to see me?

W: Yes, Peter. Come have a seat.

M: Thanks.

W: Um... Peter, I read your midterm paper and... I think you have a pretty interesting viewpoint about Millet's painting, *Angelus*.

M: Oh, yes, ma'am. I... well, when I took a trip to France last year, I got to see the painting at the Louvre Museum, and I... well, I had this eerie feeling while I was looking at it. I didn't know what that feeling was, and I wanted to find out why it gave me that feeling. While I was researching, I found out that the basket of potatoes in between the man and the woman was originally a basket of their dead baby... like I wrote in my paper... and that the couple were actually praying for their dead baby in sorrow, not praying because they were thankful for the harvesting.

W: Did you also refer to the book of Salvador Dali?

M: Yes, I did, and I included it in my list of references.

W: That's very insightful. I can see you've grasped the symbolism behind his painting. Um, one more thing. I noticed you also mentioned the use of an X-ray in your paper, and that's what I wanted to talk to you about. Actually, we were supposed to discuss the use of X-rays in order to distinguish whether an art piece is genuine or not in our next class. But since you've already covered this in your paper, I'd like you to gather up some more information and make a presentation next week about Millet's painting and the use of X-rays. If you do a good job, I might give you a good grade on your participation.

M: Really? Wow... Thank you, Professor Keaton. Do you want my presentation to be in a certain way, or can I organize it on my own?

W: It doesn't matter, really. You can do it whichever

way you want. Although, try to make it as a 10-minute oral presentation with visuals, and give students something to think about and discuss for 20 minutes.

M: 안녕하세요, 키튼 교수님. 절 보자고 하셨다고요?

W: 그래요, 피터. 들어와서 앉아요.

M: 감사합니다.

W: 음 … 피터, 중간 고사 보고서를 읽어봤는데, 밀레의 그림 "만종"에 대해 독특한 견해를 가지고 있더군요.

M: 아, 맞아요. 작년에 프랑스로 여행을 갔을 때 루브르 박물관에서 그 그림을 봤는데, 보면서 이상한 느낌이 들었거든요. 그 느낌이 무엇인지 몰랐고 왜 그런 느낌이 들었는지 알아보고 싶었어요. 조사하는 동안, 남자와 여자 사이의 감자 바구니가 실제로는 그들의 죽은 아기가 들어있는 바구니라는 걸 알게 되었어요. 보고서에 써 놓은 것처럼. 그리고 그 부부는 죽은 아기를 위해 슬픔에 잠겨 기도하는 것이지, 수확의 기쁨에 대해 기도하는 것이 아니라는 것도 알게 되었어요.

W: 혹시 살바도르 달리의 책도 참조했나요?

M: 네, 그래서 참고문헌 리스트에 포함시켰어요.

W: 상당히 통찰력이 있군요. 밀레의 그림에 숨어있는 상징성을 잘 잡아낸 것 같네요. 하나만 더 얘기하자면. 보고서에 엑스레이의 사용을 언급한 것 같던데. 그 얘기를 하려고 했어요. 사실, 다음 시간에 예술품이 진품인지 아닌지를 구별하는 방법으로 엑스레이를 사용한다는 것에 대해 얘기하려고 했어요. 그런데 피터가 이미 이 내용을 보고서에서 다루었으니까, 좀 더 많은 정보를 모아서 다음 주에 밀레의 그림과 엑스레이의 사용에 대해 발표를 하면 어떨까요? 발표를 잘 하면 참여 점수를 높게 줄 수도 있어요.

M: 정말요? 감사합니다. 키튼 교수님. 원하시는 특정 발표 방법이 있으신가요, 아니면 제 마음대로 구성해도 되나요?

W: 별로 상관 없어요. 원하는 대로 해도 돼요. 하지만 시각 자료를 제시하면서 10분 정도 구술 발표를 한 후에, 학생들로 하여금 20분 정도 생각하고 토론할 수 있는 시간을 갖게 하세요.

Exercise

P.1	1. D	2. C	3. D		
P.2	1. C	2. D	3. B		
P.3	1. B	2. B	3. A		
P.4	1. C	2. 참조			
P.5	1. C	2. C	3. B	4. B	5. C

Passage 1

1. D　　**2.** C　　**3.** D

M: Hey, Sandy! How's it going?

W: Hey, Patrick. You know, everything's so hectic around here these days.

M: Oh? What's up?

W: Well, remember last time when I told you about how busy I was because of my part-time job at the cafeteria? I had to work on three 20-page-papers for my classes but they wanted me to work more time.

M: Yeah, I remember. So? Did you get a promotion or something?

W: I wish, but no. I've been working at least five hours a day at the cafeteria Monday through Friday, right? Well, last time, I barely managed to finish my papers, but my workload is piling up because right after I get home from work, I just don't have any energy left to study. I just feel like I sit through my classes without understanding anything! I really need help with my time management.

M: Uh-oh, we've got a problem there. Um... you know, I think I can give you a hand regarding your situation.

W: Really?

M: Yeah. You remember my ex-roommate, Robert?

W: Yeah, sure. What about him?

M: Well, he was in the same situation as yours, right? He was working at the professor's office as an RA for, like, somewhere around five hours a day, and he was the head of some kind of a student organization or something... so he was pretty busy as you are right now.

W: Really?

M: Yeah, and his GPA was getting lower and lower... so he went to the Student Center to get some help.

W: What do they have at the Student Center?

M: Robert told me that there were counselors who advised him how to manage his free time. When you wanna fill a jar with rocks, pebbles, and sand, you're supposed to put the rocks in first, then pebbles, and then sand. You've heard about this, right? It's the same with managing time. Well, this is the general idea, but I don't know the exact details on how to manage your time better, so... why don't you go make an appointment with some of the counselors there?

W: That's a great idea, Patrick! Why didn't I think about this before?

M: 어이, 샌디! 별일 없어?

W: 안녕, 패트릭. 요즘 너무 바빠.

M: 그래? 왜?

W: 저번에 식당에서 파트타임 일을 하는 것 때문에 바쁘다고 했던 것 기억나? 20페이지짜리 보고서를 세 개나 작성해야 했는데 식당에선 일을 더 하라고 했거든.

M: 그래, 기억나. 그래서? 진급이라도 했어?

W: 그랬다면 좋았겠지만, 아냐. 월요일에서 금요일까지 하루에 5시간씩 식당에서 일을 하고 있거든. 지난번엔 보고서를 간신히 작성하긴 했지만, 일 끝나고 집에 오면 공부할 여력이 없기 때문에 공부량이 계속 쌓이고 있어. 수업 시간에 아무것도 이해 못하고 그냥 앉아만 있는 것 같아. 시간 조절하는 데 도움이 필요해.

M: 이런, 그거 문제네. 음... 그 문제에 대해 도움을 줄 수 있을 것 같아.

W: 정말?

M: 그래. 내 옛날 룸메이트 로버트 기억하지?

W: 그럼. 근데 그 친구가 뭐?

M: 로버트가 지금 나랑 비슷한 상황에 있었거든. 교수 사무실에서 RA로 하루에 거의 5시간씩 일했고 무슨 학생 단체에서 회장도 맡았고... 지금 너처럼 상당히 바빴어.

W: 그래?

M: 응. 그리고 학점은 계속 낮아지기만 해서 학생 센터에 가서 도움을 청했지.

W: 학생 센터에 뭐가 있는데?

M: 로버트 말로는, 자유 시간을 어떻게 관리하는지 조언해 준 상담원들이 있다고 했어. 병에다 돌과 조약돌, 그리고 모래를 넣으려면 먼저 돌을 넣고 그 다음에 조약돌을 넣고 마지막으로 모래를 넣어야 한다는 얘기는 들어봤지? 시간을 관리하는 것도 똑같아. 뭐, 전체적인 얘기는 이렇지만 시간 관리에 대한 자세한 사항은 나도 잘 모르겠으니까 거기 상담원들과 약속을 잡는 게 어때?

W: 좋은 생각이야, 패트릭. 왜 진작에 이 생각을 하지 못했을까?

❶ What is the woman's problem?

"I really need help with my time management"라는 여학생의 말에서 정답을 알 수 있다.

❷ Why does the man talk about his ex-roommate?

남학생은 옛날 룸메이트가 비슷한 문제로 고민하다가 학생 센터에서 도움을 받았다고 언급함으로써 여학생이 가지고 있는 문제를 해결할 수 있는 방법을 제시하고 있다.

❸ What will the woman probably do next?

남학생이 "Why don't you go make an appointment with some of the counselors there?"이라고 제안하자 여학생은 "That's a great idea, Patrick! Why didn't I think about this before?"이라고 한다. 따라서 여학생은 학생 센터에 가서 상담원과 약속을 잡을 것임을 유추할 수 있다. 선택지 A와 C는 본문의 내용과 관련이 없으며, 지금 하는 아르바이트를 그만두겠다는 말도 없으므로 선택지 B도 답이 아니다.

W: Hi, Keith, come on in. ❷ So, how's it going with your applying to graduate school? Did you make up your mind yet about which school you want to apply to?

M: Actually, not yet. This must be the most difficult and painful decision in my life!

W: I know what you mean. Trust me, I've been there, you know.

M: Um, speaking of which... could you give me some advice? I'm really desperate.

W: Sure, that's what I'm here for. Go ahead, spill it out.

M: Well, at first, I had several schools in mind... I've done all the research about their field of study, school ranking, faculty, neighborhood, everything. But I can only afford applying to three schools. I'm having a hard time deciding which three.

W: ❸ Well, first of all, based on your GPA and extracurricular activities, I'm pretty sure you're gonna get into all three schools. So take it easy.

M: Thanks for those kind words, Dr. Dalton, but it's really not that big of a deal.

W: I mean it. And secondly, you wanna choose a school that's famous for your field of interest. Of course, I believe you've already done that.

M: Uh-huh.

W: 안녕, 키쓰, 들어와요. 대학원 지원하는 건 어떻게 되어가고 있나요? 어느 학교에 지원할지 결정했어요?

M: 실은 아직요. 제 평생 가장 어렵고 힘든 결정인 것 같아요!

W: 무슨 말인지 알아요. 나도 경험을 했으니까요.

M: 아, 말이 나와서 말인데요. 조언 좀 해 주시겠어요? 정말 간절해요.

W: 물론이죠. 그래서 내가 여기 있는 거니까요. 말해봐요.

M: 처음엔 마음에 두고 있는 학교가 몇 군데 있었어요. 그 학교의 전공 분야, 순위, 교수진, 주변 환경 등 모든 것에 대해 조사를 해봤어요. 하지만 세 군데만 지원할 수 있을 것 같아요. 어느 세 군데를 정해야 할지 결정하기가 힘들어요.

W: 우선, 학점과 과외활동 기록으로 볼 때, 분명 세 군데 모두에 합격할 수 있을 거예요. 그러니까 마음을 편하게 가져요.

M: 친절한 말씀 고맙습니다. 달튼 박사님. 그렇지만 그렇게 대단하지는 않아요.

W: 진심이에요. 그리고 두 번째로는 자신이 관심을 갖고 있는 분야에서 유명한 학교를 골라야 해요. 물론 이미 그렇게 했겠지만요.

M: 네, 그렇죠.

❶ Why does the student advisor want to see the student?

"So, how's it going with your applying to graduate school? Did you make up your mind yet about which school you want to apply to?"라는 부분에서 정답을 알 수 있다.

❷ What does the student advisor imply when she says this:

"I've been there"이라는 표현은 "내가 (물리적으로) 그곳에 갔다 왔다"라는 뜻도 되지만, "내가 그것을 겪어봤다"라는 뜻도 된다. 여자는 학생이 대학원에 지원하는 것에 어려움을 겪는 것을 보고, 자신도 대학원에 지원시 결정을 내리는 것이 쉽지 않았다며 학생과 공감한다.

❸ Why does the student say this:

여자가 학생의 성적과 과외 활동이 훌륭하다며 학생을 칭찬하자 학생은 별 것 아니라며 겸손하게 답한다. 따라서 정답은 선택지 B 이다.

---

1. B   **2.** B   **3.** A

M: Maggie, where are you going?

W: Oh, hey, Chad. I'm going to the Engineering Building. I have a meeting there in 20 minutes.

M: You're always busy. Oh, by the way, did you move to that apartment yet?

W: Actually, not yet... I didn't even make up my mind yet.

M: Why, what's wrong? I thought you hated living in the dormitory.

W: I really am tired of living in the dorm — I just can't stand all those roaches popping up everywhere in my room! But that apartment, Rowland Hills, is... just insanely expensive.

M: Well, how much is it?

W: Their studio with a kitchen and a bathroom is $810 a month. The same room at the dorm is only $600 a month. I mean, $210 is a lot to me — that can pay a month's meal for me, you know?

M: Yeah, but you always complained that the dorm building was so far away from your school building.

W: I know. Well, I guess that's why the dorm's cheaper... Rowland Hills keeps raising the rent each year because it's located right in front of the school building.

M: Well, I'm really sorry to hear that... hey, wait a

minute. Um... do you mind living with a roommate?

W: Not really. I don't have one right now, but I've lived with two other roommates last year. Why?

M: Actually... it just hit my mind... I have a cousin who lives off-campus. She's a doctoral candidate at the business school, and she does have a roommate now, but the roommate is supposed to be graduating and leaving in a couple of months. So, if you're interested...

W: Really? Well, how much is the rent? How far is her place from school?

M: Well, I'm not really sure about the rent, but her place is... well, a good 10-minute-walk from your school building.

W: That's not bad at all. After all, I use my bicycle to go to school anyways. As long as it's not infested with roaches...

M: Oh, you don't have to worry about that. Believe me — she always freaks out when she sees roaches, so she told me that she has exterminators come over and fumigate the house every month!

W: Wow, that's a relief.

M: Uh, I'm supposed to have lunch with her in a couple of hours... would you like to join us?

W: Sure, why not? When and where are you guys gonna meet?

M: At noon, in front of the school book store.

W: Cool, I'll see you in two hours, then. Thanks a lot, I owe you big time. I'll see you later.

M: 매기, 어디 가고 있는 중이니?

W: 안녕, 채드. 엔지니어링 건물에 가고 있어. 20분 후에 거기서 미팅이 있거든.

M: 넌 늘 바쁘구나. 그나저나, 그 아파트로 아직 이사 안 했어?

W: 응, 아직... 아직 결정도 못 했어.

M: 왜, 무슨 일인데? 네가 기숙사에 사는 걸 싫어하는 줄 알았는데.

W: 맞아, 기숙사에서 사는 게 정말 지겨워. 방 여기저기에서 바퀴벌레가 나오는 것도 이젠 못 참겠어! 하지만 로랜드 힐 아파트는 임대료가 터무니없이 비싸.

M: 얼만데 그래?

W: 부엌과 화장실이 딸린 스튜디오가 한 달에 810달러야. 기숙사에 있는 똑같은 방은 한 달에 600달러 밖에 안 하거든. 210달러는 내게는 큰 돈이야 – 한 달 식비라서 말야.

M: 그래, 하지만 넌 항상 기숙사 건물이 학교에서 너무 멀다고 불평했었잖아.

W: 알아. 그래서 기숙사가 저렴한 건가 봐. 로랜드 힐은 학교 바로 앞에

CHAPTER **1** ▪ Main Idea   83

있어서 매년 임대료를 인상하거든.

M: 정말 유감이네... 아, 잠깐만. 너 혹시 룸메이트랑 같이 살아도 괜찮겠니?

W: 괜찮아. 지금은 룸메이트랑 같이 살고 있지 않지만, 작년엔 룸메이트 두 명이랑 함께 살았었거든. 왜?

M: 실은 방금 생각난 건데 말이야. 캠퍼스 밖에서 사는 사촌 누나가 있거든. 경영 대학원에서 박사 과정 중이야. 지금은 룸메이트가 있는데, 그 룸메이트가 몇 달 후면 졸업하고 이사를 가야 해. 그러니까 만약 네가 관심 있다면...

W: 정말이야? 임대료는 얼만데? 집은 학교랑 얼마나 멀어?

M: 임대료가 얼마인지는 잘 모르겠지만, 집은 네 학교 빌딩에서 걸어서 10분 거리에 있어.

W: 나쁘지 않네. 어차피 학교에 갈 땐 자전거를 타고 가거든. 방에 바퀴벌레만 없다면야...

M: 그건 걱정 안 해도 돼. 날 믿어 – 누나도 바퀴벌레만 보면 경악을 하기 때문에 매달 해충 구제업자를 불러서 온 집안을 방역한다고 했거든!

W: 와, 그거 다행이네.

M: 몇 시간 있다가 사촌 누나랑 점심 먹기로 했는데, 너도 같이 갈래?

W: 그래. 좋지. 언제 어디서 만날 건데?

M: 12시에 학교 서점 앞에서.

W: 좋아. 그럼 2시간 후에 만나자. 정말 고마워. 이번에 큰 신세지게 됐네. 나중에 보자.

❶ **What is the woman's problem?**

"I just can't stand all those roaches popping everywhere in my room! But that apartment, Rowland Hills, is... just insanely expensive"라는 여학생의 말에서 정답을 알 수 있다. 해충 구제업자(exterminator)와 문제가 있는 것이 아니므로 선택지 A는 정답이 아니며, 바퀴벌레에 대한 여학생의 "공포"가 문제가 아니므로 선택지 C 역시 오답이다. 선택지 D는 본문에서 언급된 바가 없다.

❷ **What can be inferred about the man's cousin?**

남학생의 사촌은 경영대에서 박사 과정을 밟고 있을 뿐, 학생들을 가르친다는 직접적인 언급은 없으므로 선택지 A는 바른 답이 아니다. 또한 그녀는 현재 룸메이트와 살고 있지만 룸메이트가 몇 달 뒤 방을 비울 것이다. 그녀의 집은 여학생의 학교 빌딩에서 적어도 10분 이상은 걸리는 곳이며 학교 바로 옆에 있는 것은 아니므로 D 역시 답이 아니다. 매달 해충 구제업자를 불러서 집을 방역한다는 것을 볼 때 매우 깔끔한 성격임을 알 수 있으므로 정답은 B이다.

❸ **What will the woman probably do next?**

20분 후에 엔지니어링 빌딩에서 미팅이 있으므로 곧 그곳에 가야 한다. 따라서 정답은 A이다. 오후 12시에 만나자는 남학생의 말에 2시간 후에 만나자는 여학생의 대답으로 미루어 보아, 이 대화가 이루어지는 시간은 대략 오전 10시 전후임을 알 수 있다. 따라서 남학생의 사촌과 서점 앞에서 만나는 것은 여학생이 미팅에서 나온 이후의 일이다.

1. C   **2.** 참조

Statement	Yes	No
Upload the thesis abstract.	✔	
Register at the library information desk.		✔
Type in thesis title and student information and upload file.	✔	
Log in and click online thesis submission button.	✔	
Print out confirmation form, then click submission complete button.		✔

W: Umm, hi, I'm a graduate student here, and.. I'm a little confused about uploading my thesis file on the online library.

M: Okay, I can help you with that. Have you registered on the online library?

W: Oh, I didn't know we had to do that.

M: Well, yes, that's the first thing you need to do. After you register online, log in and click on the online thesis submission button right here, you see?

W: Let me write that down real quick. Okay. And then, what do I have to do?

M: Type in your thesis title, your major and student number and then upload your file.

W: Umm, my thesis is about 120 pages. Do I need to compress it into a smaller file?

M: No, that won't be necessary. Most of the thesis goes well over 100 pages in length.

W: Okay, that sounds simple enough.

M: Oh, one more thing. Don't forget to upload your abstract. It's the last step in the online thesis submission system, but I've seen many students skip it. Your thesis submission won't be completed unless you upload your abstract.

W: Okay, I'll remember that.

M: After you upload everything, click on the submission complete button on the bottom, and print out the confirmation form. You have to get it signed by your advisor and submit that to the department office.

W: 어, 안녕하세요, 여기 대학원생인데요, 온라인 도서관에 논문 파일을 올리는 것이 좀 헷갈려서요.

M: 좋아요. 제가 도와드릴 수 있어요. 온라인 도서관에 등록은 하셨나요?

W: 아, 등록을 해야 하는지 몰랐어요.

M: 그걸 가장 먼저 하셔야 해요. 온라인에 등록한 후 로그인을 하시고

여기에 보이는 온라인 논문 제출 버튼을 클릭하시면 돼요. 보이시죠?

W: 잠깐 받아 적을게요. 네, 그 다음엔 어떻게 하면 되죠?

M: 논문 제목과 전공 과목, 그리고 학생 번호를 입력하신 후에 파일을 올리시면 돼요.

W: 제 논문은 약 120페이지 정도 되는데, 파일 용량을 압축해야 할까요?

M: 아니요, 그러실 필요 없어요. 대부분의 논문들이 100페이지는 훌쩍 넘어가니까요.

W: 네, 간단한 것 같네요.

M: 아, 한 가지 더요. 논문 개요를 올리는 것도 잊지 마세요. 온라인 논문 제출 과정 중 마지막 단계인데, 많은 학생들이 그냥 넘어가더라고요. 논문 개요를 올리지 않으면 논문 제출이 완료되지 않아요.

W: 네, 기억해 둘게요.

M: 전부 올린 후 밑에 있는 제출 완료 버튼을 누르시고 확인서를 출력하세요. 그 확인서에 지도 교수의 서명을 받아서 과 사무실에 제출하시면 돼요.

❶ Why does the woman want to talk with the man?

"I'm a little confused about uploading my thesis file on the online library"라는 여학생의 말과 "Okay, I can help you with that"라는 남자의 대답에서 정답(선택지 C)를 알 수 있다. 자신의 논문을 올려달라고 부탁하기 위해 찾은 것이 아니므로 D는 답이 될 수 없다.

❷ Based on the information in the conversation, indicate whether the following statements are information about uploading the thesis file on the online library.

온라인 도서관에 논문을 게재하려면 먼저 온라인 도서관에 등록을 하고 로그인을 한 후, 온라인 논문 게재 단추를 눌러야 한다.

Passage 5

1. C   **2.** C   **3.** B   **4.** B   **5.** C

M: Professor Simmons, I heard that you wanted to see me?

W: Yes, David, please come in.

M: Thank you.

W: ❷ Well, first of all, I wanted to tell you that I enjoyed your presentation last week at the student conference at Irvine Hall. Your topic was very interesting and I liked your point of view on Actualism.

M: Really? Oh, thank you so much! I was extremely nervous that day, you know.

W: Yes, you did stammer a little bit and went off topic sometimes, but I guess making a

presentation that day really paid off, huh?

M: What do you mean?

W: I just came back from the dean's office. I recommended you as a junior presenter of the Geology Conference held this October in Prague.

M: Junior presenter?

W: Yes, I'm supposed to make a presentation at that conference, and every presenter can recommend a student as a junior presenter. What you're going to do is make a presentation in front of a group of senior presenters after the main events are over. They will choose three junior presenters and recommend them as scholarship recipients to their schools. If you're in the final three, it might actually be advantageous for you when you apply for graduate school, you know.

M: A... Are you serious?

W: Of course.

M: But... I was so nervous at the student conference held in our school... but in Prague? This is huge! D... Do you think I can do well?

W: Don't worry, David, we still have months to prepare for that conference. Now, what I want you to do is to write an article on Actualism. Try to make it around 40 pages including pictures, graphs, and reference lists. Oh, and, uh, you're going to have to write an abstract as well.

M: 40 pages?

W: Yes, we still have about six months, so there's plenty of time. Um, what's your plan for the summer, by the way?

M: Well, I... I was thinking about going back home and get a part-time job or something.

W: All right, then you might want to start gathering your references now. You know my e-mail address, so send me your draft every other week, okay? I'll try to give you as much feedback as I can.

M: 시몬스 교수님, 절 보자고 하셨다고요?

W: 그래요, 데이빗. 들어와요.

M: 고맙습니다.

W: 자, 먼저, 지난주 얼바인 홀에서 있었던 학생 컨퍼런스에서의 발표가 참 좋았다고 말해주고 싶었어요. 주제가 굉장히 흥미로웠고 헌실주의에 대한 견해가 마음에 들었어요.

M: 정말요? 정말 감사합니다! 실은 그날 많이 긴장했거든요.

W: 그래요, 조금 더듬거리기도 하고 가끔 주제에서 벗어난 말을 하기도 했지만, 그날 발표를 한 게 좋은 성과를 거둔 것 같지요?

M: 무슨 말씀이신가요?

W: 방금 학장실에서 돌아오는 길이에요. 이번 10월에 프라하에서 열리는 지질학 컨퍼런스에서 주니어 발표자로 학생을 추천하고 왔어요.

M: 주니어 발표자요?

W: 그래요, 그 컨퍼런스에서 내가 발표를 해야 하는데, 모든 발표자들이 주니어 발표자로 학생 한 명씩을 추천할 수 있어요. 학생이 해야 하는 일은 발표가 모두 끝나고 난 후 시니어 발표자들 앞에서 프레젠테이션을 하는 거예요. 그들이 3명의 주니어 발표자들을 뽑아서 그들의 학교에 장학생으로 추천할 거예요. 그 3명 안에 들면 나중에 대학원에 진학할 때에도 유리하게 작용할 수 있어요.

M: 정말이세요?

W: 물론이죠.

M: 하지만... 전 우리 학교에서 개최된 학생 컨퍼런스에서도 그렇게 긴장했었는데... 프라하에서라뇨? 굉장한데요! 제가 잘 할 수 있을까요?

W: 걱정 말아요, 데이빗. 컨퍼런스 준비할 시간이 아직 몇 달이나 남았으니까. 자, 우선은 현실주의에 대해 소논문을 작성하도록 해요. 사진과 그래프, 그리고 참고서적 리스트까지 합쳐서 약 40페이지 정도로 작성하고, 아, 그리고 논문 개요도 써야 할 거예요.

M: 40 페이지요?

W: 그래요. 아직 6개월이나 남아있으니까 시간은 충분할 거예요. 그나저나, 이번 여름방학 계획이 어떻게 되죠?

M: 저... 저는 그냥 집에 돌아가서 아르바이트나 할까 하고 생각하고 있었는데요.

W: 좋아요, 그러면 지금부터 참고서적을 준비하기 시작해야겠네요. 내 이메일 주소는 아니까 2주일에 한번씩 원고를 보내세요. 알겠죠? 최대한 피드백을 해 줄게요.

❶ Why does the professor want to talk to the student?

교수는 먼저 얼바인 홀에서 있었던 학생의 발표가 좋았다고 칭찬하며, 그로 인해 학생이 프라하의 컨퍼런스에서 발표할 수 있는 기회를 얻게 되었다고 설명한다. 따라서 정답은 C이며, 오직 얼바인 홀에서의 발표를 칭찬하기 위해서 학생을 부른 것이 아니므로 선택지 D는 답이 될 수 없다.

❷ What does the professor mean when she says this:

"Pay off"라는 표현은 "(어떤 노력 등이) 좋은 성과를 얻다"라는 뜻으로, 선택지 C가 답이 된다. 얼바인 홀에서의 학생의 발표로 프라하에서 발표할 수 있는 기회를 얻었기 때문이다. 얼바인 홀에서의 발표로 장학금을 받는 것이 아니므로 선택지 D는 틀린 선택이다.

❸ What can be inferred about the student?

"But... I was so nervous at the student conference held in our school... but in Prague? This is huge! D... Do you think I can do well?"이라는 학생의 말에서 정답을 알 수 있다. 선택지 A는 지문의 내용에서 알 수 없으며, 선택지 C와 D는 본문의 내용과 반대되는 내용이므로 올바른 선택이 아니다.

❹ According to the professor, what will junior presenters do in order to prepare for the conference?

주니어 발표자는 발표가 모두 끝나고 난 후 시니어 발표자들 앞에서 프레젠테이션을 하게 된다. 따라서 소논문을 작성하고 발표를 준비할 것임을 알 수 있다. 정답은 선택지 B이다.

❺ What will the student mostly probably do during the summer vacation?

학생의 원래 여름방학 계획은 집에 돌아가서 아르바이트를 하는 것이었지만, 교수는 이제부터 참고서적 준비를 시작하고 원고를 2주일에 한 번씩 보내라고 하면서 원고 작성을 시작하라고 한다. 따라서 정답은 선택지 C이다.

Vocabulary Test

1. d   **2.** a   **3.** c

4. a   **5.** a   **6.** c

7. b   **8.** d

2 Supporting Detail

W: 오늘 발표 때문에 너무 긴장돼.

M: 맞아. 오늘 한슨 교수님 시간에 구두 발표를 하기로 했다고 그랬지? 왜 그래. 아직 준비가 안됐니?

W: 준비는 됐지만... 너도 알다시피 한슨 교수님은 혹독하게 비판하고 지적하시는 걸로 유명하시잖아. 오늘 고생 좀 할 것 같아.

M: 교수님께서 비판하는 것으로 악명이 높긴 하지만, 말을 더듬지 않고 발표 주제에 대해서 잘 알고 있다면 분명히 점수를 잘 주실 거야. 그리고 나중에 생각해 보면, 지적해 주신 부분이 주제에 대해 더 많이 이해할 수 있도록 도와줄 거야.

W: 그래, 네 말이 맞는 것 같아. 하지만 어쨌든 긴장되는 건 어쩔 수 없어.

Strategy Focus

1. B   **2.** C   **3.** D   **4.** B

1. B

W: You told me you're going to the library, right?

M: That's right.

W: Can I ask you a favor?

M: Sure, go ahead.

W: Could you turn in these books for me? I'm in a real hurry.

M: No problem. Is there anything else I can do for you?

W: Um... no. Oh, wait, actually... oh, never mind.

M: Come on, tell me, is it something I can do, or what?

W: Um, I need to borrow some other books, too.

M: Oh, I can do that. I'm going to the library to see if they have some books that I need as well. Do you have the list?

W: Yeah. Here you go.

M: Hmm. Seems like we're going to be checking out the same books. I hope they have multiple copies.

W: Oh, if they're out of copies, then you can just borrow your own. Just let me share the books later, okay?

M: We can do that. So, if I get to borrow the books, how do I give them to you?

W: Um... do you have class today?

M: Yeah, Beckman Hall at three. I get out at four thirty.

W: Great. I'll see you at Beckman Hall lounge around four thirty, then. Hey, thanks a lot.

M: No problem, see you then.

W: 너 도서관에 간다고 했었지?

M: 응. 맞아.

W: 부탁 좀 해도 될까?

M: 그럼. 얘기해.

W: 이 책 좀 반납해 줄래? 내가 정말 바빠서 그래.

M: 그럴게. 다른 건 없어?

W: 없어. 아, 잠깐만... 아니, 신경 쓰지 마.

M: 왜 그래. 말해봐. 내가 할 수 있는 거니?

W: 음, 실은 다른 책도 빌려야 하거든.

M: 내가 빌려다 줄게. 나도 도서관에 필요한 책이 있는지 보려고 가는 중이거든. 빌려올 책 목록은 있어?

W: 응. 여기 있어.

M: 흠. 우리가 같은 책을 빌리는 것 같네. 여러 권 있어야 할 텐데.

W: 만약 없으면 네 것만 빌려. 그냥 나중에 빌려줘. 알았지?.

M: 그래도 되지. 책을 빌릴 수 있으면, 너한테 어떻게 전해줄까?

W: 음... 오늘 수업이 있니?

M: 응. 3시에 베컴홀에서 있어. 4시 30분에 끝나.

W: 좋아. 그럼 베컴홀 라운지에서 4시 30분쯤에 보자. 정말 고마워.

M: 천만에. 그때 봐.

2. C

M: Excuse me, Professor Kinney, do you have a minute? I have a question about the Language and Gender final project you gave us last week.

W: Sure, David, come in. It'll have to be quick though, I have a faculty meeting in 10 minutes.

M: Oh, okay. Well, I know that we're supposed to pick an item from the mass media and analyze how it depicts gender role, so I was thinking about choosing one magazine each from girls' magazine and guys' magazine, and analyzing them.

W: Hmm, that sounds pretty interesting. Do you have any particular magazines in mind?

M: Well, that's actually what I wanted to talk to you about. I have tons of magazines at home, you know... but they're all copies of one magazine I subscribe called *Men's Health*, and I don't think that it clearly shows dichotomized gender roles of men and women. It just shows how to eat healthy and work out effectively.

W: Well, if I could make a suggestion, I think that's gonna work just fine. It clearly shows the idea that men should be fit and strong, and have a six-pack on their abs, right?

M: Come to think of it, you're right, professor.

W: And some of the girls' magazines, such as *Cosmo* and *Vogue*, often talk about what a woman should do in order to get a man's attention, so maybe you can analyze that as well.

M: Well, thank you so much for your help. I've been so worried about choosing the right kind of magazine for the project. I really need the grade, you know.

W: I'm glad I could be of help, David. Now, I really have to run along.

M: 실례합니다. 키니 교수님, 시간 좀 있으세요? 지난주에 주신 언어와 성별에 대한 기말 프로젝트에 대해 질문이 좀 있는데요.

W: 그래요, 데이빗, 들어와요. 하지만 10분 후에 교수진 미팅이 있기 때문에 빨리 해야 될 거예요.

M: 네, 알겠습니다. 대중 매체에서 아이템을 골라 그것이 성역할을 어떻게 묘사하는지를 분석해야 한다는 건 알고 있는데요. 그래서 여성 잡지와 남성 잡지 각각 하나씩을 골라서 분석을 해보려고 생각하고 있었어요.

W: 흠, 꽤 흥미로울 것 같네요. 생각해 둔 잡지라도 있나요?

M: 실은 그것 때문에 교수님께 상의드리고 싶었어요. 집에 잡지가 많긴 한데요, 사실 전부 제가 구독하는 "멘스 헬스"라는 잡지뿐이거든요. 그런데 이 잡지는 남성과 여성의 성역할을 이분법적으로 분명하게 보여주지 않는 것 같아요. 그냥 어떻게 하면 건강에 좋은 음식을 먹고 효율적으로 운동을 할 수 있는지 보여줄 뿐이에요.

W: 내 의견으로는 그것도 괜찮을것 같네요. 그 잡지는 남성은 몸이 좋고 건강하며 복근이 있어야 한다는 믿음을 심어주고 있지 않나요?

M: 생각해 보니 교수님 말씀이 맞네요.

W: 그리고 "코스모"나 "보그"와 같은 일부 여성 잡지들은 남성의 관심을 사로잡기 위해 여성들이 어떻게 해야 하는지를 자주 다루니까 그것에 대해 분석해도 좋을 것 같아요.

M: 와, 도와주셔서 정말 감사합니다. 프로젝트에 맞는 잡지를 고르는 것에 대해 많이 고민했거든요. 이번 점수가 정말 중요해서요.

W: 내가 도움이 돼서 기쁘네요, 데이빗. 자, 나는 이제 가봐야겠어요.

3. D

M: Hi, is Professor Ronalds here? I need to talk to him about the midterm paper.

W: Sorry, he's not in today. He went to attend a conference in Chicago.

M: Oh... umm, then who can I talk to about the paper? It's really urgent.

W: You can talk to me. I'm his T.A., Janet.

M: Oh, thank god. He gave us a list of topics to choose from at the beginning of the semester, and ...well, I thought I had it in my file, but I just can't seem to find it! I've looked everywhere for it!

W: I've had more than a dozen students come in for the list. Don't worry about it, I have the list right here.

M: Great. Whew~! You saved my life.

W: Make sure your paper is at least ten pages, double-spaced, 12 points. The professor is pretty strict about the format, you know.

M: I'll keep that in mind. Thanks a lot!

M: 안녕하세요, 로날즈 교수님 계신가요? 중간고사 리포트 때문에 상의를 드려야 하는데요.

W: 죄송해요, 오늘은 안 계세요. 회의에 참석하러 시카고에 가셨거든요.

M: 아... 그러면 리포트와 관련해서는 누구와 얘기해야 하나요? 굉장히 급한데요.

W: 저한테 말씀하시면 돼요. 저는 교수님 조교 자넷이라고 해요.

M: 아, 다행이네요. 교수님께서 학기 초반에 저희가 골라야 하는 주제 목록을 주셨는데요, 파일에 갖고 있는 줄 알았는데 도저히 찾을 수가 없어요! 사방으로 찾아봤거든요.

W: 그 목록을 달라는 학생이 열 명도 넘게 찾아왔어요. 걱정하지 마세요, 여기 있어요.

M: 아, 다행이네요. 휴! 제 생명의 은인이세요.

W: 리포트 분량은 적어도 10장 이상 되어야 하고, 더블스페이스에 글자 크기는 12 포인트로 하는 것 잊지 마세요. 아시겠지만 교수님께서는 형식에 매우 엄격하시거든요.

M: 명심할게요. 정말 고맙습니다!

4. B

M: Hi. Can I help you?

W: Hi. Is this where I can get a new student ID?

M: Yes, you've come to the right place. Can I have your driver's license please?

W: Umm, actually, I lost my license along with my student ID. Someone took my wallet from my desk at the library when I went to the bathroom.

M: Sorry to hear that. Well, then... unless you have your passport, you won't be able to get your student ID reissued today. We need a photo identification for all renewals.

W: Yeah, I thought so. I did bring my passport just in case. Here it is.

M: Alright. Let me just make a photocopy of your passport. Please fill out this form while I'm gone. This will only take a few minutes.

M: 안녕하세요, 뭘 도와드릴까요?

W: 안녕하세요, 여기서 학생증을 새로 발급받으면 되나요?

M: 네, 맞게 찾아 오셨어요. 운전면허증을 보여주시겠어요?

W: 어, 실은, 학생증과 함께 면허증도 잃어버렸어요. 도서관에서 화장실에 간 사이에 누가 지갑을 가져갔거든요.

M: 안됐네요. 그렇다면... 여권이 없는 이상 오늘 학생증을 재발급 받으실 수

는 없을 것 같네요. 재발급을 받으시려면 사진이 들어간 신분증이 있어야 하거든요.

W: 그럴거라 생각했어요. 혹시나 해서 여권을 가져왔어요. 여기 있습니다.

M: 좋아요. 여권을 복사 좀 할게요. 그동안 이 서류를 작성해 주세요. 몇 분 안 걸릴 겁니다.

Exercise

P.1	**1.** B	**2.** C	**3.** C
P.2	**1.** B	**2.** A	**3.** C
P.3	**1.** D	**2.** D	**3.** B
P.4	**1.** D	**2.** C	**3.** A
P.5	**1.** A	**2.** A, B	**3.** B	**4.** C	**5.** B

Passage 1

1. B　　**2.** C　　**3.** C

W: Hi, Howard, come in, have a seat.

M: Hi, Dr. Reynolds. You wanted to talk to me about something? I hope this isn't about my grades...

W: No, no. It's actually about the foreign exchange student program that you applied for.

M: Oh, okay. Umm... Is there any problem?

W: Well, I just got a letter from the school you applied for... It seems that their dormitory is under construction and they can't provide housing for foreign exchange students this semester. You should find an off-campus apartment or a homestay on your own.

M: Oh, no, really? Can't they find an apartment for me?

W: I'm sorry, but I don't think so...

M: Oh, man.... Um, then can I get a refund for the housing fee?

W: ❶ Well, I've contacted them about that, but unfortunately, they can't give you a full refund for the housing.

M: <u>Are you serious?</u> Why?

W: They say that's the rule. They can only give you 50% of your housing fee back, and give you a full refund if you decide not to go to that school at all.

M: Oh, geez. What should I do then?

W: I guess your best option is to go study at another French college or a language institution that's cheaper and offers housing. I know that you wanted to go there because their linguistics program's one of the best, but as you know, housing problems are one of the most important issues for foreign exchange students. I'd advise you to take a detour and start looking at other schools and programs.

M: Aww, this is ridiculous... and I spent all these years getting prepared for that exchange student program... If I can't go to that school, I don't know where I want to go!

W: 하워드, 들어와서 앉아요.

M: 안녕하세요, 레이놀즈 교수님. 제게 하실 말씀이 있으시다고요? 성적 문제는 아니겠죠.

W: 아니 아니. 실은 신청했던 해외 교환 학생 프로그램 때문이에요.

M: 아, 네... 무슨 문제라도 있나요?

W: 지원한 학교로부터 방금 편지를 받았는데, 그 학교의 기숙사가 공사 중이라 이번 학기에는 해외 교환 학생들에게 숙소를 제공할 수 없다고 하는군요. 캠퍼스 밖에 있는 아파트나 홈스테이를 직접 찾아봐야 할 것 같아요.

M: 아, 이런, 정말요? 그쪽에서 아파트를 찾아줄 순 없는 건가요?

W: 유감이지만 그건 안될 것 같아요…

M: 이런… 그러면 주거비는 환불을 받을 수 있나요?

W: 그 문제로 그쪽에 연락을 해봤는데, 안타깝게도 주거비 전액 환불은 불가능하다고 하네요.

M: 정말이세요? 왜 그런 건가요?

W: 그게 규정이라고 해요. 주거비의 50%만 돌려줄 수 있고, 그 학교에 등록하지 않겠다고 결정하는 경우에만 전액 환불을 해준다고 해요.

M: 오.. 이런… 그럼 전 이제 어떻게 하면 되죠?

W: 가장 좋은 대안은 좀 더 저렴한 다른 프랑스 대학이나 어학원으로 가는 거예요. 그 학교가 언어학 프로그램이 훌륭한 곳 중 하나라서 가고 싶어하는 건 알겠지만, 알다시피 주거 문제는 해외 교환 학생들에게 있어서 가장 중요한 문제 중 하나거든요. 다시 고려해 보고 다른 학교와 프로그램을 알아보는 게 좋겠어요.

M: 오, 이건 정말 말도 안돼요… 지금까지 오랫동안 그 학교의 교환 학생 프로그램을 준비해 왔는데… 그 학교에 갈 수 없다면 가고 싶은 곳이 어디인지 모르겠는걸요!

❶ Why does the man say this:

학생이 가고자 하는 학교의 기숙사가 공사 중인데, 주거비가 환불이 안된다는 지도교수의 말에 학생은 놀라움과 당황스러움을 표시한다. "Are you serious?"라는 표현은 "진담이세요?"라는 뜻도 되어 선택지 A와 헷갈릴 수 있지만, 학생은 몰랐던 정보에 놀라움을 표시하는 것이므로 B가 더 나은 답이다.

❷ Why is the man upset with the foreign exchange student program?

"Aww, this is ridiculous... and I spent all these years getting prepared for that exchange student program... If I can't go to that school, I don't know where I want to go"라는 학생의 말에서 정답을 찾을 수 있다. 즉, 학생은 가고자 하는 학교에 갈 수 없게 되어서 당황스러워 하는 것이다.

❸ What can be inferred about the man?

지원한 학교의 교환 학생 준비를 하느라 오랜 시간이 걸렸다며 그 학교가 아니면 어떤 학교에 가야 할지 모르겠다는 남학생의 말에서, 이 교환 학생 프로그램 외에 다른 학교를 준비하지 않았다는 것을 유추할 수 있다. 따라서 선택지 C가 정답이며, 나머지 선택지들은 이 지문만으로는 알 수 없다.

Passage 2

1. B   **2.** A   **3.** C

W: Professor Loven, can I come in?

M: Oh, yes, Patricia. Please have a seat.

W: Thank you.

M: Okay. Uh, I just wanted to see if you're doing well with your pre-med courses. Um... you told me last semester that you're taking pre-med courses because you wanted to go to medical school, right?

W: Yes, sir, but I kind of changed my mind.

M: Oh, you did? What made you change your mind?

W: Um... I just... came to think that becoming a doctor is not my calling.

M: Well, then what do you want to do?

W: Well, I was thinking about it very hard these days, and... well, when I was a child, I always thought that I wanted to become a lawyer. So... I thought I should go to law school after I graduate.

M: Hmm, that's not a bad idea. But you took so many pre-med courses until now. If you want to go to law school, you should have taken pre-law courses — such as constitutional law, business law, criminal justice, and so on.

W: I know. Do you think I have to take those courses now?

M: Not necessarily. Most, if not all law schools will accept students from any fields of study. However, it would definitely have helped if you took any of those courses I just mentioned to you.

W: 로벤 교수님, 들어가도 될까요?

M: 그래요, 패트리샤. 앉아요.

W: 감사합니다.

M: 음, 의대 선수 과목을 잘 듣고 있는지 얘기해 보려고 오라고 했어요. 저번 학기에 의대를 가고 싶어서 의대 선수 과목을 듣는다고 했었죠?

W: 네, 하지만 생각을 바꿨어요.

M: 그래요? 왜 생각을 바꾸게 되었나요?

W: 그냥... 의사가 되는 게 천직이 아닌 것 같다는 생각을 하게 됐거든요.

M: 그러면 뭘 하고 싶은데요?

W: 요새 생각을 많이 해 봤는데요, 음... 어렸을 때 전 늘 변호사가 되고 싶었거든요. 그래서 대학 졸업 후 법대를 가는 게 좋을 것 같아요.

M: 흠, 나쁜 생각은 아니에요. 하지만 여태 의대 선수 과목을 많이 들었잖아요. 법대를 가고 싶으면 헌법, 상법, 형사법 같은 법대 선수 과목을 들었어야 해요.

W: 알고 있어요. 지금 그 과목들을 들어야 하나요?

M: 꼭 그런 것은 아니에요. 전부는 아니지만 대부분의 법대들은 모든 분야의 학생들을 선발하니까요. 하지만 내가 방금 말해준 과목들을 들으면 분명히 도움이 될 거예요.

❶ Why does the professor want to talk to the woman?

"I just wanted to see if you're doing well with your pre-med courses"라는 교수의 말에서 정답을 알 수 있다.

❷ What does the student say about becoming a doctor?

학생은 의사가 되는 것이 천직이 아닌 것 같다며 어렸을 때부터 되고 싶었던 변호사로 길을 바꾸겠다고 한다. 따라서 정답은 A이다.

❸ According to the professor, what can be said about law schools?

법대 선수 과목을 수강하면 법대 대학원 진학에 도움이 될 것이라 했으므로 법대 대학원이 선수 과목을 수강한 학생들을 선호한다는 것을 알 수 있다.

Passage 3

1. D   **2.** D   **3.** B

M: Excuse me, Professor Johnson. You wanted to see me?

W: Hi, Joey. I wanted to talk to you about your paper.

M: Uh-oh. Did I do something wrong?

W: Well, Joey, I've noticed that you didn't use the proper paper-writing standard. That's why I couldn't give you a high score.

M: The proper writing standard? What do you mean?

W: You've heard of the APA format, right?

M: APA format? Um, I'm sorry, professor. I don't

think I've ever heard of it.

W: Hmm, that explains it. Well, APA format is basically a format that's commonly used among scholars to cite sources within the social sciences, but you're expected to use this format in college writing as well. Most high schools teach this format — that's why I didn't think it was necessary to mention it in class.

M: ❷ I... never heard about it. <u>Oh no, does this mean that I can get in trouble for plagiarizing or something?</u> Because I didn't cite the references properly?

W: Well, no, not exactly. This is a common mistake from many freshmen. But you should be really careful from now on, because some students did get expelled for plagiarizing dissertations and published articles.

M: Oh, boy, I'll keep that in mind. What... what can I do?

W: Well, I'll give you three days to re-do your paper this time. Of course it's going to be on another topic. And this time, make sure you use the APA format. Go to the university bookstore and look up the APA manual, or go on the Internet and and look for the format.

M: Thank you so much professor. I'll go look it up right now.

M: 실례합니다, 존슨 교수님. 절 보고 싶어하셨다고요?

W: 안녕, 조이. 보고서에 대해서 얘기 좀 나눌까 해서 불렀어요.

M: 이런, 제가 무슨 잘못이라도 했나요?

W: 글쎄요, 조이. 적절한 보고서 작성 기준을 지키지 않았더군요. 그래서 높은 점수를 줄 수 없었어요.

M: 적절한 보고서 작성 기준이요? 무슨 말씀이신가요?

W: APA 형식에 대해 들어는 봤겠지요?

M: APA 형식이요? 교수님, 죄송하지만 들어본 적이 없는 것 같은데요.

W: 음, 왜 그 형식을 따르지 않았는지 이제 이해가 되네요. APA 형식은 기본적으로 사회학 분야에서 학자들이 출처를 언급할 때 일반적으로 사용하는 방식이에요. 그렇지만 대학 보고서에서도 이 형식을 사용해야 해요. 고등학교에서도 대부분 이 형식을 가르치기 때문에 수업 시간에 따로 언급하지 않아도 될 거라 생각했어요.

M: 한번도 들어본 적이 없어요. 이런, 그럼 제가 표절과 같은 문제로 곤란해 질 수도 있다는 건가요? 출처를 제대로 언급하지 않아서요?

W: 꼭 그런 것은 아니에요. 많은 1학년 학생들이 흔히 저지르는 실수거든요. 하지만 이제부터는 정말로 조심해야 해요. 몇몇 학생들이 논문이나 이미 출판된 논설을 표절해서 실제로 퇴학 당한 사례가 있거든요.

M: 휴, 그렇군요. 명심하겠습니다. 그럼 이제 어떻게 하면 되나요?

W: 이번에는 보고서를 다시 작성할 수 있도록 사흘 정도 시간을 줄게요. 물론 다른 주제를 다루어야 하고요. 이번 보고서는 반드시 APA 형식을 사용하도록 하세요. 대학 서점에 가서 APA 매뉴얼을 찾아보거나 인터넷에서 찾아보도록 해요.

M: 정말 감사합니다. 교수님. 지금 바로 가서 찾아볼게요.

❶ **Why does the professor give a poor grade on the student's paper?**

올바른 작성 기준을 지키지 않아서 높은 점수를 줄 수 없었다고 했으므로 정답은 D이다.

❷ **How does the student feel when he says this:**

"Oh, no"라는 학생의 표현과 말투에서 알 수 있듯, 학생은 자신이 다른 사람들의 저작물을 적절한 인용 없이 사용한 것 때문에 문제가 되지 않을까 걱정하고 있음을 알 수 있다. 따라서 정답은 D이다. 선택지 B와 C는 관련이 없으며, 선택지 A에서와 같이 학생이 "APA 형식을 좀 더 일찍 알았으면 좋았을 걸"이라고 생각할 수는 있지만 다시 듣는 부분에는 아쉬움보다는 걱정하는 마음이 더 크게 담겨있다.

❸ **What kind of penalty does the professor say some students received when they committed plagiarism?**

"Some students did get expelled for plagiarizing dissertations and published articles"라는 교수의 말에서 선택지 B가 정답임을 알 수 있다.

Passage 4

1. D   **2.** C   **3.** A

W: Hi, can I help you with something?

M: Yes, a lot, actually. See, I... I've got a small problem with my roommates.

W: Oh, with your roommates. Actually, I'm not in charge of complaints regarding roommate problems. The person in charge is on leave today.

M: Yeah, I know. I talked with him last time, but it's kind of urgent. I need to talk to you.

W: Well... All right, if you could explain it to me, I'll make sure the person in charge receives your complaint. So, what's the problem?

M: Uh... I live with two other roommates who are actually great guys. One is the best cook I've ever seen, and the other's like the smartest guy I've known so far. He actually tutors me in Calculus.

W: Well, it seems like you have the best roommates you could ever wish for, no?

M: Well, maybe, but what's really bothering me

is that none of them seem to be interested in studying — and the biggest problem is that they're trying to lure me into their habit.

W: What do you mean?

M: Well, they're like the biggest game freaks I've ever seen. They play video games all night long. I've asked them to turn off the game when I'm studying, but they keep asking me to play with them even when I refuse. It's very distracting, you know. I'm having trouble with my studies right now and if I don't get good grades this semester, I don't think I can make it to grad school.

W: Well, I understand how you might feel since you share the same room with two other people. But, you see, I don't think that's a problem that any of us can solve for you. You're gonna have to find a solution on your own.

M: Excuse me?

W: What I'm saying is that, we can only help you when your roommates are not cleaning up the house or are making extreme noises at night and seriously disturbing other people's sleep. You didn't mention your roommates making noises, so I guess the biggest problem you have here is them trying to make you play video games with them. These types of personal problems, we cannot help you with, I'm afraid.

M: Oh, man.... Then, what should I do? Where can I find help?

W: Well, let me tell you what I would do if I were in your shoes. I'd go to the library and study there all night until your roommates go to sleep. The Bronz Library opens up 24 hours a day. Or you can make a study group for the exams to help you with your studies.

M: Well, my roomies usually play games at night and go to sleep in the morning. I think I should consider that. Thanks anyways.

W: My pleasure. How do your roommates get by with their studies, though? Now that's a mystery.

W: 안녕하세요. 도와드릴 거라도 있나요?

M: 네, 사실은 도와주실 게 많아요. 제 룸메이트들과 문제가 좀 있어서요.

W: 룸메이트들요? 실은 저는 룸메이트 문제와 관련한 불만 사항을 담당하지 않아요. 담당자는 오늘 휴가세요.

M: 네, 알아요. 지난번에 그 분과 얘기했었어요. 하지만 좀 급해서 꼭 말씀드려야 돼요.

W: 글쎄요.... 알았어요. 저에게 설명해 주시면 담당자가 불만 사항을 접

수할 수 있도록 해드릴게요. 문제가 무엇인가요?

M: 룸메이트 두 명과 살고 있는데, 사실 참 괜찮은 애들이에요. 하나는 제가 아는 최고의 요리사이고 다른 하나는 지금껏 만난 사람들 중 가장 똑똑해요. 저에게 미적분을 가르쳐주고 있어요.

W: 음. 최고의 룸메이트를 만난 것 같은데요?

M: 그럴 수도 있죠. 하지만 진짜 문제는 두 명 다 공부에는 신경쓰지 않는다는 거예요. 그리고 더 큰 문제는 자기들 습관에 저를 끌어들이려고 한다는 거죠.

W: 무슨 말인가요?

M: 그들은 제가 본 최고의 게임광이에요. 밤새도록 비디오 게임을 해요. 제가 공부할 때는 좀 꺼달라고 했는데. 싫다고 하는데도 계속 같이 하자고 권해요. 정말 신경쓰여요. 요즘 공부하느라 힘들고 이번 학기에 좋은 점수를 받지 못하면 대학원도 못 갈 것 같아요.

W: 두 사람과 같은 방을 쓰고 있다니 어떤 기분인지 알겠어요. 하지만 저희가 해결할 수 있는 문제는 아닌 것 같네요. 스스로 해결책을 찾으셔야 해요.

M: 무슨 말씀이세요?

W: 무슨 말이냐면, 저희는 룸메이트가 청소를 안하거나 밤에 큰 소음을 내서 다른 사람의 잠을 방해하는 등의 경우에만 도와드릴 수 있어요. 룸메이트들이 시끄럽다고는 안했으니까. 학생이 가장 힘들어하는 이유는 룸메이트들이 비디오 게임을 같이 하자고 하는 것 같은데요. 이런 개인적인 문제들의 경우에는 죄송하지만 저희쪽에서 도와드릴 수가 없어요.

M: 이런... 그럼 전 어떻게 해야 하죠? 어디서 도움을 받을 수 있나요?

W: 만약 제가 학생이라면 어떻게 할지 말씀드릴게요. 저라면 룸메이트들이 잠을 때까지 도서관에 가서 공부하겠어요. 브론즈 도서관은 하루 24시간 열거든요. 아니면 공부에 도움이 되도록 스터디 그룹을 만들던가요.

M: 제 룸메이트들은 보통 밤새도록 게임을 하고 아침에 잠들긴 해요. 한번 고려해 봐야겠네요. 어쨌든 고맙습니다.

W: 천만에요. 그런데 룸메이트들은 어떻게 학점을 받는 건가요? 신기하군요.

❶ According to the conversation, what is the man's problem?

남자는 밤새 비디오 게임을 하고, 거절하는데도 불구하고 함께 하자고 설득하는 룸메이트들 때문에 고민하고 있다. 선택지 C와 D가 혼동될 수 있지만. 그의 궁극적인 문제는 비디오 게임을 하는 룸메이트들 때문에 공부에 집중할 수가 없는 것이므로, D가 정답으로 적절하다.

❷ What does the woman say about the man's problem?

여자는 남자의 문제가 개인적인 문제이므로 도와줄 수 없다고 한다. 따라서 정답은 선택지 C이다.

❸ Why does the woman mention the Bronz Library?

여자는 만약에 자신이 남학생의 입장에 있었다면 룸메이트들이 잠들 때까지 도서관에서 공부하겠다고 하며 24시간 문을 여는 도서관을 소개시켜 주었으므로 정답은 선택지 A이다.

1. A **2.** A, B **3.** B **4.** C **5.** B

M: Hi, can I help you?

W: Yes, hi... um, my laptop computer broke down, and I don't know how to fix it.

M: All right. Did you bring your computer along?

W: Sure, here you go.

M: Okay... first, could you explain the problems you're having with your computer?

W: Um, I think it started about a week ago... I was writing my term paper, and suddenly the power just went off. I thought it was because my laptop caught a virus or something, so I activated an anti-virus system, but it kept on turning off. I didn't even backup my term paper and I need to retrieve it from my laptop, but the computer keeps turning off every three minutes — it's extremely frustrating.

M: Well, it seems like your cooling fan's out of order. If the computer is overheated, it may severely damage the CPU and everything you have in the hard drive might just be erased.

W: Oh, are you serious? Do you think you can you fix it?

M: Well, we can fix desktop computers in no time, but when it comes to laptop computers, it takes some time.

W: How long?

M: About a month.

W: Oh, no, that long? I'm going to be out of town in two weeks!

M: All we can do is detect the problem of the machine. It takes time because we have to send it to the manufacturing company which will take several days, and usually manufacturing companies take their time in fixing their products. If you need it to be fixed faster, you may call the manufacturing company, ask them if they have customer service offices that fix laptops right away. I kind of doubt that they have these offices around here, though.

W: Well, do you have any other recommendations?

M: ❺ Um, if you want to use your laptop for the time being without fixing it, <u>you might want to put your laptop over this cooling pad when you use it.</u> It's gonna function as a small cooling fan, but it won't last that long. Another thing you might want to consider is to supply cool air to the hot components as directly as possible. Maybe turn an electric fan on while you're using the computer.

W: I'll try that.

M: I don't recommend you using your laptop for a long time without fixing your cooling fan, though. As soon as you get your data out of the laptop, turn it off and ask the manufacturing company to fix it, or bring it to us. We can ship the laptop to where you're staying after it's fixed.

M: 안녕하세요. 무엇을 도와드릴까요?

W: 예, 안녕하세요. 제 랩탑 컴퓨터가 고장났는데, 수리 방법을 몰라서요.

M: 알겠습니다. 컴퓨터는 가져오셨나요?

W: 네, 여기 있어요.

M: 네... 우선, 컴퓨터에 어떤 문제가 있는지 말씀해 주시겠어요?

W: 음, 한 일주일 전부터 문제가 생긴 것 같아요... 학기 보고서를 쓰는데 갑자기 전원이 꺼졌어요. 처음엔 바이러스 때문에 그런가 싶어서 백신 시스템을 실행시켰지만 계속 꺼지는 거예요. 학기 보고서를 저장도 안해서 랩탑에서 빼내서 옮겨야 되는데, 3분마다 꺼져요. 정말 짜증나요.

M: 음, 냉각기가 고장난 모양이군요. 컴퓨터가 과열되면 CPU를 심하게 훼손시키고 하드 드라이브 안에 있는 데이터가 전부 지워질 수도 있어요.

W: 정말요? 고칠 수 있으신가요?

M: 데스크탑은 금방 고치지만, 랩탑의 경우 시간이 좀 걸릴 거예요.

W: 얼마나 걸리나요?

M: 한 달 가량요.

W: 이런, 그렇게 오래요? 2주 후에 여행을 갈 건데요!

M: 저희가 할 수 있는 건 단지 기계의 문제를 진단하는 것 뿐이에요. 제조사에 제품을 보내야 하는데 그 기간이 며칠은 걸릴 것이고, 제조사는 대부분 고치는 데 여유를 두기 때문에 시일이 좀 걸릴 거예요. 좀 더 빨리 수리받고 싶다면, 제조사에 전화를 해서 랩탑을 바로 고칠 수 있는 고객 서비스 센터가 있는지 여쭤보세요. 하지만 이런 지점이 근처에 있을 것 같지는 않아요.

W: 그럼, 다른 대안은 없나요?

M: 일단 수리를 받지 않고 랩탑을 당분간 사용하고 싶으면, 랩탑을 사용할 때 이 냉각 패드 위에 대고 해 보세요. 이 냉각 패드가 작은 냉각기처럼 작용하겠지만 오래가진 않을 거예요. 또 한 가지 방법으로 뜨거운 부위에 최대한 찬 바람을 직접 보내는 거예요. 선풍기를 튼다던지 해서요.

W: 한 번 해볼게요.

M: 그래도 냉각기를 고치지 않고 장시간 랩탑을 사용하지는 마세요. 랩탑에서 데이터를 빼자 마자 전원을 끄고 제조사에 수리를 맡기거나 제게 가져오세요. 랩탑을 고친 후 계신 곳으로 배달해 드릴게요.

❶ What is the purpose of the conversation?

여자의 랩탑 컴퓨터가 고장이 나서 컴퓨터 수리업자에게 가져가서 문의하고 있으므로 정답은 선택지 A이다. 선택지 B는 이 대화와 관련이 없으며, 제조사에 랩탑 컴퓨터를 보내라고 권유하는 것이 대화의 목적은 아니므로 선택지 C 역시 오답이다. 여자는 컴퓨터가 오작동을 일으키는 이유를 처음에는 몰랐으므로 선택지 D 역시 올바른 답이 아니다.

❷ **Which of the following were mentioned as alternative recommendations for the woman to use the laptop?**

남자는 임시적으로 랩탑을 사용하기 위해 냉각 패드를 사용하거나, 직접 찬 바람을 쐬이는 방법을 제안했다.

❸ **How does the woman feel about the current situation with her computer?**

여자는 학기 보고서를 저장하지 않아서 랩탑 컴퓨터에서 빼야 하는데 컴퓨터가 계속 꺼지기 때문에 짜증난다고 말한다. 따라서 정답은 선택지 B이다.

❹ **According to the conversation, why does it take a long time to fix a laptop computer?**

랩탑을 고치는 경우 한 달 정도가 소요되는 이유는 제품을 보내는 기간이 며칠 걸리며 제조사가 제품을 고칠 때 대부분 여유를 두고 한다는 남자의 말에서 정답(선택지 C)을 알 수 있다.

❺ **Why does the man say this:**

"You might want to..."라는 표현은 무언가를 권유할 때 사용하는 표현이다. 남자는 컴퓨터를 고치지 않고 당분간 사용하려면 냉각 패드 위에 놓고 사용할 것을 권하고 있으므로 정답은 B이다.

Vocabulary Test

1. c	**2.** a	**3.** b
4. a	**5.** d	**6.** b
7. a	**8.** d	

3 Content

W: 안녕하세요. 어떻게 도와드릴까요?

M: 안녕하세요. 전에 이 체육관 회원이었는데, 회원권이 만기되었어요. 그래서 주차권을 환불하고 싶어서요.

W: 알겠습니다. 전에 갖고 다니시던 회원 카드와 주차권을 가져오셨나요?

M: 네, 여기 있습니다.

W: 네, 이 서류를 좀 작성해 주시겠어요?

M: 그러죠. 무슨 서류인가요?

W: 손님의 현재 주소와 낮에 연락 가능한 전화번호입니다. 환불 금액을 개인 수표로 보내드리기 위해서지요. 2, 3주 내에 우편으로 받으실 수 있습니다.

M: 아, 그렇군요. 그런데 저는 현금으로 바로 환불받을 수 있다고 생각했는데요.

W: 두 달 전에 정책이 변경되었거든요. 이제는 모든 환불건은 이렇게 처리됩니다.

Strategy Focus

1. D   **2.** D   **3.** C   **4.** C

1. D

M: Lois! Wait up!

W: Oh, hi, Josh! I haven't seen you for a while. Where have you been?

M: You know, my basketball team was on a tour game, so I had to miss a couple of weeks of class. So, how are you?

W: Fine, fine, everything's good. Oh, by the way, Professor Johnson gave us an assignment. You haven't heard about this, right?

M: Uh-oh, he did? I can't believe I missed it! What's the assignment?

W: Well, we went on a field trip last week to observe some of the oldest buildings in Philadelphia. Philly has many old-fashioned houses and buildings, you know. So, you're supposed to team up with another classmate, pick a house that represents one of the old styles we've learned so far, draw a rough sketch on it, and analyze why it represents that style. Got it?

M: Yeah, barely. But where do I get a partner?

W: Um, I think you should talk to Professor Johnson first. Maybe he knows another student without a partner. I'm sorry I already have a teammate.

M: That's okay. Maybe I'll send him an e-mail and

schedule an appointment or something. By the way, when's this project due?

W: Next week.

M: That's not that bad. If I hurry up, I think I can make it. Thanks for the tip, Lois. I owe you big this time.

W: No problem, Josh. Just a cup of coffee would do fine.

M: 로이스! 기다려!

W: 아, 안녕, 조쉬! 진짜 오랜만이네. 어디 갔다왔어?

M: 농구팀이 원정 경기를 다녀왔거든. 그래서 수업을 몇 주 빠졌어. 넌 잘 지내니?

W: 그럼, 잘 지내고 있지. 그나저나 존슨 교수님께서 과제를 내주셨어. 이 얘기 못 들었지?

M: 이런, 그랬어? 그걸 놓쳤다니! 과제가 뭔데?

W: 저번 주에 필라델피아의 가장 오래된 건물을 조사하기 위해서 현장 학습을 갔었거든. 너도 알다시피 필리에는 고전 양식의 집과 건물들이 많잖아. 그래서 다른 학우와 팀을 짜서 우리가 지금까지 배운 고전 양식을 대표하는 집을 골라서 더략적인 그림을 그리고, 그것이 왜 그 스타일을 대표하는지를 설명해야 해. 이해되니?

M: 응, 대충. 그럼 팀원을 어디서 구하지?

W: 음, 일단 존슨 교수님과 상의해 보는 게 좋을 것 같아. 팀이 없는 학생을 알고 계실지도 모르니까. 미안하지만 난 이미 팀원이 있어.

M: 괜찮아. 이메일을 보내서 약속을 잡아봐야겠다. 아, 그런데 이 프로젝트 기한은 언제까지야?

W: 다음 주야.

M: 나쁘진 않네. 서두르면 할 수 있을 것 같아. 알려줘서 고마워, 로이스. 큰 신세졌어.

W: 천만에, 조쉬. 커피 한 잔이면 돼.

2. D

M: Student Service Office. How can I help you?

W: Um, hi... my name is Joyce Williams. I'm a student at the School of Nursing, and um, I'm here to ask about my student I.D. Uh, I lost my I.D. yesterday so I went to the Franklin Building to get a new I.D., but they wouldn't let me in. So...

M: Well, you could have showed the security guard your driver's license. They can look your name up on the system and confirm.

W: The thing is, I lost my wallet itself so I lost every type of I.D. I have along with it.

M: I see. Um... well, you're gonna need a photo I.D. in order to prove that it is you... to, uh, get a new student I.D. Uh, do you happen to have a passport?

W: I do... but I have it back at home.

M: Well, when you come back here later, you can bring

it along.

W: No, no, I mean, back at home... my parents' home. Not where I live right now.

M: Oh, well... is your hometown far away from here?

W: Kind of. It's like at least two hours' flight.

M: Well, this is a difficult situation. We're not allowed to issue any I.D. unless we confirm the person with a photo I.D., you know.

W: Oh, wait a minute. I have a credit card back in my room. Is that gonna be okay?

M: Does it bear your photo?

W: Uh... I don't think so.

M: I'm sorry, but we can't take that. Do you have a debit card with your photo?

W: I lost that with my wallet.

M: Well, what I advise is that you call your parents to ship your passport through... uh, Fedex or Express Mail or something right away. As soon as you receive your passport, please bring it to us so that we could issue a new student I.D. for you.

W: Okay. Can I ask one more thing?

M: Sure, go ahead.

W: I think that's gonna take at least a couple of days, but I have classes tomorrow and the day after tomorrow. I'm supposed to show my student I.D. in order to enter the building... what should I do?

M: Well, in that case, you can always ask your professors to write you a note that states that you're in the class. As long as the note has the professor's signature on it, most security guards will allow you to enter the building.

W: Really? Thank you so much!

M: 학생 서비스실입니다. 무엇을 도와드릴까요?

W: 안녕하세요. 제 이름은 조이스 윌리엄스이고 간호대학 학생입니다. 학생증 때문에 왔는데요, 어제 학생증을 잃어버려서 프랭클린 빌딩에 새 학생증을 발급받으려고 갔는데 학생증이 없다고 건물에 못 들어가게 하더라고요. 그래서...

M: 음, 그런 경우에는 경비원에게 운전면허증을 보여주면 됐을 텐데요. 시스템에서 찾아보고 확인해 줄 수 있거든요.

W: 사실은 제가 지갑을 잃어버려서 학생증 말고도 가지고 있던 다른 신분증을 전부 잃어버렸어요.

M: 그렇군요. 음... 학생 본인이라는 걸 증명하기 위해선 사진이 붙은 신분증이 필요해요... 학생증을 새로 발급받으려면 말이죠. 혹시 여권은 갖고 있으신가요?

W: 네, 그런데 집에 있어요.

M: 그러면 나중에 다시 오실 때 가져오시면 되겠네요.

W: 아뇨, 그게 아니라, 집에 있다고요... 그러니까 부모님 댁에요. 지금 사는 곳

말고요.

M: 아... 고향이 여기서 먼가요?

W: 그런 편이에요. 비행기로 2시간 정도 걸리니까요.

M: 상황이 좀 어렵게 됐네요. 사진이 붙은 신분증으로 본인 확인을 하지 않으면 학생증을 만들어 드릴 수가 없거든요.

W: 아, 잠깐만요. 제 방에 신용카드가 있는데요, 그걸로는 안될까요?

M: 사진이 붙어 있나요?

W: 그런 것 같지는 않아요.

M: 그러면 죄송하지만 안 될 것 같네요. 사진이 붙은 현금카드는 없나요?

W: 그건 지갑 속에 있어서 잃어버렸어요.

M: 그럼 부모님께 연락을 해서 페덱스나 특급우편으로 여권을 바로 보내달라고 하세요. 여권을 받는대로 저희에게 오시면 새로 학생증을 발급해 드릴게요.

W: 네, 한 가지만 더 여쭤봐도 될까요?

M: 그럼요. 말씀하세요.

W: 여권이 오려면 적어도 며칠은 걸릴 텐데, 내일과 모레에 수업이 있거든요. 수업이 있는 건물에 들어가려면 학생증을 보여줘야 하는데, 어떻게 하죠?

M: 그런 경우에는 교수님께 부탁드려서 학생이 그 교수님의 수업을 듣는다는 확인서를 써달라고 하세요. 그 확인서에 교수님의 서명만 있다면 대부분의 경비원들이 건물로 들어가게 해줄 거예요.

W: 정말요? 감사합니다!

3. C

M: Um... Professor Higgins, may I come in? Is this a bad time?

W: Oh, Mr. Woods. No, not at all. Please, come in and have a seat.

M: Thank you.

W: Okay. So... I didn't see you participate in class a lot yesterday. What happened?

M: Well, ma'am, actually... that's why I'm here.

W: Hmm?

M: Actually, uh... the reading assignment that you gave us last week, ma'am. I couldn't get the book, so I didn't do it. So...

W: Oh, I see. Well, I'm not surprised at all that you couldn't get the book.

M: I mean, I did go to the school bookstore and the other bookstores nearby, but none of them had a copy! And, and... and I tried the school library, but all the copies were checked out.

W: Well, you don't have to give excuses, Mr. Woods. The university bookstore frustrates me all the time. They always bring in the required books late, and they don't bring in the exact number of the copies of the books. See, when I order 30 copies, they only bring in 20.

M: Why would they do that?

W: Well, obviously, they think that a lot of students end up dropping the class. What they don't know is that the student number might actually increase. That's what happens all the time. I don't understand — they're the university bookstore! Oh, well, anyways, Mr. Woods.

M: Yes, ma'am.

W: You could have asked your classmates to share the book, or at least tried the Interlibrary Loan if you couldn't find the book at the library.

M: I'm sorry, ma'am. I should have thought about that. I promise this will never happen again.

W: That's okay. But you know how important it is to actively participate in class, right?

M: Sure, ma'am.

W: That's good. Well, fortunately, I do have several copies of the book, so... here, let me lend you one. You can... either just keep it for the next couple of weeks or make a photocopy of it and return it to me. What would you like to do?

M: Um, I'd better make a photocopy and return it to you in class next week. I need to write notes in the book and highlight important parts when I read.

M: 히긴스 교수님, 들어가도 되나요? 시간 괜찮으세요?

W: 아, 우즈 군. 괜찮아요. 들어와서 앉아요.

M: 감사합니다.

W: 어제 수업에서 참여를 잘 안하던데, 무슨 일이 있나요?

M: 교수님, 실은 그것 때문에 왔어요.

W: 흠?

M: 어, 실은... 지난 주에 교수님께서 내 주신 읽기 과제 말인데요. 책을 구할 수가 없어서 과제를 못했거든요. 그래서...

W: 아, 그렇군요. 책을 못 구했다는 게 전혀 놀랍지는 않네요.

M: 학교 서점이랑 가까운 다른 서점들에 갔는데도 그 책이 한 권도 없었어요! 그리고 학교 도서관에도 가봤는데 모두 대출중이었고요.

W: 변명하지 않아도 돼요, 우즈 군. 학교 서점 때문에 나도 자주 짜증이 난답니다. 필요한 책은 항상 늦고, 주문한 부수대로 책을 구비하지도 않아요. 30부를 주문하면 한 20부 정도만 가져오거든요.

M: 왜 그런 건가요?

W: 많은 학생들이 수업을 도중에 그만둔다고 생각하는 것 같아요. 그런데 서점에서 모르는 건, 학생 수가 오히려 증가할 수도 있다는 거지요. 항상 그렇게 되거든요. 정말 이해가 안돼요. 학교 서점인데 말이죠. 어쨌든, 우즈 군.

M: 네, 교수님.

W: 같은 수업을 듣는 친구한테 책을 빌려달라고 물어보거나 도서관에서 책을 찾을 수 없다면 도서관 상호 대출 제도를 통해 알아봤어야죠.

M: 죄송합니다, 교수님. 그 생각을 해야 했었는데. 다시는 이런 일이 없도록 하겠습니다.

W: 괜찮아요. 하지만 수업에 활발하게 참여하는 게 얼마나 중요한지 알죠?

M: 네, 그럼요.

W: 좋아요. 다행히도 나한테 그 책이 몇 권 있어요. 자, 한 권 빌려줄게요. 다음 몇 주 간 가지고 있거나 복사한 후 나에게 돌려줘도 돼요. 어떻게 하는 게 편하겠어요?

M: 복사를 하고 다음 주 수업 시간에 돌려드리는 게 나을 것 같아요. 저는 책을 읽을 때 필기를 하고 중요한 부분에 표기를 해야 하거든요.

4. C

M: Hey, Jackie. How come you didn't show up at the lounge?

W: What are you talking about?

M: We were supposed to meet at the student lounge at 4 today, remember?

W: What?

M: You know, to discuss our topic for our presentation next month.

W: Oh, my gosh! Michael, I am so sorry! I totally forgot!

M: Well, you stood me up for half an hour, so you're gonna have to buy lunch tomorrow. Ha-ha! By the way, what got into you? You usually don't forget what you're supposed to do.

W: I don't know, I guess my mind's been elsewhere these days.

M: What's the matter, are you sick?

W: No. Um.. I just can't seem to concentrate in class.

M: Huh?

W: Well, let me give you an example. I had a class this morning, like, 10 am at Bringham Hall, right?

M: Uh-huh.

W: We were supposed to read like five articles, summarize each of them shortly, and then compare the different viewpoints of the authors. Well, I did read all the articles very thoroughly and I wrote down all the important points on a piece of paper. But when I was in a group discussion, my brain just shut down. I just didn't understand what they were talking about the whole two hours. This has been happening for the past week. Is there something wrong with me?

M: Well, Jackie... I know you're a good reader and you're smart, so this doesn't make any sense. Um... do you get enough sleep before you go to class?

W: Well... I've been working on my resume these days, so... last night, at least, I didn't get to have a good night's sleep.

M: Ah-ha! That's the reason. Sleep deprivation!

W: Are you serious?

M: Jackie, I'm not a psychiatrist, but this I know for sure — when you don't get enough sleep, your brain functions very slowly. Isn't this too obvious?

W: Hey, nobody's perfect, all right? Well... come to think of it, I have been stressed out a lot these days because of my resume and job applications.

M: Man, just take it easy. If you need any help, just ask me, all right?

W: Thanks a lot, Michael. I really appreciate it.

M: 이봐, 재키. 오늘 왜 휴게실에 안왔어?

W: 무슨 소리야?

M: 오늘 4시에 학생 휴게실에서 만나기로 했었잖아. 기억 안 나?

W: 뭐라고?

M: 다음달 우리 프레젠테이션의 주제에 대해 얘기하기로 했었잖아.

W: 오, 이런! 마이클, 너무 미안해! 까맣게 잊고 있었어!

M: 30분 동안 바람 맞혔으니까 내일 네가 점심 사. 하하! 그나저나, 무슨 일 있어? 넌 해야 할 일은 잘 잊어버리지 않잖아.

W: 모르겠어. 요즘 머리가 복잡해.

M: 무슨 일이야. 어디 아프니?

W: 아니. 그냥 요즘에 수업 시간에 집중이 잘 안돼.

M: 응?

W: 예를 들어서, 오늘 아침에 브링엄 홀에서 수업이 있었거든, 10시 쯤에.

M: 응. 그런데?

W: 기사를 다섯 개 읽고 각각 짧게 요약한 후 저자들의 서로 다른 관점을 비교해야 했어. 그래서 다섯 개를 전부 자세하게 읽고 종이에 중요한 요점도 다 적어놨는데 그룹 토론 시간에 머릿속이 새하얗게 되면서 아무 생각도 안 나는 거야. 2시간 내내 다른 애들이 무슨 얘기를 하는지 알아들을 수가 없었어. 지난주 내내 이랬어. 혹시 나한테 무슨 문제가 있는 걸까?

M: 글쎄, 재키... 넌 평소에 책도 많이 읽고 똑똑한 애라서 잘 이해가 안 되는데. 수업에 들어가기 전에 잠은 충분히 자고 가니?

W: 글쎄... 요즘 이력서를 작성하고 있거든. 그래서 적어도 어젯밤에는 그다지 잘 못잤어.

M: 아하! 그게 이유구나. 수면부족!

W: 진심이야?

M: 재키, 난 정신과 의사는 아니지만, 이건 확실히 알아 – 잠을 충분히 자지 않으면 뇌 기능이 저하돼. 당연한거 아니니?

W: 이봐, 누구도 완벽하진 않잖아. 흠... 생각해 보니까 요즘 이력서와 취직 문제 때문에 스트레스를 많이 받은 것 같기도 해.

M: 마음을 편하게 가져. 도움이 필요하면 언제든지 말하고, 알았지?

W: 정말 고마워. 마이클.

Exercise

P.1	**1.** 참조	**2.** B	**3.** B	**4.** C
P.2	**1.** D	**2.** C	**3.** B	
P.3	**1.** A	**2.** A, B	**3.** C	
P.4	**1.** C	**2.** A	**3.** B	
P.5	**1.** C	**2.** B	**3.** A	

Passage 1

1. 참조　**2.** B　**3.** B　**4.** C

	Yes	No
Take a tour around the studios	✔	
Meet the residents		✔
Meet the housing manager	✔	
Sign the contract	✔	
Pay three months' rent in advance		✔

W: Hi, I don't know if I'm in the right place, but… um, ❹ I'm planning to move out of the dorm and move to an on-campus studio. Uh, could you help me find one?

M: Well, you did come to the right place. We're also in charge of on-campus housings. Well, let me look up on the system first… Ah, yes, we do have several studios left. Two of them are on 21st and Locust Street, and five of them are on 47th and Gerard Street. Which one would you like?

W: Um… is that all you have? I mean, isn't any studio available on 34th street?

M: I'm afraid all the on-campus housings are on 21st and 47th streets.

W: Well… if it has to be one of those two streets, I prefer 21st and Locust Street. My school building is on 36th street, you know. Um, then, how much is the rent?

M: All studios are $500 a month.

W: Five hundred dollars… that's a little bit steep.

M: It might look as if it's too steep for students, but the buildings are relatively new compared to the undergrad dorm buildings, and they're safe. Oh, and all maintenance fees are included, like electricity, water, TV cable, and the Internet.

W: Well, I do like the fact that the buildings are quite new and safe. Um, what do I have to do to sign a contract?

M: Before you sign a contract, we recommend

you to take a tour around the rooms and choose which one you would like to rent. If you'd like, we'll arrange a tour later this afternoon or some time this week.

W: That'd be great. I'm free all afternoon today.

M: All right. After the tour, you'll read a leasing contract with the housing manager and then sign the contract. You're gonna have to tell us the specific date you'll be moving in so we can arrange carts and your new keys.

W: How do I pay the rent?

M: When you sign your contract, you must pay two months' rent in advance, so that'd be a $1000. One month's rent will be held as security money, which means that you will start paying your rent 30 days after you sign your contract. Do you follow me?

W: Yes, I got it. Um, do I get to receive my security money back when I move out, though?

M: Sure. When you decide to move out, you must inform us 30 days in advance so that we can arrange another resident in time. If you fail to do so, 50% of your security money will be reduced.

W: All right. Um… do I have to pay the rent with check, or can I use my credit card?

M: We recommend you to write a check to us.

W: That sounds okay. What time do I come back today, then?

W: 안녕하세요. 제가 제대로 찾아온 건지 모르겠는데요… 기숙사에서 나와서 캠퍼스 내 원룸으로 이사 하려고 하거든요. 방을 찾는 것을 도와주실 수 있나요?

M: 네, 잘 찾아오셨네요. 저희는 캠퍼스 내 주거도 담당하거든요. 우선 컴퓨터에서 좀 찾아볼게요… 아, 네, 지금 남은 원룸이 몇 개 있네요. 21번가와 로커스트가에 두 개가 있고 47번가와 제라드가에 다섯 개가 있어요. 어느 쪽으로 하시겠어요?

W: 어… 그게 전부인가요? 그러니까, 34번가에는 남은 방이 없나요?

M: 죄송하지만 모든 캠퍼스 내 원룸들은 21번가와 47번가에만 있답니다.

W: 그 두 곳에서만 선택해야 한다면, 21번가와 로커스트가가 낫겠네요. 학교 건물이 36번가에 있거든요. 음, 그러면, 임대료는 얼마인가요?

M: 원룸은 전부 한 달에 500달러입니다.

W: 500달러라… 좀 비싸네요.

M: 학생들에게는 비싸 보일 수 있지만, 학부생 기숙사와 비교했을 때 상대적으로 신축 건물이고 안전해요. 그리고 전기, 수도, TV 케이블, 그리고 인터넷 등의 관리비가 모두 포함되어 있죠.

W: 신축 건물이고 안전하다는 점이 마음에 들기는 하네요. 계약서를 작성하려면 어떻게 해야 하죠?

M: 계약서를 작성하기 전에 어느 방을 임대하고 싶은지 먼저 둘러보시는 게 어떠세요. 원하시면 오늘 오후나 이번 주 내로 둘러보실 수 있도록 약속을 잡을게요.

W: 네, 좋아요. 오늘은 오후 내내 시간이 있어요.

M: 좋습니다. 둘러보신 후에 주거 매니저와 함께 임대 계약서를 읽어보시고 서명하실 거예요. 이사에 필요한 카트와 새 열쇠를 준비할 수 있도록 정확한 이사 날짜를 정해주셔야 해요.

W: 임대료는 어떻게 내나요?

M: 계약서를 작성하면 두 달치 임대료를 선불로 내셔야 해요. 그러니까 1000달러가 되겠죠. 그 중에서 한 달치 임대료는 보증금이니까 계약서 작성 후 30일 이후부터 임대료를 내시면 돼요. 이해되시죠?

W: 네, 알겠습니다. 음, 그런데 이사를 나갈 때 계약금은 돌려받나요?

M: 그럼요. 이사를 하기로 결정하시면 30일 이전에 저희에게 알려주셔야 해요. 그래야 시간에 맞게 저희가 다른 임대인을 찾으니까요. 만약에 그렇지 않으면 계약금의 50%가 깎일 거예요.

W: 알겠습니다. 음… 임대료는 수표로 내야 되나요, 아니면 그냥 신용카드로 내도 되나요?

M: 수표를 저희 앞으로 적어주시는 게 나아요.

W: 괜찮네요. 그러면 오늘 몇 시에 올까요?

❶ **The student and the university housing manager discuss signing the contract for an on-campus housing. Indicate whether each phrase below is a step in the process.**

계약을 하기 전에 먼저 원하는 방을 둘러본 후 주거 매니저와 임대 계약서를 읽어보고 서명을 하면 된다. 주거자들을 만나보는 것은 언급되지 않았으며, 임대료는 두 달치만 선불로 내면 된다.

❷ **What will the woman probably do next?**

"If you'd like, we'll arrange a tour later this afternoon or some time this week."이라는 매니저의 말에 여학생은 "That'd be great. I'm free all afternoon today."라고 한다. 또한 여학생은 마지막에 "What time do I come back today, then?"이라고 물어보고 있으므로, 지금 이 자리를 떠났다가 오후에 시간에 맞춰 돌아올 것임을 알 수 있다. 따라서 정답은 B이다.

❸ **Why does the woman go to see the university housing manager?**

여자는 현재 살고 있는 기숙사에서 나와 캠퍼스 내의 원룸으로 이사가고 싶어한다. 따라서 정답은 B이다.

❹ **Why does the woman say this:**

21번가와 47번가에 원룸이 있다는 매니저의 말에 여자는 34번가에는 원룸이 없느냐며 묻는다. 따라서 정답은 C이다.

Passage 2

1. D **2.** C **3.** B

W: Hi, can I ask you something real quick?

M: Yeah, sure. What can I do for you?

W: Well, I was working out on the second floor and saw the poster about some marathon event next month, and I just thought I should drop by and get some more information...

M: Oh, you mean, the Spring Marathon at Stanton River?

W: Yes, that's right, at Stanton River.

M: So, what is it that you're curious about?

W: Um, first of all, I think the poster said that you could participate if you're a member of the gym.

M: That's correct. Are you interested in running at the marathon?

W: Well... I am, but I know a friend who would like to run the marathon as well, but he's not a member of this gym, so...

M: Oh, I see. In that case, your friend should pay the participation fee which is $35. It's free for all the gym members to run in the marathon as long as they register beforehand.

W: Oh, really? Well, that's a relief... um, how can I register for the event, then?

M: You can just log on to our website and click "Spring Marathon Event" at the top right. You need your gym membership card so that you can put in your membership number.

W: Okay. Um, what about my friend? Does he have to register on-line as well?

M: No, your friend has to come over to the information desk with a photo I.D.

W: All right. Uh... I heard that the Spring Marathon has two courses... is that right, two courses?

M: Yes, a 5-mile-course and a 10-mile-course. You can choose whichever you like, according to your running abilities.

W: Okay, thanks. Um, is there anything else I should be aware of?

M: Well, you might want to wear something light of course, but you should also bring a warm jacket, since it's still gonna be chilly, especially if you run alongside the river. Oh, and you don't have to bring water since there will be plenty of bottled waters available on the spot.

W: Thank you so much.

M: No problem. Good luck with the marathon.

W: 안녕하세요, 잠깐 뭐 좀 여쭤봐도 될까요?

M: 네, 그럼요, 뭘 도와드릴까요?

W: 2층에서 운동을 하다가 다음달에 열리는 마라톤 대회에 관한 포스터를 봤거든요. 그래서 정보를 좀 얻을까 해서 왔어요...

M: 아, 스탠튼 강에서 열리는 봄철 마라톤 대회 말씀이신가요?

W: 네, 맞아요. 스탠튼 강이요.

M: 네, 무엇이 궁금하신가요?

W: 우선 포스터에는 체육관 회원이면 참가할 수 있다고 되어 있던데요.

M: 맞아요. 마라톤에 참여하실 생각이 있으신가요?

W: 네, 그런데 마라톤에서 뛰고 싶어하는 친구가 있는데 그 친구는 여기 회원이 아니라서요...

M: 아, 그렇군요. 그런 경우에는 친구분께서 참가비용 35달러를 내시면 돼요. 체육관 회원들은 미리 등록만 하면 무료로 참여할 수 있고요.

W: 아, 정말요? 다행이네요... 그러면 대회에는 어떻게 등록하죠?

M: 저희 인터넷 웹사이트에 로그인 하시고 상단 오른쪽에 있는 "봄철 마라톤 대회"를 클릭하시면 돼요. 회원 번호를 입력해야 하니까 체육관 회원카드를 준비하시고요.

W: 알겠습니다. 제 친구는요? 친구도 온라인으로 등록해야 되나요?

M: 아니요, 친구분께서는 사진이 부착된 신분증을 가지고 직접 안내 데스크로 오셔야 해요.

W: 네, 알겠습니다. 어... 봄철 마라톤에 두 가지 코스가 있다고 들었는데 그게 맞나요?

M: 네, 5마일 코스와 10마일 코스가 있어요. 본인 능력에 따라 원하시는 대로 고르시면 돼요.

W: 네, 고맙습니다. 또 알아두어야 하는 것은 없나요?

M: 글쎄요, 물론 가볍게 입으셔야겠지만, 그맘때도 계속 날씨가 쌀쌀할 것 같고 특히 강변을 따라 뛰려면 더 추울 테니 따뜻한 재킷을 가져오시는 게 좋을 거예요. 아, 그리고 현장에 물이 많을 테니 물은 따로 가져 오지 않으셔도 돼요.

W: 고맙습니다.

M: 뭘요. 마라톤 잘 뛰세요.

❶ Why does the woman want to talk with the man?

여자는 2층에서 운동을 하다가 다음달에 있을 마라톤 대회에 대한 포스터를 봤다면서 그 대회에 대한 정보를 얻으려고 왔다고 말한다. 따라서 정답은 D이다. 체육관의 회원권을 받으려고 온 것이 아니기 때문에 A는 오답이며, 마라톤 대회에 대한 정보를 얻으려고 온 것이지 처음부터 대회에 등록하기 위해서 온 것이 아니므로 B 또한 틀렸다. C는 이 지문의 내용과는 관련이 없다.

❷ Why does the woman mention her friend?

여학생은 일단 자신은 마라톤에 참가할 것이며, 체육관의 회원이

아닌 다른 친구도 참가할 수 있는지를 묻고 있으므로 정답은 C이다. 나머지 선택지들은 본문의 내용과는 관련이 없다.

❸ What can be inferred about the courses at the Spring Marathon?

5마일과 10마일의 두 가지 코스가 제공되며 본인의 능력에 따라 선택하면 된다고 했으므로 정답은 B이다. 나머지 선택지의 내용은 본문에서 나온 바가 없다.

(Passage 3)

1. A   **2.** A, B   **3.** C

M: Hi, I'd like to check out these books, please.

W: Okay, can I see your student I.D.?

M: Sure, here you go.

W: All right... thank you. Is that all?

M: Actually, there was another book I was looking for but I couldn't find it. Could you check whether you have a copy or not?

W: Sure. What's the name of the author?

M: John Flavell and Scott Miller.

W: Flavell and Miller... okay. Um, is this it, *Handbook of Child Psychology*?

M: No, it's *Cognitive Development*.

W: Oh, here we go. Um, it looks like we have seven copies of this book, and they're all checked out right now. Sorry.

M: Aww, really? When will it come in?

W: Um, one should be coming in next Monday.

M: Next Monday, that's too far away. Well, then, can you check these books? I'm supposed to write a book report on either one of these four books.

W: Of course. Let me see the authors... okay. Uh, you can find copies of *Developmental Psychology* and *Human Development* on the fourth floor, but every copy of *Infant Behavior and Development* is checked out.

M: Well, at least I can find those two. Thanks a lot.

W: Sure.

M: 안녕하세요, 이 책들을 빌리려고 하는데요.

W: 네, 학생증을 보여주시겠어요?

M: 네, 여기 있습니다.

W: 좋아요... 고맙습니다. 이게 다인가요?

M: 실은 찾던 책이 한 권 있는데 찾을 수가 없었어요. 그 책이 있는지 좀 봐주시겠어요?

W: 그러죠. 작가 이름이 뭔가요?

M: John Flavell하고 Scott Miller요.

W: Flavell과 Miller라... 이건가요, *Handbook of Child Psychology*?

M: 아뇨, *Cognitive Development*이에요.

W: 아, 여기 있네요. 이 책이 7권이 있는데, 모두 대출중이네요. 죄송합니다.

M: 아, 그래요? 언제쯤 들어오나요?

W: 다음 주 월요일에 한 권이 들어올 거예요.

M: 다음 주 월요일이면 너무 늦네요... 그럼 이 책들도 알아봐 주시겠어요? 이 4권 중 하나로 보고서를 써야 하거든요.

W: 물론이죠. 작가를 좀 볼게요... *Developmental Psychology*하고 *Human Development*는 4층에 있지만, *Infant Behavior and Development*는 모두 대출중이에요.

M: 어쨌든 적어도 그 두 권은 찾아서 다행이네요. 고맙습니다.

W: 천만에요.

❶ What does the woman say about the book, *Cognitive Development*?

도서관에 이 책이 7부가 있지만, 현재 모두 대출중이라고 했으므로 정답은 A이다. B는 "이 도서관에는 이 책이 없지만 다른 도서관에는 있을지도 모른다"는 내용이므로 지문의 내용과 다르며, C 역시 "예전에는 도서관에 있었지만 모두 처분해 버렸다"는 내용으로 지문과 다른 내용이다. *Cognitive Development*는 7부가 있지만 모두 대출중이라고 했으므로 D는 오답이다.

❷ According to the woman, which books are currently available at the library?

"Uh, you can find copies of *Developmental Psychology* and *Human Development* on the fourth floor"라는 여자의 말에서 정답을 알 수 있다.

❸ What will the man probably do next?

"Well, at least I can find those two books. Thanks a lot."이라는 학생의 말에서, 현재 4층에 있는 책 두 권 (*Developmental Psychology*와 *Human Development*) 을 찾으러 갈 것임을 알 수 있다. 따라서 정답은 C이다.

Passage 4

1. C **2.** A **3.** B

M: Hello, how can I help you?

W: Hi, um, I'm trying to find a plane ticket to Boston. Could you check if there are any seats available, please?

M: Sure. Um, are you flying alone or do you have another company?

W: I'm gonna travel alone.

M: All right. Uh, roundtrip?

W: Yes.

M: Okay. Uh, when would you want to travel, miss?

W: Two weeks from now — uh, that's Friday, April 6th, and I'll be coming back on Saturday, April 14th.

M: And that's coach, right?

W: Yeah.

M: All right, hold on a minute, please. Oh, I'm sorry, but all the tickets are sold out.

W: Oh, my God — are you serious? Oh no... um, then, can you check other dates, please? Like, uh... uh... Thursday or Saturday?

M: Sure... Uh-oh, seems like all seats are booked. I'm sorry.

W: Oh, gosh... I don't believe this...

M: Actually, Miss, it'd be better if you purchased the ticket at least two months before Spring Break actually starts. Everyone wants to get out of town during Spring Break.

W: Oh... I know, this was clearly my mistake. I keep procrastinating until the last minute. What should I do?

M: Well, actually... they do have some business class seats left... would you like to take it?

W: Really? I don't think I have another choice... how much is it?

M: It's $950.

W: 950 dollars? The coach seats are only $200 for roundtrip! I can't believe this!

M: Well, if you don't want to take the business class, I'm afraid you're gonna have to drive or take the train which will probably cost you $400 anyways.

W: But I don't have a car and the train's gonna take forever.

M: Well, it usually takes five to six hours.

W: Oh, my God... and it takes less than an hour to fly to Boston... Um, I think I'm gonna have to think about this a little more.

M: Well, do as you please, Miss, but they only have a few seats left for the business class, and you never know whether they'll be available tomorrow.

W: Well, you know what — I think I'll have to call my parents, so... let me just talk to my father first. Um... can I use your phone, please?

M: Sure, go ahead.

W: Thanks.

M: 안녕하세요. 어떻게 도와드릴까요?

W: 안녕하세요. 보스턴행 비행기표를 구하고 있어요. 남은 좌석이 있는지 봐주시겠어요?

M: 네, 알겠습니다. 혼자 가시나요, 아니면 동행이 있으신가요?

W: 혼자 가요.

M: 알겠습니다. 왕복이고요?

W: 네.

M: 네. 언제 가실 예정이신가요?

W: 2주 후에요. 그러니까, 4월 6일 금요일에 떠나서 4월 14일, 그 다음주 토요일에 돌아오는 걸로 해주세요.

M: 일반석 맞으시죠?

W: 네.

M: 잠시만 기다려 주세요... 아, 죄송하지만 표가 매진되었네요.

W: 이런, 정말요? 어, 그러면 다른 날짜를 좀 알아봐 주시겠어요? 음, 목요일이나 토요일로요.

M: 네 그러죠. 이런, 모든 좌석이 마감된 것 같습니다. 죄송합니다.

W: 이런... 믿을 수가 없군요...

M: 실은 봄 방학이 시작되기 적어도 두 달 전에는 비행기표를 구입하시는 게 좋습니다. 봄 방학에는 모두들 떠나고 싶어하니까요.

W: 알아요... 제가 정말 실수했네요. 마지막까지 늑장을 부렸거든요. 이제 어떻게 하면 될까요?

M: 사실 비즈니스석이 남아 있긴 한데요... 이 자리라도 하시겠어요?

W: 그래요? 별다른 방도가 없네요... 얼마인가요?

M: 950달러입니다.

W: 950달러요? 일반석은 왕복에 200달러 밖에 안하는데요! 믿을 수가 없군요!

M: 비즈니스석을 구매하지 않으시면 직접 운전하거나 기차를 타는 방법밖에 없는데, 이것도 어차피 400달러는 들 거예요.

W: 하지만 전 차도 없고 기차를 타면 너무 오래 걸리잖아요.

M: 음, 보통 대여섯 시간 걸리기는 하죠.

W: 이런 세상에... 비행기를 타고 보스턴에 가면 한 시간도 안걸리는데... 어, 조금 더 생각해 봐야겠어요.

M: 원하시는 대로 하세요. 하지만 비즈니스석도 얼마 안 남아서 내일까지 남아있을지는 확실하지 않습니다.

W: 음, 부모님께 전화를 해 봐야겠어요. 먼저 아버지께 전화를 해 볼게요. 전화 좀 써도 될까요?

M: 그럼요. 쓰세요.

W: 고맙습니다.

❶ According to the conversation, why was the woman late in purchasing her plane ticket?

"I know, this was clearly my mistake. I keep procrastinating until the last minute."이라는 여자의 말에서 답을 찾을 수 있다.

❷ What does the woman say about taking the train to Boston?

"But I don't have a car and the train's gonna take forever."라는 여자의 말에서 정답을 알 수 있다.

❸ What will the woman probably do next in order to get to Boston?

학생은 일단 차가 없으므로 운전해서 갈 수가 없으며, 비행기를 타면 한 시간 이내에 갈 수 있는 보스턴에 대여섯 시간이 걸리는 기차를 타고 갈 생각이 없다. 따라서 먼저 아버지에게 전화를 해서 상의를 한 다음 결정할 것임을 알 수 있다. 그러므로 가장 좋은 정답은 B이다. A와 D는 운전하는 것과 기차를 타는 것이 포함됐으므로 지워야 하며 다른 날짜의 일반석은 모두 마감됐으므로 C 역시 틀린 답이다.

(Passage 5)

1. C   **2.** B   **3.** A

M: Dr. Weinstein, is this a bad time for you?

W: Oh, hello, Lenny. It's okay, come in and have a seat. So... what brings you to my office today?

M: Well, I wanted to talk to you about my time management.

W: Your time management? What do you mean?

M: ❶ Well, I'm having a real hard time following my studies right now. I can't seem to find time to study, and... I don't know, I'm really distracted.

W: What's the matter? Is something wrong?

M: Well... actually, it's my part-time job at the newsstand.

W: Your part-time job? I didn't know you had a part-time job.

M: Yes, um... I used to work three hours a day three days a week, and that didn't actually hurt my study time that much. But the owner opened up a restaurant somewhere in downtown, and he asked me if I could work another two, three hours every day of the week. He said I would get a pay raise, so I said okay... I kind of regret it, though.

W: All right, now I understand. Working six hours a day and five days a week as a full-time student — that's not an easy thing to do.

M: Exactly. I'm practically a full-time worker there now. I know if I quit the job, I'm gonna have more time to focus on my studies, but I really depend on this job because of the good pay. What I do now is... I get off at 6 pm, grab a quick dinner and start studying. But that still gives me only 3 or 4 hours of study every day. I don't know what to do — I really need help with my time management.

W: Well, Lenny... You know your field of study requires an enormous amount of effort — you have tons of papers and books to read and essays to write as well. I can help you with your time management on the premise that you're a fully devoted student, but if you work 30 hours a week at the newsstand, you're gonna have to deal with that on your own. What I recommend you to do is that you cut back the times you work there. I know it's going to hurt your financial status for now, but I'll talk with the dean to see if there's any scholarship available for you.

M: Are you serious, Dr. Weinstein? Oh, thank you so much!

M: 와인스틴 박사님, 시간 괜찮으세요?

W: 아, 안녕, 레니. 괜찮아요, 와서 앉아요. 연구실에는 무슨 일로 왔나요?

M: 제 시간 관리 때문에 상담을 좀 드릴까 해서요.

W: 시간 관리요? 무슨 말이에요?

M: 요즘 수업을 따라가기가 정말 힘들어요. 공부할 시간도 없고... 모르겠어요. 집중을 못하겠어요.

W: 무슨 일이에요? 무슨 문제라도 있는 건가요?

M: 사실은 신문 가판대에서 아르바이트 하는 것 때문이에요.

W: 아르바이트? 아르바이트를 하는 줄은 몰랐네요.

M: 네, 예전에는 하루에 3시간씩 일주일에 사흘만 일했고, 그건 공부 시간을 그다지 방해하지 않았거든요. 그런데 사장님께서 시내 어딘가에 레스토랑을 개업하셔서 주중 매일 두어 시간씩 더 일해줄 수 있냐고 물어보셨어요. 급여도 인상해 준다고 해서 알았다고 했는데... 좀 후회하고 있어요.

W: 알았어요. 이제 이해가 되는군요. 정규 학생이 하루에 6시간씩 일주일에 닷새를 일한다는 건 쉬운 일이 아니에요.

M: 맞아요. 그곳에서 거의 전업으로 일하고 있는 셈이에요. 일을 그만두면 공부에 시간을 더 많이 할애할 수 있다는 건 알지만, 급여가 좋아서 이 일에 많이 의존하고 있거든요. 요즘에는 오후 6시에 일을 끝낸 후 저녁을 간단히 먹고 공부를 하기 시작해요. 하지만 그렇게 해도 하루에 서너 시간 밖에 공부를 못해요. 어떻게 해야 할지 모르겠어요. 시간 관리에 대한 도움이 필요해요.

W: 글쎄요. 레니... 지금 전공하는 것이 얼마나 많은 노력을 필요로 하는지는 알고 있겠죠 – 논문과 책을 많이 읽어야 하고 써야 할 에세이도 많아요. 공부에만 집중한다는 전제 하에서는 시간 관리에 대해 조언해 줄 수 있지만, 신문 가판대에서 일주일에 30시간씩 일한다면 그건 본인이 해결해야 할 문제예요. 내가 해줄 수 있는 조언은 거기서 일하는 시간을 줄이라는 거예요. 지금 당장은 금전적인 문제가 생기겠지만, 학장님과 얘기해서 받을 수 있는 장학금이 있는지 알아볼게요.

M: 정말이세요. 와인스틴 박사님? 정말 감사합니다!

❶ How does the man feel when he says this:

학생은 시간이 없어서 공부하기가 힘들다며 힘든 심정을 토로한다. 지도 교수의 말을 이해하지 못하는 것이 아니며 교수의 무관심에 기분이 상한 것도 아니다. 교수가 학생에게 열심히 노력하라고 격려하고 있는 것 또한 아니므로 정답은 C이다.

❷ What can be inferred about the man's current part-time job?

학생은 현재 아르바이트 때문에 공부할 시간이 없지만, 높은 임금 때문에 쉽게 그만둘 수가 없다고 한다. 따라서 학생의 일은 높은 임금을 준다는 것을 알 수 있다. 선택지 A와 C는 본문의 내용과 상반되는 내용이며, 웨이터로 일하는 게 아니라 신문 가판대에서 일하는 시간을 늘린 것이기 때문에 D는 틀린 내용이다.

❸ Why does the woman mention talking to the dean?

지도 교수는 학생에게 공부가 우선이므로 아르바이트 시간을 줄이라고 조언한다. 그리고 학장과 얘기해서 학생에게 줄 수 있는 장학금이 있는지 알아보겠다고 한다. 따라서 정답은 A이다.

Vocabulary Test

1. d	**2.** c	**3.** a
4. c	**5.** a	**6.** d
7. b	**8.** b	

4 Stance

Sample

W: 짐, 오늘 왜 미팅에 나오지 않았나요?

M: 음... 러셀 교수님. 무슨 말씀이신가요... 무슨 미팅이요?

W: IHT 미팅 있는 걸 깜빡했나요?

M: IHT 미팅이요?

W: 지미, 인터내셔널 하우스 튜터 미팅 말이에요. 수업이 어떻게 진행되고 있는지 이야기하기로 했잖아요. 기억나요?

M: 오, 이런... 제가 대체 어떻게 된 걸까요. 믿을 수가 없네요!

W: 이제 기억나요? 오지 않아서 걱정했거든요.

M: 네... 오, 정말 죄송합니다. 러셀 교수님. 일정을 적어두지 않으면 늘 이래요. 자주 깜빡하거든요.

Strategy Focus

1. C   **2.** A   **3.** B   **4.** C

1. C

W: Hi, Dr. Urban, can I come in?

M: Oh, yes, Laura... I was expecting you. So... you told me last time that you wanted to go to medical school, right?

W: That's right.

M: I wanted to recommend some pre-med classes that you might want to take next semester.

W: Ugh, do you mean there are classes that I need to take even before applying to medical school? I'm still just a freshman though!

M: Well, it's kind of like a prerequisite, because most medical schools prefer biology or chemistry majors. It's gonna be a tremendous help for your studies at medical school.

W: I understand... um, then, what courses should I take next semester?

M: Well, fortunately, you took some biology courses this semester, so... why don't you take some chemistry courses next semester? For example, General Chemistry I and II, and Organic Chemistry.

W: That sounds interesting but very difficult.

M: Well, as long as you don't idle away and do what you're supposed to do on time, you'll be fine. By the way, in order to go to a med school, you'd want to keep your GPA over 3.8.

W: 3.8? It means no B's or C's allowed! I've never been a straight A student before!

W: 안녕하세요, 어번 박사님. 들어가도 될까요?

M: 아, 네. 로라... 기다리고 있었어요. 지난번에 의학 대학원에 가고 싶다고 했죠?

W: 네.

M: 다음 학기에 들을 만한 예비 의대 관련 수업을 추천해 주려고 해요.

W: 의학 대학원에 지원하기도 전에 들어야 할 수업이 있다는 말씀이신가요? 전 아직 1학년인데요!

M: 필수 과목이나 다름없어요. 왜냐하면 대부분의 의학 대학원은 생물학이나 화학 전공자들을 선호하거든요. 나중에 의학 대학원에서 공부할 때 도움이 많이 될 거예요.

W: 알겠습니다... 그러면 다음 학기에 어떤 수업을 들으면 되나요?

M: 이번 학기에 다행히 생물학 수업을 몇 개 들었으니까 다음 학기에는 화학 수업을 듣는 게 어때요? 예를 들어 일반 화학 I, II와 유기화학 같은 것요.

W: 흥미로울 것 같긴 한데 굉장히 어려울 것 같아요.

M: 게으름을 피우지 않고 해야 할 일만 제 때에 한다면 괜찮을 거예요. 그나저나, 의학 대학원에 가려면 학점을 3.8 이상은 유지해야 해요.

W: 3.8이요? B나 C는 받아서는 안된다는 말이잖아요! 전 이제까지 전과목 A를 받아본 적이 한 번도 없어요!

2. A

W: Did you decide which class you should take next semester, Josh?

M: Not yet. I was thinking about going to dental school, so I had to take pre-dental courses, like biochemistry and biology this semester. The thing is... I don't think I'm good at any of those anymore.

W: Aww, come on, Josh. You've been doing so well, and you've been taking pre-dental courses for four semesters. You don't wanna give up now. What's the matter?

M: It's really embarrassing, but.... I got a C in a couple of my classes.

W: You did? I always saw you studying until late at night at the library, so I never thought you'd get a C. What happened?

M: Well, I'm having a hard time with my neurophysiology classes. I do my readings and study all night for exams, but somehow I can't follow the concepts well.

W: Well, that does sound like a pain in the neck. But, Josh, you've been trying so hard to get into dental school and if you switch your major, it's gonna take extra time and money. If I were you, I'd still try for dental school and get some help for the neurophysiology class.

M: Get some help? What do you mean?

W: Why don't you talk to your academic advisor and ask her if she can find a private tutor for you? Or you can visit the Student Academic Center — they have a student tutor system. Most of the tutors are graduate students, so I think you can get a lot of help from them.

M: Are you serious? Geez, thanks, Melinda. How come I never thought of that before?

W: 다음 학기에 뭘 들을지 생각해 봤니, 조쉬?

M: 아직, 치대를 갈 생각이어서 이번 학기에는 생화학이나 생물학 같은 치대 코스를 들어야 했어. 문제는… 그런 과목에 소질이 없는 것 같다는 거야.

W: 이런, 조쉬. 지금껏 잘해왔고 벌써 4학기 동안 예비 치대 과정을 들어왔잖아. 지금와서 포기하면 안돼. 문제가 뭔데 그래?

M: 좀 창피한데… 몇 과목에서 C를 받았어.

W: 그랬어? 항상 밤 늦게까지 도서관에서 공부하는 걸 봐서 네가 C를 받을 거라곤 생각도 안했는데. 어떻게 된 거야?

M: 신경 생리학 수업 때문에 고생하고 있어. 책도 다 읽고, 밤새 시험 공부도 하는데 도대체 개념을 이해하지 못하겠단 말야.

W: 정말 고생스럽겠다. 하지만 조쉬. 치대에 가려고 그렇게 열심히 준비했는데 이제 와서 전공을 바꾼다면 시간과 돈이 더 들 거야. 내가 너라면 계속 치대 준비를 하면서 신경 생리학 수업에 대한 도움을 받겠어.

M: 도움을 받는다고? 무슨 말이야?

W: 지도 교수님이랑 상담을 하고 개인 교사를 찾아달라고 하지 그래? 아니면 학생 센터에 가봐. 학생 개인교사 시스템이 있거든. 개인 교사들 대부분이 대학원생이니까 도움이 많이 될 거야.

M: 정말이야? 정말 고마워, 멜린다. 이제껏 왜 그 생각을 못했을까?

3. B

W: Hi, un… I'd like to ask you about something.

M: Sure, how can I be of help?

W: Um, my parking permit is going to be expired next week. I was wondering if I could park my car here for a week or two without having to renew the parking permit.

M: Well, you know that we don't allow one-day parking here, don't you? Only monthly parkings are allowed.

W: I know, but, the thing is… I'm going to be moving into the undergrad dormitory soon and I won't need my car anymore. I'm selling my car in a couple of weeks. I need a place to park until I move into the dorm and sell my car. I only need to use the parking lot about a week or two more… I know it's a lot to ask, but…

M: Ohhhhh…. Well, all right, let me see what I can do for you. Um, have you tried the street meter parking?

W: I have, but you know there's practically no space during the weekdays. If you find a spot available after 8 o'clock in the morning, that's a miracle.

M: What about the street parking on 10th street, then?

W: Oh, you mean the residence area?

M: Yeah.

W: I did try to park there before, but they said that only residents of that area could park their cars. My car was almost towed last time I parked there.

M: Oh, well… you know I shouldn't be doing this, but… let me talk to the manager first, all right? Can you wait here for a second? I'll be right back.

W: Thank you so much!

W: 안녕하세요, 뭣 좀 여쭤보려고 하는데요.

M: 네, 뭘 도와드릴까요?

W: 제 주차권이 다음 주에 만료되는데요, 주차권을 갱신하지 않고 여기에 1, 2주 정도 주차해도 될지 궁금해서요.

M: 저희는 일일 주차는 허용하지 않는다는 거 아시죠? 월별 주차만 됩니다.

W: 네, 알아요, 하지만 전 얼마 안 있으면 학생 기숙사로 들어가게 되고 차가 더이상 필요없게 되거든요. 몇 주 내로 차를 팔 거예요. 기숙사에 들어가고 차를 팔기 전까지 주차할 곳이 필요해요. 주차장을 1, 2주만 더 사용하면 되거든요… 좀 과한 부탁인건 알지만요.

M: 이런… 알겠어요. 방법을 찾아봅시다. 도로 미터제 주차는 생각해 보셨나요?

W: 네, 하지만 주중에 자리가 거의 없다시피 하잖아요. 아침 8시 이후에 주차 자리를 찾는 게 기적일 정도로요.

M: 10번가에 있는 길거리 주차는 어때요?

W: 아, 주거 지역 말씀이신가요?

M: 네.

W: 예전에 한번 거기에 주차하려고 했었는데 그 지역 주민들만 주차할 수 있다고 했어요. 지난 번에 그곳에 주차했을때 견인 당할 뻔 했다니까요.

M: 이런… 이래서는 안되지만… 일단 매니저한테 얘기를 해 볼게요. 여기서 잠깐만 기다리실래요? 금방 올게요.

W: 정말 감사합니다!

4. C

W: So… as I was saying, Ken, bring me your written proposal on the topic next week.

M: Okay, ma'am. Um, by the way, can I ask you one more question, Professor McCaine?

W: Sure, what is it?

M: Um, this has nothing to do with the proposal, but… **I heard that the Engineering building will turn off the heater beginning at 5 pm from next month. Is that true?**

W: Well, unfortunately, yes.

M: Well… because, my study group members and I study at this building all the time, sometimes until the building closes at 10 o'clock. It's still winter and it gets especially cold after sunset. I don't think it's going to get warmer in two or three weeks.

W: Well, Ken, I understand what you're saying, but the school has been concerned about the theft and vandalism going on in the building recently. It's for the students' sake, you know.

M: I understand, but I don't know where to do the study group meeting anymore. I've been to the library but they're short of study rooms... and the reservation is full. I can't find a spot until after April.

W: Well, if you really need a place to study, why don't you use the Graduate Student Center?

M: The Graduate Student Center? But isn't that place just for graduate students?

W: Well, technically, it is — but they also allow undergrad students and faculty who have the proper school ID to study there. They have plenty of study rooms but not many people know about this place. I'm sure you'll be able to find a spot there.

M: Oh, really? I have never heard of this before. Uh, where can I find this place?

W: It's near Beckham Hall. It's a relatively small building, but they're always open until 10 pm, and I believe they run the heating system until they close at night.

M: Gee, thank you, Professor McCaine. Now, I think I should get going... I'll see you in class next week.

W: 그래서, 켄, 내가 말한대로 다음 주에 그 주제에 대한 계획서를 작성해서 가져오세요.

M: 알겠습니다. 저, 그런데 한가지 더 여쭤봐도 될까요, 맥케인 교수님?

W: 물론이죠. 뭔데요?

M: 이건 계획서와는 관련 없는 건데요... 엔지니어링 건물이 다음달부터 오후 5시부터 난방을 끈다고 하던데, 사실인가요?

W: 아쉽게도 그래요.

M: 왜냐면요... 저와 스터디 그룹 멤버들이 항상 이 건물에서 공부하거든요. 가끔은 10시에 건물이 닫을 때까지 있을 때도 있어요. 아직 겨울이고 해가 지면 특히 더 추워져요. 2, 3주안에 날씨가 풀릴 것 같지는 않은데요.

W: 켄, 무슨 말을 하는 건지는 이해하지만, 건물 내에서 최근 일어나고 있는 도난 사건과 물건 파괴 행위 때문에 학교에서 골머리를 앓고 있어요. 학생들을 위한 방침이라고 생각하세요.

M: 이해는 하지만, 이제 어디에서 스터디 그룹 미팅을 해야 할지 모르겠어요. 도서관에 가봤지만 스터디룸도 부족하고 예약도 꽉 차 있거든요. 4월 이후까지는 자리가 없대요.

W: 공부할 곳이 정말로 필요하다면, 대학원생 센터에 가 보지 그래요?

M: 대학원생 센터요? 하지만 거긴 대학원생 전용 아닌가요?

W: 이론적으로는 그렇지만 학생증만 있으면 학부생도 들어갈 수 있고 신분증이 있으면 교수진도 거기서 공부할 수 있어요. 거기에는 스터디룸이 많지만 알고 있는 사람들이 많지 않더라구요. 그곳이라면 공부할 장소는 분명 찾을 수 있을 거예요.

M: 정말요? 금시초문인데요. 거기가 어딘가요?

W: 베크먼 홀 근처에 있어요. 비교적 작은 건물이긴 하지만 항상 저녁 10시까지 열고 밤에 닫기 전까지 난방을 하는 걸로 알고 있어요.

M: 고맙습니다. 맥케인 교수님. 전 이제 가봐야겠어요. 다음 주 수업 시간에 뵙겠습니다.

Exercise

P.1	1. C	2. D	3. C		
P.2	1. A	2. D	3. C		
P.3	1. A	2. B	3. C		
P.4	1. D	2. C	3. A		
P.5	1. A	2. C	3. A	4. C	5. D

Passage 1

1. C   **2.** D   **3.** C

M: Hello, what can I do for you, miss?

W: Um, hi... uh, I was wondering about your car lease program.

M: All right, would you like to have a seat?

W: Thank you.

M: ❶ Okay. Um, first of all, which leasing program are you interested in?

W: Excuse me? Which program? Do you have, like, multiple leasing programs here?

M: Of course. We have two short-term programs, which is three months and six months respectively, and two long-term programs, each one year and three years.

W: Oh, um... you know, I only need the car for the next semester, so... I guess, the six-month program.

M: All right. Well, for the six-month leasing program, we have five different cars available.

W: Oh, I thought I can choose whichever car I like.

M: No, not really. That's for the long-term leasing program.

W: Oh, I see...

M: So, what are you planning to use the car for — commute, leisure, or everyday use? The car depends on your main use.

W: Um, well, I need the car for my internship for the next semester — I get to work as a student teacher at a school in Hollyfield, so, I will be mostly commuting.

M: All right. Then... your choice is narrowed down to two conpact cars. Here's the pamphlet... which one would you like? Both cars have about the same mileage and are in good condition.

W: Well, I like this silver car. I'll go with this one.

M: Excellent. Now, about the mileage... um, we have two different mileage programs as well — 6,000 miles and 12,000 miles. The one with the 12,000 miles is a bit more expensive, though. Which one would you like?

W: Oh, geez... Um, you know... the school is, like, 30 miles away from my place, but I won't be using the car on weekends or on holidays. Since I'm not planning a long trip for the next six months, I'll go with the 6,000 miles.

M: Okay, Miss. Can I see your driver's license, please?

W: Sure, here you go.

M: Thank you. Um, your lease is $350 a month plus the short-term insurance.

W: Insurance? Uh, could you take out the insurance, please? Because I'm already on the school insurance policy.

M: Actually, insurance is mandatory if you want to lease the car. It's the law. And I don't think your school insurance applies to car insurance.

W: Oh.... Well, well then... okay.

M: Excellent. Now, uh, read this contract here and fill out the form while I make a copy of your driver's license.

M: 안녕하세요, 손님. 뭘 도와드릴까요?

W: 안녕하세요. 어, 차량 대여 프로그램에 관심이 있는데요.

M: 알겠습―다. 앉으시겠어요?

W: 고맙습니다.

M: 좋습니다. 우선 어떤 대여 프로그램에 관심이 있으신가요?

W: 네? 어떤 프로그램이요? 대여 프로그램이 여러 개인가요?

M: 물론이지요. 3개월짜리와 6개월짜리 단기 프로그램이 있고 1년짜리와 3년짜리 장기 대여 프로그램이 있답니다.

W: 아... 다음 학기에만 차를 사용하면 되니까 6개월짜리로 할게요.

M: 알겠습―다. 6개월 프로그램으로는 다섯 대의 차량이 대여 가능합니다.

W: 아, 제가 원하는 차를 고를 수 있는 줄 알았는데요.

M: 아닙니다. 그건 장기 대여인 경우에만 가능합니다.

W: 그렇군요...

M: 그럼, 차를 어떤 용도로 주로 사용하실 건가요 – 출퇴근, 레저, 혹은 일상 생활용 중에서요? 주된 용도에 따라 차가 결정됩니다.

W: 음, 다음 학기 인턴십 때문에 차가 필요하거든요. 홀리필드에 있는 학교에서 교생 실습을 할거라서요. 그러니까 주로 출퇴근용이겠네요.

M: 좋습니다. 그러면 차량 선택이 소형차 두 대로 압축되네요. 여기 팸플릿이 있는데, 어떤 것이 마음에 드세요? 두 대 모두 마일리지가 비슷하고 상태도 좋습니다.

W: 이 은색 차가 좋은데요. 이걸로 할게요.

M: 좋습니다. 자, 이제 마일리지를 선택하셔야 하는데요. 저희는 마일리지 프로그램이 2개 있거든요. 6천 마일과 만2천 마일 중에 고르세요. 하지만 만2천 마일짜리가 좀 더 비쌉니다. 어느 걸로 하시겠어요?

W: 이런... 제가 일할 학교는 집에서 약 30마일 정도 떨어져 있어요. 하지만 주말이나 휴일에 차를 사용할 것 같지는 않아요. 다음 6개월 동안 장거리 여행 계획이 없으니까 6천 마일로 할게요.

M: 알겠습니다. 운전면허증을 보여 주시겠어요?

W: 네, 여기 있습니다.

M: 고맙습니다. 대여비는 한 달에 350달러이고 단기 보험금이 추가됩니다.

W: 보험이요? 그 보험은 빼 주시겠어요? 학교 보험에 이미 가입되어 있거든요.

M: 실은 차를 대여하려면 보험은 필수입니다. 법이거든요. 그리고 차량 보험에는 학교 보험이 적용이 안될 거에요.

W: 아... 그렇다면 그렇게 해 주세요.

M: 좋습니다. 자, 그럼 운전면허증을 복사하는 동안 이 계약서를 읽어 보시고 서류를 작성해 주세요.

❶ Why does the woman say this:

어떤 대여 프로그램에 관심이 있냐고 묻는 남자에게 여자는 놀란 듯 대여 프로그램이 한 개가 아닌 여러 개가 있느냐며 확인한다. "Excuse me?"라고 했다고 무조건 못 들었으니 다시 말해달라는 것이 아니기 때문에 선택지 A는 틀린 선택이며, 화가 난 것 또한 아니므로 B도 맞는 선택이 아니다. 본인에게 가장 잘 맞는 프로그램이 어떤 것인지 물어보는 것 역시 아니기 때문에 D도 아니다. 따라서 가장 좋은 선택은 C이다.

❷ What can be said about the woman?

여자는 앞으로 교생 실습을 대비해서 차를 대여하려고 한다. 아직 일을 하고 있는 것은 아니므로 선택지 A는 정답이 아니며, 주말이나 휴일에 차를 이용하지도 않고 장거리 여행 계획이 별로 없으므로 B 또한 틀린 답이다. 또한, 여자가 일을 하게 될 학교는 30마일이 떨어져 있는 것이지 30분 거리에 있는 것이 아니므로 C도 답이 아니다.

❸ How does the woman feel about the short-term insurance?

"Uh, could you take out the insurance, please? Because I'm already on the school insurance policy."라는 여자의 말에서 정답을 알 수 있다.

1. A　　**2.** D　　**3.** C

M: Hi, is this the Student Employment Center?

W: Yes, can I help you with anything?

M: Yes, uh.... I'm looking for a part-time job that I can start, like, immediately.

W: Well, what kind of job are you looking for, on-campus or off-campus?

M: Well, anything, actually, as long as I can start working as soon as possible.

W: Wow, you must be really desperate there.

M: Yeah, kind of. My budget for the rest of the semester has already hit the bottom, you know.

W: Well, that's what happens to many students. Let's see... well, it seems like there's an opening for a cashier at Burger Place just outside the campus, but the pay is pretty low — 5 dollars an hour.

M: Well, I was hoping for something like 7 or 8 bucks an hour.

W: All right... let me look up on the system a little bit more... Uh, Coffee House in Levine Hall is looking for an experienced coffee brewer. Do you have any background in coffee brewing?

M: I'm afraid not...

W: That's all right. Um... okay, you might be interested in this... are you interested in housing manager?

M: Housing manager?

W: Yeah. There's an opening for a housing manager at the college dormitory.

M: Um, what do you do as a manager there?

W: Well, you basically sit in front of the desk at the building entrance, take care of spare keys, sign up guests and stuff. But the thing is...

M: What is it?

W: Well, the shift is at night, so... you're gonna have to work from 11 pm to about 5 in the morning. The pay is pretty good, though — they pay you double the normal shift, so the pay would be somewhere between $16 and $20 an hour.

M: Wow... that is somewhat tempting.

W: Yeah, and if you think about it, there aren't many people coming into the building or going out of the building in the middle of the night, so you pretty much have the early morning time all to yourself.

M: ❷ Well, I don't know if I can stay up until morning since I'm a morning person and I always go to sleep around 10 at night, but... <u>I can't really be picky about my job right now.</u>

M: 안녕하세요, 여기가 학생 취업 센터인가요?

W: 네, 무엇을 도와드릴까요?

M: 네, 곧바로 시작할 수 있는 아르바이트를 찾고 있어요.

W: 어떤 일을 찾고 계신가요? 캠퍼스 내? 캠퍼스 외?

M: 사실 아무거나 괜찮아요, 일을 곧바로만 시작할 수 있다면요.

W: 와, 많이 급하신가 보네요.

M: 네, 그런 편이에요. 이번 학기 예산이 벌써 바닥났거든요.

W: 많은 학생들이 겪는 일이죠. 자, 그럼 한번 볼까요. 캠퍼스 바로 밖에 있는 버거 플레이스에서 계산원을 구하고 있는데, 임금이 좀 적네요... 시간당 5달러예요.

M: 저는 시간당 7, 8달러 정도로 생각하고 있었는데요.

W: 알겠습니다. 시스템에서 좀 더 찾아보죠... 르바인 홀의 커피하우스에서 경험 있는 커피 제조자를 찾고 있어요. 혹시 커피를 제조해 본 경험이 있으신가요?

M: 아니요...

W: 괜찮아요. 어... 아, 이건 관심이 있으실 것 같은데... 혹시 주거 매니저에는 관심 있으세요?

M: 주거 매니저요?

W: 네, 대학생 기숙사의 주거 매니저 자리가 있어요.

M: 거기서 매니저로 무슨 일을 하나요?

W: 기본적으로 건물 입구의 책상에 앉아서 여분의 열쇠를 관리하고 방명록을 작성하고 그래요. 하지만 문제는...

M: 뭔데요?

W: 근무 시간대가 밤이에요. 그러니까... 밤 11시에서 새벽 5시까지 일해야 해요. 그래도 급여 수준은 꽤 괜찮은 편이에요. 일반 시간대보다 두 배를 주니까 급여는 시간당 16달러에서 20달러 사이가 될 거예요.

M: 와, 구미가 당기긴 하네요.

W: 네, 그리고 생각해 보면, 한밤중에 건물 내외로 출입하는 사람이 많지 않으니까 새벽 시간대 대부분은 거의 개인 시간이나 다름없어요.

M: 제가 아침형 인간이라 항상 밤 10시면 자기 때문에 아침까지 깨어 있을 수 있을지 잘 모르겠지만... 그래도 지금은 일자리 찾는데 이것 저것 따질 때가 아닌 것 같네요.

❶ How does the man feel about the job opening at Burger Place?

버거 플레이스 아르바이트 자리의 시간당 수당이 5달러 밖에 안된다고 하자 남자는 그보다는 좀 더 높은 수준의 급여를 원한다고 한다. 따라서 정답은 A이다.

❷ How does the man feel when he says this:

남자는 근무 시간대 때문에 기숙사의 주거 매니저 일을 마음에 들어하지는 않지만 시급 때문에 구미가 당긴다며, 지금은 까다롭게 이것저것 가릴 때가 아니라고 한다. 선택지 A와 B는 대화의 내용과 다른 선택이며, 자신이 직업을 선택하는 것에 대해 언제나 까다로웠다고 느끼는 것도 아니므로 C도 정답이 아니다.

❸ What kind of part-time job will the man probably get?

남자는 내키지는 않지만 기숙사의 주거 매니저 일을 하게 될 것이다. 커피 제조 경험이 없으므로 커피하우스에서 일을 하지는 않을 것이며, 시급이 너무 적으므로 버거 플레이스에서 일하지도 않을 것이다. 또한 D는 지문에서 언급된 바가 없다.

Passage 3

1. A   **2.** B   **3.** C

W: Hi, Professor Ross. I heard that you wanted to talk to me.

M: ❷ Oh, hello, Phoebe. Yes, please come in.

W: Thank you. Um... is it because of my thesis proposal? Was there any mistake or anything?

M: Mistake? Oh, no, no... it's not that, don't worry... actually, I thought your proposal was exceptional.

W: Really? Do you really think so?

M: Yes. I believe your proposal was about a research on high school dropouts, right?

W: Yes, sir. I'm supposed to interview and study 50 high school dropouts, analyze the reason why they made that decision, and design a prevention program that might be effective for some of the school districts in the city.

M: ❸ Well, I'm glad to inform you that your research may receive the dean's support.

W: Um... I... get to receive the dean's support? I'm... I'm sorry, but can you explain it a little bit more, please?

M: What I'm saying is that you can apply for the dean's financial support for your research. You know, in order to write your thesis, you might have to meet and interview those dropouts, transcribe the voice-recorded interview, and so on. You can request all your financial expenses to the dean and he'll support your research. Am I making myself clear?

W: Wow... are you serious, Professor? This is unbelievable! Thank you so much!

M: Well, I'm glad that one of my finest students

is being recognized by the dean. So, in order to request the support, calculate your budget first. I have your proposal here, so I'll submit it to the dean along with my recommendation letter.

W: Thank you so much!

M: Oh, and, uh... one more thing... if you want to research more on your subject, you can go visit Brown University's main library. I'll write you a note so that you can enter the building.

W: 안녕하세요, 로스 교수님. 절 보자고 하셨다고요.

M: 아, 안녕, 피비. 들어와요.

W: 고맙습니다. 어... 제 논문 제안서 때문에 부르신 건가요? 제가 무슨 실수라도 했나요?

M: 실수? 아, 아니에요, 그건 아니니까 걱정하지 말아요... 실은 피비의 제안서가 매우 훌륭하다고 생각했어요.

W: 정말요? 진짜 그렇게 생각하세요?

M: 그래요. 고등학교 중퇴자들을 조사하는 것에 대한 제안서였죠?

W: 네, 고등학교 중퇴자들 50명을 인터뷰하고 조사하고요, 왜 중퇴를 결정하게 됐는지를 분석하고 시내 교구들에 도움이 될 수 있는 중퇴 방지 프로그램을 고안해 보려고 해요.

M: 피비의 연구가 학장의 지원을 받게 됐다는 소식을 전해주게 돼서 기쁘군요.

W: 어... 제가 학장의 지원을 받게 된다고요? 죄송하지만, 조금 더 자세히 설명해 주시면 안될까요?

M: 무슨 말이냐면 피비의 연구가 학장님으로부터 재정적 지원을 받게 됐다는 거예요. 논문을 쓰기 위해서는 중퇴자들을 만나서 인터뷰하고, 녹음된 인터뷰 내용을 나중에 받아 적고 해야 하겠죠. 필요한 모든 비용을 학장님에게 요구할 수 있고 연구를 학장님이 지원해 주시는 거예요. 이해되나요?

W: 와... 정말이세요, 교수님? 믿을 수가 없어요! 정말 고맙습니다!

M: 똑똑한 제자들 중 한 명이 학장님에게 인정을 받게 되어서 기뻐요. 자, 그러면 지원을 요청하기 위해서 먼저 예산을 산출해 보세요. 피비의 제안서는 내가 가지고 있으니 추천서와 함께 학장님께 제출하도록 할게요.

W: 정말 감사합니다!

M: 아, 그리고 한가지만 더... 주제에 대해 더 찾아보고 싶으면 브라운 대학 중앙 도서관에 가 보세요. 건물에 들어갈 수 있도록 편지를 써줄게요.

❶ What is the purpose of the conversation?

교수는 학생의 연구가 학장의 지원을 받게 되었다는 소식을 전해주기 위해 불렀으므로 정답은 A이다.

❷ Why does the woman say this:

학생은 교수가 자신을 부른 것이 논문 제안서에 문제가 있기 때문이라고 생각했지만, 논문 제안서가 마음에 들었다는 교수의 말에 놀라며 안심한다. 교수의 말에 도전하려는 것이 아니며, 교수가 방금 무슨 말을 했는지 듣지 못해 다시 말해달라고 하는 것도 아니다. 또한 본인의 논문 제안서에 있는 실수들을 덮으려고 하는 것도 아니기 때문에 가장 좋은 답은 B이다.

❸ How does the woman feel when she says this:

다시 들려주는 부분의 바로 뒤에 나오는 "I... I'm sorry, but can you explain it a little bit more, please?"라는 여자의 말에서 정답을 알 수 있다. 즉, 여학생은 교수가 하는 말을 잘 이해하지 못했기 때문에 다시 한번 설명해 달라고 한다.

(Passage 4)

1. D　　**2.** C　　**3.** A

M: Hi, um, I'd like to ask you something about these books.

W: Yes, what is it?

M: Well, I checked out these books 3 months ago, and I believe that they're allowed to be checked out for 6 months. But, uh... I got an e-mail from the library yesterday that I should return these books. So, I just wanted to know what happened...

W: Oh, actually, you're right — you can keep them for 6 months, but, uh... this professor at the School of Design needs those books urgently for his research.

M: Oh, so that's what happened. But I think it's unfair for me to return the books just because the professor needs them. I mean, I need these books, too, you know.

W: I understand. Well, the professor told us that he's gonna be using the books for just 2 weeks, so if you returned them now, you can check them out again later.

M: Really? But what if other people check them out before I do?

W: Don't worry — we'll make sure you're the one who checks them out.

M: Oh, geez... I need to refer to some parts of these books for my thesis. I can't afford two weeks without them.

W: ❸ If that's the case, then... uh, well, I'm not supposed to do this, but I'll let you make a photocopy of the chapters you need. Would that be okay?

M: Well... yeah, but...

W: Alright. Then, now, keep in mind that if you don't turn those books in by 7 o'clock today, you'll be fined a late fee of $2.50 per day.

M: What? You're joking! Man, that's too unfair!

W: I'm sorry, but that's the rule. Uh, if you'd like to

check those books out two weeks from now, you can fill out this form and come back in two weeks.

M: 안녕하세요. 이 책들에 대해서 좀 여쭤볼 게 있는데요.

W: 네, 뭔데요?

M: 3달 전에 이 책들을 빌렸어요. 6개월 동안 빌릴 수 있는 걸로 알고 있는데요. 어제 도서관에서 이메일을 받았는데 책들을 반납하라고 하더라고요. 그래서 어떻게 된 건지 알아보려고요.

W: 아, 실은 학생이 맞아요. 6개월 동안 가지고 있어도 되는 건데, 디자인 대학원의 교수님 한 분이 연구 때문에 그 책들을 급하게 필요로 하시거든요.

M: 아, 그런 거였군요. 하지만 단지 교수님께서 필요로 한다고 해서 책을 반납하는 건 불공평한 것 같아요. 저도 그 책이 필요하거든요.

W: 이해해요. 교수님께서는 한 1주 정도만 그 책들이 필요하다고 하셨어요. 그러니까 지금 책을 반납하시면 나중에 또 빌릴 수 있게 해 드릴게요.

M: 정말요? 하지만 제가 다시 빌려가기 전에 다른 사람이 빌려가면 어쩌죠?

W: 걱정 마세요. 학생이 빌려갈 수 있게 조치를 취할게요.

M: 이런... 저는 논문 때문에 이 책들을 참조해야 되거든요. 책이 없이 2주나 있을 수는 없을 것 같아요.

W: 음, 그렇다면... 어... 원래 이렇게 하면 안되지만, 책에서 필요한 부분을 복사할 수 있게 해 드릴게요. 그러면 될까요?

M: 글쎄요... 네. 하지만...

W: 좋아요. 그럼 오늘 저녁 7시까지 반납하지 않으시면 하루에 연체대금을 2달러 50센트씩 내셔야 한다는 걸 유의하세요.

M: 뭐라고요? 말도 안돼요! 너무 불공평하잖아요!

W: 죄송하지만 이게 방침이라서요. 지금부터 2주 후에 이 책들을 다시 대출하고 싶으시면 이 서류를 작성하시고 2주 후에 오세요.

❶ Why does the man want to talk with the woman?

학생은 어제 도서관으로부터 받은 이메일의 내용을 확인하기 위해 찾아왔다고 말하고 있다.

❷ Why does the man need to return the books earlier than the original due date?

도서관 사서는 학생이 빌린 책을 디자인 대학원의 교수가 급하게 필요로 하기 때문에 반납해야 한다고 한다. 따라서 정답은 C이다.

❸ How does the man feel when he says this:

필요한 부분을 복사하도록 해 주겠다는 사서의 제안을 마지못해 받아들이고 있다. 학생의 상황과 말투로 미루어 보아 정답은 A임을 알 수 있다.

1. A　　**2.** C　　**3.** A　　**4.** C　　**5.** D

M: Professor Manning, may I come in?

W: Ah, Mr. Gilbert. I was waiting for you. Come in and have a seat.

M: Yes, ma'am.

W: All right. Um... the reason I wanted to talk to you was because of your midterm paper.

M: My midterm paper, ma'am?

W: Yes. Obviously, you didn't understand the guideline of writing the paper.

M: Um... I... I don't understand. Did I do anything wrong?

W: Well... let's put it this way: Your paper is... well, not complete. But I guess you didn't know that, did you?

M: No, ma'am. ❷ Um... could you... could you explain what kind of mistakes I made? I mean, why is my paper incomplete? I thought I had to analyze and write a 3-page report on one of the articles on English teaching methods.

W: That is true; but I believe I handed out a model review in class. If you took a look at that model paper, you would have had the idea as to how to write your article review.

M: Oh, I think I was absent when you gave out the handout. Um, I got permission from the TA to be excused from the class, like, 3 weeks ago when I caught a bad flu.

W: ❺ Hmm... Yes, I remember when you were sick. You came to the class early before I was there and talked to Marianne, right? She should have given you the handout when you talked to her that day. She's usually good at those things... I don't know what got into her.

M: I... obviously didn't know that there was gonna be a handout that day, so...

W: All right. As long as you didn't know the exact format of the paper... Um, so, let me go through the paper with you. It's gonna take a while since we have to go over all 15 sections. Um, do you have to be somewhere now, or...?

M: Oh, I'm free for 2 hours, ma'am. I have a class at 4 o'clock today.

W: That's great. So... first, the citation part... the part where you should cite the article that you

analyzed, you did it right according to the APA format. So I gave you a point for that.

M: Okay.

M: 매닝 교수님, 들어가도 되나요?

W: 아, 길버트 군, 기다리고 있었어요. 들어와서 앉아요.

M: 네.

W: 좋아요... 오늘 보자고 한 건 길버트 군의 중간고사 레포트 때문이에요.

M: 제 중간고사 레포트요?

W: 그래요. 보니까 레포트를 쓰는 가이드라인을 잘 이해하지 못한 것 같더군요.

M: 어... 무슨 말씀이신지 잘 모르겠는데요. 제가 뭘 잘못했나요?

W: 이렇게 표현하는 게 좋겠네요 – 길버트 군의 레포트는 미완성이에요. 잘 몰랐나 보군요?

M: 네, 몰랐어요. 어떤 실수를 했는지 말씀해 주시겠어요? 그러니까, 제 레포트가 왜 미완성인가요? 영어 교수법에 대한 논설을 분석한 후에 3페이지짜리 레포트를 써야 하는 줄 알았는데요.

W: 맞아요. 하지만 수업 시간에 모델 레포트를 나눠줬던 것으로 기억하고 있는데요. 그 모델 레포트를 봤다면 논설 분석을 어떻게 썼어야 했는지 감을 잡을 수 있었을 거예요.

M: 아, 그 유인물을 나눠주셨을 때 결석했던 것 같아요. 3주 전 쯤에 독감에 걸렸을 때 조교한테서 수업에서 빠져도 된다는 허락을 받았거든요.

W: 흠... 네, 아팠던 것이 기억나는군요. 내가 수업에 들어가기 전에 미리 와서 메리앤하고 얘기했었죠? 그날 메리앤하고 얘기했을 때, 유인물을 줬어야 했는데. 메리앤은 평소에 이런 일을 잘 챙기던데 그날은 어떻게 된 건지 모르겠군요.

M: 저는 그날 유인물이 있을 줄 전혀 모르고 있었어요.

W: 좋아요. 레포트의 정확한 형식을 몰랐다니 어쩔 수 없군요... 자, 그럼 레포트를 같이 봅시다. 15개 섹션을 모두 훑어야 하기 때문에 시간이 좀 걸릴 텐데. 지금 시간이 괜찮은가요?

M: 아, 2시간 동안은 괜찮습니다. 오늘은 4시에 수업이 있거든요.

W: 잘됐네요. 자, 그럼 우선 인용 부분을 보죠. 본인이 분석한 논술을 인용하는 부분은 APA 형식에 따라 잘 썼기 때문에 1점을 줬어요.

M: 알겠습니다.

❶ **Why does the student go to see his professor?**

학생의 중간고사 레포트 때문에 교수가 할 말이 있어서 부른 것이므로 선택지 A가 정답이 된다.

❷ **How does the student feel when he says this:**

학생은 레포트의 요구 사항을 충족시켰다고 생각하기 때문에 자신의 레포트가 미완성이라는 교수의 말을 이해하지 못한다. 따라서 자신의 레포트가 미완성이라는 말에 당황스러워하며 교수에게 그 이유를 묻는다. 가장 좋은 답은 선택지 C이다.

❸ According to the conversation, why did the student miss receiving the model review handout?

학생은 교수가 수업에서 모델 레포트 유인물을 나눠주던 날 아파서 조교에게 말하고 수업에 불참했다고 했으므로 정답은 선택지 A이다.

❹ According to the professor, why is the student's paper incomplete?

대화의 초반에서 교수는 남학생이 레포트를 쓰는 가이드라인을 잘 이해하지 못한 것 같다며 그의 레포트가 미완성이라고 말한다. 따라서 정답은 C이다. 남학생은 영어 교수법에 대한 논설을 분석한 후 3페이지 분량의 레포트를 써야 한다는 것은 이해했지만 정확한 가이드라인을 알지 못한 것이므로 선택지 A와 B는 오답이며, 남학생이 APA 형식에 따라 논술을 인용하는 부분을 써서 1점을 받았기 때문에 D 또한 틀렸다.

❺ What does the professor mean when she says this:

교수는 메리앤이 평소에 유인물을 챙기는 일을 잘 하는데 그 날엔 왜 그랬는지 모르겠다고 말한다. "I don't know what got into her"은 "그 사람에게 무엇이 들어갔는지 모르겠다"가 아니라 "그 사람에게 무슨 일이 있었는지 모르겠다"는 뜻이다. 따라서 정답은 D이다.

Vocabulary Test

1. b	**2.** d	**3.** c
4. a	**5.** c	**6.** d
7. a	**8.** c	

5 Function

Sample

W: 다음 수업에 제출할 보고서는 잘 되고 있어?

M: 무슨 말이야?

W: 지난주에 배운 유명한 조각상들에 대해서 5페이지짜리 보고서를 제출해야 하잖아, 기억나?

M: 확실해? 난 왜 몰랐지?

W: 지난주에 수업에 안왔어?

M: 갔었지만 내가 있을 때는 교수님께서 보고서에 대해서는 아무 말씀 없으셨는데.

W: 수업이 끝나기 직전에 말씀해 주셨어. 그날 오전에 수업에 왔다면 왜 그 얘기를 못 들은건지 모르겠네.

M: 이런. 아르바이트에 늦어서 수업 끝나기 5분 전에 나갔거든. 더 있을걸 그랬네!

W: 이제라도 알게 되었으니 다행이네. 제출할 때까진 아직 3일이나 남았어.

Strategy Focus

1. C   **2.** B   **3.** B   **4.** D

1. C

M: Hello. Welcome to the Student Information Center. What can I do for you?

W: Hello, I'm a freshman at the School of Arts and Sciences, and I was supposed to be at the school orientation, but unfortunately I couldn't make it because of personal reasons. And...

M: Uh-huh.

W: And I was wondering if I could get some of the information here.

M: Well, you came to the right place. First of all, are you staying on-campus or off-campus?

W: On-campus. I'll be staying at Quadrangle Square.

M: Okay. Uh... if you're staying at Quadrangle Square, then you might want to log onto the school's Internet website and download a pamphlet first. Just so you know, you're expected to move in from August 22nd to the 23rd.

W: That's it? Only two days are allowed to move in? Geez, I didn't know that... Um, can't I just move in a couple of days later? I don't think I could make it on that date.

M: I'm sorry, but freshmen are allowed to move in only during those two days. It's because they're trying to avoid confusion and disorder at the dormitory.

Available carts are short in number as well. If you'd like to move in at a later date, you should write a letter to the housing manager and get a written permission.

W: Oh, I see...

W: 안녕하세요. 학생 정보 센터에 잘 오셨습니다. 무엇을 도와드릴까요?

W: 안녕하세요. 저는 인문학부 1학년생인데요. 학교 오리엔테이션에 참석했어야 했는데 개인 사정으로 참석하지 못했거든요.

M: 네, 그러셨군요.

W: 그래서 여기에서 정보를 좀 얻을 수 있을까 해서 왔어요.

M: 잘 찾아오셨네요. 우선 기숙사에 계신가요, 아니면 학교 밖에서 사시나요?

W: 기숙사요. Quadrangle Square에 들어갈 거예요.

M: 알겠습니다. Quadrangle Square에서 계실 거면, 먼저 학교 인터넷 홈페이지에 들어가셔서 팸플릿을 다운 받으세요. 혹시나 해서 말씀드리는 건데, 8월 22일에서 23일 사이에 이사를 하셔야 해요.

W: 그게 다예요? 이사하는 데 겨우 이틀만 준단 말인가요? 이런... 그건 몰랐어요... 그냥 며칠 후에 이사하면 안될까요? 그 날은 안될 것 같거든요.

M: 죄송합니다만 1학년생들은 그 날에만 이사올 수 있게 돼 있어요. 기숙사 내의 혼잡과 혼란을 피하기 위해서예요. 그리고 이삿짐을 나를 수 있는 카트도 갯수가 적고요. 만약에 좀 늦게 이사하고 싶으시다면 기숙사 매니저에게 편지를 써서 서면으로 허락을 받으셔야 해요.

W: 아, 그렇군요... 알겠습니다.

2. B

M: Hi. I'd like to make a reservation to use the tennis court at Huntington Hall. I have a friend visiting me and I want to have a tennis match with her.

W: Okay. Could you tell me the date and time you prefer, please?

M: Um, I was wondering whether I could, uh, make a reservation for tomorrow. I know it's kind of short notice, but...

W: Hmm. I'll have to look it up. Usually, students need to make a reservation at least 3 days in advance — especially during this time of year. You know, it's tennis season and many students want to use the court.

M: Yeah, I'm sorry for the inconvenience.

W: That's okay. Um, let's see... Hmm, okay, there is a spot available tomorrow at court 17, from 3 to 5. How does that sound?

M: That sounds great. Thank you so much. Um, is there anything that I should be aware of?

W: Not really. I believe you're gonna be wearing tennis shoes, right? We don't allow students wearing any other types of shoes. And, uh, just in case you don't have tennis rackets, you can always rent one from the sports shop on the first floor at Huntington Hall.

M: All right, thanks a lot.

M: 안녕하세요, 헌팅턴 홀의 테니스 코트를 예약하러 왔는데요. 친구가 저를 방문하러 오는데 함께 테니스를 치고 싶거든요.

W: 알겠습니다. 원하시는 날짜와 시간을 말씀해 주시겠어요?

M: 어, 혹시 내일로는 예약이 안될까요? 좀 급박한 걸 알지만요...

W: 흠, 한번 봐야 할 것 같네요. 보통 적어도 3일 전에는 예약을 해야 되거든요. 특히 지금 같은 시기에는 말이죠. 아시겠지만 요즘이 테니스 시즌이라서 많은 학생들이 코트를 사용하고 싶어해요.

M: 네, 번거롭게 해 드려서 죄송합니다.

W: 괜찮아요. 봅시다... 좋아요, 내일 17번 코트에 3시부터 5시까지 빈 자리가 있네요. 어떠세요?

M: 좋아요, 정말 고맙습니다. 제가 또 알아야 하는 사항이 있나요?

W: 별로 없어요. 테니스화를 신으실 거죠? 다른 신발을 신는 것은 허용하지 않거든요. 그리고 테니스 라켓이 없으면 헌팅턴 홀 1층에 있는 스포츠 용품점에서 빌리실 수 있어요.

M: 알겠습니다. 고맙습니다.

3. B

W: Hi, can I help you with anything?

M: Yes, hi... Um, I'm supposed to be moving out of the dorm a week from now, and I was just wondering what I should do with my room key and the building key.

W: Oh, you can just bring it to me after you finish moving out.

M: Oh, okay... that was simple. Um, another question I'd like to ask... um, I have a lot of stuff in my room and I think I'll need a cart or something like that.

W: Well, in that case, you should sign up for the cart use here in advance. You're lucky you came here before you actually moved out — it's gonna be pretty hectic on that day so I don't think carts will be available for everyone.

M: Really?

W: Yeah. Um, just fill out this form, and... can I see your school I.D. please?

M: Sure.

W: 안녕하세요, 도와드릴까요?

M: 네, 안녕하세요. 1주일 후에 기숙사에서 이사를 나가기로 했는데요. 기숙사 방 열쇠와 건물 열쇠는 어떻게 해야 하는지 궁금해서요.

W: 아, 방을 비우신 후에 그냥 저한테 가져오시면 돼요.

M: 아, 네... 간단하네요. 또 한 가지 묻고 싶은게 있는데요... 제 방에 물건이 많아서 카트 같은 게 필요할 것 같거든요.

W: 그런 경우에는 미리 카트 사용을 예약하셔야 해요. 이사 가시기 전에 여기 오시기 잘하셨네요 - 그 날은 많이 혼잡해서 모두가 카트를 이용할 수 있을 것 같지는 않거든요.

M: 정말요?

W: 네, 이 서류를 작성하시고요. 학생증 좀 보여주시겠어요?

M: 네.

4. D

M: Hey, Erika, how's it going with your graduate school application?

W: Oh, hi, Dr. Stevens. It's going okay. My GPA's not that bad and my GRE score is pretty high. The only problem I have right now is my recommendation letters — I don't know whom I should ask for.

M: Well, sounds like someone's done with her essay, huh?

W: Yeah, thanks to you, Dr. Stevens.

M: My pleasure. Um, and about the recommendation letter, how many letters did you receive so far?

W: None, actually. I did ask Professor Hudson to write me a recommendation letter, but I need to get two more. Do you think I should ask other professors here?

M: Well, that's a tricky question, Erika. **Usually, graduate schools don't require work experience in that field, but some areas do, right? Like communications, where you're trying to work on. You're more likely to be accepted to the school if you have work experience in that field — about a year or two, at least.**

W: Um... I don't think I follow you.

M: Well, what I'm trying to say here is that those people with work experience usually get their recommendation letters from their professors and bosses whom they worked for.

W: Oh, so you mean that I should get a job before I apply to graduate school?

M: No, not really. Actually, you can get a recommendation from the boss you worked for during your summer internship.

W: Oh, that's right. Why didn't I think of that before? Thank you, Dr. Stevens.

M: Don't mention it. I'm sorry I can't write you a recommendation, though. I don't think any of the professors here know about you and your academic achievements as much as I do.

M: 에리카, 대학원 입학 신청은 잘 돼가고 있어요?

W: 아, 안녕하세요, 스티븐스 박사님. 잘 되고 있어요. 학점이 그다지 나쁘지 않고 GRE 시험 점수도 꽤 높게 나왔거든요. 지금 문제가 있다면 추천서인데, 누구에게 부탁을 해야 할지 모르겠어요.

M: 그렇게 말하는 걸 보니 에세이는 다 쓴 모양이군요?

W: 네, 다 박사님 덕분이에요.

M: 천만에요. 음, 추천서 말인데, 지금까지 몇 통이나 받아났어요?

W: 실은, 한 통도 못 받았어요. 허드슨 교수님께 추천서를 써달라고 부탁드리긴 했는데, 두 분께 더 받아야 하거든요. 여기 계신 다른 교수님들께 부탁해볼까요?

M: 그게 좀 미묘한 문제예요, 에리카. 보통 대학원들은 그 분야의 경력을 요구하긴 않지만, 어떤 분야들은 요구하기도 하거든요. 에리카가 지원하려고 하는 커뮤니케이션 같은 곳이 그래요. 적어도 1, 2년 정도의 직장 경력이 있으면 대학원에 합격하기가 더 쉽지요.

W: 음, 무슨 말씀이신지 잘 모르겠어요.

M: 무슨 말이냐면, 직장 경력이 있는 사람들은 보통 함께 일했던 교수나 직장 상사한테서 추천서를 받는다는 거예요.

W: 아, 그러면 대학원에 가기 전에 먼저 취직을 해야 한다는 말씀이신가요?

M: 아니, 그런 건 아니에요. 여름 인턴십 때 함께 일했던 상사에게서 추천서를 받을 수도 있다는 거죠.

W: 아, 그렇네요. 왜 그 생각을 진작 못 했을까요? 고맙습니다, 스티븐스 박사님.

M: 천만에요. 어쨌든 내가 추천서를 써줄 수가 없어서 아쉽네요. 에리카의 인품이나 성적에 대해서는 여기 있는 어떤 교수들보다도 내가 더 잘 알고 있는 것 같은데 말이죠.

Exercise

P.1	1. B	2. C	3. C	
P.2	1. B	2. A	3. D	
P.3	1. C	2. A	3. B	
P.4	1. A	2. B	3. D	
P.5	1. B	2. C	3. B	4. A 5. D

Passage 1

1. B   **2.** C   **3.** C

W: Hi, Dr. Lansing. Uh, I was wondering if I could talk to you for a minute — should I wait outside?

M: Oh, hello, Yasmine. I'm free right now — please come in.

W: Thank you.

M: So, what brings you here, Ms. Blaire?

W: Um, I just wanted to turn in my homework for this week's class. I know it's a bit early, but I'm gonna be out of town that day, so...

M: Hmm, now that's interesting. You've never missed any of my classes so far, now, have you? What's the occasion?

W: ❸ It's a family emergency — my grandmother is... she's really sick right now, and... the family wanted me to be there right away.

M: Oh... I'm sorry to hear that. Is she in a critical condition?

W: I don't know. My father called a couple of days ago and told me that I should be at her side before she passes away.

M: Again, I'm very sorry to hear that. <u>Uh... now... about your homework.</u>

W: Yes, sir.

M: I think I told you to write about ten pages, no less than eight pages, including the references. Now, I do see ten pages, but the last three pages are blank. What happened?

W: Uh... what? Um, can I take a look at that?

M: Sure, go ahead.

W: Oh, my gosh. I think it's my printer! I promise, Dr. Lansing — I wrote nine and a half pages including the references!

M: Well, Yasmine, if you say that you wrote nine and a half pages, then you wrote nine and a half pages. You can either print it out somewhere and drop it in the mailbox outside my door, or e-mail it to me as soon as you go back home.

W: I'll print it out and drop it in about an hour.

M: Okay, I'll be in a class by the time you come back. Oh, and since you're gonna be missing this week's session, let me give you this sheet of paper... let me see...

W: What is it?

M: Well, it's an article that you can refer to while doing next week's reading assignment. I was going to pass it out this week.

W: Thank you.

W: 안녕하세요, 랜싱 교수님. 잠깐 말씀 좀 나누고 싶은데요, 밖에서 기다릴까요?

M: 아, 야스민. 지금은 시간이 있으니까 들어와요.

W: 고맙습니다.

M: 어쩐 일로 여기까지 왔죠, 블레어 양?

W: 이번 주 숙제를 제출하려고요. 좀 이른 감이 있지만, 수업날에 어딜 좀 가야 하거든요...

M: 흠, 흥미롭네요. 지금까지 수업을 한 번도 빠진 적이 없었죠? 무슨 일인가요?

W: 집안에 급한 일이 있어요. 저희 할머니께서 많이 편찮으셔서 가족들이 저에게 당장 오라고 했거든요.

M: 저런, 안됐군요. 상태가 많이 안 좋으신가요?

W: 모르겠어요. 아버지께서 며칠 전 전화하셔서 할머니께서 돌아가시기 전에 제가 곁에 있어 드리는 게 좋겠다고 하셨어요.

M: 정말 유감이네요. 자, 그럼... 숙제 얘기를 좀 해볼까요.

W: 네, 교수님.

M: 참고서적 리스트까지 포함해서 적어도 8페이지에서 10페이지 정도를 작성하라고 한 것 같은데, 야스민의 숙제는 10페이지가 맞긴 한데, 마지막 3페이지는 백지네요. 어떻게 된 거죠?

W: 네? 어... 좀 봐도 될까요?

M: 그럼요.

W: 이런... 프린터 때문인 것 같아요! 정말이에요. 랜싱 교수님 – 참고서적 리스트까지 합쳐서 아홉 장 반을 썼어요!

M: 아홉 장 반을 썼다면 아홉 장 반을 쓴 게 맞겠죠. 다른 곳에서 출력해서 내 연구실 밖에 있는 우편함에 넣어두거나, 집에 가자마자 나에게 이메일로 전송해 줘요.

W: 1시간 이내로 출력해서 가져올게요.

M: 좋아요, 돌아올 때 쯤이면 난 수업에 들어가 있을 거예요. 아, 그리고 이번 주 수업을 빠진다고 했으니까, 이걸 줄게요. 어디 보자...

W: 이게 뭔가요?

M: 다음 주에 읽을 과제를 하면서 참고할 수 있는 소논문이에요. 이번 주에 나눠주려고 했었거든요.

W: 고맙습니다.

❶ Why does the student want to talk to the professor?

이번 주 숙제를 제출하기 위해서 교수를 찾아간 것이므로 정답은 B이다.

❷ What does the professor say about the woman's homework?

학생이 가져온 숙제를 보고 교수는 원래 8페이지에서 10페이지 정도 작성해야 하는데 학생의 숙제는 10페이지 중 마지막 3페이지가 백지라고 말하며 정해준 분량을 채우지 않았다고 말한다. 따라서 정답은 선택지 C이다.

❸ Why does the professor say this:

학생의 할머니에 대한 이야기에서 학생의 숙제로 주제를 바꾸기 위해 언급한 것이므로 정답은 C가 된다.

1. B   **2.** A   **3.** D

M: Hi, I'm having a problem with my dorm phone.

W: All right, um, which building are you in?

M: Cambridge West building, room 1815.

W: Okay. Uh... now, did you say that you're having a problem with your dorm room phone? What exactly is the problem?

M: Well, whenever I try to call other places, I hear a loud static and other people's voices. I think the lines are crossed. Funny thing is, this doesn't happen when I receive a call.

W: All right. Um, are you sure it's not the problem with your telephone itself? 'Cause that can happen especially when you use a cordless phone.

M: No, I'm sure it's not my phone. I used the phone jack in my roommate's room and I didn't hear any other noises. Plus, I don't use a cordless phone.

W: Okay... just let me check the system for a moment... Uh... I don't see any problem with your room. The signal's clear — I don't see any other problems on the computer, at least.

M: Well, but this is driving me crazy, you know. I spend a lot of time talking on the phone, and it really bothers me when I hear other people talking on the phone.

W: Well, how long have you been experiencing this static and other noises?

M: It was okay for the first two months since I moved into my dorm room, so, I guess about three months.

W: All right... you know, you should have let us know as soon as you noticed something wrong with your phone.

M: Yeah, I know, but I thought it would go away soon, so...

W: Okay. Um.... Well, there's nothing I can do to help you here — the computer system says that there's nothing wrong with your phone line. See?

M: Oh... then, what should I do?

W: We'll send you a technician some time this week or next week. Maybe he can detect what's wrong with your phone. Uh, when are you available this week?

M: I have classes in the morning, so any time after 1 o'clock is fine with me.

W: Okay, um, does this Friday sound okay? At two o'clock?

M: Yeah, why not. Actually, it'd be better if he could come over as quick as possible.

W: Well, that's the fastest time we can arrange for you. Um, so, what's gonna happen is that the technician will pay you a visit, check what's wrong with your phone jack... I think it's probably your phone jack on the wall that's causing all the problem... and, uh, he'll decide what to do afterwards.

M: Sounds good. ❸ Uh, how much do you think it's going to cost me?

W: That depends—if it's the phone jack, then he'll probably change it for free. If it's a bigger problem that I can't even imagine, he's going to send you a bill later.

M: I see. Hopefully it's not a big problem, though. Thanks a lot.

W: No problem.

M: 안녕하세요, 제 기숙사 전화가 말썽이라서 왔는데요.

W: 알겠습니다. 어느 건물에 계신가요?

M: 캠브리지 웨스트 빌딩 1815호예요.

W: 네, 어... 기숙사 전화가 말썽이라고 하셨죠? 문제가 정확히 뭔가요?

M: 다른 곳에 전화만 하면 잡음 소리가 크게 나고 다른 사람들 목소리가 들려요. 전화가 혼선이 되는 것 같아요. 이상하게도 전화를 받으면 이런 현상이 없어요.

W: 알겠습니다. 전화기 자체에 문제가 있는 건 아니고요? 왜냐하면 무선전화기를 사용하면 그런 문제가 발생하기도 하거든요.

M: 아니요, 전화기 문제가 아닌 건 확실해요. 룸메이트 방에 있는 전화잭을 사용해 봤는데 다른 소리가 안 들렸거든요. 게다가 저는 무선전화기를 이용하지 않아요.

W: 알겠습니다... 잠깐만 시스템상에서 확인해 볼게요. 어... 학생의 방에는 문제가 없는 걸로 나오네요. 신호도 선명하고, 적어도 컴퓨터상에서는 문제가 보이지 않아요.

M: 하지만 이것 때문에 미치겠는걸요. 저는 전화를 많이 쓰는데 다른 사람의 목소리가 들리면 정말 거슬려요.

W: 잡음과 다른 소리가 들린 지 얼마나 되었나요??

M: 기숙사 방에 들어간 지 처음 두 달은 괜찮았으니까, 한 3개월 정도 된 것 같아요.

W: 알겠습니다... 전화기에 뭔가 문제가 생겼다는 걸 알자마자 저희한테 연락을 주셨으면 좋았을 텐데요.

M: 네, 알아요, 하지만 금방 괜찮아질 줄 알았어요...

W: 네, 음... 지금 여기서 도와드릴 수 있는 건 없는 것 같네요. 컴퓨터 시스템상에서는 전화선에 문제가 없다고 나오니까요.

M: 아... 그러면 어떻게 하면 되나요?

W: 이번 주나 다음 주 중에 저희쪽 기술자를 보내드릴게요. 기술자가 전화에 무슨 문제가 있는지 알아낼 수 있을 거예요. 이번 주엔 언제 시간이 되세요?

M: 수업이 아침에 있으니까 오후 1시 이후면 아무때나 돼요.

W: 좋아요. 이번 금요일 2시 괜찮으세요?

M: 네, 좋아요. 실은 좀 더 빨리 오실 수 있으면 좋을 것 같아요.

W: 저희가 잡아드릴 수 있는 것 중 제일 빠른 시간이에요. 어, 그러니까, 기술자분이 학생의 방에 가서 전화책에 무슨 문제가 있는지를 확인하실 거예요... 제 생각에는 벽에 있는 전화책이 문제인 것 같은데요. 그리고 그 다음에 어떻게 해야 할지는 기술자분이 결정하실 거예요.

M: 좋아요. 비용은 얼마나 들까요?

W: 상황에 따라 다를 거예요. 만약에 전화책이 문제라면 아마 무료로 교체해 주실 거예요. 상상은 안되지만 그보다 더 큰 문제라면 나중에 청구할 거고요.

M: 알겠습니다. 큰 문제가 아니면 좋겠네요. 고맙습니다.

W: 천만에요.

❶ What can be inferred about the man?

학생에 따르면 처음 기숙사로 옮긴 첫 두 달 동안에는 괜찮다가 그 후로 3개월 정도 전화기 문제가 지속되었다고 한다. 따라서 학생은 기숙사에서 지금까지 5개월 정도 살았다는 것을 알 수 있다. 지문의 내용상 학생은 기숙사에서 룸메이트와 다른 방을 쓰고 있으므로 원룸 스튜디오에서 사는 것이 아님을 알 수 있으며 선택지 C와 D는 지문의 내용에서 알 수 없다.

❷ Why does the man mention his roommate?

룸메이트 방의 전화책을 사용했더니 문제가 없었다며, 자신의 전화기에 문제가 없음을 설명하고 있다. 따라서 정답은 선택지 A가 된다.

❸ What does the man mean when he says this:

더 큰 문제가 있으면 요금 청구가 될 것이라는 직원의 말에 큰 문제가 아니었으면 좋겠다고 한다. "Hopefully..."라는 표현은 "~이었으면 좋겠다"라는 뜻이므로 선택지 A는 답이 아니며, 선택지 B는 지문의 내용과 반대이므로 이 역시 정답이 아니다. 선택지 C는 지문의 내용에서 알 수 없다. 그러므로 가장 좋은 답은 선택지 D이다.

Passage 3

1. C   **2.** A   **3.** B

W: Hi, um, can I ask you something?

M: Of course.

W: Um, I have a friend coming over tomorrow, and I'd like to use the rock climbing facility in the Athletic Center with her. Um, do I, do I have to make a reservation for something like that?

M: Oh, actually, I'm not in charge of making reservations, so... you can go ahead to the office right across the hallway and ask them there. It's kind of short notice, but I think you can make a reservation for tomorrow.

W: Okay. And, uh, what if she's not from this university? I mean, um, is she gonna be allowed to enter the building at all?

M: Well, in that case, you're gonna have to make a guest pass.

W: A guest pass?

M: Yeah.

W: Well, can I make it now?

M: I'm sorry we can't do that for you. Your friend's gonna have to be here and show her I.D.

W: Really? Well, do you think it's gonna take long?

M: Not that long — only a couple of minutes.

W: Okay... uh, if she makes that guest pass, can she use it for the whole time she's here?

M: No, you can only make a guest pass once a day. So, if your friend wants to use any of the Athletic Center facilities, she's gonna have to make it everytime she comes here.

W: Aww, that sounds so inconvenient! We're gonna be using the facility the whole time she's here! Can't you make an exception and just make one guest pass that's usable for at least a week? Please?

M: I'm sorry, but I can't do that. Oh... and I almost forgot. ❸ Um, in order for your friend to use the facility in the Student Athletic Center, she has to pay the daily fee.

W: Excuse me?

M: Well, we can't just let anybody use the facility for free, you know.

W: Well, I'm a student here, but I don't pay for the facility.

M: That's because the fee is included in your tuition.

W: Oh... all right, how much is the daily fee, then?

M: It's $15 per day for using the entire facility.

W: 15 dollars? But we're only gonna use the rock climbing facility. Can't you make it a little bit cheaper?

W: Well, I'm sorry, but that's the rule. Whether your friend uses only the rock climbing facility, the treadmill, or other equipment, she's gonna still have to pay $15.

W: 안녕하세요, 뭣 좀 여쭤봐도 될까요?

M: 네, 물론이죠.

W: 내일 방문하는 친구가 있는데 체육 센터에 있는 암벽 등반 시설을 같이 이용했으면 하거든요. 예약 같은 걸 해야 하나요?

M: 실은 제가 예약 담당이 아니라서요... 복도 저 맞은편에 있는 사무실에 가서 물어보세요. 시간이 촉박하긴 하지만, 내일 예약은 가능하실 것 같아요.

W: 네, 그리고요, 제 친구가 여기 대학 출신이 아닌데... 그러니까 그런 경우에도 건물에 들어갈 수 있나요?

M: 그런 경우에는 방문증을 만드셔야 해요.

W: 방문증이요?

M: 네.

W: 지금 만들 수 있나요?

M: 죄송하지만 그렇게는 안돼요. 친구분께서 직접 신분증을 가져 오셔야 해요.

W: 정말요? 오래 걸리나요?

M: 그다지 오래 걸리진 않아요, 몇 분 정도 밖에 안 걸려요.

W: 네, 그 방문증을 만들면 친구가 여기 있는 동안 계속 써도 되는 건가요?

M: 아니요, 방문증은 하루에 한 번만 만들 수 있어요. 그러니까 만약 친구분께서 체육 센터의 시설을 이용하시려면 오실 때마다 만드셔야 하는 거죠.

W: 아, 그건 너무 불편할 것 같은데요! 친구가 여기 있는 내내 함께 시설을 사용할 거거든요! 이번만 예외로 해 주시고 최소 일주일간 사용할 수 있는 방문증을 만들어 주시면 안될까요? 부탁드려요.

M: 죄송하지만 그건 안돼요. 아, 그리고 잊어버릴 뻔 했는데, 친구분께서 체육 센터의 시설들을 이용하려면 일일 사용요금을 내셔야 해요.

W: 뭐라고요?

M: 아무나 공짜로 시설을 사용하게 할 수는 없으니까요.

W: 저는 여기 학생이지만 시설을 이용할 때 돈을 안내는데요.

M: 그건 요금이 학비에 포함되어 있기 때문이에요.

W: 알겠습니다. 그러면 일일 사용요금이 얼마인가요?

M: 시설을 전부 이용하는 데 하루에 15달러예요.

W: 하지만 저희는 암벽 등반 시설만 이용할 건데요? 좀 더 싸게 해 주시면 안될까요?

W: 죄송하지만 그게 규칙이라서요. 친구분이 암벽 등반 시설만 이용하든, 런닝머신을 이용하든 다른 시설을 사용하든간에 여전히 15달러를 내셔야 해요.

❶ What can be inferred about the woman's friend?

지문의 내용상 여자의 친구는 암벽 등반 시설을 방문 기간 내내 사용할 것임을 알 수 있다. 방문 기간 동안 암벽 등반 시설 외의 다른 시설은 사용할 의도가 없다고 했으므로 선택지 A는 정답이 아니며, 선택지 B와 D는 지문의 내용만으로는 알 수 없다.

❷ What does the man say about the university students' Athletic Center use?

자신은 이 대학의 학생이지만 체육 센터의 시설을 이용할 때 전

혀 요금을 안낸다고 하자 남자는 학생들의 이용 요금이 학비에 이미 포함되어 있기 때문에 따로 돈을 낼 필요가 없는 것이라고 한다. 따라서 정답은 선택지 A이다.

❸ Why does the woman say this:

친구가 체육 센터의 시설을 이용하기 위해서는 일일 사용요금을 내야 한다는 남자의 말에 여자는 자신은 돈을 내지 않고도 시설을 이용한다면서 반박한다. 정답은 선택지 B이며, 나머지 선택지들은 본문의 내용과 관련이 없다.

Passage 4

1. A   **2.** B   **3.** D

M: Hi, Dr. Phillips. Can I come in?

W: Hello, Paul, I was waiting for you. So... you told me that you would like to join the Student Study Abroad Program, right?

M: That's right.

W: All right. Let me check my file here... ah, here it is. Okay. Uh, now, since you major in European History, I believe you're more interested in European countries rather than in Australia or other Asian countries, right?

M: Yes, actually, my first choice is France.

W: That's a good choice. Um, let me ask you this first — did you take AP French before you came to college?

M: Well, I did, but I barely got a B.

W: Well, why I'm asking you this is because the qualification for a French college is higher than those of any other countries because they don't provide English classes. You're supposed to have gotten at least an A- for your AP French. You're supposed to take classes with other French students in French, and they usually require excellent language proficiency. Of course, they have one of the best history courses in Europe, and the French education system is exceptional — you can learn a lot from them.

M: Oh... well, I'm not that good with French... I'm too intimidated now.

W: Well, you don't have to be intimidated. Let's talk more about your other choices, shall we? What are your second and third choices?

M: England and Spain. Actually, no... Spain would be my second choice and England my third.

W: That's fine. Um, Spanish colleges don't require high Spanish language proficiency because they do provide courses in English. ❸ **The university is in Madrid, and you might be able to enjoy the excellent weather and the culture as well. Actually, I do recommend you go to Spain, since I've been there myself already... but it's all up to you, so... Anyways.** Um, England colleges won't be that difficult since the education systems there are quite similar to those in the United States. The only thing is the living expense — it's going to cost you a lot to go live in London for six months.

M: Oh, gee... now I don't know which country to choose. They all sound good, but now I'm confused.

W: Well, take your time and think it over. Here, take a look at this pamphlet and compare the expenses and programs. Actually, there's not much difference in programs... they're all excellent. What you want to consider the most here is the money and the country you'd like to stay in.

M: 안녕하세요, 필립스 박사님. 들어가도 될까요?

W: 안녕, 폴, 기다리고 있었어요. 지난번에 학생 해외 교육 프로그램에 가입하고 싶다고 했었죠?

M: 네, 맞아요.

W: 좋아요, 파일을 먼저 확인해 볼게요... 아, 여기 있네요. 좋아요. 어, 유럽 역사를 전공하고 있으니까 호주나 다른 아시아 국가들보다 유럽 국가에 더 관심이 가졌죠?

M: 네, 실은 제 1지망이 프랑스예요.

W: 좋은 선택이네요. 먼저 이걸 좀 물어 볼게요 – 대학에 지원하기 전에 AP 프랑스어 과목을 들었나요?

M: 네, 듣기는 했는데 간신히 B학점을 받았어요.

W: 내가 이걸 왜 물어보냐면, 프랑스 대학에 가는 자격 기준이 다른 나라들보다 더 높아서 그래요. 프랑스에서는 영어로 하는 수업을 제공하지 않거든요. AP 프랑스어 과목에서 적어도 A-를 받았어야만 해요. 다른 프랑스 학생들과 프랑스어로 수업을 들어야 하기 때문에 그쪽에서는 일반적으로 높은 프랑스어 실력을 요구하죠. 물론, 그 학교의 역사 수업이 유럽에서 가장 뛰어난 수업들 중 하나이고 프랑스의 교육 체계는 매우 훌륭해서 많이 배울 수 있긴 하지만요.

M: 아... 저는 프랑스어를 그다지 잘하진 못하는데요... 이제 너무 부담스럽네요.

W: 겁낼 필요 없어요. 다른 선택들에 대해 더 얘기해 볼까요? 2지망, 3지망은 어디죠?

M: 영국이랑 스페인이에요. 아, 그게 아니라, 스페인이 2지망이고, 영국이 3지망이에요.

W: 좋아요. 스페인 대학들은 영어 수업도 제공하기 때문에 그다지 높은 스페인어 실력을 요구하지는 않아요. 대학은 마드리드에 있고 그곳의 멋진 날씨·문화도 즐길 수 있어요. 사실, 스페인으로 가라고 권하고 싶네요. 나도 거기에 다녀왔거든요. 물론 폴의 선택에 달린 거지만요. 어쨌든, 어, 영국 대학들은 교육 체계가 미국과 비슷하기 때문에 그다지 어렵지

않을 거예요. 한가지 문제가 있다면 생활비인데, 런던에서 6개월 동안 산다면 생활비가 많이 들 거예요.

M: 이런... 이제 어느 나라를 선택해야 할지 모르겠어요. 전부 좋은 것 같은데, 헷갈리네요.

W: 시간을 두고 잘 생각해 보세요. 자, 여기 팸플릿을 가져가서 비용이랑 프로그램을 비교해 보세요. 사실, 프로그램 자체에는 큰 차이가 없어요... 다 좋으니까. 생각해 봐야 할 것은 비용과 어느 나라에 있고 싶은지일 거예요.

❶ **How is the information in the conversation organized?**

학생이 학생 해외 교육 프로그램을 가기 위해 지망하려고 하는 나라별로 이야기를 하고 있으므로 정답은 선택지 A이다.

❷ **Why does the academic advisor mention AP French?**

지도 교수는 프랑스 대학으로 가려면 AP 프랑스어 과목에서 적어도 A-를 받았어야 한다며 학생이 자격이 되는지를 묻는다. 따라서 가장 좋은 답은 선택지 B이다.

❸ **Why does the academic advisor say this:**

지도 교수는 자신이 스페인으로 다녀왔다며 그곳으로 가라고 권유하면서 스페인에 대해 이야기를 하다가 영국으로 대화의 주제를 바꾼다. 따라서 가장 좋은 정답은 선택지 D이다.

Passage 5

1. B **2.** C **3.** B **4.** A **5.** D

M: Housing Service, what can I do for you?

W: Yes, hi, um... can I ask you something really quick?

M: Sure, what is it?

W: Um, I'm having a small problem with my kitchen sink so I called you a few days ago for a plumber.

M: All right, can I have your name, please?

W: It's Sarah O'Donnell.

M: Okay, Ms. O'Donnell.... Um, room 203?

W: That's right.

M: All right, Ms. O'Donnell... um, the plumber will be there next Tuesday at 3:15 to take a look at your sink.

W: Actually, I wanted to postpone that. I have to leave for New York next Monday for a job interview, and I won't be back until Thursday morning. I was wondering whether the plumber could come, like, Thursday afternoon or any time on Friday.

M: Well, I'm sorry but we can't do that. The plumber

has a full schedule — if you want to change the appointment to a later time, I'm afraid that he won't be able to make it until two weeks after that.

W: Two weeks after that? Do you mean, like, three weeks from now?

M: I'm afraid so.

W: ❸ Oh, gee.... This is a very important interview for me, but I can't live with my kitchen sink clogged for three whole weeks! I can't afford to miss my interview... what should I do?

M: Well, you don't have to worry about that — the plumber has keys to all the dorm rooms, so, if you're not there, with your permission, he can get in, fix the problem, and leave a note.

W: Oh, is that true? But what if I wanted to explain the problems that I was having?

M: Don't worry about that either — the plumber's been working with us for more than 15 years and is very experienced. I'm sure he's going to detect exactly what the problem is and fix it. If you'd like, you can write down the problems on a piece of paper and leave that note on the sink.

W: Well... All right. I don't actually like people coming into my house when I'm not there, but I don't think I have any other choice.

M: 주거 서비스입니다. 무엇을 도와드릴까요?

W: 네, 안녕하세요. 뭣 좀 빨리 여쭤봐도 될까요?

M: 그럼요, 무슨 일이세요?

W: 어, 부엌 싱크대가 고장이 나서 며칠 전에 배관공을 불러달라고 전화 드렸거든요.

M: 알겠습니다, 성함이 어떻게 되시죠?

W: 사라 오도넬이에요.

M: 네, 오도넬 양... 203호 맞으시죠?

W: 맞아요.

M: 좋습니다. 오도넬양. 배관공은 다음 주 화요일 3시 15분에 싱크대를 보수하러 방문할 거예요.

W: 실은 그 시간을 좀 미루려고요. 다음 주 월요일에 뉴욕에서 취업 면접이 있어서 가야 하는데, 목요일 아침에나 돌아오거든요. 목요일 오후나 금요일 아무때나 와 주실 수 있을까요?

M: 죄송하지만 그렇게는 안 될 것 같은데요. 배관공의 스케줄이 꽉 차서 나중으로 약속을 미루시려면 그 날짜부터 2주 후에나 될 것 같아요.

W: 그 날짜부터 2주 후라고요? 그러니까 지금으로부터 3주 후란 말씀이세요?

M: 죄송하지만 그래요.

W: 이런... 이 인터뷰는 저한테 정말 중요하거든요. 그렇지만 부엌 싱크대가 3주일이나 막혀 있는 채로 살 수도 없는데요! 인터뷰를 놓칠 수는

없고.. 어떻게 하면 좋죠?

M: 그것에 대해서는 걱정하지 않으셔도 돼요. 배관공이 모든 기숙사 방의 열쇠를 갖고 있기 때문에, 학생이 방에 없는 경우에는, 허락을 한다면 직접 들어가서 문제를 고치고 메모를 남겨놓을 거예요.

W: 아, 정말요? 하지만 제가 직접 문제를 설명하고 싶다면요?

M: 그것도 걱정하지 마세요. 그 배관공은 저희랑 15년이 넘게 일해왔고 경험도 풍부하답니다. 그가 문제를 정확하게 짚어내고 고칠 거예요. 만약 원하시면 문제가 무엇인지 적어서 그 메모를 싱크대에 두시면 될 거예요.

W: 알겠습니다. 원래 전 제가 없을때 사람들이 집에 들어오는걸 별로 좋아하진 않지만, 다른 방도가 없을 것 같네요.

❶ Why does the woman want to talk with the man?

학생은 배관공을 불렀지만 배관공이 올 시간에 자신이 집에 없을 거라며 스케줄을 바꾸고 싶어한다. 정답은 선택지 B이다.

❷ What does the man say about the plumber?

"The plumber's been working with us for more than 15 years and is very experienced"이라는 남자의 말에서 정답을 알 수 있다. 뉴욕으로 가는 것은 학생이기 때문에 선택지 A는 틀린 답이며, 약속을 미루면 2주 후에나 다시 올 수 있다는 남자의 말로 미루어보아 선택지 B 역시 틀린 내용임을 알 수 있다. 선택지 D는 지문의 내용에서 알 수 없다.

❸ What does the woman mean when she says this:

"Afford to~"란 "~을 할 수 있는 여유가 있다"는 뜻으로, 여자의 말은 "인터뷰가 너무 중요해서 빠질 수 없다"와 "뉴욕까지 가는 여비가 너무 비싸서 이번에 놓치면 다시 갈 수가 없다"로 해석할 수 있겠지만, 여기에서는 내용상 전자로 해석해야 한다. 따라서 가장 좋은 정답은 선택지 B이다.

❹ What kind of problem does the woman have with her kitchen sink?

3주 동안 부엌의 싱크대가 막혀 있는 채로 살 수는 없다는 여자의 말에서 정답을 알 수 있다.

❺ What can be inferred about the woman?

자신이 집에 없을 때 사람들이 집에 들어오는 것을 별로 좋아하진 않는다는 여자의 말에서 정답을 알 수 있다. 나머지 선택지들은 대화의 내용만으로는 알 수 없다.

Vocabulary Test

1. a	**2.** d	**3.** d
4. a	**5.** c	**6.** d
7. a	**8.** c	

PART 3 · ACTUAL TEST

Set 1

P.1	1. A	2. C	3. B	4. D	5. B
P.2	1. B	2. B, D, E	3. C		
	4. B	5. D	6. 참조		
P.3	1. C	2. A	3. B		
	4. D	5. D	6. C		
P.4	1. B	2. D	3. C	4. C	5. C
P.5	1. A	2. C	3. C		
	4. D	5. B	6. 참조		
P.6	1. B	2. C	3. B		
	4. B, D	5. A	6. B		

Passage 1

1. A **2.** C **3.** B **4.** D **5.** B

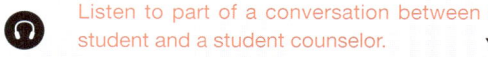

Listen to part of a conversation between a student and a student counselor. ▼

W: Hi, what can I do for you?

M: Hi, my name is Jason Hopkins, and, uh... I'd like to ask you something about a volunteer job that I might do on campus.

W: All right. Um, what kind of volunteer job are you looking for?

M: Well, since I major in education, it'd be better if it has something to do with teaching.

W: Which subjects are you interested in?

M: Actually, I'd prefer teaching English language to ESL students or literature to junior high students.

W: ❸ Okay, Mr. Hopkins, just a minute, please... Ah, the International House is looking for an English instructor for ESL students. Are you interested in this job?

M: Um, could you read the job description for me, please?

W: Well, uh... I was going to print it out for you later, but... well, okay. Uh, it seems like it's a part-time volunteer job, so there's no pay involved, and, uh, the instructor gets to teach English conversation

to about five students from different countries for two hours a day. The session goes on for the whole semester.

M: Hmm, I was thinking more of, like, teaching three days a week.

W: Oh, then you might be interested in this... Um, the ISC people are looking for a leader and an instructor for their new English chatting group.

M: ISC? What's that?

W: International Student Center. Not many American students know about this, but most of the international students from all over the world who need help with their English skills or just want to make some friends outside of their classrooms come over and hang around.

M: Oh, so it's something like a student lounge, right?

W: Yes, kind of.

M: Um, then, what's the English chatting group? I mean, what do they do exactly?

W: Well, in short, it's a group meeting where people get to chat in English. Actually, ISC has several other language chatting groups, such as Italian, Spanish, and Japanese, but no English chatting group at all, so they decided to organize one earlier this semester. I don't think they found any group leader, though.

M: I see. Um, what does the group leader do, then?

W: Well, basically, the group leader gets to lead the chat. On the first day, you write down the members' names and their e-mail addresses. The group meetings would be held twice a week, Mondays and Thursdays at 2 pm and would go on for about an hour, so a day before the meeting, you will have to send the members a reminder via e-mail.

M: Okay, so I basically write down their names and e-mail addresses and send them an e-mail twice a week. Got it.

W: Exactly. Well, it's a simple chatting meeting, so you won't need any textbooks or English articles from newspapers or magazines — just start off by exchanging greetings and asking each other how they're doing... you know, those basic stuff.

M: No problem.

W: All right. Um, but you're going to have a hard time

leading the chatting group, since there are already 9 students who enrolled in English chatting and they expect more to come.

M: I understand — more than 9 international students with only one native speaker sounds pretty bad.

W: Exactly. They're actually looking for two group leaders, but the chatting group can start as soon as one of the leaders is fixed.

M: Well, if you don't mind, can I recommend my roommate? He's my classmate as well, and he was looking for a volunteer job, too.

W: Is he a native English speaker?

M: Yeah — although, he has a Boston accent.

W: That's fine. Just tell him to come over to my office as soon as he can, okay?

M: All right. So, when do I get to start?

W: Well, in order to become a chatting group leader, you'll have to register at the ISC counter first. It's going to take a couple of days, so if you register at the counter today, you'll be able to start working from next week.

M: All right, I think I'll do that right away.

W: So, you are planning to take the job, right? Because I have to notify the ISC counter first.

M: Sure, definitely. Um, I don't know about my roommate, though. Let me talk with him first and I'll send him to you later.

W: 안녕하세요? 뭘 도와드릴까요?

M: 안녕하세요. 제 이름은 제이슨 홉킨스인데요. 학교 내에서 할 수 있는 자원봉사에 대해서 문의하려고 왔어요.

W: 알겠습니다. 음, 어떤 자원봉사 일을 찾고 계신가요?

M: 교육학을 전공하기 때문에 가르치는 것과 관계된 일이라면 좋겠어요.

W: 어떤 과목을 가르치고 싶으세요?

M: 실은, 외국인 학생들에게 영어를 가르치거나 중학생들에게 문학을 가르쳤으면 해요.

W: 알겠습니다, 홉킨스씨, 잠시만 기다려 주세요... 아, 인터내셔널 하우스에서 외국인 학생들에게 영어를 가르칠 수 있는 강사를 찾고 있는데요, 관심 있으세요?

M: 업무 내용을 좀 읽어주시겠어요?

W: 음, 나중에 프린트해 드리려고 했는데... 예, 알겠습니다. 어, 파트타임 자원봉사 일이라서 보수는 없고요, 강사는 서로 다른 나라에서 온 국제 학생들에게 영어 회화를 하루에 2시간씩 매일 가르치게 돼요. 수업은 한 학기 동안 계속되고요.

M: 흠, 저는 좀 더 시간이 적게 드는 일을 원했거든요. 그러니까 일주일에 사흘 정도 가르치는 걸 생각했는데요.

W: 아, 그러면 이게 좋겠네요... ISC에서 개설된 영어 채팅 그룹의 리더 겸 강사를 찾고 있어요.

M: ISC요? 그게 뭐죠?

W: 국제 학생 센터예요. 미국 학생들 대부분은 잘 모르지만, 영어 실력 향상에 도움이 필요하거나 교실 밖에서 친구를 사귀고 싶어하는 전 세계에서 온 대부분의 국제 학생들은 이곳에 와서 시간을 보내곤 하죠.

M: 아, 그러니까 학생 라운지 같은 거네요, 그렇죠?

W: 네, 그런 셈이죠.

M: 음, 그러면 영어 채팅 그룹은 뭔가요? 그러니까, 정확하게 하는 일이 뭔가요?

W: 간단히 말하면, 사람들이 영어로 대화를 할 수 있는 그룹 미팅이에요. 사실, ISC에는 이탈리아어, 스페인어, 그리고 일본어와 같은 다른 언어로 대화하는 그룹 미팅이 있긴 한데 영어는 없거든요. 그래서 이번 학기 초에 영어 채팅 그룹을 만들기로 결정했는데 아직까진 그룹 리더를 찾지 못한 것 같아요.

M: 그렇군요. 그러면 그룹 리더는 뭘 하게 되죠?

W: 기본적으로 그룹 리더는 대화를 이끌게 돼요. 첫날에는 멤버들의 이름과 이메일 주소를 적고요. 그룹 미팅은 일주일에 두 번씩, 월요일과 목요일 오후 2시에 있는데, 1시간 정도 지속되거든요. 그러니까 미팅 전날 그룹원들에게 이메일을 보내서 확인시켜주면 돼요.

M: 네, 그러니까 이름과 이메일 주소를 적고 일주일에 두 번씩 이메일을 보내면 되는거죠, 알겠습니다.

W: 좋아요, 이것은 단순한 채팅 미팅이니까 교재나 혹은 신문이나 잡지의 기사를 준비하실 필요는 없어요. 그냥 서로 안부를 묻고 어떻게 지내는지 묻는 그런 기본적인 것부터 시작하시면 돼요.

M: 알겠습니다.

W: 좋아요, 하지만 벌써 등록한 학생이 9명이나 되는데다 더 등록할 것이라고 예상되기 때문에 채팅 그룹을 이끌기 좀 힘드실 거예요.

M: 이해되네요, 원어민이 혼자인데 9명 이상의 국제 학생이 있는 것은 꽤 힘들 것 같아요.

W: 맞아요, 사실 ISC에선 두 명의 그룹 리더를 찾고 있긴 한데, 리더가 한 명이라도 확정되기만 하면 바로 시작할 수 있다고 해요.

M: 혹시 괜찮다면 제 룸메이트를 소개해도 될까요? 저랑 같은 수업을 듣는데 그 친구도 자원봉사 일을 찾고 있거든요.

W: 룸메이트도 원어민인가요?

M: 네, 보스턴 억양이 있긴 하지만요.

W: 괜찮아요, 나중에 시간 되는대로 제 사무실로 오시라고 전해 주세요.

M: 네, 그러면 언제부터 시작하죠?

W: 채팅 그룹의 리더가 되기 위해서는 우선 ISC의 카운터에서 등록하셔야 해요, 며칠 걸리니까 오늘 등록하시면 다음 주부터는 시작할 수 있을 거예요.

M: 알겠습니다, 바로 할게요.

W: 그럼, 이 일을 하시는 거죠? 왜냐하면 ISC 카운터에 통보해 줘야 하거든요.

M: 그럼요, 물론이죠. 하지만 제 룸메이트는 아직 잘 모르겠어요. 먼저 그 친구랑 얘기해보고 방문하라고 할게요.

❶ Why does the man want to talk with the woman?

"I'd like to ask you something about a volunteer job that I can do on campus"라는 학생의 말에서 정답(선택지 A)을 찾을 수 있다.

❷ What can be inferred about the man?

교육학을 전공하고 있는 학생은 자신의 전공을 살려 영어 교육과 관련된 일을 하고 싶어한다. 따라서 앞으로도 영어 교육과 관련된 업종에 종사하고자 한다고 추론할 수 있다. 선택지 A와 D는 지문의 내용에서 알 수 없으며, 학생의 룸메이트는 같은 수업을 듣는 학생이지 교사가 아니므로 선택지 B 역시 답이 아니다. 또한 학생은 자원봉사직을 찾고 있으므로, 고소득을 목적으로 하는 것이 아니다. 가장 좋은 답은 C이다.

❸ How does the woman feel when she says this:

인터내셔널 하우스의 자원봉사직이 어떤 것인지 업무 내용을 읽어 달라는 학생의 말에 여자는 "나중에 프린트해서 주려고 했는데..." 라며 약간 주저하는 모습을 보이다가 그냥 읽어준다. 따라서 가장 좋은 답은 선택지 B이다.

❹ How does the man feel about the job at the International House?

수업이 하루에 2시간씩 매일 있다는 여자의 말에 학생은 일주일에 세 번 정도 일을 하는 것을 원한다고 한다. 따라서 학생은 인터내셔널 하우스에서의 자원봉사직이 업무 시간에 있어 부담이 너무 크다고 느낀다는 것을 알 수 있다.

❺ What is the man most likely to do next?

채팅 그룹의 리더가 되기 위해서는 먼저 ISC의 카운터에서 등록해야 한다는 여자의 말에 학생은 "All right, I think I'll do that right away"라고 말한다. 따라서 학생은 곧바로 ISC로 가서 카운터에서 등록할 것임을 알 수 있다.

> Passage 2

1. B **2.** B, D, E **3.** C **4.** B **5.** D **6.** 참조

	sfumato	chiaroscuro
It means "lightdark" in Italian.		✓
Its root word means "smoke" in Italian.	✓	
It uses sharp contrast of light and shadow.		✓
It uses infinite transitions between color areas.	✓	
It contributes to the famous question of Mona Lisa's smile.	✓	

Listen to part of a discussion in an art history class. The professor is discussing Leonardo da Vinci. ▼

P(W): *The Vitruvian Man. Mona Lisa. The Last Supper.* These are the names of famous paintings of a genius painter, sculptor, architect, engineer, inventor, and scientist. Who do you think this is?

M: Oh, this is easy... it's Leonardo da Vinci.

P: That's correct. He was born on April 15, 1452, in the small Tuscan town of Vinci, near Florence. As all of you might already be aware of, he is known to be one of the greatest masters of the High Renaissance. The course of Italian art was heavily influenced by da Vinci's innovations in the field of painting. Da Vinci also held great interest in science, especially in the fields of anatomy, optics, and hydraulics. His scientific studies came before many of the modern scientific developments.

W: Professor, um, you said that da Vinci was also a scientist... then, um, did he... did he ever come up with a scientific theory, like Newton's gravity theory or something like that?

P: That's a good question, Cindy. Well, he didn't actually publish his ideas, despite some important scientific discoveries. Interesting, isn't it?

M: I read in the last week's reading assignment... uh, the list of his paintings in that book was not as much as I had expected. Well, you mentioned that he was like the forerunner of the High Renaissance, right? In order to be considered such an important position of an era, I think one might have to have painted dozens of paintings. Yet, he has only a handful of paintings on the list. Why is this?

P: Well, that's because da Vinci actually didn't finish many of his paintings. During his early years, his style closely resembled that of his teacher, Andrea del Verrocchio. Verrocchio treated his figures quite stiffly and tight, but da Vinci gradually departed from his teacher's characteristic and developed a more evocative and atmospheric handling of composition. You remember Verrocchio from last class, right? He's the painter of *Madonna with Child* and *The Baptism of Christ* — He's also a famous sculptor whose works include the bronze statue of David and many other statues in bronze and marble. Anyways, like I mentioned before, several of his most famous works are *The Last Supper* and *Mona Lisa*. Let's talk about *The Last Supper* first. In this painting... well, uh... uh...why... you know what, let's, um, let's first look at the picture here... it's gonna help you understand better than just having to listen to my explanation. Well, so, here, you can see his stylistic innovation. The twelve apostles are grouped in dynamic units of three instead of being portrayed as individual figures. The figure of Christ, on the other hand, is isolated in the center of the picture, composing a calm nucleus among others' animated response.

Now, let's turn our attention to the *Mona Lisa*. Let's look at this picture here... ah, yes. Who can tell me the technical characteristics of this famous masterpiece?

W: Um, the, uh, the painting looks somewhat cloudy.

M: Yeah, and then, um, her upper body is bright but also has shadows.

P: Very good. The characteristic Cindy pointed out is due to a technique called sfumato, and what Will pointed out is related to chiaroscuro. Actually, the *Mona Lisa* is considered a consummate example of both techniques. The term, sfumato, was used by da Vinci himself to refer to a painting technique which is characterized by subtle, almost infinitesimal transitions between color areas. This creates a delicately atmospheric haze or smoky effect, like you see here in the picture. In Italian, sfumato means "vanished." It also has connotations of "smoky" and it's derived from the Italian word fumo, which means "smoke." Got it? Well, da Vinci himself described sfumato as "without lines or borders, in the manner of smoke or beyond the focus plane."

W: Does sfumato have anything to do with whether *Mona Lisa* is smiling or not?

P: Good point, Cindy. ❺ Yes, uh, the use of sfumato around her mouth arouses a mystery as to whether the shadows are a result of a smile or if the smile is a result of the shadows. Art historians and critics still debate over this — is she smiling, or is she not? Now, let's talk about chiaroscuro. The word chiaroscuro means "lightdark" in Italian. It's the technique of defining forms through bold contrasts of light and shadow.

P: "비트루비안 맨", "모나리자", "최후의 만찬", 이는 천재적인 화가이자 조각가, 건축가, 기술공, 발명가이며 또한 과학자이도 했던 사람의 유명한 작품들입니다. 누구일 것 같나요?

M: 쉽네요... 레오나르도 다빈치예요.

P: 맞았어요. 그는 1452년 4월 15일, 플로렌스 근처의 작은 토스카나 마을인 빈치에서 태어났어요. 모두들 알다시피 그는 르네상스 황금기의 위대한 인물 중 하나이죠. 이탈리아의 미술 영역은 다빈치의 혁신으로 인해 큰 영향을 받았어요. 다빈치는 또한 과학, 특히 해부학, 광학 그리고 수력학 등에 큰 관심을 가지고 있었어요. 그의 과학 연구 다수는 현대의 과학 개발 이전에 이루어졌어요.

W: 교수님, 다빈치가 과학자이기도 했다고 하셨는데요... 그럼... 다빈치도 뉴턴의 중력의 법칙과 같은 과학적 이론을 제시했나요?

P: 좋은 질문이에요, 신디. 그는 중요한 과학적 발견을 했음에도 불구하고 실제로 자신의 아이디어를 발표하지는 않았어요. 흥미롭죠?

M: 저번 주 독서 과제에서 읽었는데요. 그 책에 나와 있는 그의 그림 목록이 생각보다 적었어요. 그가 르네상스 황금기의 선구자라고 하셨잖아요. 특정 시기에 그렇게 중요한 위치를 차지하기 위해선 수십 점 이상의 그림을 그렸어야 할 것 같은데요. 그렇지만 그의 목록에는 몇 개의 그림 밖에 없어요. 왜 그럴까요?

P: 그건 다빈치가 자신의 그림 대다수를 완성하지 않았기 때문이에요. 그의 스타일은 초반에는 스승인 안드레아 델 베로키오와 비슷했어요. 베로키오는 다소 딱딱하고 정적인 인물 구도를 연출했지만 다빈치는 점차적으로 스승의 이러한 구도에서 벗어나 주변 환경과 사물을 연상할 수 있는 분위기 있는 그림을 추구하게 되었어요. 지난 주에 배웠으니 베로키오에 대해서는 기억 나죠? "성모와 아기", 그리고 "그리스도의 세례"라는 그림의 화가이자 청동으로 만든 다비드상 외에 다양한 청동 및 대리석 조각상을 만든 조각가이기도 하죠. 자, 어쨌거나 아까 말한대로, 다빈치의 유명한 작품 중 몇 점이 바로 "최후의 만찬"과 "모나리자"입니다. 먼저 "최후의 만찬"에 대해 얘기해 보죠. 이 그림에선...아. 먼저 여기 그림부터 봅시다. 내 설명을 듣는 것보다 그림을 보는 게 더 쉽게 이해가 될 거예요. 여기서 그의 혁신적인 형식을 볼 수가 있어요. 그는 열두 사도를 개인으로 묘사하는 게 아닌, 역동적인 3명 단위로 그렸어요. 반대로 예수의 형상은 그림 한가운데에 위치하여, 다른 이들이 활동적인 반응을 보이는 데 반해 정적인 중심을 유지하고 있죠.

이제 "모나리자"를 봅시다. 자, 여기 이 그림을 보죠. 누가 이 유명한 걸작의 기술적 특징을 말해볼까요?

W: 음, 그림이 조금 뿌옇게 보여요.

M: 네, 그리고 상체가 밝은데 그림자도 있어요.

P: 좋아요. 신디가 말한 특징은 스푸마토라는 기법 때문에 생긴 것이고, 윌이 말한 것은 명암법과 관련이 있어요. 사실, 모나리자는 두 기술의 결합된 예라고 할 수 있죠. 스푸마토란 레오나르도 자신이 색감 사이의 섬세하고, 매우 미묘한 변환을 특징으로 갖는 예술적 기술을 일컫기 위해 사용한 용어예요. 이 기술은 여기 그림에서 볼 수 있듯이 섬세하고 흐릿한 효과를 내죠. 이탈리아어로 스푸마토는 '사라진다'는 뜻을 가지고 있어요. 또한 '흐릿한'이라는 뜻을 내포하고 있고, '연기'라는 뜻의 이탈리아어인 fumo에서 유래했죠. 이해됐나요? 다빈치 스스로 스푸마토를 "경계나 선이 없는, 연기와 같은 혹은 초점 너머"라고 표현했어요.

W: 스푸마토가 "모나리자"가 미소짓는지 아닌지와 관계 있나요?

P: 좋은 지적이에요, 신디. 네, "모나리자"의 입 주위의 스푸마토의 사용은 미소 때문에 그림자가 생긴 것인지 아니면 그림자 때문에 미소짓는 것처럼 보이는지에 대해 신비감을 제공해요. 미술 역사가들과 비평가들은 여전히 이것에 대해 논쟁을 벌이고 있죠 – 그녀가 미소를 짓고 있는 걸까요, 아닌 걸까요? 자, 이제 명암법에 대해 알아봅시다. 명암법이라는 단어는 이탈리아어로 "밝은 어둠"이라는 뜻이에요. 빛과 어둠의 대담한 대비를 통해 형상을 그리는 기술이지요.

❶ **What is the discussion mainly about?**

교수는 먼저 레오나르도 다빈치에 대해 간략하게 소개하며 스푸마토와 명암법 등 다빈치의 그림에 사용된 기법들을 설명한다. 선택지 A, C, D는 본문에 잠깐 언급된 제한적인 내용을 담고 있으므로 정답이 아니다.

❷ **Which of the following were mentioned as Leonardo da Vinci's drawings?**

"*The Vitruvian Man. Mona Lisa. The Last Supper.* These are the names of famous paintings of a genius painter, sculptor, architect, engineer, inventor, and scientist"라는 교수의 말에서 정답을 알 수 있다. *Madonna with Child*와 *The Baptism of Christ*는 다빈치의 스승인 베로키오의 작품이다.

❸ **What can be said about Leonardo da Vinci's *The Last Supper*?**

교수는 다빈치가 초반에는 베로키오의 화풍과 유사했지만 점차적으로 자신만의 화풍을 추구하게 되었다고 설명했으며, 최후의 만찬이라는 작품에서 이러한 혁신적인 모습을 볼 수 있다고 말하였으므로 이 작품에서 다빈치는 베로키오의 스타일과는 다른 자신만의 화풍을 보여주었다는 것을 알 수 있다. 따라서 정답은 C이다. 선택지 A는 본문의 내용과 반대되는 내용임을 알 수 있다. 선택지 B와 D는 지문에서 언급된 바가 없다.

④ **Why does the professor mention Verrocchio?**

교수에 따르면 다빈치가 스승 베로키오에게서 초기에 영향을 받았으나 점차 그의 화풍에서 독립하였다는 것을 설명하기 위해 베로키오를 언급하였다. 따라서 가장 좋은 답은 선택지 B이다.

⑤ **Why does the professor say this:**

교수는 모나리자가 웃고 있는지 아닌지는 미술 역사가들과 비평가들 사이에서 계속적으로 논란이 되고 있는 주제라고 말한다. 직접적으로 학생들에게 질문을 하는 것이 아니므로 가장 좋은 답은 선택지 D이다.

⑥ **Indicate whether each sentence below describes sfumato or chiaroscuro.**

스푸마토는 "연기"라는 뜻인 이탈리아어에서 유래했으며 미묘한 색감의 차이와 흐릿한 효과를 갖는 기술이다. 명암법은 이탈리아어로 "밝은 어둠"이라는 뜻이며 빛과 어둠의 명확한 대비가 그 특징이다.

> **Passage 3**

1. C   **2.** A   **3.** B   **4.** D   **5.** D   **6.** C

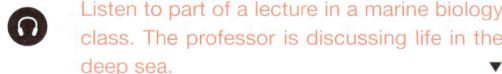

Listen to part of a lecture in a marine biology class. The professor is discussing life in the deep sea. ▼

P(M): If we could, uh, if we could all be seated now... all right. Okay, now, let's start for today. Um... today, we'll be discussing life in the deep sea. Over 60 percent of our planet is covered by water·more than a mile deep. Well, as we could easily imagine, life in the deep sea confront harsh living conditions and must adapt to these conditions such as low or no light, high pressure, low energy, and near-freezing or superheated temperatures. It's not easy for us, humans, to explore the deep sea creatures because of this adverse condition — no wonder less than one percent of the deep sea has been explored. Because little or no light penetrates to the deep sea, it is also called the aphotic zone, of which many organisms mainly rely on a food chain based on chemosynthesis rather than photosynthesis.

Before we move on to the life in the deep sea, we should first know how the ocean is vertically divided.

The pelagic zone is also known as the open-ocean zone, and is part of the open sea comprising of water column, other than that near the coast or the sea floor. Got it? Let's take a look at this diagram here... okay. Well, this pelagic zone is divided into several sub-sections according to the function of depth and different ecological characteristics. The epipelagic zone, which is from the surface of the water down to about 200 meters, has much light which makes it possible for sea creatures to photosynthesize. Due to this condition, it has large concentration of plants and animals. The food chains here primarily start with phytoplankton. You can see lots of animals here... tuna, porpoises, sharks, and much more. The mesopelagic zone, from 200 meters down to about 1000 meters, is also called the twilight zone. A little bit of light penetrates to this zone, but not sufficient for photosynthesis. Although it is somewhat arguable, these two zones, the epipelagic zone and the mesopelagic zone together comprise the open ocean's photic zone.

Now, let's talk about the aphotic zone and some of the creatures that live here. Listen carefully — otherwise, you'll be lost. All right, now... the area from 1000 meters down to around 4000 meters is called the bathypelagic zone where the ocean is entirely dark and no living plants could be found. The only light that could be found is from some occasional bioluminescent organisms that emit light as a result of a chemical reaction. Most animals here are known to survive by consuming the marine snow — um, the detritus of other organisms falling from the zones above, or by preying upon others. Giant squid can be found at this depth, and deep-living sperm whales hunt the giant squid. Okay, so... next, um, abyssopelagic zone goes down from 4000 meters to above the ocean floor. This zone is also called the midnight zone. You'd easily notice that absolutely no light would penetrate this deep, huh? Most creatures that live here are blind and colorless. It is known that creatures like the Black swallower, tripod fish, deep-sea angler fish, that are able to withstand the immense pressures of the ocean depths, live here. It is continuously cold in this area... somewhere between 43 degrees Fahrenheit to 32 degrees Fahrenheit, and it lacks nutrients. Oh, and about the pressure... well, pressure usually increases 1 atmosphere for each 10 meters in depth, so the deep sea pressures may vary anywhere between 100 atmosphere to more than 1,000. Deep sea creatures have evolved in order to adapt to this harsh environment... you see, they have developed bodies with no excessive cavities such as swim bladders that could collapse under immense pressure. So, if these creatures were to be taken out of the water where there is no pressure, their organs might actually expand and possibly explode. Well, and... last but not least... right below this abyssopelagic zone lies the hadopelagic zone, where its name came from the Greek word Hades meaning the underworld. More than 90 percent of this deep water in ocean trenches is unknown but what we do know is that very few species live here... well, at least, in the open areas.

Until pretty recently, the deep sea environment was largely unexplored like I explained before. However, thanks to advances in deep sea submersibles and image capturing technologies, marine biologists are more and more being able to observe and uncover the mysteries of the deep sea which were previously unknown. Let's talk about this a little bit more and move on to our discussion.

자, 모두 앉읍시다. 좋아요. 이제 오늘 강의를 시작해 보죠. 오늘은 심해 생물에 대해 얘기해 보겠습니다. 우리가 사는 지구의 60퍼센트 이상이 수심이 1마일이 넘는 물로 덮여 있습니다. 우리가 쉽게 상상할 수 있듯이, 심해 생물은 혹독한 생활 조건과 맞서야 하는데, 예를 들어 빛이 매우 적거나 없고, 수압은 높고 에너지가 적으며 영하에 가깝거나 매우 높은 온도 등의 조건에 적응해야만 하죠. 이러한 악조건들 때문에 우리 인간이 심해를 탐사하기란 쉬운 일이 아닙니다. 심해의 1 퍼센트 이하만이 인간에 의해 탐사되었다는 건 놀라운 일이 아니죠. 심해까지는 빛이 매우 조금만 통과되거나 아예 닿지 않기 때문에 무광대라고도 불리는데요. 이 무광대의 많은 생물들은 광합성이 아닌 화학합성에 기반을 둔 먹이 사슬에 의존하고 있습니다.

심해 생물에 대해 더 자세히 살펴보기 전에, 먼저 바다가 수직으로 어떻게 구분되는지 알아봅시다. 원양대는 중심해지역이라고도 알려져 있는데, 이곳은 해변가나 해저를 제외한, 바다를 구성하는 대해의 일부입니다. 이해됐나요? 이 도표를 봅시다. 이 원양대는 수심에 따른 해수 기능의 차이와 서로 다른 생태적 특징에 따라 몇 개의 하부 구역으로 나뉘어집니다. 바다 표면에서 약 200미터 깊이까지의 표해수층은 태양빛을 많이 받기 때문에 이곳에 서식하는 생물들로 하여금 광합성을 할 수 있게 합니다. 이러한 조건 때문에 표해수층에 동식물이 가장 많이 살지요. 이곳의 먹이 사슬은 식물성 플랑크톤에서 시작합니다. 여기에서는 참치, 돌고래, 상어 등 많은 동물들을 볼 수 있습니다. 200미터에서 1000미터까지 되는 중심해층은 미광수층이라고도 불리우는데, 빛은 조금밖에 닿지 않으며 광합성을 할 정도로 충분하지는 않습니다. 어느 정도 의견이 분분하긴 하지만, 표해수층과 중심해층. 이 두 층을 합쳐 대양의 유광대라고 합니다.

자, 이제 무광층과 여기에 서식하는 생물들에 대해 알아봅시다. 잘못하면 헷갈릴 수 있으니까 잘 들으세요. 심해 1000미터부터 약 4000미터 정도까지는 점심해수층이라고 불리우는데, 이곳은 아주 어둡고 살아 있는 식물은 발견할 수 없습니다. 여기서는 가끔씩 화학적 반응으로 빛을 내는 발광 생물들에게서만 빛을 구경할 수 있는데요. 이 층에서 사는 대부분의 동물들은 바다눈, 즉 다른 층에서 떨어지는 생물들의 사체를 먹고 살거나 다른 동물들을 습격해 잡아 먹고 삽니다. 대왕오징어를 이 정도 깊이에서 찾아볼 수 있으며 심해에 서식하는 향유고래가 대왕오징어를 먹고 삽니다. 자, 좋아요... 다음은 심해수

층인데요, 이는 심해 4000미터부터 바닥까지의 지역을 이릅니다. 이 지역은 암흑층이라고 불립니다. 이 암흑층에는 빛이 전혀 닿지 않는다는 걸 쉽게 알 수 있겠죠? 여기에 사는 대부분의 생물들은 눈이 보이지 않고 색깔도 없습니다. Black swallower이나 삼발이고기, 심해 아귀와 같이 깊은 바다의 엄청난 수압을 견딜 수 있는 생물들만이 이 심해수층에서 서식하지요. 이 지역은 화씨 43도와 32도 사이 정도의 온도로 항상 수온이 차고 영양분 또한 없습니다. 아, 그리고 수압에 대해서는... 보통 표면에서 10미터 아래로 내려갈 때마다 수압은 1기압씩 올라가기 때문에, 심해의 수압은 100기압에서 1000기압이 넘을 수도 있습니다. 심해의 생물들은 이러한 가혹한 환경에 적응할 수 있도록 진화했는데요, 이 생물들의 몸에는 높은 기압에서 터질 수 있는 부레와 같은 기관이 없습니다. 따라서 이 생물들을 수압이 없는 바깥으로 꺼내면 이들의 기관들이 팽창하고 터질 수도 있지요. 자, 마지막으로, 이 심해수층 바로 아래에 hadopelagic zone이 있는데요, 이 이름은 지하세계를 뜻하는 그리스어인 하데스에서 유래된 것입니다. 바다의 해구에 있는 이 지역의 90퍼센트 이상은 우리에게 알려져 있지 않지만, 우리가 알고 있는 것은 여기에 사는 생물종은 극히 드물다는 겁니다. 적어도 좀 트인 공간에서는요.

앞서 설명했듯이, 최근까지 심해 환경은 인간의 탐사 손길이 닿지 않았지만, 심해 잠수함과 사진을 찍을 수 있는 과학 기술의 발달로 해양 생물학자들은 기존에는 알려지지 않았던 심해의 수수께끼를 관찰하고 파헤쳐 낼 수 있게 되었습니다. 이것에 대해 조금만 더 얘기해 보고 토론으로 넘어갑시다.

❶ What is the main topic of the lecture?
이 강의는 심해의 수직적 구분과 각 해양대에 사는 심해생물에 대한 것이다. 선택지 A, B, D는 강의에서 잠깐 언급된 제한적인 내용이므로 정답이 될 수 없다.

❷ According to the professor, why does the epipelagic zone have a large concentration of plants and animals?
교수는 수면에서 약 200 미터 깊이까지의 지역인 표해수층에는 태양빛을 많이 받아 바다 생물들로 하여금 광합성을 할 수 있게 하기 때문에 동식물이 많이 서식한다고 한다. 정답은 선택지 A이다.

❸ What does the professor say about deep sea animals when they are taken out of the water?
심해어는 극심한 수압에서 견딜 수 있도록 적응했으므로 수압이 없는 곳에 나오게 되면 내부 장기들이 팽창하여 터질 수 있다고 한다. 따라서 정답은 B이다.

❹ Which of the following is true about the aphotic zone?
참치와 돌고래는 표해수층에서 발견될 수 있으며, 또한 표해수층의 먹이사슬이 식물성 플랑크톤에서 시작한다고 하였으므로 선택지 A와 C는 잘못된 정보임을 알 수 있다. 또한 무광수층은 암흑의 세계이며 살아 있는 식물을 발견할 수 없다고 했으므로 선택지 B 역시 오답이다.

❺ Why does the professor mention marine snow?
무광층의 생물들은 바다눈, 즉 다른 층에서 떨어지는 생물들의 사체를 먹고 살거나 다른 동물들을 습격해서 잡아 먹는다고 교수의 설명에서 정답은 선택지 D임을 알 수 있다.

❻ How does the professor organize the lecture?

교수는 바다의 가장 얕은 부분인 표해수층으로부터 시작해서 가장 깊은 곳인 hadopelagic zone까지 차례대로 지역을 설명하며 그 지역에 사는 생물과 서식환경 등을 설명한다. 따라서 가장 좋은 정답은 선택지 **C**이다. 각 지역에 서식하는 생물을 언급하기는 하지만 생물을 주로 설명하는 것이 아니므로 선택지 **A**는 틀린 답이다.

Passage 4

1. B　　**2.** D　　**3.** C　　**4.** C　　**5.** C

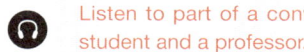 Listen to part of a conversation between a student and a professor.　▼

W: Hi, Professor Edmonton, can I come in? Is this a bad time?

M: Oh, hello, Clara. It's okay, please come in.

W: Thank you.

M: So, Clara, I didn't see you in class yesterday.

W: Well, actually, sir, I went to the doctor. I thought I could make it to your class, but the waiting line was unexpectely long, so...

M: You went to the doctor? Are you all right?

W: Yes, actually, my eyes started hurting a couple of days ago so I went to see my opthalmologist. He thinks I accidentally rubbed my eyes while sleeping and somehow hurt my cornea. Hopefully I'll get better in a few days.

M: That's good to hear. So, is it because of your absence yesterday that you came to see me?

W: Yes. Um, I knew that you were supposed to talk about the life of the mid-1800's in America. I read the assigned part of the book already, but there were some points that I didn't understand very well. So, I was wondering if you could, uh, sort of sum up the whole lecture for me, if it's not too much.

M: Well, the whole lecture? The lecture went on for an hour and a half, you know... Well, I'll try. Before that, let me give you this handout... wait a second... ah, here it is. Here, these three pages are the basic outline of the lecture, and this last page is a list of articles that you might wish to use as a reference.

W: Thank you.

M: So... yesterday's lecture was about the technological and economic growth during the 1840's and the 1850's. What do you know about this, Clara?

W: Uh... better sewing machines were invented and, uh, the steam engine, the cotton gin, the reaper, the telegraph all helped America's economy expand. Um, what I don't understand here, sir, is whether all of those machines were invented in America or not.

M: Well, not exactly. Some of those came from Europe but Americans invested in others' inventions and perfected their own.

W: Oh, I see.

M: Also, there was some advancement in agriculture as well. I talked about agriculture in the prairies and the woodlands, like some parts of Ohio, Kentucky, Michigan, Indiana, and Illinois... it's in the second page of the handout.

W: Okay.

M: It was really difficult for people to break the matted soil or plant anything, but in 1837, John Deere invented a steel-tipped plow that halved the labor required to clear prairie for planting. Soon after that, settlement occurred rapidly, because there was sufficient supply of timber for housing and fencing.

W: Interesting. Um, what about the railroad growth? The book says that by 1850 an ordinary American could travel on a train, but how does this connect with the growth of economy?

M: At the end of the 1860s, the United States had more track than rest of the world, which spearheaded the revolution of transportation. See, not only people traveled using the train, but commercial goods as well. Canals were still used for carrying goods, but it wasn't as fast as the railroad and it was vulnerable to winter freezes, so the value of goods transported by railroads quickly exceeded that carried by canals. ❹ **Cities started to boom thanks to the railroad, like Chicago, Chattanooga, and Atlanta.**

W: Chicago? Gee, I didn't know that.

M: **I thought so — you didn't read this in the textbook, right? That's why you can't afford to miss any of my classes. The book doesn't actually elaborate on the details very much.**

W: I know — I really regret that I missed yesterday's class. I'm sorry, sir.

M: You don't have to apologize, Clara. Now, let's move on.

W: 안녕하세요, 에드먼튼 교수님. 들어가도 될까요? 잠깐 시간 있으세요?

M: 아, 안녕, 클라라. 괜찮아요, 들어오세요.

W: 고맙습니다.

M: 클라라, 어제 수업시간에 안보이더군요.

W: 아, 실은 병원에 다녀왔어요. 수업에 갈 수 있을 줄 알았는데 대기자가 생각보다 많았거든요...

M: 병원에 다녀왔다고요? 괜찮은가요?

W: 네, 실은 며칠 전부터 눈이 아프기 시작해서 안과에 다녀왔어요. 자는 동안 눈을 잘못 비벼서 각막에 상처가 난 것 같다고 의사가 그러더라고요. 며칠 내로 나았으면 좋겠어요.

M: 다행이네요. 그럼 어제 수업에 빠진 것 때문에 찾아온 건가요?

W: 네, 어제 교수님께서 1800년대의 미국에 대해 수업하기로 하신 걸 알고 있었어요. 책에서 숙제로 내 주신 부분을 읽었지만 이해가 잘 안되는 부분들이 있거든요. 그래서 교수님께서 괜찮으시다면 강의 전체를 요약해 주시면 안될까 해서요.

M: 강의 전체를요? 한 시간 반 동안이나 했는데요... 한번 해 보죠. 그 전에 먼저 프린트물을 줄게요. 잠시만요... 아, 여기 있군요. 자, 여기 세 페이지는 강의의 기본적인 개요이고, 마지막 페이지가 참고할 만한 소논문 목록이에요.

W: 감사합니다.

M: 자, 어제 수업은 1840년대와 1850년대의 기술과 경제 성장에 대한 것이었어요. 이 주제에 대해 무엇을 알고 있나요, 클라라?

W: 어... 더 성능이 좋은 재봉틀이 발명됐고 증기 엔진이랑 조면기, 수확기, 그리고 전신기 등이 미국의 경제를 확장시키는데 기여했어요. 제가 여기서 이해가 안되는 건요, 교수님, 그 기계들이 모두 미국에서 발명된 것인지 아닌지예요.

M: 꼭 그런 건 아니에요. 이들 중 몇몇은 유럽에서 건너왔지만 미국인들이 다른 이들의 발명품에 투자해서 자신들에게 잘 맞는 것으로 완성시킨 거지요.

W: 아, 알겠어요.

M: 그리고 농업 분야에서도 발전이 있었는데 오하이오, 켄터키, 미시건, 인디애나, 일리노이주 등의 대초원과 삼림지에서의 농업에 대해 언급했어요. 이것은 나눠 준 프린트물의 두 번째 페이지에 있어요.

W: 알겠습니다.

M: 딱딱하게 들러붙은 농토를 부수거나 무언가를 심는 것이 매우 힘들었지만 1837년에 존 디어라는 사람이 끝이 강철로 된 쟁기를 발명해서 대초원을 경작할 수 있는 땅으로 만드는 데 드는 노력이 반으로 줄게 되었어요. 곧이어 이주가 급격하게 일어났어요. 집을 짓고 울타리를 만들 수 있는 목재가 충분해서였죠.

W: 흥미롭네요. 철도 성장은 어떤가요? 책에서는 1850년에 이르렀을 때 일반 미국인이 기차로 여행할 수 있었다고 하는데, 그것이 경제 성장과 어떻게 연관이 되어 있나요?

M: 1860년대 말에 미국에는 세상에서 가장 많은 철도가 건설되어 있었는데 이것이 교통의 혁명을 가져왔어요. 사람들만 여행하기 위해 기차를 이용한 게 아니라 상품들도 철도로 운반이 되었죠. 상품을 운반하는데 운하가 계속 사용되긴 했지만 철도만큼 빠르진 않은데다가 겨울에 강이 얼면 문제가 됐기 때문에 운하로 운반되는 상품보다 철도로 운반되는 상품의 가치가 훨씬 더 높아졌어요. 철도 덕택에 시카고, 차타누가, 그리고 아틀란타 같은 도시도 성장하기 시작했고요.

W: 시카고요? 그런 건 몰랐는데요.

M: 그럴 줄 알았어요. 이 내용은 책에 안 나와 있죠? 그래서 수업에 출석해야 하는 거예요. 책에는 이러한 세부적인 사항들이 자세하게 나와 있지 않거든요.

W: 알아요. 이번 수업을 빠진 게 정말 후회돼요. 죄송합니다, 교수님.

M: 미안해 할 것 없어요, 클라라. 자, 계속해 보죠.

❶ Why does the student want to talk with the professor?

학생은 병원에 가느라 수업에 결석했으며, 수업 내용을 요약해 달라는 부탁을 하기 위해 교수를 찾아왔으므로 정답은 B이다.

❷ What does the professor say about the technological development during the 1840's and the 1850's?

"Some of those came from Europe but Americans kind of invested in others' inventions and perfected their own"라는 교수의 말에서 정답을 알 수 있다. 유럽에서 수입해온 기계들을 수입해서 필요한 대로 개조해서 사용했기 때문에 선택지 A는 정답이 아니며, 농업 위주로 기술 발전이 된 것이 아니므로 선택지 B 역시 틀린 답이다. 선택지 C는 본문의 내용과 다르다.

❸ According to the professor, why was the railroad used more often than canals to transport commercial goods in the 19th-century America?

운하가 계속 이용되긴 했지만 철도만큼 빠르지 않으며 겨울에 강이 얼면 운하를 이용할 수가 없었기 때문에 운하보다 철도가 훨씬 더 많이 이용됐다는 교수의 말에서 답을 찾을 수 있다.

❹ What does the professor mean when he says this:

교수는 이렇게 말한 후 "That's why you can't afford to miss any of my classes. The book doesn't actually elaborate the details very much"라고 말하며, 책에 나오지 않은 세부사항들을 자신의 수업에서 많이 얘기해주기 때문에 수업에 잘 참석하라고 말한다. 여학생이 책을 잘못 읽었거나(선택지 A) 교수의 강의를 이해할 수 있는 지식이 없다고 하는 것(선택지 B)도 아니다. 또한 읽어야 할 책을 여학생이 제대로 읽지 않은 것(선택지 D)도 아니다. 가장 좋은 정답은 선택지 C이다.

❺ What can be inferred about the professor and his lectures?

책에는 세부적인 내용이 잘 나와있지 않기 때문에 수업에 잘 참석하라는 교수의 말에서 정답을 알 수 있다. 선택지 A와 D는 본문의 내용에서 알 수 없으나 B의 내용은 본문에서 보이는 교수의 태도를 봤을 때 너무 극단적인 내용이다.

Passage 5

1. A **2.** C **3.** C **4.** C **5.** B **6.** 참조

Order	Sentence
First	C
Second	A
Third	D
Fourth	B

 Listen to part of a lecture in a psychology class. The professor is discussing cognitive development of infants. ▼

P(M): All right, let's get started. Uh... today, we will discuss cognitive development in terms of mathematics learning. But first of all, let's start off with the nature of mathematical knowledge and skill... who here has struggled with math during high school?

Yeah, just as I expected — lots of you. Actually, end-of-the-year assessments frequently expose the fact that many students graduate high school without sufficient knowledge of math. School officials and scholars wonder what they're doing wrong, or what kind of teaching method they should apply.

Well, most of us think that children start learning mathematic skills when they start elementary school... uh, some prodigies, maybe a little bit earlier than preschool. But what most people don't know is the fact that mathematic skills can develop as early as when a child is 5 or 6 months old... you know, that infants can count long before they can demonstrate that skill to their parents or guardian. Amazing, huh? So, let's discuss the four sections of a child's math-learning phases: the infancy and preschool periods, the elementary school period, the middle school period, and finally, the high school period. Let's talk about the infancy first.

Nativist psychologists say that infants come into the world equipped with concepts such as number, space, and causality. Because babies who are six months or seven months old are neither verbal nor adept at pointing, researchers had to design special experiments that could support their theory. One of the three methodologies used here is called habituation. Habituation, basically, um, explains when the same picture is shown over and over again, the infant looks at it less and less as if she's saying, "I've seen that before and I'm bored." Get it? In an experiment based on this methodology, researchers showed a picture with two dots and another picture with three dots to several 6-month-old infants. After the picture with two dots was flashed 15 times the other picture with three dots was flashed. The researchers found that the infants gave longer looks on trial sixteen. This study suggests that the ability to subitize is present very early and seems to be innate. Subitizing is the perception-based ability to rapidly, accurately, and confidently determine the number of objects present without counting them. For example, most people can immediately tell whether there are four dots or less without counting, but if there are more than four, many of them have to start counting in order to decide how many there are. However, it's also possible to conclude that the infants in the study gave a longer look on trial sixteen when the picture changed because they just knew that there was something different.

Now, um, let's talk about the second methodology which can be called the surprise methodology. In a 1992 article featured in the Nature, Karen Wynn explained her experiment involving Mickey Mouse dolls and 5-month-old infants. The experiment went on like this: first, the doll was placed on a small stage in front of an infant and a screen rose to hide the doll. Then, a hand holding another doll went behind the screen and came out empty as if it placed the doll behind the screen. Lastly, the screen rolled down to show the dolls on the stage. Now, there were two events involved here — the possible event and the impossible event. The possible event was when the screen was lowered and revealed two dolls sitting there, and the impossible one was when there was only one doll on the stage or even three dolls. Does everyone follow me? Okay. ❺ **Well, of course, in the impossible event, one of the dolls was removed or another one was placed without the infant knowing it. And what was the result? Well, what do you know — it turned out that the infants looked longer at the impossible event than they did at the possible event, suggesting they were doing some mental addition.**

All right, now, let's move on to the third and last methodology here which involves a visual expectation procedure. Here, an infant sees a picture being flashed two or three times in a row on the left side of a screen. And then, the picture is flashed on the right side. Over time, the infant starts to follow the left-left-right pattern with his eyes. If he fixates at the left side until the second one flashes, then moves his eyes to the right to look for the picture to appear, that seems to suggest that he's counting the ones on the left before looking to the right.

The experiments I just explained suggest two possible

interpretations. First, the Nativists might be right after all. You know, infants might be born with some math concepts and procedures. Second, infants actually do not understand such high-level math ideas but rather they possess brain structures that are implicitly sensitive to patterns in the environment. Which one is right? Only additional research and theorizing will reveal the answer. Now, let's move on to the next phase, the preschool period.

좋아요, 이제 시작합시다. 아, 오늘은 수학 습득과 관련된 인지발달에 대해 논해 보도록 하겠습니다. 하지만 먼저 수학적 지식과 기술의 특징부터 시작해 보죠. 고등학교 시절 수학 때문에 골머리를 앓아 본 사람 혹시 없으세요? 네, 생각했던 대로 여러명이 겪어봤군요. 사실 연말에 보는 시험 결과에 따르면 많은 학생들이 충분한 수학적 지식 없이 고등학교를 졸업한다고 하더군요. 학교 관계자들과 학자들은 혹시 자기들한테 문제가 있는 것인지, 아니면 어떤 교육 방법을 적용해야 하는지 생각하기도 하지요.

우리들 대부분은 어린이들이 초등학교 때부터 수학적 기술을 배우기 시작한다고 생각합니다. 어떤 신동들은 유아원에 가기 조금 전부터 시작하기도 하고요. 하지만 대부분의 사람들이 모르는 사실은 수학적 기술은 빠르면 생후 5~6개월 때부터 발달할 수 있다는 겁니다. 영아들은 부모나 보호자에게 말이나 행동으로 그 기술을 가지고 있다고 보여줄 수 없을 정도로 어릴 때부터 수를 셈할 수 있다고 해요. 신기하죠? 자, 그럼 어린이의 수학 습득 네 가지 단계에 대해 살펴봅시다 – 영유아기 시절, 초등학교 시절, 중학교 시절, 그리고 마지막으로 고등학교 시절이 바로 그것이지요. 먼저 영아기부터 살펴봅시다.

선천론 심리학자들은 영아들이 숫자와 공간, 그리고 인과관계와 같은 개념을 미리 가지고 태어난다고 말합니다. 생후 6개월이나 7개월 된 아기들은 말을 할 수도 없고 손으로 가리킬 수 있는 능력도 없기 때문에 연구자들은 그들의 이론을 뒷받침할 수 있는 특별한 실험을 해야만 했지요. 여기에서 사용된 세 가지 방법 중 하나가 바로 습관화입니다. 기본적으로 습관화에서는 같은 그림이 지속적으로 반복해서 보여지게 되면, 영아는 마치 "나 그거 벌써 봐서 지루해요"라고 말하는 듯이 점점 그 그림을 보는 횟수가 줄어듭니다. 이해되죠? 이 방법론에 기반을 둔 한 실험에서 연구자들은 6개월 된 몇 명의 아기들에게 두 개의 점이 있는 그림 하나와 세 개의 점이 그려져 있는 다른 그림 하나를 보여줬습니다. 두 개의 점 그림을 15번 보여준 후 세 개의 점 그림이 보여주었습니다. 연구자들은 영아들이 16번째 시도에 조금 더 오랜 기간 시선을 보냈다는 것을 발견했지요. 이 연구는 순간적으로 사물을 파악할 수 있는 능력(subitize)이 아주 어린 아기들에게도 있다는 것과, 이것이 선천적인 것 같다는 것을 말해줍니다. 순간적으로 파악하는 것이란 물체의 수를 세지 않고 빠르게, 정확하게, 그리고 자신있게 그 수를 결정하는 능력을 말합니다. 예를 들어, 대부분의 사람들은 세지 않고 네 개나 그 이하의 점의 수를 곧바로 알아낼 수 있지만, 점이 네 개 이상이 되면 많은 사람들이 몇 개의 점이 있나 보기 위해 수를 세기 시작해야 한다는 것입니다. 하지만 이 연구에서의 아기들이 그림이 바뀐 16번째 시도에서 조금 더 시선을 길게 준 이유는 무언가가 달랐기 때문에 그랬을 수도 있다고 결론지을 수도 있습니다.

이제 놀람 방법론이라고 불리는 두 번째 방법론에 대해 얘기해 봅시다. 1992년에 "네이처"지에 실렸던 소논문에서 캐런 윈은 미키마우스 인형과 5개월 된 영아들과의 실험을 설명했는데요. 이 실험은 이렇게 진행됐습니다. 먼저, 영아 앞에 설치된 작은 무대에 인형을 놓고, 스크린이 올라와서 인형을 가립니다. 다음으로 다른 인형을 들고 있는 손이 스크린 뒤로 들어가고 마치 인형을 스크린 뒤로 놓았다는 듯이 빈 손으로 나옵니다. 그리고 나서 스크린이 다시 내려가고 무대 위의 인형들을 보여줍니다. 자, 여기에서는 두 가지의 사건이 있었는데요. 하나는 가능적 사건이고 다른 하나는 불가능적 사건입니다.

가능적 사건은 스크린이 내려갔을 때 두 개의 인형이 무대 위에 있는 경우이고, 불가능적 사건은 단 한 개나 심지어 세 개의 인형이 무대 위에 올려져 있는 경우를 말합니다. 모두 이해됩니까? 좋아요. 물론, 이 불가능적 사건에서는 영아 몰래 인형 하나가 치워졌거나 새로 하나가 더 놓아진 것입니다. 이 실험의 결과는 어땠을까요? 신기하게도 영아들은 가능적 사건을 본 것보다 불가능적 사건을 더 오래 바라봤습니다. 이것은 이 영아들이 머릿속으로 셈을 했다는 것을 제시합니다.

자, 이제 시각적 기대 절차인 세 번째이자 마지막인 방법론으로 가 봅시다. 여기에서는 한 영아가 스크린의 왼쪽에서 그림이 연속으로 두 번이나 세 번 켜졌다 꺼졌다 하는 것을 보게 됩니다. 그리고 그림은 오른쪽에서 깜빡이지요. 시간이 지나면서 아기는 왼쪽-왼쪽-오른쪽 패턴을 눈으로 쫓기 시작합니다. 만약 아기가 그림이 두 번째 깜빡일 때까지 왼쪽으로 눈을 고정시키고 그림이 나타나는지 보기 위해 눈을 오른쪽으로 돌린다면, 이것은 아기가 오른쪽을 보기 이전에 왼쪽에서 깜빡이는 횟수를 세고 있었다는 것을 뒷받침해 줍니다.

제가 방금 설명한 실험들로 두 가지의 해석을 할 수 있습니다. 먼저, 선천론 심리학자들의 이론이 맞을지도 모른다는 것이지요. 영아들은 수학 개념과 절차 방법을 선천적으로 가지고 태어나는지도 모릅니다. 둘째, 영아들은 실제로는 고차원적인 수학 개념은 알지 못하지만 환경의 패턴에 대해 내재적으로 민감한 뇌구조를 가지고 있을지도 모른다는 것입니다. 이 중에서 어느 것이 맞는 것일까요? 앞으로 더 연구를 하고 이론화 해야만 답을 얻을 수가 있겠죠. 이제 그 다음 단계인 유아기 시절로 넘어갑시다.

❶ What is the lecture mainly about?

"Today, we will discuss cognitive development in terms of mathematics learning"와 "Let's talk about the infancy first"라는 교수의 말에서 정답을 알 수 있다.

❷ According to the lecture, why do most people think that children's ability to learn mathematics skills start from elementary school?

5, 6개월 된 영아들은 부모나 보호자가 알 수 있을 만큼 그들의 수학적 능력을 보여줄 수 있는 표현 방법을 모르므로 대부분의 사람들이 초등학교 시절부터 수학적 능력이 발달된다고 생각한다는 것을 알 수 있다. 따라서 정답은 선택지 C이다.

❸ Which of the following would Nativist psychologists probably agree with?

선천론 심리학자들은 사람은 숫자, 공간과 인과관계와 같은 개념을 가지고 태어난다고 믿는다고 했으므로 정답은 선택지 C이다.

❹ According to the professor, what does the term subitizing mean?

"Subitizing is the perception-based ability to rapidly, accurately, and confidently determine the number of objects present without counting them"라는 교수의 설명에서 정답을 알 수 있다.

❺ What does the professor imply when he says this:

"What do you know"라는 표현은 "당신은 무엇을 알고 있습니까"라는 뜻도 되지만, "신기하다"며 놀라움을 나타내는 표현도 된다. 여기에서 교수는 영아들에게 실행된 실험의 결과가 놀랍다고 생각한다는 것을 알 수 있다. 그러므로 정답은 선택지 B이다.

❻ Based on the information in the lecture, indicate the order of the given sentences.

실험은 먼저 영아 앞에 설치된 작은 무대 위에 인형이 놓아지는 것에서 시작된다. 스크린이 올라와서 인형을 가린 후, 다른 인형을 든 손이 스크린 뒤로 들어가고 빈 손으로 나온다. 그리고 나서 스크린이 내려져 무대 위에 있는 인형을 보여준다.

(Passage 6)

1. B　　**2.** C　　**3.** B　　**4.** B, D　　**5.** A　　**6.** B

🎧 Listen to part of a discussion in an environmental studies class. ▼

P(W): All right, uh, let's all settle down. Okay, um... today, we're gonna talk about animal species that are in jeopardy as a result of human activity and its consequences. ❸ I believe you all have researched some of those endangered species, right? Tom?

M: Um.... I, uh... um....

P: What about you, Kevin?

M: I, I, I did find some species that are in danger... um, like, the polar bear?

P: Okay, that can be one species. What about other animals?

M: Um....

P: Well, folks, in order to follow my class, you've got to do what you're asked to do.

M: I'm sorry, Dr. Cena.

P: Well, make sure it doesn't happen again next time. Okay, well, let's, uh, let's talk about the polar bear first and then we'll move on to some other animal species, all right? Okay. Now... Kevin, tell me why you think polar bears are in danger because of human activity.

M: Um, it's because their habitat, which is the Arctic, is melting due to global warming.

P: That's correct. The sea ice they live on is thinning due to global warming. What other reasons can you think of?

M: What about overhunting by hunters, development and pollution of the area, and growing tourism? I guess they may all affect the dropping population of polar bears.

P: Good. Actually, it might be more suitable to address polar bears as imperiled or threatened species rather than endangered species... at least for now, since the endangered category is used more for species highly likely to become extinct. However, there are signs that indicate that polar bears are dropping in numbers and weight in the Arctic.

Polar bears usually live in Greenland and Norway, and about a quarter of them live mainly in Alaska and travel to Canada and Russia. It is amazing when you think about a living animal able to live in such a harsh environment — they are well-adapted to the habitat with their thick blubber and fur that insulate them against the extreme cold. Also, the translucent fur that appears white or cream-colored can camouflage them from their prey. Because of their physical conditions, they cannot live in a warm environment... you might have seen them in zoos during the summer time, right? Um, or pictures of polar bears swimming in ice water or hugging a big chunk of ice.

M: Yeah, I've seen one eating ice cubes when I went to the San Diego Zoo last summer.

P: Exactly. Now, if we move on to what polar bears prey on... they, um, primarily hunt seals but also eat anything they catch, such as birds, rodents, crabs, shellfish, beluga whales, and young walruses. They might even kill and eat each other. They are excellent swimmers and, surprisingly, hunt efficiently on land due to their prodigious speed, so they can easily outrun a human on land.

M: Interesting.

P: It is, isn't it? However, their body can quickly overheat when they run a long mile, so they usually stay on the ice. Now, if we go back to our topic today, as I reiterate, the destruction of their habitat of the Arctic ice, the melting of the ice due to global warming, and other reasons seriously threaten polar bears' existence. Some researchers even fear that they might become extinct within the century. The Polar Bear Specialist Groups of the World Conservation Union which is based in Switzerland has estimated that the polar bear population in the Arctic is somewhere between 20 to 25 thousand, but the population will decrease by 30 percent over the next 45 years. It also expects that sea ice will decrease 50 to 100 percent over the next 50 to 100 years.

M: That's pretty scary... it means that the sea level will dramatically go up and affect the human beings as well. Um, professor, does overhunting and other human activities other than global warming pose serious danger on the existence of polar bears?

P: Well, this is quite arguable and controversial. The government is trying to regulate human activities that might affect polar bears' habitat, such as oil and gas exploration, commercial shipping, releases of toxic contaminants, or climate-affecting pollution. However, at the same time, it does not want to curtail coastal and offshore oil and gas searches in Alaska... it's all related with the country's interests. See? Also, the government says that the oil and gas activity in that area doesn't pose a threat to the polar bear population. Interestingly enough, so do other hunting activities of Alaskan natives who hunt the bears as part of their subsistence diet. All right, enough about polar bears for now — what else?

P: 좋아요, 모두 시작할 준비합시다. 자, 오늘은 인간의 활동과 그 영향으로 인해 멸종 위기에 처한 동물 종에 대해 이야기해 보겠어요. 이러한 멸종 위기 동물들에 대해 다들 조사해 왔겠지요? 탐?

M: 어... 저는, 어....

P: 케빈은 어떤가요?

M: 저, 저는 위기에 처한 종을 좀 찾기는 했는데요... 그러니까, 북극곰 같은 거요?

P: 좋아요, 북극곰도 그 중 하나일 수 있어요. 다른 동물은 어떤가요?

M: 그게....

P: 자, 여러분, 내 수업을 잘 따라오려면 해 오라는 건 잘 해 와야 할 거예요.

M: 죄송합니다, 세나 교수님.

P: 다음 번엔 이런 일이 없도록 합시다. 좋습니다. 먼저 북극곰에 대해 얘기해 보고 다른 종으로 넘어가도록 해요. 자, 케빈, 북극곰이 왜 인간 활동에 의해 멸종 위기에 처했다고 생각하는지 얘기해 보세요.

M: 왜냐하면 그들의 서식지인 북극 지역이 지구 온난화로 인해 녹고 있기 때문이에요.

P: 맞았어요. 북극곰이 서식하는 북극해의 얼음이 지구 온난화 때문에 얇아지고 있지요. 또 생각나는 다른 이유로는 무엇이 있나요?

M: 사냥꾼에 의한 과도한 사냥이나 서식지의 개발과 오염, 그리고 관광객의 증가는 어떤가요? 이런 것 모두 북극곰의 개체수를 떨어뜨리는 원인이 될 것 같은데요.

P: 맞아요. 사실 적어도 지금은 북극곰을 멸종 위기 동물이라고 부르기 보다는 위험에 처한 종이라고 부르는 게 더 맞을 것 같아요. 멸종 위기 목록은 실제로 멸종할 것 같은 종을 위해 남겨두는 것이니까요. 하지만 북극 지역에서 북극곰의 개체수와 몸무게가 줄고 있다는 것을 나타내는 조짐이 있어요.

북극곰들은 그린란드와 노르웨이에서 주로 서식하는데, 이들 중 1/4 가량은 주로 알래스카에서 살고 캐나다와 러시아로 이동해요. 살아있는 생물이 그렇게 가혹한 환경에서 살아갈 수 있다는 건 생각만 해도 참 신기한데요, 북극곰들은 두꺼운 지방층과 털을 가지고 있어 바깥의 강추위로부터 몸을 보호할 수 있도록 환경에 적응했어요. 또한 흰색 혹은 크림색으로 보이는 반투명의 털은 북극곰이 포식동물에게 노출되지 않도록 위장해 주죠. 이러한 신체적 조건들 때문에 북극곰은 따뜻한 지역에서는 살 수 없어요. 여름에 이들을 동물원에서 본 적이 있었죠? 아니면 북극곰이 얼음물에서 수영하거나 커다란 얼음 덩어리를 안고 있는 사진을 보았거나요...

M: 네, 지난 여름에 샌디에고 동물원에 갔을 때 북극곰 한 마리가 얼음조각을 먹고 있는 걸 봤어요.

P: 맞아요. 자, 이제 북극곰의 먹이로 넘어가 보죠. 북극곰은 주로 물개를 사냥하지만 새, 설치류, 게, 갑각류, 흰돌고래나 어린 해마 등 사냥하는 것 아무거나 닥치는대로 먹어요. 심지어 서로를 죽여서 잡아먹을 수도 있답니다. 북극

곰은 수영을 매우 잘하고, 놀랍겠지만 속도가 매우 빠르기 때문에 육지에서도 효율적으로 사냥을 한답니다. 북극곰은 육지에서 쉽게 사람을 따라잡을 수 있어요.

M: 흥미롭네요.

P: 그렇죠? 하지만 오래 뛰면 체온이 급격히 상승할 수 있기 때문에 주로 얼음 위에서 생활해요. 자, 이제 주제로 돌아가보면, 다시 한 번 말하지만 북극곰의 서식지인 북극 얼음의 파괴와 지구 온난화로 인해 얼음이 녹는 것, 그리고 다른 이유들이 북극곰의 생존을 심각하게 위협하고 있어요. 어떤 연구자들은 이번 세기 안에 북극곰이 멸종할 것이라고 걱정하기도 하죠. 스위스에 기반을 둔 세계보전연맹의 북극곰 전문단체는 북극 지역의 북극곰 개체수가 2만마리에서 2만5천마리 사이가 될 것이라고 예측했지만, 앞으로 45년간 그 개체수는 30퍼센트 정도 감소할 것이라고 보고 있어요. 이 단체는 또한 앞으로 50년에서 100년 사이에 바다 얼음이 50퍼센트에서 100퍼센트 감소할 것이라고 해요.

M: 생각해 보면 무시무시하네요... 그 말은 즉 해수면이 급격하게 상승해서 인간에게도 영향을 줄 것이라는 거잖아요. 교수님, 지구 온난화 외에도 과잉 사냥과 인간의 다른 활동들이 북극곰의 생존에 심각하게 영향을 주나요?

P: 글쎄요, 그것은 상당히 논쟁의 여지가 있는 문제예요. 정부는 석유와 가스 탐사, 상업적 해운업, 독극물의 방류, 혹은 기후에 영향을 주는 오염 등, 북극곰의 서식지에 영향을 줄 수 있는 인간 활동을 규제하려고 노력하고 있어요. 하지만 동시에 알래스카 연안과 앞바다에서의 석유와 가스 탐사를 줄이고 싶어하지는 않아요. 이 모두가 국가의 이익과 관련이 되는 문제라서 말이지요. 또한, 정부는 그 지역에서의 석유와 가스 탐사 활동이 북극곰의 개체수에 그다지 큰 위협을 가하고 있지는 않다고 합니다. 흥미로운 것은, 북극곰을 주식으로 사냥하는 알래스카 원주민들의 활동 또한 북극곰에게 그다지 큰 위협이 되지 않는다고 하는군요. 자, 북극곰은 여기에서 마칩시다. 다른 동물은 또 없을까요?

❶ What is the discussion mainly about?

"Today, we're gonna talk about animal species that are in jeopardy as a result of human activity and its consequences"라고 말한 후 "let's talk about the polar bear first and then we'll move on to some other animal species"라고 말하며 인간 활동과 그 결과로 인한 북극곰의 생태적 위험에 대해 설명한다. 따라서 가장 좋은 정답은 선택지 B이다. 선택지 A와 D는 너무 제한적인 내용이며 반대로 선택지 C는 너무 광범위한 내용이다.

❷ Why does the professor mention imperiled or threatened species?

교수는 북극곰을 imperiled or threatened species라고 부르는 것이 낫다고 하는데, 그 이유는 비록 개체수가 감소하고 있는 추세이기는 하지만 아직까지 실제로 멸종 위기에 처한 것은 아니기 때문이다. 따라서 정답은 선택지 C이다. 교수는 북극곰의 현재 상황에 대해 심사숙고 해보라고 이러한 용어를 제시한 것은 아니므로 선택지 A는 답이 될 수 없다.

❸ How does the professor feel when she says this:

교수는 멸종 위기에 처한 종이 무엇이 있는지 학생들에게 물어보지만 아무도 시원하게 대답하지 못하자 준비를 잘 해오라며 학생들을 나무란다. 화가 났다기 보다는 강의 준비를 철저하게 하지 않은 학생들의 모습에 다소 실망한 것이므로 선택지 A 보다는 B가 답으로 적절하다. 학생들의 불복종에 무관심한 것도 아니므로 D

역시 답이 아니다. 마찬가지로 학생들이 주제에 대해 잘 알지 못하는 것에 기뻐하는 것도 아니므로 C 역시 답이 될 수 없다.

❹ **According to the professor, what physical feature of a polar bear makes it easier to withstand the extreme cold?**

북극곰이 극심한 추위를 견딜 수 있는 것은 두꺼운 지방층과 빽빽한 털 때문이다. 추위와 북극곰의 털 색깔, 그리고 지상에서 빨리 뛸 수 있는 능력과는 관련이 없다.

❺ **Which of the following is true about the effect of human activity on polar bears?**

"The destruction of their habitat of the Arctic ice, the melting of the ice due to global warming, and other reasons seriously threaten polar bears' existence"라는 교수의 말에서 정답(선택지 A)을 알 수 있다. 선택지 B와 C는 지문의 내용과 다르며, 선택지 D는 지문에서 언급된 바가 없다.

❻ **What will the professor probably discuss next?**

처음에 "Let's talk about the polar bear first and then we'll move on to some other animal species"라는 교수의 말에서 먼저 북극곰에 대해 논한 후 다른 종으로 주제를 옮겨 갈 것을 알 수 있다. 또한 "All right, enough about polar bears for now — what else?"라는 교수의 말에서 이제 북극곰에 대해 그만 이야기하고 멸종 위기에 처한 다른 종으로 넘어 갈 것임을 알 수 있다. 따라서 정답은 B이다.

Set 2

P.1	1. B	2. A	3. C	4. C	5. D
P.2	1. D	2. C	3. B		
	4. D	5. A, D	6. A		
P.3	1. C	2. A	3. C		
	4. B	5. A	6. 참조		
P.4	1. D	2. A	3. B	4. D	5. C
P.5	1. C	2. A	3. D		
	4. B	5. A, D	6. B		
P.6	1. C	2. A, B	3. B		
	4. A	5. D	6. C		

(**Passage 1**)

1. B   2. A   3. C   4. C   5. D

 Listen to part of a conversation between a student and a staff at the school transportation office. ▼

W: Hello, what can I do for you?

M: Hi, I'm a freshman here, and I was wondering how to get to the nearest airport from here.

W: Okay. Um, is this the first time you're trying to get to the airport?

M: Yes, my father drove me here when I first came here, so I don't know where the airport is.

W: That's understandable — a lot of freshmen do that, actually, because they have to bring in their stuff. Um, there are several ways to get to the airport. Um, do you have... do you have a car? Because that's the easiest way to get there.

M: Uh, unfortunately, no, I don't have a car.

W: Oh. Well, if you drove on your own, it would have taken you only about 30 minutes, and you could always use the self-parking lot near the airport, but... well, since you don't have a car, then you might as well call a cab. It will probably cost you about $50.

M: Fifty dollars? Gee, my plane ticket only cost me a hundred bucks — I don't want to spend that money on a taxi fare. Besides, I don't have any extra baggage to carry along because I'll be gone only for a week. ❸ Um, is there any other transportation that I could use? I don't care how long it takes to get to the airport... It's no sweat being the early bird.

W: Well, if that's the case, you can either take the public transportation, or take the airport shuttle bus. Mind you, though — the airport shuttle bus runs only once every two hours, so if you miss it by one second, you're going to have to take the public transportation.

M: As long as I know what time the shuttle bus comes, I'm pretty sure I can take it.

W: Okay, here's the time schedule for the shuttle bus.

M: Thank you. Um, where do I take the bus?

W: If you go out to 42nd and Windsor Street, you can find a post that says "Airport Shuttle." You can't miss it.

M: How long does it take to get to the airport if I take the shuttle bus?

W: The shuttle circles around the city, so it'll take you about 50 minutes.

M: Thanks a lot. Um, just in case I miss the shuttle bus... could you tell me what public transportation I should take?

W: Sure, but you're going to have to transfer twice. Uh, go down Windsor Street until you meet 36th Street. Take the bus number 605 there, get off at 10th and Windsor, and take the subway to Marshall Hall. If you get off at Marshall Hall, ask a personnel there... uh, ask them where you should take the Redding Bus. The Redding Bus should travel all the way to the airport.

M: Oh, wow... it's pretty complicated... let me just write this down a little bit... I'm sorry.

W: It's okay, take your time. By the way, it will take you nearly an hour and a half to get to the airport this way, so you want to make haste. They say that you should arrive at the airport at least two hours before your flight, since the security has been increased these days.

M: I'll keep that in mind. Thank you so much. I really appreciate it.

W: 안녕하세요, 무엇을 도와드릴까요?

M: 안녕하세요. 이곳 1학년생인데요. 여기에서 가장 가까운 공항으로 어떻게 가는지 궁금해서요.

W: 네. 공항에 가시는 게 이번이 처음이신가요?

M: 네, 여기 처음 왔을 때는 아버지께서 차로 데려다 주셨기 때문에 공항이 어디 있는지 몰라요.

W: 이해해요. 사실 많은 1학년 학생들이 그렇게 와요. 물건을 가져와야 하니까요. 공항에 가는 방법은 몇 가지가 있는데, 혹시 차가 있나요? 왜냐하면 그 방법이 공항에 가기에 가장 쉽거든요.

M: 아쉽지만 차가 없어요.

W: 그렇군요. 직접 운전한다면 30분 정도 밖에 안걸리고 공항 근처의 셀프 주차장을 이용할 수 있는데... 차가 없으시다니 택시를 이용하시면 되겠네요. 요금이 아마 50달러 정도 들거예요.

M: 50달러요? 이런. 비행기표가 100달러 밖에 안되는데요... 그렇게 많은 돈을 택시비로 낭비하고 싶진 않아요. 게다가 일주일만 다녀올 거라서 가져갈 짐도 없거든요. 다른 교통 수단은 이용할 만한 게 없을까요? 시간은 얼마든지 걸려도 상관 없어요. 일찍 일어나는 건 문제가 아니거든요.

W: 그렇다면 대중교통을 이용하거나 공항 셔틀버스를 이용하시면 돼요. 그런데 공항 셔틀버스는 2시간에 한 번씩밖에 안오니까 그걸 놓치면 대중교통을 이용하셔야 된다는 점 기억하세요.

M: 셔틀버스가 몇 시에 오는지만 알면 탈 수 있을 거예요.

W: 좋아요, 여기 셔틀버스 시간표를 드릴게요.

M: 고맙습니다. 어, 셔틀버스는 어디에서 타면 되나요?

W: 42번가와 윈저가로 나가시면 "공항 셔틀"이라는 표지판이 있을 거예요. 쉽게 찾으실 거예요.

M: 셔틀버스를 타면 공항까지 얼마나 걸리나요?

W: 셔틀버스가 시내를 돌아서 보통 50분 정도 걸려요.

M: 고맙습니다. 셔틀버스를 놓칠 경우에는 어떤 대중교통을 이용해야 하는지 알려주시겠어요?

W: 물론이에요. 하지만 두 번 갈아타셔야 해요. 윈저가를 쭉 따라서 36번가까지 가세요. 거기서 605번 버스를 타고 10번가와 윈저가에서 내리시고요. 거기에서 마셜 홀까지 지하철을 타세요. 마셜 홀에서 내리시면 레딩 버스를 어디서 타야 하는지 직원한테 물어보세요. 레딩 버스가 공항까지 가니까요.

M: 와... 좀 복잡하네요. 잠시 적을게요. 죄송합니다..

W: 괜찮아요. 천천히 하세요. 그나저나. 그렇게 가시면 공항까지 거의 1시간 반 정도가 걸리니까 서두르셔야 할 거예요. 요즘 공항 보안이 엄격해져서 비행기 시간 2시간 전에는 도착해야 한다고 하더군요.

M: 명심할게요. 정말 고맙습니다.

❶ Why does the man want to talk to the woman?

"I'm a freshman here, and I was wondering how to get to the nearest airport from here"라는 남자의 말에서 정답을 알 수 있다.

❷ What does the man imply about taking a taxi to the airport?

공항까지 택시를 타고 가면 약 50달러 정도 요금이 나온다는 여자의 말에 남자는 비행기값이 100달러 들었다고 말하며 그렇게 많은 돈을 낭비하고 싶지는 않다고 말한다. 따라서 정답은 선택지 A 이다.

❸ What does the man mean when he says this:

"Be the early bird"는 "일찍 일어나다"라는 뜻이며 "it's no sweat"은 "문제 없다"라는 뜻이다. 즉, "일찍 일어나는 것은 문제 없다"라는 것이므로 정답은 선택지 C이다.

❹ How does the man feel about taking the public transportation?

대화의 내용으로 보아, 학생은 셔틀버스를 타고 싶어하지만, 혹시라도 놓치게 되면 대중교통을 이용해도 상관 없다고 생각한다는 것을 알 수 있다. 따라서 정답은 선택지 C이다. 셔틀버스를 타면 공항까지 50분 정도 걸리지만 대중교통을 타면 1시간 반 정도가 걸리므로 선택지 D는 틀린 선택이다.

❺ Why does the woman recommend the man to arrive at the airport 2 hours before his flight?

"They say that you should arrive at the airport at least two hours before your flight, since the security has been increased these day"라는 여자의 말에서 정답을 알 수 있다.

Passage 2

1. D **2.** C **3.** B **4.** D **5.** A, D **6.** A

 Listen to part of a lecture in a literature class. The professor is discussing the history of Latin literature. ▼

P(W): All right, are we all settled? ... Okay. Um, before we go on with our lecture today, I'd like to make an announcement first... uh, this Thursday's class will be canceled because I will be speaking at a conference in Temple University on Friday. I'll be flying to Philadelphia tomorrow and be back on Saturday. The makeup class will be some time next week... uh, now, I'll hand out this piece of paper with three different dates, so please choose the date and time you prefer for the make-up class. We will go by majority of the votes. Here you go, Brian.

Okay, now, let's, uh, let's start for today. Um, for the last couple of weeks, we've been discussing female writers from Latin America. Um... we, we talked about Juana Ines de la Cruz from the colonial period, Avellaneda from Cuba, and Turner from Peru. However, uh, I'd like to say that the true female literature in Latin America was formed after the Modernismo, or, in English, the Modernism movement. We're going to talk about female writers such as Teresa de Parra and several others, but before that, I'd like to turn your attention on Modernismo in Latin America.

Latin literature was introduced to European countries due to Modernismo. Before the Modernismo movement, many Romanticists tried to create a new literature that would fit with the new independent countries, but, uh, because of the various countries in Latin America, their effort was futile. Octavio Paz once said that in order for literature to exist, a place is necessary where writers and their productions could be discussed. This critical place started off with the introduction of the Modernismo movement in Latin America. Well, for the first time in Latin American history, some novels and poetry began to be read across the border in other continents.

Now, when we talk about Modernismo in Latin America, we can't leave out the Nicaraguan poet, Ruben Dario, the Father of Modernismo, also known as the Prince of Spanish Literature. He participated in... or I should say, was the leader of many literary movements in some of the Latin countries such as Nicaragua, Chile, Spain, and Argentina. Well, before him, the Spanish-language poetry was usually monotonous, stale, moribund... well, you get the idea. Dario introduced musicality and prosodic virtuosity to Spanish poetry, reinvigorating it. The vocabulary was equally diverse, and included borrowings from antique words and his own coinages. With exotic and vibrant style, he expressed passion and strong emotions in his poems.

Another characteristic of his works is the destruction of the traditional rules of versification. He used free verse to express values such as individualism and freedom by mixing traditional poetic style and new innovative rhythmic and metric structure. The work that made him most famous was his first full-length collection of poems — Azul... which means Blue in English. Here, he incorporated a timeless, mythic world of fairies, princesses and artists in pursuit of an aesthetic ideal.

Well, now, let's talk about Dario's life a little bit. He was born in the Nicaraguan town of Metapa in 1867, which is now named Ciudad Dario. Quite contemporary, huh? As a young child, he was raised in poverty and absence of family. He began to display his talents as a poet at a very young age — he started reading at the age of three and already published poems when he was only 12. No wonder why he was called El Nino Poeta or the poet child. His first major collection of poems, Azul... was published in 1888 when he was 21 years old in Chile. Well... let's consider this here, first... I already mentioned that Dario destroyed the traditional rules of versification, right? What do you think other poets who already had great influence in Latin American poetry would have thought about Dario's poetry? At first, many poets and critics disparaged Dario's works... you know, their reactions were extremely hostile. However, a powerful Spanish critic, Juan Valera, recognized his talents and launched the poet's career. Later in 1903, Dario was named Ambassador of Nicaragua in Paris. In 1914, he fell ill to pneumonia, and died later that year. Well, Modernismo had ended with the death of Ruben Dario, but its influence continued well into the 20th century.

Uh… so…. ❻ Some say that in Spanish, there is poetry before and after Dario. The poetic revolution led by this poet spread across the Spanish-speaking world and extended to all of literature. But you should keep in mind that Dario did not influence poetry only. Modernismo, which we say started off by works of Dario, had an immense influence on other things from ornaments to interior design, from furniture and fashion. <u>His voice can also be heard in lyrics of popular Spanish love songs.</u> Interesting, isn't it?

좋아요, 모두 준비됐나요? 음, 오늘 강의를 시작하기 전에 먼저 발표 하나만 할게요. 이번 주 목요일 수업은 금요일에 템플 대학에서 열리는 회의에 강사로 초빙되었기 때문에 휴강을 하겠어요. 내일 필라델피아로 가서 토요일에 돌아오거든요. 보충 수업을 다음 주 정도에 할 텐데. 세 가지 날짜가 적혀 있는 종이를 줄 테니, 보강을 원하는 날짜와 시간을 고르도록 하세요. 다수결로 하겠어요. 자, 여기 있어요, 브라이언.

자, 그럼 이제 시작합시다. 지난 몇주간 우리는 라틴 아메리카의 여류작가들에 대해 얘기했어요. 식민지 시대의 후아나 이네스 데 라 크루즈, 쿠바의 아베야네다, 그리고 페루의 터너가 있었죠. 하지만 라틴 아메리카의 진정한 여류문학은 모데르니스모, 즉 영어로 모더니즘 운동 이후에 생겼다고 할 수 있어요. 테레사 데 빠라를 포함하여 몇몇 여류문학가에 대해 얘기해 볼 텐데. 그 전에 라틴 아메리카의 모데르니스모에 대해 먼저 알아보도록 합시다.

라틴 문학은 모데르니스모로 인해 유럽에 소개되었어요. 모데르니스모 운동 이전에 많은 낭만주의자들은 새로운 독립 국가에 적절한 새로운 문학을 만들려고 했지만, 라틴 아메리카의 다양한 국가들로 인해 그들의 노력은 성과가 없었어요. 옥타비오 빠스는 문학이 존재하기 위해서는 작가와 그들의 작품에 대한 논의가 이뤄질 공간이 있어야 한다고 했어요. 이 중요한 공간은 라틴 아메리카의 모데르니스모 운동이 소개되면서 시작되었어요. 라틴 아메리카 역사상 처음으로, 소설과 시 등이 다른 대륙으로 전파되기 시작한 것이죠.

라틴 아메리카의 모데르니스모에 대해 논할 때는 모데르니스모의 아버지이자 스페인 문학의 왕자라고도 알려진 니카라과의 시인 루벤 다리오를 빼놓을 수가 없어요. 그는 니카라과, 칠레, 스페인과 아르헨티나 등 많은 라틴 국가의 문학 활동에 참여했어요. 아니, 사실 지도자인 셈이었지요. 다리오 이전의 스페인어 시는 대부분 단조롭고, 건조하고, 죽어가고 있었어요… 어떤 상태였는지 이해가 되죠? 다리오는 스페인 시에 운율과 작시법적 다양성을 도입했는데, 이는 스페인 시를 되살려 놓았어요. 다양한 어휘가 사용되는데, 여기에는 고대어에서 차용된 단어와 직접 만든 신조어도 포함되었어요. 이국적이면서도 빛나는 스타일로, 그는 열정과 강한 감정을 자신의 시에서 표현했어요.

그의 작품의 또 다른 특징은 바로 작시의 전통적 구조의 파괴예요. 그는 개인주의와 자유 등의 가치를 표현하기 위해 전통적인 시의 형식과 새롭고 혁신적인 운율과 계량적인 측면을 혼합하는 자유시를 사용했어요. 그를 가장 유명하게 만든 작품은 그의 첫 시 모음집인 "Azul…"인데, 이는 영어로 파랗다는 뜻이에요. 여기서 그는 미적인 이상을 추구하면서 시간을 초월하는 요정과 공주, 그리고 예술가들의 신화적인 세계를 도입했어요.

자, 그러면 이제 다리오의 삶에 대해 좀 더 얘기해 봅시다. 그는 1867년에 메타파라는 니카라과의 마을에서 태어났는데, 이곳은 오늘날 다리오시라고 불

려요. 꽤 현대적이지요? 어렸을 때 그는 가족도 없이 가난하게 자랐어요. 그는 시인으로서의 재능을 매우 어린 나이에 보이기 시작했는데, 3살 때부터 책을 읽고 12살밖에 안 됐을 때 시를 출판했죠. 그가 시 신동이라고 불리던 것도 당연하지요. 그의 첫 시집인 "Azul…"은 그가 21살이었을때 1888년 칠레에서 출간됐어요. 자, 이걸 먼저 생각해 봅시다. 다리오가 작시의 전통적 법칙을 파괴했다는 것은 이미 얘기했었죠? 이미 라틴 아메리카 시에 커다란 영향을 주었던 시인들이 다리오의 작품에 대해 어떻게 생각했을까요? 처음엔 많은 시인과 비평가들이 다리오의 작품을 혹평했어요. 그들의 반응은 무척 적대적이었지요. 하지만 영향력 있는 스페인 비평가인 후안 발레라가 그의 천재성을 읽고 시인으로서의 길을 열어주었어요. 그 이후 1903년에 다리오는 파리에서 니카라과 대사관으로 임명되었지만, 1914년에 폐렴에 걸려 그 해에 숨을 거두었어요. 모데르니스모는 루벤 다리오의 죽음과 함께 끝났지만, 그 영향력은 20세기에까지도 지속적으로 영향을 주었죠.

어떤 이들은 스페인 문학권에는 다리오 이전의 시가 있고 그 이후의 시가 있다고 해요. 이 시인이 이끈 시적 혁명은 스페인어권 전역에 퍼져서 문학 전반에 영향을 미쳤어요. 다리오가 시에만 영향을 준 것이 아니라는 것을 기억해야 해요. 다리오에 의해 시작되었다고 말하는 모데르니스모는 장식에서 내부 장식, 가구와 패션에 이르기까지 다양한 것에 큰 영향을 미쳤어요. 그의 목소리는 또한 유명한 스페인 연가의 가사에서도 들을 수 있죠. 흥미롭지 않아요?

❶ What is the main topic of the lecture?

교수는 먼저 "I'd like to turn your attention on Modernismo in Latin America"라고 말하며 라틴 아메리카의 모더니즘 하면 빼놓을 수 없는 인물인 루벤 다리오를 소개한다. 따라서 정답은 선택지 D이다.

❷ Why does the professor mention Temple University in Philadelphia?

교수는 템플 대학에서 초청강사로 초대되었기 때문에 이번 목요일 수업은 휴강이라고 말하며 다음주에 보충수업을 할 것이라고 한다. 그러므로 정답은 선택지 C이다.

❸ According to the lecture, what can be said about Modernismo in Latin America?

"Modernismo, which we say that started off by works of Dario, had an immense influence on other things from ornaments to interior design, from furniture to fashion"이라는 교수의 말에서 선택지 A는 잘못된 내용임을 알 수 있으며, "Dario introduced musicality and prosodic virtuosity to Spanish poetry, reinvigorating it"이라는 부분에서 선택지 C 역시 틀린 것임을 알 수 있다. 또한 라틴 아메리카에 모더니즘 운동을 도입한 사람은 옥타비오 빠스가 아니라 루벤 다리오이다. 다리오는 스페인 문학에 음악성과 작시법적 다양성을 도입해서 스페인 문학에 활력을 불어넣었다고 하는 교수의 말에서 선택지 B가 정답임을 알 수 있다.

❹ What was the initial response of the Latin American literary men on *Azul…*?

전통에서 탈피한 다리오의 시집에 대한 라틴 아메리카 문인들의 반응이 초반에는 매우 적대적이었다는 교수의 말에서 정답을 알 수 있다.

❺ According to the lecture, what subject matter did Dario adopt in his collection of poems, *Azul...*?

"Here, he incorporated a timeless, mythic world of fairies, princesses and artists in pursuit of an aesthetic ideal"이라는 강의 부분에서 정답(선택지 A, D)을 알 수 있다.

❻ What does the professor mean when she says this:

여기에서 "voice"는 물리적인 "목소리"라기 보다는 "루벤 다리오의 시구" 정도로 해석할 수 있다. 즉, 유명한 스페인 연가들이 다리오의 시에서 가사를 빌려왔다는 것을 알 수 있다. 정답은 선택지 A이며, 나머지 선택지들의 내용은 지문에서 알 수 없다.

Passage 3

1. C   **2.** A   **3.** C   **4.** B   **5.** A   **6.** 참조

	Plinian	Hawaiian
It may produce wide lava lakes.		✔
It is under the category of effusive eruptions.		✔
Its lava moves extremely fast and destroys everything in its path.	✔	
Its lava is relatively low in viscosity and gas content.		✔
It bursts out columns of smoke and ash high into the air.	✔	

 Listen to part of a discussion in a geology class. ▼

P(M): Uh, before we start today's class... um, let's, uh, let's take a little bit of time recapping what we've been discussing for the last few weeks. Audrey, could you tell us what volcanoes are?

W: Well, basically, volcano is an opening or rupture in the Earth's surface... um, which basically, uh, lets out hot rock, ash, and gases...

P: Okay, if a volcano is a fissure in the Earth's surface, then what forms the mountains or features like mountains?

W: Well... basically it's because of the volcanic activity which involves effluence of rock and lava.

P: Thank you, Audrey. I asked you to be careful with your use of basically within your sentences last time, right? It doesn't make you sound that academic.

W: Oh, yes, um, I'm trying to stop using the word basically when I'm talking, but... it's not that easy, so...

P: That's fine. You can try harder. All right, moving on...

James, can you tell me the difference between lava and magma?

M: Um, magma is the material that's inside the Earth... um, fluid, molten rock. Magma is partially solid and partially gaseous. According to the plate tectonics theory, the lithosphere is divided into several large crustal plates. Lithosphere is a layer which is composed of the crust and the upper part of the mantle. So, um, these plates are continually moving to different directions because of the moving mantle below which makes the plates to spread from the center and sink at the edges. And then, uh, because the edges of the plates move against each other, magma is produced much more here than it is in other places. And that's why volcanic activities and earthquakes happen much more frequently in this region. When, uh, magma comes out to the Earth's surface and flows, now we call that lava.

P: Very good, James. Well, I guess you all did your study, huh? Very well. Now that we've covered the plate tectonics and locations of volcanoes, let's move on to this question: Why does magma erupt at all? Well, in order to explain this phenomenon, we've got to go back to the material that constitutes magma. We already know that the material that forms magma contains a lot of dissolved gases, right? The pressure of the surrounding rock, which is greater than the vapor pressure of the gas, confines the gas and keeps it in the dissolved state. Simply put, there's a balance between the gas and the surrounding rock. But once this balance is altered and vapor pressure becomes greater than the confining pressure, then the dissolved gas expands and makes small gas bubbles in the magma. These bubbles are called vesicles. Well, this happens when either one of the following two things happens... one is when the magma is decompressed, in other words, the pressure of the magma is decreased. The other one is when the vapor pressure increases due to the cooling of the magma which involves a crystallization process. Do you all follow me?

All right. In either case, magma gets filled with tiny gas bubbles. The magma surrounding the gas bubbles has much higher density. Because of this, the gas bubbles try to push out to escape from the magma. Um... let me give you an example... ah, yes. ❸ **Uh, what happens when you shake a soda can and open it afterwards?**

W: Um, basically, the soda inside will burst out, creating a disaster. <u>Oh... I'm sorry.</u>

P: That's okay, you don't have to be self-conscious too much, but that was a good answer. Carbonized soda will burst out when you decompress the soda by opening the bottle, because the tiny little gas bubble push out and escape. Okay, now, let's move on to several typical eruption types. First of all, there are two broad eruption categories — effusive and explosive. Well, usually, effusive lava... because it moves really slowly after it escapes from the Earth, doesn't cause considerable danger to human beings. Of course, it may seriously affect the wildlife and manmade structures, though. On the other hand, explosive volcanoes are extremely dangerous because they launch materials into the air. What goes up must come down, right?

Within those two categories, there are several eruption varieties. First, let's talk about Plinian eruptions. If you have a Plinian eruption, you'll witness columns of smoke and ash extending high into the air. It is devastating and powerful. Uh, you might all be familiar with the eruption that buried Pompeii, right? That was a Plinian eruption. Um... short eruptions can end in less than a day, but longer events can take more than several days... sometimes even months. It produces a towering, sustained eruption pillar which deposits a large amount of tephra on surrounding areas. The lava flows created from the Plinian eruption are extremely fast that it can destroy everything in their path.

Next, Hawaiian eruptions. This type of eruption is relatively gentle and low level, and it's named for the volcanoes of Hawaii. Um, they... uh, they don't throw much pyroclastic material into the air. Its lava is low in viscosity and gas content, and it moves relatively slowly. The Hawaiian eruption can generally take several different forms, one of which is the fire fountain, jet-like incandescent orange lava pouring hundreds of feet in the air. The more typical eruption involves a steady lava flow from a central vent which ponds in craters or broad depressions to make wide lava lakes. Lava lakes are... well, ponds of lava that are formed in craters or other depressions. The Kilauea volcano, one of the five shield volcanoes that together form the island of Hawaii, is one of the examples of this type of eruption.

P: 자, 오늘 수업을 시작하기 전에... 저번 주에 논의하던 부분에 대해 조금 복습해 봅시다. 오드리, 화산이 뭔지 말해주겠어요?

W: 화산은 기본적으로 지구 표면의 개구 혹은 파손 부분이에요... 뜨거운 돌, 재, 가스를 내뿜죠...

P: 좋아요. 만약 화산이 지구 표면의 균열이라면, 산 혹은 산의 형태의 것은 무엇으로 인해 생성되죠?

W: 어... 기본적으로 돌과 용암을 분출하는 화산 활동 때문에 생겨요.

P: 고마워요. 오드리. 저번에도 기본적으로라는 말을 쓸 때 조심하라고 했지요? 그다지 학구적으로 들리지 않거든요.

W: 아, 네, 말할 때 기본적으로라는 말을 안 쓰려고 하지만... 쉽지가 않아요...

P: 괜찮아요. 좀 더 노력하면 돼요. 좋아. 계속합시다. 제임스, 용암과 마그마의 차이를 얘기해 볼까요?

M: 마그마는 지구 내에 있는 물질인데... 녹아 있는 액체 상태의 돌이에요. 마그마는 부분적으로 단단하고 부분적으로 기체이고요. 판 구조 이론에 의하면, 지각은 여러 개의 큰 층으로 나뉜다고 해요. 지각은 지각과 맨틀의 상부로 이루어졌어요. 이 판들은 지속적으로 다른 방향으로 움직이는데, 그 이유는 판의 아래에 있는 움직이는 맨틀로 인해 판이 중앙에서 퍼져서 끝부분이 가라앉기 때문이에요. 판의 경계가 서로 부딪히기 때문에 이곳에서는 다른 곳에서보다 마그마가 훨씬 더 많이 생성되죠. 그래서 이러한 지역에서 화산 활동과 지진이 더 빈번하게 발생하게 되어요. 마그마가 지구 표면으로 나와서 흐르게 되면 이것을 용암이라고 불러요.

P: 아주 잘했어요. 제임스. 모두들 공부를 한 것 같군요. 좋습니다. 판 구조론과 화산의 위치를 알았으니, 다음 질문으로 넘어갑시다 — 마그마는 왜 분출되는 걸까요? 이 현상을 설명하기 위해서 우선 마그마를 구성하는 물질들을 살펴봅시다. 우리는 이미 마그마를 구성하는 물질이 많은 양의 용해 가스를 포함하고 있다는 것을 알고 있죠? 주변에 있는 암석의 압력이 가스의 수증기 압력보다 높기 때문에 가스를 안에 가두고 용해된 상태로 유지해요. 간단히 말해 가스와 주변 암석 간의 균형이 있는 것이지요. 하지만 이 균형이 변해 수증기 압력이 주변 압력보다 높아지면, 용융 가스가 팽창해서 마그마 내에 작은 기포를 만들어요. 이 기포는 소낭이라고 불리고, 이것은 다음과 같은 두 가지 중 하나가 발생하면 일어나요. 하나는 마그마의 압력이 낮아지는 경우예요. 또 하나는 기체 압력이 증가하는 경우인데, 이는 마그마가 수정화 과정으로 인해 식을 때 발생하게 되어요. 모두 이해되나요?

좋습니다. 어느 쪽이든, 마그마에는 작은 가스 거품이 가득 차게 되어요. 이 가스 거품을 감싸고 있는 마그마는 밀도가 훨씬 높죠. 그렇기 때문에 가스 거품이 마그마로부터 탈출하기 위해 밀어내는 것이에요. 음... 예를 들어보죠... 아. 소다 캔을 흔든 후 열면 어떻게 되지요?

W: 음. 기본적으로 내부에 있는 소다가 터지고 엉망진창이 돼요. 아, 죄송합니다.

P: 괜찮아요. 그렇게 의식할 필요는 없어요. 어쨌든 좋은 대답이에요. 탄산 소다는 소다 뚜껑을 열어 압착이 풀리면 터져나오는데, 이는 작은 기포들이 밀려나와 탈출하려 하기 때문이에요. 자, 이제 몇 가지 전형적인 분출 형태에 대해 알아봅시다. 먼저, 두 개의 넓은 분출 유형이 있는데요, 바로 분출형과 폭발형입니다. 일반적으로 분출형 용암은 용암이 지구 내부를 탈출한 후 매우 천천히 움직이기 때문에 사람에게 그리 위험적이진 않습니다. 반대로, 폭발형 화산은 매우 위험한데 물질을 공중으로 뱉어내기 때문입니다. 올라간 건 내려와야만 하니까요.

이 두 개의 유형 안에 또 다시 여러 개의 분출 유형이 있는데, 우선은 플리니언 분출에 대해 알아봅시다. 플리니언 분출의 경우에는 연기와 재 기둥이 하늘 높이 솟아오르게 됩니다. 위험적이고 강력하지요. 폼페이를 묻어버린 화산 폭발에 대해서 모두 알고 있지요? 그게 바로 플리니언 분출이었어요. 짧은 분출은 하루도 안 걸리지만, 긴 경우 며칠을 가고 심지어 몇 달씩 가기도 합니다. 이는 높은 분출 구름 기둥을 만들며 많은 양의 테프라가 주변에 쌓이게 됩니다. 플리니언 분출로 인해 형성된 용암은 매우 빠르게 흐르기 때문에 진로에 있는 모든 것을 파괴할 수 있어요.

다음은 하와이언 분출이에요. 이 종류의 분출은 상대적으로 고요하고 강도가 낮으며, 하와이의 화산에서 이름을 딴 것입니다. 이러한 형태의 분출은 화쇄

류 물질을 다량으로 공중으로 뿜지 않아요. 이 분출의 용암은 점도가 낮고 가스 함량이 적으며 천천히 흘러요. 하와이언 분출은 일반적으로 몇 개의 다른 형태를 지닐 수 있는데, 이 중 하나는 불기둥형으로, 밝은 오렌지색 용암을 수백 피트 상공으로 분출하죠. 보다 전형적인 분출은 중앙에서 지속적으로 용암을 분출하여 넓은 구멍을 만드는데, 이것은 분화구나 다른 움푹 들어간 곳에 흘러들어가서 용암호를 형성해요. 하와이를 구성하는 5개의 방패 화산중 하나인 킬라우에아 화산은 이런 분출의 예입니다.

❶ **What is the discussion mainly about?**

교수는 먼저 지난 수업에 배웠던 내용을 간략하게 소개하고 다음 주제인 마그마 분출로 넘어간다. 따라서 정답은 선택지 C이다.

❷ **According to the professor, why do vesicles form?**

소낭(vesicle)이란 마그마에 생기는 기포이다. 이러한 기포는 주변 기압이 낮아질 때 생기거나 마그마가 식으면서 기체 압력이 높아지면 수정화 작업이 이루어져 마그마의 가스 성분이 높아질 때 생긴다. 따라서 정답은 선택지 A이다.

❸ **Why does the student say this:**

토론 초반에 교수는 "basically"라는 표현을 너무 자주 사용하는 것에 대해 학생에게 지적을 하는데, 다시 들려준 부분에서 학생이 "basically"라는 표현을 또 사용한다. 학생이 이를 스스로 깨닫고 미안하다고 사과하고 있으므로 정답은 선택지 C이다.

❹ **What does the professor say about explosive eruptions?**

"On the other hand, explosive volcanoes are extremely dangerous because they launch materials into the air. What goes up must come down, right?" 이라는 교수의 말에서 정답(선택지 B)을 알 수 있다. 선택지 A의 내용은 본문의 내용과 다르며, 선택지 C와 D는 effusive lava에 대한 설명이다.

❺ **Why does the professor mention the Kilauea volcano of Hawaii?**

교수는 하와이언 분출에 대해 설명하며 킬라우에아 화산을 예로 제시하고 있다.

❻ **According to the information in the discussion, indicate whether each sentence below describes Plinian eruptions or Hawaiian eruptions.**

플리니언 분출은 폭발형으로, 매우 빠른 마그마를 분출하여 진로에 있는 모든 것을 파괴하기도 하고, 연기와 재의 기둥이 하늘 높이 솟아오른다. 반면에 하와이언 분출은 일반적으로 분출형(effusive)이며 넓은 용암호를 만들기도 한다. 또한 하와이언 분출의 용암은 점도와 가스 함량이 낮다.

Passage 4

1. D **2.** A **3.** B **4.** D **5.** C

 Listen to part of a conversation between a student and a university gym employee. ▼

W: Hi, can I get some help, please?

M: Oh, sure, what can I do for you, miss?

W: Um, I was thinking about joining the gym.

M: All right. Would you like to join the gym today?

W: Uh-huh. Um, how much is the membership?

M: It's $250 for the annual membership, and $150 for six months.

W: Hmm, I guess I'll sign up for the annual membership — it's a bit cheaper, I guess.

M: Then fill out this form for me... how are you going to pay — credit card, personal check, or cash?

W: I'll pay with credit card.

M: That's fine.

W: Here you go.

M: Thank you.

W: ❸ Oh, I can't wait to start working out... I'm so excited at the fact that I could finally take the yoga class!

M: Oh, yeah, speaking of which — would you like to sign up for the yoga class now?

W: Uh, wh- what do you mean? Do I have to sign up for the yoga class? You don't just walk in?

M: Of course not. Yoga classes are provided for gym members and are usually done over a four-month period. It's $100 to join the class, but you don't have to bring your yoga mat... we already have a bunch of them here at the gym.

W: W-wait a second... I thought if I joined the gym, all the classes were free, like, the yoga class, pilates, swim class... everything!

M: Of course not. You know, those instructors are pretty expensive, especially the yoga instructor. He's like the best known yoga instructor in town. I mean, $100 for four months is not that expensive... and you get to take the class three times a week. So, if you sign up for the gym and the yoga class at the same time, you get to use all the gym equipment for free, plus you get to take the yoga class.

W: Well, but I didn't know that... that's not fair. I mean, I don't think I'll ever get to use the gym equipment like the treadmill or the cycle... I'm not interested in cardio or lifting weights... I only want to take the yoga class! Um... okay, what if I didn't sign up for the gym but only the yoga class? Do you think I could do that?

M: I'm sorry, but no can do. It's gym policy — only gym members can take additional classes, you know... sorry.

W: Awww, I don't believe this! It's just a total waste of money! Well, I'm not blaming you... sorry about that.

M: Don't worry about it. So... uh, what do you want to do, then?

W: Well, I don't think I have a choice, do I?

M: All right, then... uh, the total amount is $350. Um, if you're done filling out that form, choose a level for your yoga class. Is this your first time doing yoga?

W: Actually, no... I've learned yoga for a year before, but that was such a long time ago.

M: All right, then... I guess, the instructor's going to have to check your level.

W: Do you mean I have to do yoga in front of him?

M: No, no, no, um, I'm going to schedule an appointment for you to meet with him. All you have to do is tell him how long you've been doing yoga, and whether your level is intermediate or advanced... well, he's the professional so I guess he can figure out your level at the interview.

W: That's fine with me.

M: Well, when you're done with filling out that form, just let me know, okay? I'll take care of this credit card. Hang on to that pen, because you have a bunch of signing to do.

W: 안녕하세요, 뭣 좀 여쭤봐도 될까요?

M: 그럼요, 어떻게 도와드릴까요?

W: 음, 체육관 회원 등록을 하려고 생각 중인데요.

M: 네, 그럼 오늘 등록하시겠어요?

W: 네, 회원권이 얼마죠?

M: 연간 회원권으로 하시면 250달러고요, 반년짜리는 150달러예요.

W: 흠, 연간 회원권이 좀 더 저렴하니까 그걸로 할게요.

M: 그럼 이 양식을 작성해 주세요... 지불은 뭘로 하시겠어요–신용 카드, 개인 수표, 아님 현금?

W: 신용카드로 할게요.

M: 좋습니다.

W: 여기 있습니다.

M: 고맙습니다.

W: 빨리 운동을 시작했으면 좋겠어요... 드디어 요가를 할 수 있어서 정말 신나요!

M: 아, 그 말이 나와서 말인데요, 지금 요가반도 같이 신청하시겠어요?

W: 무슨 말씀이세요? 요가반도 신청해야 되나요? 그냥 알아서 들어가는 게 아니고요?

M: 물론이죠, 요가반은 회원들에게만 제공되고 보통 4개월 코스예요, 등록 비용은 100달러인데, 요가 매트는 가져오실 필요 없어요, 체육관에 이미 많이 있거든요.

W: 자... 잠깐만요... 전 그냥 체육관에 등록하면 요가, 필라테스, 수영 등 모든 것이 다 무료인 줄 알았는데요!

M: 물론 아니에요, 아시겠지만 강사들 급여가 정말 비싸거든요, 특히 요가 강사는 더욱 그렇죠, 인근에서 제일 유명한 요가 강사거든요, 그러니까 제 말은, 4개월에 100달러면 그렇게 비싼 편은 아니에요, 일주일에 3번씩 수업을 하니까요, 체육관이랑 요가반을 동시에 등록하면 체육관 내 모든 시설을 무료로 사용할 수 있고 요가도 할 수 있어요.

W: 하지만 전 그건 몰랐어요... 불공평해요, 전 런닝머신이나 싸이클 같은 기구는 안 쓸건데... 유산소 운동이나 웨이트 운동은 흥미 없고 요가반만 하고 싶거든요! 좋아요, 그럼 체육관 등록을 하되 요가반만 할 순 없나요? 그렇게는 되나요?

M: 죄송하지만 그렇게는 안됩니다, 체육관 정책이거든요–체육관 회원만 추가반을 수강할 수 있어요... 죄송합니다.

W: 이런, 믿을 수 없어요! 정말 돈 낭비잖아요! 당신을 비난하는 건 아니에요... 죄송합니다.

M: 괜찮아요, 음, 그러면 어떻게 하시겠어요?

W: 선택의 여지가 없는 것 같은데요?

M: 좋습니다, 그럼... 총 비용은 350달러이고요, 양식을 다 작성하시면 요가반 등급을 정해 주세요, 요가는 처음이신가요?

W: 아니요, 예전에 1년동안 배웠는데, 너무 오래돼서요.

M: 알겠습니다, 그러면 강사가 손님의 수준을 테스트 해 봐야 할 것 같네요.

W: 그럼 그 분 앞에서 요가를 해야 된단 말씀인가요?

M: 아뇨, 아뇨, 강사와 만날 수 있도록 약속을 잡아둘게요, 그냥 얼마나 요가를 했고, 수준이 중등인지 고급인지만 말씀해 주시면 돼요, 강사가 전문가이니 면담 후 손님의 수준을 결정할 수 있을 거예요.

W: 네, 괜찮은 것 같아요.

M: 다 작성하시면 말씀해 주세요, 이 신용 카드는 제가 처리할게요, 서명할 게 많으니 펜은 들고 계세요.

❶ Why does the woman want to join the gym?

여자는 요가 수업을 듣기 위해 체육관에 등록하고 싶어한다. 따라서 정답은 D이다.

❷ What does the woman imply about her use of other gym equipment?

여자는 런닝머신이나 싸이클 같은 체육관 내의 다른 시설들을 사용하지 않을 것이라고 말하며, 유산소나 웨이트 운동이 아닌 요가에만 관심 있다고 말한다. 따라서 정답은 A이다.

❸ How does the woman feel when she says this:

체육관에 등록만 하면 요가반이나 기타 다른 수업을 공짜로 들을 수 있다고 생각했었는데, 따로 등록을 해야 한다는 말에 놀란 것이므로 가장 좋은 답은 선택지 B이다.

4 **Why is the woman upset about the gym policy?**

요가반을 들으려면 체육관에 등록을 해야 하며, 체육관 회원만이 추가반을 수강할 수 있다는 체육관의 정책을 마음에 들어하지 않는다. 또한 체육관의 다른 시설을 일체 사용하지 않을 것인데 체육관에 등록하는 것이 돈낭비라고 생각한다. 따라서 정답은 D이다.

5 **What does the man say about the yoga class provided at the gym?**

"He's like the best known yoga instructor in town"라는 남자의 말에서 정답을 알 수 있다. 선택지 A의 내용은 지문에서 알 수 없으며, 요가반이 그렇게 비싸지 않다고 하였으므로 선택지 B 또한 오답이다. 또한 요가반은 4달 동안 일주일에 3번 제공된다.

Passage 5

1. C   **2.** A   **3.** D   **4.** B   **5.** A, D   **6.** B

 Listen to part of a discussion in a health science class. The professor is discussing anorexia. ▼

P(W): Well, before we get started, let's take a look at this picture first. This is a picture of a model... uh, who is extremely skinny. What comes into your mind when you see this picture?

M: Um, she's a model, and usually, models are supposed to be really skinny, so she might have been on an extreme diet.

P: Okay, that's a good answer, George. What else?

W: I think she has some kind of an eating disorder, like some of those really skinny Hollywood actresses. Like... she's on an extreme diet by not eating a sufficient amount of food to sustain her metabolism.

P: Very good, Anastasia. Well, people usually use the term anorexia interchangeably with one of its subtypes, anorexia nervosa, which is an eating disorder where people basically starve themselves by not eating sufficient amount of food and exercising excessively. It usually happens in young people around the onset of puberty, but adults can also have this eating disorder. People who suffer from anorexia experience extreme weight loss. An interesting fact about these people is that, uh, although they are as skinny as a twig, they are convinced that they're still overweight.

M: Professor, uh, how do people with anorexia control what they eat? Um, do they simply not eat at all, or eat a very small portion? Or are there some other methods to control their body weight? Because I've been on a diet myself, but I found that it's extremely difficult to lose weight at all.

P: Good question, George. Well, primarily, people with anorexia try to control their weight by purging and vomiting, excessive exercise, diet pills... which are known to be harmful for your heart, by the way... um, what else... uh... taking laxative pills or diuretic drugs, or not eating at all. You know... basically straining their body. Uh... now, I already mentioned that anorexia occurs primarily among adolescents, but more to girls than boys. What does this suggest?

W: That teenage girls are more self-conscious about becoming fat?

P: That's right. Most of the anorexics have an intense fear of becoming... well, fat. Like I said, anorexics continue to think they are overweight even after they become extremely thin, which may lead to illness or even death. In the Western world, approximately 10 percent of people diagnosed with anorexia eventually die due to related factors such as failure of the heart and cardiovascular system, um, slow heart rate, immune dysfunction, muscle weakness, and so on.

M: Why do people have anorexia anyways?

P: Well, there is no single clear reason for developing anorexia.. it's very complicated, actually. Many researchers believe that it results from a complex mixture of social, psychological and biological factors.

W: Biological factors? What do you mean?

P: Well, more like, physiological factors. Let's talk about social factors first. Uh... the thin images of models and celebrities shown on TVs and magazines are one of the core contributors of anorexia among young females. Any questions? Okay, now, physiological factors... well, researchers say that people can develop anorexia due to genetic factors such as genes influencing personality, emotion, eating regulation, and so on. And there's neurobiological factors. Uh, this is quite complicated, but, let's just say, um, that the disturbed neurotransmitter serotonin has something to do with dysfunction of anxiety, mood, appetite, and impulse control. Now, psychological factors.... Well, I already told you that people with anorexia think that they are overweight and unattractive even though they are extremely thin, right? The behavior of considering oneself as fat and unattractive is supported by cognitive biases and changes the person's way of evaluating herself.

But just being thin is not the only symptom of anorexia. You should be careful when you suspect someone as anorexic or not because although there are many symptoms of the eating disorder, some individuals might not experience all of them. Of course, one of the most common symptoms is being seriously underweight... you know, being about 15 percent below normal weight or extremely skinny. You can also suspect anorexia if a person doesn't want or refuses to eat in public. Women may skip at least three consecutive menstrual periods, or may experience anxiety, weakness, brittle skin, or shortness of breath, or be obsessive about the calories they take and consume.

M: ❸ That sounds dangerous... um, what happens when you have anorexia, besides... uh... eventually dying?

P: Didn't I already explain that? No? Oh, I thought I already did. Wait, I did mention dysfunction of the heart and the immune system... Oh, well, let me recap again. Or let's just move on to the medical consequences of anorexia, okay? Um, just think about the consequences of not eating properly... anorexics might experience bone shrinkage, mineral loss, irregular heartbeat, or fail to grow normally. They are highly likely to develop osteoporosis and bulimia nervosa. Also, when a female is pregnant, she might end up miscarrying the baby.

W: Uh, you mentioned bulimia nervosa... is that... is that related with anorexia nervosa? What is bulimia nervosa?

P: Well, bulimia nervosa is another type of eating disorder, but this time, you can describe it as the diet-binge-purge disorder. Get the idea? Let's say that a person diets, becomes hungry, and binges voraciously in response to powerful cravings and feelings of deprivation. While the person's eating, she helplessly feels out of control. But after binging, she feels guilty or feels somehow getting fat, so usually vomits, misuses laxatives, or fasts in order to get rid of the calories. It's a vicious circle.

P: 자, 시작하기 전에 먼저 이 사진을 봅시다. 이것은 매우 마른 모델의 사진이에요. 이 사진을 보면 어떤 생각이 드나요?

M: 어, 이 여자는 모델인데, 모델들은 보통 매우 말라야 되니까 극단적인 다이어트를 했을 것 같아요.

P: 좋은 대답이에요, 조지. 또?

W: 무슨 섭식 장애가 있는 거 같아요, 마치 헐리웃의 마른 배우들처럼. 그러니까... 신진대사를 유지하기 위해 필요한 적정량을 먹지 않는 극단적 다이어트를 하고 있는 중인 거죠.

P: 잘했어요, 아나스타샤. 사람들은 일반적으로 거식증이라는 용어를 신경성 무식욕증과 혼환해서 사용하고 있어요. 신경성 무식욕증이란 거식증의 하위 종류인데, 기본적으로 음식을 충분히 섭취하지 않고 극단적으로 운동을 해서 영양 결핍 상태에 이르게 되는 섭식 장애예요. 거식증은 주로 사춘기에 막 들어선 젊은이들에게서 나타나는데, 어른들도 걸릴 수 있어요. 거식증을 앓는

사람들은 극단적으로 체중이 감소하게 돼요. 흥미로운 것은 이들이 실제로는 나뭇가지처럼 말랐는데, 여전히 스스로가 뚱뚱하고 생각한다는 거예요.

M: 교수님, 거식증에 걸린 사람들은 먹는 걸 어떻게 조절하나요? 전혀 먹지 않거나 굉장히 조금만 먹나요? 아니면 체중 조절을 하는 다른 방법이 있나요? 저도 다이어트를 해 봤는데, 살을 빼기가 정말 어렵던데요.

P: 좋은 질문이에요, 조지. 거식증에 걸린 사람들은 굶거나 토하고, 과도하게 운동을 하거나 심장에 해롭다고 알려져 있는 다이어트약을 먹으면서 체중 조절을 해요. 음... 그 외에도 설사약이나 이뇨약을 먹을 수도 있고, 아예 아무것도 먹지 않을 수도 있어요. 그러니까 결국 몸에 무리를 가하는 것이죠. 자, 거식증은 보통 사춘기 청소년들에게 생긴다고 했는데, 일반적으로 남자 아이들보다 여자 아이들에게 더 많이 생겨요. 이건 뭘 뜻하는 것일까요?

W: 사춘기 여자 아이들이 뚱뚱한 것에 더 예민하다는 것 아닐까요?

P: 맞아요. 대부분의 거식증 환자들은 뚱뚱해지는 것에 공포감을 갖고 있어요. 앞서 말했듯이 거식증 환자들은 자신이 극도로 마른 후에도 과체중이라고 생각하기 때문에 질병이나 죽음에 이르기도 해요. 서구 사회에서는 거식증 환자의 약 10퍼센트가 심장 마비나 심혈관 계통 질환, 느린 심박수, 면역력 저하, 근력 약화 등의 관련 질환으로 결국 사망하게 돼요.

M: 그런데 거식증에는 왜 걸리는 것인가요?

P: 음, 거식증 발병의 간단한 원인은 없어요. 실은 매우 복잡하죠. 많은 연구자들은 거식증이 사회적, 심리학적, 생물학적 요인이 복합되어서 발생한다고 믿고 있어요.

W: 생물학적 요인이요? 무슨 말씀이신가요?

P: 생물학적이라기 보다는 생리학적 요인이라고 생각하면 돼요. 사회적 요인 먼저 살펴보죠. TV와 잡지에 자주 나오는 모델과 연예인들의 마른 이미지가 젊은 여성 사이의 거식증을 부추기는 원인 중 하나예요. 질문 있나요? 자, 심리학적 요인은... 연구자들은 사람들이 거식증에 걸리는 원인을 유전적 요인에서 찾아요. 예를 들어 성격, 감정, 음식 조절 등에 영향을 미치는 유전자 등이 관련이 있는 것이죠. 그리고 신경 생물학적 요인도 있어요. 이건 매우 복잡한데, 간단히 말해 신경분비 물질인 세로토닌의 장애가 불안, 기분, 식욕과 충동 억제 조절에 이상을 일으킨다고 생각하면 되겠어요. 이제 신경학적 요인으로 가 보면, 거식증에 걸린 사람들은 매우 말랐음에도 불구하고 스스로를 뚱뚱하고 볼품없다고 생각한다고 말했죠? 자신이 뚱뚱하고 매력이 없다고 생각하는 행동은 인지적 선입견에 의해 뒷받침되는데, 이는 스스로를 평가하는 것에 변화를 가져와요.

하지만 단지 마른 것만이 거식증의 유일한 증상은 아니에요. 거식증에 걸렸는지 아닌지를 판별할 때는 조심해야 해요. 왜냐하면 비록 거식증은 여러 가지 증상이 있지만 어떤 사람들은 이 증상들이 전부 나타나지 않을 수 있기 때문이에요. 가장 흔한 증상 중 하나는 물론 심각한 저체중인데요, 그러니까 정상 체중보다 15%정도 적게 나간다거나 극도로 말랐을 경우에 해당되어요. 또한 공공 장소에서 먹는 것을 원하지 않거나 거부하는 경우에도 거식증을 의심할 수 있어요. 여성의 경우 최소한 세 번의 월경기를 연속으로 놓친다거나, 불안함, 나른함, 거친 피부, 혹은 짧은 호흡 등을 경험할 수 있고 섭취하는 음식의 칼로리 계산에 집착할 수 있어요.

M: 위험하게 들리네요. 거식증에 걸리면... 결국 죽게 되는 것 외에 무슨 일이 발생할 수 있나요?

P: 그건 이미 설명하지 않았나요? 안 했어요? 아, 이미 한 줄 알았네요. 잠깐. 심장 질환과 면역 저하는 언급했고... 아예 다시 설명할게요. 아니면 그냥 거식증의 의학적 결과로 넘어가도록 하죠. 자, 잘 먹지 않는 경우의 결과를 한 번 생각해 봅시다... 거식증 환자들은 뼈의 수축, 미네랄 손실, 불규칙한 심장박동 혹은 정상적으로 성장하지 않는 것을 경험할 수 있어요. 또한 골다공증과 신경성 과식증에 걸릴 확률이 높죠. 임산부의 경우에는 유산할 수도 있고요.

W: 신경성 과식증이라고 하셨는데, 거식증과 연관이 있나요? 신경성 과식증이 무엇인가요?

P: 신경성 과식증은 식욕 장애의 또 다른 종류지만, 식욕조절—폭식—구토 장애라고 보면 돼요. 이해되나요? 어떤 사람이 다이어트를 하는데 적게 먹어서 배고파지고, 강한 식욕과 박탈감 때문에 폭식을 한다고 칩시다. 먹는 동안에는 스스로의 제어를 잃어요. 하지만 폭식을 하고 난 후에는 죄의식을 갖거나 왠지 살이 찐다는 느낌에 사로잡혀. 주로 토하거나 설사제를 남용하고, 혹은 칼로리를 없애기 위해 굶지요. 끔찍한 악순환인 거죠.

❶ What is the discussion mainly about?

거식증, 신경성 과식증과 같은 섭식 장애의 증상과 원인에 대해 토론하고 있다. 선택지 A, B, D는 너무 제한적인 내용이어서 정답이 될 수 없다.

❷ Why does the professor show a picture of a model?

교수는 매우 마른 모델의 사진을 보여주며 오늘의 주제인 섭식 장애를 시각적으로 소개한다. 따라서 정답은 A이다.

❸ How does the professor feel when she says this:

학생의 질문의 답인 거식증의 결과를 이미 설명한 것으로 혼동하고 있으므로 정답은 선택지 D이다. 교수 자신이 모르는 질문을 한 것이 아니므로 선택지 B는 정답이 아니며, 이미 설명한 것을 학생이 기억하지 못해서 실망한 것도 아니므로 선택지 C 역시 답이 될 수 없다.

❹ How does the professor explain medical consequences of anorexia?

교수는 "Um, just think about the consequences of not eating properly... shrunken bones, mineral loss, low body temperature, irregular heartbeat, permanent failure of normal growth, development of osteoporosis and bulimia nervosa. Also, when a female is pregnant, she might end up miscarrying the baby"라고 말하며 거식증의 의학적 결과를 예를 들며 열거한다. 따라서 정답은 B이다. 실제로 거식증에 걸린 사람을 언급하거나 정확한 정의를 내리는 것이 아니다. 또한 다른 병의 증상과 비교하는 것도 아니다.

❺ What does the professor say about the reason for developing anorexia?

교수는 거식증이 여러가지 원인이 복합적으로 일어날 때 발생한다고 하는데, 성격 등을 좌우하는 유전적 요인(선택지 A)과 TV와 잡지 등에 자주 나오는 마른 모델들의 이미지(선택지 D) 등이 그 원인으로 언급됐다. 젊은 여성들 사이에서 서로 받는 사회적 압력(선택지 B)이나 가족이나 친구에게서 관심을 덜 받는 것(선택지 C)은 언급된 바가 없다.

❻ According to the discussion, how is bulimia nervosa different from anorexia nervosa?

신경성 과식증은 체중 조절을 하다가 과식을 한 후, 먹은 음식을 토해낸다는 점에서 먹는 것을 거부하는 거식증과 다르다. 따라서 정답은 선택지 B이다.

Passage 6

1. C **2.** A, B **3.** B **4.** A **5.** D **6.** C

 Listen to part of a discussion in a linguistics class. ▼

P(M): All right, let's begin. Um... last week's assignment was to read the Nichols article in *Sociolinguistics and Language Teaching*. Today's presenter is Jack Andrews. Jack, are you ready?

M: Uh, yes, but I can't find the button to lower the screen here.

P: Oh, let me get that for you. Here you go, now, are we all set? All right, Jack, it's all yours now. First of all, let's see what your main subject is.

M: Uh... okay. Well, today, I'll be talking about what pidgin language is and where it came from. I will give you some examples of pidgin language and, uh, fortunately, I obtained a video clip of an interview with a woman who lives in Louisiana who can only speak pidgin.

P: Excellent.

M: Um, I will also talk about creole language as well. Next, I will move on to AAVE... African American Vernacular English and assess the difficulties many AAVE speakers are confronted with.

P: That sounds good.

M: Okay. Um... first of all, let's discuss pidgin language and where it comes from. A pidgin language is a new language variety which spontaneously develops when groups of people who speak different languages try to communicate with one another on a regular basis. For example, when people from tribe A and tribe B who use different languages from each other try to do some trading, they need to communicate with each other but have no means of communication, right? So, uh... they mix their language with uh, another common language, such as English.

P: Yes, this process is called pidginization. Let me go through the condition of pidginization real quick. First of all, as Jack mentioned, a prolonged, regular contact between two or more communities that use different languages is required. Second, a need to communicate between the different language groups is required, in this case, the need to trade between tribe A and tribe B. Also, there should be no shared interlanguage.

M: That's right. Um... I think it's gonna be better if I

move on and explain creole languages here...

P: Go on.

M: Okay. Um, basically, when two people who speak different languages but both speak pidgin get married and speak pidgin to each other, the pidgin spoken at home is learned by their children as a mother language. Usually, pidgins have a very simple, crude language structure and vocabulary, but creoles have a more complicated structure and expanded vocabulary.

Creoles often replace the existing mixture of languages and become the native language of a community. It's no longer a contact language. However, that doesn't always happen because pidgins can die out and become obsolete. All right, now, let me talk about the superstrate and substrate languages. First, superstrate or superstratum is the language that has become the basis of pidgin or creole — in other words, the language of an invading people that is imposed on an indigenous population and contributes features to their language. Usually, superstrate is the language of the socio-economically dominant group in the society. Substrate language is the counterpart of superstrate... um, it is the native language of the people who make pidgin. And, uh... I need to talk about the lexifier... um, Professor Schiffman, could you explain the lexifier real briefly?

P: Sure. Lexifier language is the source of most of the vocabulary. Since most vocabulary is borrowed from the dominant group of the society, so you can say that a lexifier language is equivalent to the superstrate language.

M: Thank you. Um, does anybody have any questions so far?

W: Yeah, um, you talked about the difference between pidgins and creoles... like, pidgins have less complicated language structure and vocabulary, right? What does that specifically mean — less complicated?

P: Well, let me explain this for you, Katie. It might be easier to put it this way — pidgins don't have a stable vocabulary... you know, different people may prefer to use different words, especially those from their own language. Also, pidgins usually have simplified grammar systems and don't have complicated structures such as embedded clauses and so on. Does this answer your question?

W: Yes, thank you.

P: ❺ All right. Now, Jack, uh, we're running out of time, but I remember you were supposed to talk about AAVE speakers, right?

M: Yes, I'll make it quick. Basically, AAVE or Ebonics is a specific language variety that is spoken by many African Americans. Some researchers like Rickford and Dillard have suggested that AAVE is a decreolized form of a slave Creole. Decreolization is a process where a creole language becomes more like the standard language form from which most of its vocabulary comes. AAVE also has pronunciation, grammatical structures, and vocabulary similar to various West African languages... which, uh, are somewhat different from those of the Standard American English. Like I just mentioned, AAVE is spoken by many African Americans in the States and is a strong marker of ethnic identity. Because of this linguistic discrepancy between AAVE and Standard English, many AAVE speakers tend to get low grades at school and eventually drop out. Um, now, I would like to ask you to pair up in groups of four or five and discuss the questions you see on the screen regarding pidgins, creoles, and AAVE speakers and their problems. I'm sorry I couldn't play my video clip... uh, hopefully we'll have some time after we're done with the discussion.

P: 자, 시작합시다. 지난 주 과제가 사회언어학과 언어 교육 교재에서 니콜스의 소논문을 읽어오는 거였죠. 오늘 발표자는 잭 앤드류입니다. 잭, 준비됐나요?

M: 네, 그런데 화면을 내릴 수 있는 버튼을 못 찾겠어요.

P: 아, 내가 대신 해 줄게요... 자, 됐습니다. 준비 다 됐나요? 좋아요, 잭, 시작하세요. 우선, 주제가 뭔지 한번 볼까요.

M: 네, 오늘은 혼성어가 무엇이며 어디에서 유래했는지 발표하겠습니다. 혼성어의 예시를 보여드릴 텐데요. 운 좋게도 루이지애나에서 거주하고 혼성어만 할 줄 아는 여성을 인터뷰한 영상자료를 구했습니다.

P: 좋아요.

M: 또한 크리올 언어에 대해서도 얘기하겠습니다. 다음으로, AAVE, 즉 미국 흑인 영어로 넘어가서 많은 AAVE 사용자들이 직면하고 있는 문제에 대해서 진단해 보겠습니다.

P: 네, 좋습니다.

M: 네, 어... 우선, 혼성어에 대해 토론하고 그 유래를 살펴보겠습니다. 혼성어는 다른 언어를 사용하는 사람들이 주기적으로 의사소통을 해야 할 때 자연스럽게 발생하게 되는 새로운 언어의 형태입니다. 예를 들어, 서로 다른 언어를 사용하는 A 부족과 B 부족의 사람들끼리 상품 거래를 할 때, 서로간에 의사소통을 해야 하지만 적절한 수단이 없었습니다. 그래서 이들은 그들의 언어와 영어와 같은 다른 공통 언어를 섞어서 사용하게 되었습니다

P: 맞아요. 이 과정을 혼성어화 과정이라고 하죠. 혼성어화 과정의 조건에 대해 간단히 설명할게요. 우선 책이 말했듯이 서로 다른 언어 사회간의 장기적이고 주기적인 접촉이 있어야 해요. 두번째로는 서로 의사소통할 필요성이 있어야 되는데, 이 경우에는 A와 B 부족간의 무역의 필요라고 할 수 있겠죠. 또한, 공통적으로 사용되는 중간 언어가 없어야 해요.

M: 네, 맞습니다. 음... 이어서 크리올 언어를 설명하는 게 좋을 것 같습니다..

P: 계속 하세요.

M: 네. 간단히 말하자면 각자 다른 언어를 사용하지만 둘다 혼성어를 사용하는 두 사람이 결혼을 하고, 서로 혼성어를 사용하면, 자녀들은 가정에서 혼성어를 모국어로 습득하게 됩니다. 보통 혼성어는 매우 단순하고 조잡한 언어 구조와 단어를 갖고 있지만, 크리올 언어는 좀 더 복잡한 구조와 확장된 단어를 가지고 있습니다.

크리올 언어는 종종 현존하는 언어의 혼재를 대신해서 한 사회의 새로운 모국어가 되기도 합니다. 더 이상 목적을 위한 언어가 아닌 것이 되는 것이죠. 하지만 혼성어가 사라져서 폐어가 될 수도 있기 때문에 항상 그런 것은 아닙니다. 그럼 이제 상층언어와 하층언어에 대해 알아보겠습니다. 우선, 상층언어는 혼성어나 크리올 언어의 모태가 된 언어입니다. 즉, 후에 침략한 국민의 언어가 원주민의 언어에 영향을 미친 것입니다. 상층언어는 주로 사회경제학적으로 우월한 집단의 언어라고 할 수 있겠습니다. 하층언어는 상층언어의 상대어인데요, 어, 혼성어를 만드는 이들의 모국어입니다. 그리고 lexifier에 대해서도 이야기를 해야 하는데요... 시프먼 교수님, lexifier에 대해 간략하게 설명해 주실 수 있을까요?

P: 물론이에요. Lexifier 언어는 대부분의 어휘의 출처가 되는 언어예요. 대부분의 어휘를 사회의 지배층 언어에서 차용하기 때문에 lexifier 언어는 상층언어와 동일하다고 할 수 있습니다.

M: 감사합니다. 음, 여기까지 질문 있는 분 계신가요?

W: 네, 혼성어와 크리올어의 차이에 대해 이야기를 했는데, 그러니까 혼성어는 보다 덜 복잡한 언어 구조와 어휘를 갖고 있다고 했죠? 그게 정확히 무슨 뜻인가요? 덜 복잡하다는 것인가요?

P: 이건 내가 설명해야 할 것 같군요, 케이티. 이렇게 얘기하는 편이 이해하기 쉬울 거예요 – 혼성어는 안정된 어휘가 없어요. 즉, 사람들은 서로 다른 단어, 특히 자기 모국어의 단어를 사용하길 선호해요. 또한 혼성어는 대부분 간단한 문법 체계를 갖고 있고 삽입절과 같은 복잡한 문법 구조는 없는 경우가 대부분이에요. 질문에 대한 답이 되었나요?

W: 네, 고맙습니다.

P: 좋아요. 잭, 시간이 다 되가는데, AAVE를 사용하는 사람들에 대해서도 이야기 하기로 했었죠?

M: 네, 간략하게 할게요. 간단히 말해 AAVE 혹은 Ebonics(흑인 영어)는 미국의 많은 흑인들이 사용하는 특정 언어의 형태입니다. 릭포드와 딜러드 같은 일부 연구자들에 따르면 AAVE는 노예 크리올 언어가 비크리올화된 것이라고 합니다. 비크리올화란 크리올어가 표준 언어가 되어 대부분의 어휘가 차용되는 과정을 의미합니다. 또한 AAVE의 발음, 문법 구조, 단어 등이 서부 아프리카의 다양한 언어와 유사하다고 하는데요, 이는 표준 미국 영어와는 약간의 차이가 있습니다. 방금 설명했듯이, 미국의 많은 흑인들이 AAVE를 사용하고 있고, 이는 인종적 정체성을 뚜렷하게 나타내는 역할을 합니다. AAVE와 표준 영어와의 차이점으로 인해 많은 AAVE 사용자들이 낮은 성적을 받고 결국에는 자퇴를 하는 경향이 있습니다. 자, 이제 4명이나 5명씩 한 조로 나눠서 혼성어, 크리올어, 그리고 AAVE 사용자들의 문제점과 특징에 대해 토의하도록 하겠습니다. 가져온 영상 자료를 틀어드리지 못해서 죄송합니다. 토의가 끝난 후 시간이 나면 틀도록 하겠습니다.

❶ What is the main topic of the discussion?

오늘의 주제는 혼성어와 크리올어, 그리고 그 형성에 관한 것인데, 혼성어란 우세한 언어에서 파생된 원시적인 언어이며 크리올어란 혼성어가 모국어화된 것이다. 크리올어가 조금 더 복잡한 구조와 넓은 어휘를 가지고 있지만 원시적 언어에 가깝다고 볼 수 있다. 따라서 정답은 C이다.

❷ According to the discussion, which of the following is required in order for a pidgin language to develop?

혼성어가 형성되려면 서로 다른 언어를 사용하는 집단들간에 지속적인 접촉이 있어야 하며 그 집단간에 의사소통에 대한 필요성이 있어야 한다. 따라서 답은 A, B이다.

❸ What is mentioned in the discussion about a creole language?

선택지 A는 혼성어(pidgin)에 대한 설명이며, 선택지 C와 D는 본문의 내용과 상반되는 내용이므로 정답이 될 수 없다. "When two people who speak different languages but both speak pidgin to each other, the pidgin spoken at home is learned by their children as a mother language"라는 학생의 말에서 선택지 B가 정답임을 알 수 있다.

❹ What can be inferred about the lexifier language?

"Superstrate is the language of the socio-economically dominant group in the society"와 "Lexifier language is the source of most of the vocabulary"와 "Lexifier language is equivalent to the superstrate language"라는 지문의 내용에서, lexifier를 사용하는 집단은 한 사회에서 사회경제학적으로 우위에 있다는 것을 유추할 수 있다. 따라서 정답은 선택지 A이다.

❺ Why does the professor say this:

교수는 "AAVE를 사용하는 사람들에 대해서도 이야기 하기로 했었죠"라고 말하면서 간접적으로 AAVE 사용자들에 대한 주제로 넘어가라고 지시한다. 따라서 정답은 선택지 D이다.

❻ What will the students probably do next?

"Um, now, I would like to ask you to pair up in groups of four or five and discuss the questions you see on the screen regarding pidgins, creoles, and AAVE speakers and their problems"에서 정답을 알 수 있다. AAVE 사용자에 대한 동영상은 토론이 끝난 후 틀어줄 것이므로 선택지 B는 틀린 선택이다.

MEMO

MEMO